The Handbook of
Educational Linguistics

Blackwell Handbooks in Linguistics

This outstanding multi-volume series covers all the major subdisciplines within linguistics today and, when complete, will offer a comprehensive survey of linguistics as a whole.

Already published:

The Handbook of Child Language
Edited by Paul Fletcher and Brian MacWhinney

The Handbook of Phonological Theory
Edited by John A. Goldsmith

The Handbook of Contemporary Semantic Theory
Edited by Shalom Lappin

The Handbook of Sociolinguistics
Edited by Florian Coulmas

The Handbook of Phonetic Sciences, Second Edition
Edited by William J. Hardcastle and John Laver

The Handbook of Morphology
Edited by Andrew Spencer and Arnold Zwicky

The Handbook of Japanese Linguistics
Edited by Natsuko Tsujimura

The Handbook of Linguistics
Edited by Mark Aronoff and Janie Rees-Miller

The Handbook of Contemporary Syntactic Theory
Edited by Mark Baltin and Chris Collins

The Handbook of Discourse Analysis
Edited by Deborah Schiffrin, Deborah Tannen, and Heidi E. Hamilton

The Handbook of Language Variation and Change
Edited by J. K. Chambers, Peter Trudgill, and Natalie Schilling-Estes

The Handbook of Historical Linguistics
Edited by Brian D. Joseph and Richard D. Janda

The Handbook of Language and Gender
Edited by Janet Holmes and Miriam Meyerhoff

The Handbook of Second Language Acquisition
Edited by Catherine J. Doughty and Michael H. Long

The Handbook of Bilingualism
Edited by Tej K. Bhatia and William C. Ritchie

The Handbook of Pragmatics
Edited by Laurence R. Horn and Gregory Ward

The Handbook of Applied Linguistics
Edited by Alan Davies and Catherine Elder

The Handbook of Speech Perception
Edited by David B. Pisoni and Robert E. Remez

The Blackwell Companion to Syntax, Volumes I–V
Edited by Martin Everaert and Henk van Riemsdijk

The Handbook of the History of English
Edited by Ans van Kemenade and Bettelou Los

The Handbook of English Linguistics
Edited by Bas Aarts and April McMahon

The Handbook of World Englishes
Edited by Braj B. Kachru; Yamuna Kachru, and Cecil L. Nelson

The Handbook of Educational Linguistics
Edited by Bernard Spolsky and Francis M. Hult

The Handbook of Clinical Linguistics
Edited by Martin J. Ball, Michael R. Perkins, Nicole Müller, and Sara Howard

The Handbook of Pidgin and Creole Studies
Edited by Silvia Kouwenberg and John Victor Singler

The Handbook of Language Teaching
Edited by Michael H. Long and Catherine J. Doughty

The Handbook of Language Contact
Edited by Raymond Hickey

The Handbook of Language and Speech Disorders
Edited by Jack S. Damico, Nicole Müller, Martin J. Ball

The Handbook of Educational Linguistics

Edited by

Bernard Spolsky and Francis M. Hult

WILEY-BLACKWELL

A John Wiley & Sons, Ltd., Publication

Library of Congress Cataloging-in-Publication Data

The handbook of educational linguistics / edited by Bernard Spolsky and Francis M. Hult.
    p. cm. — (Blackwell handbooks in linguistics)
  Includes bibliographical references and index.
  ISBN 978-1-4443-3104-2 (paper)
  ISBN 978-1-4051-5410-9 (hardcover : alk. paper) 1. Language and education.
I. Spolsky, Bernard.   II. Hult, Francis M.

  P40.8.H36 2008
  306.44—dc22
      2007030476

A catalogue record for this book is available from the British Library.

Set in 10/12pt Palatino by Graphicraft Limited, Hong Kong

1 2010

And this is what Rabbi Chanina said: "I have learned much from my teachers, and from my colleagues more than from my teachers, but from my students more than from them all."

Babylonian Talmud, Tractate *Taanit*, 7a

Contents

Notes on Contributors   x

1 Introduction: What is Educational Linguistics?   1
   BERNARD SPOLSKY
2 The History and Development of Educational Linguistics   10
   FRANCIS M. HULT

Part I Foundations for Educational Linguistics   **25**

3 Neurobiology of Language Learning   27
   LAURA SABOURIN AND LAURIE A. STOWE
4 Psycholinguistics   38
   WILLIAM C. RITCHIE AND TEJ K. BHATIA
5 Linguistic Theory   53
   RICHARD HUDSON
6 Sociolinguistics and Sociology of Language   66
   RAJEND MESTHRIE
7 Linguistic Anthropology   83
   STANTON WORTHAM
8 The Political Matrix of Linguistic Ideologies   98
   MARY MCGROARTY
9 Educational Linguistics and Education Systems   113
   JOSEPH LO BIANCO

Part II Core Themes   **127**

Linguistically and Culturally Responsive Education
10 The Language of Instruction Issue: Framing an Empirical
    Perspective   129
    STEPHEN L. WALTER

11   Bilingual and Biliterate Practices at Home and School   147
     ILIANA REYES AND LUIS C. MOLL
12   Vernacular Language Varieties in Educational Settings:
     Research and Development   161
     JEFFREY REASER AND CAROLYN TEMPLE ADGER
13   Linguistic Accessibility and Deaf Children   174
     SAMUEL J. SUPALLA AND JODY H. CRIPPS
14   Identity in Language and Literacy Education   192
     CAROLYN MCKINNEY AND BONNY NORTON
15   Post-colonialism and Globalization in Language Education   206
     HYUNJUNG SHIN AND RYUKO KUBOTA

Language Education Policy and Management
16   Levels and Goals: Central Frameworks and Local Strategies   220
     BRIAN NORTH
17   Language Acquisition Management Inside and Outside
     the School   233
     RICHARD B. BALDAUF JR., MINGLIN LI, AND SHOUHUI ZHAO
18   Language Cultivation in Developed Contexts   251
     JIŘÍ NEKVAPIL
19   Language Cultivation in Contexts of Multiple
     Community Languages   266
     M. PAUL LEWIS AND BARBARA TRUDELL
20   Ecological Language Education Policy   280
     NANCY H. HORNBERGER AND FRANCIS M. HULT
21   Education for Speakers of Endangered Languages   297
     TERESA L. MCCARTY, TOVE SKUTNABB-KANGAS, AND
     OLE HENRIK MAGGA
22   The Impact of English on the School Curriculum   313
     YUN-KYUNG CHA AND SEUNG-HWAN HAM

Literacy Development
23   Literacy   328
     GLYNDA A. HULL AND GREGORIO HERNANDEZ
24   Vernacular and Indigenous Literacies   341
     KENDALL A. KING AND CAROL BENSON
25   Religious and Sacred Literacies   355
     JONATHAN M. WATT AND SARAH L. FAIRFIELD
26   Genre and Register in Multiliteracies   367
     MARY MACKEN-HORARIK AND MISTY ADONIOU

Acquiring a Language
27   Order of Acquisition and Developmental Readiness   383
     KATHLEEN BARDOVI-HARLIG AND LLORENÇ COMAJOAN
28   Language Socialization   398
     KATHLEEN C. RILEY

29 Interlanguage and Language Transfer   411
    PETER SKEHAN
30 Second Language Acquisition and Ultimate Attainment   424
    DAVID BIRDSONG AND JEE PAIK
31 Explicit Form-Focused Instruction and Second
    Language Acquisition   437
    ROD ELLIS

Language Assessment
32 Language Assessments: Gate-Keepers or Door-Openers?   456
    LYLE F. BACHMAN AND JAMES E. PURPURA
33 Diagnostic and Formative Assessment   469
    ARI HUHTA
34 Accountability and Standards   483
    ALAN DAVIES
35 Scales and Frameworks   495
    NEIL JONES AND NICK SAVILLE
36 Nationally Mandated Testing for Accountability:
    English Language Learners in the US   510
    MICHELINE CHALHOUB-DEVILLE AND CRAIG DEVILLE

Part III   Research–Practice Relationships   **523**

37 Task-Based Teaching and Learning   525
    TERESA PICA
38 Corpus Linguistics and Second Language Instruction   539
    SUSAN M. CONRAD AND KIMBERLY R. LEVELLE
39 Interaction, Output, and Communicative Language Learning   557
    MERRILL SWAIN AND WATARU SUZUKI
40 Classroom Discourse and Interaction: Reading Across
    the Traditions   571
    LESLEY A. REX AND JUDITH L. GREEN
41 Computer Assisted Language Learning   585
    CAROL A. CHAPELLE
42 Ecological-Semiotic Perspectives on Educational Linguistics   596
    LEO VAN LIER
43 The Mediating Role of Language in Teaching and Learning:
    A Classroom Perspective   606
    FRANCIS BAILEY, BEVERLEY BURKETT, AND DONALD FREEMAN
44 A Research Agenda for Educational Linguistics   626
    PAOLA UCCELLI AND CATHERINE SNOW

Author Index   643
Subject Index   659

Notes on Contributors

Carolyn Temple Adger directs the Language in Society Division at the Center for Applied Linguistics in Washington, DC. She has conducted several studies of classroom discourse and interaction among teachers in a professional development setting and has applied linguistic research in work with teachers of English language learners. Her publications include *Dialects in Schools and Communities* (with Walt Wolfram & Donna Christian, 2007) and *What Teachers Need to Know about Language* (co-edited with Catherine E. Snow & Donna Christian, 2002).

Misty Adoniou is a lecturer in literacy and ESL in the School of Teacher Education and Community Services at the University of Canberra in Australia. Her research interests include multimodality in literacy teaching and children's out-of-school literacy practices.

Lyle F. Bachman is Professor and Chair of Applied Linguistics at the University of California, Los Angeles. His publications include *Fundamental Considerations in Language Testing* (1990), *Interfaces between Second Language Acquisition and Language Testing Research* (co-edited with Andrew Cohen, 1998), *Language Testing in Practice* (with Adrian S. Palmer, 1996) and *Statistical Analyses for Language Assessment* (2004). His current research interests include validation theory, epistemological issues in Applied Linguistics research, and issues in assessing the academic achievement and English proficiency of English language learners in schools.

Francis Bailey is Associate Professor of Second Language Education at the School for International Training, Brattleboro, Vermont, USA. His research interests include the role of semantic memory in the learning of elementary school children.

Richard B. Baldauf, Jr. is Associate Professor of TESOL at the University of Queensland. He is coauthor, with Robert B. Kaplan, of *Language Planning from Practice to Theory* (1997) and *Language and Language-in-Education Planning in the*

Pacific Basin (2003), and is co-editor with Robert B. Kaplan of the "Language Policy and Planning" polity study series published by Multilingual Matters. His interests include language policy and planning and TESOL curriculum related studies.

Kathleen Bardovi-Harlig is Professor of Second Language Studies at Indiana University. Her books include *Tense and Aspect in Second Language Acquisition* (2000), *Interlanguage Pragmatics: Exploring Institutional Talk* (with Beverly Hartford, 2005), and *Pragmatics and Language Learning* (with César Félix-Brasdefer and Alwiya Omar, 2006). She has published in *Language Learning*, *Studies in Second Language Acquisition*, and *TESOL Quarterly*, and is a former editor of *Language Learning*.

Carol Benson is based at the Centre for Teaching and Learning at Stockholm University. Her PhD is in Social Sciences and Comparative Education, and her research and consulting focus on mother tongue based schooling in multi-lingual countries.

Tej K. Bhatia is Professor of Linguistics and Director of South Asian Languages at Syracuse University. He has been Director of the Linguistic Studies Program and Acting Director of Cognitive Sciences at his university. His publications include three handbooks with William C. Ritchie. His authored books include *Colloquial Hindi* (2007, revised edition), *Advertising in Rural India: Language, Marketing Communication, and Consumerism* (2000), *Colloquial Urdu* (2000), *Colloquial Hindi* (1996), *Negation in South Asian Languages* (1995), *Punjabi: A Cognitive-Descriptive Grammar* (1993), and *A History of the Hindi Grammatical Tradition* (1987). Email: tkbhatia@syr.edu

David Birdsong is Professor of French Linguistics at the University of Texas, with a specialization in second language acquisition. He has held visiting positions at Georgetown University and at the Max Planck Institute for Psycholinguistics. He has published articles relating to age and second language acquisition in such journals as *Language, Journal of Memory and Language*, and *Studies in Second Language Acquisition*.

Beverley Burkett is Project Leader for Language Education at Nelson Mandela Metropolitan University, Port Elizabeth, South Africa. She has spent 22 years in teacher development and is currently team leader of a longitudinal research study that is focusing on additive bilingualism.

Yun-Kyung Cha is Professor of Education at Hanyang University in Korea. He received his doctorate in the Sociology of Education at Stanford University (USA) and was awarded a National Academy of Education Spencer Fellowship (1991). His research interests focus on the comparative and sociological analysis of school curricula, and the institutionalization of teacher education and lifelong education programs.

Micheline Chalhoub-Deville is a Professor in the Educational Research Methodology Department at the University of North Carolina, Greensboro. She has published in journals such as *Language Testing, Language Learning, Annual Review of Applied Linguistics,* and *World Englishes.* Her most recent edited book is entitled *Inference and Generalizability in Applied Linguistics: Multiple Research Perspectives* (co-edited with Carol A. Chapelle & Patricia A. Duff, 2006). Her main interest in second/foreign language testing includes performance-based assessment, computerized testing, ELL testing, as well as admissions and exit proficiency testing.

Carol A. Chapelle, Professor of TESL/Applied Linguistics at Iowa State University in the United States, is past president of the American Association for Applied Linguistics (2006–7) and former editor of *TESOL Quarterly* (1999–2004). Her research explores issues at the intersection of computer technology and applied linguistics. Her books on this area are *Computer Applications in Second Language Acquisition: Foundations for Teaching, Testing, and Research* (2001), *English Language Learning and Technology: Lectures on Applied Linguistics in the Age of Information and Communication Technology* (2003) and *Assessing Language through Computer Technology* (with Dan Douglas, 2006).

Llorenç Comajoan holds a PhD in Linguistics from Indiana University and is a professor at the University of Vic, Catalonia (Department of Philology, School of Education). His interests include the interrelationship of discourse and semantic features in second language acquisition as well as language attitudes by children of immigrant origin in Spain. He has published articles in *Language Learning, Catalan Review,* and *Caplletra.* His contribution was funded by a grant to the Department of Linguistics of the University of Barcelona (C-RED 2005).

Susan M. Conrad is Professor of Applied Linguistics at Portland State University in Portland, Oregon, USA. Her co-authored book projects in corpus linguistics include *Corpus Linguistics: Investigating Language Structure and Use* (1998), *Longman Grammar of Spoken and Written English* (1999), and *Variation in English: Multi-Dimensional Studies* (2001).

Jody H. Cripps is a doctoral student in the Second Language Acquisition and Teaching Interdisciplinary Program at the University of Arizona. His research interests are second language processing and second language use with a specialty in literacy.

Alan Davies is Emeritus Professor of Applied Linguistics at the University of Edinburgh. His books include: *The Native Speaker: Myth and Reality* (2003), *A Glossary of Applied Linguistics* (2005), and *Assessing Academic English: Testing English Proficiency 1950–2005 – the IELTS solution* (2007). One-time editor of *Applied Linguistics* and of *Language Testing,* his main research interests are in language assessment and in the construct of the native speaker.

Craig Deville currently serves as the Director of Psychometric Services with Measurement Inc. His interests include language testing, educational achievement assessment, computerized testing, and validation. He has published widely, including in such journals as *Language Testing* and *Applied Psychological Measurement*, and has contributed chapters in numerous edited volumes. His most recent co-authored chapter appeared in the fourth edition of *Educational Measurement* (ed. R. L. Brennan, 2006).

Rod Ellis is currently Professor in the Department of Applied Language Studies and Linguistics at the University of Auckland, New Zealand. His published work includes *Understanding Second Language Acquisition* (awarded the BAAL prize in 1986), *The Study of Second Language Acquisition* (awarded the Duke of Edinburgh Prize in 1995), *Task-Based Learning and Teaching* (2003), and (with Gary Barkhuizen) *Analyzing Learner Language* (2005).

Sarah L. Fairfield teaches Sociology and Humanities at Geneva College, and is a doctoral student in the Social and Comparative Analysis of Education at the University of Pittsburgh.

Donald Freeman is Professor and Director of the Center for Teacher Education, Training, and Research at the School for International Training, Brattleboro, Vermont, USA. His research focuses on teacher education designs and the connections between teacher and student learning.

Judith L. Green is Professor of Education in the Gevirtz Graduate School of Education, University of California, Santa Barbara. Her research focuses on the social construction of knowledge in classrooms with linguistically and culturally diverse students. She is currently editor of the *Review of Research in Education (30),* and co-editor of two recent handbooks: *Complementary Methods for Research in Education* (2006, for the American Education Research Association) and *Multidisciplinary Perspectives on Literacy Research* (2005, for the National Conference for Research on Language and Literacy). Email: green@education.ucsb.edu

Seung-Hwan Ham is a doctoral student in educational policy at Michigan State University. His academic interests are in cross-national and historical analyses of curricular changes and associated transformations in schooling and teacher training.

Gregorio Hernandez received his PhD in Education in Language, Literacy, and Culture at the University of California, Berkeley. He is a member of the Transnational Literacy Researchers Group, in the Center for the Americas, Vanderbilt University. His research focuses on literacy practices in and out of school, Hispanic migration in the US, and the politics of literacy education in Mexico and Latin America.

Nancy H. Hornberger is Professor of Education at the University of Pennsylvania, where she also convenes the annual Ethnography in Education

Research Forum. Her research interests are multilingual language education policy and practice, with a focus on indigenous and immigrant heritage language education. Her recent and forthcoming volumes include *Continua of Biliteracy: An Ecological Framework for Educational Policy, Research, and Practice in Multilingual Settings* (2003), *Language Loyalty, Language Planning, and Language Revitalization: Recent Writings and Reflections from Joshua A. Fishman* (2006, with Martin Pütz), *Can Schools Save Indigenous Languages? Policy and Practice on Four Continents* (in press), and the *Encyclopedia of Language and Education* (in press).

Richard Hudson is Emeritus Professor of Linguistics at University College London. His 12 books include *Language Networks: The New Word Grammar* (2007) and *Teaching Grammar: A Guide for the National Curriculum* (1992). His website is www.phon.ucl.ac.uk/home/dick/home.htm.

Ari Huhta works as a researcher at the Centre for Applied Language Studies at the University of Jyväskylä, Finland. He specializes in foreign and second language assessment, and has participated in a number of national and international research and development projects in the field (e.g., IEA Language Education Study, DIALANG, EALTA); he has published in several journals, such as *Language Testing*.

Glynda A. Hull is Professor of Education in Language, Literacy, and Culture at the University of California, Berkeley. Her research focuses on literacy and new media, identity formation, and urban education. Her books include *Changing Literacy, Changing Workers: Critical Perspectives on Language, Literacy, and Skills* (1997), *School's Out: Bridging Out-of-School Literacies with Classroom Practice* (co-edited with Katherine Schultz, 2002), and *The New Work Order* (co-authored with James Paul Gee and Colin Lankshear, 1996).

Francis M. Hult is Assistant Professor of Applied Linguistics in the Department of Bicultural-Bilingual Studies at the University of Texas at San Antonio. He has also taught at Lund University and the University of Pennsylvania. He is the founder and manager of the Educational Linguistics List (Edling-L). His research explores processes of language planning and curriculum development that attempt to manage the status of national languages with respect to minority and foreign languages in multilingual polities. His current work focuses on the positions of English and Swedish as they relate to language policy, linguistic culture, and language education in Sweden. His publications have appeared in the journals *World Englishes* (with Kendall King and E. Cathrine Berg), *Language Policy*, and *Current Issues in Language Planning*. He holds a PhD in educational linguistics from the University of Pennsylvania.

Neil Jones holds an MSc and PhD in Applied Linguistics from the University of Edinburgh (UK) on the application of item response theory. He has extensive experience as teacher and director of studies in several countries including Poland and Japan, where he set up English teaching departments at university level. In Cambridge ESOL he works on innovative developments including item banking and computer-based testing.

Kendall A. King is Associate Professor of Linguistics at Georgetown University. Her work addresses ideological, interactional, and policy perspectives on second language learning and bilingualism. Her publications include *Language Revitalization Processes and Prospects: Quichua in the Ecuadorian Andes* (2000) and articles in the *Journal of Sociolinguistics, International Journal of the Sociology of Language, Journal of Language, Identity, and Education*, and *Journal of Child Language*. She is editor (with Elana Shohamy) of the journal *Language Policy*.

Ryuko Kubota is Professor in the School of Education and the Department of Asian Studies at the University of North Carolina at Chapel Hill. Her research interests are in critical pedagogies, culture, politics, and race in second language education. Her publications appear in such journals as *Canadian Modern Language Review, Foreign Language Annals, Journal of Second Language Writing, TESOL Quarterly, World Englishes*, and *Written Communication*.

Kimberly R. LeVelle is a doctoral student in Applied Linguistics and Technology at Iowa State University. She completed her MA in TESOL at Portland State University. Her research interests include language pedagogy, assessment, and corpus linguistics.

M. Paul Lewis (paul_lewis@sil.org) holds a PhD in Linguistics from Georgetown University and did field work with SIL International in Central America from 1975–90 and 1994–6. He was International Sociolinguistics Coordinator for SIL International from 1996 to 2003 and is an International Sociolinguistics Consultant for that organization. His publications include: *K'iche': A Study in the Sociology of Language*, the volume *Assessing Ethnolinguistic Vitality: Theory and Practice* (edited with Gloria Kindell), and various articles, contributions to edited volumes, and electronic papers. He was general editor of SIL's Publications in Sociolinguistics series and is currently a consulting editor of SIL's Publications in Language and Education series as well as editor of *Ethnologue: Languages of the World*.

Minglin Li is Associate Professor in EFL at Ludong University in China and is currently undertaking a PhD at the School of Education, University of Queensland. Her research interests are EFL teaching and teacher education, language education policy and planning in China.

Joseph Lo Bianco is Professor of Language and Literacy Education at the University of Melbourne. His recent books include *Australian Policy Activism in Language and Literacy* (2001, with R. Wickert), *Australian Literacies: Informing National Policy on Literacy Education* (2001, with P. Freebody), *Voices from Phnom Penh: Development and Language* (2002), *Teaching Invisible Culture: Classroom Practice and Theory* (2003, with C. Crozet), and *Site for Debate: Australian*

Language Planning (2004). His current research projects include English and Identity in China and New Theorization in Language Planning.

Mary Macken-Horarik is Senior Lecturer in Language and Literacy Education at the University of Canberra, Australia. She has published widely in the field of systemic functional linguistics. Her recent publications include "Negotiating Heteroglossia" (a special issue of *Text*, edited with J. R Martin) in 2003. She is currently writing a book about systemic functional semiotics in school English.

Ole Henrik Magga is Professor in Saami linguistics at the Saami University College (Sámi allaskuvla) in Guovdageaidnu (Kautokeino), Norway. His research has been mostly on Saami syntax, but he has also studied aspects of onomastics, language teaching and language planning. He has for several decades been active in defense of the rights of indigenous peoples, including their rights to education, both on national and international levels as the first chairman of the Saami Parliament in Norway and the first chairman of the UN Permanent Forum on Indigenous Issues. Email: ole-henrik.magga@samiskhs.no.

Teresa L. McCarty is the Alice Wiley Snell Professor of Education Policy Studies at Arizona State University. Her research, teaching, and service focus on Indigenous language education, language policy, and ethnographic studies of American Indian education. Her recent books include *A Place To Be Navajo: Rough Rock and the Struggle for Self-Determination in Indigenous Schooling* (2002), *Language, Literacy, and Power in Schooling* (2005), and *"To Remain an Indian": Lessons in Democracy from a Century of Native American Education* (with K. T. Lomawaima, 2006).

Mary McGroarty is Professor in the Applied Linguistics Program of the English Department at Northern Arizona University, where she received the 2006 Teaching Scholar Award that recognizes sustained use of research in all levels of teaching. Editor of the *Annual Review of Applied Linguistics*, her research interests include language policy, pedagogy, and assessment, with recent articles in *Language Policy* (2006) and *Language Testing* (2005).

Carolyn McKinney is a senior lecturer in the School of Education, University of Witwatersrand, South Africa. She has published on research methods in language and literacy, critical literacy, identity/subjectivity and learning, as well as critical pedagogy. Her research interests focus on language, race, and gender in education and youth identities. Email: carolyn.mckinney@wits.ac.za

Rajend Mesthrie is Professor of Linguistics at the University of Cape Town. He is currently President of the Linguistics Society of Southern Africa. He has published widely in sociolinguistics, with special reference to variation and contact in South Africa, including *Language in South Africa* (2002).

Luis C. Moll is Professor of Language, Reading, and Culture and Associate Dean for Academic Affairs at the College of Education of The University of Arizona. His main research interest is the connection among culture, psychology, and education, especially as it relates to the education of Latino children in the US. Among other studies, he has analyzed the quality of classroom teaching, examined literacy instruction in English and Spanish, studied how literacy takes place in the broader social contexts of households and community life, and attempted to establish pedagogical relationships among these domains of study. His recent book, a co-edited volume titled *Funds of Knowledge: Theorizing Practices in Households, Communities, and Classrooms* (with N. González & C. Amanti), was published in 2005. He was elected to membership in the US National Academy of Education in 1998.

Jiří Nekvapil teaches sociolinguistics, discourse analysis and general linguistics at the Department of Linguistics at Charles University, Prague. He has published extensively in these areas. His current research focuses on language planning in Europe, Language Management Theory, and the impact of the economy on the use of languages.

Bonny Norton is Professor and Distinguished University Scholar in the Department of Language and Literacy Education, University of British Columbia, Canada. She is also Honorary Professor in the School of Education, University of Witwatersrand, South Africa, and Visiting Senior Research Fellow at King's College, University of London, UK. Her award-winning research addresses identity and language learning, education and development, and critical literacy. Recent publications include *Identity and Language Learning* (2000), *Gender and English Language Learners* (2004, with A. Pavlenko), and *Critical Pedagogies and Language Learning* (2004, with K. Toohey). Her website can be found at http://lerc.educ.ubc.ca/fac/norton/

Brian North is Head of Academic Development at Eurocentres, the language school foundation, and recently elected Chair of EAQUALS (European Association for Quality Language Services). He is co-author of the Council of Europe *Common European Framework of Reference for Languages: Learning, Teaching, Assessment* (2001).

Jee Paik is a PhD candidate in French linguistics at the University of Texas. Her dissertation research concerns the expression of emotion in the first and second language.

Teresa Pica is a professor at the University of Pennsylvania. Her research addresses questions on classroom practice in light of second language acquisition theory and research.

James E. Purpura (mailto: jp248@columbia.edu) is Associate Professor of Linguistics and Education in the TESOL and Applied Linguistics Programs at Teachers College, Columbia. He teaches courses in language assessment. In addition to several articles, his recent books include *Assessing Grammar* (2004) and *Learner Strategy Use and Performance on Language Tests* (1999). His research interests include the assessment of grammatical ability, the cognitive underpinnings of language tests, and measuring second language acquisition. He is currently President of the International Language Testing Association.

Jeffrey Reaser is an assistant professor in the teacher education and linguistics programs at North Carolina State University in Raleigh, NC. His primary research interest is developing, implementing, and measuring the effects of dialect awareness programs in public schools. He is co-author of curricular materials supporting the PBS documentary "Do You Speak American?" and the Voices of North Carolina dialect awareness curriculum. Email: jlreaser@ncsu.edu

Iliana Reyes is an assistant professor in the Department of Language, Reading, and Culture, and a member of the faculty in the Interdisciplinary Graduate Program in Second Language Acquisition and Teaching at the University of Arizona. Her research focuses on bilingual and biliteracy development, language socialization, and child development. She is the principal investigator of a longitudinal research study that focuses on emergent biliteracy and literacy practices in immigrant families in the US Southwest. Her most recent publications have appeared in the *Journal of Early Childhood Literacy*, *Bilingualism: Language and Cognition*, and the *International Journal of Bilingualism*.

Lesley A. Rex is Associate Professor in the School of Education at the University of Michigan, where she is Co-Chair of the Joint PhD Program in English and Education and Faculty Leader for Secondary Teacher Education. Her main research focus is literacy teaching and learning. She is particularly interested in classroom interaction and discursive construction of literacy knowledge and student participation, complicated by issues of class, ethnicity, language, culture, and disability. Her most recent book is a collection of studies that demonstrate interactional ethnography as a research approach for understanding how learning opportunities are created and limited: *Discourse of Opportunity: How Talk in Learning Situations Creates and Constrains* (2006). You can reach her and her work through www.umich.edu/~rex/

Kathleen C. Riley is a part-time faculty member of the Departments of Linguistics and of Sociology and Anthropology at Concordia University, Montreal, Canada. She conducted her doctoral research in French Polynesia and post-doctoral work in the suburbs of Paris (Université de Paris X, Nanterre) and has published articles in the *Bulletin de la Société des Etudes Océaniennes* (1996), the *HRAF Encyclopedia of Sex and Gender* (2003), as well as in several edited volumes. A forthcoming article will appear in *Language and Communication*.

William C. Ritchie is Associate Professor of Linguistics at Syracuse University. His publications include an edited volume entitled *Second Language Acquisition Research: Issues and Implications* (1978) and three handbooks co-edited with Tej K. Bhatia: *The Handbook of Child Language Acquisition* (1999), *The Handbook of Second Language Acquisition* (1996), and *The Handbook of Bilingualism* (2004).

Laura Sabourin is a research associate in the Brain Development Lab at the University of Oregon. She completed her BA in Linguistics at McGill, and gained her MSc in Psycholinguistics from the University of Alberta and her PhD in Neurolinguistics from the University of Groningen, The Netherlands. She is currently editing a special issue of the journal *Second Language Research* on "Brain imaging techniques in the investigation of second language acquisition."

Nick Saville is Director of Research and Validation for the University of Cambridge ESOL Examinations. He represents Cambridge ESOL in the Association of Language Testers in Europe (ALTE) and has close involvement with other European initiatives, including the Council of Europe's Common European Framework of Reference (CEFR). Currently he is Associate Editor of *Language Assessment Quarterly* and is on the editorial board of *Language Testing*.

Hyunjung Shin is a PhD candidate in second language education at the Ontario Institute for Studies in Education of the University of Toronto, Canada. Her research interests include transnationalism, globalization and language education, ethnographic approaches to language research, sociolinguistics, and critical pedagogies. Her works have appeared in *Critical Inquiry in Language Studies*.

Peter Skehan is Professor of Applied English Linguistics at the Chinese University of Hong Kong. He researches in the areas of task-based instruction and foreign language aptitude. He authored *A Cognitive Approach to Language Learning* (1998). E-mail: pskehan@arts.cuhk.edu.hk

Tove Skutnabb-Kangas, Emerita, Guest Researcher at Department of Languages and Culture, University of Roskilde, Denmark; "docent" (visiting professor) at Åbo Akademi University, Dept of Education, Vasa, Finland. Her latest books in English include *Linguistic Genocide in Education: Or Worldwide Diversity and Human Rights?* (2000), *Sharing A World of Difference: The Earth's Linguistic, Cultural, and Biological Diversity* (2003, with Luisa Maffi and David Harmon), *Imagining Multilingual Schools: Languages in Education and Glocalization* (2006, co-edited with Ofelia García and María Torres Guzmán). For more publications, see http://akira.ruc.dk/~tovesk/

Catherine Snow is the Henry Lee Shattuck Professor of Education at the Harvard Graduate School of Education. She has published several books and many articles in refereed journals and chapters in edited volumes. Snow chaired the National Research Council Committee on Preventing Reading Difficulties in Young Children, the RAND Reading Study Group that produced the volume *Reading for Understanding: Towards an R&D Agenda*, and the National Academy of Education committee that produced the 2005 volume *Knowledge to support the teaching of reading*. For more information: http://gseweb.harvard.edu/~snow/

Bernard Spolsky retired from Bar-Ilan University in 2000 as Emeritus Professor. He has written and edited two dozen books, including *Educational Linguistics: An Introduction* (1978), *Conditions for Second Language Learning* (1989), *The Languages of Jerusalem* (1991), *Measured Words* (1995), *Sociolinguistics* (1998), *The Languages of Israel* (1999), *Concise Encyclopedia of Educational Linguistics* (1999), and *Language Policy* (2004), as well as about 200 articles and chapters. He was founding editor of three journals, *Applied Linguistics*, *Journal of Asia TEFL*, and *Language Policy*. He lives in the Old City of Jerusalem where he is writing a monograph on fundamentals of language management. http://www.biu.ac.il/faculty/spolsb/

Laurie A. Stowe is an associate professor of Linguistics at the University of Groningen in the Netherlands. Her research focuses on the neurological basis of language investigated with neuroimaging methods like event-related potentials and regional blood flow change, publishing in such journals as *NeuroImage* and *Cognitive Brain Research.* She graduated from the University of Wisconsin at Madison and from Cornell University.

Samuel J. Supalla is Associate Professor of Sign Language/Deaf Studies in the Department of Special Education, Rehabilitation, and School Psychology at the University of Arizona. His research has been funded through the National Institutes of Health, US Department of Education, and James S. McDonnell Foundation. The focus of his research is on understanding modality-specific attributes of signed language structure and addressing instructional and assessment considerations in terms of accessibility for deaf children. The development of measures for language and literacy skills deemed appropriate for deaf children are included in Dr. Supalla's research agenda along with considerations for ramifications on policy for deaf education.

Wataru Suzuki is a PhD candidate in the Second Language Education program at the Ontario Institute for Studies in Education of the University of Toronto, Canada. His research interests include applied linguistics and psycholinguistics (particularly cognitive and sociocultural theories of second language acquisition). Email: wsuzuki@oise.utoronto.ca

Merrill Swain is Emeritus Professor in the Second Language Education Program at the Ontario Institute for Studies in Education of the University of Toronto, Canada. Her interests include bilingual education (particularly French immersion education) and communicative second language learning, teaching, and testing. Her recent research is about languaging and second language learning. She has published widely. Email: mswain@oise.utoronto.ca

Barbara Trudell (barbara_trudell@sil.org) holds a PhD from the University of Edinburgh's Centre of African Studies. She has worked in local-language literacy and education since 1982, in both South America and sub-Saharan Africa. She is currently the Director of Academic Affairs for SIL International,

Africa Area. Recent publications and research interests focus on language policy implementation, language-in-education issues, local agency, and the various aspects of language development in the sub-Saharan African context. Her current research is on local-language literacy programs in rural Senegalese communities.

Paola Uccelli is a Postdoctoral Fellow at the Harvard Graduate School of Education. She received her BA in Linguistics from the Pontificia Universidad Católica in Lima, Perú, and her EdD in Human Development and Psychology from the Harvard Graduate School of Education. She has taught Spanish at the Harvard Romance Languages and Literatures Department, and has carried out research on grammatical and discourse development. Her current research focuses on reading comprehension with a particular interest in designing diagnostic assessments and effective interventions for English language learners. Her research is being conducted in collaboration with CAST (Center for Applied Special Technology), and CAL (Center for Applied Linguistics) and it is supported by the Institute of Education Sciences.

Leo van Lier is Professor of Educational Linguistics at the Monterey Institute of International Studies. His books include *Interaction in the Language Curriculum: Awareness, Autonomy and Authenticity* (1996) and *The Ecology and Semiotics of Language Learning: A Sociocultural Perspective* (2004). He is the Editor of the *Modern Language Journal*.

Stephen L. Walter (steve_walter@gial.edu) received his PhD in linguistics from the University of Texas at Arlington and is currently Department Chair and Associate Professor in the Department of Language Development of the Graduate Institute of Applied Linguistics in Dallas, Texas. His most recent publication is *Eritrea National Reading Survey: A Research Report on the Status of Mother Tongue Education in Eritrea* (2006). Currently, he is the senior researcher on a longitudinal, international study of multilingual education in minority language communities in developing countries.

Jonathan M. Watt is Associate Professor of Biblical Studies at Geneva College (Beaver Falls, PA). He is the author of *Code-Switching in Luke and Acts* (1997) and various articles on sociolinguistics and religion.

Stanton Wortham is the Judy and Howard Berkowitz Professor at the University of Pennsylvania Graduate School of Education. He also has appointments in Anthropology, Communications and Folklore. His research applies techniques from linguistic anthropology to study interactional positioning and social identity development in classrooms. He has also studied interactional positioning in media discourse and autobiographical narrative. Publications include: *Acting Out Participant Examples in the Classroom* (1994), *Narratives in Action* (2001), *Education in the New Latino Diaspora* (2002, co-edited with Enrique Murillo and Edmund Hamann), *Linguistic Anthropology of Education* (2003, co-edited with Betsy Rymes), and *Learning Identity* (2006). More information about his work can be found at http://www.gse.upenn.edu/~stantonw.

Shouhui Zhao is Research Fellow of the Centre for Research in Pedagogy and Practice at Nanyang Technological University. His research interests include Chinese applied linguistics and language planning.

1 Introduction: What is Educational Linguistics?

BERNARD SPOLSKY

First named as a field 30 years ago (Spolsky, 1974b) and defined in two introductory books (Spolsky, 1978; Stubbs, 1986), educational linguistics has rapidly expanded and has become widely recognized in reference texts (Corson, 1997; Spolsky, 1999) and in university programs and courses. With the growing significance of language education as a result of decolonization and globalization, more and more educational systems are appreciating the need to train teachers and administrators in those aspects of linguistics that are relevant to education and in the various subfields that have grown up within educational linguistics itself.

I first proposed the term "educational linguistics" because of my dissatisfaction with efforts to define the field of applied linguistics. In the narrowest definition, courses and textbooks on applied linguistics in the 1960s dealt with the teaching of foreign languages; in the widest definition (for example, in the scope of subjects covered in the international congresses starting to be organized by AILA) it came to include all of what Charles Voegelin had called "hyphenated linguistics," that is to say, everything but language theory, history, and description. One of the central issues of debate was the relationship between theoretical or mainstream linguistics and the applied field. It was becoming clear, particularly with the failure of the audio-lingual method on the one hand and the refusal of transformational linguistics to accept responsibility for practical issues on the other, that the simplistic notion that applied linguistics was simply linguistics applied to some practical question was misleading.

Applied linguistics as it had developed seemed to me to be a fairly soulless attempt to apply largely irrelevant models to a quite narrow range of problems, especially in teaching foreign languages. It produced a couple of potential monsters in language teaching: the deadening drills of the audio-lingual method, and the ungoverned chaos of the early natural approach. I saw the challenge in this way:

Many linguists believe that their field should not be corrupted by any suggestion of relevance to practical matters; for them, linguistics is a pure science and its study is motivated only by the desire to increase human knowledge. Others, however, claimed that linguistics offers a panacea for any educational problem that arises and quickly offer their services to handle any difficulties in language planning or teaching. Each of these extreme positions is, I believe, quite wrong, for while it is evident that linguistics is often relevant to education, the relation is seldom direct. (Spolsky, 1978: 1)

In a review of a recent Festschrift dealing with applied linguistics, Davies (2006) suggested a distinction between those like Henry Widdowson who argued for a dictionary definition of the field, maintaining that there is "an applied linguistics core which should be required of all those attempting the *rite de passage*" and those who prefer the approach by ostensive definition, "if you want to know about applied linguistics, look around you." He correctly places me somewhere in this latter camp, although in the case of educational linguistics, which I argue is more focused, I think I have less trouble in finding a core, in the interactions between language and education. It was the very lack of a core in applied linguistics that led me to propose educational linguistics. On the analogy of educational psychology, I hoped it would be possible to define a field relevant to education but based on linguistics.

It soon became clear that the term is necessarily ambiguous: it includes those parts of linguistics directly relevant to educational matters as well as those parts of education concerned with language. This turns out to be a pretty wide scope, as most parts of education do involve language: we found for instance the measured competence in mathematics of new immigrant students in Israel was lowered by their limited Hebrew proficiency. But more recent thought, following at least a decade of research and publication in the area of language policy, has given me a clearer view of how to locate educational linguistics, which I now see as providing the essential instruments for designing language education policy and for implementing language education management. Language policy, I argue, exists within all speech communities (and within each domain inside that community), consisting of three distinct but interrelated components: the regular language practices of the community (such as choice of varieties); the language beliefs or ideology of the community (such as the values assigned to each variety by various members of the community); and any language management activities, namely attempts by any individual or institution with or claiming authority to modify the language practices and language beliefs of other members of the community.

Tracing the history of language management, the earliest activities were those aiming to preserve sacred texts (the work of the Sanskrit, Arabic, and Hebrew grammarians, for instance) or to translate them into new languages. Later, with the establishment of the Spanish and French academies, the emphasis moved to preserving the purity of standard varieties. To this, the French Revolution added, and the German Romantics confirmed, the emphasis on defining a centralized standard language variety in order to assert national identity. This task, concentrating on language status and supported by puristic language cultivation (or corpus planning), was the central management activity in newly developed independent nations in the nineteenth century and again with the end of colonialism after World War II. While this had obvious effects on education (especially on the choice of language of instruction), the recognition that language acquisition policy was a key component of language management had to wait until it was suggested by Cooper (1989). While it is true that most students of language policy continue to focus on decisions concerning status at the level of the nation-state, it is starting to be recognized that the major changes in language practices and beliefs are the results of management activities concerning education.

An obvious example is the way that decisions concerning language of instruction have been the major cause in Africa and other former colonies of the downgrading and extinction of minority languages. Similarly, pressures are now developing in Asia and elsewhere to introduce English into primary schools, either alongside the local language or replacing it as medium of instruction especially for science subjects. In South America, the destruction of indigenous languages was virtually guaranteed by Spanish refusal to admit them into the educational system. In the Soviet Union, the better facilities provided to Russian-medium schools raised the status and importance of the language and threatened the territorial languages. In New Zealand, the change from Maori to English in the 1870s in the Native Schools was the beginning of the suppression of language, and the movement for Maori language regeneration of the last two decades has been focused on the schools. It is reasonable to claim then that the most important language management activities are now those taking place within the school system.

A parenthetical word of concern may, however, not be out of place. Recently, especially in the field of language assessment, there has been a growing recognition of the issue of ethical responsibility for the use of language tests. Whereas at one stage language testers spent most of their time studying and talking about the reliability and validity of a test, they are now more likely to be concerned with test use and misuse. Strong alarm has been expressed, for example, about the use of language tests to exclude asylum seekers or to control immigration. Similarly, the growing employment of national standardized tests to ensure accountability of education systems is interfering with efforts to provide education suitable for minorities and new immigrants.

This sense of responsibility and ethical disquiet has also moved to language management, in part as a result of the criticism of the contribution of imperialist and colonialist policies to language endangerment and also as a result of widespread recognition of the need to apply principles of human rights to language policy. It is clear that language management can be directed toward socially and morally inappropriate goals, such as the homogenization and suppression of minority languages. Many scholars hold that the contrary pressure, toward the revival of fading languages or toward giving power to minority languages, is necessarily good and to be encouraged – a common argument makes an analogy between biological and linguistic diversity that remains debatable.

By definition, however, any language management is the application of power coming from authority, and has totalitarian overtones. It assumes that the language manager (government or activist or scholar) knows best and it is thus in essence patriarchal. Taking a liberal or pluralistic point of view, one would argue that people should be allowed free choice of language, as of religion, provided only that they do not interfere with or harm others. On this principle, individuals should also be offered an opportunity to acquire the language in which national and civic activities are undertaken, and the language or languages which will provide them with access to economic success. A language education policy which denies such access (such as the ban on English in the Maori *Kura kaupapa*) needs very strong justification.

At the same time, one may question the demands made by ethnic language revival movements that all members of the ethnic group must use only the ethnic language, granting rights to the group, or even worse, to a specific language as an object, at the cost of individual freedom to choose. This is an example of conflict of values: identity with a large group (family, ethnic group, religion, or nation) is valuable, but so is the right to choose one's own language. From a pluralist point of view, there is no obvious way to apply a higher value to one or the other, leaving a free choice accompanied of course by a price. But what gives me (the putative language manager) the authority to make decisions for others? Can I point to some ideal society in which utopian pluralism has been achieved, or simply to the many failures of efforts to manage languages? I can be comfortable with what I might call language accommodation: providing all citizens with linguistic access to civic life but defending their freedom to choose also which language best represents their social, cultural, and religious identity.

Questioning language management like this may seem to move us beyond the spheres of language policy and educational linguistics into fundamental questions of identity and philosophy, but it is a reasonable step in a study of both fields. At the same time, it is only fair to note that most scholars in the field tend toward activist positions, assuming that their expertise in various aspects of educational linguistics gives them responsibility as well as ability to attempt to manage language education. In editing this handbook, we too accept this responsibility, if with a continuing modicum of skepticism and modest doubt.

In planning the book, we selected what we considered the more central areas of educational linguistics and added other fields in which there has been relevant research and publication over the last few decades. We divided the 44 commissioned chapters into three clusters. For each chapter, we invited the scholar we believed could give the best description of the development, current state, and future prospect of the topic. We also encouraged contributors to choose a colleague to add a wider perspective. This reflected our decision on joint editorship, and the fact that Francis M. Hult has written the second chapter recounting and analyzing the history of the field, which I personally found very revealing.

The first cluster of chapters presents the foundational background, setting out the knowledge derived from neurobiology, linguistic theory, psychology, sociology, anthropology, and politics relevant to educational linguistics and the educational systems in which it operates. Language, it has come to be realized especially since the work of Chomsky, is embodied in the brain, and growing knowledge of the brain is therefore relevant if not yet directly applicable (Schumann, 2006). Thus the section opens with a chapter on neurobiology by Laura Sabourin and Laurie A. Stowe, further developed in the chapter on psycholinguistics by Tej K. Bhatia and William C. Ritchie. Basically, a central principle of all the chapters in this section is the realization that the core fields do not have direct application but rather set possibilities and have implications for activity. Applied linguists, I suggested earlier (Spolsky, 1970), are somewhat like little boys with hammers looking for something to hit; one notes the ease with which some of them moved from structurally based language textbooks to transformational exercises. A much more reasonable discussion of the relevance of linguistic theory to education is presented in the chapter by Richard Hudson. At the same time, as the work of Labov and other sociolinguists has shown us, all varieties of language and their uses are contextualized in social settings, depending on common co-construction and the interplay of social and linguistic structures and patterns. That gives importance to the fields of sociolinguistics and sociology of language presented by Rajend Mesthrie. Much of the understanding of social contextualization was also a result of work in the foundation field of linguistic anthropology, discussed in the chapter by Stanton Wortham. The inevitable effect of code choice on power relationships, the realization that choice of language for school and other functions has major power to include or exclude individuals, has taught many people to take what is often called a "critical" approach and ask who benefits from decisions about choice. Thus, while educational linguistics tries like most other disciplines to achieve a measure of scientific objectivity, it is often committed and regularly interpreted as being on one side or the other in the politics of education. These aspects are discussed in a chapter on the political matrix of linguistic ideologies by Mary McGroarty. It is finally important to note that linguistics is not the sole core area, but educational linguistics draws equally on such other relevant fields as anthropology, sociology, politics, psychology, and education itself. This opening section is tied together by an essay by Joseph Lo Bianco on educational linguistics and education systems.

In the centre of the volume, we include 25 chapters dealing with specific themes or sub-areas of educational linguistics that show the synthesis of the knowledge from the theoretical foundations in Part I. The first group of papers in this part picks up my original question about the nature of the language barrier between home and school (Spolsky, 1971, 1974a). A chapter by Stephen L. Walter reviews the evidence concerning the choice of language of instruction in schools: all major empirical studies support the UNESCO-proclaimed belief in the value of initial instruction in the language that children bring with them from home, and suggest that it takes at least five or six years of careful preparation in some model of bilingual education before most pupils are ready to benefit fully from instruction in the national official school language. Unfortunately, the reality is far different, with the majority of governments and education departments satisfying themselves with at most one year of preparation before launching into teaching in a standard language.

Other chapters look at the home–school gap. Iliana Reyes and Luis C. Moll focus on cultural as well as linguistic differences between home and school. Jeffrey Reaser and Carolyn Temple Adger tackle the difficult situation that arises when the home language is stigmatized as a dialect or nonstandard. In the next chapter, Samuel J. Supalla and Jody H. Cripps consider the relevance of the language barrier to the education of the Deaf, a group now increasingly recognized by some as analogous to a linguistic or ethnic minority. In a chapter by Carolyn McKinney and Bonny Norton, new definitions of literacy are shown to be related to developments of multiple identities in modern societies. In the final chapter in this group, dealing with postcolonialism and globalization in language education, Hyunjung Shin and Ryuko Kubota attempt to analyze causes, looking at the effects of colonization and its aftermaths and the growing pressure of globalization.

The second group of chapters in this part deals specifically with language education policy and management. The chapter by Brian North describes work in Europe to define common goals for foreign language teaching, the major effort to revise language teaching in Europe in response to the development of the European Community. The second chapter in the section, by Richard B. Baldauf, Jr., Minglin Li, and Shouhui Zhao, considers language teaching inside and outside schools. The third chapter, on language cultivation in developed contexts by Jiří Nekvapil, presents the theories and practices of language management cultivation initially developed by the Prague School of linguists who were interested in the elaboration of developed literary languages at a time when the American school of language planning was tending to concentrate on the issues faced by previously underdeveloped languages. M. Paul Lewis and Barbara Trudell next describe the work continuing with language cultivation in underdeveloped contexts, such as the development of writing systems, the choices involved in adapting vernacular languages to school and other uses, and the sharing of functions with standard languages. In a chapter on ecological language education policy, Nancy H. Hornberger and Francis M. Hult explore specific directions for the application of the ecology of language approach to the study of language policy and planning in education. Writing about education for speakers of endangered languages, Teresa L. McCarty, Tove Skutnabb-Kangas, and Ole Henrik Magga look at the extreme cases, presenting arguments for the involvement of education systems in the preservation of endangered languages. The final chapter in this section by Yun-Kyung Cha and Seung-Hwan Ham adds a note of realism or sounds the tocsin, presenting evidence of the rapid invasion of primary education throughout the world by the spread of English and its impact.

In the third group of articles in this part, the central theme is literacy. Thirty years ago, one might have been satisfied with a chapter on the teaching of reading, but now there is separate treatment of literacy in general by Glynda A. Hull and Gregorio Hernandez, vernacular and indigenous literacies by Kendall A. King and Carol Benson, religious and sacred literacies by Jonathan M. Watt and Sarah L. Fairfield, and the particular approaches to multiliteracies that have developed out of M. A. K. Halliday's alternative view of linguistic theory in a chapter on genre and register in multiliteracies by Mary Macken-Horarik and Misty Adoniou. Literacy is much more than reading, as studies of the various functions and varied literacy environments is starting to show.

The fourth group of papers in Part II picks up major themes in second language acquisition, a term, coined after the transformational revolution, that is perhaps crying out for a new name as it adds social context to psycholinguistic models. Kathleen Bardovi-Harlig and Llorenç Comajoan tackle the problem of the order of acquisition that started to be studied in the light of Chomsky's claim that language was innate rather than learned. Kathleen C. Riley takes a different perspective, looking at research encouraged by anthropology into the process of language socialization. The next three chapters cover what have become traditional second language acquisition themes: the nature of interlanguage and the influences one language has on learning another language (Peter Skehan); the extent to which the language learner is able to reach the proficiency or competence level of the native speaker and whether this is biologically or otherwise determined (David Birdsong and Jee Paik); and the continuing debate as to whether natural exposure to a new language must be supplemented by explicit teaching and focus on forms (Rod Ellis).

The last five chapters in this part deal with language assessment, not just as 20 years ago they might have done by simply describing various kinds of language testing, but now starting with a sociologically anchored and ethically informed discussions of language assessment for inclusion or exclusion (immigrants, asylum seekers, minorities) with Lyle F. Bachman and James E. Purpura asking whether language assessment acts as Gate-Keeper or Door Opener. The chapter by Ari Huhta describes recent work in diagnostic and formative assessment, the difficulty of which is slowly being made clear. In the next chapter, Alan Davies discusses ethical approaches to accountability and standards, recognizing the tensions that remain unresolved. Next, the potential of scales and frameworks, increasingly used but still challenged, is discussed by Neil Jones and Nick Saville. Finally, the effects of attempts at national standardization particularly in the United States, are analyzed by Micheline Chalhoub-Deville and Craig Deville. The recurring interest in language use and policy relevance is evident.

The third part of the book has a number of chapters exploring the relationship between research and practice. Teresa Pica summarizes recent work on task-based learning, moving emphasis from form to use. Susan M. Conrad and

Kimberly R. LeVelle outline developments in instructional approaches that take advantage of current work in corpus linguistics: taking advantage of the computer, we now have access to information about language use that would once have taken decades of painstaking work to obtain. Interaction, output, and communicative language learning are described in a chapter by Merrill Swain and Watara Suzuki. Lesley Rex and Judith Green look at actual language use inside the classroom. Carol Chapelle describes current trends in computer-assisted language learning, a field I was working on 40 years ago in Bloomington but that has grown with the greater power of computers. The final chapters open wider perspectives. Leo van Lier presents an ecological perspective on educational linguistics within the context of semiotics. There are two concluding and summarizing chapters. Frances Bailey, Beverley Burkett, and Donald Freeman present a classroom agenda in which they tackle the complex question of what educational linguistics the language teacher should know. In the final chapter, Paola Uccelli and Catherine Snow propose a research agenda for the field, identifying gaps that remain untackled.

This is an appropriate place to express thanks and appreciation to the people (Ada Brunstein, Sarah Coleman, Danielle Descoteaux, and Haze Humbert) at Blackwell Publishing, now incorporated in John Wiley & Sons, for the idea of this series and this volume, and for all their help in producing it. Especial thanks to my co-editor, Francis Hult, who took a full share of planning the volume and a larger measure of the detailed tasks of seeing it through to press. Of course, our greatest debt of gratitude is to the contributors: presented with a title and a suggestion of scope, they have written fascinating chapters which do not merely describe but also advance significantly their piece of the field.

This handbook describes and celebrates 30 years of research and publication in the field of educational linguistics relevant to language education management. The individual chapters trace the breadth of interest and offer innovative views of past developments and possible future trends. While there are probably good pragmatic reasons why the field will never be fully institutionalized (there are programs in educational linguistics at only a few pioneering universities), the book will provide guidance for those working in a variety of academic departments and especially for those training others to participate.

Looking at the history of the last century, it is encouraging to note that there has been improvement in the number of people with access to education, especially in less developed parts of the world and in particular for women. But it is regrettable that this increase in quantity has not been reflected in any dramatic improvement in quality. A good deal of the blame falls, we argue, on the failure to deal with the language barrier to education and the matching failure to remedy the effects of hegemonic monolingual education in a language not well enough known by the richly pluralistic pupils in schools. The field of educational linguistics offers a way to tackle this issue, and the increasing professionalization of the field signaled among other things by the publication of this handbook is an important step in this process.

REFERENCES

Cooper, Robert L. (1989). *Language Planning and Social Change*. Cambridge: Cambridge University Press.

Corson, David (ed.) (1997). *Encyclopedia of Language and Education* (8 vols.). Dordrecht, The Netherlands: Kluwer Academic Publishers.

Davies, Alan (2006). Review of *Directions in Applied Linguistics: Essays in honour of Robert B. Kaplan*. *Applied Linguistics*, 27(3), 534–537.

Schumann, John H. (2006). Summing up: Some themes in the cognitive neuroscience of second language acquisition. *Language Learning Journal*, 56(s1), 313–319.

Spolsky, Bernard (1970). Linguistics and language pedagogy: Applications or implications? In James E. Alatis (ed.), *Twentieth Annual Round Table on Languages and Linguistics* (pp. 143–155). Washington, DC: Georgetown University Press.

Spolsky, Bernard (1971). The language barrier to education. In George E. Perren (ed.), *Interdisciplinary Approaches to Language* (pp. 8–17). London: CILT.

Spolsky, Bernard (1974a). Linguistics and the language barrier to education. In Thomas A. Sebeok, Arthur S. Abramson, Dell Hymes, Herbert Rubenstein, Edward Stankiewicz, & Bernard Spolsky (eds.), *Current Trends in Linguistics: Linguistics and adjacent Arts and Sciences* (vol. 12, pp. 2027–2038). The Hague: Mouton.

Spolsky, Bernard (1974b). The Navajo Reading Study: an illustration of the scope and nature of educational linguistics. In J. Quistgaard, H. Schwarz, & H. Spong-Hanssen (eds.), *Applied Linguistics: Problems and Solutions: Proceedings of the Third Congress on Applied Linguistics, Copenhagen, 1972* (vol. 3, pp. 553–565). Heidelberg: Julius Gros Verlag.

Spolsky, Bernard (1978). *Educational Linguistics: An Introduction*. Rowley, MA: Newbury House.

Spolsky, Bernard (ed.) (1999). *Concise Encyclopedia of Educational Linguistics*. Amsterdam/New York: Elsevier.

Stubbs, Michael (1986). *Educational Linguistics*. Oxford/New York: Basil Blackwell.

2 The History and Development of Educational Linguistics

FRANCIS M. HULT

Introduction

Educational linguistics is an area of study that integrates the research tools of linguistics and other related disciplines of the social sciences in order to investigate holistically the broad range of issues related to language and education (Hornberger, 2001; Spolsky, 1978). As an area of inquiry, educational linguistics is young. Its naissance occurred in the early 1970s with the work of Bernard Spolsky. The history of educational linguistics is inextricably linked to applied linguistics, with which it continues to have a symbiotic relationship. At the same time, educational linguistics has developed a unique niche in its directed focus on language and education. This chapter recounts the emergence of this niche and the development of the nature and scope of educational linguistics.

Applied Linguistics and the Precursors of Educational Linguistics

Applied linguistics as an articulated field of study is itself only about 60 years old, although Phillipson traces the concept to the work of nineteenth-century scholars such as Rasmus Rask and Jan Baudouin de Courtenay (Phillipson, 1992: 175). Markee (1990, citing Howatt, 1984) and Phillipson (1992: 175) report that the term has been used since 1948 in the journal title *Language Learning: A Quarterly Journal of Applied Linguistics*. About ten years later the term is used in Britain for the first time as "a label for serious intellectual and academic activity" in naming the School of Applied Linguistics at the University of Edinburgh (Strevens, 1980: 28). In 1959, the Center for Applied Linguistics (CAL) was founded under the leadership of Charles Ferguson, with the specific mission to serve as a multidisciplinary resource base for second language learning (Center for Applied Linguistics, 2006). The Association Internationale de Linguistique Appliquée (AILA) was organized in 1964 at a colloquium in Nancy, France that featured strands in the psychology of second language learning, sociolinguistics, and contrastive linguistics (Association Internationale de Linguistique Appliquée, 2003). In 1967, the British Association for Applied Linguistics (BAAL) held its founding meeting (Mitchell, 1997: 5). As Brumfit notes, the primary areas of interest for the British association would be "the study of language use, language acquisition and language teaching, and the fostering of inter-disciplinary collaboration in this study . . ." (1996: 1, citing the BAAL constitution).

The seeds were planted for an American Association for Applied Linguistics in the early 1970s. A first attempt was made in 1973 to form a subsection for applied linguistics within the Linguistic Society of America (LSA) but the notion was ultimately not well received by the society's membership; however, a subsequent special interest group under the chairmanship of Bernard Spolsky that was formed within the Teachers of English to Speakers of Other Languages (TESOL) association proved to be more fruitful (Kaplan, 1980a: v–vi). Indeed, during a roundtable discussion on the scope of applied linguistics at the 1977 TESOL Convention, the formation of an American Association for Applied Linguistics was seriously discussed and efforts were made during the summer of 1977 to begin the process (Kaplan, 1980a: vi). The American Association for Applied Linguistics (AAAL) formally took shape with a constitutional meeting held on November 24, 1977 in tandem with the meeting of the American Council on the Teaching of Foreign Languages (ACTFL) (Kaplan, 1980a: vi). Today applied linguistics thrives around the world, as evidenced by the presence of AILA-affiliated national organizations in 34 countries.

Considering the provenance of applied linguistics as reflected in the development of professional associations it is, perhaps, no surprise that it has come to be closely associated with language pedagogy. Yet this certainly does not fully define applied linguistics. A clear definition remains somewhat elusive, however, since the field has suffered from an identity crisis as long as it has been in existence. The identity crisis seems to follow from two major concerns that have long been fundamental for applied linguists: an uneasy relationship with the discipline of linguistics and uncertainty about the precise scope of applied linguistics. These concerns were central as the field took shape (Kaplan, 1980b) and continue to be salient today (Bruthiaux et al., 2005). I will explore them each in turn here because they have both been central to the emergence of educational linguistics.

Discussions surrounding the founding of AAAL are illustrative of the disciplinary tensions. There was a common belief that "applied linguists perform a *mediating* function between theoretical disciplines and various kinds of more practical work" (Buckingham and Eskey, 1980: 2).[1] A principal concern, given the moniker applied linguistics, is the primacy of the discipline of linguistics in that process. Applied linguists have long had differing views on this issue, as reflected in the statements about the scope of applied linguistics solicited by the TESOL special interest group in 1977 (Kaplan, 1980b: 4–20). Some viewed applied linguistics as reflecting the elements of linguistics that are relevant to other disciplines while others saw applied linguistics as superseding linguistics. The conundrum faced by applied linguistics is nicely summarized in the words of Thomas Buckingham:

> First, the very name which we have chosen to identify ourselves is misleading and inadequate, both too narrow and too broad. It limits us, seemingly, to applications of linguistics to language teaching without regard for the multitude of other disciplines vital to our success – sociology, psychology, anthropology, speech pathology and speech communication, pedagogy, learning theory, philosophy, literature – on and on . . .
>
> To encompass within applied linguistics all of the disciplines which might appropriately apply, on the other hand, we risk destroying all of the meaning of the term applied linguistics: because it is everything, it is nothing. (1980: 5–6)

If applied linguistics were to be allied with linguistics alone, applied linguists would be limited to linguistics for theoretical approaches to the multitude of issues with which they are concerned. Furthermore, applied linguistics might be doomed to forever play second fiddle to the discipline of linguistics from whence all theoretical underpinnings would come (Markee, 1990: 317–318). If, on the other hand, applied linguistics could be allied with any and all disciplines which might seem relevant, would applied linguistics then be anything but a patchwork of disciplinary foundations? The debate continues today.

A close connection to the discipline of linguistics is no longer problematic for some applied linguists. In the early days of applied linguistics there was an attempt to set it apart from a limited view of language phenomena, which many scholars saw reflected in the discipline of linguistics, in order to achieve a more practical understanding that could be applied to issues in education and other domains of life (Palmer, 1980: 21–22). It must be kept in mind that applied linguistics came of age at a time when, at least in the American context, the discipline of linguistics was preoccupied with decontextualized formal elements of language (Buckingham & Eskey, 1980: 1). Applied linguistics, along with the emerging field of sociolinguistics (e.g., Labov, 1972; Hymes, 1974), set out to focus on language practices in social context in contrast to the approach of linguistics proper. Today, as Widdowson (2001) suggests, the discipline of linguistics is arguably more focused on language in context than it once was, which blurs the line between linguistics and applied linguistics such that applied linguistics must cultivate its unique perspective on language and social practice in a dynamic and complementary relationship with linguistics. Accordingly, the linear flow from theoretical linguistics to applied linguistics to practice, which applied linguists found problematic in the 1960s and 1970s, has given way to a more reciprocal view where these three areas mutually inform one another (Shuy, 1981: 457–458). As Brumfit remarks, "Applied Linguistics is emerging as an integrated discipline, feeding in to Linguistics technically sophisticated statements about language in genuine social situations, on the one hand, and responding to the needs of practitioners, on the other" (1996: 10).

A close connection to linguistics, or even any discipline, is problematic for other applied linguists. Strevens suggests that applied linguistics is best considered a "multi-disciplinary approach to the solution of language-related problems" (1989: 9, cited in Markee, 1990: 316). In his view, linguistics is one among many disciplinary foundations that are relevant to the practical work of applied linguistics. In this way, applied linguistics may draw upon or inform a variety of disciplines, but as a field it is not beholden to the theoretical underpinnings of any one discipline. By extension, this means that it is not theory, often tied to a disciplinary foundation, that drives applied linguistic research but research into practical matters that calls upon theory (Markee, 1990: 317). This notion has led another applied linguist to go even a step further. Describing his vision for applied linguistics, Halliday writes:

> "I say 'transdisciplinary' rather than 'inter-' or 'multidisciplinary' because the latter terms seem to me to imply that one still retains the disciplines as the locus of intellectual activity, while building bridges between them, or assembling them into a collection; whereas the real alternative is to supercede them, creating new forms of activity which are thematic rather than disciplinary in their orientation." (2001: 176)

Applied linguists, in this view, are ideally not fettered to any one, or even several, disciplinary orientation(s); they are free to use any and all of the research tools in which they have been trained in order to investigate a specific issue holistically. That is to say, any one researcher will have a tool kit of research and analysis methods based on her/his training. The researcher, upon identifying a specific theme or issue to be explored, then draws upon the necessary tools to construct a multi-dimensional study of that theme or issue.

The central difference between inter-/multidisciplinarity and transdisciplinarity is the starting point. In inter-/multidisciplinary inquiry a researcher begins with the epistemology of a certain set of disciplines and then seeks to make connections among them in order to arrive at a depth of understanding, beyond what would be possible in a single discipline alone, to apply to a research case. In transdisciplinary inquiry the researcher begins with a theme (an issue, concern, problem, etc.) and then draws upon relevant methodological and analytical resources to investigate it. To parrot Halliday, this approach removes the locus of intellectual activity from disciplines, superseding them to place the locus on a theme (Hornberger & Hult, 2006: 78). The concept of themes brings us to the second major concern of applied linguists: What is the scope of themes in applied linguistics?

Applied linguistics has had a broad scope since its inception, but it is language and education that has come to be dominant. As Shuy remarks, early formulations of applied linguistics in the 1950s included a wide range of topics such as "linguistic geography, usage, teaching grammar and composition, the dictionary and literature" in addition to teaching English as a second language (1981: 458). Other areas include translation, lexicography, general language planning (Spolsky, 1978: 1), rhetoric and stylistics, language for specific purposes (LSP), and forensic linguistics. It is largely through historical and political circumstances that language and education, especially as it relates to English language teaching (ELT), became prominent in applied linguistics.

While ELT was gaining momentum in the 1960s and booming by the 1970s, in large part as a result of funded efforts to promote ELT around the world, many of the other areas which were included under applied linguistics either received much less attention (e.g., linguistic geography and lexicography) or became the object of interest of other developing areas of study (e.g., usage becoming the focus of sociolinguistics) (Shuy, 1981: 458–459; Phillipson, 1992: 174–175; cf. Smith, 2003). The establishment of the Center for Applied Linguistics in 1959 was a watershed moment in US applied linguistics and certainly served to solidify a link to language education. "The major thrusts in applied linguistics in the past twenty years, then, are," Shuy comments, ". . . language teaching, dialect studies, bilingual education and foreign language learning" (1981: 459). In the 25 years since Shuy made this observation, it is clear that applied linguistics remains as diverse in its scope today as when it first emerged. One need only look at the thematic strands of the 2008 International Association of Applied Linguistics conference to see that nearly every topic originally conceived of as part of applied linguistics is still represented (see also Bruthiaux et al., 2005 for an edited volume representing the state of applied linguistics).[2] Nonetheless, the predominant notion of applied linguistics is that is serves the needs of language teaching, particularly ELT (Phillipson, 1992: 174–181; Widdowson, 2001). Still, while language and education may be a major focal area from which themes in applied linguistics come, it is certainly not the only area of research that falls under the purview of applied linguistics.

The Emergence of Educational Linguistics

The problems and controversies regarding the nature and scope of applied linguistics were driving forces in Spolsky's decision to formulate a more precise designation for the constellation of research specifically related to language and education. Reflecting on the disciplinary relationships and the broad scope of intellectual activity that were advanced under applied linguistics, Spolsky began to carve a niche for educational linguistics.

Although Spolsky alluded to the term educational linguistics in a short newsletter article (Spolsky, 1971), he first set forth his vision for its nature in a presentation at the third AILA congress in 1972, later published in its proceedings (Spolsky, 1974). He subsequently published a seminal monograph on educational linguistics (Spolsky, 1978), where he further elaborated on its nature and scope.

Spolsky (1978: vii) explains at the very beginning of his monograph that his decision to put forth the term educational linguistics grew from his 'discomfort' with the ambiguity of applied linguistics. This discomfort grew from the problems of nature and scope outlined earlier. He noted that the scope of applied linguistics as a whole encompasses a diverse array of research topics; language and education is just one among many. Accordingly, Spolsky felt that applied linguistics in its broad sense obscures the work specifically devoted to language and education. He also felt that to use applied linguistics in a narrow sense to refer to only language education research obscures the multiplicity of work being done within the field in other domains. In other words, the term applied linguistics was imprecise, disadvantaging everyone concerned.

His second major concern, echoed in applied linguistics more broadly as noted earlier, was with the position of the discipline of linguistics. Spolsky felt, like other applied linguists, that there is an implication in the term applied linguistics that linguistics is simply applied to issues of social practice. Such a unidirectional approach is undesirable and even dangerous, he noted, especially in education where attempts by linguists to insert their theories directly into practice have led to disastrous results in, for example, phonemic approaches to reading and audio-lingual approaches to general language learning (Spolsky, 1978: 2; 2003: 503). He suggested that a more dynamic and reciprocal approach would be desirable (Spolsky, 1978: 2). Moreover, disciplines other than linguistics should also be relevant to language education (Spolsky, 1978: 5).

Educational linguistics, for Spolsky, then, clearly emerged in relation to applied linguistics. Indeed, he specifies in his original paper that educational linguistics is a 'subgroup' within applied linguistics that "forms a coherent and logically unified field" (Spolsky, 1974: 554). His objective was not, as it has sometimes been misunderstood (e.g., Markee, 1990: 315; Davies, 2005: 40) to provide a new label for applied linguistics. Such misapprehensions stem from a view of applied linguistics as being solely occupied with language and education. His aim was to provide an umbrella under which research specifically about language and education, as opposed to all the other avenues of research within applied linguistics, would fit. Considering the dominance of language and education research in applied linguistics today, the delineation of educational linguistics might be especially important for establishing parity for the scholars not working in the domain of language and education!

Historical and intellectual connections to applied linguistics notwithstanding, the taxonomy of educational linguistics is somewhat less than clear. Spolsky himself variously describes it as a "*discipline-tampon* (one that mediates between theory and practice) or a *discipline-carrefour* (a crossroads or gatekeeping discipline for others)" (Spolsky, 2003: 502), a "unifying field" (1985: 3435), and, within the same monograph, as a "unified field within the wider discipline of applied linguistics" (1978: vii) and as "essentially a sub-field of linguistics" (1978: 2).

As Hornberger and Hult (2006: 76) note, rather than locating themselves within educational linguistics as a field unto its own, some researchers consider themselves to be linguists who do applied linguistics who do educational linguistics (e.g., van Lier, 1994; 1997: 95) while others view educational linguistics as an autonomous field (e.g., Christie, 1994: 97; Hornberger, 2001: 5). Much of the debate, no doubt, stems from broader discussions about the nature of the discipline of linguistics and its relationship to applied linguistics which was described earlier (cf. Brumfit, 1996).

Spolsky is clear in his foundational monograph that any and all fields and disciplines that illuminate language in education may be usefully integrated under educational linguistics, with linguistics, broadly conceived, playing a central role (Spolsky, 1978: 2–3). As such, educational linguistics brings together theoretical linguistics, sociolinguistics, psycholinguistics, and anthropological linguistics (Spolsky, 1978: 3–6; 1985: 3435) as well as neurolinguistics, clinical linguistics, pragmatics, and discourse analysis (Spolsky, 2003: 503). Many of these areas themselves represent an integration of linguistics and disciplines such as anthropology, neurobiology, psychology, and sociology. Any number of other disciplinary areas might be relevant as well, depending on the topic and/or the individual researcher.

Where educational linguistics fits academically is perhaps less important than its purpose and focus. Indeed, as Hornberger points out, it is here that educational linguistics has developed a distinctive niche: its "starting point is always the practice of education and the focus is squarely on (the role of) language (in) learning and teaching" (2001: 19). It is in the service of this objective that the nature and scope of educational linguistics have developed and continue to flourish.

Reflecting on the nature and scope of educational linguistics, Hornberger (2001) delineates three major dimensions that characterize it: it represents a reciprocal integration of linguistics and education, it provides in-depth analytical insight into a broad scope of issues related to language (and) learning, and it is problem-oriented in its focus on specific ways in which theory, research, policy, and practice inter-relate. It is this last dimension, I argue, that is the governing principle of educational linguistics. In the next section, I will discuss the importance of the problem-oriented nature, addressing how the synthesis of knowledge from multiple disciplines plays a central role. In the subsequent section I will treat the scope of educational linguistics, highlighting the reciprocal nature of research and practice.

The Nature of Educational Linguistics

In his early formulations, Spolsky (1974: 554; 1978: 2) envisioned a close relationship between educational linguistics and (applied) linguistics, much like the relationship between educational psychology and (applied) psychology. At the same time, Spolsky makes it clear in his description of educational linguistics that it must necessarily involve much more than linguistics. He writes, "language teaching takes place in a school and is closely tied to socio-logical, economic, political, and psychological factors. A good language educa-tion policy, or effective methods of implementation, will not ignore linguistics or its hyphenated fields but will represent much more than an application of linguistics" (1978: 2). Still, he notes that linguistics has a central role to play and it is in this area that most educational linguists will have their primary training. What is particularly noteworthy in Spolsky's original formulation, however, is his problem-oriented approach to doing educational linguistics (Hornberger, 2001: 9–11). It is here that educational linguistics, like applied linguistics more broadly, emerges as a transdisciplinary field (Hornberger & Hult, 2006: 77–79).

There is a striking similarity between Spolsky's problem-oriented approach and Halliday's notion of a transdisciplinary field that supersedes disciplines, "creating new forms of activity which are thematic rather than disciplinary in their orientation" (Hallilday, 2001: 176). For Spolsky, educational linguistics "start[s] with a specific problem and then look[s] to linguistics *and other relevant disciplines* for their contribution to its solution" (1978: 2, emphasis mine). This problem-oriented nature resonates with Halliday's theme-based formulation of transdisciplinarity. Likewise, Spolsky's charge to look to linguistics together with other relevant disciplines for solutions reverberates with Halliday's call to look beyond disciplines to create new forms of intel-lectual activity (Hornberger & Hult, 2006: 78). The transdisciplinary nature of educational linguistics is of importance to the individual researcher and to educational linguistics as a whole.

On the part of the individual researcher, the idea is that one does not simply apply disciplinary knowledge to a specific situation. Instead, in educational linguistics, the researcher starts with a problem (or theme) related to language and education and then "synthesizes the research tools in her/his intellectual repertoire to investigate or explore it" (Hornberger & Hult, 2006: 78). In most cases, many of the research tools to be synthesized will come from linguistics but certainly not linguistics alone (Hornberger, 2001: 8). Moreover, linguistics here does not refer only to a narrow conception of theoretical linguistics but to linguistics broadly conceived as the multiple systematic ways of studying language (Gee, 2001: 648–652). This may not be how the discipline of lin-guistics has come to be viewed in many contexts, but it follows an intellectual tradition of the *practice* of linguistics as it has been conceived by visionaries like Edward Sapir (Anderson, 1985: 219–221) and Dell Hymes (1974; 1980: 139–160). This is also fundamental to Spolsky's original vision for the role of linguistics in educational linguistics. He points to what he calls linguistics and "its hyphenated fields" (1978: 2) which, as noted earlier, have come to include a wide variety of approaches such as anthropological linguistics, clinical linguistics, discourse analysis, neurolinguistics, pragmatics, psycholinguistics, sociolinguistics, and theoretical linguistics. The individual educational linguist, trained in any number of combinations of these or other relevant areas of study, might have her or his home in a variety of different departments, including anthropology, applied linguistics, area studies, education, English, foreign languages, linguistics, psychology, and sociology. Common to all educational linguists, though, is training in critical thinking of a transdisciplinary nature (van Lier, 2004).

As Hornberger (2001: 9–11) illustrates, it is the problem-oriented nature of educational linguistics that drives it. Educational linguists are concerned with the dynamic ways in which theory, research, policy, and practice inter-relate. All work done under the rubric of educational linguistics, then, is focused on relationships not on theory, research, policy, or practice in isolation. More-over, recalling Hornberger (2001: 19), practice is the *starting point*. That is to say, educational linguists look to practice for problems or themes that need investigation and they look for ways to foster, as well as learn from, effective practice. An educational linguist is, as Rothery points out, an educator who is "likely to be sensitive to and knowledgeable about where the teacher is coming from in terms of an orientation to language and learning" (1996: 87). Moreover, as Brumfit (1997) suggests, some teachers are beginning to think of themselves as educational linguists. Practice is paramount in educational linguistics. Practice, in turn, is in a dialectic relationship with policy, so policy is also a keystone in educational linguistics. I shall return to this notion in the next section. Here I wish to highlight the importance of transdisciplinarity for the problem-oriented researcher.

In order to investigate the complex themes that emerge from educational practice, educational linguists must not only be trained in a variety of theoret-ical and analytical tools but also in critical thinking skills that prepare them to integrate these tools in systematic yet creative ways (van Lier, 2004: 188–191). As such, educational linguists are able to approach themes as they have hitherto not been approached before from bounded disciplines. Here, too, we see a difference between inter-/multidisciplinary and transdisciplinary thinking. Those who retain disciplines as the locus of intellectual activity view the integration of multiple perspectives as (potentially) problematic. For example, Widdowson writes:

> Interdisciplinarity is a notion that commands universal commendation, "a con-summation devoutly to be wished," in that it seems to provide for the possibility of seeing things more comprehensively from a diversity of perspectives at the same time. This is an appealing idea, but it is also an illusion. For it is simply not possible to see things from two different perspectives at the same time . . . [T]he requirement for disciplinary consistency and coherence must set limits on how much diversity you can accommodate, and how comprehensive your vision can be. (2005: 19)

Widdowson's argument presumes that a researcher is necessarily limited in her/his thinking, unable to creatively integrate conceptual notions in novel ways. The human spirit is not organized according to the knowledge bases of specific disciplines nor need the minds of researchers necessarily be fettered to them. To extend the metaphor of 'seeing' that Widdowson uses, perhaps the transdisciplinary researcher could be said by analogy to see with a compound eye, much like a fly on the wall. Let us not allow the limits of our metaphors to hamper our analytical thinking (Low, 2003). While we might physically *view* the objects of our research from only one vantage point at a time, we are certainly capable of *seeing* them in our minds from multiple perspectives simultaneously.

Indeed, it is training in precisely this kind of critical thinking that is an essential component of preparing educational linguistic researchers. In this regard, educational linguistics shares many characteristics with critical applied linguistics (van Lier, 2004: 188–191). *Critical* applied linguistics, as Pennycook notes, is especially concerned with "way[s] of going about applied linguistics that constantly [seek] to push our thinking in new and provocative ways" (2001: 169).[3] This, too, is the hallmark of educational linguistics. Researchers are called upon to use their intellectual repertoires in innovative ways with every new theme they investigate. This is not to suggest that individual researchers, as Widdowson holds, are not limited in how comprehensive their vision can be. Educational linguistics is decidedly diverse in both potential themes and conceptual approaches to investigating them such that few researchers, if any, could reasonably have a full command of all of them (Spolsky, 2003: 503). Each researcher can only draw upon those areas in which they have expertise. Together, though, educational linguists generate a body of knowledge greater than the sum of its parts. Here we see the importance of transdisciplinarity for educational linguistics as a whole.

In his seminal monograph, Spolsky calls for the 'reunification' of language teaching/learning, noting that "to divide it up into various curricular areas like first-language teaching, the teaching of reading, or the teaching of foreign languages leads to a serious loss of perspective" (1978: 172). In other words, myopic specialization obscures the bigger picture. As individuals, educational linguists produce a wealth of diverse transdisciplinary scholarship; however, it is important not lose sight of how the collection of this individual work forms a body of knowledge from which new ideas and implications can emerge. Individual educational linguists use their specific intellectual repertoires to seek novel interconnections between theory and practice in their research. This transdisciplinary research, when seen as a whole, may generate further novel interconnections between theory and practice than could any individual or even a subset of individuals. Educational linguistics as a transdiscipline, then, serves to generate new understandings of theory and practice beyond what is possible from specific disciplines (Martin, 1993: 141; Rothery, 1996: 88).

In all, educational linguistics as a field is multi-method in the diverse approaches individual researchers use in their work, pluricentric in the multiple academic platforms from which researchers operate, and holistic in the over-all body of knowledge produced with respect to language and education (Hornberger & Hult, 2006: 77). As a result, educational linguistics allows for

an integrated understanding of subjects that are normally seen as separate curricular areas as well as for the possibility of understanding all issues related
to language and education in a wider social context (Spolsky, 2003: 503). In
essence, as a whole educational linguistics develops in-depth knowledge on
a broad scope of themes (Hornberger, 2001: 11–18). Let us turn next to this
scope and the reflexive nature of research and practice.

The Scope of Educational Linguistics

In his original formulation, Spolsky indicates that "the primary task of the
educational linguist is to offer information relevant to the formation of
language education policy and to its implementation" (1974: 554). The focus
on educational practice, then, is both indirect and direct. On the one hand,
the knowledge generated in educational linguistics may be used to guide the
process of crafting sound educational language policy which is designed to
influence practice. On the other hand, this knowledge may be used to guide
sound teaching practice as it is implemented in relation to educational
language policy. The scope of educational linguistics, Spolsky later elaborates,
"is the intersection of linguistics and related language sciences with formal
and informal education" (1978: 2). Having already addressed the transdisciplinary nature of educational linguistics, let us turn to the focus on language
and education and the special place of policy.

The areas to which educational linguistics might be relevant are undeniably
vast. Spolsky has put forth broad areas such as "first or second language
pedagogy and the teaching of reading, spelling, writing, listening, and speaking" (2003: 503). He further suggests, following Carroll (1962), that the
ultimate goal is to arrive at an understanding of the sum total of individual,
institutional, and societal processes that factor into the learning of how to use
language for communication (Spolsky, 2003: 503). It follows from this notion
that educational linguists variously investigate a host of themes related to
individuals, the institutions they inhabit, and the societies in which both are
situated, all as they relate to language and education. The range of themes is
clearly great, as reflected, for example, in the *Encyclopedia of Language and
Education* (Corson, 1997; Hornberger, in press). The range of themes might
usefully be considered in terms of wider, though not necessarily mutually
exclusive, core themes like linguistically and culturally responsive education,
literacy development, acquiring a language, and language assessment, as
they have been grouped in this volume. Regardless of the theme, though, the
purpose is always to inform or to be informed by educational practice,
either directly or indirectly. Recalling the policy–practice dialectic alluded to
previously, let us return to the role of policy in educational linguistics.

Language policy as an area of study might be characterized as a quintes-
sential example of applied linguistics at work (Spolsky, 2005). Within language
policy is educational language policy, with which educational linguists are

primarily concerned. Educational language policy forms a part of wider national language planning, focusing specifically on the educational sector as "the transmitter and perpetuator of culture" (Kaplan & Baldauf, 1997: 123). It is, as such, a rather high stakes area of language planning that serves political, social, and economic agendas (Shohamy, 2006: 77). Education is a domain where children spend many years of their lives under systematic obligatory government control; thus, it is a domain unique in its ability to influence lifelong language behavior (Fishman, 2006: 321). The values and beliefs that are pervasive in public discourses find their way into educational language policies (McGroarty, 2002: 19–22). Educational linguists must seek to understand the societal implications of policies designed to influence education by exploring how language education policies affect both dominant and minority groups, how policies can be tools for equality, inequality, marginalization, and integration (Tollefson, 2002: 3–4).

These points of concern also serve to highlight the particular importance of educational linguistics for diverse societies where multiple languages and cultures are in contact. In today's globally inter-connected world, there is effectively no place on earth that is not in some way affected by multilingualism (Calvet, 1999). In most cases, it is an illusion to believe that a language education policy targets a truly monolingual situation (Spolsky, 1978: 170–171).

All of this is not to suggest that every educational linguist is a language policy researcher, nor that educational linguistics is subsumed by the field of language policy. The point is that all work in educational linguistics, the research conducted by individual scholars and the knowledge generated by the field as whole, must be relevant to educational practice as it is envisioned in policy and implemented in teaching and learning. Educational linguists must be committed to working with policymakers and educators to ensure that the needs of all students are met by informed, linguistically responsible pedagogy. In order to achieve this, every educational linguist must have a vision for their work that includes a broader understanding of where it fits in relation to the work of other scholars as well as how it serves to advance education.

Conclusion

With its roots in the controversies of applied linguistics, educational linguistics has grown into a thriving field of inquiry focused on language (and) education. Its transdisciplinary nature has allowed it to flourish in a wide range of disciplinary climates. While this wide range has resulted in an impressively diverse body of knowledge with great potential to influence educational practice, it has also made it challenging to develop a sense of cohesion for educational linguistics as a whole. Now is the time for educational linguists to take stock of the field, develop mutual understanding for each others' work, and consider how the current body of knowledge can be put to use strategically.

NOTES

1   The mediating function of applied linguistics remains central for many applied linguists. See Widdowson (2001) for a thorough discussion.
2   See the thematic strands of the International Association of Applied Linguistics online at http://www.aila2008.org/en/thematic-strands.html
3   Widdowson also espouses a similar kind of critical thinking, though he views it primarily as a tool for mediating between disciplinary discourses, not superseding them. For Widdowson, to be critical means "taking a plurality of perspectives into account so as to mediate between them, seeking points of reciprocity and correspondence as a basis for accommodation" (2001: 16).

REFERENCES

Anderson, S. R. (1985). *Phonology in the Twentieth Century: Theories of Rules and Theories of Representations*. Chicago: The University of Chicago Press.

Association Internationale de Linguistique Appliquée (2003). History of AILA. Retrieved on June 10, 2006 from http://www.aila.info/about/history/index.htm

Brumfit, C. (1996). Educational linguistics, applied linguistics and the study of language practices. In G. M. Blue & R. Mitchell (eds.), *Language and Education* (pp. 1–15). Clevedon, UK: British Association for Applied Linguistics and Multilingual Matters.

Brumfit, C. (1997). The teacher as educational linguist. In L. van Lier & D. Corson (eds.), *Encyclopedia of Language and Education, Vol. 6: Knowledge about Language* (pp. 163–172). Boston: Kluwer Academic Publishers.

Bruthiaux, P., Atkinson, D., Eggington, W. G., Grabe, W., & Ramanathan, V. (eds.) (2005). *Directions in Applied Linguistics*. Clevedon, UK: Multilingual Matters.

Buckingham, T. (1980). No title. In R. B. Kaplan (ed.), *On the Scope of Applied Linguistics* (pp. 5–7). Rowley, MA: Newbury House.

Buckingham, T. & Eskey, D. E. (1980). Toward a definition of applied linguistics. In R. B. Kaplan (ed.), *On the Scope of Applied Linguistics* (pp. 1–3). Rowley, MA: Newbury House.

Calvet, L.-J. (1999). *Pour une écologie des langues du monde* [Towards an Ecology of the World's Languages]. Paris: Plon.

Carroll, J. B. (1962). The prediction of success in intensive foreign language training. In R. Glaser (ed.), *Training Research and Education* (pp. 87–136). Pittsburgh, PA: University of Pittsburgh Press.

Center for Applied Linguistics (2006). *History*. Retrieved on September 29, 2006 from http://www.cal.org/about/history.html

Christie, F. (1994). Developing an educational linguistics for English language teaching: A systemic functional linguistic perspective. *Functions of Language* 1(1): 95–127.

Corson, D. (ed.) (1997). *Encyclopedia of Language and Education* (vols. 1–8). Boston: Kluwer.

Davies, A. (2005). *A Glossary of Applied Linguistics*. Mahwah, NJ: Lawrence Erlbaum.

Fishman, J. A. (2006). Language policy and language shift. In T. Ricento (ed.), *An Introduction to Language Policy: Theory and Method* (pp. 311–328). Malden, MA: Blackwell.

Gee, J. P. (2001). Educational linguistics. In M. Arinoff & J. Rees-Miller (eds.), *The Handbook of Linguistics* (pp. 647–663). Malden, MA: Blackwell.

Halliday, M. A. K. (2001). New ways of meaning: The challenges to applied linguistics. In A. Fill & P. Mühlhäusler (eds.), *The Ecolinguistics Reader: Language Ecology and Environment* (pp. 175–202). New York: Continuum. First published in *Journal of Applied Linguistics* 6 (1990), pp. 7–36.

Hornberger, N. H. (2001). Educational linguistics as a field: A view from Penn's program on the occasion of its 25th anniversary. *Working Papers in Educational Linguistics* 17(1–2): 1–26.

Hornberger, N. H. (in press). *Encyclopedia of Language and Education* (vols. 1–10). New York: Springer.

Hornberger, N. H. & Hult, F. M. (2006). Educational linguistics. In K. Brown (ed.), *Encyclopedia of Language and Linguistics* (2nd edn, pp. 76–81). Oxford: Elsevier.

Howatt, A. P. R. (1984). *A History of English Language Teaching*. Oxford: Oxford University Press.

Hymes, D. H. (1974). *Foundations in Sociolinguistics: An Ethnographic Approach*. Philadelphia: University of Pennsylvania Press.

Hymes, D. H. (1980). *Language in Education: Ethnolinguistic Essays*. Washington, DC: Center for Applied Linguistics.

Kaplan, R. B. (1980a). Introduction. In R. B. Kaplan (ed.), *On the Scope of Applied Linguistics* (pp. v–viii). Rowley, MA: Newbury House.

Kaplan, R. B. (ed.) (1980b). *On the Scope of Applied Linguistics*. Rowley, MA: Newbury House.

Kaplan, R. B. & Baldauf, R. B. (1997). *Language Planning: From Practice to Theory*. Clevedon, UK: Multilingual Matters.

Labov, W. (1972). The study of language in its social context. In J. B. Pride & J. Holmes (eds.), *Sociolinguistics: Selected Readings* (pp. 180–202). Harmondsworth: Penguin.

Low, G. (2003). Validating metaphoric models in applied linguistics. *Metaphor & Symbol* 18(4): 239–254.

Markee, N. (1990). Applied linguistics: What's that? *System* 18(3): 315–323.

Martin, J. (1993). Genre and literacy: Modeling context in educational linguistics. *Annual Review of Applied Linguistics* 13: 141–172.

McGroarty, M. (2002). Evolving influences on educational language policies. In J. W. Tollefson (ed.), *Language Policies in Education: Critical Issues* (pp. 17–36). Mahwah, NJ: Lawrence Erlbaum.

Mitchell, R. (1997). Notes on the History of the British Association for Applied Linguistics: 1967–1997. British Association for Applied Linguistics. Retrieved on June 10, 2006 from http://www.baal.org.uk/about_history.pdf

Palmer, J. D. (1980). Linguistics in *medias res*. In R. B. Kaplan (ed.), *On the Scope of Applied Linguistics* (pp. 21–27). Rowley, MA: Newbury House.

Pennycook, A. (2001). *Critical Applied Linguistics: A Critical Introduction*. Mahwah, NJ: Lawrence Erlbaum.

Phillipson, R. (1992). *Linguistic Imperialism*. Oxford: Oxford University Press.

Rothery, J. (1996). Making changes: Developing an educational linguistics. In R. Hasan & G. Williams (eds.), *Literacy in Society* (pp. 86–123). London: Addison Wesley Longman.

Shohamy, E. (2006). *Language Policy: Hidden Agendas and New Approaches*. New York: Routledge.

Shuy, R. (1981). Educational linguistics. *Die Neueren Sprachen* 80(5): 455–468.

Smith, R. C. (ed.) (2003). *Teaching English as a Foreign Language, 1912–1936: Pioneers of ELT* (vols. 1–5). London: Routledge.

Spolsky, B. (1971). The limits of language education. *The Linguistic Reporter* 13(3): 1–5.

Spolsky, B. (1974). The Navajo reading study: An illustration of the scope and nature of educational linguistics. In J. Quistgaard, H. Schwarz, & H. Spong-Hanssen (eds.), *Applied Linguistics: Problems and Solutions: Proceedings of the Third Congress on Applied Linguistics, Copenhagen, 1972* (vol. 3, pp. 553–565). Heidelberg: Julius Gros Verlag.

Spolsky, B. (1978). *Educational Linguistics: An Introduction*. Rowley, MA: Newbury House.

Spolsky, B. (1985). Educational linguistics. In T. Husén & T. N. Postlethwaite (eds.), *International Encyclopedia of Education* (pp. 3095–3100). Oxford: Pergamon.

Spolsky, B. (2003). Educational linguistics. In W. J. Frawley (ed.), *International Encyclopedia of Linguistics* (vol. 1, pp. 502–505). Oxford: Oxford University Press.

Spolsky, B. (2005). Is language policy applied linguistics? In P. Bruthiaux, D. Atkinson, W. G. Eggington, W. Grabe, & V. Ramanathan (eds.), *Directions in Applied Linguistics* (pp. 26–36). Clevedon, UK: Multilingual Matters.

Strevens, P. D. (1980). Who are applied linguists and what do they do? A British point of view offered upon the establishment of AAAL. In R. B. Kaplan (ed.), *On the Scope of Applied Linguistics* (pp. 28–36). Rowley, MA: Newbury House.

Strevens, P. D. (1989). *Applied Linguistics: An Overview*. Mimeo.

Tollefson, J. W. (2002). Introduction: Critical issues in educational language policy. In J. W. Tollefson (ed.), *Language Policies in Education: Critical Issues* (pp. 3–15). Mahwah, NJ: Lawrence Erlbaum.

van Lier, L. (1994). Educational linguistics: Field and project. In J. E. Alatis (ed.), *Georgetown University Roundtable on Language and Linguistics 1994* (pp. 197–209). Washington, DC: Georgetown University Press.

van Lier, L. (1997). Apply within, apply without? *International Journal of Applied Linguistics* 7(1): 95–105.

van Lier, L. (2004). *The Ecology and Semiotics of Language Learning: A Sociocultural Perspective*. New York: Kluwer Academic Publishers.

Widdowson, H. G. (2001). Coming to terms with reality: Applied linguistics in perspective. *AILA Review* 14: 2–17.

Widdowson, H. G. (2005). Applied linguistics, interdisciplinarity, and disparate realities. In P. Bruthiaux, D. Atkinson, W. G. Eggington, W. Grabe, & V. Ramanathan (eds.), *Directions in Applied Linguistics* (pp. 12–25). Clevedon, UK: Multilingual Matters.

Part I Foundations for Educational Linguistics

3 Neurobiology of Language Learning

LAURA SABOURIN AND LAURIE A. STOWE

Introduction

Some of the current issues in the field of language research include how language is organized in the brain, how we learn our first language (L1) as a child, whether we learn other languages (L2s) differently as we grow older, whether there are effects of critical or sensitive periods on our ability to learn language and on how we learn language, and how brain damage and atypical development affect language representation and processing. These issues are of interest to researchers in the fields of psychology, linguistics, education, neuroscience and speech language pathology, among others. In this chapter we hope to bring together research approaches and results from all of these fields in the belief that it is only through cross-disciplinary collaboration that answers to language questions can be answered. As background we will first discuss how language is organized in the brain and then we will discuss the four main techniques that are being used today to investigate language processing in the brain. We will then proceed to discuss the research issues with a focus on neuroimaging evidence and the potential importance of this type of evidence for the field of educational linguistics.

The Neurobiology of Language

According to the classical view, language is represented in the left hemisphere of the brain (for the majority of people) and two main brain regions are specialized for language functions; Broca's area (located in the inferior frontal lobe) and Wernicke's area (located in the posterior temporal lobe). The evidence for this view came largely from studies of brain damaged patients with language deficits. In early studies autopsies following death showed that portions of the left hemisphere of the brain were damaged while right hemisphere areas were intact. In 1865, Broca concluded from his patients that the left frontal lobe is responsible for speech. These patients had difficulty with language production. The specific area described as the locus (the left inferior frontal gyrus) is now called Broca's area. In 1874, Wernicke described two patients with profound deficits in language comprehension. The damaged brain area for these patients was found to be in the posterior part of the superior temporal gyrus of the left hemisphere. This region is now known as Wernicke's area. These production and comprehension sites are connected via the arcuate fasciculus. Later studies using Computed Tomography and Magnetic Resonance have confirmed these earlier studies using living patients (for a review see Price, 2000).

More recently, however, it has become clear that this view is too narrow for a full understanding of how language is processed in the brain. These new views come from advances in neuroimaging techniques. Instead of studying brain damaged patients, it is now possible to study language processing in the healthy human brain. In particular, it is now possible to see which areas in the brain normal volunteers activate while processing language by using haemodynamic techniques and to determine when these processes are taking place by using electrophysiological techniques. Localization techniques, summarized below, have provided a lot of support for involvement of the classical areas in language processing; electrophysiological methods have confirmed that a number of clearly separable processes occur during language processing. However, many findings also strongly suggest that the classical model needs to be updated, as the functions assigned to the classical language areas have been oversimplified and many other areas contribute to normal processing (for a review see Stowe, Haverkort, & Zwarts, 2005).

Brain Imaging Techniques

Neuroimaging methods provide a window into online processing of the brain during language tasks. Different techniques are sensitive to different aspects of language processing in the brain.

Where Techniques are haemodynamic (or blood flow) techniques such as functional magnetic resonance imaging (fMRI) and positron emission tomography (PET), which allow us to see where brain activity changes depending on the nature of the input or task being carried out. The logic behind studies using these techniques is that task demands cause increases in neuronal activity in those regions within the brain which support that aspect of cognition, causing an increase in the demand for blood to supply glucose and oxygen to the area. It is this regional change in blood flow that is measured. This is an indirect measure of neural processing, and since the increase in blood flow takes a few seconds to become visible after neuronal activity is initiated, the time resolution of blood flow change techniques are severely limited. These techniques are used to investigate issues of where particular aspects of language are processed. They have been used to address issues about whether different neural resources are needed to process language depending on the modality of the language (signed vs. auditory languages), for acquiring second languages (at different timelines), and to determine where language is processed in atypical populations. Although these techniques are most suitable to demonstrate qualitatively different neural organization (e.g., the use of a different set of anatomical regions to support language processing in these different populations), they can also address the issue of whether there are quantitative changes (e.g., relatively more or less use of a particular anatomical resource by different groups). We will return to how such differences have been interpreted below.

When Techniques are encephalographic techniques such as event-related potentials (ERP), which makes use of the electroencephalogram (EEG) measuring the electrical activity of neurons and the magnetoencephalogram (MEG) measuring the magnetic field generated by neuronal activity. These techniques are capable of fine temporal resolution. This allows researchers to see when different processes occur. As these techniques reflect the online activity of neurons, they provide a more direct measure of neural activity than the *where* techniques, but since the task-related signal change is very small relative to the amount of electrical and magnetic activity generated by the brain as a whole, they can only record the activity of large groups of neurons which are aligned with each other.

The signal to noise issue also means that to find ERP and MEG components many trials of a condition must be averaged together to find a part of the waveform time-locked to the event type of interest. The timelocked ERP waves include various positive and negative wave deflections. The ERP component is best thought of as an electrical current, which has one positive end and one negative end; both are integral to the signal and what can be measured on the surface of the scalp depends purely on the orientation of the flow of the current. ERP components are generally described in terms of their polarity (whether the voltage charge is positive or negative) and by their latency (the point in time, in milliseconds, at which the component begins or reaches its maximum). Other important aspects of ERP components are their amplitude and their scalp distribution. The scalp distribution reflects the location of the group of neurons which generates the signal. Although that location cannot be fully determined from the scalp distribution, when two different aspects of processing have a different scalp distribution, they cannot be generated by exactly the same brain sources.

These *when* and *where* techniques can be combined to determine when different aspects of language are processed and whether there are qualitative differences in the manner in which they are processed in terms of the underlying brain organization. Comparing different groups of language learners (L1, L2, and atypically developing groups), we can investigate whether there are qualitative differences in processing between groups (e.g., responses of a different type), or whether there are instead quantitative changes such as delays in time or in the size of the signal change. Furthermore, fine grained questions about the parameters of the groups can be investigated such as the role of age of acquisition or proficiency.

The developmental timecourse of language processing in the brain and the circumstances under which language learners show the typical adult L1 ERP responses will be presented below. There are three primary ERP components associated with normal adult language processing: the N400, the LAN, and the P600. The N400 is a negative component, peaking about 400 ms after presentation of a word, which is sensitive to semantic variables. The amplitude of the N400 component increases as a function of the difficulty of identifying a word and of integrating the critical word with a context. It is normally largest for unrelated or anomalous words or for non-words. The LAN (Left Anterior Negativity) is a negative component that is sensitive to syntactic effects and is somewhat variable in time of onset. Ungrammatical sentences elicit a larger LAN than grammatical sentences. The P600, a positive component peaking at around 600 ms after presentation of a word, is also sensitive to syntactic effects and is larger to grammatical violations and complex structures than to canonical sentences. For a more complete review of ERP results, see Kutas and Schmitt (2003). These three components will be discussed below in terms of their development in first and second language acquisition.

The Neurobiology of First Language Acquisition

During typical first language (L1) development, a child is able to acquire, within a few years, the phonology, lexicon, and syntax of any natural language that they are exposed to. This is done without any explicit instruction. Understanding the development of language is very important from both a scientific and societal viewpoint. The overall level of language ability that is obtained by individuals has a profound impact on their success in many other aspects of life. Improving our understanding of normal language development and how to optimize it, as well as how to treat and help those with language development disorders or with atypical development, will greatly help society. Here we will discuss different levels of language acquisition from a neurodevelopmental perspective. In this section we will focus on typical language development and processing followed by a section on the effects of delayed exposure on language acquisition.

Infants apparently come equipped at birth for the task of phonological acquisition with some perceptual processing biases which allow them to, among other things, discriminate both native and non-native phonetic contrasts. Within the first year, they show processing biases for well-formed syllables, the beginnings of word segmentation, and they are able to distinguish closed and open class words. During the first year of language development, following exposure to the ambient language, there is a progression from language-general to more language-specific speech sound discrimination. This language-general ability becomes refined as a function of listening experience, resulting in improved discrimination of native phonetic contrasts and poorer discrimination of non-native distinctions. For a discussion of infant phonological development see Werker and Tees (2005).

While much of the research leading to these conclusions has come from behavioral research, there is currently an influx of research at the neuroimaging level that supports these findings as well as adding more precise characterization of how phonological acquisition occurs. ERPs are also useful for investigating the finer points of the developmental trajectory, since they are relatively easy to collect from young children and continue to be measurable over a wider time range than most behavioral methods (e.g., high amplitude sucking and head turn paradigms). Recent ERP research suggests that the "decline" in non-native speech perception may actually not be a decline in discrimination of non-native phonemes, but rather an increase in neural responsiveness to native language speech sounds (Kuhl et al., 2006). This suggests that the possible mechanism for "tuning in" to the native language may work by augmenting the linguistic distinctions in the environment rather than, as was thought based on the behavioural findings, that infants actually "lose" the ability to perceive differences in non-native speech contrasts.

Infants clearly begin to acquire lexical knowledge within the first year of life. However, there is clear development in their sensitivity to phonological distinctions within words over the second year of life. Mills et al. (2004) demonstrated that 14-month-olds show clear N400-like responses to non-words as opposed to known words when the non-words are clearly distinct from the words. However, at 14 months, they do not distinguish known words from non-words which are phonologically very similar. This ability develops over the following months, with clear N400-like responses by the time the infants are 20 months old. By this age, children also show an N400-like effect to words which are semantically compatible with a picture context as opposed to incongruous with it (Friedrich & Friederici, 2005).

Syntactic perception also begins within the first year. It has been shown that 1-year-olds are capable of recognizing patterns of co-occurrence within even a relatively small set of input (i.e., an artificial grammar), which suggests that they are capable of recognizing such dependencies in natural language as well (Gomez & Gerken, 1999). The development of semantic and syntactic aspects of language proceeds over a much longer time than phonological perception. Children by around age 3 seem to have most of the language systems in place, in the sense that they in general produce lexical items in syntactically correct sequences, although learning will continue in both domains. However, that is not to say that their processing is completely adult-like even for those words and syntactic structures which they already know. The early effects discussed above differ considerably from the adult patterns in amplitude, latency, and sometimes even scalp distribution. In terms of the development of the N400 (which is sensitive to lexical and semantic processes), children show an adult-like pattern by age 6, though the onset of the effect continues to decrease with age, suggesting that processing becomes more efficient and less time-consuming

(Hahne, Eckstein, & Friederici, 2004). However, the development of syntactic processing seems to progress more slowly. At age 6, children do show a delayed reduced P600 effect to grammatical violations, but they do not yet reliably show the early negativity found in adult processing (although see Oberecker, Friedrich, & Friderici, 2005, for evidence that the effect can sometimes be seen quite early). The early negativity has been linked to efficient automatized processes, while the P600 may reflect effortful integration (Kaan et al., 2000), which again suggests that the automatization of language processing requires time. It is still not clear when syntactic processing becomes completely adult-like. Language proficiency may depend heavily on the degree to which learners are able to automatize. Examining the course of the acquisition of linguistic processes may eventually provide an interesting diagnostic for educational purposes. This path is currently being investigated in a number of projects on early identification of dyslexia (e.g., Espy et al., 2004).

It is clear from the discussion above that language acquisition takes place in stages, with some indications that phonological development normally precedes lexical and semantic acquisition and with complete syntactic development lagging behind. One of the important issues about the neurobiology of language development is the relationship between brain development and language acquisition. It is clear that the human brain is by no means fully developed at birth. There is considerable development of the brain after birth, with dendrites developing at least up to 5 years and chemical processes until the end of puberty (Uylings, 2001). Some systems are relatively well developed earlier than others; phonological processing may precede the other systems because it is relatively mature at birth. This suggests that the genetic predisposition for localization of functions within the brain and their developmental trajectory is central to the time course of language development. Conversely, language learning is frequently considered not to be as optimal after certain stages of brain development (critical or sensitive periods), just like the development of vision. The claim is that the brain becomes less plastic after some aspect of development is complete, so that late learning is less successful (sensitive period) or impossible (critical period). Since their developmental trajectories differ, it is possible that the different aspects of language have different sensitive periods. We will discuss this issue below. A third issue is the extent to which the presence of input determines brain development.

Effects of Delayed Language Exposure

The hypothesis of critical or sensitive periods for certain aspects of language acquisition raises the issue of the effects of receiving language input at times other than those optimum periods. When learning a second language (L2) later in life, there is no delay in exposure to language, but the exposure to the L2 is not within the normal period for language development. Here it is possible to investigate such effects as the role of language transfer and whether the same brain regions are recruited in first and second language learning. In the unfortunate case of deaf children that were unable to typically acquire a first language, language may not be available at all within the sensitive period.

There is both lesion and ERP evidence consistent with a critical link between input and brain development (Thal et al., 1991; Neville, Mills, & Lawson, 1992). The early lesion evidence also argues for a developmentally limited neural plasticity; early damage does have negative consequences, but they are not nearly as bad as later lesions in the same areas. Given the evidence presented above that different aspects of language have different developmental time courses, this suggests that different subsystems of language may be more vulnerable to disruption at different stages. Knowing when different functional subsystems are most vulnerable to damage and most open to experience is very important for educators.

Second language acquisition (SLA)

These days more and more of the world's population are learning second and foreign languages later in life, and knowing how the brain deals with this type of linguistic input would ideally help in focusing programs of language training. Compared to L1 acquisition, L2 acquisition rarely results in native-like fluency, possibly due to sensitive period effects. An alternative is that L1 interferes with L2 learning and leads to a less optimal result. Simply investigating the off-line language behavior of L2 speakers cannot decide between these two hypotheses. Using neuroimaging techniques that can tell us when and where language processing is occurring will bring us closer to answering this question.

This research area has produced very inconclusive results so far. Part of the complexity in determining whether L1 and L2 make use of the same neural resources is due to the difficulty in disentangling the effects of age of acquisition, level of proficiency, (dis)similarity between the L1 and L2, and whether the L2 was learned in a naturalistic manner or in a classroom. Adding to this difficulty is the fact that all of these effects are graded. Despite these difficulties there are some trends in the research. We will start with adult SLA, as it is clear that this group has acquired the L2 after any proposed sensitive period.

Recent reviews of language localization studies (Stowe & Sabourin, 2005; Indefrey, 2006) suggest that the normal language areas, including Broca's and Wernicke's, are also used to process L2. Thus it does not seem likely that totally different learning mechanisms are employed in SLA, which might have been predicted by a version of the critical period hypothesis in which the learning mechanisms cease to be available at all after a certain stage of brain development. This seems to be true independent of age of acquisition, and largely independent of proficiency as well.

However, L2 does appear to lead to quantitatively more activation in some of these areas, which under the logic of this sort of experiment suggests that the areas need to work "harder" to deal with L2. Under a different version of the sensitive period hypothesis we might argue that the regions of the brain that are optimally suited for language processing have been optimized for L1 processing during the sensitive period and thus are less available and less efficient for L2 processing. Such a view is consistent with needing to acquire input during a sensitive period in order to optimize processing, but is also a specific version of the L1 interference hypothesis.

The N400, which is sensitive to lexical and semantic factors, can be seen very early during L2 acquisition. After only 14 hours of instruction, learners showed a difference between words and non-words and after an average of 63 hours of instruction they showed semantic relatedness effects as well (McLaughlin, Osterhout, & Kim, 2004). These results suggest that L2 learners continue to acquire word phonology and semantics in a manner comparable to the first language. However, Hahne (2001) showed that relatively advanced Russian L2 learners of German showed less advantage in the N400 from a predictive sentence context (less decrease in N400 for predictable words) than native speakers and that the N400 effect elicited by unexpected words was clearly delayed. This latter result is similar to that found for children learning their L1 and can also be interpreted as being due to a lack of optimization for L2 processing. It is also compatible with the localization evidence that L2 requires more work than L1.

For syntactic processing, even relatively straightforward syntactic rules appear to be difficult to process in a completely native-like way. Sabourin (2003) showed that the relatively late P600 effect in response to ungrammaticality can be seen in relatively advanced L2 speakers. How native-like the response is appears to depend more on whether the grammatical structure involved is similar to one found in the native language than on general level of proficiency in the L2. As with the N400, the P600 is typically reduced and delayed for L2 learners, and may not appear at all for non-native structures. There is little evidence for the development of the LAN effect in any group of adult learners (Hahne, 2001).

Although adult L2 learners do not process their L2 in a totally native-like way, the patterns which they exhibit are in fact fairly similar to those found during the earlier stages of L1 acquisition. The LAN is difficult to find in early acquisition, and the N400 and P600 are delayed. In this sense, late learners do not show a qualitatively different acquisition pattern from normal L1 acquisition. As discussed above, for L1 learners the changes in these responses over time may reflect automatization of linguistic processes; this interpretation is thus equally valid for L2 learners.

This leads to the question whether L2 learners who have reached (near-)native levels of attainment would show adult L1 patterns in their syntactic processing, particularly if their L1 is similar to the L2. Despite the difficulty of finding late L2 speakers of a sufficient level of expertise, this question is well worth pursuing. It also brings up the issue of whether L2 learning during the sensitive period would lead to a more native-like processing pattern.

The most extensive study of which we are aware on this issue was carried out by Weber-Fox and Neville (1996), who compared six subject groups:

monolingual English speakers and Chinese L2 learners of English who began acquisition at 1–3, 4–6, 7–10, 11–13, and after 16 years. All groups showed clear N400 effects of semantic incongruency. However, the latency of the effect was delayed for the two later groups and latency and amplitude both correlated with age of acquisition. Similarly, the LAN and P600 effects were not substantially different from those found in the monolinguals for those groups that acquired their L2 at earlier ages (<11). We can conclude from these data that the mere existence of an L1 is not sufficient to prevent substantially native-like processing, which is incompatible with the account of L2 deficits which appeals to L1 interference as the only explanatory factor.

To sum up, both localization and ERP evidence are compatible with the view that the same brain structures and mechanisms are involved in acquisition of a first and a second language, both during and after the hypothesized sensitive periods. However, these areas do not appear to be used as efficiently in acquisition or processing of the L2. This is compatible with a view under which the automatization of using L1 proceeds optimally during the sensitive period and/or interferes with the optimization of L2. It should be noted however, that the effects of age of acquisition are not limited to L2; L1 words which are acquired later show similar signs of less efficient processing (Fiebach et al., 2003).

A delay in first language acquisition

Based on SLA research only, it is difficult to determine if changes due to neural maturation determine the optimum period of language acquisition. The unfortunate case of deaf children not being exposed to a language until they are taught a sign language allows us to investigate the effects of delayed exposure to language without the added confound of interference from a previously known language. Behavioral results suggest that late first language acquisition, as seen in the case of many deaf children acquiring American Sign Language (ASL) as a first language later in life, has a significant effect on proficiency (for discussion see Newport, 2002). However, here, as in SLA, semantics, as measured by the N400 ERP component, can be processed in a native-like manner while syntax, as measured by the LAN, is less native-like and is only evident in individuals who had acquired ASL before the age of 10 (see Neville, 2006 for an overview). These findings support the idea that automatic syntactic processing, indexed by the LAN, is particularly vulnerable to delays of language input. If there is a sensitive period for lexical semantics, it appears to be much more extensive.

The language processing of deaf adults who have learned ASL at varying times in their life does show effects of age of acquisition on their grammatical skills, even though they may not actually have knowledge of any other language. This suggests that the interference hypothesis for SLA does not apply to all cases of late language acquisition; there is something important about being exposed to a first language at a very early age.

Discussion and Future Directions

In this chapter, we have focused on issues related to brain and language development. Neuroimaging techniques can also be used to carry out research directed toward more practical issues. First, as discussed above, ERPs in particular provide a good method for examining the success of L2 learning. An issue of interest for educators is the extent to which various learning situations and training techniques affect success. This can be tested "in the wild," as in the studies discussed above, with all the uncontrolled variables of experience and motivation that learning a natural language entails. However, these studies contain many uncontrolled factors. Studies employing artificial grammars or mini-languages provide a more controllable option for investigating these issues.

Second, we mentioned that these methods have been used to examine the nature of language processing deficits in groups with developmental problems such as dyslexia. A very promising direction for future research is the application of these techniques to investigate the effectiveness of intervention programs geared toward improving language in young children at risk for language delay as well as child second language learners. It will be important here to look at patterns of brain activation both before and after these interventions to provide not only information about the efficacy of the language interventions, but also to help determine the effects of these interventions on brain organization.

REFERENCES

Espy, K. A., Molfese, D. L., Molfese, V. J., & Modglin, A. (2004). Development of auditory event-related potentials in young children and relations to word-level reading abilities at age 8 years. *Annals of Dyslexia*, 54(1), 9–38.

Fiebach, C. J., Friederici, A. D., Müller, K., Von Cramon, D. Y., & Hernandez, A. W. (2003). Distinct brain representations for early and late learned words. *NeuroImage*, 19, 1627–1637.

Friedrich, M. & Friederici, A. D. (2005). Phonotactic knowledge and lexical-semantic processing in one-year-olds: Brain responses to words and nonsense words in picture contexts. *Journal of Cognitive Neuroscience*, 17(11), 1785–1802.

Gomez, R. L. & Gerken, L. (1999). Artificial grammar learning by 1-year-olds leads to specific and abstract knowledge. *Cognition*, 70(2), 109–135.

Hahne, A. (2001). What's different in second-language processing? Evidence from event-related brain potentials. *Journal of Psycholinguistic Research*, 30(3), 251–266.

Hahne, A., Eckstein, K., & Friederici, A. D. (2004). Brain signatures of syntactic and semantic processes during children's language development. *Journal of Cognitive Neuroscience*, 16(7), 1302–1318.

Indefrey, P. (2006). A meta-analysis of hemodynamic studies on first and second language processing: Which suggested differences can we trust and what do they mean? *Language Learning*, 56, 279–304.

Kaan, E., Harris, A., Gibson, E., & Holcomb, P. (2000). The P600 as an index of syntactic integration difficulty. *Language and Cognitive Processes*, 15(2), 159–201.

Kuhl, P. K., Stevens, E., Hayashi, A., Deguchi, T., Kiritani, S., & Iverson, P. (2006). Infants show a facilitation effect for native language phonetic perception between 6 and 12 months. *Developmental Science*, 9(2), F1–F9.

Kutas, M. & Schmitt, B. M. (2003). Language in microvolts. In M. T. Banich & M. Mack (eds.), *Mind, Brain, and Language: Multidisciplinary Perspectives* (pp. 171–209). Mahwah, NJ: Lawrence Erlbaum.

McLaughlin, J., Osterhout, L., & Kim, A. (2004). Neural correlates of second-language word learning: Minimal instruction produces rapid change. *Nature Neuroscience*, 7(7), 703–704.

Mills, D. L., Prat, C., Zangl, R., Stager, C. L., Neville, H. J., & Werker, J. F. (2004). Language experience and the organization of brain activity to phonetically similar words: ERP evidence from 14- and 20-months olds. *Journal of Cognitive Neuroscience*, 16(8), 1452–1464.

Neville, H. J. (2006). Different profiles of plasticity within human cognition. In Y. Munakata & M. Johnson (eds.), *Processes of Change in Brain and Cognitive Dvelopment: Attention and Performance XXI* (pp. 287–314). Oxford: Oxford University Press.

Neville, H. J., Mills, D. L., & Lawson, D. S. (1992). Fractionating language: Different neural subsystems with different sensitive periods. *Cerebral Cortex*, 2(3), 244–258.

Newport, E. L. (2002). Critical periods in language development. In L. Nadel (ed.), *Encyclopedia of Cognitive Science* (pp. 737–740). London: MacMillan/Nature Publishing Group.

Oberecker, R., Friedrich, M., & Friederici, A. D. (2005). Neural correlates of syntactic processing in two-year olds. *Journal of Cognitive Neuroscience*, 17(10), 1667–1678.

Price, C. J. (2000). The anatomy of language: Contributions from functional neuroimaging. *Journal of Anatomy*, 197, 335–359.

Sabourin, L. (2003). Grammatical gender and second language processing: An ERP study. Unpublished doctoral dissertation, University of Groningen, The Netherlands.

Stowe, L. A. & Sabourin, L. (2005). Imaging the processing of a second language: Effects of maturation and proficiency on the neural processes involved. *IRAL*, 43, 329–353.

Stowe, L. A., Haverkort, M., & Zwarts, F. (2005). Rethinking the neurological basis of language. *Lingua*, 115, 997–1042.

Thal, D. J., Marchman, V., Stiles, J., Aram, D., et al. (1991). Early lexical development in children with focal brain injury. *Brain and Language*, 40(4), 491–527.

Uylings, H. B. M. (2001). The human cerebral cortex in development. In A. F. Kalverboer & A. A. Gramsbergen (eds.), *Handbook on Brain and Behaviour in Human Development* (pp. 63–80). Dordrecht: Kluwer Academic Press.

Weber-Fox, C. & Neville, H. J. (1996). Maturational constraints on functional specializations for language processing: ERP and behavioral evidence in bilingual speakers. *Journal of Cognitive Neuroscience*, 8(3), 231–256.

Werker, J. F. & Tees, R. C. (2005). Cross-language speech perception: Evidence for perceptual reorganization during the first year of life. *Infant Behavior & Development*, 25, 121–133.

4 Psycholinguistics

WILLIAM C. RITCHIE AND
TEJ K. BHATIA

The traditional domain of psycholinguistic research has been language acquisition in the child and language use in the adult, primarily in the monolingual context. However, psycholinguists have also turned their attention to bilingual and multilingual language processing (see, e.g., de Bot & Kroll, 2002: 133). The general recognition that bilingualism is not an exceptional phenomenon but is, in fact, a growing global trend, has presented new challenges for language researchers in general and psycholinguists in particular. This chapter approaches psycholinguistics primarily from the perspective of bi-/multilingualism. Such an approach is particularly imperative for educational linguistics because bilingualism and bi-dialectalism are fundamental issues in an educational setting. Since many of the central questions in psycholinguistics have been posed in terms of the study of monolingual language acquisition and use, the discussion of the monolingual case will serve as a basis for comparison with the bilingual case.

The key questions for psycholinguistics concerning bilingual language acquisition and use, then, are as follows:

- How does monolingual acquisition of the knowledge of a language proceed? Once attained, how is knowledge of a language actually put to use in the processes of production and comprehension of speech utterances?
- How do children attain bilingualism? How does the process of a child's acquisition of two (or more) languages compare with that of monolingual acquisition?
- How is early bilingualism different from late bilingualism (that is, child second language acquisition) and adult second language acquisition?
- What are the psychological and social determinants of language choice once one has mastered a second language? How do bilinguals activate and deactivate the languages in their verbal repertoire?
- How does the bilingual brain keep its two languages separate; how is accommodation to interlocutors achieved through mixing/integrating the two languages?

Understanding a speech utterance – even in one's native language – is an immensely complicated affair. From a speech signal that is, physically, a continuous stream of sound, the hearer extracts the sounds, the words and word parts composed of these sounds, the sentence structures into which they enter, and the meaning of the whole utterance – all at the rate of approximately 20 sounds per second. The acquisition of one's native language is no less remarkable. By the age of 4 or 5 years normal children master the basic structures of their language in spite of the tremendous complexity and intricacy of these structures, having "picked up" the language with virtually no instruction. The conclusion seems inescapable that human beings are innately endowed with the capacity for language.

And yet there are cases – for example, when a child struggles to learn to read and write or an adult strives unsuccessfully to achieve native proficiency in a second language – where mastery of a language or language-related skill seems anything but natural. It is in these cases that instruction is essential and educators play a crucial role. There is now little doubt that attainment of literacy and (relative) success for adults in acquiring a second language benefit from instructional intervention. Though research in psycholinguistics cannot provide any "silver bullets" that will ensure success in these instructional endeavors, it does make available information about the learner's natural abilities that may make it possible to design instruction so that it will work *with* these abilities rather than against them.

The body of research that addresses the issues referred to above is vast – so much so that anything like a detailed survey is far beyond the scope of this chapter. Nonetheless, we will address the main themes and key ideas in the field that are of most interest to educators. In the process, we will attempt to integrate the research on monolingual and bilingual acquisition and use. The first section is an overview of the central properties of linguistic knowledge and use as well as language acquisition, using monolingual acquisition and use as a model case. The second section focuses on bilingual language acquisition and use while presenting similarities to and differences from the monolingual case. The third section is a conclusion.

Monolingual Language Use and Acquisition: An Introduction

Monolingual linguistic knowledge and linguistic behavior

Psycholinguists, like linguists, generally distinguish between knowledge of a given language variety (the language user's *linguistic competence*) and the use of that knowledge in actual speaking and listening (the user's *linguistic performance*). (The distinction between competence and performance extends to writing and reading in the case of literacy or signing and sign comprehension in the case of the sign languages of the deaf.) A central aspect of the knowledge of a particular language variety consists in its grammar – that is, in *implicit* (or tacit or subconscious) knowledge of the rules of pronunciation (phonology), of word structure (morphology), of sentence structure (syntax), of certain aspects of meaning (semantics), and of a lexicon or vocabulary. Speakers of a given language variety are said to have an implicit *mental grammar* of that variety consisting of these rules and lexicon. It is this mental grammar that determines in large part the perception and production of speech utterances. Since the mental grammar plays a role in actual language use, we must conclude that it is represented in the brain in some way.

The detailed study of the language user's mental grammar is generally regarded as the domain of the discipline of linguistics, whereas the study of the way in which the mental grammar is put to use in the actual comprehension and production of speech in linguistic performance has been a major concern of psycholinguistics. Henceforth, we will refer to the cognitive system that consists of the language user's mental grammar along with accompanying performance processes of comprehension and production as the language user's *language system*.

There are a number of features of language use that are worth noting at this point; these will figure into the discussion below. First, language use is enormously *creative*. With the exception of greetings and other formulaic expressions, few utterances in a language variety are ever repeated. Second, the language system is, as noted earlier, *implicit* (or tacit or subconscious) as opposed to *explicit* (or conscious). Third, the language system is an autonomous component of the mind. Differences between the kinds of rules and principles found in mental grammars and those found in, say, the capacity for vision or music perception (see, e.g., Jackendoff, 1994) have led to the conclusion that the human mind/brain is *modular* – that is, that it is not a single, undifferentiated information processor, but rather consists of distinct systems of principles (distinct *modules*), each module dedicated to the processing of information from a different domain of experience. These modules then interact in the actual cognitive functioning of the organism. The language system is one of the modules.

Monolingual language acquisition

We turn now to questions concerning the acquisition of the language system in the relatively simple case of monolingual acquisition. We may conceive of the acquisition of a mental grammar as the result of interaction between the language learner's experience with a language (input in the form of utterances from the language) on one hand with the innate capacity of the human child for grammar acquisition on the other.

With respect to the learner's experience, one important result of careful research is that, in general, children are not receptive to (and, in fact, seem unable to take advantage of) explicit correction. The example in (1) (McNeill, 1966) is a well-known case:

(1) Child: Nobody don't like me.
     Mother: No, say "nobody likes me".
     Child: Nobody don't like me.
              (eight repetitions of this dialog)
     Mother: No, now listen carefully; say "nobody likes me".
     Child: Oh! Nobody don't likes me.

Research on actual caregiver reaction to children's speech (e.g., Brown & Hanlon, 1970; Pinker, 1984) has shown that explicit correction of grammar is generally either non-existent or ineffective in first language acquisition; most caregiver corrections concern the truth value of the child's utterances, not their grammar. In fact, instruction in general plays little, if any, role in first language acquisition. Children acquire a given structure when they are developmentally ready to and not before, and they do so on the basis of hearing and processing the utterances that occur around them – not by having their "errors" corrected.

As implied by the lack of effectiveness of correction in moving children through the process of language acquisition, this process is determined to a remarkable extent by internally-determined staging rather than by the environment.

The systematic character of the utterances at each stage of acquisition and the difference between the child's utterances and those of the environment indicate that children have their own language systems at each stage in their development, though, of course, these systems differ (in some instances quite radically) from those of adult native speakers of the language until late in the process of acquisition.

Although every normal child acquires at least one language during his or her lifetime, there is considerable evidence that the capacity for full, native acquisition of the language system for one's first language is confined to a period ranging between approximately 2 and 13 years of age (Lenneberg 1967). Though the case is controversial, Genie, a girl who was isolated from language input between the ages of 20 months and 13 years and 8 months and who never progressed in language development past the stage in syntactic development of a normal child at the age of $2^{1}/_{2}$ years (Curtiss, 1977), is often cited as a case in point. The period during which a first language is fully acquirable is called *the critical period for language acquisition*.

Sentence production and comprehension

We turn now to an area that has also been a central concern of psycholinguistic research: How are speech utterances produced and comprehended?

That is, in the case of production, how does a speaker convert a message into a syntactic, morphological, and phonological structure in the process of producing an utterance and, in comprehension, how does the language user assign a structure and meaning to a speech utterance of his/her language?

Speech errors have been used extensively as evidence for and against specific hypotheses about sentence production. One type of error that is frequently found is termed a *reversal* or *exchange* error – see the examples in (2), where the (a) example is the intended utterance and the (b) example is the actual one.

(2)   a.   It pays to wait.
      b.   It waits to pay.

Note that the error in (2b) consists in the reversal of the positions of the forms *pay* and *wait* in contrast with the correct form in (2a). Because of the fact that, in errors like this, verbs and nouns are reversed but functional elements like *it*, *-s*, and *to* in (2) are not, it is hypothesized that, at an early stage in the planning of an utterance, the speaker implicitly formulates a "planning frame" consisting of functional elements in the correct order (in the case of (2), the frame is *It ___-s to ___.*). The forms of verbs and nouns are then added at a single later stage, when the possibility of a reversal arises and is sometimes realized. (See Fromkin, 1973; Garrett, 1988; and Levelt, 1989 for detailed discussion.)

Of course, as noted above, language users not only produce speech utterances, they comprehend them as well, as noted above. Just as there is a cognitive process of the sort noted above for production of utterances, there are also processes of utterance comprehension that enter into language use. Detailed discussion of these processes is beyond the scope of this chapter. (See Pisoni & Remez, 2005 for a thorough treatment.)

The Psycholinguistics of Bilingualism

Having discussed the key concepts and issues involving monolingual acquisition of spoken language as a basis for comparison, let us now turn to second language acquisition and bilingualism. The discussion will proceed from cases of simultaneous acquisition of two languages from birth (resulting in early bilingualism) to sequential acquisition of two languages in childhood (late bilingualism) to adult second language acquisition.

With respect to the capacity for acquisition, we will note changes in the capacity for acquisition at different ages that have been investigated in the research literature and discuss features of the sequence of language systems that constitute the process of acquisition.

Input and language separation in simultaneous bilingual acquisition

In some cases, children are exposed to and acquire two languages from birth. Such cases are referred to as instances of simultaneous bilingual acquisition.

The child's task in simultaneous bilingual acquisition seems even more complex than that of the monolingual child. The problem of acquisition for bilingual children is shown diagrammatically in Figure 4.1. The two diagrams in this figure are intended to represent, in a simplified way, two ways in which caregivers often plan to manage input to the child in the two languages. The top diagram (a) is the "one person/one language" scheme, under which one person in the child's environment speaks one language and another person speaks the other; the lower diagram (b) is the "mixed input" scheme, under which no provision is made for allocating input from the two languages to particular individuals. However, even in cases in which the caregivers intend to keep input from the two languages separate, they may unwittingly provide mixed language input to the child.

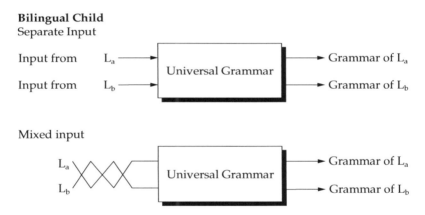

Figure 4.1 Input conditions for bilingual children (adapted from Bhatia & Ritchie, 1999)
(a)   Separate input
(b)   Mixed input

The major issue that has been addressed in research on simultaneous acquisition is whether the two language systems (that is, the mental grammars and processing strategies for the two languages) are separated in the child's mind or not. Two hypotheses have been proposed to address this issue: The Unitary System Hypothesis (Volterrra & Taeschner, 1978; and others) and the Dual System Hypothesis (De Houwer, 1990; and Meisel, 2006, among others).

According to the Unitary System Hypothesis (also termed the Initial One-System Hypothesis), bilingual children undergo a stage of 'confusion'

Bilingual Child

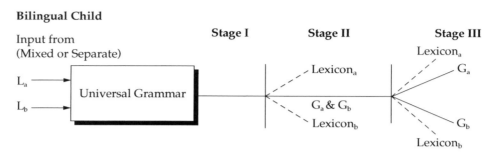

Figure 4.2   The Unitary Hypothesis (adapted from Bhatia & Ritchie, 1999)

before separating the two language systems. Under this hypothesis, in the initial stage of acquisition, children have no reliable mechanism for separating two linguistic systems to accommodate the two distinct sets of input utterances. The model is summarized in Figure 4.2. Research findings have generally shown that the three-stage model of bilingual language development represented in Figure 4.2 suffers from serious shortcomings on both empirical and methodological grounds.

The Dual System Hypothesis claims that children do not undergo a stage of confusion; rather they separate both the lexical and the grammatical systems as early as age 2 or before, based on their access to Universal Grammar and the acquisition of major differences between the two languages.

The evidence based on subsequent research lends support not only to the Dual System Hypothesis, but also to the claim that simultaneous bilingualism is similar to monolingual first language development in other respects. For example, the acquisition of negative structures in the well-studied case of an English-French bilingual child (Paradis & Genesee, 1996) showed the same process of acquisition in each language that appears in English and French monolinguals, even though the two languages differ significantly in the structure of their negative sentences. For a detailed review of this research, see Bhatia and Ritchie (1999) and Meisel (2006).

Sequential and adult bilingualism: Age, the critical period hypothesis, and input environment for learners from age 5 to adulthood

We turn now to the case of second language acquisition – that is, sequential childhood bilingualism (i.e., acquisition of a second language between the age of 5 years and puberty) or adult second language acquisition (i.e., acquisition of a second language after puberty). As noted above, the age of 5 years is significant in language development, since this is the age by which the language system of the child is well established. As will become evident from the following discussion on sequential childhood bilingualism and adult second language acquisition, bilinguals are not always "two monolinguals in one brain" (Grosjean, 1989).

Research on sequential or successive bilingualism and adult second language acquisition reveals that children who acquire language after the age of 5 but before puberty fall in the middle of the continuum with respect to the relative ease and success of language acquisition between those who undergo simultaneous bilingual acquisition on one hand and those who acquire second languages as adults on the other.

With regard to the overall process of acquisition, young children have been observed (Saville-Troike, 1988, among others) to begin their time in a second language setting by simply using their first language. Once they discover that others are not speaking their language, many children enter a "silent period," during which they produce few or no utterances in the presence of speakers of the second language. This is typically followed by single-word utterances and, eventually, genuinely creative language. Bilingual children have also been observed to become silent even in the environment of one of their languages, if that environment is unfamiliar (Leopold, 1939–49). Adults also appear to go through a silent period when they are allowed to do so (Sorenson, 1967) and may benefit from delay in oral production (Postovsky, 1977) when such delay is feasible.

Just as we did for the case of monolingual and simultaneous bilingual language acquisition, we may conceive of the acquisition of a language system for a second language as the result of interaction between the language learner's experience with the second language (input in the form of utterances from the second language) and the capacity for language acquisition of the second language learner. As in the case of the monolingual and simultaneous-bilingual learner, the second language learner moves through a sequence of stages of acquisition, each stage consisting in a language system. For the process of second language production, see Poulisse (1997); for perception processes in second language performance, see Kroll and Dussias (2006); for stages in the process of second language acquisition see Pica, this volume.

Second language learners exhibit a number of crucial differences from the simultaneous bilingual. First, since they have a well-established language system for their first languages, some form of that system will be the initial language system in the sequence that makes up the process of second language acquisition, accounting for *transfer* of features (or "foreign accent" – including morphological and syntactic features) from the first language to performance in the second language. Second, since the learner is more mature than a simultaneous bilingual, his/her capacity for acquisition may affect the second language learner's *ultimate attainment* of the second language (that is, the final result of acquisition); recall the notion of a critical period for language acquisition referred to above (Birdsong, 1999; this volume). Third, the second language learner is older and may therefore be learning the language in a set of circumstances quite different from that of a monolingual or simultaneous bilingual learner.

For the implicit knowledge and use of major structures (the language system for questions, negation, etc.), the stages of acquisition are, for the most part, shared across monolingual learners, simultaneous bilinguals, and second language learners – with the exception of the effects of initial (and, perhaps, permanent) transfer in the case of second language learners. This is true even for acquisition in instructional contexts. We emphasize that this is true for the *implicit* language system of the second language learner. We return to the issue of explicit knowledge – particularly in the case of the adult learner – below.

Although second language learners pass through essentially the same stages as other learners, they do so more quickly than either monolingual or simultaneous bilingual learners. On the other hand, with respect to ultimate attainment, older learners are at a disadvantage in the long run. Even though they move more quickly than younger learners through the early stages, they tend to "plateau" earlier as well (Krashen, Long, & Scarcella, 1979); whereas younger (prepubertal) learners generally attain full native language systems, the ability to achieve native pronunciation begins to decrease when the learner begins learning the second language at 6 years of age or more; likewise, the capacity for achievement of native proficiency in morphology and syntax begins to decrease significantly when the learner begins to learn at about 15 years of age or older (Long, 1990).

As for experience or input, in comparison with younger learners, learners between 5 years of age and puberty are likely to respond to correction in very much the same way as younger learners do. However, when learners reach puberty they are better able to think abstractly about the contents of their own minds and, therefore, to master abstract rules that can be used to regulate their own behavior (e.g., Inhelder & Piaget, 1958). In such cases, then, the learner can internalize rules that are the consequences of correction; however, there is evidence that these rules are not part of the implicit language system but, rather, serve as elements in a self-monitor or self-editor – as explicit knowledge *about* the language rather than implicit knowledge *of* the language (Schwartz, 1993; White, 2003). As the capacity to acquire the full native language system diminishes around puberty, the adult can, to some extent, compensate for this loss by internalizing such monitoring rules.

For a summary of the major differences among simultaneous bilingual acquisition, child second language acquisition between ages 5 and puberty, and adult second language acquisition that we have discussed, see Table 4.1.

We turn now to issues in the study of the bilingual's capacity for the separation and mixing of his/her two languages.

Bilingual modes of language use: Separation and integration of two linguistic systems

Unlike the monolingual who has access to a single set of mutually intelligible styles, bilinguals/multilinguals control styles in each of two or more languages;

Table 4.1 Summary of similarities and differences among types of language acquisition

	Monolingual and simultaneous bilingual acquisition	Second Language Acquisition	
		Sequential acquisition between age 5 and puberty	*Postpubertal (adult) acquisition*
Transfer in initial stages of acquisition?	No	Yes	Yes
Speed of initial learning	Gradual	Faster than in monolingual or simultaneous bilingualism	Faster than either simultaneous or sequential pre-pubertal
Ultimate attainment of implicit native-like knowledge?	Yes	Some non-native features	Many non-native features when self-monitoring is not operative
Results of explicit correction	None	Little or none	Some; contributes to a self-editor but doesn't change the implicit mental grammar

neither of their languages is mutually intelligible with the other(s). Not only do bilinguals have tacit knowledge for keeping the two linguistic systems apart – which enables them to activate and deactivate/suppress languages with efficiency and accuracy – but they also exhibit a higher level of cognitive skill to draw from the two systems for production both between and within sentences.

Whenever needed (e.g., speaking to a monolingual), bilinguals can restrict themselves to a monolingual mode (either Language A or B but not both); or they can switch into bilingual mode (i.e., activation of both Language A and B) while interacting with a bilingual. The process of language choice is not random; bilingual pragmatic competence, which consists in a complex set of implicit socio-psychological rules (formulated in terms of, e.g., participant roles and relationships, situational and message-intrinsic factors, and socio-psychological language association, among others), determines the bilingual's choice of one language over the other. (See Ritchie & Bhatia, 2006 on social determinants of language choice.)

The key question is the bilingual's control of his or her two languages and the ability to switch from one to the other. On the basis of research on bilingual aphasia, Green (1986) proposed the Inhibitory Control Model in order to explain the regulation/production of two or more languages by polyglots. The model attempts to address the key issue of control to account for the normal bilingual's ability to successfully regulate language use by making an appropriate language choice. A bilingual aphasic, in contrast, lacks such control, resulting in language mismatching, translational disorder, or diminished ability to language switch. For details about the neurological aspects of control, see Ijalba, Obler, and Chengappa (2006).

Social-psychological determinants of language choice reveal the complexity of the procedures of language activation and deactivation. The Markedness Model (Myers-Scotton, 1999) claims that "humans are innately disposed to exploit code choices as negotiations of position." For instance, English-Hindi bilinguals or English-Swahili bilinguals may activate Hindi or Swahili to mark in-group membership and local identity, whereas they may choose English to mark objectivity, neutrality, and identity as participants in the wider world. Similarly, the bilingual's language organization is quite different from that of monolinguals; whereas the different styles of the monolingual are associated with different social domains of use (e.g., intimate versus distant or private versus public), it is the different languages of the bi-/multilingual that are so associated. These schemas can activate or deactivate a particular language in the process of a language switch. In a multilingual setting in India, for example, advertisers are likely to use four languages – English, Hindi/regional language, Persian, and Sanskrit – to create associations of modernity, locality, royalty, and deep-rooted cultural appeal, respectively. The challenge for psycholinguists and social psychologists is how to capture such associations in the modeling of bilingual language production and processing/comprehension. (See Costa, 2006; and Kroll & Dussias, 2006 for details.)

Let us now consider the ability of the bilingual to mix languages within a single sentence. Like monolinguals, bilinguals' implicit language systems not only enable them to produce or comprehend, in principle, an infinite number of mixed sentences, but also to create mixed sentences which they have not encountered before. This phenomenon is termed *code-switching* (or by some *code-mixing*), and is an integral part of bilingual linguistic competence and performance. Language mixing on the part of bilinguals is largely implicit and systematic. This knowledge also enables them to arrive at well-formedness judgments of mixed utterances as exemplified below (switches prefixed by an asterisk '*' are ill-formed):

(3)   Monolingual Hindi
       merii patnii saaRii cun   -egii
       my   wife   saree choose -Fut.3.Sg. fem
       'My wife will choose a saree.'

(4) Hindi-**English** code-switching/mixing
  merii patnii saaRii **choose -egii*
  my   wife   saree   choose -Fut.3.Sg. fem
  'My wife will choose a saree.'

(5) Monolingual Hindi
  *merii patnii saaRii cun(na)   <u>kar</u> -egii
  my   wife   saree   choose (inf.) do -Fut.3.Sg. fem
  'My wife will choose a saree.'

(6) Hindi-**English** code-switching/mixing
  *merii patnii saaRii **choose** <u>kar</u> -egii*
  my   wife   saree   choose do -Fut.3.Sg. fem
  'My wife will choose a saree.'

Monolingual Hindi shows no ill-formedness when the tense/agreement element *-egii* is suffixed to the Hindi verb stem *cun*. The ungrammaticality of (4) shows that the Hindi tense/agreement element cannot be suffixed directly to the switched English verb *choose*. The grammaticality of (6) shows that the switched English verb requires a semantically light verb *kar-naa* 'to do' (underlined) in order for the code-switched sentence to be grammatical. The tense/agreement element *-egii* is attached to the Hindi light verb in the switched utterance, whereas this attachment with the dummy verb in a monolingual Hindi utterance yields ungrammatical output, as in (5).

The search for explanations of cross-linguistic generalizations about the phenomenon of code-mixing (particularly, code-mixing within sentences) in terms of independently justified principles of language structure and use has taken two distinct forms. One approach – represented by, e.g., Belazi, Rubin, and Toribio (1994) and MacSwan (2005) – is formulated in terms of the theory of linguistic competence. The other approach – as best exemplified by the Matrix Language Frame (MLF) model (Myers-Scotton, 1993; Myers-Scotton & Jake, 1995) – is grounded in the theory of sentence production (particularly that of Garrett, 1988 and Levelt, 1989 and others). In simplified terms, the MLF model claims that the planning frame for an utterance comes from one of the bilingual's languages and the lexical items in the utterance come from the other language. (For further development of these ideas and a critique, see Bhatia & Ritchie, 2001 and MacSwan, 2005.)

Communication Accommodation Theory, developed by Howard Giles and his research team, views code-mixing as a form of accommodation or modification of one's speech to match that of an interlocutor. Despite the unfavorable social evaluation of mixed speech by prescriptivists (and, often, educators), bilinguals cannot resist language mixing. Lawson and Sachdev (2000) found that, in spite of its generally perceived low prestige, "students reported using this language style pervasively" because it carries "covert prestige" (Sachdev & Giles, 2006: 360) – that is, prestige that is unrecognized or is even denied by bilinguals themselves. Additionally, it has been shown in the research on bilingual language acquisition that Spanish-English bilingual mothers employ language mixing for paraphrasing purposes, which enhances input quality in the process of bilingual language acquisition. Bilingual teachers consciously or unconsciously employ language mixing/switching in the classroom setting to overcome social asymmetry and accommodate the child's more dominant language, thereby offering the child learning strategies such as paraphrasing, summarizing, reinforcement, and explanation. See Martin-Jones (1995) for a review of two decades of work on code-switching in the classroom.

Conclusions

We have discussed various facets of monolingual and bilingual language acquisition and use – production, acquisition, learning, use, and comprehension. In the process we have attempted to focus particularly on those key notions and salient features of linguistics and psycholinguistics that are of value to practitioners of educational linguistics, while suggesting at the same time that the scope of research in psycholinguistics is far greater than we could possibly review in the space available here. Drawing the distinction between implicit and explicit linguistic knowledge and use (e.g., implicit and explicit language learning, determinants of language choice and mixing in bilinguals), we argue that both kinds of linguistic knowledge and learning need to be exploited to the greatest extent possible in classroom interaction and material development among other aspects of the educational linguistic enterprise. A recent shift in psycholinguistic research – to include research on bilingualism as well as monolingualism – is a step toward making psycholinguistic research more relevant to the concerns of educators. Nevertheless, the study of the bilingual language mode continues to pose serious challenges for both psycholinguists and educational linguists.

REFERENCES

Belazi, Heidi M., Rubin, Edward J., & Toribio, Almeida J. (1994). Code switching and X-bar theory: The functional head constraint. *Linguistic Inquiry*, 25(2), 221–237.

Bhatia, Tej K. & Ritchie, William C. (1999). The bilingual child: Some issues and perspectives. In William C. Ritchie & Tej K. Bhatia (eds.), *Handbook of Child Language Acquisition* (pp. 569–643). San Diego: Academic Press.

Bhatia, Tej K. & Ritchie, William C. (2001). Language mixing, typology, and second language acquisition. In Peri Bhaskarrao & Karumuri V. Subbarao (eds.), *The Yearbook of South Asian Languages and Linguistics* (pp. 37–62). New Delhi: Sage Publications.

Birdsong, David (ed.) (1999). *Second Language Acquisition and the Critical Period Hypothesis.* Mahwah, NJ: Lawrence Erlbaum.

Brown, Roger & Hanlon, Camille (1970). Derivational complexity and order of acquisition in child speech. In John R. Hayes (ed.), *Cognition and the Development of Language* (pp. 11–53). New York: John Wiley & Sons.

Costa, Albert (2006). Speech production in bilinguals. In Tej K. Bhatia & William C. Ritchie (eds.), *The Handbook of Bilingualism* (pp. 201–223). Oxford: Blackwell.

Curtiss, Susan (1977). *Genie: A Psycholinguistic Study of a "Wild Child."* New York: Academic Press.

de Bot, Kees & Kroll, Judith F. (2002). Psycholinguistics. In Norbert Schmitt (ed.), *An Introduction to Applied Linguistics* (pp. 133–149). London: Arnold.

De Houwer, Annick (1990). *The Acquisition of Two Languages from Birth: A Case Study.* Cambridge: Cambridge University Press.

Fromkin, Victoria (1973). *Speech Errors as Linguistic Evidence.* The Hague: Mouton.

Garrett, Merrill F. (1988). Processes in language production. In Fredrick Newmeyer (ed.), *Language: Psychological and Biological Aspects. Linguistics: The Cambridge Survey III* (pp. 69–96). Cambridge: Cambridge University Press.

Green, David W. (1986). Control, activation, and resources: A framework and a model for control of speech in bilinguals. *Brain and Language*, 27, 210–223.

Grosjean, François (1989). Neurolinguists, beware! The bilingual is not two monolinguals in one person. *Brain and Language*, 36, 3–15.

Ijalba, Elizabeth, Obler, Loraine K., & Chengappa, Shyamla (2006). Bilingual aphasia. In Tej K. Bhatia & William C. Ritchie (eds.), *The Handbook of Bilingualism* (pp. 71–89). Oxford: Blackwell.

Inhelder, Barbara & Piaget, Jean (1958). *The Growth of Logical Thinking from Childhood to Adolescence.* New York: Basic Books.

Jackendoff, Ray S. (1994). *Languages of the Mind.* Cambridge, MA: MIT Press.

Krashen, Stephen, Long, Michael, & Scarcella, Robin (1979). Age, rate, and eventual attainment in second language acquisition. *TESOL Quarterly*, 13, 573–582.

Kroll, Judith F. & Dussias, Paola E. (2006). The comprehension of words and sentences in two languages. In Tej K. Bhatia & William C. Ritchie (eds.), *The Handbook of Bilingualism* (pp. 169–200). Oxford: Blackwell.

Lawson, Sarah & Sachdev, Itesh (2000). Code-switching in Tunisia: Attitudinal and behavioral dimensions. *Journal of Pragmatics*, 32, 1343–1361.

Lenneberg, Eric (1967). *Biological Foundations of Language.* New York: Wiley.

Leopold, Werner (1939–49). *Speech Development of a Bilingual Child: A Linguist's Record* (4 vols.). Evanston: Northwestern University Press.

Levelt, Willem (1989). *Speaking: From Intention to Articulation.* Cambridge, MA: MIT Press.

Long, Michael (1990). Maturational constraints on language development. *Studies in Second Language Acquisition*, 12(3), 251–285.

MacSwan, Jeff (2005). Remarks on Jake, Myers-Scotton & Gross's response: There is no "Matrix Language." *Language and Cognition*, 8(3), 277–284.

Martin-Jones, Marilyn (1995). Code-switching in the classroom: Two decades of research. In Lesley Milroy & Pieter Muysken (eds.), *One Speaker, Two Languages* (pp. 90–111). Cambridge: Cambridge University Press.

McNeill, David (1966). Developmental psycholinguistics. In Frank Smith & George Miller (eds.), *The Genesis of Language* (pp. 15–84). Cambridge, MA: MIT Press.

Meisel, Jurgen M. (2006). The bilingual child. In Tej K. Bhatia & William C. Ritchie (eds.), *The Handbook of Bilingualism* (pp. 91–113). Oxford: Blackwell.

Myers-Scotton, Carol (1993). *Duelling Languages: Grammatical Structures in Codeswitching.* Oxford: Clarendon Press.

Myers-Scotton, Carol (1999). Explaining the role of norms and rationality in code-switching. *Journal of Pragmatics*, 32(9), 1259–1271.

Myers-Scotton, Carol & Jake, Janice (1995). Matching lemmas in a bilingual language competence and production model: Evidence from intrasentential code-switching. *Linguistics*, 33, 981–1024.

Paradis, Johanne & Genesee, Fred (1996). Syntactic acquisition in bilingual children. *Studies in Second Language Acquisition*, 18, 1–25.

Pinker, Steven (1984). *Language Learnability and Language Development*. Cambridge, MA: Harvard University Press.

Pisoni, David B. & Remez, Robert E. (2005). *The Handbook of Speech Perception*. Oxford: Blackwell.

Postovsky, Valerian (1977). Why not start speaking later? In Marina Burt, Heidi Dulay, & Mary Finocchiaro (eds.), *Viewpoints on English as a Second Language* (pp. 17–26). New York: Regents.

Poulisse, Nanda (1997). Language production in bilinguals. In Annette M. B. de Groot & Judith F. Kroll (eds.), *Tutorials in Bilingualism: Psychological Perspectives* (pp. 201–224). Mahwah, NJ: Lawrence Earlbaum.

Ritchie, William C. & Bhatia, Tej K. (2006). Social and psychological factors in language mixing. In Tej K. Bhatia & William C. Ritchie (eds.), *The Handbook of Bilingualism* (pp. 336–352). Oxford: Blackwell.

Sachdev, Itesh & Giles, Howard (2006). Bilingual speech accommodation. In Tej K. Bhatia & William C. Ritchie (eds.), *The Handbook of Bilingualism* (pp. 353–378). Oxford: Blackwell.

Saville-Troike, Muriel (1988). Private speech: Evidence for second language learning strategies during the "silent" period. *Journal of Child Language*, 15, 567–590.

Schwartz, Bonnie (1993). On explicit and negative data effecting and affecting competence and "linguistic behavior." *Studies in Second Language Acquisition*, 15, 147–163.

Sorenson, Arthur (1967). Multilingualism in the Northwest Amazon. *American Anthropologist*, 69, 674–684.

Volterra, Virginia & Taeschner, Traute (1978). The acquisition and development of language by bilingual children. *Journal of Child Language*, 5, 311–326.

White, Lydia (2003). *Second Language Acquisition and Universal Grammar*. Cambridge: Cambridge University Press.

5 Linguistic Theory

RICHARD HUDSON

Linguistic Theory and Education

The links between education and language are fundamental and obvious:

- Language is the main medium of education.
- Literacy, a mode of language, is one of the foundations of education.
- Verbal intelligence is one of the most-used predictors of educational success.
- Foreign or second languages are traditionally an important part of the school curriculum.
- Education has a profound effect on language.

Given these connections, one might expect equally close links between the relevant research communities – educationalists watchful for useful new ideas about how language grows and works, and linguists looking for educational uses (or validation) of their theories. But reality is different. Educationalists typically find theoretical linguistics abstruse and irrelevant, while linguists generally see no link between their work and education. Needless to say, I disagree with both these views. This chapter will try to explain why. It is based on a somewhat longer article addressed primarily to linguists (Hudson, 2004).

Linguistic Theory

Linguists generally contrast *theory* and *description*. Description comprises the details of vocabulary, grammar, pronunciation, and so on of particular languages whereas theory covers more general ideas about how language works and about how we might study it. For instance, how speakers of a language pronounce the word that means 'dog' is a matter of description; but more general questions about how pronunciation is related to meaning belong to theory, as do questions about how to study pronunciations and meanings. This chapter is concerned with theory rather than description, so it says nothing about the contribution of works such as dictionaries and descriptive grammars in education. They are clearly important, but they raise different issues from theory and deserve separate treatment.

It is helpful to divide theory into two areas which I have previously called 'ideas' and 'models' (Hudson, 2004); for example, we can contrast the idea that language is constantly changing with the various models of how and why it changes. Ideas can be controversial, but a great many of them are accepted by every linguist and provide the common framework of assumptions that allows rational debate at the frontiers of research. In the early 1980s I collected 83 "issues on which linguists can agree" (Hudson, 1981; Brookes & Hudson, 1982), all of which are ideas in this sense. Many of these ideas that linguists take for granted are important precisely because they clash with 'common sense'; for example, the linguists' view of language as constantly changing contrasts with the popular view of language as fixed and unchanging. Moreover, ideas tend to be simple and easily understood, so the main obstacles to wide acceptance are prejudice and emotion rather than comprehension.

In contrast, models exist at the frontiers of research, so, almost by definition, they attract controversy and they are complicated and hard to explain. Among linguists, it is the models rather than the ideas that are the live issues that deserve attention and debate, which may give the impression to outsiders that linguistic theory has nothing to offer except models. This is regrettable because the individual ideas are at least as important, and much safer. Outsiders have neither the time nor the expertise to evaluate models in relation to the available research evidence, so an educationalist may adopt a model of language without being aware of the research evidence against the model. Unfortunately one very general model of language (systemic functional linguistics) has become very influential in education on this basis, as I explain briefly at the end of this chapter.

In short, linguistic models should be treated with caution, but linguistic ideas are tried, tested, and agreed; so 'linguistic theory' will now mean ideas rather than models except where I say otherwise.

Why Education Needs Linguistic Theory

Before we explore the ideas of linguistics in more detail it will be helpful to distinguish the needs of different areas of education, starting with the main participants: teachers and pupils. The least ambitious claim is that teachers do need to understand explicitly how language works, but pupils do not; but I shall make the more ambitious claim that this understanding is important for pupils as well. In the UK, teachers and education managers have adopted the very useful term 'knowledge about language', often abbreviated to KAL, as the name for this explicit knowledge of facts and principles informed by the ideas of linguistics (Carter, 1990). My argument is that pupils should be taught KAL and that they need it for different reasons in different subject areas.

There are good reasons for starting with mother tongue teaching. This is obviously where KAL should start precisely because the mother tongue is what pupils know already. But why is KAL sufficiently important to deserve a serious place in the curriculum? There are two main arguments for teaching KAL.

- The most obvious answer, at least to a linguist, is that a deeper understanding of language deserves a place in any liberal curriculum because of its long-term intellectual benefits; if it is important for children to understand their bodies and their social environment, it is at least as important for them to understand the faculty which makes social life possible. Moreover, most people find language interesting. Unfortunately these arguments put language in competition with philosophy, economics, art, history, and all the other undoubtedly important and interesting areas of life, so it is important to be able to demonstrate more concrete benefits of KAL.
- The strongest possible justification for KAL is the argument that it improves the language skills of writing, reading, speaking, and listening. Unfortunately, this argument has not been deployed recently because of a perceived conflict with both linguistic theory and research in education which I evaluate below.

According to Noam Chomsky, the world's most influential linguist, language is an 'organ' that grows unaided, regardless of instruction, so that teaching is as irrelevant to the growth of the mother tongue as it would be to growing taller or reaching puberty (Chomsky, 1986). This 'nativist' view is highly controversial and is challenged directly by a large number of linguists and psycholinguists who believe that language is mostly learned from experience of usage rather than inherited genetically (Barlow & Kemmer, 2000; Tomasello, 2003). Nativism is not one of the ideas that unites linguists. In any case, it misses the point of mother tongue teaching: even if nature can be left to look after 'natural' language development, society has decided that the outcome is not good enough. Children also need not only the very 'unnatural' skills of reading and writing, but also the entire linguistic competence of a mature educated person – a range of grammar and vocabulary that goes well beyond what is needed in normal dealings with friends and family. In short, mother tongue teaching takes over where 'nature' stops. In the days of traditional grammar it tried to 'improve' the natural product, but at least in the UK the main aim is now to enlarge it, to extend the "functional potential of language" (Halliday, 1978: 100). KAL offers the intellectual underpinnings for this expansion.

A long tradition of research in education also raises questions for the claim that KAL improves language skills. This research focused on one particular area of KAL – knowledge about grammar – and one particular skill – writing – and asked whether grammar teaching had any positive effect on pupils' writing. A number of reviews of this research literature have drawn negative conclusions (Andrews et al., 2004; Elley, 1994; Wyse, 2001), and this negative view has become the received wisdom; but the research evidence is actually much less clear than these surveys imply. For one thing, all the relevant research showed a positive effect for 'sentence combining', an exercise in which pupils combine a number of simple sentences into a single complex or compound sentence (Hillocks & Mavrognes, 1986). For another, the other studies tended to separate the teaching and testing in both time and content; why should a lesson on classifying nouns and verbs every Monday afternoon affect the students' use of relative clauses at the end of the term? More recent research has shown a clear positive effect on writing of more focused grammar teaching; for example, Bryant and Nunes and their colleagues found that instruction about how to use possessive apostrophes had a positive effect on children's use of them (Bryant et al., 2002) and that the study of morphology improved their spelling (Nunes, Bryant, & Olsson, 2003). The answer seems therefore to be that under the right circumstances explicit grammar teaching can have a positive effect on writing skills. There is also some research evidence for a similar effect on reading skills: teaching pupils about complex sentence structure improved their ability to read and understand complex sentences (Chipere, 2003). However more research is urgently needed before we can be sure how best to use KAL in the development of writing and reading (not to mention the much less teachable skills of speaking and listening).

One particular type of mother tongue teaching which deserves special mention is the teaching of linguistic minorities, and especially of those which have no recognised status within mainstream education. For example, London boasts about 300 languages distributed among its schools, most of which are spoken by recently arrived immigrants. Many of the larger communities provide ad hoc mother tongue teaching out of regular school hours, but there is no central control or evaluation and no machinery for ensuring that linguistic theory plays the role it should. KAL is just as necessary for these 'Saturday schools' as for other mother tongue teaching – perhaps more so since the issues are more complex. For example, if children are to grow up proud of their community's language they need to be aware of its linguistic similarities to the dominant language.

Apart from mother tongue teaching, the other subject which obviously needs linguistic theory is the teaching of foreign languages. One rather obvious idea of linguistics is that different languages are all manifestations of a single phenomenon called 'language', so foreign languages and the mother tongue are drawn from the same stock. If schools took this idea seriously, foreign languages would be closely linked to the mother tongue, using the same ideas and technical metalanguage. This ideal is very different from historical reality in many countries (including the UK), though we have recently seen very encouraging references to mother tongue teaching in official documents for foreign language teaching in England (Anon., 2005). When foreign language teaching follows this principle, it recycles the insights learned initially in mother tongue lessons and thereby reinforces the insights in much the same way that physics or geography use and strengthen the numeracy skills first developed in mathematics. This idea of a unified approach to language has been brewing in the UK for several decades under the title 'language awareness', a term which deliberately implies explicit knowledge tied to a metalanguage (Hawkins, 1999). In this view, learners should be aware of how language works in general and also of at least some of the specific patterns that they are learning; and they should be able to discuss these issues. This raises the same question as with first-language teaching: Does explicit teaching improve performance? This has been a major preoccupation of applied linguistics over the last few decades, where the research evidence seems to have swung in favor of explicit teaching – what is sometimes called 'focus on forms' (Hawkins & Towell, 1996; Norris & Ortega, 2000). It is still a matter of debate why focusing on forms should help – for example, it may help the learner to benefit from experience (Renou, 2001), and this may be especially true when a learner encounters a pattern for the first time (Ellis, 2002). Whatever the explanation, the benefits of explicit attention to forms are clear, and they show how important it is for teaching to be underpinned by good linguistic ideas.

Ranging more widely, there are yet more parts of education which need linguistics. Language is fundamental to every subject, and not just to those subjects where it is the primary object of study. Every subject has its terminology and its presentation styles – for example, a science report is linguistically different from a history essay – and pupils are expected to learn each of these registers. Arguably explicit teaching is as helpful here as in mother tongue teaching, and linguists should be able to describe the registers more efficiently than the non-linguist specialist teachers themselves.

However deeper issues arise as well. It is important for teachers to understand how the use of language helps children to learn; for example, how talking about new ideas from geography helps children to integrate them into their existing knowledge. One influential theory, called Language Across the Curriculum, considers "students' language, especially their informal talk and writing, as the key learning resource in the classroom" (Corson, 1994). Similarly, we can ask how the teacher's language use helps or hinders their learning; this question embraces all aspects of the teacher's language from choice of vocabulary and grammar to discourse features such as the use of questions (Stubbs, 1986: ch. 3). These questions about the language of the classroom arise for every subject, and may require different answers for different subjects. It should be obvious that they also require a good understanding of language founded on reliable linguistic theory.

Finally I should like to mention two 'new' curriculum subjects which have recently appeared in the UK curriculum: citizenship and thinking. No doubt other countries recognize the same subjects under different names. Citizenship

in the UK secondary curriculum covers three topics: social and moral responsibility, community involvement, and political literacy. It is easy to find links
to linguistic theory in all these themes. The following are some of the more
obvious linguistic topics which could arise in citizenship classes: bias (e.g.,
sexism, racism) in language, linguistic markers of communities, bilingualism,
language and ideology. These are all important and relevant topics and need
the theoretical underpinnings of linguistics.

The particular skills that are recognized in the UK as 'thinking' are: information processing, reasoning, enquiry, creativity, and evaluation. Linguists have
been arguing for some time that linguistics is particularly well suited as a
vehicle for teaching thinking skills, and in particular scientific thinking (Honda
and O'Neil, 1993; Hudson, 1999). One advantage of language as an area of
inquiry is that vast amounts of data are easily available either by introspection
or by observation, so children can easily formulate and test hypotheses about
their language system. Another advantage is that language is an important
tool for thinking, so children can explore thought processes such as classification and reasoning via the language that they use for expressing the processes.
A number of small-scale projects have developed these ideas. For example,
trial groups of mixed ability seventh- and eleventh-graders were tested for
their ability to reason scientifically both before and after a period spent exploring the grammar of their own language (English) by inducing rules from
examples (Honda, 1994). The results showed a significant improvement, which
is all the more remarkable for the fact that their experience of linguistics lasted
a mere two weeks. Even more encouragingly, the children enjoyed it and
described it as fun.

All these suggestions about introducing linguistic theory into schools raise
serious questions, of course, about teacher education. In an ideal world, schools
would teach easy linguistic ideas to pupils, who would then deepen and
develop these ideas at university before returning as teachers to pass their
mature understanding on to the next generation. Where the reality falls short
of this ideal, as it does in the UK, change may have to be spread over a
generation or so, with teachers gradually becoming familiar with a widening
range of ideas. It is neither realistic nor necessary to expect teachers to become
familiar and confident overnight with everything in the new world of linguistic theory. Where planners can help is in deciding priorities and interconnections so that ideas are introduced in a helpful order.

My conclusion, therefore, is that education needs linguistics in several different curriculum subjects and even, arguably, in all curriculum subjects. I
am not suggesting that linguistics should be added as a separate curriculum
subject for all pupils; that certainly would be unrealistic because the UK
curriculum is already over-full and no doubt the same is true in other
countries. Rather, what I am suggesting is that linguistic theory can help to
strengthen all the existing language subjects, and that one of the by-products
of this strengthening will be a much more coherent approach to language
throughout the school.

Some Important Linguistic Ideas

Most of the relevant ideas that emerge from linguistic theory can conveniently be expressed as a series of conceptual distinctions. The following list includes the most important of these distinctions.

Description or prescription

Prescription tries to change language by proscribing some forms that are in fact used and prescribing alternatives, whereas description accepts all forms that are used. Linguistics is based on description and favours it in school teaching.

This does not mean that linguists believe that 'anything goes'; far from it, because a description of what is inside a language implies that everything else is outside it and (for that language) wrong – for example, the phrase *those books* is inside English, but outside French. The same logic applies to dialects of the same language: the form *them books* is allowed by some dialects of English, but not by Standard English; and conversely, the standard form *those books* is outside the limits of those dialects. Regional dialects of English are not failed attempts at Standard English any more than English is a bad attempt at Latin or French; they are simply different and equal.

However, the descriptive principle raises moral issues because the reality being described is often unfair; descriptive linguists frequently find themselves campaigning to change the world. For example, if a dialect has low social status, prejudice against the dialect turns into unfair prejudice against its speakers; and in some cases the speakers themselves may share the rest of society's low opinion of the way they speak. Describing these facts of social psychology is often a prelude to action aimed at changing the facts; for example, teachers can try to change students' prejudices by discussion. To take a different kind of example, many linguists are concerned about the areas of language where a description reveals social bias such as racism and sexism; here too, description means starting with the present facts, but not necessarily accepting those facts as inevitable. Paradoxically, therefore, description means studying the linguistic facts objectively, but may in itself lead to attempts to change the facts.

Variation or uniformity

Another important (and related) idea is variation, the idea that a language may vary across groups (geographical and social variation) and across time (developmental and historical variation), and that a given individual will speak or write differently in different social contexts. It contrasts with the assumption that a language is uniform – a single dialect using a single style. When this assumption is confronted with the obvious reality of variation, it can be rescued by prescription which condemns any deviation from some imagined golden age or ideal purity. Healthy language education celebrates variation in all its forms as manifested in dialects, genres, styles, historical periods, and languages, and encourages learners to enrich their 'language repertoire'. Largely thanks to the work on variation of Halliday and his colleagues in Australia (Halliday, 1978) variation is now central to England's National Curriculum for English (Anon., 1999).

Form or function

Every unit of language combines a form with a function; for example a word combines a pronunciation and spelling (form) with a meaning (function). These two aspects of a unit are conceptually distinct so they can be studied separately and it is important not to confuse them. For example, a word's classification as noun, adjective, or whatever is distinct from the function it plays in building a sentence as subject of the verb, modifier of a noun, and so on; the function identifies the part it plays in the current sentence, whereas the word class identifies its range of potential parts. For instance, consider the word *garden* in the phrase *long garden wall*, where grammarians would agree that although *garden* is modifying *wall* in much the same way as *long*, *garden* and *long* must belong to different word classes because they have very different potentials (e.g., *The wall is long* but not *The wall is garden*). Forms and functions are distinct but complementary and deserve equal attention in education.

Synchrony or diachrony

A synchronic fact applies to a single point in time whereas a diachronic fact involves change through time; for example, from a synchronic point of view, the words *solicitor* and *solicit* have nothing to do with each other's meaning, but diachronically one is derived from the other in a way that used to make sense. Diachrony includes etymology, an important topic for education, and most of the interest of etymology lies precisely in the fact that the words it connects are not related synchronically.

Texts or systems

The written and spoken texts in a language are conceptually distinct from the system of stored rules and vocabulary that make them possible; in linguistic terms, performance is distinct from competence. For example, the fact that eighteenth-century novels used complicated sentences (texts) does not mean that the system of eighteenth-century grammar was complicated. Texts provide evidence for the system and the system explains the texts. The system is more abstract, so teachers may be tempted to concentrate on texts; but this misses the point of language education.

Lexemes or inflections

In linguistics, the words *dog* and *dogs* are different inflections of the same lexeme, DOG. This distinction is fundamental in education because of dictionaries: the richer the system of inflections is, the harder it is to use a dictionary. How does a beginner find *hablamos* in a Spanish dictionary, or even *misunderstood* in an English one?

Sounds or letters

Written characters (letters) are much easier to talk and think about than sounds, so the two are often confused not only by young children but also by their teachers (and indeed most other adults, including linguistics undergraduates); for instance, people talk about 'the sound th' being pronounced differently in *thin* and *then*. This is particularly damaging in a language where sounds and letters match as poorly as they do in English. Linguists and phoneticians solve the problem by providing a visual notation for sounds which is distinguished unambiguously from the writing system by the surrounding brackets. For example, we use <Ann> for the written form in contrast with /an/ or [an] for the spoken. School teachers would benefit enormously from some such convention.

Words or meanings

As with sounds and letters, words are often confused with their meanings; for example, an analysis of *fox* might describe it as both a noun (word) and a mammal (meaning). Here too it would be helpful to have a visible distinction such as the one used by many linguists which uses italics for words and quotation marks for meanings (e.g., *fox* is a noun but 'fox' is a mammal).

Punctuation or grammatical structure

Like meanings and sounds, grammatical structure is much harder to talk and think about than the punctuation marks which signal it, so there is a great temptation to confuse the two – e.g., to define a sentence as a sequence of words bounded by a capital letter and a full stop, rather than as a sequence held together by grammar. It is clearly a waste of time, or worse, to exhort children to put full stops at the end of their sentences before they have some understanding of grammatical sentence-hood.

A general conclusion that emerges from this list is that popular culture already has a kind of 'linguistic theory' for thinking and talking about language. This is heavily influenced by literacy, which provides visual objects (spellings and punctuation) that are much easier to handle conceptually than the invisible things that they stand for – sounds, meanings, grammatical structures, and so on. For all its undeniable benefits, literacy promotes a number of undesirable tendencies:

- to give higher status to the written form and to forms that are written;
- to project the uniformity of spelling onto the rest of language;
- to confuse the current language with its earlier stages;
- to focus on form rather than function;
- to focus on text rather than system;
- to confuse lexemes and inflections;
- to confuse the visual object with the thing it stands for, whether this is sound, meaning, or grammatical structure.

In contrast, professional linguistic theory is more or less successful in avoiding all these tendencies (although it undoubtedly shows residual effects of literacy).

Some Linguistic Models

As I explained earlier, linguistic theory also includes what I called 'models', which are complex packages of tightly interconnected claims. These models are essential for progress at the level of research, but they are much less relevant to education. Education does of course need models – models of learning and teaching, of psychological growth and social needs, and so on. And of course, among the models that education needs are models of language structure, use, and change. Unfortunately, linguistics does not yet have any such model which commands the same general support of the profession as the ideas that I listed above. Instead, it includes a number of approaches, each of which has some valuable insights for education.

I finish with a thumb-nail survey of the main approaches. These might be called 'super-models' as they comprise large bundles of assumptions about the aims and methods of linguistics, taking us into the higher realms of ideology and even politics.

- Generative linguistics produces very detailed and often dauntingly technical analyses of small areas of individual languages combined with extremely abstract generalizations about all languages. Its leading figure is Noam Chomsky, whom many people believe to have turned linguistics into a science by showing that grammars are theories to be confirmed or disconfirmed by data – what he called 'generative grammars'. His ideas lie behind the attempts mentioned earlier to use school-level linguistics as an introduction to the scientific method. Chomsky himself has tended to discourage applications to education by claiming that language is a unique 'mental organ' which develops under its own innate momentum (like puberty) rather than through learning or teaching.

- Systemic linguistics (also known as 'systemic functional linguistics') is led by Michael Halliday, and is strongly oriented towards education – the direct opposite of generative linguistics. Its adherents tend to avoid the technical questions about the formal structure of language that dominate generative linguistics and not to engage with adherents of other linguistic theories, so its claims regarding the structure of language should be taken with caution. However, education has been enriched by important ideas such as textual coherence, genre and register variation, and social meaning.
- Cognitive linguistics, which is newer and has no single leader, brings together a number of general models which are united in rejecting the generative idea that language is unique and innate. In contrast, cognitive linguists claim that language is similar to other areas of cognition, and that it grows gradually through vast amounts of experience. This new super-model has not yet had much impact on education, but it has a great deal to offer in the areas of both learning and structure.

It is unfortunate that one of these super-models, systemic linguistics, has achieved a near monopoly of influence on education. For one thing, fellow linguists have raised serious objections to the systemic theory of language which have never been answered, so this theory may well be wrong (Hudson, 1986). For another, language is enormously complex so it is likely to be many decades before we have a single model which brings together all its complexity; at this stage it would be much wiser for education to focus on single good ideas wherever they come from rather than signing up to a complete package of ideas. And finally, it would be a shame if allegiance to a single super-model distracted education either from good ideas such as the ones I listed above, or from the excellent language descriptions that are now available – dictionaries, grammars, phonologies, sociolinguistic analyses, and so on.

REFERENCES

Andrews, Richard, Beverton, Sue, Locke, Terry, Low, Graham, Robinson, Alison, Torgerson, Carole, & Zhu, Die (2004). The effect of grammar teaching (syntax) in English on 5 to 16 year olds' accuracy and quality in written composition. 2004. Unpublished manuscript.

Anon. (1999). *The National Curriculum for England: English.* London: Department for Education and Employment and the Qualifications and Curriculum Authority.

Anon. (2005). *Key Stage 2 Framework for Languages.* London: Department for Education and Skills.

Barlow, Michael & Kemmer, Suzanne (2000). *Usage Based Models of Language.* Stanford: CSLI.

Brookes, Arthur & Hudson, Richard (1982). Do linguists have anything to say to teachers? In R. Carter (ed.), *Linguistics and the Teacher* (pp. 52–74). London: Routledge & Kegan Paul.

Bryant, Peter, Devine, M., Ledward, A., & Nunes, Terezinha (2002). Spelling with apostrophes and understanding possession. *British Journal of Educational Psychology*, 67, 91–110.

Carter, Ron (1990). *Knowledge about Language and the Curriculum: The LINC Reader*. London: Hodder & Stoughton.

Chipere, Ngoni (2003). *Understanding Complex Sentences: Native Speaker Variation in Syntactic Competence*. London: Palgrave Macmillan.

Chomsky, Noam (1986). *Knowledge of Language: Its Nature, Origin and Use*. New York: Praeger.

Corson, David (1994). Language across the curriculum. In R. E. Asher (ed.), *Encyclopedia of Language and Linguistics* (pp. 1932–1933). Oxford: Pergamon.

Elley, Warwick (1994). Grammar teaching and language skill. In R. E. Asher (ed.), *Encyclopedia of Language and Linguistics* (pp. 1468–1471). Oxford: Pergamon.

Ellis, Nick (2002). Frequency effects in language processing: A review with implications for theories of implicit and explicit language acquisition. *Studies in Second Language Acquisition*, 24, 143–188.

Halliday, Michael (1978). *Language as Social Semiotic*. London: Arnold.

Hawkins, Eric (1999). Foreign language study and language awareness. *Language Awareness*, 8, 124–142.

Hawkins, Roger & Towell, Richard (1996). Why teach grammar? In Dulcie Engel & Florence Myles (eds.), *Teaching Grammar: Perspective in Higher Education* (pp. 195–211). London: AFLS and Centre for Information on Language Teaching.

Hillocks, George & Mavrognes, N. (1986). Sentence combining. In George Hillocks (ed.), *Research on Wrtten Composition: New Directions for Teaching* (pp. 142–146). Urbana, IL: NCTE.

Honda, Maya (1994). Linguistic inquiry in the science classroom: "It is science, but it's not like a science problem in a book." *MIT Occasional Papers in Linguistics*, 6, 1–262.

Honda, Maya & O'Neil, Wayne (1993). Triggering science-forming capacity through linguistic inquiry. In Kenneth Hale & Samuel J. Keyser (eds.), *The View from Building 20: Essays in Linguistics in Honor of Sylvain Bromberger* (pp. 229–255). Cambridge, MA: MIT Press.

Hudson, Richard (1981). Some issues on which linguists can agree. *Journal of Linguistics*, 17, 333–344.

Hudson, Richard (1986). Systemic grammar. Review of Halliday, M. A. K. (1985) *An Introduction to Functional Grammar*, London: Edward Arnold , and Butler, C.S. (1985) *Systemic Linguistics: Theory and Applications*, London: Batsford in *Linguistics*, 24, 791–815.

Hudson, Richard (1999). Grammar teaching is dead – NOT! In Rebecca S. Wheeler (ed.), *Language Alive in the Classroom* (pp. 101–112). Westport, CT: Greenwood.

Hudson, Richard (2004). Why education needs linguistics (and vice versa). *Journal of Linguistics*, 40, 105–130.

Norris, John & Ortega, Lourdes (2000). Effectiveness of L2 instruction: A research synthesis and quantitative meta-analysis. *Language Learning*, 50, 417–528.

Nunes, Terezinha, Bryant, Peter, & Olsson, Jenny (2003). Learning morphological and phonological spelling rules: An intervention study. *Scientific Studies of Reading*, 7, 289–307.

Renou, Janet (2001). An examination of the relationship between metalinguistic awareness and secondlanguage proficiency of adult learners of French. *Language Awareness*, 10, 248–267.

Stubbs, Michael (1986). *Educational Linguistics.* Oxford: Blackwell.

Tomasello, Michael (2003). *Constructing a Language: A Usage-Based Theory of Language Acquisition.* Cambridge, MA: Harvard University Press.

Wyse, Dominic (2001). Grammar for writing? A critical review of empirical evidence. *British Journal of Educational Studies,* 49, 411–427.

FURTHER READING

Brumfit, Christopher (2001). *Individual Freedom in Language Teaching: Helping Learners to Develop a Dialect of Their Own.* Oxford: Oxford University Press.

Hasan, Ruqaiya, Matthiessen, Christian M. I. M., & Webster, Jonathan (2005). *Continuing Discourse on Language: A Functional Perspective.* London: Equinox.

Heath, Shirley B. (2000). Linguistics in the study of language in education. *Harvard Educational Review,* 70, 49–59.

6 Sociolinguistics and Sociology of Language

RAJEND MESTHRIE

What is Sociolinguistics?

Linguistics studies language from various vantage points, most significantly focusing on language structure, acquisition, use, and change. Whilst the subfield of Sociolinguistics touches on all these aspects, its main concern is with 'use'. The subfield studies how language is socially embedded, paying attention to the social background and intentions of speakers, issues pertaining to their social characteristics and identities, as well as to the social context of speaking. This context incorporates matters like who is authorized to speak, what counts as appropriate language in different circumstances, and how speakers from different backgrounds may have different cultural assumptions and norms whilst ostensibly using 'the same language'. The main locus of enquiry is thus not the structure of a language for its own sake, as recorded in descriptive linguistic grammars; or the acquisition of language by individuals, which is primarily the domain of psycholinguistics; or the abstract mental capacity underlying all languages, which falls under the jurisdiction of cognitive and generative linguistics. Rather, the main focus in Sociolinguistics falls on language use within a speech community. Sociolinguistics is generally characterized by close attention to the actual speech of representative sections of a community, rather than the somewhat static and idealized patterns one finds in formal writing. Sociolinguistics thus adopts a non-prescriptive approach to its subject matter, avoiding subjective judgments about whether some aspect of language is 'better' than another. It stresses that frequently there are variable norms within the same community, with different instances of this variation characteristic of different subgroups of speakers or different contexts of using language. Thus the same speaker may say *Damn!* in one context, and *What a pity!* in another. Furthermore sociolinguists as professionals do not pass easy judgments in debates like "Which is preferable: *She spoke to John and I* or *She spoke to John and me*?" In this instance current patterns are genuinely variable. Looking up an old grammar book or consulting a figure of authority like a schoolteacher will not resolve the issue. Amongst the questions that a sociolinguist would initially pose are: Is the one variant characteristic of particular groups of speakers (social class)? In which style (formal/informal) is it used? In which modality (e.g., speech or writing)? Are other pragmatic factors involved (politeness)?, and so on. Likewise, the current spread of English features like *I'm like . . .* and *I go . . .* (followed by direct speech) is of immense linguistic interest: Why are these new 'quotative' forms so widespread? Are they more frequently used by young females than young males? Are there ethnic and class differences within societies in which it is found?, and so on. The orientation of Sociolinguistics is thus firmly 'bottom-up' rather than 'top-down'.

Where several languages coexist in a society, sociolinguists note that these languages frequently influence each other. Words from one language may be adopted into another (a process called borrowing), a sound from one language may gradually be adopted into another by bilingual speakers, etc. Again, sociolinguists avoid making purist judgments like 'foreign words spoil a language'. In some societies languages are hierarchically arranged, with relatively clear consensus about which language is used in which contexts. However, in other societies speakers may use more than one language in what appears to be the same speech event. Such code-switching is an area of considerable research, showing that it can be considered a social and linguistic skill. Speakers do not mix words randomly; rather there are specific grammatical points at which one may (or more frequently, may not) switch to another language. Moreover, switching is used to achieve subtle strategic effects, like to change the 'tone' of the conversation, to distance oneself from what is being said, to evoke a greater sense of authority or rapport, etc.

We may sum up the sociolinguistic approach by saying that it is generally:

- non-prescriptive and non-purist,
- appreciative of variation,
- considerate of speech and conversational norms,
- sympathetic towards multiculturalism and multilingualism 'on the ground',
- mindful of the interactive nature of speech,
- attentive to attitudes and norms of different subgroups within a society,
- receptive to change in language,
- responsive to broader contextual issues relating to power, culture, and identity.

These themes will be explored in the rest of the chapter, which will also show that whilst the emphases outlined above may not seem to gel too easily with educational practice (which sometimes by necessity tends to be formal, top-down, and/or homogenizing), there is considerable room for dialogue between Sociolinguistics and Education. Furthermore, the idealist orientation of Sociolinguistics has sometimes to be matched by *realpolitik* when some sociolinguists turn 'applied', in advising governments on language policy, devising educational materials, writing down a language for the first time, etc. This time the approach has to be more top-down, approaching language matters in relation to the concerns of governments, educational policies, state resources, etc. It is customary to label this area 'the Sociology of Language'. Broadly conceived, Sociolinguistics spans both bottom-up 'Microsociolinguistics' as well as the Sociology of Language.

Variation: Dialect, Style, Practice, Change

The study of linguistic variation focuses on the form of speakers' utterances rather than the content of the communication. Even while primarily concerned with the communicative function of language, a speaker will inevitably give off signals concerning his or her social and personal background. Language is accordingly said to be *indexical* of one's social class, status, region of origin, gender, age group, etc. The term 'index' here is drawn from semiotic theory (or the science of signs), in which it refers to a particular relation between a sign and the object it stands for. In the sociolinguistic sense 'index' refers to certain features of speech (including accent), which indicate an individual's social group (or background). The use of these features signals (or indexes) that the individual has access to the lifestyles that support that type of speech.

Some variation studies are concerned with style, situation, and function. They deal with the importance of contextual factors in determining different 'registers', styles, and genres. They also deal with the use of language in specific domains and functions such as in advertising, religion, business, and emailing. The notion of a domain is a particularly useful one. Fishman (1965) defined it as a sphere of activity arising from combination of specific times, settings, and role relationships, which results in a specific choice of language or style. The notion of 'register' is a linguistic counterpart of the sociological concept of domain. A register (Halliday, Macintosh, & Strevens, 1964) refers to variation according to the context in which language is used. Relatively well-defined registers include the language of the law, the language of science, and the language of Hip Hop or jazz.

Whereas register studies focus upon language use, relatively independent of the users, social dialectology does the reverse. In modern sociolinguistics, dialects and social groups are central to an understanding of language variation and change. The emphasis in this tradition falls upon the finely nuanced differences within a language according to social groupings, especially class, gender, ethnicity, and region. Variation theory, as developed by William Labov (1966), studies the relationship between region of origin, age, and – especially – social status and characteristic ways of using language. Variationists use correlational techniques in revealing the relationship between linguistic variables (e.g., a vowel sound that has different variants that result in different accents) and social variables (age, gender, class, etc.). This is a vibrant and rigorous branch of Sociolinguistics – to the extent that many characterize it as 'core Sociolinguistics' or 'Sociolinguistics proper'.

Prior to Labov's work in the early 1960s, dialectology had scored its main successes in studies of regional differentiation. Researchers had certainly been aware of linguistic distinctions of a social nature within a region, but had not developed systematic ways of describing them. Earlier explanations of nonregional variation fell into one of two categories: dialect mixture or free variation. 'Dialect mixture' implies the coexistence in one locality of two or more dialects, which enables a speaker to draw on one dialect at one time and on the other dialect(s) on other occasions. 'Free variation' refers to the random use of alternate forms within a particular dialect (e.g., two pronunciations of *often* (with or without the /t/ sounded)). Both views relegate variation to an extralinguistic domain, and mistakenly identify structure with homogeneity. Labov argued, instead, that language involved 'structured heterogeneity'. While he was not the first to point to the interplay between social and linguistic determinants of certain linguistic alterations (e.g., Fischer had discussed the social implications of the use of *-in* versus *-ing* in a New England setting in 1958), Labov was the initiator of an elaborate body of work which broke new ground in understanding language in its social context, accounting for linguistic change, and broadening the goals of linguistic theory. An important motivation in his early work was to understand one of the unsolved problems of historical linguistics – how changes in pronunciation are effected, as when a sound like [p] at one phase of a language may be later replaced by a sound like [f]. He also wondered how, if a language has to be structured in order to function efficiently, people continue to talk while language changes. The problem was shown to be less intractable once one invoked the idea of systematic variation among different groups of speakers within a speech community. In a famous study Labov showed that, contrary to previous beliefs, the use of postvocalic-*r* in New York City was not random ('postvocalic -*r*' refers to the sound [r] after a vowel in words like *park* or *bird*). For it to be random there should be no way of predicting in what contexts and by whom it was pronounced and when it was not. By undertaking detailed interviews with a cross-section of the city's mother tongue speakers of English, Labov was able to show a finely graded sociolinguistic patterning of [r]. The two important parameters were the social class of the speaker and the level of formality of the communication. Speakers from all social groups in the 1960s tended not to pronounce postvocalic-*r* in their most casual styles, except for the upper middle classes whose score for its presence was just under 20 percent. This feature was therefore associated with the prestige of the upper middle classes. In more careful styles within the interview all speakers showed a higher proportion of the presence of postvocalic [r], and in reading out a passage and a list of words at the end of the interview the proportion increased even further. The variable was thus sensitive to the dimension of style, as well as social class. This is what Labov meant by 'structured heterogeneity' in language. Under certain circumstances variation in language leads to change, as when the influence of the 'overt prestige' of middle-class usage is transferred from the formal styles of the other social classes to their more casual styles. Postvocalic [r] is called a linguistic variable and its different realizations in speech, variants (in this case whether it is pronounced or not).

Other sociolinguists were able to demonstrate the reverse effect in some societies – namely, the 'covert prestige' or solidarity value of working-class culture and speech. Although working-class language is frequently denigrated, sometimes by speakers themselves when asked to comment on their language, the persistence of these norms calls for alternative explanations. Trudgill (1978) shows how working-class pronunciations of certain vowels (in words like *nose, road, moan*) in Norwich, UK, exerted a counter-influence on males who were higher up in the social scale. Women were less susceptible to the 'covert prestige' of male working-class norms. The theme of gender differences in the realization of variables is, in fact, a prominent one in sociolinguistics. Gender and class appear to interact in complex ways (see Mesthrie et al., 2000: 106– 107). Likewise, ethnicity may be a prominent social variable that results in differential realization of specific linguistic variables. In the New York City study African American speakers followed the same patterns of usage for postvocalic [r] as other speakers. But an ethnic effect could be seen in a related variable – the use of [r] between two vowels (or intervocalic [r]) in words like *Carol* and *Paris*. In this instance dropping the [r] is an option for African American speakers, but not for other groups in the city. Age too is a prominent social variable.

Interaction

The Labovian tradition revolutionized our understanding of language variation and dialect use. It did this by focusing on social categories and salient linguistic elements. Labov's methods were statistical and correlational. By analyzing large numbers of words containing a variable of interest in the speech of large samples of speakers and correlating them with different social groups, Labov demonstrated how a society was organized in terms of speech behavior. In this section alternate ways of approaching variation are discussed, mainly from a perspective that has come to be called 'interactional sociolinguistics'. Interactionists tend to take neither language nor social groups as 'given', rather they see them as constantly created and recreated, on the basis of personal interaction between people. Although Interactional Sociolinguistics is primarily associated with the work of John Gumperz (1982), there are many approaches that can be called interactional. I will give an overview of some of these.

Like that of Bakhtin, the Russian linguist/critic writing in the 1920s to the 1940s, Gumperz's work stresses that the linguistic sign is 'dialogic', and hence best studied in context, and not in isolated interview utterances. (The term 'dialogic' was, however, used by Bakhtin (1981), not Gumperz.) Language is socially grounded, existing in context-bound encounters between individuals.

Social and cultural forces, together with grammar and lexicon, constrain what can be said and how it can be said. An important part of this work concerns the identification of 'contextualization cues'. These are constellations of features of the verbal (e.g., vocabulary, prosody, syntactic choices) and non-verbal (e.g., gestures, facial expressions) configurations which in the light of previous experience signal what kind of speech activity interlocutors consider themselves to be engaged in (e.g., banter, negotiating a loan, telling a story). The cues help establish social relations, set the frame for what will come next, fill in implicit information, and make inferences about the nature of the speech act.

Speech accommodation is a particular perspective upon communicative competence that fosters variation in speaker style. Giles and Powesland (1975) held that speakers tune their communicative style in relation to their interlocutor. The basic forms of accommodation are convergence and divergence, depending on the relative status of the speakers and the intended social relations. Bell's (1984) 'audience design' framework elaborates this scheme, taking into account the speaker and the audience. He stresses that we tailor our language not just according to our class or gender position, and to style, but to suit both the interlocutor (the person we are speaking to) and the audience. Speech may be adapted (deploying different realizations of different variables) depending on whether there are authorized participants, overhearers, eavesdroppers, a displaced mass audience on radio, television, etc.

The work of Le Page and Tabouret-Keller forms a bridge between Labov's emphasis on linguistic variables and the interactional emphasis on the role of interlocutors. For Le Page and Tabouret-Keller (1985: 14) linguistic behavior is "a series of *acts of identity* in which people reveal both their personal identity and their search for social roles." In this view identity and language use are potentially fluid; and individuals have priority – well-defined social groups may or may not exist beforehand. In the highly multilingual and heterogeneous communities they studied in the Caribbean, the researchers found it necessary to pay attention to the processes of emergence and disintegration of identities in relation to linguistic processes of focusing and diffusion. The terms 'focusing' and 'diffusion' are based on the metaphor of cinematic projection of images. Speech acts are acts of projection: the speaker projects his inner universe via a common language (with its nuances of grammar, vocabulary and accent) or via a particular choice of language where choices exist (in multilingual settings). The speaker implicitly invites others to share his projection of the world, insofar as they recognize his language as an accurate symbolization of the world, and to share his attitudes towards it (Le Page & Tabouret-Keller, 1985: 181). The feedback he receives from those with whom he talks may reinforce his perceptions, or may cause him to modify his projections, both in their form and content. To the extent that his speech forms are reinforced, his behavior in that context may become more regular, more focused; to the extent that he modifies his behavior to accommodate others, it may for a time become more variable, more diffuse. In time, however, the behavior of the group – that is, he and those with whom he is trying to identify – will become focused. The individual thus creates for himself patterns of linguistic behavior so as to resemble those of the group or groups which he wishes to be identified at different times. Le Page stressed four provisos to this hypothesis:

1   that one can identify the groups,
2   that one has adequate access to the groups and the ability to analyze their behavioral patterns,
3   that the motivation for joining the group must be sufficiently powerful and is either reinforced or lessened by feedback from the group,
4   that one has the ability to modify one's behavior.

Le Page and Tabouret-Keller's model thus teases out the kind of variation evident in a society from its historical moments: is it a society in the making or in flux (diffuse), or is it, historically speaking, focused?

Gender, Ethnicity, and Network

Le Page and Tabouret-Keller's approach is made more concrete in a complementary approach to the study of linguistic variation, social network theory, which utilizes both variation and interactional insights. Linguistic work utilizing the social networks of speakers was pioneered by Leslie Milroy (1980). Rather than study individual speakers as part of an abstract social group defined by social class, Milroy looked at how their speech behavior correlated with the nature of their everyday social contacts. She outlined two different types of social networks: close-knit and loose-knit ones. These are determined by two factors. First, 'density' or the number of contacts one has within the network: a maximally dense network relationship is one in which one has regular contacts with all members. One's friends' acquaintances are one's own too. A minimally dense equivalent is when one does not have much contact with one's friends' acquaintances. The second factor is whether the relationships within the network are multiplex or not. A 'multiplex' relation is one in which one interacts with another member in several roles. A neighbor might also be a friend, a co-worker, and a member of the same religious group. Milroy demonstrates convincingly that close-knit networks require loyalty to the local ways of speaking, whereas loose-knit networks have more diffuse norms and are more open to linguistic innovations.

The interactional approach has informed much recent work on language and gender in Linguistics. In earlier gender and language research (see Lakoff, 1975) the main aim was to demonstrate a broad linguistic split between the sexes. Subsequent researchers went beyond the descriptive framework to an action-research mode that popularized the argument that languages could be sexist – that is, they could discriminate against women by presenting things from a male perspective (see, e.g., Spender, 1990). Language thus not only reflects existing inequalities, but also helps to sustain and reproduce them, unless challenged. Subsequent gender research has increasingly become more nuanced. Eckert (1989) stresses the interplay between gender and social class in setting up various overlapping identities. From Anthropology and Gay Studies has come the notion that a simple two-way dichotomy is misleading; that there are differing degrees of masculinity and femininity (Johnson & Meinhof, 1997; Kulick, 2000). Within network analysis, certain gendered patterns of work are seen to foster differences in linguistic behavior between men and women. For example, if men from a close-knit network all work at the same locale, whilst the women stay at home and do not have as intense contacts with each other, the men's speech might be more 'focused' upon a local norm, while the women's speech might be more diffuse. The strength of this analysis is that it is not gender per se which generates specific accents and styles of talking, but the nature of the interaction within the network. As Milroy (1980) showed, a change in employment patterns (say with male unemployment causing more women to work outside the neighborhood) would alter both network structure and, eventually, linguistic behavior.

Similar arguments hold for sociolinguistic approaches to ethnicity. In some societies, ethnicity may be more salient than class stratification and language may play a key role in reflecting and indeed in maintaining and 'reproducing' an ethnic identity. Ethnicity is notoriously difficult to define and may not be as objective a phenomenon as sometimes assumed. Edwards (1985: 8) quotes Weber (1968), who regards ethnic groups as "those human groups that entertain a subjective belief in their common descent . . . it does not matter whether or not an objective blood relationship exists. Ethnic membership . . . differs from the kinship group precisely by being a *presumed* identity." Sociolinguists therefore argue against the notion of a 'primordial ethnicity' which one sometimes finds in the literature on language maintenance. After all, group identity can survive language shift (when a community gradually changes its primary language), and frequently does. On the other hand it is difficult to imagine a sense of ethnicity that does not entail significant differences in language use (e.g., religious and cultural vocabulary, and nuances of accent are well attested in ethnic dialects). Post-modern urban people of the twenty-first century frequently have multiple identities, playing out a number of roles in a single day, each of which may require different language choices.

Multilingualism and Language Contact

Many countries, especially in the West, attach special significance to one language over others, adhering to an ethos of 'one state, one language'. Many of the states of Europe arose in a period of intense nationalism, with accompanying attempts to make national borders co-terminous with language (and vice versa.) The dominance of European powers in modern history has made this seem a desirable situation, if not an ideal one. The non-aligned sociolinguist would, instead, point to the essentially multilingual nature of most human societies, and the fact that there are almost no countries in the world – even in Western Europe – where everyone speaks, or identifies with, one language. In statistical terms, Grosjean (1982: vii) estimates that about half the world's population is bilingual. Romaine (1989: 8) points out further that there are about 30 times as many languages as there are countries. Even countries like France and England that we are tempted to think of as monolingual have, in fact, a vast array of languages within their borders. In France, for example, the following languages are still in use: French, Breton, Flemish, Occitan, Catalan, Basque, Alsatian, and Corsican.

While multilingualism is not uncommon throughout the world, many schools have a policy that recognizes (and replicates) the hierarchy of relations within a territory and in the world as a whole. Only a small proportion of the 5,000 or so languages of the world are used at high school level as media of instruction, and still fewer at university level. Schools have often downplayed the value of the 'vernaculars' by minimizing their use in classrooms or recognizing them only as means of facilitating competence in the dominant language(s). Since the 1950s, and more especially since the 1970s, Western educationists have begun to recognize that multi-culturalism is not a transient phenomenon. Sociolinguists are generally sympathetic to an approach that gives recognition to and valorizes as many of a society's languages as possible. This is in keeping with a holistic approach that is sensitive to the needs of children from different backgrounds ('bottom-up'), and not just the bureaucratic needs of the state ('top-down').

The subfield of Language Contact stresses the reality that societies are rarely monolingual; languages exist amidst other languages. The idea of a pure and self-contained language is a poor simplifying assumption compared to the challenges of studying the ways in which speakers of different languages influence each other; how new languages (e.g., pidgins and creoles) are borne out of struggle and how multilingualism is 'managed' by speakers at a micro level and by societies at a macro level. In some multilingual societies a child may be said to have several native languages, with the order of acquisition not being an indicator of ability. Multilingual speakers may switch languages according to situation in a way that monolingual speakers switch styles of the same language 'natively' (Scotton, 1985). For many New English speakers monolingualism is the marked case, a special case outside of the multilingual prototype. Today's ideal speaker lives in a heterogeneous society (stratified along increasingly globalized lines) and has to negotiate interactions with different people representing all sorts of power and solidary positions on a regular basis. What is this ideal speaker a native speaker of, but a polyphony of codes/languages working cumulatively (and sometimes complementarily), rather than a single, first-learned code?

Studies of code-switching reinforce the notion that communicative competence goes beyond that of the monolingual's mastery of syntax. Accounts of the social and contextual motivations for code-switching have proven a necessary complement to purely structural approaches seeking to account for where in the sentence a speaker may (or may not) switch to another language (Myers-Scotton, 1993). Interaction between speakers, degrees of convergence and divergence, and intentions to alter the rights and obligations associated with one code rather than another have all been fruitfully employed to account for the facility that fluent bilinguals show in switching between languages. 'Crossing' is a particular kind of code-switching in which speakers use a variety which is not generally associated with their group (Rampton, 1995). It permits speakers from one group to overcome social boundaries and build links with members of what may be otherwise seen as an 'outgroup'. Crossing may have an accommodative and emblematic function. But it can also emphasize boundaries if the code used in the crossing reflects stereotypes about the outgroup's language use, rather than their actual practice. Crossing, which is done mainly by adolescents or post-adolescents, is one way of calling into question set identities associated with older generations. The notion of identity is crucial in Sociolinguistics, in which emphasis falls more on small self-selected groups or larger groups tied to a regional identity, rather than on national identities.

A 'Community of Practice' is a collection of people who engage in a common activity on an ongoing basis. The value of the concept, introduced into Sociolinguistics by Eckert and McConell-Ginet (1992), lies in the identification of a social grouping not on the basis of shared abstract characteristics (class, ethnicity, etc.), but on the basis of shared practice. The Community of Practice concept thus mediates between the vernacular (and its basis in early learnt, localized forms of language) and officialese/bureaucratese/transactional language. A focus on the domains of usage and code choice pertaining to those domains necessitates an examination of language in its more bureaucratic modes.

The field of Language Planning deals with the management of language resources of a state or other political entity. A formal language policy may be the outcome of language planning. Language policy may also refer to the norms of the speech community in its characteristic choices of language items or language varieties in relation to some conscious or unconscious ideology. Whereas one policy or another may have significant influence on the fate of a language, the field of language maintenance and shift shows that language legislation is seldom sufficient to halt the decline of a language. Factors to do with perceived economics and prestige amongst speakers and would-be speakers are equally important.

An area in which sociolinguists work with anthropologists and theoretical linguists is in studies of language maintenance and shift in minority communities, and of language endangerment. It is predicted that the vast majority of the world's languages will face a struggle to survive in the present century (Krauss, 1992), as regionally and globally more powerful languages spread. The very cultural and linguistic diversity that sustained small and less powerful communities and which formed the core concerns of Sociolinguistics and

Anthropology is under threat. Recording, cataloging, archiving, and even teaching languages to communities who have few or no native speakers left has become of vital concern in Linguistics (see Grenoble & Whaley, 1998; Nettle & Romaine, 2000).

Sociolinguistic Applications in Education

The chief contribution of sociolinguistics in educational settings has been to draw attention to the differences between language use in the classroom and in students' homes and communities. Because it is important to teaching and learning, language is heavily regulated in classrooms. *Teacher talk* is the name given to the special register that teachers use. It is a means of inducting pupils into specific topics and approaches and imparting instruction. Like all registers, Teacher Talk has developed certain conventions and properties. It typically comprises longer and more complex utterances than the teacher expects from the pupils. And the discourse is usually stacked in the direction of the teacher, who asks the questions, regulates responses, and so forth. Teacher–student exchanges are not randomly constructed but organized in terms of a three-part *IRE* sequence (Initiation, Response, Evaluation, as identified by Mehan, 1979), exemplified below:

INITIATION (teacher):	*Who can tell me where penguins live?*
RESPONSE (pupil):	*In Antarctica.*
EVALUATION (teacher):	*That's right, Jill. Now where else can they be found?* (new sequence initiated).

Classroom discourse uses IRE as its backbone, whilst elaborating, modifying, and extending it as needed. Yet this simple sequence is not a 'universal', readily understood convention. Leap (1993) stresses that since questions may have different significance in different cultures, pupils need to initially come to grips with classroom language conventions before grasping the content of lessons. Amongst the Northern Ute people that Leap worked with, asking a question is permissible if it is known that the addressee knows the answer – hence, a pupil being asked a question feels obliged to answer. In an example from classroom language Leap shows how this tradition forces a novice pupil to supply an answer to a teacher's question, rather than admit that he doesn't yet have one (see Leap & Mesthrie, 2000: 356–361). This can lead to misunderstandings on the side of pupil or teacher, and be a hindrance to progress in the lesson. The ethnographic sensitivity needed to come to terms with understanding the role of primary education is amplified in Shirley Brice-Heath's (1983) acclaimed study of differences in the 'ways with words' between middle-class white, working-class white, and working-class black communities in rural South Carolina. Because middle-class white parents spend time with their children reading stories out aloud and discussing them, children are attuned to being asked 'teacherly' kinds of questions, 'revoicing' (having one's words paraphrased, modified, and extended) and other features of teacher talk that they encounter in the classroom. Amongst the working-class whites, however, a different kind of reading socialization is offered, with less focus on interaction: the parents read the story and children absorb it. This makes it initially difficult for pupils to cope with the approach they face in the class-room, where the emphasis is more on forming opinions and making predictions from the stories, rather than accurate retellings alone. In the working-class black communities that Heath studied, stories were more oral, rather than literacy-based: there is less reading and more oral performance. Such different orientations to verbalization are common the world over. The sociologist Basil Bernstein (1974) had earlier hypothesized that there was a disjuncture between working-class and middle-class norms in more than just storytelling modes. Rather, he saw two different cognitive modes of operation amongst the working and middle classes of England, which were realized linguistically as different codes, which he termed the *restricted* and *elaborated codes*. An elaborated code was more characteristic of pupils from a middle-class background, using language that Bernstein believed to be more precise, creative, and expressive, and relatively decontextualized. He characterized working-class pupils as coming from a culture that emphasized the opposite: shared understanding that required less explicit language, and greater authoritarianism in the home amongst parents, requiring more direct use of language. Sociolinguists in the US and UK did not concur with such a bipolar assessment of language differences according to class. Labov (1969) stressed that a relatively elliptical style could be appropriate in certain contexts, while an elaborated code could be unnecessarily verbose in certain contexts. Moreover, Bernstein's characterization of language itself was not that of a specialist: actual linguistic examples were rather rare in his studies. By contrast, linguistics at that time was stressing the relations between 'universal' deep structure and surface manifestations in different languages and different dialects of the same language system (Chomsky, 1965). Dialect differences which seem large scale to the non-specialist or prescriptively trained analyst are often minor in the overall context of the language system. A famous demonstration of this was Labov's account of copula deletion in Black English of the US. The copula is the linking element in language, expressed in English by the verb *to be* (and its realizations as *am/is/are/were*, etc.), as in *She is smart* or *He is my uncle*. Black English and some other dialects of English tend to delete the copula (*She smart*, *He my uncle*). Labov showed how this surface difference concealed a great deal of underlying, logical similarity. He first noted that there were contexts when the copula couldn't be deleted in Black English, e.g., at the end of a sentence (*How smart you are!*, not *How smart you!*). This variability, far from being defective, mirrored a rule of standard English which allows the copula to occur in contracted form (*She's smart*; *He's my uncle*). The most compelling part of the analysis showed that contraction is disallowed in certain contexts in standard English: e.g., in the sentence *How smart you're!* From the viewpoint of set theory and logic, the rules of Black English and standard English turn out to be parallel: the set of potential sentences in which Black English permits deletion is precisely that in which standard English permits contraction. Although some details of Black English copula deletion have since been modified (see Baugh, 1980), Labov's account signaled the quiet demise of theories of linguistic deficit, amongst linguists at least.

However, there are aspects of Bernstein's work that remain relevant to educational linguistics. Bernstein drew attention to the ways in which the norms of the school favored the one code over the other. Educational intervention is thus potentially open ended: either the school should adapt to accommodate the norms of its pupils or it should provide the opportunities for the pupils to adapt more easily to the orientations of the school. Whereas Labov's demonstrations of equivalence were on structural grounds, education is much more of a 'discursive activity'. Habitual ways of using language and organization into patterns larger than the sentence take us from structure into discourse. And here, though different dialects are equal in potential, the actual standing of a dialect depends on the extent to which it is used in the relevant registers. Ultimately, this depends on power relations within societies, habits of history, and degrees and kinds of literacies that operate within communities. In this regard the work of Heath cited above is particularly salient.

These issues about the status and capacities of dialects in educational settings and the needs, attitudes, and expectations of their speakers came to the fore in the Ann Arbor trial over the possibility of using Black English (now termed *African American English*) in the classroom. A group of parents and community activists brought suit against the Martin Luther King Junior Elementary School (Ann Arbor School District), charging that the education system did not address the cultural, social, and economic situation of the pupils. Sociolinguists like Labov and Geneva Smitherman testified to the regularity of African American English, citing evidence that the features considered to be defective by schoolteachers were in fact widely occurring regularities in the dialect (see Labov, 1982 for details). The presiding judge decided in favor of the plaintiffs, concluding that the children's home language is not in itself a barrier, but becomes one when it is not taken into account in teaching standard English. The Ann Arbor school board was directed to prepare a plan to help teachers use the pupils' fluency in the dialect as a foundation for developing standard English skills. A training program was devised by the school district to familiarize teachers with the details of African American English. However, it was terminated after two years as there was considerable uncertainty about ways to make this knowledge relevant to classroom instruction.

The uncertainty continued into the 1990s, culminating in what has become known as the Ebonics debate. This time it was a school in Oakland, California that raised the issue of the legitimacy of African American English (called *Ebonics*, after *Ebony + phonics*) and the need to incorporate it into school programs. The Oakland school board stressed the independent histories of Black and White varieties of English, and suggested that something akin to a bilingual school program was needed to ensure greater levels of success than was the case at that time in schools having large numbers of African American children. Although the Linguistic Society of America strongly supported the recognition of the variety spoken by African American children, public reaction nationally was mixed (see Leap & Mesthrie, 2000: 376–381). A majority of commentators from diverse sectors (including some African American parents and leaders) criticized the proposals heavily. As a result, the issue gradually faded from the public eye. The Oakland school board retreated to a compromise position that called for programs that focused on the acquisition and mastery of standard English skills, while simultaneously respecting the legitimacy and richness of the language that students bring to the school. The Ann Arbor and Ebonics debates show how important language issues are to education. But they also show that other less purely linguistic factors are fully implicated too – e.g., the status of language varieties, the attitudes of speakers, and the existing power relations in the wider society.

Just as complex an issue is the choice of which language(s) to use in classrooms in multilingual settings, especially ones in which inequality between the status and position of different languages coexists with limited resources. A basis for this discussion is the report of 1953 of the committee of specialists commissioned by UNESCO to investigate the choice of languages in educational settings worldwide (the document is reprinted in Fishman, 1968). The report stressed the importance of using the pupil's mother tongue in developing his/her power of self expression to the full. This applied to the early years of formal education. The mother tongue should be used for as long as the supply of books and materials permitted. The report recommended that where a child's language is not the official language of the country concerned, or is not a world language, she/he needs to learn such a second language. It also stresses (contrary to many parents' belief) that a knowledge of a second language can be gained without using it as a medium of instruction. These are valuable guidelines, though practical circumstances (e.g., a school with a high multilingual intake) and the availability of educational resources may make these ideals less viable (see Bull, 1964; and Fasold, 1984). The concerns of the UNESCO report were brought into focus in the work of James Cummins (1979), who studied different types of bilingual programs in Canada. Cummins argued that children can attain educational success in a second language provided that first-language development is also heeded, particularly in developing vocabulary and concepts relevant to the school. Children in immigrant communities often speak a language that has little of the support that dominant languages enjoy. Cummins argued that in such cases the home–school mismatch leads to a delay in the acquisition and development of the second language, and hence of the education provided in that language. He proposed that the child has to reach a certain level in the first language before she/he could succeed in the second language. This is known as the 'threshold hypothesis'. The levels attained in each language would then lead to knowledge accumulated in the one reinforcing the other – the 'interdependence hypothesis'. Cummins's arguments are attractive, but have remained hypotheses, difficult to prove outside the rather special case of French-English bilingual programmes in Canada. Critics argue that success in bilingual education is dependent on many more factors that the relationship between first and second language. For example, motivational, emotional, financial, and sociopolitical factors are also involved. The Ebonics efforts can be seen as an attempt to build inter-dialect interdependence of the sort promulgated in Cummins's work. An even greater challenge is to build such a relation between languages, where the one does not have the status or the resources associated with a more powerful language of wider communication. What if the home language is not written, and is receding in that not all members of the community use it anymore? See Leap (1993) for a discussion of a bilingual education program in the northern Ute reservation facing just these issues.

Conclusion

Whilst at first sight the interest of sociolinguists in colloquial speech may not seem to have much in common with the concerns of teachers, who frequently teach more formal registers of language, there is, in fact, ample room for cross-fertilization. Sociolinguistics forces us to recognize the priority of speech in peoples' lives and its basis for the more formal registers that school success is predicated upon. It is also important for educationists to recognize that variation is a normal part of human linguistic behavior, and is involved in subtle 'identity' work. Requiring children to change their way of speaking is not just a language directive, but a social one as well. It is more reasonable to try to add to a speaker's stylistic repertoire, rather than replace the vernacular, since style shifts are part of normal linguistic behavior. Likewise, a validation of multilingual practices, including code-switching and borrowing, is necessary in certain classrooms. Hopefully we are a long way away from the demeaning punishments imposed in colonial schools upon children who dared to use their home languages and dialects in class or in the playground (see Romaine, 1989; Mesthrie, 2002).

REFERENCES

Bakhtin, M. M. (1981). *The Dialogic Imagination*, edited by M. Holquist, trans. C. Emerson and M. Holquist. Austin: University of Texas Press.

Baugh, J. (1980). A re-examination of the Black English copula. In W. Labov (ed.), *Locating Language in Time and Space: Quantitative Analyses of Linguistic Structure* (vol. 1, pp. 83–106). New York: Academic Press.

Bell, A. (1984). Language style as audience design. *Language in Society*, 13(2), 145–201.

Bernstein, B. (1974). *Class, Codes and Control*, vol. 1. London: Routledge.

Bull, W. (1964). The use of vernacular languages in education. In D. Hymes (ed.), *Language in Culture and Society* (pp. 527–533). New York: Harper & Row.

Chomsky, N. (1965). *Aspects of the Theory of Syntax*. Cambridge, MA: MIT Press.

Cummins, J. (1979). Linguistic interdependence and the educational development of bilingual children. *Review of Educational Research*, 49, 221–251.

Eckert, P. (1989). Gender and sociolinguistic variation. In J. Coates (ed.), *Language and Gender: A Reader* (pp. 64–75). Oxford: Blackwell.

Eckert, P. & McConnell-Ginet, S. (1992). Communities of practice: Where language, gender and power all live. In K. Hall, M. Buchholtz, & B. Moonwomon (eds.), *Locating Power: Proceedings of the 1992 Berkeley Women and Language Conference* (pp. 89–99). Berkeley: Berkeley Women and Language Group. Reprinted in J. Coates (ed.) (1998), *Readings in Language and Gender*, Oxford: Blackwell.

Edwards, J. (1985). *Language, Society, and Identity*. Oxford: Blackwell.

Fasold, R. (1984). *The Sociolinguistics of Society*. Oxford: Blackwell.

Fishman, J. A. (1965). Who speaks what language to whom and when. *La Linquistique*, 2, 67–88.

Fishman, J. A. (ed.) (1968). *Readings in the Sociology of Language*. The Hague: Mouton.

Giles, H. & Powesland, P. F. (1975). *Speech Style and Social Evaluation*. London: Academic Press.

Grenoble, L. A. & Whaley, L. J. (eds.) (1998). *Endangered Languages: Current Issues and Future Prospects*. Cambridge: Cambridge University Press.

Grosjean, F. (1982). *Life with Two Languages: an Introduction to Bilingualism*. Cambridge, MA: Harvard University Press. vii.

Gumperz, J. J. (ed.) (1982). *Language and Social Identity*. Cambridge: Cambridge University Press, Cambridge, UK.

Halliday, M. A. K., Macintosh, A., & Strevens, P. (1964). *The Linguistic Sciences and Language Teaching*. London: Longman.

Heath, S. B. (1983). *Ways with Words: Language, Life and Work in Communities and Classrooms*. Cambridge: Cambridge University Press.

Johnson, S. & Meinhof, U. H. (1997). *Language and Masculinity*. Oxford: Blackwell.

Krauss, M. (1992). The world's languages in crisis. *Language*, 68, 4–10.

Kulick, D. (2000). Gay and lesbian language. *Annual Review of Anthropology*, 29, 243–285.

Labov, W. (1966). *The Social Stratification of English in New York City*. Washington, DC: Center for Applied Linguistics.

Labov, W. (1969). Contraction, deletion and inherent variability of the English copula. *Language*, 45(4), 715–762.

Labov, W. (1982). Objectivity and commitment in linguistic science: The case of the Black English trial in Ann Arbor. *Language in Society*, 11, 165–201.

Lakoff, R. (1975). *Language and Woman's Place*. New York: Harper & Row.

Leap, W. (1993). *American Indian English*. Salt Lake City: University of Utah Press.

Leap, W. & Mesthrie, R. (2000). Sociolinguistics and education. In R. Mesthrie, J. Swann, A. Deumert, & W. Leap (2000). *Introducing Sociolinguistics* (pp. 354–383). Edinburgh: Edinburgh University Press.

Le Page, R. B. & Tabouret-Keller, A. (1985). *Acts of Identity: Creole-Based Approaches to Language and Ethnicity*. Cambridge: Cambridge University Press.

Mehan, H. (1979). *Learning Lessons*. Cambridge, MA: Harvard University Press.

Mesthrie, R. (2002). Building a new English dialect: South African Indian English and the history of Englishes. In P. Trudgill & R. Watts (eds.), *The History of English: Alternative Perspectives* (pp. 111–133). London: Routledge.

Mesthrie, R., Swann, J., Deumert, A., & Leap, L. (2000). *Introducing Sociolinguistics.* Edinburgh: Edinburgh University Press.

Milroy, L. (1980). *Language and Social Networks* (1st edn.; 2nd edn. 1987). Oxford: Blackwell.

Myers-Scotton, C. (1993). *Social Motivations for Code Switching: Evidence from Africa.* Oxford: Clarendon.

Nettle, D. & Romaine, S. (2000). *Vanishing Voices: The Extinction of the World's Languages.* Oxford: Oxford University Press.

Rampton, B. (1995). *Crossing: Language and Ethnicity among Adolescents.* London: Longman.

Romaine, S. (1989). *Bilingualism.* Oxford: Blackwell.

Scotton, C. M. (1985). "What the heck, Sir": Style shifting and lexical colouring as features of powerful language. In R. L. Street, Jr. & J. L. Cappella (eds.), *Sequence and Pattern in Communicative Behaviour* (pp. 103–119). London: Arnold.

Spender, D. (1990). *Man Made Language.* London: Pandora.

Trudgill, P. (1978). Sex, covert prestige, and linguistic change in the urban British English of Norwich. *Language in Society*, 1, 179–196.

Weber, M. (1968). *Economy of Society.* New York: Bedminster.

7 Linguistic Anthropology

STANTON WORTHAM

Linguistic anthropologists investigate how language use both presupposes and creates social relations in cultural context (Silverstein, 1985; Duranti, 1997; Agha, 2006). Theories and methods from linguistic anthropology have been productively applied in educational research for the past 40 years. This chapter describes key aspects of a linguistic anthropological approach, reviews research in which these have been used to study educational phenomena, and illustrates how researchers can analyze educational data from this perspective. Readers should also consult Chapter 28, Language Socialization, by Kathleen Riley, later in this volume, for a discussion of linguistic anthropological research in the language socialization tradition.

The linguistic and paralinguistic signs that compose educational language use communicate both referential and relational messages. When educators and learners speak and write, they communicate not only about the subject matter they are learning but also about their affiliations with social groups both inside and outside the speech event. These affiliations, some of which are created in educational events and institutions themselves, can shape students' life trajectories and influence how they learn subject matter. For both theoretical and practical reasons, then, educational researchers need to understand how language use both creates and presupposes social relations during educational activities.

Linguistic anthropology provides a useful set of tools for studying how educational language use reinforces and creates social relations (Wortham & Rymes, 2003). Linguistic anthropology is an interdisciplinary field – a recognized subdiscipline within American anthropology that also draws on linguistics (e.g., Eckert, 2000), qualitative sociology (e.g., Goffman, 1981; Mehan et al., 1996), cultural anthropology (e.g., Street, 2005), and European "linguistic ethnography" (e.g., Blommaert, 1999; Rampton, 2005). Linguistic anthropologists study how signs communicate referential and relational messages as they are used in social and cultural contexts. In doing so they draw on four key concepts, comprising what Silverstein (1985) has called the "total linguistic fact" – that is, four aspects of language use that must be analyzed to understand how linguistic signs have meaning in practice – *form*, *use*, *ideology* and *domain*.

Linguistic anthropologists use linguists' accounts of phonological, grammatical and other systematically distributed categories of language *form*. Unlike formal linguists, however, linguistic anthropologists are not primarily interested in how linguistic signs have meaning apart from contexts of use. Instead, they study how such signs come to have both referential and relational meanings in social and cultural context (Hymes, 1964; Duranti, 1997). The meaning of any linguistic sign in *use* cannot be determined by decontextualized rules, whether linguistic or social. No matter how robust the relevant regularities, speakers and hearers can use signs in unexpected yet meaningful ways (Goffman, 1981; Silverstein, 1992). Linguistic anthropologists study how speech comes to have sometimes-unexpected meanings in local contexts. As important as local context is, however, the meaning of any linguistic sign cannot be understood without also attending to more widely circulating models of the social world. Linguistic anthropologists often construe these models as *ideologies* of language – models of linguistic features and the speakers who characteristically use them, which people draw on as they interpret the social relations signaled through language use (Silverstein, 1985; Schieffelin, Woolard, & Kroskrity, 1998). These ideologies are not evenly distributed across social space, but have a *domain* – the set of people who recognize the indexical link between a type of sign and the relevant ideology (Agha, 2006). Linguistic anthropologists study how models of language and social relations move from event to event, across time and across social space, and how such movement contributes to local and historical change in both language and society. This chapter describes how "linguistic anthropologists of education" – those who use a linguistic anthropological approach to study educational phenomena (Wortham & Rymes, 2003) – have applied the concepts of form, use, ideology, and domain in educational research.

Form and Use

The basic question facing both participants in and analysts of verbal interaction is: What does a given sign or utterance communicate about the events being described and enacted (Garfinkel & Sacks, 1970; Silverstein, 1992; Erickson, 2004)? From a linguistic anthropological perspective, we cannot answer this question unless we attend to form, use, ideology, and domain. As I discuss these four aspects across the next several sections, I will refer to an example taken from my own work in American high school classrooms. I offer brief analyses of these data both to exemplify my conceptual sketch of linguistic anthropology and to illustrate a methodological approach often taken by linguistic anthropologists. Space limitations prevent an adequate description of either the data or the methodological approach. See Wortham (2004, 2006) for the former and Wortham (2001; Wortham & Locher, 1996) for the latter.

These data come from a ninth grade combined English and history classroom in an urban American school. The following example concerns a student whom I call Tyisha. This example occurred in January, at an important time for the emergence of Tyisha's social identity in this classroom. She had begun the academic year, in both the teachers' and other students' estimation, as one of the good students in the class. In November and December, however, the teachers began to identify her as disruptive, as more concerned with pushing her own opinions than with contributing to class discussion. On January 18, the class was discussing Aristotle's *Politics* and exploring his definition of "courage." In the following passage Tyisha offers herself as an example, and this discussion becomes an important turning point in teachers' and students' emerging identification of Tyisha as disruptive. ("TYI" stands for Tyisha, "T/B" for Mrs Bailey, one of the teachers, and "FST" for an unidentified female student. Transcription conventions are in the appendix.)

```
        TYI:   okay, I(hhh)- I had a friend. and she was like,
               sneaking out with a boy, and she lied and said that she was
               going with her friends. (hh) a(h)nd she told me, if my
  270          mother call, to tell her she was at the zoo with her friend
               Stacey. now that took her courage to te(h)ll me.
        FST:   (hhh)[
        TYI:         [ and it took c(hh)oura(h)ge for me to tell her
               mother that.
  275   FST:   mhm
        T/B:   did it take courage for[ her to tell her mother tha[t?
        FST:                          [ no                        [I
               don't think so
```

Throughout the chapter, I will use this example to illustrate a linguistic anthropological approach to educational processes. Further excerpts from subsequent class discussion of this example appear below. Note for the moment that Tyisha's example puts both cognitive and interactional issues into play. After Tyisha gives this example, teachers and students might ask: Does the example illuminate Aristotle and relate it to students' own lives? Does the fact that Tyisha lied to her friend's mother make her morally suspect and/or less promising as a student?

Linguistic anthropologists attend to linguistic *form*. For many decades, however, linguistic anthropologists have moved away from a linguistic emphasis on referential meaning and decontextualized regularities to a more ethnographic emphasis on appropriate communication in cultural contexts (Gumperz, 1982; Hymes, 1964). Early work on education described students from non-mainstream language communities employing norms of appropriate communication from their home communities, and showed how mainstream educators often misinterpreted this language use as "uneducated" (Cazden, John, & Hymes, 1972). This research attended systematically to linguistic form, but it did so in order to understand how linguistic patterns interconnect with local cultural models of social relationships and appropriate demeanor, and the emergent organization of speech events. Contemporary linguistic anthropology of education continues to offer systematic analyses of various linguistic patterns, ranging from studies of phonological variation across groups (e.g., Eckert, 2000; Bucholtz, 2001; Stocker, 2003) to studies of grammatical and lexical patterns that distinguish dialects and registers (e.g., Jaffe, 1999; Kiesling, 2001), in order to illuminate the cultural significance of language in use.

In Tyisha's example, participants and analysts need to know certain things about syntax and semantics in order to understand what is being communicated. For instance, Tyisha's example represents her friend's speech. Like all languages, English provides grammatical categories used to represent speech. In line 268, Tyisha uses the metapragmatic verb "lie," as well as the verb "say." These verbs come from a specific paradigmatic set, and they distribute in regular ways. Tyisha also quotes her friend's speech, from lines 269–271, using a blended version of quoted speech, in which some of the deictics ("my" in line 269) shift to the perspective of the quoted speaker, as in direct quoted speech, while others remain from the perspective of the quoting speaker ("she" and "her" at line 270). This variant of "indirect freestyle" (Banfield, 1982; Lee, 1997) allows a speaker to move what Jakobson (1957/1971) calls the "narrated event" closer to the "event of speaking," thus heightening the immediacy of the example.

From the beginning, linguistic anthropology of education has moved beyond a study of form to emphasize the study of language in *use*. Hymes (1972) argues that speech can have multiple functions and that educational researchers must examine how utterances come to serve particular functions in context. Instead of presenting speakers as following decontextualized linguistic and pragmatic rules, Gumperz (1982) and Hymes (1972) describe speakers drawing on diverse resources and creating novel responses in context. Erickson and Shultz (1982) provide an extended study of creative language use, in which they explore the "socially and culturally organized improvisation" that occurs in conversations between academic counselors and students from non-mainstream backgrounds. Erickson and Shultz do not argue simply that non-mainstream students and mainstream counselors experience a "mismatch" of discursive styles, resulting in counselors' misjudgments about students. They show how counselors and students use various resources to create, override, resist, and defuse such mismatches. Non-mainstream students are often disadvantaged by their non-standard habits of speaking and by mainstream counselors' assumptions about these "deficits," but such disadvantage does not happen simply through a clash of monolithic styles. Erickson and Shultz find that "situationally emergent identity" explains more about the outcome of a "gatekeeping" encounter than demographically fixed identity, and they show how speakers use linguistic and cultural resources in context both to reproduce and to overcome disadvantage.

The general point here, as described systematically by Silverstein (1992), is that signs indicate social relations only in context. When a speaker uses a less formal term, for instance – say, "lawyer" or "ambulance-chaser" instead of "attorney" – this can indicate that the speaker is poorly educated or unrefined, but it can also signal solidarity or humor. Tokens of such a sign only come to have determinate meaning when hearers understand them against the background of relevant context. "Context," however, potentially includes an enormous number of sometimes contradictory pieces of information. When I said "ambulance-chaser" just now, were you aware of the fact that I had recently been victimized by an unscrupulous lawyer, or the fact that I am organizing a movement to rescue our government from the legal-lobbyist complex, or the fact that I know you are married to one? Any or all of these (perhaps hypothetical) aspects of the context could have been made salient by earlier interaction, or they could be facts we know about each other. Depending on which features of the context are salient at the moment of utterance, participants will interpret the sign differently. This is what Silverstein calls "contextualization," the fact that signs come to have meaning only as they and co-occuring signs index aspects of the context. Cultural knowledge is crucial to interpreting the relational meaning of utterances, but we can only interpret that meaning by examining how utterances get contextualized in use. Instead of establishing a list of cultural beliefs, styles or rules that allegedly suffice to determine meaning, linguistic anthropologists study how speakers select from among many potentially relevant beliefs, styles, and rules, and sometimes ignore or change them, in actual events of language use.

Contemporary work in the linguistic anthropology of education has shown how attention to language use in this sense can illuminate educational processes. Rampton (2005), for instance, describes language "crossing" in urban, multiethnic groups of adolescents. Crossing is the use of words or other linguistic features from other languages in the course of an utterance. Rampton studies the use of Panjabi, Carribean Creole, and Stylized Asian English by white, South Asian, and Carribean youth in the UK. He does not argue simply that minority languages are devalued and used to stigmatize non-mainstream youth, nor that such youth use their home languages to resist such discrimination. Both of these processes, among others, do occur, but Rampton studies how these and other functions are accomplished in practice. The use of terms from a minority language does not have one or two fixed meanings – like stigma or resistance – because particular uses involve contestation, teasing, resistance, irony, and other stances. Like Erickson (2004; Erickson & Shultz, 1982), Rampton is deeply concerned about how the cultural politics of difference can disadvantage minority youth, and he describes the larger social and political forces regimenting language, identity, and politics in the UK. But he does not reduce disadvantage to predictable forms of identity politics, in which signs of identity routinely signal negative stereotypes. He shows instead how youth use language to navigate among the conflicting forms of solidarity and identity available to them in multiethnic Britain.

He (2003) and Rymes (2001) also attend closely to creativity and indeterminacy in particular speech events. Like Rampton, they first describe habitual patterns of language use which serve as background against which creative uses happen. He (2003) shows how Chinese heritage language teachers often use predictable three-part "moralized directives" in order to control disruptive behavior. Rymes (2001) describes typical "dropping out" and "dropping in" autobiographical stories, through which alternative school students construct senses of self and reject or embrace formal education. But He and Rymes go on to show how educators and learners use and sometimes transform these habitual patterns as they construct particular stances in context. He (2003) shows how the Chinese heritage language teacher's authority waxes and wanes during a lesson, as she uses moralized directives in various ways and as students react to these uses. Rymes (2001) shows how students from the alternative school reproduce, contest, and ridicule typical dropping out and dropping in stories. Sometimes they even contest the distinction between students who have embraced and rejected school, thereby positioning themselves in unpredictable ways with respect to linguistic, ethnic, and economic stereotypes. This work shows that, in order to study the social relations established through education, we must attend to both predictable and unexpected ways that marginalized and mainstream speakers talk in and about school.

Tyisha's example and the subsequent classroom discussion, like all discourse, contain many indexical signs through which speakers both draw on and reformulate widely circulating stereotypes. Tyisha's example gives teachers and students an opportunity to explore Aristotle's definition of courage, by discussing whether Tyisha's lying to her friend's mother was in fact courageous. But the example also presents both her friend and herself as flouting parents' moral injunctions against lying and illicit dating. This positions Tyisha against adults like the teacher. In fact, Tyisha skillfully constructs the example to create interactional problems for the teachers. Because the example involves immoral behavior (at least from an adult's point of view), if Tyisha's behavior was in fact courageous then the teachers would have to acknowledge her courage while condemning her behavior. Tyisha thus both adopts and revels in an oppositional identity, as an adolescent who helped her friend get away with illicit dates and who also manages to talk about this in an academic discussion – perhaps even in such a way that her oppositional behavior could be classified as courageous.

As the classroom discussion continues, the teachers try to convince Tyisha and other students that her behavior was not courageous, that it would instead have been courageous to tell her friend's mother the truth. Tyisha acknowledges that this latter alternative would have been courageous, but she insists that lying to her friend's mother also required courage. ("T/S" is Mr Smith, one of the two teachers running the discussion).

> **TYI:**   if I lyin'- If I'm sittin' here lying in another person
>   <u>mo</u>ther <u>face</u>, that took courag(h)e. [and if I'm
> **T/S:**   [why?

315 **TYI:** telling her, be<u>cause</u> you don't-
    FST lies.
    T/S have you never <u>lied</u> to your mother?
    FST: hnuh
    TYI: no- not- not to no one <u>else</u>'s momma, <u>no</u>.
320 **T/S:** have you ever <u>lied</u> to a <u>tea</u>cher who is a mother?
    FST: uh(hhh)
    TYI: that's <u>different</u>.
    FST: aw <u>man</u>.
    STS: [2 seconds of laughter]
325 **TYI:** that's <u>very</u> different um- I mean that's <u>different</u>. I'm
    always over there visiting this <u>friend</u> and her mother, might
    have had trus- trust in me and I come over and tell her this
    big, <u>bold</u> faced lie.

At line 320 Mr Smith cites "a teacher who is a mother." This clearly indexes the other teacher, Mrs Bailey, who, as everyone in the room knows, has an adolescent daughter herself. Mr Smith's question highlights the interactional tension that Tyisha's example raises. Tyisha acts proud of the fact that she lied to her friend's mother, even though Mrs Bailey and other adults would identify with the friend's mother and consider this wrong. Mr Smith thus seems to be pointing out that Tyisha opposes Mrs Bailey and people like her. In use, then, the discussion of Tyisha's example has positioned her not only as a potentially unethical adolescent but also as opposed to one of the teachers who is sitting right there in the room (and who is probably at that moment worrying about her own daughter's friends doing the same thing to her).

Tyisha revels in this oppositional identity, as illustrated in the sequence of increasingly colorful metapragmatic verbs that she uses to describe her lie. She started by using the verb "tell" to describe what she said to her friend's mother (at line 270). In segments not presented here (see Wortham, 2004, 2006), Mr Smith reframed it as a "lie" at line 288, and opposed such lying to "telling the truth" (line 298). Another student spiced up the characterization: "so you gonna sit there and lie to her face" (line 297). Tyisha herself embraces this characterization at lines 312–313: "I'm sitting here lying in another person mother face." And she ends up with: "her mother might have had trust in me and I come over and tell her this big bold-faced lie" (lines 326–328). Far from euphemizing what she did, Tyisha embraces the oppositional character of her action and proudly flaunts social norms. This clearly opposes her to Mrs Bailey.

This evolving set of metapragmatic verbs illustrates how a linguistic anthropologist of education can use grammatical categories to help uncover the emerging social identity of a student like Tyisha. Tyisha's use of more and more highly presupposing verbs, together with her example of illicit adolescent behavior, opposes her to the teachers. This contributes to the shift in her local classroom identity, from "good student" toward "disruptive student" (see Wortham, 2006). Only by attending to language in use, to the indexical signaling accomplished by discussion of Tyisha's example, can we uncover how Tyisha and the teachers do this relational work.

Power and Ideology

Erickson and Shultz (1982), He (2003), Rampton (2005), and Rymes (2001) all attend both to the unpredictable character of local interactions and to the larger social regularities that provide resources for such interaction. Other linguistic anthropologists of education attend less to the creative potential of language in use, focusing instead on the power relations bound up with language and education. Before moving on to the concept of language *ideology*, I will briefly review several studies that show how linguistic anthropologists have attended to questions of *power*.

Heller (1999) and Blommaert (1999) both describe language planning and education within multilingual nation states. They acknowledge the unexpected meanings that can emerge in particular events, but they do not focus on creativity within discursive interactions. Instead, they provide more detailed accounts of how state and institutional language policies can differentially position diverse populations. Heller studies how French Canadians' arguments for ethnic and linguistic legitimacy have shifted over the past few decades – from proclaiming the authenticity of their culture and asserting their rights as a minority group to emphasizing the benefit of French as an international language. This shift in models of "Frenchness" has changed the value of French Canadians themselves, with bilinguals valued more than monolinguals and Standard French valued more than vernaculars. Heller explores how this shift plays out in a French language high school in Anglophone Ontario. Blommaert (1999) describes how the Tanzanian state has used language planning for nation building. He traces the attempt to make a common nation out of a multilingual society by establishing Swahili as the index of a homogeneous Tanzania and as the primary language of education. In the process, language planners create "symbolic hierarchies" between languages and language varieties. Blommaert shows how institutions like schools (and the media, science, etc.) do this work.

Collins and Blot (2003) describe how literacy practices are embedded in global processes, like colonialism and neo-liberalism, and institutionally anchored power relations. They analyze interdependencies between local literacies and larger sociohistorical movements, describing the hegemony of the literate standard and arguing against the common assumption that schooled literacy will provide intellectual and economic salvation in all cases. Like Collins and Blot, Eckert (2000) argues for a "practice" approach to language and power. Using arguments similar to those offered by Rampton (2005), Silverstein (1992), and others who work on language in use, Eckert argues that apparently stable macrosocial categories are more variable than most theories of power assume

– "masculinity," "heterosexuality," "sluttiness," and other social categories are constructed in practice. Eckert does not abandon macrosociological variables, but she explores how they are deployed in unexpected ways. She describes the divergent phonological patterns of peer groups at a suburban high school, revealing complex relations among students' social positions and their habitual phonology.

As linguistic anthropologists have moved toward practice-based accounts that attend both to language in use and to power relations, many have used the concept of language *ideology* (Schieffelin, Woolard, & Kroskrity, 1998). Silverstein (1985) describes an ideology as a metapragmatic model of language and social relations that regiments particular uses. Because of indeterminacy about what a sign might mean in context, speakers and hearers must draw on models of linguistic forms and the speakers who typically use them. When one such model becomes salient, from among the many that might be relevant to interpreting the meaning of a given utterance, it "regiments" the values of indexical signs. When I called lawyers "ambulance-chasers," for instance – and you were unsure whether I was upset about a recent legal experience, crusading to overhaul the legal-lobbyist system, or insulting you and your spouse – you needed to know more about the relevant context to know what my utterance meant. Each of these models (aggrieved victim of legal misconduct seeking sympathy, political crusader seeking a convert, aggressive interlocutor) might frame the event we were engaged in, and in doing so fix the indexical value of "ambulance-chaser" (and neighboring signs). As Silverstein (1992) argues, any account of the social meanings of language use must describe such models and explain how they become salient in practice, as configurations of indexical signs come to mutually presuppose one model as most relevant.

Many linguistic anthropologists have noted that such models, often called "language ideologies," systematically associate types of speech with socially located types of speakers. Language ideology has become an important concept, allowing linguistic anthropologists to explore relations between the emergent meanings of signs in use, socially circulating ideologies, and broader social structures. Language ideology has also been important for the linguistic anthropology of education, because schools are important sites for learning (and legitimating) associations between types of speakers ("educated," "authoritative," "at-risk," etc.) and types of language use.

Jaffe (1999) traces the policies and practices involved in the recent revitalization of Corsican. She describes one ideology that values French as the language of logic and civilization, another that values Corsican as the language of nationalism and pride, and a third that embraces multiple languages and multiple identities. Her analyses show how schools are a central site for the struggle among these ideologies – with some trying to maintain the centrality of French in the curriculum, some favoring Corsican language revitalization and the displacement of French, and others wanting some Corsican in the schools but resisting a new "standard" Corsican as the official language of schooling. Kiesling (2001) uses "language ideology" to understand peer relations and ethnic stereotypes among white middle-class fraternity brothers, exploring how racially linked features of their speech both serve local inter-actional functions and reproduce social hierarchies. He describes fraternity brothers asserting their intellectual or economic superiority over each other by marking interlocutors as metaphorically "black." But he also shows how they assert physical prowess over each other by themselves speaking like black men, thus inhabiting a stereotype of physical masculinity. The fraternity brothers use and reinforce ideologies of Black English Vernacular speakers as less rational, economically distressed, and physically imposing.

Stocker (2003) describes a monolingual Spanish-speaking group in Costa Rica that is believed to speak a stigmatized dialect – despite the fact that their language is not linguistically distinguishable from their neighbors' – because they live on an artificially bounded "reservation" and are perceived as "indigenous." She shows how high school language instruction reinforces this ideology. Berkely (2001) describes Mayan speakers going to school to learn how to write "authentic" local stories in their language. He shows how this brought two ideologies into conflict – a literate ideology that valued the authority of the (young, female) teacher and treated literacy as an "auto-nomous" skill (Street, 2005), and a local ideology that presented older men as empowered to tell stories on behalf of others. Berkely shows how the teacher and the elders creatively navigated this conflict, with older men telling stories that younger people learned to write down.

With respect to Tyisha's example, I have already mentioned various lan-guage ideologies that became relevant to interpreting the social implications of the discussion. Students and teachers have at least two different models available to understand an adolescent who lies about illicit dates: an imma-ture, rebellious, unethical person who should be disciplined and grow up; and a heroic person who resists the illegitimate authority of adults and helps adolescents to be autonomous. The teachers try to establish that Tyisha's behavior fits the former model, while Tyisha tries to evoke the latter and win fellow students to her side. As we have seen in the section on language use, such models always get adjusted or modified in context, as participants use them for various interactional purposes and tailor them to the situation. Nonetheless, participants cannot understand what signs mean in context without attending to the more widely circulating models or ideologies that provide a starting point for local interactional work.

Domain and Trajectory

Work on language ideology shows how language in use both shapes and is shaped by more widely circulating social models and power relations. We must be careful, however, not to cast this as a simple two-part model – sometimes called the "micro-macro dialectic" – in which events create structures and structures are created in events. In fact, there are many scales of social organization relevant to understanding language in use (cf. Wortham, 2006). In their study of "untracking" as an educational reform, Mehan et al. (1996) move beyond a simple combination of local events and larger social patterns. They explore various realms that influence "at-risk" students' school success – ranging from the student him- or herself, to parents, family, the classroom, the school, peer groups, the community, as well as national educational policy and broader socioeconomic constraints. Instead of describing "micro" and "macro," Mehan and his colleagues describe how resources from many different spatial and temporal scales combine to facilitate or impede students' academic success. They give a more complex account of how "intelligence" and "educational success" are constructed in practice, describing how various resources work together to facilitate a given student's path.

Agha (2006; Agha & Wortham, 2005) describes the diverse spatial and temporal scales that allow language to signal social relations. Any model that associates linguistic features with an identifiable type of speaker has what he calls a *domain*. Models are used and recognized only by a subset of any linguistic community, and this subset changes as the model moves across time and space. There is no one "macro" set of models or ideologies, universal to a group. Instead, there are models that circulate densely in communities ranging from pairs, to local groups, to groups at various spatial and temporal scales all the way up to global language communities. The task is not to relate micro to macro, but to describe the various relevant resources – likely drawn from several different spatial and temporal scales – that facilitate a phenomenon of interest, and to describe the "intertextual" links across events through which models move as they are used to characterize people (Agha & Wortham, 2005; Wortham, 2006).

Rogers (2003) applies this approach to trace an individual student's trajectory across two years, as the student and her family negotiate with authorities about whether she is "disabled." Rogers shows how both institutionalized and local models facilitate the transformation of this student from "low achieving" to "disabled," and she follows the intertextual links among official texts, conferences, tests, family conversations, and other events that helped constitute this student's trajectory. Wortham (2006) traces the emergence of individual students' social identities across an academic year in one ninth grade classroom. This analysis tracks the development of classroom-specific models that identify different types of "student" one might be in this classroom, showing the distinctive gendered models that emerge across several months. These local models both draw on and transform more widely circulating models, and they are used in sometimes-unexpected ways in particular classroom events. The analysis shows how two students' identities emerge as speakers transform widely circulating models of race and gender into local models of appropriate and inappropriate studenthood, and as they contest these identities in particular interactions.

Crucial to this analysis is the local, classroom-specific domain within which models of identity emerge and become recognizable. The local model of Tyisha – as a disruptive force in class discussion, as someone who should be cast out from the group of teachers and students who contribute productively to discussion, and as a student who is thus "unpromising" – would not be immediately recognized by people outside the classroom, although it is constructed using resources from models of identity that have broader domains. "Macro" and "micro" thus do not suffice to analyze this example, because we must attend to intermediate domains like the one including only teachers and students in this classroom.

As the discussion of Tyisha's example ends, she has failed in her attempt to enlist other students. She skillfully embedded a defense of illicit adolescent behavior within an academic discussion of Aristotle. But she did not get other students to take her side and identify themselves as adolescents who will not accept the authority of adults like the teachers. ("LIN" is Linda, pseudonym for another student in the class.)

	LIN:	I don't think that's <u>cou</u>rage to go and steal a <u>can</u>dy bar
385		[because <u>cou</u>rage- right
	MST:	[it's stupid
	LIN:	cause courage, the virtue of courage, what we read
		of courage was to <u>do</u> something- something <u>good</u>, not to
		do <u>some</u>thing and go and do <u>some</u>thing [evil.
390	TYI:	[that's <u>not</u>
		true
	FST:	[yeah that's
		right
	TYI:	<u>cou</u>rage is not just doing something <u>good</u>.
395		[students talking at once]
	TYI:	if I go[shoot you in the <u>head</u>
	T/B:	[shhhhhh
		[students arguing]
	T/B:	ahh, if we <u>can</u>- if we <u>can</u> talk about courage as being
400		something good, the virtue of <u>cou</u>rage, and go back to that
		definition, and I know you <u>never</u> bought into <u>it</u>, but the rest
		of us <u>seem</u> to be, using this as a definition, so <u>there</u>fore,
		we'd ask you to kind of go a<u>long</u> with it.
	FST:	okay.
405	T/B:	the idea of <u>cou</u>rage, was not just doing things you're
		a<u>fraid</u> to do, but doing things <u>that</u>- overcoming your fear
		for a <u>good</u> reason. <u>Lin</u>da?
	LIN:	I was saying what Tyisha said, if you go shoot
		somebody in the <u>head</u>, you gonna call that courage? or you
410		is gonna call that <u>stupid</u>?

The other students side with the teachers here, opposing Tyisha's argument and calling her behavior "stupid." At lines 399–403 Mrs Bailey also uses a clear opposition between "us" (the teachers and students other than Tyisha, who are trying to have a productive discussion of Aristotle) and "you" (Tyisha, who is disrupting their discussion), and she makes it clear that Tyisha is outside the core group of cooperative students.

In Wortham (2006), I show how, in addition to the concept of domain, we need the concept of "trajectory" (Dreier, 2000) to analyze what happens to Tyisha across the year. Instead of analyzing language ideologies as if they occurred in stable form across a homogeneous group, we must explore their domains and describe how they move across both local and global scales. Similarly, instead of assuming that individuals are identified in stable ways, we must explore how their identities emerge and change across a trajectory of events in which these identities solidify and re-form.

Conclusions

Linguistic anthropologists of education study language form, in use, as organized by ideologies, as those ideologies move across social domains and come to identify individuals. A linguistic anthropological approach is thus characterized by its refusal to adopt simple accounts of educational processes and institutions. Instead of studying either the referential or the social functions of language, linguistic anthropologists study how speakers deploy both grammatical categories and social indexicals to accomplish reference, social identification, and other functions. Instead of emphasizing either institutions and power relations or events in which social relations are constructed – or a simple combination of the two – linguistic anthropological approaches show how both "macro" and "micro" are abstracted from a continuum of potentially relevant resources that together constrain and facilitate the functions of speech. By attending to form, use, ideology, and domain, linguistic anthropologists provide a more complex picture of educational language use.

NOTE

This is a revised and significantly expanded version of the chapter "Linguistic Anthropology of Education," previously published in the *Encyclopedia of Language and Linguistics*, general editor Nancy Hornberger, vol. 3: Marilyn Martin-Jones & Anne Marie de Mejia (eds.) (2007). *Discourse and Education*. New York: Springer Verlag. Copyrighted portions are reproduced with the permission of the publisher.

Appendix: Transcription Conventions

-       abrupt breaks or stops
?   rising intonation

.   falling intonation
–   (underline) stress
[indicates simultaneous talk by two speakers, with one utterance represented on
         top of the other and the moment of overlap marked by left brackets
[. . .] transcriber comment
,   pause or breath without marked intonation
(hh)   laughter breaking into words while speaking

REFERENCES

Agha, Asif (2006). *Language and Social Relations*. New York: Cambridge University Press.
Agha, Asif & Wortham, Stanton (eds.) (2005). *Discourse across Speech-Events: Intertextuality and Interdiscursivity in Social Life*. Special issue of the *Journal of Linguistic Anthropology*, 15(1).
Banfield, Ann (1982). *Unspeakable Sentences: Narration and Representation in the Language of Fiction*. Boston, MA: Routledge & Kegan Paul.
Berkley, Anthony (2001). Respecting Maya language revitalization. *Linguistics and Education*, 12, 345–366.
Blommaert, Jan (1999). *State Ideology and Language in Tanzania*. Cologne: Rüdiger Köppe Verlag.
Bucholtz, Mary (2001). The whiteness of nerds: Superstandard English and racial markedness. *Journal of Linguistic Anthropology*, 11, 84–100.
Cazden, Courtney, John, Vera, & Hymes, Dell (eds.) (1972). *Functions of Language in the Classroom*. New York: Teachers College Press.
Collins, James & Blot, Richard (2003). *Literacy and Literacies*. New York: Cambridge University Press.
Dreier, Ole (2000). Psychotherapy in clients' trajectories across contexts. In Cheryl Mattingly & Linda Garro (eds.), *Narrative and the Cultural Construction of Illness and Healing* (pp. 237–258). Berkeley: University of California Press.
Duranti, Alessandro (1997). *Linguistic Anthropology*. New York: Cambridge University Press.
Eckert, Penelope (2000). *Linguistic Variation as Social Practice: The Linguistic Construction of Identity in Belten High*. Malden, MA: Blackwell Publishers.
Erickson, Frederick (2004). *Talk and Social Theory: Ecologies of Speaking and Listening in Everyday Life*. Cambridge: Polity Press.
Erickson, Frederick & Schultz, Jeffrey (1982). *Counselor as Gatekeeper: Social Interaction in Interviews*. New York: Academic Press.
Garfinkel, Howard & Sacks, Harvey (1970). On formal structure of practical actions. In J. McKinney & A. Tiryakian (eds.), *Theoretical Sociology* (pp. 338–366). New York: Appleton Century Crofts.
Goffman, Erving (1981). *Forms of Talk*. Philadelphia: University of Pennsylvania Press.
Gumperz, John (1982). *Discourse Strategies*. Cambridge: Cambridge University Press.
He, Agnes (2003). Linguistic anthropology and language education. In Stanton Wortham & Betsy Rymes (eds.), *Linguistic Anthropology of Education* (pp. 93–119). Westport, CT: Praeger.
Heller, Monica (1999). *Linguistic Minorities and Modernity*. Paramus, NJ: Prentice-Hall.

Hymes, Dell (1964). Introduction: Toward ethnographies of communication. *American Anthropologist*, 66(6), 1–34.

Hymes, Dell (1972). Introduction. In Courtney Cazden, Vera John, & Dell Hymes (eds.), *Functions of Language in the Classroom* (pp. xi–lvii). New York: Teachers College Press.

Jaffe, Alexandra (1999). *Ideologies in Action: Language Politics on Corsica*. Berlin: Mouton de Gruyter.

Jakobson, Roman (1957/1971). Shifters, verbal categories, and the Russian verb. In R. Jakobson, *Selected Writings* (vol. 2, pp. 130–147). The Hague: Mouton.

Kiesling, Scott (2001). Stances of whiteness and hegemony in fraternity men's discourse. *Journal of Linguistic Anthropology*, 11, 101–115.

Lee, Benjamin (1997). *Talking Heads: Language, Metalanguage, and the Semiotics of Subjectivity*. Durham, NC: Duke University Press.

Mehan, Hugh, Villanueva, Irene, Hubbard, Lea, & Lintz, Angela (1996). *Constructing School Success: The Consequences of Untracking Low Achieving Students*. New York: Cambridge University Press.

Rampton, Ben (2005). *Crossing* (2nd edn.). Manchester, UK: St. Jerome Publishing.

Rogers, Rebecca (2003). *A Critical Discourse Analysis of Family Literacy Practices: Power in and out of Print*. Mahwah, NJ: Lawrence Erlbaum.

Rymes, Betsy (2001). *Conversational Borderlands: Language and Identity in an Alternative Urban High School*. New York: Teachers College Press.

Schieffelin, Bambi, Woolard, Kathryn, & Kroskrity, Paul (eds.) (1998). *Language Ideologies: Practice and Theory*. New York: Oxford University Press.

Silverstein, Michael (1985). On the pragmatic "poetry" of prose. In D. Schiffrin (ed.), *Meaning, Form and Use in Context* (pp. 181–199). Washington, DC: Georgetown University Press.

Silverstein, Michael (1992). The indeterminacy of contextualization: When is enough enough? In Aldo DiLuzio & Peter Auer (eds.), *The Contextualization of Language* (pp. 550–575). Amsterdam: John Benjamins.

Stocker, Karen (2003). Ellos se comen las eses/heces. In Stanton Wortham & Betsy Rymes (eds.), *Linguistic Anthropology of Education* (pp. 185–211). Westport, CT: Praeger.

Street, Brian (ed.) (2005). *Literacies across Educational Contexts: Mediating Learning and Teaching*. Philadelphia: Caslon Publishing.

Wortham, Stanton (2001). *Narratives in Action: A Strategy for Research and Analysis*. New York: Teachers College Press.

Wortham, Stanton (2004). From good student to outcast: The emergence of a classroom identity. *Ethos*, 32, 164–187.

Wortham, Stanton (2006). *Learning Identity: The Joint Emergence Identification of Social and Academic Learning*. New York: Cambridge University Press.

Wortham, Stanton & Locher, Michael (1996). Voicing on the news. *Text*, 16, 557–585.

Wortham, Stanton & Rymes, Betsy (eds.) (2003). *Linguistic Anthropology of Education*. Westport, CT: Praeger.

8 The Political Matrix of Linguistic Ideologies

MARY MCGROARTY

Language Ideologies as Expressions and Consequences of Sociopolitical Conditions

This chapter identifies some of the political and social factors that shape language ideologies, the belief systems that determine language attitudes, judgments, and, ultimately, behavior (Spolsky, 2004). These represent "the socially and culturally embedded *metalinguistic* forms of language and language use" including "conceptions of 'quality,' value, status, norms, functions, ownership, and so forth" (Bloemmert, 2006: 241). Language ideologies have both personal and societal valence. For any user of language, it would be impossible *not* to have some ideology of language, however inchoate; as Silverstein notes, "people have ideologies of language . . . [as] a necessary entailment of the fact that language, like any social semiotic, is indexical in its most essential modality" (1998: 130). Hence, all users of language and all speech communities possess ideological frameworks that determine choice, evaluation, and use of language forms and functions. Some political influences on linguistic ideology can be observed directly, as when one language or language variety is promoted or proscribed; more must be inferred, and are not always susceptible to direct investigation of discrete communicative events.

A brief nod to historical disciplinary roots: anthropology and linguistics emerged during an epoch when legitimation of discrete national states was an intellectual project of enormous perceived importance and great practical consequence. Gal and Irvine point out that, in the nineteenth and early twentieth centuries, the formative period of anthropology and linguistics coincided with European nationalist movements that sought to legitimize politically unified national states. Some of the main justifications adduced for their existence occurred through various formulations of the 'one-nation, one-language' position, however inaccurate that claim might have been at the time and since. These commentators acknowledge the "growing awareness among linguists, historians, and anthropologists that our conceptual tools for understanding linguistic differences still derive from this massive scholarly attempt to create the political differentiation of Europe" (Gal & Irvine, 1995: 968). They then describe basic semiotic processes by which individuals build their understandings of social and linguistic reality; two of them, *iconicity* and *erasure*, are directly relevant to exploration of linguistic ideologies. To gloss each: *iconicity* involves assuming that any of the linguistic practices of a group are not merely contingent, but represent the essence of the group. By *erasure*, these scholars refer to "the process in which ideology, in simplifying the field of linguistic practices, renders some persons or activities or sociolinguistic phenomena invisible" (1995: 974). As we shall see, these processes, particularly iconicity and erasure, mark much contemporary discourse about language in the United States.

Some national language ideologies are directly promulgated by political authorities, generally because they are consistent with overarching political values that distinguish particular polities. Instances of contemporary nation-states with explicit language ideologies are instructive, for they demonstrate some of the reasons governments invoke to justify resources such as time and fiscal support for public instruction in a particular language. One widely discussed example of a clearly articulated language ideology is manifest in France's *loi Toubon* that gives primacy to French within France (Wright, 2006), ratifying at long last a situation that French citizens had taken for granted. Another example of explicit and clearly articulated language ideology appears in the decrees and regulations that aggressively promote the learning of Hebrew among immigrants to Israel for purposes of prompt social integration (Spolsky & Shohamy, 1999; Shohamy, 2006). A third current instance of explicit language ideology can be found in the efforts of the Chinese government to promote *pǔtōnghuà*, or the standard oral form of the national language, based on Mandarin, through such means as development of a more standardized notation system and speech contests requiring its use (Li, 2006).

More often, language ideologies remain tacit in whole or in part, and must be inferred through examination of various combinations of the actual practices and language-related decisions of speakers and institutions. Such is the case in three of the largest Anglophone countries: the United States, the United Kingdom, and Australia. Canadian linguistic ideology contrasts with these because of the legal protections accorded to French since the 1960s. Yet, even when language ideologies are largely implicit, they are typically influenced to a considerable if not fully recognized extent by prevailing political traditions and social structures. Hence, shifts in political and social factors have ramifications for language ideologies, a situation of consequence for theorists in applied linguistics, researchers, and all practitioners who use or teach language. In the following, I wish to explicate some of the political and social factors affecting language ideologies at play in the contemporary United States to demonstrate that, even in nation-states like the US lacking an officially articulated language policy, political and social factors shape the climate for individual and societal linguistic ideologies.

Political Influences on US Linguistic Ideologies and Language Practices

There are many possible lenses through which to examine political develop-ments affecting language-related beliefs and practices. The following is perforce a selective treatment of principal theoretical and empirical work that illuminates the national discourse on language and consequently contributes to national and local "policy streams" (Kingdon, 1995), wherein language-related positions are articulated, legislation is passed (or not), regulations are elaborated and adopted (or not), and decisions regarding language practices made.

Schmidt (2006) usefully reviews political theory pertinent to language policies in the US. He draws on the work of Honig (2001) to show that national mythology related to immigrants and immigration has both positive and negative aspects, each with implications for understanding related language ideology and policy issues at individual and group levels. He notes that recent increases in numbers of immigrants and perceptions that English is 'threat-ened' provide only partial explanations for the intensity of national debates related to the 'English-only' or 'English First' organizations that would pro-mote designation of English as official language and/or restrict other languages. Following Honig, he notes that the idealized notions of 'immigrants,' and 'immigrant communities' help to bolster the notion of a 'super-citizen' who can achieve the oft-touted upward mobility through hard work, in-group sup-port, and ratification of patriarchal family values, even when their contemporary experiences might lead all US residents, immigrants included, to question whether these conditions actually obtain. Recent demographic data raises doubts about the extent of upward mobility for all US workers in a labor mar-ket that is increasingly differentiated, with a small number of individuals reaping large financial returns while much larger numbers of workers in many sectors see their earning power stagnate or decline. The nostalgia inspiring uncritical admiration for the presumptive community values of immigrants serves to alleviate social anxieties based on the fraying social safety net, circumstances affecting all US residents facing uncertainties related to familial and institutional support for child-rearing, health care, attention to the elderly, and so on. Here we see current manifestations of what Gal and Irvine (1995) had labeled *iconicity* and *erasure*. These idealizing processes allow mainstream Americans to interpret the contemporary impacts and realities of immigration selectively. As long as general political rhetoric privileges the myth of the hard-working, family-oriented immigrant, who comes from a cohesive com-munity that can meet many social needs without drawing on public resources (*iconicity*), it may be reasonable to permit other immigrants to use languages other than English; however, once immigrants wish to access public benefits (including public schooling), or exercise choice or leadership in the public sphere, they should be prepared to do so in English, for these latter activities denote mainstream privileges of citizenship that ought to be realized in and through the mainstream language (*erasure* of recognition of the complexities of education and political participation). Thus, Schmidt demonstrates that political theory offers useful directions for a clearer understanding of American language issues.

It is also instructive to examine collective political behavior, specifically voting, in the US as an additional source of information about political trends potentially influencing language ideologies and policies. Glaeser and Ward's (2006) study of American voting in Presidential elections from 1840 through 2004 shows the historical depth and persistence of some of the country's major political divisions, as well as the internal heterogeneity within many of the 50 states. Their analysis suggests why political rhetoric in recent years has been more stridently partisan than could be expected based on the results of national elections, often closely contested. Economists, they use voting patterns to explore five myths related to the widely popular "red state/blue state" (i.e., Republican/Democratic) division. They find that, with regard to political behavior, the US has always been extremely diverse, and is now neither more nor less so than throughout its history. Rather, the degree of relative consensus, defined as percent of electoral votes coming from swing states, was relatively low (about 30 percent) between 1904 and 1948, but more often amounted to 50 percent or higher in the earlier (1840–1904) and later (1948–2004) periods. They thus claim that regional and cultural divisions observed throughout the last 200 years of American history are nothing new, for "diversity . . . is still the central fact of American cultural geography" (2006: 10). However, they further find that, in the last 50 years, religious and cultural issues have to some degree replaced economic self-interest in staking out political positions, so that, currently, "religion predicts party preference better than income" (2006: 26). A final result of their analysis relevant to considerations of linguistic ideology is the recent emergence of "strategic extremism" in political discourse, where this term is understood to mean a propensity for party elites to articulate positions very strongly and in ways that attract loyal supporters (each party's base) and encourage them to vote, more than it angers opponents; this amounts to the ability to send "coded messages" efficiently to supporters conveniently assembled in large social organizations such as churches or unions (2006: 31).

Given the overall political variation within individual states shown by Glaeser and Ward's analysis of voting patterns, it is relevant to examine a recent investigation that specifically addressed voters' opinions regarding language issues. Palozzi (2006) reports results of two studies in which he administered a specially constructed language attitude scale to two groups of American voters: 300 respondents from a large random sample of Colorado voters surveyed in 2002; and 333 voters enrolled as students at Indiana University, polled in 2003. Besides choosing from one of four numerical options signaling level of agreement or disagreement with the survey's 12 statements, 6 favoring a multiculturalist and 6 an assimilationist viewpoint, participants were invited to comment on survey items, and many did so. Qualitative results showed that 'American values' often served as justification for language related opinions; Palozzi notes "traditional American values may be as important to, but interpreted differently by, both assimilationists and multiculturalists" (2006: 24). Most relevant to the topic of this chapter, Palozzi's quantitative results showed that many respondents in both voter groups, the Colorado residents and the Indiana students, endorsed the importance of English while still supporting education in and use of other languages. Voters' propensities for holding these two opinions simultaneously were somewhat sensitive to age, with younger voters more likely to hold multiculturalist positions, but did not always follow party affiliation, reminding us that, as Glaeser and Ward had found with voting patterns overall, the value positions of the electorate in any state may well be much more varied than election returns in a majoritarian system would suggest. (The ability to hold seemingly contradictory opinions is also, perhaps, further evidence that voting behavior is not rational, a tenet of current political theory repeatedly cited by Glaeser and Ward and one beyond the scope of discussion here.) In sum, political theory shows that idealized conceptions of immigration and multiculturalism shape the context of contemporary American language policy; studies of voting behavior attest to the continuing contrasts between historically similar regions of the US, while reminding us that, even within each of the 50 states, the electorate is far from homogeneous; and research on language attitudes shows that many American voters accept, to varying levels, the value of English along with the value of using other languages for varied individual and social purposes. These trends do not constitute strong endorsement of a national linguistic ideology that requires exclusive use of English, which is nonetheless often assumed; rather, we find that political theory and public sentiment as expressed through voting or in opinion polls grants various degrees of possible legitimacy and utility to the use or study of other languages, although these more nuanced positions are rarely articulated in public discourse related to language unless specific local issues arise.

Linguistic Ideologies, Tacit and Explicit, in US Workplaces and Schools

We now examine two major social arenas, work and school, in the US where linguistic ideologies related to English and to the promotion, tolerance, or prohibition of other languages can be identified or inferred. Contrasting linguistic ideologies affecting workplaces and schools enables us to highlight some of the influences of past histories and contemporary governance structures as these interact with current social conditions. I do not argue that this characterization represents either universal or necessary entailments in the linguistic ideologies associated with democratic, capitalist systems. Rather, they are offered to provoke discussion, stimulate further theorizing, and invite related analyses for specific localities within the US and elsewhere.

Workplaces

Within the United States, ideologies and practices related to workplace language use have been relatively neglected by scholarship in applied linguistics and allied fields, a regrettable omission, given that most individuals spend many years of their lives in the workplace, often more years than they spend in the school systems that are the more usual foci of research. In the American system, this is a particularly telling site for elucidation of linguistic ideology, for it foregrounds two language-related aspects of the immigrant-related mythologies that underlie much public discourse, namely, the oft-expressed beliefs that (1) getting a job requires English proficiency, and (2) its frequent corollary, that improving one's English will lead to getting a better job. Social science research indicates that the accuracy of each of these propositions is highly variable. Regarding the first, there is ample evidence that many US workplaces in regions attracting the largest numbers of immigrants are segregated linguistically, with entire shifts or even whole industries dominated by workers who regularly use a non-English language and may never need to interact with English speakers on the job (Waldinger & Lichter, 2003). Regarding the second, it is also the case that fluent bilingualism may, for some positions, lead to advancement, but such a consequence is also sector- and circumstance-specific, and is neither guaranteed nor consistent over the course of a career (McGroarty & Urzúa, in press).

Most workplaces are not regulated or monitored as much as public schools, partly because (at least in principle) they involve adults at work voluntarily, and partly because of political distaste for government intervention in the private economic sphere. Depending on whether employment occurs in the private or public sector; the nature of the work done; the demographics of the clientele or customer base served; the location and size of the unit, office, or franchise, and of the entire enterprise, varying linguistic ideologies expressed through regulations or implied by typical practices may apply. Such extreme heterogeneity makes it impossible to represent workplace-related language practices in any single setting as typical. Hence, workplace language use and related community and consumer interactions are some of the prime sites in which 'unplanned' or 'micro' language policies may emerge (Baldauf, 2005), particularly in places with large linguistically diverse populations. Different regions and employment sectors respond differently to the presence of workers or customers using languages other than English. Social science research and demographic data confirm the strongly network-driven characteristics of contemporary US immigration, which brings new immigrants to places where compatriots, often from the same village or region of the sending country, have settled. In the late twentieth century, particularly after the 1965 immigration reforms, new arrivals tended to concentrate in five major metropolitan areas: New York, Chicago, Los Angeles, San Francisco, and Miami (Waldinger, 2001). More recent data has documented growing geographic dispersion along with continuing tendencies of new immigrants toward residential and occupational clustering (Lyman, 2006). Network-driven immigration creates concentrations of workers who regularly use languages other than English, and thus creates linguistic work environments that may differ, often dramatically, from those found elsewhere in the country, although such differences require further empirical specification.

In areas of high newcomer concentration, the workforce as a whole can come to be increasingly divided, in part by language, as new arrivals enter and may even come to dominate entire industries. Large numbers of workers using another language then affect the "context of reception," the actions and interpretations of members of the mainstream. The presence of workers using a non-English language also alters perforce the languages of interaction; changes in communication patterns may then affect both language ideologies, the inchoate theories brought to bear on communication, and fully articulated language policies, on the part of workers, co-workers, supervisors, and managers. As mentioned, some mainstream ideologies of language hold that getting a job requires ability to speak English, and that, once employed, a worker will have continued opportunities to develop English proficiency. Given the segmented workforce now a reality across the US, this cannot be assumed. Waldinger reminds us that an individual's personal and occupational paths are influenced by the views and expectations of one's own co-ethnics as well as those held by other social actors "who perceive and assign difference [and hence] delimit one's options. Thus, the specificities of time and place circumscribe trajectories, without necessarily locking individuals into place" (2001: 326). The incentives to use English as well as the need to use other languages at work are both influenced by the tasks done for the job, the composition of the workforce, and matters such as whether or not the job in question includes interacting with managers, employees, international colleagues, or members of the public who might regularly use other languages, all contingent and dynamic factors. Workplace language ideologies and practices, then, reflect a more varied range of rewards, levels of tolerance, types of accommodation, and sanctions than is the case in most US school systems. While some employers may seek out and celebrate the presence of multilingual and bilingual employees, others may simply tolerate the use of languages besides English, and still others may try to control or forbid the use of languages other than English at the job. Pragmatic factors related to shifts in the nature of the social organization of work and the demographics of the workforce undoubtedly play roles here, but political factors related to governmental reluctance to intervene in work arrangements should not be overlooked. The domain of the workplace, in contrast to education, is viewed as an arena where employer priorities, as identified by management, are usually perceived as the authoritative basis for decisions, although there is some consideration (generally much less, particularly as the proportion of unionized workers declines) accorded to the rights of workers as individuals or as members of particular groups protected by civil rights regulations. Public authorities in the form of the courts may become involved if conflicts related to workplace language regulations or practices arise; workplace language issues have come to the attention of scholars, including applied linguists, when a breach of a 'higher' constitutionally protected right such as the right to free expression has been alleged, and courts are then called upon to adjudicate.

In a review of recent court cases involving English-only policies, Gibson (2004) identified several relevant aspects of linguistic ideologies directly expressed or inferable in the related decisions. Most of the cases reviewed involved Spanish speakers, as might be expected, given that they represent the preponderance of workers who use a language other than English in the US. Gibson found that "the linguistic practices of the workplace . . . have been successfully dictated by the employers, not the members themselves" (2004: 2). Moreover, US courts have generally declined to view a worker's language proficiency as an aspect of ethnic identity, a protected category under the regulation of US Civil Rights law. Rather, when employers, including monolingual English-speaking supervisors, have alleged that the use of English represents "a business necessity," courts have upheld such claims even when they are weak, and even when made regarding bilingual employees who might have been hired to serve customers more comfortable in a different language. Gibson concludes that most court decisions thus reflect an ethos of the 'homogeneism' of an idealized American worker, who is not merely capable of speaking English but eager to do so.

Schools

It is in the sphere of public education in the US, specifically the K-12 level system, that linguistic ideologies and related regulations and practices have been most widely studied, particularly when provision of bilingual instruction is at issue. I have argued that "educational language policies . . . reflect social judgments not only about language but a host of factors that, at first glance, bear no relationship to language" (McGroarty, 2002: 19). The relative size and concentration and variability in linguistically diverse populations characterizing US workplaces also affect all aspects of public schooling. Unlike workplaces, however, public schools are institutions subsidized by the communities and states where they are located, subject to the public regulation of elected school boards and state departments of education. Furthermore, unlike participation in work, which is promoted but generally not required of adults, school attendance is mandatory up to a particular age. Additionally, the current political climate has promoted much greater federal influence through legislation such as No Child Left Behind (NCLB) that specifies achievement testing and sets out expected performance targets for all students, even those for whom English is a new language, although the proportion of school funding received through federal channels remains far lower (usually in the 10–15 percent range) than that received from individual states and school districts, which provide the lion's share. Many of the relevant ramifications for instruction and assessment are discussed in detail elsewhere in this volume (see, for example, Chapter 10, The Language of Instruction Issue; Chapter 32, Language Assessments); and Chapter 36, Nationally Mandated Testing for Accountability), so I will not address them further. Instead, I summarize some recent developments in political theory and proposals for educational reform that bear on matters of linguistic ideologies in US schools. Most pertinent to considerations of politics and ideologies affecting language in American public schools are recent theoretical proposals probing the entailments of multiculturalism and citizenship, two focal concepts around which ideologies related to language and a host of other factors coalesce.

Reich's (2002) analysis of multiculturalism in education speaks directly to matters of the content of, and indirectly to those of linguistic media for, instruction. He addresses one of the central tensions in education: reconciling educational approaches that seek to instill community values and mores just as they have been received, with those that would promote intellectual independence and individual autonomy. He offers a detailed critique of multicultural theorists such as Kymlicka (see Kymlicka & Patten, 2003) who have suggested various possible structural accommodations in education allowable for cohesive and historically rooted language minority groups. To allow for more pluralist education, multicultural theorists have outlined a number of accommodations that reflect various combinations of "negative" and "positive" freedoms, where the former denote the right for the education of children not to be interfered with, and the latter the right to state support and promotion of any reasonable educational approach, including one that could include special arrangements regarding content and language of instruction (Reich, 2002: ch. 4). Reich notes that these freedoms have been inconsistently defined, and that some of their logical consequences (for example, the putative right of parents not to educate children at all) are clearly unacceptable in democratic societies. Reich's most crucial language-related problem is one that resonates deeply with current treatments of language and education in applied linguistics: "multiculturalism appears to assume that individuals possess only one cultural attachment" (2002: 88), an assumption found inadequate within the realm of political theory, in which many liberal commentators "countenance the possibility, even the likelihood, that individuals may have more than one cultural attachment" (2002: 88).

That individuals have many ways of marking belonging, of noting multiple cultural affiliations (which may or many not include the use of multiple languages), is a social reality in the US as in many other countries. Some operational clues to the growing official acceptance of mixed identities appears in policies that allow a respondent to select multiple racial categories rather than one on the US Census and certain other federal forms, a practice recommended 10 years ago although still variably implemented (Gootman, 2006). (Racial categories are not linguistic categories, and I do not want to imply that they provide any kind of reliable information on language ability; the point is that now there is an official mechanism for expressing hybrid categories.) Relying only on ascriptive categories as indicators of cultural and linguistic belonging, even when those categories are self-chosen, however, underplays the influence of particular domains and situations on behavior. As shown by Palozzi's (2006) research on language-related opinions, many Americans simultaneously endorse the value of high levels of English proficiency along with the value of knowing and using other languages for individual intellectual development and for practical communication with others within or outside of the US. Reich's theoretical project culminates in the formulation of education characterized by "minimalist autonomy" (2002: ch. 5) that would prepare individuals for "democratic citizenship." Of the five guidelines suggested for school programs and practices, those most relevant to linguistics ideologies are: (1) that schools provide all students with the "skills and knowledge necessary to independent functioning and the ability to exercise the rights of citizenship" (2002: 196); and (2) "all schools should strongly encourage the teaching of foreign languages . . . and the teaching *about* [not *of*] religion" (p. 198), with these two latter areas of instruction promoted in order to allow learners to develop wider horizons though experiencing a language code different from their own and learning to appreciate a range of spiritual and ethical systems, including their own. Such laudable recommendations present the learning of another language from the perspective of majority group learners (although Reich remarks that learning a second language could "potentially encourage students to understand better the position of linguistic minorities in liberal societies" (p. 198), and elide the pedagogical use of a minority language that might be used in service of the first guideline, acquisition of ability to function independently as learner and citizen.

The multiple and undefined influences of language and linguistic ability on these two roles, that of learner and that of citizen, lie at the crux of many arguments invoked to support education in a minority language along with English. Numerous models that support the value of maintenance and development of community language have been elaborated within applied linguistics and related fields, and are presented elsewhere in this volume (see Chapter 11, Bilingual and Biliterate Practices at Home and School; Chapter 12, Vernacular Language Varieties in Educational Settings; Chapter 20, Ecological Language Education Policy; and Chapter 21, Education for Speakers of Endangered Languages), so I will deal only with ideological arguments. Probing the effect of political and social conditions on linguistic and educational ideologies, we observe that, in the US and elsewhere, political developments in education have led to educational 'reforms' following a market-driven model in which teachers, and by implication students, are cast as objects, not agents, of reforms that generally involve more monitoring, more uniformity, more detailed prespecification of a narrow set of pedagogical objectives (Tyack, 2003; Shaker & Heilman, 2004). In much scholarship on language and education and in education generally, the concept of 'citizenship' is used as an expansive metaphor for full adult participation in the social life and institutions of the dominant society. (In the US, as elsewhere, there are complex judicial and legislative issues concerning various legal categories governing attainment of citizenship – see Miller, 2000; McGroarty, 2002 – but these are beyond the purview of this discussion.) As an intriguing parallel to Honig's (2001) analysis cited in Schmidt (2006), I would like to highlight the dual faces of 'citizenship' that animate many current discussions of educational goals for students generally. In contemporary public discourse on politics as well as education, the role of 'citizen' is presented as a model of rational, responsible involvement in public affairs. But, as Glaeser and Ward (2006) have shown, social science research suggests that voting behavior itself is not rational (see also Westin, 2007). Moreover, election returns demonstrate that many American citizens do not, in fact, regularly vote in local or even national elections. Hence this idealized conception of citizenship seems to index an attitude of minimal, highly controlled civic participation, and under-represents the equally plausible notion of a role that supports the right to challenge the status quo.

What, then, is actually being proposed regarding the presumptively positive 'citizen' role when described as the objective of reform, and what might this mean for educational linguistic ideologies? Proposals by educational theorists, including experts in general learning, regularly acknowledge the linguistic hybridity characteristic of related formulations in sociolinguistics without necessarily recognizing such skills as foundations for cognitive mastery. Gardner offers a prototypical example, listing seven types of skills in service of a "possible educational regime for a global era" (2004: 253) that would, he asserts, appropriately value the typical conservatism of educational institutions while addressing the many scientific advances in learning theories emerging in a dynamic and rapidly changing environment. Like Reich, he proposes these as a foundation for "education . . . suitable for a democratic society" (Gardner, 2004: 250). Like Reich, he characterizes these new emphases in terms of individual competencies and behavioral repertoires. Of greatest relevance to this chapter are Gardner's guidelines related to understanding the global system and capacity to think analytically and creatively; ability to interact effectively with individuals with different backgrounds; respect for one's own cultural traditions, so that individuals can master "the dual process of convergence (in the instrumental domains of culture) and divergence (in the expressive domains of culture)" (p. 255); "fostering of hybrid or blended identities" that "will be increasingly indexed by multilingual competencies and transcultural sensibilities" (p. 255) and thus promote tolerance. Admirable as these are, like many such proposals, they leave unspecified the political and social compacts needed to ensure their development.

It is striking that, as in the linguistic ideologies elucidated for the US workplace, reform efforts are expressed entirely though emphases on *individual* skill profiles. The various desiderata for K-12 education in a global world (Gardner, 2004; Reich, 2002), and for adult literacy education (Stein, 2000), are framed in terms of individual competencies, leaving the impact of surrounding social and political arrangements unremarked. (To be sure, Reich notes that his proposals for development of autonomous citizens are "more partial to those cultural groups that themselves emphasize autonomy . . . and potentially corrosive for those that do not" (2002: 47.) The emphasis on the individual as the unit and object of reform is a natural consequence of a political system that ranks individualism as a central value (McGroarty, 2002; Ricento, 2006). The rhetoric of reform related to educational linguistic ideologies and related language practices is couched in abilities exhibited by omnicompetent individuals, workers or learners, in the coming epoch (which is, of course, upon us). Once again American political ideology channels proposals for change into a strongly individualist mold; as in the case of school desegregation in the 1960s and 1970s, public schools are perceived as politically appropriate arenas in which to address social challenges that affect the entire society, even though the majority of the population is not in school. The possible roles of other non-dominant languages as essential cognitive and social tools are undeveloped, except as these might constitute a supplement to more fundamental "skills and knowledge necessary to independent functioning and the ability to exercise the rights of citizenship" (Reich) and "understanding the global system" and "thinking analytically and creatively" (Gardner); these primary goals, while never labeled as achievable only through English, are left unspecified with regard to linguistic medium. Within the American system, such lack of specificity has encouraged proponents of multilingual education to frame supporting arguments mainly in terms of individual rights to education, the basis of Constitutional protections that have received some support from US courts (see May, 2006, for further discussion of other relevant theoretical concerns and international settings). Not coincidentally, this is the same basis used (with limited success, as Gibson shows) to challenge English-only workplace policies. However, concurrently in the US, the nature and entailments of "rights" in educational settings have been redefined in recent court decisions in ways that erode support for innovative language programs, including bilingual programs, which in recent decades have been undercut by "legal, regulatory, and public relations" measures that de-emphasize the value, social utility, and community relevance of other languages (Gándara, Moran, & García, 2004).

Directions for Theory and Research in Educational Linguistics

What do these varied currents of scholarly analysis and reform proposals suggest for researchers in educational linguistics? Scholarship in language ideology shows that "Singular projections of language onto national identity do not work anymore" and raises objections to the processes of oversimplifying connections between national identity, citizenship (considered literally or metaphorically), and language abilities that express such identity, which is "best seen not as one item, but as a repertoire of different possible identities ... [involving] variation between *varieties* of language, including accents, registers, styles, and genres" (Bloemmert, 2006: 249, 245). The recognition that individuals have multiple identities, and also that varying material and social conditions influence uses and evaluations of language, is now taken for granted by scholars, but presents multiple practical questions affecting language ideologies used to formulate policies and practices in workplaces and schools.

Educational linguists must recognize the urgency of related practical concerns, provide accurate information, offer critical analyses, and continue related research. Academics, policy makers, and members of the public have become impatient with reform efforts based on broad-brush social critiques that have not grappled with the operational and institutional complexities of workplaces and schools. Luke (2005) notes that "secular education systems faced with the task of opening up new life pathways and social futures" amidst "new and difficult material conditions" cannot rely only on promoting "critique and deconstruction" (p. xvi); these may constitute necessary steps, but they are insufficient to specify direct instrumental decisions or comprehensive ultimate goals. Researchers in educational linguistics have two related responsibilities when questions of language practices in social domains arise. First, they can share accurate information on current conditions: scholars can remind policy makers and the public that for instance, the linguistically differentiated American workplace constrains opportunities to learn and refine the dominant language. They can remind the public that effective innovative educational programs for English learners already exist (Genesee & Christian, 2006), and that many of these include uses of a minority language along with English to promote development of the basic cognitive capacities and cosmopolitanism described by Reich's and Gardner's reform proposals. Second, in the US and elsewhere, educational linguists have a specialized role in investigating the language processes and outcomes found in local workplaces and schools. Careful identification and continued specification of the multiple ways that language abilities are promoted, controlled, developed, encouraged, or discouraged by institutional ideologies could contribute to more conscious and conscientious public choices.

REFERENCES

Baldauf, Richard (2005). Micro language planning. In P. Bruthiaux, D. Atkinson, W. Eggington, W. Grabe, & V. Ramanathan (eds.), *Directions in Applied Linguistics: Essays in Honor of Robert B. Kaplan* (pp. 227–240). Clevedon, UK: Multilingual Matters.

Bloemmert, Jan (2006). Language policy and national identity. In T. Ricento (ed.), *An Introduction to Language Policy: Theory and Method* (pp. 238–254). Malden, MA: Blackwell Publishing.

Gal, Susan & Irvine, Judith T. (1995). The boundaries of languages and disciplines: How ideologies construct difference. *Social Research*, 62(4), 967–1001.

Gándara, Patricia, Moran, Rachel, & García, Eugene (2004). Legacy of *Brown: Lau* and language policy in the United States. *Review of Educational Research*, 28, 27–46.

Gardner, Howard (2004). How education changes: Considerations of history, science, and values. In M. Suárez-Orozco & D. Qin-Hillard (eds.), *Globalization: Culture and Education in the New Millennium* (pp. 235–258). Ewing, NJ: University of California Press. [Electronic volume]

Genesee, Fred & Christian, Donna (eds.) (2006). *Educating English Language Learners: A Synthesis of Research Evidence*. New York: Cambridge University Press.

Gibson, Kari (2004). English only court cases involving the U.S. workplace: The myths of language use and the homogenization of bilingual workers' identities. *Second Language Studies*, 22(2), 1–60.

Glaeser, Edward L. & Ward, Bryce A. (2006). Myths and Realities of American political geography. Harvard Institute of Economic Research Discussion Paper No. 2100, January. Available: http://ssrn.com.abstract=874977 (retrieved May 2006).

Gootman, Elissa (2006). U.S. proposal offers students wider way of racial identity. *The New York Times*, August 9, p. A12.

Honig, Bonnie (2001). *Democracy and the Foreigner*. Princeton, NJ: Princeton University Press.

Kingdon, John W. (1995). *Agendas, Alternatives, and Public Policies* (2nd edn.) New York: HarperCollins.

Kymlicka, Will & Patten, Alan (2003). Language rights and political theory. *Annual Review of Applied Linguistics*, 23, 3–21.

Li, David C.-S. (2006). Chinese as a lingua franca in greater China. *Annual Review of Applied Linguistics*, 26, 149–176.

Luke, Allan (2005). Foreword: On the possibilities of a post-colonial language education. In A. Lin & P. Martin (eds.), *Decolonisation, Globalisation: Language-in-Education Policy and Practice* (pp. xiv–xix). Clevedon, UK: Multilingual Matters.

Lyman, Rick (2006). New data show immigrants' growth and reach. *The New York Times*, August 15, pp. A1, A16.

May, Stephen (2006). Language policy and minority rights. In T. Ricento (ed.), *An Introduction to Language Policy: Theory and Method* (pp. 255–272). Malden, MA: Blackwell Publishing.

McGroarty, Mary (2002). Evolving influences on educational language policies. In J. W. Tollefson (ed.), *Language Policies in Education: Critical Issues* (pp. 17–36). Mahwah, NJ: Lawrence Erlbaum.

McGroarty, Mary & Urzúa, Alfredo (in press). The relevance of bilingual proficiency in U.S. corporate settings. In D. Brinton & O. Kagan (eds.), *Heritage Language Acquisition: A New Field Emerging*. Mahwah, NJ: Lawrence Erlbaum.

Miller, David (2000). *Citizenship and National Identity*. Cambridge, UK: Polity Press.

Palozzi, Vincent (2006). Assessing voter attitude toward language policy issues in the United States. *Language Policy*, 5, 15–39.

Reich, Rob (2002). *Bridging Liberalism and Multiculturalism in American Education*. Chicago: University of Chicago Press.

Ricento, Thomas (ed.) (2006). *An Introduction to Language Policy: Theory and Method*. Malden, MA: Blackwell Publishing.

Schmidt, Ronald, Sr. (2006). Political theory and language policy. In T. Ricento (ed.), *An Introduction to Language Policy: Theory and Method* (pp. 95–110). Malden, MA: Blackwell Publishing.

Shaker, Paul & Heilman, Elizabeth E. (2004). The new common sense of education: Advocacy research versus academic authority. *Teachers College Record 106*, 7, 1444–1470.

Shohamy, Elana (2006). *Language Policy: Hidden Agendas and New Approaches.* London: Routledge.

Silverstein, Michael (1998). The uses and utility of ideology. In B. Schieffelin, K. Woolard, & P. Kroskrity (eds.), *Language Ideologies: Practice and Theory* (pp. 123–145). Oxford: Oxford University Press.

Spolsky, Bernard (2004). *Language Policy.* Cambridge: Cambridge University Press.

Spolsky, Bernard & Shohamy, Elana (1999). *The Languages of Israel: Policy, Ideology, and Practice.* Clevedon, UK: Multilingual Matters.

Stein, Sondra (2000). *Equipped for the Future: What Adults Need to Know and Be Able to Do in the 21st Century.* Washington, DC: National Institute for Literacy.

Tyack, David (2003). *Seeking Common Ground: Public Schools in a Diverse Society.* Cambridge, MA: Harvard University Press.

Waldinger, Roger (ed.) (2001). *Strangers at the Gates: New Immigrants in Urban America.* Berkeley: University of California Press.

Waldinger, Roger & Lichter, Michael (2003). *How the Other Half Works: Immigration and the Social Organization of Labor.* Berkeley: University of California Press.

Westin, Drew (2007). *The Political Brain: The Role of Emotion in Deciding the Fate of the Nation.* New York: Public Affairs.

Wright, Sue (2006). French as a lingua franca. *Annual Review of Applied Linguistics, 26,* 35–60.

FURTHER READING

Appiah, Kwame Anthony (2006). *Cosmopolitanism: Ethics in a World of Strangers.* New York: Norton.

Benhabib, Seyla (2004). *The Rights of Others: Aliens, Residents, and Citizens.* Cambridge: Cambridge University Press.

Lippi-Green, Rosina (1997). *English with an Accent: Language, Ideology, and Discrimination in the United States.* London: Routledge.

Marling, William H. (2006). *How "American" is Globalization?* Baltimore: The Johns Hopkins University Press.

Sassen, Saskia (1998). *Globalization and its Discontents: Essays on the New Mobility of People and Money.* New York: The New Press.

Schieffelin, Bambi, Woolard, Kathryn, & Kroskrity, Paul (eds.) (1998). *Language Ideologies: Practice and Theory.* Oxford: Oxford University Press.

9 Educational Linguistics and Education Systems

JOSEPH LO BIANCO

Foundations

Education systems are principally the property of states. Even if authority is devolved to semi-autonomous bodies such as religious, ideological, regional-ethnic, or other parent-controlled agencies for the delivery of schooling, or higher or specialized education, states typically licence, authorize, fund, or certify educational practices. Therefore in a diverse range of ways all education systems carry the imprimatur and conditioning of political systems. State interest in educational practice is therefore governed either by overt control, by investment, or by toleration conditions. The overarching interest of states for what happens in formal systems of education is therefore deep and longstanding.

To speak comprehensively of the language activities potentially undertaken within such education systems, however they are governed, needs to transcend the mediation of the various delivery agencies. Although such agencies can condition the specific lingual characteristics of formal education, a broad depiction of the proto-typical linguistic education of young people can still be discerned. The following eight points constitute therefore state sanctioned secondary linguistic socialization:

1 extending the dialect repertoire of "majority" children's domestic language competence to include standard language literate capability (minimally reading and writing, but for elites this often involves critical and imaginative literacy as well);

2 extending the non-standard language competence of socially, regionally, and other minoritized communities to include mastery of spoken and written standard language norms;

3 inculcating mastery of the elevated linguistic registers and styles validated by national value systems and appropriate to context-reduced academic activity;

4   teaching the national standard language to non-speakers whether they are of immigrant or indigenous origin;
5   specialization of formal standard literate knowledge around the disciplinary conventions of particular fields of application, such as professions, institutions, or occupations;
6   providing standard language and literacy provision for deaf, blind and other children with language-connected special needs;
7   occasional concessions to the language backgrounds of learners, be these non-standard varieties of the national language, or languages other than the national language whether of immigrant or indigenous origin; and, finally
8   teaching prestige, strategic, or status languages.

This secondary lingual socialization differs from primary linguistic socialization (Watson-Gegeo, 2004) in its greater degree of formality, its link to certification, its systemic moderation and its material and symbolic consequences.

Religious, ideological, regional-ethnic, or other parent-controlled agencies make use of various degrees of autonomy from state direction to shape curricula, and in so doing vary and modulate this secondary linguistic socialization in particular ways.

In the context of this lingual profile which education systems aspire to produce *educational linguistics,* at least in its early conceptions (Spolsky, 1978), means something like the application of explicit linguistic knowledge to problems of teaching and learning. Its fundamental questions are: How can language be characterized, constrained, and defined in general terms? How can language learning be sequenced for teaching? How does learner processing of linguistic input influence teaching and curriculum design? How can language learning, both holistically and in its various component parts, be assessed? How does academic and context-reduced language, especially literacy and literate practice, relate to spoken language? and, crucially, How can reading and writing be sequenced, constrained and taught?

Early views of what constitutes explicit linguistic knowledge came directly from the situation-independent insights and understandings generated by the main branches of linguistic scholarship with its classical divisions of phonology, morphology, and semantics. This science of verbal communication was conceived as producing knowledge portable across context, a kind of calculus in which universally relevant knowledge was applied to the practice of language use and teaching in education systems. Education systems are ultimately formalized institutions for knowledge creation, transfer, and certification and because explicit linguistic knowledge was understood as essentially mentalist it was seen as universally applicable.

Combined, then, *educational linguistics* and *education systems* refer to the multiple ways in which formal processes of organizing the transmission of content knowledge, including knowledge of and about language, is shaped by meta-linguistic knowledge produced by a science of linguistics. In recent decades this foundational assumption has ceded space dramatically to more situationalist and constructivist paradigms in both fields, both the language sciences and the sciences of learning have made social criteria, situation, context, variability, and co-construction central tenets of their disciplines.

This change can be demonstrated in a contemporary way by reference to the 'future-person' ideology, a composite person imagined in the many policy documents issued by the supra-national agencies of Europe. In this large body of policy literature[1] is depicted the lingual capabilities of the projected and imagined future citizen of Europe, a mobile, polyglot, multicultural, literate, broad-minded, and conscientious transnational. The following is an abstraction of this idealized subject explicated from the voluminous but usually unintegrated directives, declarations, statements, pronouncements, and other desiderata issued by the agencies of the European Commission and the Council of Europe in recent decades.

The communicative capabilities and profile of this polylingual polymath can be synthesized as follows. First, *homo europaeus* would speak a primary language of identity, rooted in place and local belonging, nurtured by claims to authentic representation of Europe's primordial regions: sometimes called an autocthonous language, in New World settings called an indigenous language, or what Dante Alighieri (Lo Bianco, 2005a) called *locutio prima*. The circumscribed identity of this language is extended by mastery of a national language, what for Dante was *locutio secondaria*, and what in Europe is constituted by the formative importance of language defined statehood (Seton-Watson, 1977). In much of the discourse that underlies European official pronouncements the languages of place invoke essential personhood, primary identity, while the language of the nation transcends locality and invokes wider political citizenship. This bilingualism of place and nation is further supplemented by a wider and emergent compact of citizenship that is trans-European, so our ideal citizen would command a language that transcends his or her particular identity, and particular nationality; although technically a foreign language, it would be marked as a language of *wider European communication* and there also invoking identification and place. The realities of interconnection of global markets whose access is facilitated most easily by English also requires widespread, near-universal, mastery of English (and, realistically, Englishes). In the essentially economic and political discourses of the supra-national institutions of Europe these language competencies – local identity language, national language, language of Europe-wide communication and then global English – might also extend to include multiple, partial and temporary language skills a citizen could require during various stages of his or her professional life. All of these, of course, are intimately and ultimately associated with European literacies, possibly with different orthographic scripts, but certainly with internal language literacies such as prose writing, information or document literacy, and quantitative or numerical literacy (OECD, 1996a, b) and all of these in turn mediated by the particular literacy requirements of information and communications technologies.

This state imagined poly-lingualism needs to be nuanced to accommodate religious, regional, and citizenship diversity, so that devotional languages, ancestral languages new to Europe, and forms of speech other than spoken ones all extend the imagined communicative profile of the future European.

A central tenet of emergent Europe is the notion of mobile trans-nationality. This forging of a common European geopolitical future consciousness is forward-looking but must make amends for the past. This is why the new inclusiveness promulgated in many documents issued by the supra-national agencies of Europe contains amelioration for sub-national grievances, oppression, and alienation. Hence minorities, especially the marginalized and socially excluded, are largely defined in these statuses by the homogenizing tendencies and overwhelming power of nationality-based statehood with its past practices of neglect, assimilation, and even obliteration of differences (Gellner, 1983; Greenfeld, 1992; Hobsbawm, 1992; Smith, 1995; Hroch, 1996; Ager, 1996).

Within the foundations of educational linguistics therefore we find resonances of all these phases of how language has marked in the past and continues today to mark aspirations and history. The lingual expectations of education systems are wide ranging because they aim to produce many tools: for competing in cut-throat labor markets in a globalizing economy, for meeting the persistent demands of identity, for the refusal of national states to concede to globalization, for religious affiliation and devotion, and for marking the survival and vitality of sub-national identities; all differences marked and made possible with and through language.

Core Themes

The foundations of educational linguistics, though these are rarely elucidated, are fashioned by the interaction between languages sciences that have shifted from a universalist paradigm to a more socially situated one. In turn educational linguistics orients teachers, learners, and curriculum designers to systemic purposes inherent in compulsory education. Within compulsory education, both schooling and post-initial education, we find the historical inheritances suggested above. Curriculum can be seen as the planned learning experiences that formal institutions provide to learners, suggesting both different theories of knowledge as well as different purposes for knowing. Typically, or classically, curricula reflect orientations to knowledge, or ways that curriculum carries the primary missions, or social purposes, that underlie educational delivery. Four such frames of reasoning are proposed below to capture these overall philosophies of educating institutions. As each is described the educational linguistics they contain are discussed, drawing on the eight secondary linguistic socialization fields identified above. While educational linguistics contributes distinctive disciplinary focus, concepts, methods, and history, it also takes distinctive form in each of the following types of curriculum, which, of course, are idealizations while in practice there are many hybrid forms.

The four curriculum types are:

1 skills: how skills are transmitted and applied in economically oriented education;
2 humanist intellectualism: how eloquence and expression invoke elevated culture;
3 transcendence: how political ideology and religious devotion are cultivated; and
4 nationing: how loyal citizenship to nationality-defined states is inculcated.

Skills: An economistic-vocationally oriented curriculum

Some curricula are organized around an overarching rationale which involves the intersection of education with the skill requirements of the labor market. Curricula which aim to prepare learners for some kind of successful integration within the labor market can be either narrow or less narrow, occupationally specific or life-skills focused. In these kinds of curricula teaching aims to facilitate the acquisition of skills which are seen to be discrete or separately specifiable, and are taught via pedagogies that stress explicit teaching, identifying subskills and teaching these separately and aiming through apprenticeship to combine the subskills.

Attitudinal ideals are also invoked, usually via the development of personal qualities relevant for a working subject (diligence, professional ethics, norms and standards) to satisfy extrinsic occupationally motivated orientations or the requirements of professional certification.

Educational linguistics fashioned for the labor market focuses on the generic structures of language, the text types that typically occur, are valued, and practiced in the fields of endeavor where the skills are applied. An example of educational linguistics for skills transmission from foreign language teaching is described by Staddon (1996). In this instance the Faculties of Engineering and Arts at Monash University in Australia introduced a combined degree in Arts and Engineering. Requiring both linguistic and technical expertise of students and teachers, this kind of language for specific purposes imposed the need for interdisciplinary collaboration between linguists (French speakers) and civil engineers (English speakers). This interaction between language experts and engineering experts produced an amalgam of applied expert linguistic knowledge and the disciplinary knowledge of engineering. This intersection is precisely the domain of educational linguistics. The educational linguistics was expressed in the modes for delivering students' professional preparation through the acquisition of skills and knowledge required to use French, pragmatically and effectively, in the engineering workplace and in related social situations, showing an understanding of French engineering practices, or rather French in engineering practices. The specificity of communication practices, discourses, technical vocabulary, terms of art, and the generic organization of writing and information presentation for engineering purposes, using shared knowledge of the discourse community of engineers, etc., constitute some of this educational linguistics. Pedagogically programs of language for specific purposes work with realistic and task-based learning activities selected for their typicality, and real-world authenticity, as site-based instantiations of general principles of communication. Oral and written inter-relations are also involved since translating technical documents into oral instructions is an expected part of competently functioning as a qualified engineer working in French.

The skills curriculum has a national analogue. On a more wide-ranging basis we can identify characteristics of a systemically skills-oriented approach in the public education system as a whole. Better known perhaps as human capital based curriculum, Singapore's linguistic practices in its education systems are motivated by "linguistic instrumentalism" (Wee, 2004) or "linguistic capital" (Silver, 2005) . Analyzing the essential reasoning that underlies language education planning in the city state, these writers show how the underlying rationales, similar to what Ruiz (1984) called "policy orientations," make language education choices and adopt methodologies oriented to achieving skills outcomes, human capital, labor market applicable outcomes premised on an underlying economic rationality. Unlike Engineering French, whose more socially limited purpose is to advance domain-specific French language proficiency of engineers though an essentially English-speaking education system, the Singapore example epitomizes an entire national educational linguistics, motivated by calculations of the material outcomes of educational linguistics. It would be wrong to imagine goals of social harmony and inter-ethnic harmony are neglected in such an approach, even these are linked closely to the underlying human capital ideology; the policy settings clearly relate economic success to inter-ethnic harmony through more widely distributing social opportunity and rewards.

The educational linguistics involved ranges from choices about language of instruction through to classroom-based documentation of elementary school literacy practices and pedagogy for learners whose home language traditions involve different orthographies. Singapore's educational linguistics is one of the most explicit in the world, largely because of this level of institutionalized diversity, and gives effect to an English-knowing bilingualism (Pakir, 2003) in the service of a project of national unity based on economic instrumentalism. Although the wider discourses of linguistic instrumentalism and language capital prevail, these are combined with claims for a continuation of language-based ethnic identities. While there can be tension between non-English based ethnic identities with English based economic advantage (Lo Bianco, 2007), and while it is apparent that the non-English languages stand in diglossic inferior domain status to English, the policy has achieved extraordinary success as applied educational linguistics.

The formula of identity and advantage allocated differentially between languages is well expressed in the following statement from Mr Tharman Shanmugaratnam, appropriately the Senior Minister of State for Trade and Industry for Singapore, who during an awarding on October 13, 2002 of Most Inspiring Tamil Teacher stated that studying the "Mother Tongue":

> helps our students to imbibe values and to appreciate the accumulated know-
> ledge and wisdom contained in our cultural heritage. As bilingual learners,
> children are provided with more than one set of lens, enabling them to perceive
> the world and encoding their experiences in different ways. It allows them
> to reach a deeper understanding of their own identity, and a sense of belong-
> ing to community and country. . . . Our bilingual policy in education remains
> a key social and economic imperative for Singapore, as relevant now as it
> has been in the last few decades. Proficiency in the English language has given
> Singaporeans a key advantage in a globalised economy. It gives us relevance
> to global companies and keeps us at the intersections of global trade and
> investment. It creates good jobs for Singaporeans, now and in the future.
> (Shanmugaratnam, 2002: 1)

Eloquence: A humanistic-intellectual paradigm

When curricula are conceptualized as in some sense 'humanizing', the educa-tional linguistics which results makes use of notions of eloquence, expression, rhetoric, and elevated culture. These overarching purposes speak of a connec-tion between 'knowledge' and 'civilization'. Informing learners of time-validated canonical thought, works of art, and literature (bodies of knowledge which are elevating in cultural and even spiritual modes) distinguishes this class of curricula. The frequently encountered 'mission' of school and university curricula built from this paradigm involves claims to personal transformation and growth for individuals and sometimes for whole societies.

The educational linguistics that is deployed in curricula such as these is principally about rhetoric and historical linguistics, change in language over time, nuance in expression and verbal repertoires as expressive of either emotional, psychological, or national and cultural states.

The kinds of pedagogies adopted in curricula with overt aims of nurturing intellectualism, or advancing abstractions like 'civilization', quite often favor only the study of literary texts removed from ordinary people, their discourse, and experiences. Murphy's (1988) characterization identifies four stages of including broad cultural aims in foreign language teaching, each shaped by an educational linguistics that prevailed.

The civilization approach is the first, which assumes that a separately specified curriculum exists for culture which is taught after the language has been learned. The impact of applied linguistic research, or educational lin-guistics of different phases, then shapes the following three: Audio-lingualism assumes that there is no specific cultural aspect to language pedagogy, and instead aims to produce grammatical correctness, seeing culture as a disconnected field. Educational linguistics then leads to the promulgation of an array of teaching methods collectively called communicative, which take for granted that culture can influence communication and teach culture explicitly when it is needed to enhance communication. This is a notion of culture as non-linguistic elements required for communication. Finally, in intercultural pedagogies Murphy argues that language has come to be seen as itself a cultural practice. This assumption of inseparability of language and culture requires research between the learner's language and the target language to identify culturally infused forms and instances of language use which can then be taught directly.

The contemporary context of cultural fusion and hybridity attenuates even this sense of bounded cultures and languages, tied to single foreign countries and speaker populations. Trans-national and more critical approaches to culture itself problematize the assumptions and the practices of educational paradigms of language that appear to reinforce outmoded views of communication, cultural value, and judgmental positions about eloquence tied to the particular forms of speech of some groups. Educational linguistics here can be seen to have revolutionized pedagogical practices, based principally on the insights of variationist sociolinguistics, classically deriving from the work of dialectology (Labov, 1972; Baugh, 2000) whose systematic way to show rule-governed predictability, logic, and order in stigmatized speech forms has directly shaped education systems. Indeed in the United States a long tradition of litigation around teacher and system attitudes to non-standard speech forms has shown the power of educational linguistics, though also its controversies and failures (Krashen, 1996; Crawford, 2002).

Virtue: Paradigms of religion or social ideology

Some curricula aim to reproduce norms of life that derive from ethnicity, religious creed, or moral ideology. These politico-ideological and religious ideals are usually encapsulated in virtue, a moral paradigm rooted in the association of knowledge with ethical action. Although curricula which invoke these ideals also draw on vocational or humanistic-intellectual paradigms for organizing learning experiences, these are usually interpreted only within the ideological and systemic parameters of the 'sectional' character of the curriculum. Educational linguistics which serves educational systems premised on transcendent notions of the purposes of learning shares with all other educational linguistics the idea of making general instruction more effective, but also serves unique goals of teaching, content sequencing, assessment, and evaluation associated with modes of practice particular to the ideology of the schools involved.

A moral-religious or non-religious ethical or sectional curriculum ideal typically locates the value of knowledge (not only the selections of knowledge but how knowledge and skill are construed as 'valuable' or less so) within preexisting, or given, orders and patterns of social, ideological, or moral systems. These systems pre-date the learner, are sanctioned by systems of judgment that prevail beyond contest, and are presented as ideal behavior and identity models into which learners are to be inducted.

Although the primary purposes of these approaches to learning are reproductive, or preservationist, educational linguistics applied in these contexts is not denied its exploratory character, nor that of research and discovery. However, the political and religious values and ideals encountered in such curricula can find their way into how knowledge about applied language studies is framed, collected and valued. Reproducing patterns of life, devotional practices, particular valued languages, or reading practices that have time-honored value among new generations is the overriding goal of such curricula. Aiming therefore to reproduce intergenerationally patterns of life, ethnic identification, or religious devotion lends educational linguistics a particular functionality and occasionally a sense of urgency.

Social transformation as a curriculum paradigm can aim for one of three kinds of change. First that talented individuals have constraining circumstances removed and are enabled to acquire cultural capital for personal/individual advancement. Second, that the characteristics of the group which constitute its disadvantage are contested so that not only isolated individuals but the group as a whole is assisted; this change being the ideal that underlies the curriculum ethos. Third, and more ambitious still, that the social context is itself transformed so that it becomes defined by diversity and removes any privilege that attaches to selected groups. These more ideological parameters of curriculum ethos have a long tradition not in formal educational linguistics, but in critical studies, in the work that derives from Marxist, neo-Marxist, and Freirian (Spring, 1998) influenced views of literacy. This kind of educational linguistics today draws on critical reasoning and makes use of the ideas of sociologists, such as Bourdieu (1991), whose identification of the ways in which material advantage accrues to symbolic power, and specifically to the command of powerful registers of communicative skill, links directly educational linguistics and education systems as producers and re-producers of advantage.

Nationing: The discourse of loyal citizenship to nationality-defined states

The greatest weakening of the educational systems' classic function of inculcating identity loyalties has been the economic vocationalism of trans-national capital. Despite this, nationing, both in new nations intent on forging identities larger than regional or local ones, and in established nations intent on preserving distinctiveness, utilizes linguistic based narration, story telling about national cohesion and unity, or subliminal and continual reminders of the persistence of nationality (Billig, 1995).

In the passage from pre-national to national forms of sociality schools were transformed from their various individualistic functions and combined into education systems, under self-conscious polities interested in making nations and achieving national unity via education systems which provided the systematic, and therefore repeatable, socialization that families could not. Industrialism intensified the need for standardization of expressive culture, but added the requirement for standardized mass literacy and so nationing, and economic need, established the basic character of today's educational practice.

As early as 1791 the French nobleman and diplomat Talleyrand pronounced before the French Convention that aimed to invent a new polity to displace tradition with modernity the essential role for education: "Elementary education will put an end to this strange inequality. In school all will be taught in the language of the Constitution and the Law and this mass of corrupt dialects, these last vestiges of feudalism will be forced to disappear" (cited in Wright, 2004: 62).

For Brunot (1927), the great documenter of French linguistic consolidation, the critical moment was the state deciding that families would no longer have exclusive rights over the lingual ways of their children. The young, like the new, are a challenge to society, any society, and all societies work out ways to make the future resemble the past. Because a society must always renew itself, this renewal has a dual character: horizontal and vertical.

Horizontal cultural reproduction involves bringing in *the different from outside* the society and assimilating them. Vertical cultural reproduction involves bringing up *the young from inside* the society and socializing them. The French state decided that the school should replace the family and set up the secondary socialization of schooling: home was for learning to walk and tie shoe laces, primary socialization, but the school became the nationing instrument. When schools were individual institutions the socialization they practiced modeled the values and behaviors of their individual founders. However, self-conscious polities interested in forging bonds of national community, require more systematic action. Aiming to achieve unity via formal education Talleyrand and the French Convention organized schools into education systems to facilitate systematic and repeatable socialization.

The original target was the standard literate form of French, the language of state and law, which was spreading internationally but was unknown to many French, in villages and remote regions (Talleyrand's "strange inequality"). This disparity was perceived as a problem of families, of enduring local loyalties and of fragmented schooling, and was dealt with by instituting a formal education system tied to the explicit project of ideological language nationalism.

Research Practice

Research and practice in educational linguistics and in education systems is undergoing three major transformations. First, the researched languages from which generalizations about learning and teaching are drawn are diversifying rapidly away from dominantly Western ones. Second, what counts as literacy, and the media through which educational practice is exchanged, is being transformed dramatically by information and communications technologies. Third, education systems themselves are undergoing rapid change. Learners learn a great deal about all fields of knowledge, including language, from horizontal connections they make with age peers, unmediated by adults, whether the primary socializers of the home or the secondary socializers of the school.

Much of the literature on educational linguistics derives from First World settings, or from post-colonial national language educational planning, or at least from relatively settled relations between what counts as spoken and what counts as written language. While too many predictions of change brought about by information and communications technologies prove to be unwarranted, it is clear that the rapid advances in electronic and digital communication are changing conventions of writing. (Chat groups, for instance, disrupt traditional assumptions of temporal displacement that we have long seen as inevitable in written communication. Chat groups and other forms of digital writing which are instantaneously "consumed" resemble the more iterative and negotiated practices of spoken language.)

Many of the settings in which ideas about language have been researched are shaped by Western, or Westernized, literacy practices and the contrastive linguistic examinations that have fashioned the field have looked at binaries, learner language and target language, that are either within the Western paradigm, or that involve at least one Western language, most often English. Literacy research is often characterized by expectations of shared alphabetic roman orthographies. Looking at the titles of journals in contemporary educational linguistics shows a major diversification of sources, settings, and relationships in response to the greater diversification of societies. Research and practice in educational linguistics will also of course need to deal much more systematically with the deep and pervasive transformation of English, for which claims of its emergence as a "post-identity language" (Lo Bianco, 2005b), and its growth as "basic skill" (Graddol, 2006) indicate that relations of identity, linguistic norms, and the consequences for speakers of other languages and whole disciplines of knowledge will accelerate and diversify. And yet, perhaps the most compelling point to be made about research and practice is not that things will change, but that practice is so resistant to research. As Baynham (2003) has pointed out, researchers in adult literacy, bilingual education, and other fields of educational linguistics examine a much richer array of problems and possibilities than relatively conservative institutions of education admit and acknowledge. This research–practice gap is neither particular to educational linguistics, nor particularly unusual, and in some ways is positive. It is reflected in the wide array of curriculum ideologies discussed above, where despite what the science of educational linguistics might propound at any one time education systems draw on bodies of informing ideas, ideologies, and contesting knowledge so that the relation of educational linguistics and language education is never straightforward or unmediated.

In any case, more documentation across radically different sociolinguistic settings will impact on educational linguistics. One of its key assumptions has been that progressive kinds of educational practice emerge from the more descriptive traditions of linguistics encountered in Western academic institutions. That Asian educational practices, generally conceived as more conservative pedagogically, perform particularly well in international standardized assessments of learning is already having a washback effect onto curriculum design and educational practice within some Western societies. More documentation of multiple orthographic systems is also emerging, so that the reading and general intellectual consequences of literacy gained in different writing systems and their interaction is beginning to be felt. Hornberger's continua of biliteracy (2003: 315–339) aims to represent the wider range of language ecologies that are being researched at present and suggest that the taxonomies with which educational linguistics has operated will be called to account for more diverse settings.

Among the greatest challenges for educational linguistics will be how to accommodate cognitive attainments given the great diversity of learner backgrounds, sociological circumstances, program delivery modes, and values-centered curricula. Studies responding to this growing complexity should be collaborative endeavors undertaken between scholars trained in applied linguistics and pedagogy with colleagues who focus on sociopolitical ideology, values, and culture.

NOTE

1   European Commission (2001), Eurobarometer Report 54, *Europeans and Languages*, February 15, Brussels: European Commission; European Language Council (2001), *Universities and Language Policy in Europe*, June, Berlin: http://www.fu-berlin.de/elc; Council of the European Union (1995), *Linguistic Diversity and Multilingualism in the European Union*, Council conclusions, 1853rd Council meeting, General Affairs B, Luxembourg, 12 June; Council of the European Union (1992), *Charter of Regional or Minority Languages*, Strasbourg: Council of the European Union; Council of the European Union, *Framework Convention on National Minorities* (1995), Strasbourg: Council of the European Union; Council of the European Communities on the Schooling of Migrant Workers (1977), *Directive 77.486*; Council of Europe (2001), *Common European Framework of Reference for Languages, Learning, Teaching and Assessment*, Cambridge: Cambridge University Press; European Commission (1995), *White Paper on Education and Training – Teaching and Learning: Towards the Learning Society*, Brussels: European Commission.

REFERENCES

Ager, D. (1996). *Language Policy in Britain and France.* London/New York: Cassell.

Baugh, J. (2000). *Beyond Ebonics: Linguistic Pride and Racial Prejudice*. New York/Oxford: Oxford University Press.

Baynham, M. (2003). Adult literacy. In J. Bourne & E. Reid (eds.), *Language Education: World Yearbook of Education 2003* (pp. 109–127). London: Kogan Page.

Bourdieu, P. (1991). *Language and Symbolic Power*, trans. G. Raymond & M. Adamson. Cambridge, UK: Polity Press.

Billig, M. (1995). *Banal Nationalism*. London: Sage.

Brunot, F. (1927). *Histoire de la langue française des origins à 1900* [History of the French language from its origins to 1900], vol. 9, part 1. Paris: Armand Colin, 3–14.

Crawford, J. (2002). *At War with Diversity: US Language Policy in an Age of Anxiety*. Clevedon, UK: Multilingual Matters.

Gellner, E. (1983). *Nations and Nationalism*. Oxford, Blackwell Publishers.

Graddol, D. (2006). *English Next*. London: British Council.

Greenfeld, L. (1992). *Nationalism: Five Roads to Modernity*. Cambridge, MA: Harvard University Press.

Hobsbawm, E. J. (1992). *Nations and Nationalism Since 1780: Programme, Myth, Reality* (2nd revised edn.). Cambridge: Canto.

Hornberger, N. H. (2003). *Continua of Bi-Literacy: An Ecological Framework for Educational Policy, Research, and Practice in Multilingual Settings*. Clevedon, UK: Multilingual Matters.

Hroch, M. (1996). From national movement to the fully-formed nation: The nation-building process in Europe. In G. Balakrishnan (ed.), *Mapping the Nation* (pp. 78–97). New York/London: Verso.

Krashen, S. (1996). *Under Attack: The Case against Bilingual Education*. Culver City, CA: Language Education Associates.

Labov, W. (1972). *Sociolinguistic Patterns*. Philadelphia: University of Pennsylvania Press.

Lo Bianco, J. (2005a). Globalisation and national communities of communication. *Language Problems and Language Planning*, 29(2), 109–133.

Lo Bianco, J. (2005b). No longer a (foreign) language: The rhetoric of English as a post-identity language. *The Journal of Chinese Sociolinguistics*, 2(5), 17–41.

Lo Bianco, J. (2007). Advantage plus identity: Neat discourse, loose connection: Singapore's Medium of Instruction Policy. In V. Vaish, S. Gopinathan, & Y. Liu (eds.), *Language, Capital, Culture: Critical Studies of Language in Education in Singapore* (pp. 5–22). Amsterdam: SensePublishers.

Murphy, E. (1988). The cultural dimension in foreign language teaching: Four models. *Language, Culture and Curriculum*, 1(2) 147–163.

OECD (1996a). *Literacy, Economy and Society*. Paris: Organization for Economic Co-operation and Development.

OECD (1996b). *Lifelong Learning for All*. Paris: Organization for Economic Cooperation and Development.

Pakir, A. (2003). Singapore. In J. Bourne & E. Reid (eds.), *Language Education, World Yearbook of Education 2003* (pp. 267–280). London: Kogan Page.

Ruiz, R. (1984). Orientations in language planning. *Journal of the National Association for Bilingual Education*, 8, 15–34.

Shanmugaratnam, T. (2002). Speech by Senior Minister of State for Trade and Industry and Education, at the Tamil Murasu, Most Inspiring Tamil Teacher Award. October 13, http://www.moe.gov.sg/speeches/2002/sp14102002.htm

Silver, R. E. (2005). The discourse of linguistic capital: Language and economic policy planning in Singapore. *Language Policy*, 4(1), 47–66.

Smith, A. D. (1995). *Nations and Nationalism in a Global Era*. Cambridge: Polity Press.

Spolsky, B. (1978). *Educational Linguistics: An Introduction*. Rowley, MA: Newbury House.

Spring, J. (1998). *Education and the Rise of the Global Economy*. Mahwah, NJ: Lawrence Erlbaum.

Seton-Watson, H. (1977). *Nations and States*. London: Methuen.

Staddon, S. (1996). Engineering French: The origins, development of a French for Special Purposes subject. In J. Burston, M. Monville-Burston, & J. Warren (eds.), *Issues and Innovations in the Teaching of French*, ALAA Occasional Paper 15, 125–140.

Watson-Gegeo, K. A. (2004). Mind, language, and epistemology: Toward a language socialization paradigm for SLA. *The Modern Language Journal*, 88(3), 331–350.

Wee, L. (2004). Linguistic instrumentalism in Singapore. *Journal of Multilingual and Multicultural Development*, 24(3) 211–223.

Wright, S. (2004). *Language Policy and Language Planning: From Nationalism to Globalisation*. Basingstoke, UK: Palgrave.

Part II Core Themes

10 The Language of Instruction Issue: Framing an Empirical Perspective

STEPHEN L. WALTER

There is little dispute that formal education is primarily a language-mediated enterprise. What happens then when the child being educated does not speak the language of the classroom? While the issue of language of instruction (LoI) has begun to receive substantial attention in the research literature, we still lack an encompassing model of the role this variable plays in education. Furthermore, the extant literature is based largely on work done in developed countries. What about developing countries which are typically more linguistically diverse than the developed countries? The 1998 index of *Comparative Education Review* lists just two entries (out of approximately 1,100) on bilingual education and four more on language policy issues for the 40 years between 1957 and 1998 (Parker & Epstein, 1998). While one might suggest that this lack of attention is a result of the rise of more specialized journals as research outlets, most such journals are less than 20 years old and report research and debate primarily in developed countries.

Thomas and Collier (1997) have provided the most convincing evidence to date on the impact of the LoI variable on educational outcomes. Even though the scope and power of their research is impressive, myriad questions remain. Will the "language effect" described by Thomas and Collier be as evident when teachers and schools are weaker and communities are ambivalent on the choice of language of instruction? Is their model extensible to developing countries? Will the language effect persist when the L1 is a less developed language? What level of proficiency in L2 is adequate to eliminate or reduce the need for L1 instruction? What level of improvement in educational outcomes is needed to justify national-level changes in educational policy? Do the putative benefits of L1 instruction justify policy changes when most children leave school at the end of primary? Do the benefits of L1 instruction have lifelong implications for the individual and development consequences for entire nations?

Clearly, there is much we do not know about the consequences of LoI on either individuals or nations. The fact that many developed countries are dealing with the educational implications of massive immigration has raised the urgency of this issue. At the same time many developing countries manifest both high levels of linguistic diversity and low levels of educational performance. The purpose of this chapter, then, is twofold: (1) to make a case for the need for a more complete model of the LoI issue based on empirical evidence; and (2) to present some data suggestive of such a model.

Some Terminological and Conceptual Preliminaries

When language is the referent

The "language in education" construct is not an unambiguously defined notion. Children bring to the classroom one or more languages which they speak with varying degrees of proficiency. Following Baker (2006), it is assumed that most children enter school with one dominant language though children in cities often manifest some degree of bilingualism. Teachers may or may not speak the language(s) spoken by the students in their classrooms. The curriculum may be in a language spoken well by neither the teacher nor the students or by one and not the other. For the sake of common reference, the following terminological conventions will be used in this paper.

- Language of instruction (LoI): In any classroom, one or more languages are used by the teacher(s) to provide instruction. This instructional language will be referred to as a/the Language of Instruction.
- Subject of instruction (SoI): When a language is the subject matter of instruction – whether or not it is the medium of instruction – it will be referred to as a Subject of Instruction (SoI).
- First (or primary) language (L1): The vast majority of children entering school have an identifiable language which is that of their greatest proficiency. Many also have some level of proficiency in a second (or third) language which will be identified as an L2.
- Language of wider communication (LWC): Most linguistically diverse nations have designated a national or official language meant to be a means of communication across linguistic boundaries. Often this LWC is also the language of instruction in the classroom.

When instructional strategy is the referent

A number of terminological systems exist for describing educational processes or strategies when there is disjunction[1] between (1) the language of instruction, (2) the primary language(s) of the learners, and (3) the language(s) of the curriculum. The following typology is based primarily on the level of linguistic support provided to children in the classroom.

- *Submersion* A submersion model is one in which all elements of the educational environment are encountered in a language (largely) unknown to the learner upon entry. In submersion models it is assumed that the child will "automatically" master the language of education *during* the educational process. Level of linguistic support in this model: **none**.
- *Code-switching* In code-switching models, teachers make some use of the child's L1 – usually informally – to provide ad hoc instructional support for children who do not (yet) understand the language of instruction. Code-switching is only possible when the teacher shares a language with the learners. Level of linguistic support in this model: **minimal**.
- *Early exit programs* In early exit programs, learners receive some or much of their instruction in their primary language during the first one to three years of school. At the same time, learners either undergo second language instruction or receive some instruction in a second language – typically the future language of education. Early exit programs are predicated on the assumption that this period of L1 support is sufficient to bring children to proficiency in the language of education. Level of linguistic support in this model: **high initially, little or none subsequently**.
- *Late exit programs* Late exit programs use the language of the learner as a medium of instruction for five, six, or even more years while, at the same time, bringing the child to a level of proficiency in the L2 deemed adequate for the child to fully benefit from instruction in that second language after primary education. The logic of late exit programs rests heavily on empirical data suggesting that graduates of such programs appear to make a much stronger transition to L2 classrooms. Level of linguistic support in this model: **high throughout**.
- *Heritage language programs* Not otherwise mentioned in this paper, heritage language programs refer to an eclectic miscellany of programs in which a language other than the primary language of instruction is brought into the classroom primarily as a subject. This language typically has cultural or linguistic relevance to the learners whether as a mother tongue or as the language of the local community. Level of linguistic support in such models: **usually minimal**.

Demographic Dimensions of the LoI Issue

While it would surprise few that *small* linguistic communities exist whose primary language is not used as a LoI in formal education, it is tempting to assume that *all* of the widely spoken languages in the world are used as languages of instruction. Table 10.1 groups the languages of the world according to population size (based on data from the *Ethnologue* (Grimes, 1992)). Six population categories were used for this purpose (somewhat arbitrarily chosen), ranging from the very small – 1–4,999 – to the very large – more than 10 million speakers. The second column indicates whether the languages

Table 10.1 Use of primary languages as languages of instruction (Data distilled from the SIL *Ethnologue* and other sources by the author)

Population range	Number of languages		Total population		Percent of population having access to education in primary language
	Used in education	Not used in education	Access to education in primary language	No access to education in primary language	
No population given	0	636	0	0	0.00
1–4,999	0	2,691	0	3,428,851	0.00
5,000–49,999	7	1,857	191,497	34,446,754	0.55
50,000–249,999	18	835	2,438,515	92,911,103	2.56
250,000–9,999,999	50	653	154,586,507	901,420,392	14.64
More than 10 million	48	38	3,863,901,455	990,011,517	79.60
TOTALS	123[a]	6,709	4,021,117,974	2,022,218,617	66.54

[a] In making this count some standard needed to be adopted as to what constituted access to education in a primary language. An arbitrary choice was made to consider education available in a given language if at least one third of the school-aged speakers of that language could attend a school in which this language was used as a medium of instruction. The author is well aware that his data is incomplete with respect to the total number of languages used in education. Additional data is still being gathered with the tables and graphs being updated accordingly. For example, it is reported (Malone, personal communication) that more than 400 languages in Papua New Guinea are now being used as languages of instruction in that country alone.

[b] The numbers in this table are expressed entirely in terms of the gross population rather than actual students.

spoken by these population groups are used as media of education and subsequent columns suggest the number of people who *may* therefore have access
to education in their primary language.

Looking at the category "Over 10 million speakers," it is clear that not all
widely spoken languages are used as media of instruction in education. Of
the 86 languages having a population greater than 10 million speakers, 38
(or 44 percent) are not used as languages of instruction in education. Nearly
1 billion people speak these 38 languages. In the second category, 250,000–10
million, only 50 of 703 languages are used in education as primary media of
instruction. Collectively, one third of the world's population lacks access to
education in their primary language.

If access to education in a primary language matters at the macro level, we
should find evidence for this effect in one or more of the indicators of national
development. Consider the data in Table 10.2. In this table, the countries of the
world are categorized according to a set of developmental categories used by
UNESCO, with *Least* meaning "the least developed," and so on. Then, the data
from Table 10.1 were placed into each of these categories according to the
country in which each people group is located. The result is a "map" of the
world plotting the variable of *national development status* against the variable of
access to education in a primary language.

The 48 countries in the *Least* category collectively provide access to education in a primary language for just 38.12 percent of their populations. At the
other extreme, the *Developed* countries make education in a primary language
available to 86.42 percent of their populations. Note the steady increase in
access to education in a primary language as one traverses the development
categories from *Least* to *Developed*. Of the 2.293 billion *not* receiving L1
educational support, 2.052 billion (or 89.49 percent of the total) live in the
168 countries making up the *Least* and *Less* development categories.

Table 10.3 further examines the distributional relationship between the
variables of *access to education in L1* and *level of national development*. In this
table, the countries of the world were first ranked from low to high in terms of
whether the population groups in each country had access to education in a
primary language and then divided into four equal groups of 57 countries
each. Countries in Group 1 provide little or no education in the language(s) of
their populations. Conversely, the countries in Group 4 are the most likely to
provide education in the language(s) of their populations. After this clustering
was done the countries in each cluster were categorized according to UNESCO's
scheme for describing national development status.

A quick scan of Table 10.3 indicates a non-random relationship between the
two variables given the prominence of *Least* countries in Groups 1 and 2 and
the near absence of *In transition* and *Developed* countries in these groups. A
chi-square test confirms this observation ($\chi^2 = 59.035$; df = 9; p = 0.000000002056).
Clearly, the demographic data make a prima facie case that the LoI variable is
deeply entwined with that of national development. Even so, it is too facile to
presume that the variable of LoI operates in splendid isolation from a host of

Table 10.2 Access to education in a primary language relative to national development category

Cluster	Number of countries in this category	Total number of languages spoken in this category	Total population of all countries in this category	Population having access to education in a primary language	Percent of population having access to education in a primary language
Least	48	2,133	644,220,132	245,589,963	38.12
Less	120	5,855	4,125,288,871	2,471,608,660	59.91
In transition	31	661	435,578,075	311,228,530	71.45
Developed	29	1,358	853,610,244	737,698,139	86.42
TOTALS	228	10,007	6,058,697,322	3,766,125,292	62.16

Table 10.3 Distribution of countries into equal groups ordered by the likelihood that a country's population has access to education in a primary language

		Least	*Less*	*In transition*	*Developed*	*TOTALS*
Lowest access	Group 1	23	34	0	0	57
↑	Group 2	14	36	5	2[a]	57
↓	Group 3	7	24	13	13	57
Highest access	Group 4	4	26	13	14	57
	TOTALS	48	120	31	29	228

[a] These are both very small countries in Europe in which the official language is a closely related colloquial variant of the language of instruction. In both cases, the population is reported to be highly bilingual in both languages.

intervening variables including poverty, teacher training, language policy, sociolinguistic attitudes, and various environmental problems.

Educational Dimensions of the Language of Instruction Issue

Baker (2006) provides a good summary of the recent history of multilingual education primarily in developed countries. Dutcher (2004) summarizes much of what has been published about experience with L1 education in the developing countries. Despite the suggestiveness of the available data, the LoI question is still often subordinated to issues of political sensitivity, technical difficulties, economic limitations, societal tensions, and the established practice and inertia of national educational systems.

Even so, intrepid pioneers have launched experimental programs and published the results of their work (Lambert & Tucker, 1972; Modiano, 1973; Larson & Davis, 1981; Fafunwa, Macauley, & Sokoya, 1989; and many others). Through the work of these and more recent researchers, the linguistic dimensions of the educational process have begun to emerge. The work reported by Modiano and by Larson & Davis highlighted the many issues of language development entailed in the use of lesser-known languages as languages of instruction. The St Lambert experiment described in Lambert and Tucker (and more than 1,000 other studies) raised awareness of the importance of sociolinguistic beliefs and values in shaping educational outcomes when multiple languages of instruction are employed in the classroom. The extensive work done by Cummins (1981) has made us aware of just how linguistically proficient one must be to fully benefit from classroom instruction. Thomas and Collier (1997) have not only made a compelling case for a potent language effect in education,

Table 10.4 Summary of findings from the Thomas and Collier study (1997)

	Type of Program	Years of L1 instruction or support	Approximate number of students	Mean score (out of 100) on national test at end of Grade 11	Percentile of mean score
Program 1	Two-way developmental	6	1,200	61	70
Program 2	One-way developmental	6	3,000	52	54
Program 3	Transitional with ESL academic content	3	3,800	40	32
Program 4	Transitional with regular ESL	3	7,000	35	24
Program 5	ESL with academic content	0	5,500	34	22
Program 6	ESL pullout	0	21,500	24	11

but have also provided evidence that this effect has lifelong implications for the learner.

In the remainder of this chapter I provide empirical evidence in three categories of outcomes pertinent to understanding the educational implications of LoI. These are (1) cognitive outcomes, (2) measures of participation, and (3) cost effectiveness. While the evidence being provided derives considerable weight from having been distilled from large datasets, the reader is reminded that this evidence is still suggestive as definitive models are yet to be defined.

Cognitive outcomes

There is not yet full agreement in the literature on what constitutes evidence that one model produces outcomes superior to those of another (Rossell & Baker, 1996; Greene, 1998). Much initial research compared performance across models after a year or two with ambiguous or contradictory results. More recently the view that we must look to longitudinal evidence has been gaining traction. The logic is not complex. It takes many years for a child to become an adult. It takes even more years before one can make a reasonable assessment as to whether the quality of education received as a child mattered in the quality of one's life and work as an adult.

The best known longitudinal study is that of Thomas and Collier (1997). Launched in the late 1980s and still ongoing, the Thomas and Collier study sought to determine, "Which approach to educating limited English proficient children is most effective in terms of bringing such children to educational parity with native English-speaking children?"

To answer this question, Thomas and Collier identified six distinct strategies being used in the US to educate non English-speaking children and located schools and school districts where these six strategies were well implemented. In this way, they sought to eliminate the variable "quality of program" which had distorted results in many earlier studies. To further strengthen their study, Thomas and Collier included a large number of children (42,000) and tracked them through high school. The basis of comparison is standardized tests taken by millions of children in the US. The findings of this study are summarized in Table 10.4.

Column 3 specifies the number of years of L1 educational support received in each model. Column 5 indicates mean performance on a nationally normed standardized test of the entire research sample for each model at the end of Grade 11. The data in Table 10.4 suggest a strong relationship between years of L1 educational support and level of academic achievement. If analyzed as a simple linear correlation, we get an r of 0.94 (p = 0.002). The regression equation suggests an improvement of 6.75 percentiles for each year of L1 educational support. Note from column 6 that the only two groups to reach educational parity (mean score of 50 or higher) with native English-speaking children were those receiving six years of instructional support in L1.

Table 10.5 Career and workforce implications of the Thomas and Collier research findings

Standard deviation	NCE equivalent	English-speaking children (L1 only)	Instructional models for non-English-speaking children		Typical professional and career options associated with academic performance at this level[a]
			ESL pullouts (L2 only)	Two-way developmental (L1 AND L2)	
Above 2nd	More than 92	228	6	699	Researchers, scientists, doctors, intellectuals, poets
1st to 2nd	71–92	1,359	120	2,471	Professors, business leaders, journalists, engineers
Mean to 1st	50–71	3,413	952	3,828	Teachers, mid-level managers, skilled technicians
–1st to Mean	29–51	3,413	2,891	2,364	Factory workers, equipment operators, clerical workers
–2nd to –1st	8–29	1,359	3,710	580	Blue-collar workers, manual laborers, construction workers
Below –2nd	Less than 8	228	2,231	58	Domestics, menial labor, hard to employ

[a] Clearly, academic performance is not a certain predictor of success in life or future career. Other factors are germane – determination, maturity, creativity, social position, opportunity, personal gifting, to name just a few.

In their more recent research, Thomas and Collier have included a program type called submersion. In this program, non-English-speaking children are mainstreamed from the onset of their time in school with no L1 support of any kind. The performance of these children is essentially the same as those in Program 6 – the ESL pullout program – scoring, on average, at the twelfth percentile. This latter model most closely resembles the educational strategy used in most developing countries.

Walter (2004) sought to interpret the Thomas and Collier findings in terms of their training and career implications. In the US, as in most countries, those children who do well in primary and secondary school have the greatest likelihood of gaining access to tertiary education and thus to professional careers as doctors, lawyers, scientists, writers, engineers, teachers, researchers, etc. If a given model of education systematically precludes access to educational opportunity, it seems reasonable to suggest that such a model is inferior.

In Table 10.5, the research findings published by Thomas and Collier have been recast in terms of career or workforce implications. The numbers in the table were computed directly from the data gathered by Thomas and Collier using the normal distribution model.

The leftmost column divides the research population (or any scholastic population) into tiered groups according to test performance. The rightmost column reflects career options typically associated with a given level of academic performance (assumed to be at least somewhat predicted by test performance).

Columns 3–5 indicate the number of students out of a population of 10,000 who would be expected to perform at each level for each of the three instructional models specified in the table. Column 3 reflects expected (and measured) outcomes for native speakers of English who were educated entirely in English (their L1). Columns 4 and 5 contrast the outcomes of Programs 1 and 6, the most and least effective of the six strategies for educating non-English-speaking children investigated by Thomas and Collier.

According to the model, when education is received in the primary language (Column 3), 228 out of 10,000 students can be expected to perform at or above the second standard deviation. For those receiving education only in a second language (Column 4), only 6 of 10,000 are likely to perform at this level.

Especially stark is the distribution of students at the *lower* end of the scale. In the case of those being educated in L1, 228 children are likely to finish below the second standard deviation. However, for those being educated entirely or primarily in L2, more than 20 percent of students (2,231) will/did finish below the second standard deviation – a level corresponding to having few, if any, marketable skills. Almost 90 percent of the 10,000 students being educated in a second language only, will/did finish below the mean. The sociological and economic implications are dramatic.

It is tempting to suggest that other variables – socioeconomic status, familial support and stability, personal motivation, sociolinguistic biases – must account for this result. Recall, however, that non-English-speaking children in Program 2 (cf. Table 10.4) finished on a par with native English-speaking children. Furthermore, non-English-speaking children in two-way developmental programs (mixed cohorts of English and non-English-speaking children) significantly outperformed native English speakers (Columns 5 and 6).

In the case of the US, the Thomas and Collier data suggest that the use of submersion models to educate non-English-speaking children is producing and will continue to produce a large underclass of people capable of doing little but providing manual labor. In the case of developing countries, the data suggest that submersion models are a prescription for permanent or at least persistent underdevelopment.

Outcomes of access and participation

A second widely used measure of educational outcomes is that of participation – enrollment, pass/fail rates, repetition rates, and persistence/graduation rates. Virtually all international studies document unfavorable rates on these measures in developing countries compared to the more developed countries (Fiske, 1998; World Bank, 1988).

Thomas and Collier (1997) report that dropout rates among Hispanic children participating in two-way developmental programs (six years of L1 instructional support) are 4–6 percent compared to 30 percent for Hispanic children nationwide (Lockwood & Secada, 1999). Walter and Morren (2004) analyzed nine years of educational data from Guatemala which has been providing L1 education for some of its Mayan-speaking population using an early exit model. The data for all schools in the country suggested an advantage in promotion rates for students in Mayan-medium schools in Grade 1 and a slight advantage in Grade 6 but a negative advantage in Grades 2–4.

Given the (somewhat unexpected) ambiguity of this result, Walter and Morren disaggregated the data by the variable of ethnolinguistic density. The results of this disaggregation are set forth in Table 10.6.

This more focused comparison of promotion rates between Spanish-medium and Mayan-medium schools indicates a systematic difference of 5–9 percent favoring the Mayan-medium schools (all differences are statistically significant at the 0.000 level). Significantly, this advantage persists in Grades 5 and 6 where the medium of instruction in *all* schools is Spanish and the teacher may be either ethnic Mayan or Hispanic. Furthermore, an examination of data on enrollment in secondary indicated a strong persistent effect of L1 education at that level as well ($\chi^2 = 193.37$; p = 0.000 (5.85E-44)).

Urbanness and gender in Guatemala

Two widely cited findings about education in developing countries are (1) that urban children do (significantly) better than rural children, and (2) that male students usually do better than female students. Typically, however, this finding ignores the sociolinguistic fact that the children in rural schools are probably

Table 10.6 Comparison of promotion rates for students in highly ethnic areas of Guatemala[a] for Spanish-medium versus Mayan-medium schools

| | Spanish-medium Schools | | | | Mayan-medium Schools | | | |
| | Male students | | Female students | | Male students | | Female students | |
	Rate	School/years[b]	Rate	School/years	Rate	School/years	Rate	School/years
Grade 1	51.5	14,208	50.8	14,064	60.6	7,365	59.9	7,334
Grade 2	61.6	13,352	58.6	12,760	67.7	7,234	65.3	7,163
Grade 3	65.9	12,073	64.1	10,869	71.2	7,059	69.3	6,732
Grade 4	69.2	9,886	67.6	8,354	75.6	6,579	74.3	5,954
Grade 5	71.9	7,804	72.5	6,124	79.5	5,893	78.1	5,080
Grade 6	77.2	6,071	78.7	4,728	86.8	5,159	86.5	4,275

[a] In this analysis all schools were divided into four zones by ethnolinguistic density ranging from zones of low density (0–30 percent Mayan) to high density (90–100 percent Mayan).
[b] A school/year is the complete data for one school for one year. The data from one school for the full nine years of the study would constitute 9 school/years.

being educated in a second language while those in the city are more likely to receive their education in a more familiar (though perhaps not their first) language. Table 10.7 presents the relevant data from Guatemala.

When we compare results for the two categories of school in *urban* areas alone, we find little significant difference in terms of promotion rates. Similarly, when we compare Mayan-medium schools in urban areas with similar schools in rural areas, we find a very slight advantage for the schools in urban areas on the order of 1–3 percent. However, the Spanish-medium schools in rural areas reveal a markedly lower level of performance both with respect to Mayan-medium schools in rural areas *and* Spanish-medium schools in urban areas. The differential is on the order of 8–12 percent for both comparisons.

How do we explain these data? Sociolinguistically, it would appear that Mayan children in urban areas "function" more like Hispanic children in terms of participation in the education system. Conversely, the pattern of language usage in rural areas – children being monolingual or nearly monolingual in a Mayan language – suggests that these children have a greater likelihood of experiencing educational success when having access to Mayan-medium instruction. The data also support the hypothesis that the LoI variable accounts for most of the observed variation in performance between urban and rural schools.

Urbanness and gender in Eritrea

All primary school students in Eritrea receive their primary education in L1 (eight languages at the time of the study). Therefore, data from Eritrean schools

Table 10.7   Comparison of promotion rates for male and female students in urban versus rural schools in highly ethnic regions of Guatemala
(a)   Results for urban areas

	Spanish-medium schools				Mayan-medium schools			
	Male students		Female students		Male students		Female students	
	Rate	School/years	Rate	School/years	Rate	School/years	Rate	School/years
Grade 1	58.1	302	59.5	300	60.7	223	62.1	225
Grade 2	70.1	296	71.1	289	68.8	220	68.1	223
Grade 3	78.6	277	74.7	266	72.2	209	72.4	203
Grade 4	78.7	263	78.0	249	76.6	194	74.9	190
Grade 5	81.9	250	86.7	223	80.1	177	77.2	174
Grade 6	84.4	217	88.1	208	87.3	156	88.0	144

(b)   Results for rural areas

	Spanish-medium schools				Mayan-medium schools			
	Male students		Female students		Male students		Female students	
	Rate	School/years	Rate	School/years	Rate	School/years	Rate	School/years
Grade 1	49.4	7,727	48.6	7,638	59.7	3,646	59.1	3,626
Grade 2	59.5	7,230	56.4	6,841	66.9	3,546	65.1	3,505
Grade 3	64.2	6,447	62.2	5,717	70.6	3,460	69.5	3,272
Grade 4	67.2	5,097	64.9	4,160	74.9	3,227	74.3	2,844
Grade 5	69.4	3,915	70.4	2,857	79.0	2,866	78.9	2,407
Grade 6	74.1	2,858	74.9	2,059	86.1	2,479	86.4	1,993

should provide a good test of "conventional wisdom" on the variables of urbanness and gender. If these two variables are strong predictors of educational outcomes in a developing country (apart from the issue of LoI), this result should be clearly apparent given that Eritrea is among the poorest of the world's countries. Consider the data in Table 10.8 taken from the *Eritrea National Reading Survey* of 2002 (Walter and Davis, 2005). The data are mean test scores on a substantial test of reading skill administered as a part of the survey. The upper and lower sections of the table contain the same data rearranged by the variable of interest.

The table compares the performance of students (a stratified random sample) at three different grade levels disaggregated by gender and urbanness. When we compare students between rural and urban areas (Table 10.8a), we note

Table 10.8   Performance on graded tests of language arts knowledge and skill among Eritrean students (N = ca. 800 for each grade level)

(a)

	Rural areas		Urban areas	
	Males	*Females*	*Males*	*Females*
Grade 1	41.64	39.82	51.34	57.31
Grade 3	79.66	75.41	78.29	80.49
Grade 5	57.44	58.73	57.46	57.58

(b)

	Male students		Female students	
	Rural	*Urban*	*Rural*	*Urban*
Grade 1	41.64	51.34	39.82	57.31
Grade 3	79.66	78.29	75.41	80.49
Grade 5	57.44	57.46	58.73	57.58

fairly marked differences in Grade 1, minimal differences in Grade 3 and virtually identical performance in Grade 5.

When we compare students by gender (Table 10.8b), we note a fairly similar pattern with the differences limited primarily to Grade 1. Again, we have evidence that the effect typically ascribed to urbanness and gender in developing countries may, in fact, be largely negated when children have access to education in L1.

Cost effectiveness

Analyses of the cost effectiveness of an educational innovation can quickly immerse one in a fog of ill-defined constructs, slippery assumptions, and complex models. The case presented here is not entirely free from such encumbrances but does have the virtue of being relatively simple to present and understand. The relevant data are presented in Table 10.9.

Table 10.9 is a composite of the performance of *all* primary schools (approximately 1,000) in school districts of Guatemala which have a predominately Mayan-speaking population and which offer Mayan-medium education. The bold figures in the last row state the computed cost (based on national expenditures per school child of $145) of successfully educating one student

Table 10.9   A comparison of cost effectiveness of L1 versus L2 medium schools in highly ethnic areas of Guatemala

	Spanish-medium schools			Mayan-medium schools		
	Enrolled	*Promoted*	*Cost/grad*	*Enrolled*	*Promoted*	*Cost/grad*
Grade 1	252,728	120,279	304.67	175,608	104,028	244.77
Grade 2	139,098	83,487	241.59	118,700	80,707	213.26
Grade 3	88,090	56,918	224.41	85,300	61,009	202.73
Grade 4	54,122	35,740	219.58	57,576	42,791	195.10
Grade 5	33,231	23,256	207.19	36,755	28,320	188.19
Grade 6	19,107	14,138	195.96	19,379	15,907	176.65
	586,376		**$6,013.90**	493,318		**$4,496.83**

through Grade 6 for each model. The figure given – $6,013.90 in the case of Spanish-medium schools – encodes the actual yearly spending per child *plus* the collective wastage of the model due to dropouts, failures, and repetitions between Grade 1 and Grade 6. The differential between the models of just over $1,500 would appear to be a measure of the greater efficiency of the Mayan-medium model in educating Mayan-speaking primary school children. Since virtually all students attending both types of schools come from the same sociolinguistic and cultural background and the dataset includes such a large population (both of students and schools), the LoI variable would appear to be the primary difference between the two models.

Conclusion

The demographic data presented provide evidence that, at present, approximately one third of the world's children lack access to education in their primary language with the vast majority of these living in developing countries. At the same time, we have abundant data from research evidence that educational outcomes in developing countries are not good. Thomas and Collier have provided convincing evidence that language of instruction is a potent variable in explaining educational outcomes for language minority children.

The Thomas and Collier study, however, focused entirely on the US. Therefore, we are left with the question of the extensibility of their findings to educational practice in developing countries. To explore the question of extensibility, primary research data has been presented from programs in Guatemala and Eritrea providing evidence that the LoI variable is, indeed, a salient variable in explaining educational outcomes in these and, by extension, other developing countries.

What model theoretic insights flow from the data presented in this paper? I suggest the following:

- The impact of the LoI variable extends to education in developing countries, but the strength of its effect may be somewhat attenuated by reduced quality of instruction and the effect of local and national sociolinguistic attitudes.
- The LoI variable will be found to explain a substantial amount of the variation currently attributed to school location and some of that attributed to gender.
- The effect of the LoI variable extends well beyond primary education and is a contributing factor to underdevelopment.
- The LoI variable will eventually be associated with improved efficiency in the delivery of education.

While this list is suggestive, it barely scratches the surface of what we need to know to fully appreciate the relationship between language of instruction and educational outcomes. Not only do we need to develop, test, and refine models of this relationship, we need also to investigate myriad other issues impacting educational outcomes in linguistically complex developing countries. There is plenty of work to be done.

NOTE

1   This chapter will assume that the lack of such disjunction – i.e., full linguistic equivalence at all three levels – represents a linguistically "uncharged" educational setting where linguistic variation is not a variable having significant impact on educational outcomes.

REFERENCES

Baker, Colin (2006). *Foundations of Bilingual Education and Bilingualism* (4th edn.). Clevedon, UK: Multilingual Matters.

Cummins, James (1981b). The role of primary language development in promoting educational success for language minority students. In California State Department of Education (ed.), *Schooling and Language Minority Students: A Theoretical Framework* (pp. 3–49). Los Angeles: California State Department of Education.

Dutcher, Nadine (2004). *Expanding Educational Opportunity in Linguistically Diverse Societies*. Washington, DC: Center for Applied Linguistics.

Fafunwa, Aliu Babtunde, Macauley, Juliet, I., & Sokoya, J. A. Funnso (1989). *Education in Mother Tongue: The Ife Primary Education Research Project (1970–1978)*. Ibadan: Ibadan University Press.

Fiske, Edward B. (1998). *Wasted Opportunities: When Schools Fail*. Paris: UNESCO/Education for All.

Greene, Jay P. (1998). *A Meta-Analysis of the Effectiveness of Bilingual Education*. Austin, TX: The Tomas Rivera Policy Institute.

Grimes, Barbara F. (ed.) (1992). *Ethnologue: Languages of the World* (12th edn.). Dallas, TX: SIL International.

Lambert, Wallace E. & Tucker, G. Richard (1972). *Bilingual Education of Children: The St. Lambert Experiment*. Rowley, MA: Newbury House.

Larson, Mildred L. & Davis, Patricia M. (eds.) (1981). *Bilingual Education in Peruvian Amazonia*. Washington, DC: Center for Applied Linguistics and Dallas, TX: Summer Institute of Linguistics.

Lockwood, Anne Turnbaugh & Secada, Walter G. (1999). *Transforming Education for Hispanic Youth: Exemplary Practices, Programs, and Schools*. Washington, DC: The National Clearing-house for Bilingual Education.

Modiano, Nancy (1973). *Indian Education in the Chiapas Highlands*. New York: Holt, Rinehart, & Winston.

Parker, Christine S. & Epstein, Erwin H. (1998). Cumulative index (revised edn.), vols. 1–42, 1957–1998. *Comparative Education Review*.

Rossell, Christine H. & Baker, Keith (1996). The educational effectiveness of bilingual education. *Research in the Teaching of English*, 30, 7–74.

Thomas, Wayne & Collier, Virginia (1997). School effectiveness for language minority children. www.ncela.gwu./pubs/resource/effectiveness.

Walter, Stephen L. (2004). Does language of instruction matter? In Mary Ruth Wise & Thomas N. Headland (eds.), *Language and Life: Essays in Memory of Kenneth L. Pike* (pp. 611–635). Dallas: SIL International.

Walter, Stephen L. & Davis, Patricia M. (2005). *Eritrea National Reading Survey*. Dallas: SIL International.

Walter, Stephen L. & Morren, Ronald (2004). Twenty Years of Bilingual Education in Guatemala. Paper presented to the GIAL Academic Forum, Dallas, TX.

World Bank (1988). *Education in Sub-Saharan Africa: Policies for Adjustment, Revitalization, and Expansion*. Washington, DC: World Bank.

11 Bilingual and Biliterate Practices at Home and School

ILIANA REYES AND LUIS C. MOLL

Introduction

Across communities, members participate in social practices that influence their ways of thinking and speaking with each other. This participation not only affects learning at the individual level, but also at the collective level through the social and linguistic knowledge developed collaboratively by group members of particular communities. This knowledge develops at an early age when children start to recognize different social events that take place around them, and learn to speak and act in ways that are sensitive to the participants and to the context of such events.

In this chapter we provide an overview of the role of language and culture in such socialization practices. Our examples come primarily from the US southwest, where we have conducted our research, although we also refer to work conducted in other places. We begin with a review of the work on language socialization by discussing the social and cultural nature of language and literacy development. Then we review studies on bilingualism and biliteracy across multiple social contexts (e.g., family, school, community), and how users of two or more languages create new linguistic realities through complex bilingual practices such as code-switching and interliteracy.

We also examine the continuity and discontinuity of linguistic practices between home and school. Of particular importance here is the concept of bidirectional learning, which occurs when family members learn from each other. This bidirectionality is especially relevant in language minority or immigrant families when the child acquires greater linguistic competence than the adults in mastering the dominant language. We conclude with a discussion of the notion of language ideologies and how these impact the creation and transformation of cultural identity among community members in bilingual and multilingual settings.

Language and Literacy Practices

From a sociocultural perspective, language and literacy are viewed as socially constructed, culturally-mediated practices, and these play a vital role in the act of learning (Scribner & Cole, 1981; Taylor, 1983; Ochs, 1986). This understanding has important implications for how language and literacy develop. A first implication is the idea that those being socialized act as *agents* rather than passive *initiates*, in that practices are co-constructed (Freire, 1970; Vygotsky, 1978). A second implication is that the interaction among members of the same community is decisive in determining this development. Across cultures a common finding is the practice of caregivers – i.e., parents, other relatives, community members, teachers, and so on – providing explicit instruction to children regarding what to say and how to say something in recurrent events. Caregivers model for the young child, in many different ways, the acceptable ways of interacting in accordance with their cultural practices. For example, Andersen (1986) described how English-speaking children as young as three years old developed sociolinguistic knowledge and interacted with others during play using proper speech roles according to the situation and characteristics of the speakers (e.g., status, gender, age). Cultures, however, differ in the ways they socialize the language and literacy development of their children. For instance, the Kaluli of Papua New Guinea and Western Samoans require children to participate in lengthy speech routines and a variety of topics from an early age, which essentially adapts children to the situation at hand. The opposite is seen in middle-class families in the US where they adapt the situation to the child instead (Taylor, 1983; Andersen, 1986). These different communicative styles from adults to children point to the ways children, before they even start to speak, begin to learn specific socialization rules and roles to become competent speakers of their society (Schieffelin & Ochs, 1986; also see Hasan, 2002).

These studies have been complemented by more recent ones that have provided a wider interpretation of the concept of literacy. Traditionally, literacy has been defined as the development of a set of linguistic tools in relation to reading and writing, but in recent years literacy has been redefined as the linguistic forms and meaning developed through interactions among individuals, and where this social interaction is at the center of such development (see Whitmore et al., 2004 for a recent review). For instance, Gregory, Long, and Volk (2004) propose what they called *syncretic* literacy studies, by which they mean that children transform what they know of their languages and literacies to create new forms. For example, teachers working in classrooms and a computer club integrate resources from various contexts in the lives of students, such as popular culture, to use in writing activities (Dyson, 2003). Others have called this transformation *hybrid ways* of experiencing different forms of language and literacy. These hybrid ways shape individuals' notions of cultural identity and influence how individuals define and redefine their communities (Baquedano-López, 1997; Garrett & Baquedano-López, 2002). Moreover, within each community the *funds of knowledge* that exist are recognized and influence these hybrid ways of experiencing language and literacy. Funds of knowledge refer to the diverse bodies of knowledge existing in households and communities that develop from people's social histories and from their everyday practices (González, Moll, & Amanti, 2005).

It should be noted that historically many empirical studies exploring the development of language and literacy have suffered from three main deficiencies. First, they have often described only the relationship between caregiver and very young children, without describing the impact of peer relations and siblings on the young child. Second, the development of language and literacy has been studied in the context of monolingual communities (Schieffelin & Ochs, 1986). This is problematic because for most communities around the world, language and literacy socialization takes place in bilingual and multilingual settings, and in such settings linguistic needs may be different. Some of these needs revolve around minority language maintenance, language shift, language revitalization, and language purity versus language mixing or code-switching (Bayley & Schecter, 2003). And third, many studies have focused almost exclusively on literate societies that privilege written experiences as opposed to oral ones (Schieffelin & Ochs, 1986). The danger with this focus is that it minimizes and ignores the practices of poor communities worldwide that experience other forms of literacy. Fortunately, more recent studies have addressed these limitations and have provided a richer, more sophisticated, and ultimately more accurate, understanding of language and literacy development across communities (Bayley & Schecter, 2003).

Bilingualism and Biliteracy in Diverse Communities

The number of people worldwide who speak more than one language and the number of children being schooled in more than one language far exceed the number of monolinguals and the number of children being taught in one language (Baker & Prys Jones, 1998). Although in the past some educators and psychologists have viewed negatively the learning of more than one language during childhood, a number of studies in recent decades have revealed several advantages for bilingual children (Hakuta & Pease-Alvarez, 1992). For example, the cognitive advantages of bilingualism relative to monolingualism include greater mental flexibility when solving problems that involve distractions, and some metalinguistic advantages (Bialystok, 1997, 2001; Genesee, 2001). In terms of social and emotional development, children are able to maintain a stronger sense of their identity while developing greater sensitivity toward other people's cultures. This occurs because in developing bilingual communicative competence, children acquire knowledge of different cultural worldviews (Luykx, 2003), including the ability to incorporate other people's perspectives (Hakuta & Pease-Alvarez, 1992).

Among the unique characteristics of language and literacy practices of bilingual children, two stand out. The first is that bilingual children tend to engage in *code-switching*, a linguistic phenomenon in which children blend two languages. Although often denigrated by language purists, this phenomenon can be characterized as an effective communicative strategy and tool for understanding and clarifying meaning (Reyes, 2004a; Ervin-Tripp & Reyes, 2005). Code-switching is observed among speakers who achieve high levels of bilingualism and it becomes part of the informal linguistic repertoire children learn to use when growing up bilingual in their communities (Zentella, 1997; Reyes & Moll, 2005). The ability to code-switch has recently been studied in relation to children's literacy development. Martinez-Roldán and Sayer (2006) provide the example of Berenice, a seven-year-old Mexican girl living in the United States, who in retelling a story she had read to a bilingual interviewer, said the following in "Spanglish" (a form of code-switching between Spanish and English; Spanish is indicated in *italics*, English translations indicated in square brackets, English code-switching indicated in **bold**):

> *Y ah, y luego, um y . . . luego se fue a dormir y al otro día ellos decoraron todo.*
> *Y luego . . .* (pause) *Mm . . . decoraron todo y él-él-él se levantó y le dijeron* **Happy**
> **Birthday**. *Y le dieron sus* **presents**, *y ella, ella se sentía* **nervous**.
>
> [And um, and then, um and . . . then he went to sleep and the next day they decorated everything. And then . . . [pause] Mm . . . They decorated everything and he-he-he got up and they told him **Happy Birthday**. And they gave him his **presents** and she felt **nervous**.]

In this example, although Berenice read the text in English and the interviewer prompted the retelling in English, she began her retelling in Spanish. At the end of the read aloud, she completed her retelling in English, repeating almost verbatim the content of her Spanish retelling. Examples like the one presented here were often observed by Reyes (2004a) in second grade children's conversations. The use of equivalent words refutes the popular notion that children borrow words because they lack the vocabulary in one or both of their languages (Amastae & Elias-Olivares, 1982). In fact, this linguistic practice can be seen as a successful way for young children to link the knowledge of their native language to that of their second language as they achieve bilingual competence (Ervin-Tripp & Reyes, 2005).

A second unique characteristic of bilingual children is that their linguistic ability is not restricted to the oral and lexical levels, as in the previous code-switching example, but it extends to the syntactic level as well. In a study of young elementary children, Gort (2006) identified *interliteracy* as a transitional phase in which the grammatical rules of one language are applied to another. This interliteracy phase seems to be part of the normal literacy development of bilingual children as they make sense of the rules that apply to a specific language. The following example illustrates this point (Gort, 2006). Barbara, a first-grade English-dominant student living in the United States, was told to write a narrative recounting an event she had experienced. One of her sentences read:

Barbara: *Cuando Yo d[o]rmí [en] LiLianas casa.*
           [When I slept at Liliana's house]

In this sentence, she capitalized the pronoun *yo* (translates 'I'), a word capitalized in English but not in Spanish. Barbara also applied the English sentence structure to Spanish by using the possessive word order and by marking the "s" possessive marker. Although bilingual speakers may not always be aware of the influence that one language exerts on another, these different language and literacy practices support the development of biliteracy skills, and should be viewed by educators and teachers as valuable resources to draw upon. The linguistic funds of knowledge that children bring with them serve as a foundation for the development of literacy activities during classroom interactions. When these practices are connected to the children's background knowledge, their learning becomes more meaningful and their educational experiences more positive (González, Moll, & Amanti, 2005).

Home and School Linguistic Practices

A meta-analysis of studies on language socialization shows that home and school linguistic practices have generally been explored separately. When the findings from these studies are brought together, they reveal important continuities, especially for language majority children, and competing discontinuities, especially for language minority children. A more enlightened pedagogical practice would seek to establish a linguistic continuum from home to school to ease the transition into what can be for many children a stressful situation, especially for those students whose cultural capital differs the most from that of the school.

For example, Luykx described discourse practices in a Bolivian community where children learn Aymara, a local indigenous language, but also develop a command in Spanish because they are aware of the social stigma attached to their native language (Luykx, 2003). As Aymara families migrate to urban settings and the children learn Spanish, only the older sibling generally remains a more fluent Aymara speaker. Younger siblings tend to develop a limited competence of Aymara, or even abandon the language altogether, mostly due to pressure from school, peer culture, and popular media to embrace the dominant Spanish language and reject their ancestral one. Similarly, language minority children in the US also have found themselves torn between competing language practices at home – over 160 living languages are spoken in the US

(Gordon, 2005) – and school, where children are often required to conduct most of their studies in the dominant English language.

To assist in creating a continuity of practices, educational researchers have begun to document the various paths to literacy that language minority families employ in their daily activities (e.g., Taylor & Dorsey-Gaines, 1988; Gregory, Long, & Volk, 2004). A longitudinal study by Reyes (2006) on home literacy practices with first generation Mexican families in the US southwest, showed that family members play key roles in biliteracy development, benefiting not only the young child but each other as well. Reyes called this supporting role *bidirectional learning* because parents and children tend to develop biliteracy as they participate in different interactions with each other. This point is illustrated by Katia, a four-year-old girl whose learning was mediated by her dad and sister when they were all playing with a computer spelling game in the home's living room (Reyes, 2006):

> On a Sunday afternoon, Katia participates in a literacy event where the father helps Katia to type and spell words in English on the computer. The father is helping her daughter by pronouncing the letters in Spanish and helping her find them on the keyboard. Katia pronounces the same letters in Spanish after her Dad, and in English after typing them (the computer indicates the pronunciation in English). A few minutes later, Katia's sister joins them in the activity, and all spell together in English. The mom, watching from the dining room, is intrigued by the activity. She asks what word they are spelling and what it means in Spanish. Katia and her sister think for a second and translate the word for their mom. (Field notes, 27 April 2005)

The bidirectionality of the learning activity was highlighted in this exchange as family members participated and learned from each other. The child's learning was mediated through the process of scaffolding – that is, the use of language (by the sister and father) that is slightly above the child's level of communicative competence. However, the child also mediated the learning of those around her since she provided input in English that benefited the second language learning of her parents. An additional point to stress here is the use of the two languages at different points during this interaction. The father, in particular, used the native language as a resource to help scaffold his younger daughter's learning. In the next dialogue, Katia continued to play with the computer game by spelling in English while the father and older sister drew from Spanish to help Katia solve the activity (for further details on this case study, see Reyes, 2006):

> Scenario: The Dad (D), the Sister (S), and Katia (K) are in the living room, and Katia is typing words in a computer as part of a spelling game in English. When Katia gets the correct spelling, the computer announces "That's awesome"; when Katia misspells the word, the computer utters "Oops." Spanish is indicated in *italics*; English translations indicated in brackets; non-verbal behavior indicated in parentheses. (Video data, 27 April 2005)

S: (pointing to the right letter) *no es esa, no es esa, no debes de poner esa*
     [that's not the one, that's not the one, you shouldn't type that one]
K: *si si si* [yes yes yes]
D: *no*
S: *no es* a [that's not a (Spanish pronunciation)]
K: *mejor que diga mi apa* (papá) *porque mi apa sabe más inglés que tú*
     [It's better for my dad to tell me because he knows more English than you do]
D: (feigning) *no, yo no se inglés* [no, I don't know English]
K: *y como dices te estoy diciendo muchas palabras y si sabes*
     [and how do you know when I tell you many words and you know them]
D: *cual sigue Katia?* [Which one is next, Katia?]
K: *esa* [that one]
D: *a ver, ponla pues para que vayas aprendiendo*
     [so type the letter so you can learn]

The above example illustrates collaborative practices where siblings and adults mediate the literacy and language development of young children. These socializing practices are seen in both home and school interactions. Recent studies have found that on occasion these peer interactions serve a more important role in these processes than the interactions of adult–child at home or teacher–student in the classroom because of the large amounts of time that peers spend together and the support they provide each other (de la Piedra & Romo, 2003; Reyes, 2006).

One important finding of studies done in children's homes is the extent to which school literacy practices permeate and in some cases dominate the home context (Cairney & Ruge, 1998). The following example from Reyes' longitudinal study shows Ariel, a bilingual four-year old boy, playing the *escuelita* ('the little school') with his 10-year-old sister, an activity done on a regular basis:

Scenario: The participants are in the home's game room. Hung on the wall are two charts, one with numbers (1–100) and the other with the ABCs (in both capital and lower-case letters, but no particular language indicated).

A = Ariel, S = Sister, M = Mom, and R = Researcher. Spanish is indicated in italics; English discourse indicated in bold; English translations indicated in brackets; non-verbal behavior indicated in parentheses. (Field notes, 18 October 2005)

R: *¿aquello que es?* [what's that?]
A: **numbers**
R: **numbers** *¿pero que tipo de números?* [but what type of numbers?]
S: *hasta el* **one hundred** *llega* [it goes up to 100] (S says the number 100 in English but the rest of the sentence is in Spanish)
R: *¿cómo sabes cual es el que llega hasta el* **one hundred**? [How do you know which is the one that goes to 100?]
S: *porque el* **one hundred** *esta acá* [because the 100 is here] (S points to the number 100)
R: *ya, y el* **ABCs**? [OK, and the ABCs?]

A: (Ariel points to the other chart)

R: *Ariel ¿y tu ya te sabes todo el* **ABCs**? [Ariel, and do you already know all the ABCs?]

A: (Ariel begins to sing the ABC song in English)
      si, **A-B-C-D-** . . . (Ariel sings the entire alphabet)

R: *oye, hasta rápido lo canta, que bien* [hey, he even sings it quickly, that's great]

S: *es que yo le ayudo* [that's because I help him]

A: *mira, yo me se los números hasta el* **one hundred:** *El* **one,** *el* **two,** *el* **three** . . .
      [look, I know the numbers until 100: the one, the two, the three . . .] (Ariel continues to count in English until he reaches 100)

In this literacy event both biliteracy and mathematical knowledge are being exchanged between siblings. As children play the *escuelita* (little school) at home, they use both English and Spanish, even though the children originally experienced this literacy practice at school in English. Children, therefore, are transforming and adapting language and literacy that is used in the classroom to the language used at home. Similarly, Williams (2004) observed Wahida, a 10-year-old living in a Bangladeshi community in England, serve as a mediator of language acquisition of her younger sister. Wahida's linguistic situation is more complex than that of Ariel's, because she speaks standard English, standard Bengali, Sylheti (a dialect of Bengali), and some Arabic (learned from Islamic religious classes). Through play, Wahida helps prepare her sister to acquire some of these languages in what Vygotsky called the *Zone of Proximal Development* (ZPD). The ZPD represents the difference between what a child can learn independently and what a child can learn when provided with guidance by a knowledgeable other, be it an adult or a more capable peer. In Wahida's as in Ariel's sister's case, they worked in the ZPD by scaffolding the learning of the younger siblings, which resulted in greater learning for both the older and younger siblings (Roskos & Christie, 2001; Williams, 2004).

Moreover, out-of-school literacy is strengthened when parents and other caregivers take the children to community events (e.g., neighborhood parties, Saturday catechism school) and after-school activities (e.g., Mariachi band, classes to deepen heritage culture) where the native language and literacy are fostered (Baquedano-López, 2000; Kenner, 2004). The opportunity to participate in these literacy events provides children with different linguistic spaces where they can continue to develop and maintain their bilingualism. In terms of the classroom context, studies have found that students' ability to use a native language which is different from the dominant one is a significant source of children's support for one another (Long, Bell, & Brown, 2004). This peer support and bidirectional learning at home constitute vital strategies for improving learning in the classroom.

Language Ideologies and Identity Issues

Language and literacy practices play an important role in shaping children's identity. In any community experts and novices interact and exchange linguistic knowledge during socializing activities that promote new identities for novices as they acquire the necessary competence to fully participate in family and community activities (Rogoff et al., in press). In bilingual communities this competence occurs in two languages, but the level of bilingual competence varies from person to person depending on a host of factors, including age of arrival to host society (in the case of immigrant families), the amount of the heritage language spoken at home, the number and duration of occasions a child visits the ancestral homeland, and the language support provided by the community at large, including the school. Probably the most important institution to ensure language maintenance is the home, and the responsibility to maintain the heritage language rests mostly on the parents and other caregivers (Hinton, 1999). The caregivers' language histories and ideologies greatly shape, positively or negatively, the language experiences of the children (González, 2001). As the discourse in support of bilingualism and multilingualism becomes more widespread, minority parents become more willing to use the heritage language with their children, and find diverse ways of encouraging their children's use of it (Kondo, 1998; Luo & Wiseman, 2000; Oh, 2003). Some of the reasons given by Hispanic parents in the US for wanting their children to learn and retain Spanish are (Reyes, 2004b: 8, translations from Spanish):

> I would like for my children to communicate with our people here and there [Mexico] . . . I want them to learn about their roots there, in Mexico.

> I want for my children not to forget their Spanish. If they just talk in English they will forget and it is good if they know both [languages]. Knowing both languages allows them the opportunity to communicate with more people. [But I definitely] want them to learn English so in the future they can study and get ahead in life.

These quotes reveal that an important element in the success of heritage language maintenance is the persistent effort that parents make to support their children's bilingualism and biliteracy development (however, see Li, 2006). Sometimes the efforts are conscious and explicit, as when parents take their children to situations where they know the heritage language will be spoken. This is the case with extra-curricular activities at school. Other times it is simply part of routine transactions and habitual family activities, such as going to the store, reading the mail, visiting relatives, attending parties, and participating in community dances and festivals (Reyes, Alexandra, & Azuara, in press). The development of bilingualism and biliteracy can also be aided by particular living arrangements, as when a grandparent who does not speak the dominant language lives with the nuclear family (see Zentella, 2005, for additional examples). It is the constellation of activities that together strengthens the possibility that children will eventually become bilingual, and in some cases, biliterate.

Another institution that potentially plays a crucial role in the continuous development of competence in two or more languages is the school. In a longitudinal study of children attending a dual-language Spanish-English elementary school in the US southwest, Moll and colleagues (Moll et al., 2004; see also González & Arnot-Hopffer, 2002) found that the language ideology of the staff was crucial in promoting the use of Spanish at the school, especially in the aversive context created by English-only state policies. The school ensured the development of bilingualism for all children – both language minority and language majority students – by offering their curriculum in both languages and by creating special activities where Spanish was privileged or "unmarked." For example, particularly important was offering an hour-long period three days a week for all students that focused on language arts in Spanish, along with other popular Spanish-infused activities after school such as a Mariachi band and Mexican folk dances.

As part of an extension of this same longitudinal study, Arnot-Hopffer (2007) shadowed three students as they went into middle school. One of the students, a Mexican-American girl, was placed in a neighborhood school that, in contrast to her elementary school experiences, not only did not value her bilingual skills but also punished her and other students for speaking Spanish at school. This student and her peers, however, persisted in speaking Spanish in the playground, in what became an act of resistance, and the school eventually desisted from enforcing the English-only edict in the schoolyard, even though the ban on Spanish continued in the classrooms. Although in this case the students were able, at least to some extent, to circumvent the punitive language policies of the school, often children acquiesce to the demands or impositions of authority figures and restrain themselves from speaking their home language. Only the constant support of the home and school, as well as a host of other institutions – local, regional, and national mass media, government agencies, youth groups, and cultural groups in general – can stem the tide toward the hegemonic support of the dominant language (Fishman, 2001).

Conclusion

Cross-cultural studies on language socialization have shown the different ways children and their caregivers communicate and construct together knowledge that is vital to their learning and development. While many of these studies have focused on monolingual groups that are literate in the dominant language of the society, there is a smaller strand of research that focuses on bilingual and multilingual communities where a greater mix of literacy in both hegemonic and non-hegemonic languages occurs. To further explore these various ways of communication, there are four areas that deserve additional study:

First, working at the intersection of two or more languages or literacies, as in the case of code-switching and interliteracy, opens up new linguistic realities that enrich rather than subtract from the dialogue of two individuals. Instead of viewing these as imperfect manifestations of the standard vernacular language, they should be viewed as providing continuity in speech and a valuable extension to language use. A better understanding of how they occur and under what circumstances can greatly assist teachers and parents to help children master the rules of the languages involved, and still honor the linguistic creativity of children.

Second, the chapter underscores the importance of longitudinal studies as they analyze the evolution of language acquisition and literacy development. Given that children's developmental competence in one or more languages takes years to solidify, short-term studies tend to yield less substantive and comprehensive findings than long-term ones. Equally important is the focus on children's early years, which is when the greatest linguistic gains are witnessed.

Third, the vast majority of studies have focused on understanding how teachers, parents, and other adults influence the language socialization process of children. This unidirectional sense has failed to capture the bidirectionality (or even, multidirectionality) of this process, as when children from language minority families learn the dominant language with greater ease than their parents and end up becoming their *de facto* language instructors. Making bidirectional learning a focus of research would support the notion of learners as active generators of knowledge, a concept emphasized throughout this chapter.

And fourth, new studies are needed that go beyond the binary relationship of teacher–student or parent–child to include the larger social network in the lives of children that is instrumental in fostering language acquisition. A better sense of multiple relationships whereby numerous individuals influence each other may present a more accurate picture of language and literacy development. In language minority communities, for instance, it is not uncommon for a rich network of relatives, friends, and other community members (e.g., store owner, neighbor, other children) to participate in either promoting or subtracting – depending on a number of factors – the use of the heritage and dominant language involved. An in-depth exploration of these relationships may yield more accurate understandings of the multiple factors that help determine linguistic practices at home and school in a variety of cultural contexts.

REFERENCES

Amastae, J. & Elias-Olivares, L. (1982). *Spanish in the United States: Sociolinguistic Aspects*. Cambridge: Cambridge University Press.

Andersen, E. S. (1986). The acquisition of register variation by Anglo-American children. In B. Schieffelin & E. Ochs (eds.), *Language Socialization across Cultures* (pp. 153–164). Cambridge: Cambridge University Press.

Arnot-Hopffer, E. J. (2007). Las tres amigas: A study of biliteracy from kindergarten through adolescence. Unpublished doctoral dissertation. University of Arizona, Tucson.

Baker, C. & Prys Jones, S. (1998). *Encyclopedia of Bilingualism and Bilingual Education*. Clevedon, UK: Multilingual Matters.

Baquedano-López, P. (1997). Creating social identities through *doctrina* narratives. *Issues in Applied Linguistics*, 8(1), 27–45.

Baquedano-López, P. (2000). Narrating community in *doctrina* classes. *Narrative Inquiry,* 10(2), 1–24.

Bayley, R. & Schecter, S. R. (eds.) (2003). *Language Socialization in Bilingual and Multilingual Societies.* Clevedon, UK: Multilingual Matters.

Bialystok, E. (1997). Effects of bilingualism and biliteracy on children's emerging concepts of print. *Developmental Psychology,* 33(3), 429–440.

Bialystok, E. (2001). Metalinguistic aspects of bilingual processing. *Annual Review of Applied Linguistics,* 29, 169–181.

Cairney, T. & Ruge, J. (1998). *Community Literacy Practices and Schooling: Towards Effective Support for Students.* Canberra: Language Australia.

de la Piedra, M. & Romo, H. D. (2003). Collaborative literacy in a Mexican immigrant household. In R. Bayley & E. Schecter (eds.), *Language Socialization in Bilingual and Multilingual Societies* (pp. 44–61). Clevedon, UK: Multilingual Matters.

Dyson, A. H. (2003). *The Brothers And Sisters Learn to Write: Popular Literacies in Childhood and School Cultures.* New York: Teachers College Press.

Ervin-Tripp, S. & Reyes, I. (2005). From child code-switching to adult content knowledge. *International Journal of Bilingualism,* 9(1), 85–102.

Fishman, J. A. (ed.) (2001). *Can Threatened Languages be Saved? Reversing Language Shift, Revisited: A 21st Century Perspective.* Clevedon, UK: Multilingual Matters.

Freire, P. (1970). *Pedagogy of the Oppressed.* New York: Continuum.

Garrett, P. & Baquedano-López, P. (2002). Language socialization: Reproduction and continuity, transformation and change. *Annual Review of Anthropology,* 31, 339–361.

Genesee, F. (2001). Portrait of the bilingual child. In V. Cook (ed.), *Portraits of the Second Language User* (pp. 170–196). Clevedon, UK: Multilingual Matters.

González, N. (2001). *I am My Language: Discourses of Women and Children in the Borderlands.* Tucson: University of Arizona Press.

González, N. & Arnot-Hopffer, E. (2002). Voices of the children: Language and literacy ideologies in a dual language immersion program. In S. Wortham & B. Rymes (eds.), *The Linguistic Anthropology of Education* (pp. 214–244). Westport, CT: Praeger.

González, N., Moll, L. C., & Amanti, K. (2005). *Funds of Knowledge: Theorizing Practices in Households, Communities, and Classrooms.* Mahwah, NJ: Lawrence Erlbaum.

Gordon, R. G., Jr. (ed.) (2005). *Ethnologue: Languages of the World* (15th edn.). Dallas, TX: SIL International.

Gort, M. (2006). Strategic codeswitching, interliteracy, and other phenomena of emergent bilingual writing: Lessons from first-grade dual language classrooms. *Journal of Early Childhood Literacy,* 6(3), 323–354.

Gregory, E., Long, S., & Volk, D. (2004). *Many Pathways to Literacy: Young Children Learning with Siblings, Peers, Grandparents, and in Communities.* NY: Routledge.

Hakuta, K. & Pease-Alvarez, L. (eds.) (1992). Special issue on bilingual education. *Educational Researcher,* 21(2).

Hasan, R. (2002). Semiotic mediation and development in pluralistic societies: Some implications for tomorrow's schooling. In G. Wells & G. Claxton (eds.), *Learning for Life in the 21st Century* (pp. 112–126). Oxford: Blackwell.

Hinton, L. (1999). Involuntary language loss among immigrants: Asian-American linguistic autobiographies. *ERIC Digest.* Washington, DC, ERIC Clearinghouse on Language and Linguistics.

Kenner, C. (2004). *Becoming Biliterate: Young Children Learning Different Writing Systems.* Stoke-on-Trent, UK: Trentham Books.

Kondo, K. (1998). Social-psychological factors affecting language maintenance: Interviews with Shin Nisei university students in Hawaii. *Linguistics and Education*, 9, 369–408.

Li, G. (2006). Biliteracy and trilingual practices in the home context: Case studies of Chinese-Canadian children. *Journal of Early Childhood Literacy*, 6(3), 355–381.

Long, S. (with Bell, D., & Brown, J.) (2004). Making a place for peer interaction: Mexican American kindergarteners learning language and literacy. In E. Gregory, S. Long, & D. Volk (eds.), *Many Pathways to Literacy: Young Children Learning with Siblings, Peers, Grandparents, and in Communities* (pp. 93–104). NY: Routledge.

Luo, S. H. & Wiseman, R. L. (2000). Ethnic language maintenance among Chinese children in the United States. *International Journal of Intercultural Relations*, 24(3), 307–324.

Luykx, A. (2003). Weaving language together: Family language policy and gender socialization in bilingual Aymara households. In R. Bayley & S. R. Schecter (eds.), *Language Socialization in Bilingual and Multilingual Societies* (pp. 25–43). Cleveland, UK: Multilingual Matters.

Martinez-Roldán, C. M. & Sayer, P. (2006). Reading through linguistic borderlands: Latino students' transactions with narrative texts. *Journal of Early Childhood Literacy*, 6(3), 293–322.

Moll, L. C., Arnot-Hopffer, E., Poveda, A., & Londoño, F. (2004). Mediating Power: A Case Example of Educational Sovereignty. Paper presented at the Annual Meetings of the American Educational Research Association, April 15, San Diego, CA.

Ochs, E. (1986). *Culture and Language Acquisition: Acquiring Communicative Competence in a Western Samoan Village.* New York: Cambridge University Press.

Oh, J. S. (2003). Raising Bilingual Children: Factors in Maintaining a Heritage Language. PhD thesis, University of California, Los Angeles.

Reyes, I. (2004a). Functions of code switching in schoolchildren's conversations. *Bilingual Research Journal*, 28(1), 77–98.

Reyes, I. (2004b). Language practices and socialization in early bilingual childhood. Paper presented at the American Educational Research Association, April 15, San Diego, CA.

Reyes, I. (2006). Exploring connections between emergent biliteracy and bilingualism. *Journal of Early Childhood Literacy*, 6(3), 267–292.

Reyes, I., Alexandra, D., & Azuara, P. (in press). Literacy practices in Mexican immigrant homes. *Journal of Cultura & Educación.*

Reyes, I. & Moll, L. (2005). Latinos and Bilingualism. In I. Stavans & H. Augenbraum (eds.), *Encyclopedia Latina: History, Culture, and Society in the United States* (pp. 520–528). New York: Grolier Academic Reference.

Rogoff, B., Moore, L., Najafi, B., Dexter, A., Correa-Chavez, M., & Solis, J. (in press). Children's development of cultural repertoires through participation in everyday routines and practices. In J. Grusec & P. Hastings (eds.), *Handbook of Socialization* (pp. 211–225). New York: Guilford.

Roskos, K. & Christie, J. (2001). Under the lens: The play–literacy relationship in theory and practice. In S. Reifel (ed.), *Advances in Early Education and Day Care* (pp. 321–337). Greenwich, CT: JAI Press.

Schieffelin, B. & Ochs, E. (eds.) (1986). *Language Socialization across Cultures.* Cambridge: Cambridge University Press.

Scribner, S. & Cole, M. (1981). *The Psychology of Literacy*. Cambridge, MA: Harvard University Press.

Taylor, D. (1983). *Family Literacy*. Exeter, NH: Heinemann.

Taylor, D. & Dorsey-Gaines, C. (1988). *Growing up Literate*. Portsmouth, NH: Heinemann.

Vygotsky, L. S. (1978). *Mind in Society: The Development of Higher Psychological Processes*. Cambridge, MA: Harvard University Press.

Whitmore, K. F., Martens, P., Goodman, Y., & Owocki, G. (2004). Critical lessons from the transactional perspective on early literacy research. *Journal of Early Childhood Literacy*, 4(3), 291–325.

Williams, A. (2004). "Right, get your book bags!": Siblings playing school in multiethnic London. In E. Gregory, S. Long, & D. Volk (eds.), *Many Pathways to Literacy: Young Children Learning with Siblings, Peers, Grandparents, and in Communities* (pp. 52–65). NY: Routledge.

Zentella, A. (1997). *Growing up Bilingual: Puerto Rican children in New York*. Malden, MA: Blackwell.

Zentella, A. (2005). *Building on Strength: Language and Literacy in Latino Families and Communities*. New York: Teachers College Press; Covina: California Association for Bilingual Education.

12 Vernacular Language Varieties in Educational Settings: Research and Development

JEFFREY REASER AND CAROLYN TEMPLE ADGER

This chapter offers an overview of some important recent research on the role of vernacular varieties of English in educational domains in the United States and some applications of this kind of research to school practice. All of the studies and the applications mentioned here demonstrate that research findings from the field of sociolinguistics are useful to educational practice, and in fact essential in a number of ways. Evidence of patterned variation in language calls into question such established school traditions as teaching children to replace vernacular dialect features with standard features without also acknowledging the value of the vernacular and teaching strategies for how to switch from vernacular patterns into standard patterns when appropriate. The educational tradition of treating predictable vernacular features as errors has been evident in judgments of oral and written language, practices for diagnosing learning disabilities, and development of high-stakes tests. Because misdiagnosis of features of their dialect as error or evidence of a disability can discourage children from engaging in formal education, it has the potential to perpetuate de facto racial and class segregation, and academic failure in traditionally disfavored groups. Wiley (2005: 101) notes that poor school performance may be "more a *result* of socioeconomic problems than a *cause*." As linguists have become more concerned about the implications of widespread public misinformation about language variation and the language ideologies that go with it, it is not surprising that they have increasingly turned their attention to attempting to apply research findings to educational settings.

Research

In the US, most of the research on vernacular language varieties in educational settings has focused on African American English, both because there has been more research on this variety than on others and because of the need to understand why African American students have not fared as well academically as other groups have. However, there is some research on other varieties as well.

Sociolinguistic research on oral language development

Of special interest is a long-term program of research conducted by Holly Craig and Julie Washington and their colleagues investigating language development in children who speak African American English, and its implications for school performance. This research is reported comprehensively in Craig and Washington (2006). These researchers and their colleagues conducted a series of careful studies aimed at understanding unique features of African American English as used by children (e.g., uninflected *be*, absence of third person verbal -*s*, etc.); understanding constraints on production of these features, both static and dynamic; developing nondiscriminatory instruments and procedures for clinical evaluation of these children's language development; and understanding academic challenges related to African American English and effective methods to address them. Research participants ranged from pre-schoolers through fifth-grade students; all came from lower- through middle-income homes. This research was conducted in Michigan and may not generalize to other localities. Most of the data came from individual testing sessions at school in which children's language performance was demonstrated in a spontaneous oral language sample and on standardized assessments.

Among the questions addressed in this research program were whether, why, and how African American children who speak African American English as a first dialect acquire Standard American English. Using a measure that they term *dialect density* – the number of African American English features divided by number of words in a sample – researchers found systematic variation according to grade level: across the grades, African American English-speaking children increasingly adopted the Standard American English that is associated with schooling. Regarding morphosyntactic features (e.g., zero copula and variations in tense marking) produced in language samples, there was evidence of a pronounced shift toward the standard dialect at first grade; at third grade, there was a pronounced shift toward the standard in phonological features (e.g., final stop devoicing and consonant cluster reduction) as measured in oral reading. Furthermore, although vernacular features occurred more often at school entry in boys and in children from lower-income homes, these effects disappeared across the grades. Craig and Washington conclude that speaking African American English does not account for low academic performance by African American children, and they point to the need to better understand other language-related factors, especially those connected to learning to read.

These findings are consistent with those of Valadez, MacSwan, and Martinez (2002), who studied the speech of 6,800 students of Latino heritage in Los

Angeles who had been identified as *low achievers*, *semilinguals*, or *clinically disfluent* on prescriptive tests. The spontaneous speech of these students was found to not differ in any linguistically significant way from that of other students. The suggestion is that it is not the initial language variety that students bring to school that causes problems, but rather institutional responses to these varieties that ultimately lead to academic failure.

Sociolinguistic research on reading

A good deal of the research on the educational effects of African American English has looked at reading. For many years, African American students have scored poorly in reading on the National Assessment of Educational Progress in comparison to other groups. A number of explanations for this persistent gap have been advanced, and language issues are prominent among them (See Washington & Craig, 2001, for a comprehensive review). In essence, the argument is that differences between the grammars of African American Vernacular English and Standard American English affect reading performance. Two hypotheses have been proposed. The interference hypothesis predicts that vernacular speakers occasionally misunderstand the language of the text because it is closer to spoken Standard American English than to their own dialect. The result is usually considered to be reading error. The influence hypothesis, on the other hand, predicts that children's oral reading will include vernacular substitutions for Standard American English features, especially phonological ones (e.g., word-final consonant cluster reduction as in "res" for *rest*, and substitution of /d/ for <th> as in "dese" for *these*, etc.). Although teachers may consider vernacular features in children's oral reading to be errors, the possibility of their occurrence is predicted by the structure of their dialect, and their occurrence does not affect comprehension.

A process for estimating whether a vernacular substitution is a case of interference (i.e., a reading error) or a case of dialect influence was developed in connection with Labov and his colleagues' research program on reading and vernacular dialects (2003, http://www.ling.upenn.edu/~wlabov/Papers/WRE.html, retrieved April 15, 2006). This method involves observing what follows a dialect-related substitution in oral reading. If a substitution is a case of dialect influence, what follows it is likely to be consistent with the text. An example is a third grader's reading of *I played it cool and took a sip of my coke* as "I play it cool and took a sip of my coke." Because the second verb, *took*, was produced as written, it appears that deleting the final /d/ of *played* (and thus also the past tense marker <ed>) did not reflect the child's understanding of the verb as past tense. This study found that certain vernacular substitutions were more likely than others to be reading errors. For example, the frequency of omitting third person verbal {s} in speech correlated with dialect influence in reading: The more frequent its deletion in speech, the more likely that deletion in oral reading was not a reading error. But the more frequent the deletion of possessive {s}, the more likely that deletion in oral reading constituted a reading error. The researchers posit that this contrast is linked to the semantic information that the two inflectional morphemes carry. Thus the relationship of vernacular dialects and reading is complex.

Another careful study of African American English speakers takes a different perspective on the role of dialect in reading. Charity, Scarborough, and Griffin (2004) note that while the mismatch between written and spoken English makes learning to read challenging for young children in general, it is even more challenging for speakers of vernacular dialects, who are less likely to find predictable features of their dialects represented in print. Thus the more familiar children are with Standard American English, they hypothesized, the more likely they are to recognize what is printed. In a random sample of 217 African American children in kindergarten through second grade, drawn from a low-income population, the researchers assessed children's familiarity with Standard American English using sentence repetition tests. They analyzed phonological and morphosyntactic features of the children's performance separately, based on current understanding of essential dimensions of the reading process (Committee on the Prevention of Reading Difficulties of Young Children, 1998). Reading achievement was measured with three subtests of the Woodcock Reading Mastery Tests – Revised. Analysis showed wide variation in the degree to which the children produced Standard American English in the sentence repetition tasks (instead of replacing Standard American English with African American English variants), but reading achievement was quite clearly correlated with production of Standard American English. The results of this study support the view that African American children may have more difficulty in learning to read for reasons of dialect difference, and they raise interesting questions for further research. For example, why is it that knowledge of Standard English is so variable in the low SES (socioeconomic status) population sampled for this study, and what are the mechanisms by which increased knowledge of Standard American English favors learning to read?

Sociolinguistic research on vernacular writing

Research has also been conducted on the writing of indigenous vernacular speakers (e.g., Smitherman, 2000) and on the connection between their oral narrative and writing (e.g., Bloome et al., 2001). But we turn here to writing in another population of students whose language contrasts with that which schools expect – those who have come to North America with their families from other English-speaking countries. Several studies of students from the Caribbean detail the difficulties they encounter at school for reasons of linguistic and cultural contrasts (e.g., Coelho, 1991, but the extent of these difficulties and their nature is not well understood. There are also descriptions of high quality programs to support their school success and help them learn a standard North American English (e.g., Fischer, 1992). Typically, though, schools have not educated children from other English-speaking regions appropriately. Often they are placed in English as a second language (ESL) classes, despite the fact that these students are likely to be proficient in English or an English-based creole and to have gone to a (primarily) English-speaking school in their home country. Thus their English vocabulary far outstrips that of children who are learning English in ESL classes, and they are far more able than students learning English to interact orally in the classroom.

To understand the challenges in educating students from Anglophone West Africa (the Gambia, Ghana, Sierra Leone, Liberia, and Nigeria) in a large school district on the East Coast of the United States, a group of linguists and ESL researchers, teachers, and administrators convened as a study group. They first surveyed ESL teachers in order to understand their view of the problems these students were experiencing. Out of this effort came a study of writing, the modality in which language differences had the greatest effect on students' school success, according to the survey. Writing samples collected from 98 secondary school students were analyzed, and the teachers' estimate that syntax was the area of greatest difficulty was borne out (de Kleine, 2006). Analysis focused on the grammatical structures for which deviation from standard American written English occurred most frequently. For nouns, these include unmarked plural and possessive forms, and zero article (e.g., "all my relative," "my best friend mother," "in USA"); for verbs, zero subject-verb agreement (e.g.,"She participate in school activity"), unmarked past tense (e.g., "They all help me when I was little"), *will* in place of Standard American English *would* (e.g., "If my dreams came true, I will be so happy"), and zero copula (e.g., "It a market scene"). Contrasting conventions for preposition use (e.g., "In the other hand") were frequent too (de Klein, 2006: 214–220). All of these frequently occurring features in the students' writing are found in West African Pidgin English, the term applied to the restructured varieties of English spoken in West Africa (McArthur, 2003), and some of them in West African Standard English. For example, Holm (2000) notes that grammatical possession is signaled by juxtaposition of possessor and possessed (e.g., "Kevin car" as opposed to *Kevin's car*) in many pidginized and creolized varieties.

Implications of this research for the school district are not straightforward. De Kleine (2006) recommends explicit instruction in Standard American English, using contrastive analysis: comparing the grammatical patterns of vernacular or creole varieties to those of standard English. But she notes that this requires training teachers in the predictable features of their students' English, a tall order for teachers of students from many parts of the world. And the training should not be limited to ESL teachers: mainstream classroom teachers also need to support Standard American English instruction if that is what the school district determines is needed. Despite the challenges in instituting the study's conclusions, it represents an important contribution in an under-researched domain of language education.

Application of Sociolinguistic Research on Vernacular Dialects in Education

Hudson (2004: 105) has argued that "One of the fundamental questions on which we linguists disagree is whether or not our subject is useful for education." We argue that sociolinguistic findings are highly relevant to education, since there is no doubt that the major questions in the field (e.g., ethnicity, identity, gender, class, language prejudice) underlie issues of social inequity that persist in education. Despite its relevance, however, dissemination of linguistic research to the field of education and applications to issues of social inequity encountered there seem rather paltry, given the volume of research in the field. There are, of course, reasons for this. For one thing, relatively few sociolinguists participate in education research on language-related issues, and fewer still have first-hand experience in schools, working as or with teachers and administrators. As a result, they do not share the background knowledge and assumptions of educators, and they may not have the time and the connections that are essential to partnerships with educators. Further, linguistic outreach to education, which has the potential to benefit schools in dramatic ways, may not benefit the sociolinguist to the same extent. In terms of promotion and tenure, the benefit of such time- and resource-consuming projects remains minimal, despite universities' efforts to consider service in the review process (Hall, 2002). Nonetheless, extending the findings of dialect research to education remains an important obligation for researchers (Labov, 1982; Wolfram, 1993).

One way in which research is made relevant to education is in reports and learning materials written specifically for this audience. Clearly, research must be reported to those in the field of education differently than it is to linguists, and it must be differentiated further depending on who will read it. Education researchers who need linguistic research may not fully share the disciplinary background that can be assumed in writing for an audience of linguists. Thus writing for this audience requires attention to clarifying assumptions and specialized terminology. Teachers and other practitioners, on the other hand, generally seek information that they can use instructionally. The challenge in this case is likely to involve reaching two audiences – teachers and their students. It includes developing learning materials for students and preparing enough background information of the right kind for teachers so that they can maintain an authoritative role in teaching material in which they are not expert.

Materials development is also complicated by the fact that educators are likely to share the entrenched language ideologies that are evident throughout society (Lippi-Green, 1997). Dialect discrimination remains endemic in educational and social systems because, as Fairclough (2001) notes, language ideology is largely invisible, which is a result of relatively few people recognizing the fact that language can and must be studied scientifically. This invisibility results in the perpetuation of discrimination based on language, which is "so commonly accepted, so widely perceived as appropriate, that it must be seen as the last back door to discrimination. And the door stands wide open" (Lippi-Green, 1997: 73). Therefore, one of the first steps to any educational outreach project about language must be to convince teachers that language can be studied scientifically and that doing so is beneficial to the social and academic well-being of students.

There is a precedent for doing so in the field of English language arts, where the influential, well-respected National Council of Teachers of English (NCTE) includes among its standards (i.e., learning goals) having "Students develop an understanding of and respect for diversity in language use, patterns, and dialects across cultures, ethnic groups, geographic regions, and social roles" (1996: 3). The National Council for the Accreditation of Teacher Education (NCATE) has created a detailed list of the knowledge that all English language arts teacher candidates should acquire during their teacher preparation courses. The list includes the need to understand language variation. In addition to having "in-depth knowledge of the evolution of the English language" and "in-depth knowledge of semantics, syntax, morphology, and phonology," teacher candidates are expected to know "how and why language varies and changes in different regions, across different cultural groups, and across different time periods, and incorporate that knowledge into classroom instruction and assessment in ways that acknowledge and show consistent respect for language diversity" (NCTE/NCATE, 2003: 11–12).

Despite the fact that NCTE and NCATE both advocate including linguistics in the school curriculum and the teacher education curriculum, there is not a robust tradition of scientific study of language in schools. Many educators (teachers, administrators, and curriculum developers) continue to subscribe to the entrenched myths about language variation that sociolinguistics have identified. Wolfram and Schilling-Estes (2006: 7–8) outline six commonly held myths: the notion that there are some people who do not speak a dialect; that "dialects always have highly noticeable features that set them apart"; that dialects are only spoken by socially disfavored groups; that dialects are the result of unsuccessful (or incomplete) learning of the standard language; that dialects are not patterned; and that all dialects carry negative social connotations (or are simply "bad language"). Dissemination and application of sociolinguistic knowledge in educational contexts must focus on countering these barriers to linguistic education.

Dialect awareness curricula

In recent years, curricular materials have been developed for students and teachers that counter prevalent language myths by introducing sociolinguistic research findings, methods, and perspectives. These materials take an inductive approach to learning. For teachers and their students, being told about how and why language ideologies are at odds with research and corrosive to the social order can be interesting, but it takes knowledge of the workings of the ideologies and the workings of language to change views. Discovery learning is far more effective than lecture in effecting long-lasting changes in perceptions and knowledge (Bligh, 2000).

One of the central goals of discovery-based language awareness curricula for schools is illuminating the bond between language varieties and the culture and history of the groups that use them. If these connections are foregrounded, the reasons that language variation persists become more apparent. This also helps teachers shape their responses to (and assumptions about) vernacular-speaking students. Examining language scientifically, within cultural and historical contexts, it becomes apparent that dialect diversity reflects the richness of the human condition and that it is worthy of admiration instead of condemnation.

The center of dialect awareness curriculum development in the US has been the North Carolina Language and Life Project at North Carolina State University, directed by Walt Wolfram. Since 1993, the Project has conducted community research on language in North Carolina, and its members have sought ways of using the knowledge gained through research to give back to the community. A number of projects have been developed, including a dialect awareness curriculum for middle school students. Wolfram and his colleagues have taught experimental versions of this curriculum to eighth graders on Ocracoke Island for a number of years.

This curriculum, *Voices of North Carolina: Language and Life from the Atlantic to the Appalachians* (Reaser & Wolfram, 2005) is an expansion of the *Dialects and the Ocracoke Brogue* curriculum (Wolfram, Schilling-Estes, & Hazen, 1997), which was based in part on Wolfram, Adger, and Detwyler (1992). A significant development in this most recent version of the curriculum is that it is designed to be taught by regular classroom teachers without the support of professional linguists. In order to accomplish this, the curriculum draws on the Project's rich video and audio collection to include 12 video vignettes and 24 audio tracks compiled on two DVDs. These materials serve as a catalyst for classroom discussions and activities and, along with a teacher's manual, help build teachers' linguistic knowledge.

The curriculum leads students to investigate various assumptions about language and challenges myths through discovery learning. They see and hear representative speech samples of regional, class, and ethnic varieties, and they work with linguistic data to uncover the patterns that underlie vernacular features at several levels, including phonology, syntax, semantic, and pragmatic. Finally, students look at examples of language change over time and discuss the possibility that dialect differences represent change in progress. Early testing of the curriculum reveals promising results in that classroom teachers are able to teach students about language on their own and that students' attitudes about language variation become more positive.

Following the North Carolina lead, linguists in Alabama, Georgia, Michigan, Pennsylvania, and West Virginia have created outreach organizations of their own to bring language awareness to their local schools and communities.

Several other recent projects make sociolinguistic research accessible to students and teachers. A dialect awareness curriculum for younger children (Sweetland, 2004) makes use of children's literature that features accurate use of African American English (Sweetland & Rickford, 2004), and it uses contrastive analysis techniques to highlight differences between African American English and Standard English features in the literary texts. This curriculum was pilot tested in six upper elementary school classrooms. Analysis revealed a positive effect of the curriculum in terms of teachers' attitudes. Teachers who taught the curriculum showed nearly double the gain in positive attitudes toward African American English compared to those who participated only in the related professional development workshops. This curriculum is written in accessible language and follows standard conventions for lesson plans and learning outcomes so that it is compatible with teachers' expectations.

Teaching code-switching

These two dialect awareness curricula are aimed at introducing teachers and their students to a scientific perspective on language variation and some results of sociolinguistic research, making language ideologies visible, and influencing unwarranted attitudes toward vernacular dialects and their speakers. Sociolinguistic knowledge is used also in a program for teaching Standard English to speakers of minority dialects, by way of contrastive analysis (Wheeler & Swords, 2006). The focus here is on the writing of elementary school children, and the target is several inflectional morphological features (possessive *-s*, plural *-s*, etc.) that may be deleted in African American English, as well as other highly stigmatized items. A similar approach is used by the Academic English Mastery program in Los Angeles, CA (LeMoine, 2001). Children are taught the intricacies of the vernacular patterns and strategies to help them switch to the equivalent academic English feature. For example, vernacular speakers sometimes mark possession through proximity as opposed to an inflectional morpheme (e.g., *that is the dog_ bowl*). Students learn to apply the "formal" or "academic" English rule, owner + 's + owned, to produce the Standard English sentence, *that is the dog's bowl.* Large-scale research is needed to determine the program's effects on student performance, and on student and teacher attitudes.

Because the Sweetland dialect awareness curriculum and the Wheeler and Swords code-switching instructional approach are both intended for elementary school children and are not tied to a geographic region as the *Voices of North Carolina* dialect awareness curriculum is, it appears that they might be used together. The result might help students learn the academic English forms they need to succeed in school, as well as accurate perceptions of language variation and respect for vernacular English dialects and their speakers.

Applied reading research

Building on the rich body of research into African American English and on his research into reading and African American English cited above, Labov and his colleagues have developed a program to help raise the reading levels of minority children in Philadelphia. They developed a teacher's manual (Labov & Baker, 1999) that includes diagnostic readings; an introduction for tutors on basic letter–sound correspondences in English; strategies for focusing children's attention on the elements of word structures with complex onsets, nuclei, and codas (mostly consonant clusters), as well as letters and sounds that are particularly problematic (e.g., the "silent-*e* rule"); narrative texts for children with themes that engage their interests and evoke their world; and diagnostic tests to evaluate children's comprehension of reading materials and the accuracy of their pronunciation in oral reading.

The results from an early piloting of the program are encouraging (Labov & Baker, 2001). Twenty-nine children in grades 2–5 who were at least one grade behind in reading level participated in this program. These children showed significant decreases in reading errors after 10–12 hours of tutoring over 20–24 sessions throughout the school year. They performed better on reading tests than a similar group of students who participated in a "balanced literacy" approach taught by America Reads work/study students. Although the program is costly in that it requires one-on-one tutoring with one instructor responsible for four students at most, and tutor training by linguists, this approach should be viewed as a promising one for helping vernacular dialect-speaking students improve their reading skills. Further materials development might lessen the need for professional linguist support and increase the number of students that each tutor can assist.

Applying dialect research to speech/language services

For many years, there has been concern with understanding normal patterns of vernacular language development and identifying ways to distinguish structural features associated with developmental delay from those associated with normal vernacular development (Craig & Washington, 2006). Conducting equitable assessment of vernacular-speaking children has been difficult because the procedures and the standardized assessment batteries have not taken into account the contrasts between vernacular dialects and the standard dialect on which assessments have been predicated. But now, several products using dialect research make it possible to conduct language development assessments more fairly. One of these is the *Michigan Protocol for African American Language* that was developed with the research program discussed above (Craig & Washington, 2006). This model is applied in stages – screening, identification, and assessment. Each stage includes several traditional measures and subtests that were developed and validated in the research program. Another product can be used to increase speech/language pathologists' knowledge: *African*

American English: Structure and Clinical Implications (Adger & Schilling-Estes, 2003). This resource includes a CD with structural descriptions of morpho-syntactic and phonological features of the dialect, and a list of contrastive discourse features. It was written to be accessible and usable by non-linguists.

Conclusion

Critique of traditional models of teaching language arts and recognition of the need for teaching materials on dialect awareness (e.g., Carpenter, Baker, & Scott, 1908; Marckwardt, 1966) predates the proliferation of sociolinguistic research on language variation from the 1960s and 1970s. The importance of sociolinguistic information in teacher preparation became clearer in the late 1970s with the work of Geneva Smitherman and others on the Ann Arbor Black English Case. And gradually, materials on language varieties have become developed for educational audiences. However, much more is needed, both for the education of teachers and for the education of students in the schools. Materials on language variation for students at various grade levels and in different regions are needed in order to give teachers a range of attract-ive and appropriate options for instruction. There has been and continues to be strong teacher interest in pedagogical materials that are practical and not overwhelmingly theoretical. Fortunately, it appears that now more than ever there is sincere interest on the part of linguists in the US and around the world in working collaboratively with educators to produce materials that help teachers with the language-related problems they perceive and to introduce ideas and information about language that they would not have encountered otherwise.

REFERENCES

Adger, Carolyn Temple & Schilling-Estes, Natalie (2003). *African American English: Struc-ture and Clinical Implications*. Rockville, MD: American Speech-Language-Hearing Association.

Bligh, Donald A. (2000). *What's the Use of Lectures?* (2nd edn.). New York: John Wiley.

Bloome, David, Champion, Tempii, Katz, Laurie, Morton, Mary Beth, & Muldrow, Ramona (2001). Spoken and written narrative development: African American preschoolers as storytellers and storymakers. In Joyce L. Harris, Alan G. Kamhi, & Karen E. Pollock (eds.), *Literacy in African American Communities* (pp. 45–76). Mahwah, NJ: Lawrence Erlbaum.

Carpenter, George Rice, Baker, Franklin T., & Scott, Fred Newton (1908). *The Teaching of English in the Elementary and Secondary School*. New York: Longmans, Green.

Charity, Anne H., Scarborough, Hollis S., & Griffin, Darion M. (2004). Familiarity with school English in African American children and its relation to early reading achievement. *Child Development*, 75(5), 1340–1356.

Coelho, Elizabeth (1991). *Caribbean Students in Canadian Schools*, vol. 2. Markham, Ontario: Pippin.

Committee on the Prevention of Reading Difficulties of Young Children (1998). *Preventing Reading Difficulties in Young Children.* Washington, DC: National Research Council, National Academy Press.

Craig, Holly & Washington, Julie (2006). *Malik Goes to School: Examining the Language Skills of African American Students from Preschool–5th Grade.* Mahwah, NJ: Lawrence Erlbaum.

de Kleine, Christa (2006). West African World English speakers in U.S. classrooms: The role of West African Pidgin English. In Shondel J. Nero (ed.), *Dialects, Englishes, Creoles, and Education* (pp. 205–232). Mahwah, NJ: Lawrence Erlbaum.

Fairclough, Norman (2001). *Language and Power* (2nd edn.). London: Longman.

Fischer, Karen (1992). Educating speakers of Caribbean English in the United States. In Jeff Siegel (ed.), *Pidgins, Creoles and Nonstandard Dialects in Education* (Occasional Paper No. 12, pp. 99–123). Melbourne: Applied Linguistics Association of Australia.

Hall, Donald E. (2002). *The Academic Self: An Owner's Manual.* Columbus: Ohio State University Press.

Holm, John (2000). *An Introduction to Pidgins and Creoles.* Cambridge: Cambridge University Press.

Hudson, Richard (2004). Why education needs linguistics (and vice versa). *Journal of Linguistics*, 40, 105–130.

Labov, William (1982). Objectivity and commitment in linguistic science. *Language in Society*, 11, 165–201.

Labov, William & Baker, Bettina (1999). *The Individualized Reading Manual: A Textbook for Tutors and Children.* Philadelphia: University of Pennsylvania Press.

Labov, William & Baker, Bettina (2001). Testing the effectiveness of an individualized reading program for African-American, Euro-American and Latino inner city children. Poster presented at the meeting of Interagency Educational Research Initiative Project. Washington, DC.

LeMoine, Noma R. (2001). Language variation and literacy acquisition in African American students. In Joyce L. Harris, Alan G. Kamhi, & Karen E. Pollock (eds.), *Literacy in African American Communities* (pp. 169–194). Mahwah, NJ: Lawrence Erlbaum.

Lippi-Green, Rosina (1997). *English with an Accent: Language, Ideology, and Discrimination in the United States.* New York: Routledge.

Marckwardt, Albert H. (1966). *Linguistics and the Teaching of English.* Bloomington: Indiana University Press.

McArthur, Tom (2003). *Oxford Guide to World English.* Oxford: Oxford University Press.

NCTE (1996). *Standards for the English Language Arts.* Urbana, IL: National Council of Teachers of English.

NCTE/NCATE (2003). *NCTE/NCATE Program Standards: Program for the Initial Preparation of Teachers of Secondary English Language Arts.* Urbana, IL: National Council of Teachers of English.

Reaser, Jeffrey & Wolfram, Walt (2005). *Voices of North Carolina: Language and Life from the Atlantic to the Appalachians.* Raleigh, NC: North Carolina State University Press.

Smitherman, Geneva (2000). African American student writers in the NAEP, 1969–88/ 89. In Geneva Smitherman (ed.), *Talkin that Talk: Language, Culture and Education in African America* (pp. 163–176). New York: Routledge.

Sweetland, Julie (2004). *Sociolinguistic Sensitivity in Language Arts Instruction: A Literature and Writing Curriculum for the Intermediate Grades.* Palo Alto, CA: Stanford University.

Sweetland, Julie & Rickford, John R. (2004). Using children's literature to support linguistically-informed language arts instruction. Poster presented at New Ways of Analyzing Variation, 33. University of Michigan.

Valadez, Concepcion M., MacSwan, Jeff, & Martinez, Corinne (2002). Toward a new view of low achieving bilinguals: A study of linguistic competence in designated "semilinguals." *Bilingual Review*, 25(3), 238–248.

Washington, Julie A. & Craig, Holly K. (2001). Reading performance and dialectal variation. In Joyce L. Harris, Alan G. Kamhi, & Karen E. Pollock (eds.), *Literacy in African American Communities* (pp. 147–168). Mahwah, NJ: Lawrence Erlbaum.

Wheeler, Rebecca & Swords, Rachel (2006). *Code-Switching: Teaching Standard English in Urban Classrooms.* Urbana, IL: National Council of Teachers of English.

Wiley, Terrence G. (2005). *Literacy and Language Diversity in the United States* (2nd edn.). Washington, DC: Center for Applied Linguistics.

Wolfram, Walt (1993). Ethical considerations in language awareness programs. *Issues in Applied Linguistics*, 4(2), 225–255.

Wolfram, Walt & Schilling-Estes, Natalie (2006). *American English: Dialects and Variation* (2nd edn.). Malden, MA: Blackwell.

Wolfram, Walt, Adger, Carolyn Temple, & Detwyler, Jennifer (1992). *All About Dialects.* Washington, DC: Center for Applied Linguistics.

Wolfram, Walt, Schilling-Estes, Natalie, & Hazen, Kirk (1997). *Dialects and the Ocracoke Brogue.* Raleigh, NC: North Carolina State University Press.

FURTHER READING

Nero, Shondel (ed.) (2006). *Dialects, Englishes, Creoles, and Education.* Mahwah, NJ: Lawrence Erlbaum.

Wolfram, Walt & Ward, Ben (eds.) (2006). *American Voices: How Dialects Differ from Coast to Coast.* Malden, MA: Blackwell.

13 Linguistic Accessibility and Deaf Children

SAMUEL J. SUPALLA AND
JODY H. CRIPPS

Signed languages are generally deemed as having inherent advantages for deaf populations of a given society. This is because the language is processed through the visual/gestural modality (as opposed to vocal/aural for spoken language). American Sign Language (ASL) may serve as a good example of an accessible language for deaf children, but its role in deaf education does not necessarily reflect this fact. The ramifications of English as a spoken language for deaf children are also not fully appreciated (see Singleton et al., 1998 for further discussion on the distinction between the two languages, signed and spoken). English literacy is best described as elusive, especially when deaf children do not enjoy auditory access to the language involved. Yet, they are 'expected' to possess spoken language knowledge and develop phonetic skills for reading development purposes. The field of deaf education is now besieged by a number of issues ranging from the overrated value of spoken language to the creation of a signed version of English that is not on par with ASL or any naturally evolved signed language.

The conceptualization of linguistic accessibility can provide direction for whatever action is necessary to fulfill the educational potential of deaf children. Reform in deaf education is justified based on the new emphasis in American public education for accountability and effective reading instruction. This is especially true concerning how reading difficulties reported for deaf children (e.g., Paul & Quigley, 1987; Padden and Ramsey, 1998; Paul, 2003) indicate a strong relationship between reading instruction and disability. It is common knowledge among educators working with deaf children that the more hearing loss a child suffers, the more difficult reading becomes for this child. Research with the use of measures (reading-specific and reading-related) and degrees of hearing loss have validated such effects of deafness (e.g., Conrad, 1979; Karchmer, Milone & Wolk, 1979). Adding to the urgency of the matter involved, Marschark, Lang, and Albertini (2002: 7) have acknowledged that "if there is a problem, it is much more likely to be found in the way we teach and what we expect from deaf students than in the students themselves."

A stumbling block to reading instruction lies in how deaf children's knowledge in signed language has not yet connected to reading development in English. If anything, the value of ASL is misunderstood. The signed language is frequently described as simply another language in comparison with English when it is not – modality differences should be taken into account concerning ASL and English. A lack of understanding persists among educators on how signed language works and how signed languages relate to spoken languages. Typological considerations are proposed as the key to understanding signed languages and will help determine how English should be introduced in the classroom with deaf children. Language and literacy are two important attributes for the education of any child. Deaf children are no exception as they deserve a model that accounts for their needs. The question is then how deaf education got its start despite the noted weaknesses in theory and practice. Insights into how educators viewed signed language and what they looked for are critical to understanding their historical journey.

Signed Language and Deaf Education

Given the barriers associated with deafness for spoken language and in reading development, the first attempts in creating public education for deaf children are remarkable. The United States was part of a groundbreaking deaf education movement with strong roots in the Enlightenment that originated in Europe. The 'dark' notion that spoken language constitutes the only avenue for education was challenged when deaf education became a reality. Signing was conceived as an important tool for discourse in the classroom. This early conceptualization of deaf education took place in France in the eighteenth century, and this country became an international center for the proliferation of deaf education (Lane, 1980; Van Cleve & Crouch, 1989). Upon the founding of the first permanent American school for the deaf in Hartford, Connecticut in 1817, it is not surprising that Laurent Clerc, a deaf Frenchman who signed, served as the school's first teacher (Lane, 1984). By all accounts, the American public was 'enlightened' as expressed with their funding and support for schools for the deaf across the country.

Missing in the early deaf education model, however, was how signing should interact with language (what works or does not work). This is especially true concerning how Methodical Sign dominated deaf education right from the start. One must understand that Natural Sign was developed among deaf populations, and was readily available at the time. Yet educators were quick to come up with Methodical Sign, developed based on the structure of the French language. This structure was different from how deaf people normally signed. It seems clear that educators were 'aware' of the linguistic differences between the French language and Natural Sign and proceeded with the development and use of Methodical Sign. The notion of deaf children being able to learn and use French through the signed medium was attractive. According to Supalla and McKee (2002), the status of a 'working language' as found with Natural Sign should precede deaf children's need in learning whatever language is being used in the society. Methodical Sign's failure as a sign system lies, in part, with the effects of the visual/gestural modality in shaping the language structure. Unfortunately, this way of thinking only occurred recently in the history of deaf education.

With the advent of signing in deaf education, the situation for deaf children spiralled downwards as misconceptions were created about human language in general. For example, the notable French educator Roch-Ambroise Bebian made a rather crude argument for why signed language was structured as it was. This educator published a critical essay on the education of deaf children in 1817, the same year the first American school for the deaf was established (Bebian, 1984). Bebian adamantly opposed the choice of Methodical Sign over Natural Sign, but he was not effective in explaining his position. The French educator criticized the language planning effort with Methodical Sign by stating that spoken language was 'corrupted' with rules and grammar. That is, the French language was not natural and thus would not be suitable for the signed medium. Natural Sign (what French Sign Language was called back then) was described as a language in its 'pure' form as compared to spoken language. This was part of the French educator's attempt to refute Methodical Sign and favor Natural Sign. In fact, Bebian's statement that "the formation of signs is not determined by any principle and does not follow any fixed rule" (p. 141) was not helpful. Although he did observe structural deficiencies associated with Methodical Sign, no linguistic explanation was provided. What this suggests is that Bebian (or rather any educator) could have made a better argument favoring Natural Sign had a linguistic framework been created.

Unfortunately, serious erosion of support for the signed medium ensued. Given that only spoken language was thought to have linguistic structure, educators understandably began to believe that deaf children were entitled to learn and use 'language'. Thus it was assumed that deaf children needed to be language competent through spoken language in order to become literate. Speech therapy and auditory training became critical components of language intervention. This coincided with the concept of language impairment determining, in part, the educational potential of deaf children (see McAnally, Rose & Quigley, 1987 for the use of a language impairment framework with deaf children). The notion that signed language was essential in ensuring that deaf children develop a strong language base did not prevail. Without the consideration for signed language, the menace of low expectations became real within the field of deaf education (e.g., Johnson, Liddell & Erting, 1989). With the misconceptions concerning signed language, educators were left with no choice but to teach deaf children spoken language 'at all costs'. The tone set for deaf education was filled with strife and controversy. Although some educators had continued to advocate the mode of signing (with or without consideration for Natural Sign), they were no longer a force in the field of deaf education (see Moores, 1996 for a review on the historical division of oralism and manualism in deaf education).

In retrospect, the difference in language modalities (i.e., spoken and signed) is a factor for the confusion in deaf education. Although signing made deaf education possibile, a clear course for signed language was never set. The fact that the mainstream language scholars could not easily identify themselves with the study of signed languages has been a historical problem. Language in the visual/gestural modality made analysis using the speech-based International Phonetic Alphabet impossible, for example. This tool was made available as early as 1886, with the capacity of transcribing any spoken language (MacMahon, 1991). What was known for the spoken medium could not be used to investigate the signed language structure, at least explicitly. Thus a parallel form of linguistic investigation was belatedly done to compare the two major language types known to humans: spoken and signed.

The Discovery of American Sign Language

In the 1960s, American Sign Language was first formally examined as a human language through the work of William C. Stokoe (e.g., Stokoe, 1960; Stokoe, Casterline & Croneberg, 1965). By this time, Gallaudet University was established along with a national network of schools for the deaf. Stokoe was employed as a faculty member at the higher education institution, and he had to learn how to sign in order to teach deaf students there. Unlike the schools, Gallaudet University was more supportive of signing as a medium for instruction (Van Cleve & Crouch, 1989). It was there that the pioneering linguist was confronted with unanswered questions about signed language. While deaf people relied on different signed languages around the world, no one could confirm, at least scientifically, that the signed language used in the United States was different from British Sign Language, for example. Although non-deaf citizens of the United States and Great Britain spoke a common language, this was not the case with deaf citizens. What Stokoe found during his early years at Gallaudet is that signed language had no name other than its generic term (e.g., 'the sign language' or 'the language of signs'; Eastman, 1980; Maher, 1996).

Moreover, it was Stokoe who worked with his colleagues to break down signs into parts, and the rest is history. What was uncovered is that ASL has lexicon much like words in English as far as phonology is concerned. Contrary to what had been said in the past, signs were analyzable. Certain components and subcategories were identified; i.e., handshape, location, and movement. With this information, a transcription for the ASL lexicon was developed with 55 primary symbols, and a dictionary for signed language was created. Hundreds of signs were organized based on the 'alphabetic' order Stokoe determined for written signs (i.e., locations and handshapes in symbols are ordered for the purpose of a dictionary). The publication was justly titled as *A Dictionary of American Sign Language on Linguistic Principles* (Stokoe et al., 1965).

According to Meier (2002), research conducted on ASL was thrown into high gear in the 1970s and 1980s. This paid off with the language being accepted as a full-fledged human language (e.g., Klima & Bellugi, 1979; Wilbur, 1979; Valli & Lucas, 2001). Equally important is how the original findings with ASL were successfully repeated with a number of signed languages used in various parts of the world, notably Europe (Brennan & Hayhurst, 1980; Hansen, 1980; Mottez & Markowicz, 1980; see Sutton-Spence & Woll, 2003 for a comprehensive linguistic review of British Sign Language). The prevailing emphasis was on making generalities in regard to how signed languages share linguistic properties found in spoken languages. Information regarding what is unique to signed language was still needed. This is especially true concerning the struggle over Methodical Sign and the failure of educators to understand the complications surrounding the relationship between signed and spoken languages.

Only recently did Zeshan make the claim that "signed languages are of great typological importance by virtue of their visual-gestural modality, which makes them stand out as a distinct language type in opposition to the entirety of spoken languages" (2002: 153). What this suggests is that linguists have begun to feel comfortable addressing whatever modality-specific attributes there may be for signed language. The linguistic status of signed languages is not to be disputed, but rather the relationship between the two language types (signed and spoken) needs to be clarified. Cross-linguistic studies with the signed languages are seen as necessary, as well as more detailed comparisons with spoken language structure (see Meier, 2002 for further discussion on the modality-specific issues concerning signed language structure).

Brennan (1986) reported that Stokoe himself not only demonstrated how signs are well organized, but that they are organized differently from spoken words. Stokoe described the organization of ASL signs as 'simultaneous' as opposed to 'sequential' (typical for spoken words). When looking at individual signs closely, they can be described as monosyllabic. The signs do not resemble how spoken words are organized (i.e., sequential units of distinctive sound features). Coulter (1982) is the linguist who made this observation, and linguists are now following the direction set by Stokoe more closely (e.g., Brentari, 1995, 2002; Channon, 2002). The current trend indicates that the increasingly sophisticated models of signed language phonology are no longer a simple transformation of spoken language models. This is where the notion has emerged that signed language has different phonological representations than those found in spoken language (Meier, Cormier & Quinto-Pozos, 2002). Whatever happens at the word level is expected to create an impact on the rest of the language structure (e.g., phonological, morphological, and syntactic).

Now that that Methodical Sign is no longer in existence, the contemporary English-based sign systems provide an opportunity for investigating their status as a linguistic system. A language planning effort similar to what took place in France was conducted in the United States in the 1960s and 1970s.

This time, English, not French, was targeted for the development of a number of sign systems (e.g., Seeing Essential English, Signing Exact English, Linguistics of Visual English, and Signed English). Manually Coded English (MCE) is the term describing all of these English-based sign systems. The revival of signing in the classroom with deaf children can be attributed to the linguistic work done on ASL. The new concept that emerged was that language is not confined to speech. Because of this, educators were forced to re-evaluate the educational value of signing in general. Research findings also indicate a positive effect of signed language proficiency (i.e., ASL) on reading and academic achievement (see Chamberlain & Mayberry, 2000 for a review of studies on the superior school performance of deaf children who sign). Yet it is the educators who chose MCE over ASL as essential for the education of deaf children. This interpretation of research findings is what led to a change in policy in deaf education (i.e., a shift back to manualism from oralism).

The critical assumption that signing can include the structure of a spoken language prevailed. What is different now is the availability of linguistic knowledge on signed language accumulated to date. This includes a number of psycholinguistic studies as well as cross-linguistic studies done on signed languages and spoken languages. Language acquisition studies have demonstrated both the patterns and effectiveness of ASL and MCE. The linguistic description of ASL will play a key role in understanding what constitutes a signed language. The typological considerations in particular are expected to help determine whether a sign system approximating the structure of a spoken language (English or French) is feasible.

Understanding Signed Language Structure

To a novice signer, two persons using ASL to communicate with each other would appear to be very articulate and their signing very language-like. In order to break down the stream, one would need to find the 'words' themselves. A sign functions very much the same as a word does in spoken language. Structurally, a sign requires the use of handshape, which must move one way or another. Without the handshape, there would be no physical way of showing movement internal to sign. Additionally, a handshape without movement would mean a 'static' sign falling short of what a word should look like in the signed medium. As critical as handshape and movement are to the formation of signs, they are only two of the three parameters that Stokoe identified for the ASL lexicon. The third parameter, location, is also important for sign formation. A sign would not be appropriate if produced 'all over the place'. There are location possibilities in the signing space (in front of the signer's body) as well as on the signer's body to correctly form a sign.

When all three parameters are in use, the lexicon in ASL has additional constraints to indicate what a sign should look like. For example, a sign cannot have more than one handshape (see Battison, 1978 for further discussion on

Figure 13.1 WATCH

the typology of the ASL lexicon). Figure 13.1 shows an example from ASL: WATCH. The single handshape is produced for the duration of the entire word in the signed medium. The sign moves from one location closer to the signer's body to one further away. The sign falls within the constraints associated with locations; that is, the number of locations is two, the highest a sign can possess.

In a study by Channon (2002), a total of five signed languages were examined for their word structure: ASL, Japanese Sign Language, IndoPakistan Sign Language, Mayan Sign Language, and Israeli Sign Language. The data indicate that signs are consistently made of a single segment and repeated only in a rhythmic pattern. Reduplication can be seen as a mechanism underlying the rhythmic pattern. WATCH as a sign (in ASL) is best described as short and does not have any rhythmic pattern. Yet, there are a number of signs that fit with the description for the reduplicated word type in the signed medium. Figure 13.2 shows a relevant example from ASL: WORK. As part of a monosyllabic word structure, the sign's handshape moves down to the location of the other hand and constitutes one syllable, but the movement is then repeated to indicate a reduplication. The downward movement of WORK is made twice as a result.

With words studied in a large number of spoken languages, Channon found that they can have more than one segment (or unrelated syllables to form words) as in the English examples of 'permit' or 'understand'. This is

Figure 13.2 WORK

something that signed languages do not include in their lexicon. Owing to the unique organization of signs, there is a possibility that the boundaries are salient to the point where a person can easily perceive the beginning and ending of signs. This is especially true concerning how consistent or predictable sign formation is when it comes to single segments and with reduplication. In comparison, spoken word boundaries are, in fact, non-salient. Pinker (1994: 160) remarked that this characteristic of words ". . . become[s] apparent when we listen to speech in a foreign language: it is impossible to tell where one word ends and the next begins."

There is an experimental study that examines how word segmentation works in the signed medium. The participants were asked to decide whether an example of signing viewed on the videotape was one or two words. Supalla (1990) confirms the overt saliency for word boundaries in the signed medium as both novice signers and ASL signers were able to reliably segment the sign stream. The sequenced signs presented were derived from a different signed language, not ASL. Yet, the 'unintelligible' signs were successfully segmented based on how signs are formed phonologically. To repeat, the signs were easily identified regardless of the fact that the individuals participating in the experiment did not sign or knew a different signed language.

The next question is what role the word structure as described for the signed medium has for the morphological operations. Affixation is an excellent area of investigation for the additional modality-specific attributes. Both linear and non-linear affixation types have been identified in spoken languages in broad terms. English can be described as predominantly linear in its morphological process. Non-linear affixation is more common in other spoken languages. Semitic languages rely heavily on non-linear affixation as a morphological process, for example. What is important is that spoken language has two typological possibilities for affixation. This is not necessarily true for signed languages based on how words are formed in the signed medium (Supalla & McKee, 2002). A signed language would have a strong, if not exclusive inclination for one affixation type (i.e., non-linear; see Sandler, 1990 for further discussion on the linearity and non-linearity of morphology in signed and spoken languages).

To demonstrate, the citation form of WATCH is affected upon non-linear affixation according to two different morphological rules in ASL. For verb agreement, the verb is subject to person and case marking. Understanding that the two locations have been identified through movement for the verb's citation form (Figure 13.1), the endpoints of the movement are strictly phonological. They are meaningless as expected for any phonological structure. Upon inflection, however, the same endpoints become meaningful by adopting different locations in the signing space. Figure 13.3 shows how the verb's initial endpoint starts (on one side of the signer in the illustration) and its final endpoint is in a third person location (on the other side of the signer in the illustration). The initial endpoint also marks the third person as subject with the final endpoint marking the third person object.

Figure 13.3   WATCH undergoing non-linear affixation for verb agreement

Figure 13.4   WATCH undergoing non-linear affixation for temporal aspect

What is interesting is that the inflected form of WATCH above is consistent with how signs are formed in general. That is, no new segment(s) are added to the stem or in a position where unrelated syllables are produced. The patterns of non-linear affixation and meeting the structural constraints are repeated for the temporal aspect in ASL. Figure 13.4 shows how the same verb is subject to marking 'for a long time' (see Klima & Bellugi, 1979 for further description of the signed language's morphological subsystem for temporal aspect and number). The changes to the citation form include reducing the number of locations from two to one to allow for movement to occur in a circular fashion. The single handshape remains intact throughout the production of the inflected sign. Although the verb WATCH consists of a single syllable, the morphological rule has affected the word structure. The reduplication through circular movement is now similar to the citation form of WORK.

With both verb agreement and temporal aspect, a person is most likely to perceive inflection as occurring within the boundaries of WATCH. This conclusion has some important assumptions. Given that simple signs are made of a single segment (or are monosyllabic in nature), it is easy to imagine how such phonological structure would create word boundaries in an explicit way. The existence of multiple segments in spoken words cannot allow for such an outcome. For example, a person listening to a stream (of an unknown spoken language in use) would not be able to segment in a reliable way as the words vary in length and number of segments. In contrast, the pattern of signs will mark themselves as words at the phonological level. With the word boundaries being salient, non-linear affixation would be deemed as the appropriate morphological process for the signed medium (see Supalla, 1990 for further discussion on word structure in the signed medium and its relationship with the morphological operations). Had linear affixation been adopted as a morphological process, the result would be disastrous in terms of language processing. The linear affixes would fall outside the word boundaries and fail to be part of the word according to the signed medium.

Considerations for Manually Coded English

Understanding that non-linear affixation is adopted as the morphological process for ASL, it is not possible to observe any of the predictions concerning linear affixation. However, insights can be made with MCE, especially for the adverse effects on language acquisition when it relies heavily on linear affixation as a morphological process. Deaf children have been subject to MCE for language acquisition and frequently as their sole linguistic input. To be exact, the English-based sign systems rely on the use of invented prefixes and suffixes, to be used along with roots (borrowed from ASL). Figure 13.5 shows WATCH, this time, affixed in a linear fashion. The signed bound morpheme -ING is

Figure 13.5   WATCH undergoing linear affixation for present progressive tense

produced after the verb to indicate WATCHING. As an independent phonological unit, the present progressive tense involves a specific handshape with an extended pinkie, outward rotation of the forearm, and a final orientation of the palm facing away from the signer's body.

Upon analysis, the form of WATCHING appears to violate how the structure of phonology and morphology should operate in signed language. The number of handshapes used in the inflected sign is two, and they are not related to each other (e.g., opening or closing as found in some ASL signs). The first handshape (for WATCH) involves an opening through the extension of index and middle fingers, and the second handshape (for -ING) is also opened with the pinkie. The linear affix has its own movement and locations. At this point, it is clear that the linearly affixed sign consists of more than one segment and its structure (in WATCHING) is not rhythmic. For these reasons, the root and affix are essentially split according to the signed medium. The effects on MCE are profound, resulting in a structural deficiency alien to the perception and processing underlying any human language.

In fact, linear affixation used in MCE has led to a serious case of misanalysis by deaf children who tried to acquire English through the signed medium. They had trouble in recognizing a linear affix as part of the root (e.g., SANTA-CLAUS COME TO TOWN ING or WRITE THAT NAME ING THERE, Maxwell, 1987: 331). Linear affixes being bound morphemes were treated as if they were free morphemes (or full signs). This kind of error indicates that deaf children are not able to learn the rule of the present progressive tense in English by using MCE. In contrast, children who can hear and learn spoken English do not experience the learning difficulty described here (see Supalla & McKee, 2002 for further discussion on the limitations of MCE). What this suggests is that MCE is not comparable to the language (i.e., English) that it intends to duplicate for the benefit of deaf children. The structural violations leading to the production of distorted sentences is thus real and undermines their capacity for language acquisition.

The acquisition studies with ASL, on the other hand, indicate that deaf children are able to learn the language (e.g., Newport & Meier, 1985; Meier, 1991; Petitto, 2000). There is no learning difficulty or structural deficiency in the literature reported for the signed language. The fact that ASL is a morphologically rich language does not stop deaf children from acquiring the language. The favorable evidence for ASL as a 'working' language also lies in how psychometric measures have been developed to capture deaf children's level of native signed language proficiency (Maller et al., 1999; Singleton & Supalla, 2003). Similar measures for MCE would not be possible. The prospect of deaf children becoming native users of English through MCE has not been reported in the literature. In fact, the literature reports on their lack of mastery with the English language (e.g., Marschark, Lang, & Albertini, 2002; Yoshinaga-Itano, Snyder, & Mayberry, 1996; Quigley, Wilbur, & Montanelli, 1976). It seems safe to consider English, signed or not, to be inherently inaccessible owing to the impact of hearing loss.

Discussion and Conclusion

As part of understanding linguistic accessibility for deaf children, the structure of signed language must meet the cognitive prerequisites for perception and processing in the visual/gestural modality. A signed linguistic system as in the case of English through MCE does not suffice. A similar conclusion could be made for French and Methodical Sign as well. The linguistic system must be free in adopting a structure best suited to its modality. An adoption of the spoken language structure (for the signed medium) will only lead to the linguistic system losing its learnability variable. The range of structural options known for spoken languages is not univocally the same for signed languages (see Brentari, 1995 for further discussion on typologies concerning signed and spoken languages). Some of the options for language are not appropriate for the signed medium, whereas others are. For this reason, signed languages conform to the constraints according to their type (e.g., monosyllabic for the word structure and non-linear affixation adopted as a morphological process), thus allowing themselves to be part of the human language family.

Recall that the motivation for MCE is strong with its morphosyntactic structure being consistent with English print. MCE is supposedly helpful when deaf children can map 'word for word' between the print and signing (e.g., Mayer & Wells, 1996; Mayer & Akamatsu, 1999). This argument can be considered only if MCE works as a linguistic system. If deaf children are not learning English through MCE, they cannot make a connection with print as anticipated. There is also a criticism made on linking MCE to reading theory. Speech-based phonetic skills are still missing and deaf children using MCE would not be able to decode words in English text (LaSasso & Metzger, 1998). Educators supporting MCE may respond that speech therapy and auditory training go 'hand in hand' with the signing component of English (better known as Total Communication or Simultaneous Communication). The debate is commonplace in deaf education where futile attempts cause educators to 'run in circles'.

Language modality is what matters and it suggests that a formal distinction needs to be made between spoken languages and signed languages. A number of issues can be revisited under this new light. For example, bilingual education as advocated by some educators as a model to consider for deaf education in recent years (e.g., Strong, 1988, 1995) would not be appropriate. Paul and Quigley (1987) argued that the reading process according to bilingual education is problematic for deaf children. Children who can hear enjoy auditory access to the spoken form for reading development purposes as well as repetition of the learning process whereby two languages are in the same modality (e.g., Spanish and English). The closest comparison to bilingual education for deaf children would be when two signed languages are considered (e.g., ASL and Japanese Sign Language). The educational situation for deaf children is different with one being a signed language and the other a spoken language.

What deaf education can do is to account for reading instruction by requiring the combination of two languages; with ASL serving as the 'oral' language and English at the 'print' end. Drastic measures need to be adopted, especially if deaf children are fully capable of acquiring and mastering a language. A cross-linguistic arrangement is necessary given that deaf children need to draw on their signed language knowledge to support reading development in English (Supalla, 2003). The resulting design requires the use of special literacy tools and instructional procedures to facilitate the transition from ASL to English. This is where deaf children can make a connection with English print based on what they know in the signed language (Supalla, Wix, & McKee, 2001).

According to Supalla and Blackburn (2003), the reading formula proposed for deaf children follows the national and state reading standards, yet by-passes the sound prerequisites to English and reading. In this model, teaching English would occur simultaneously with reading. What this means is that a systematic teaching of English must occur in the same fashion as found with reading. When looking at the language arts standards, they refer primarily to broad categories of literacy (e.g., reading and writing). The standards do not explicitly list competencies in the area of English grammar (Blackburn et al., 2000). Yet the use of special literacy tools and instructional procedures with deaf children would provide information for English more precisely than is known for second language learners (i.e., those who can hear are expected to capitalize on learning English through the spoken form). In any case, the development of various measures will help validate the cross-linguistic approach to reading instruction and close the disability-deduced gap to English literacy (see Cripps & Supalla, 2004 for further discussion on the assessment under development and for deaf children's phonetic skills in ASL as part of making a transition to English literacy).

The relationship between ASL proficiency and reading achievement needs to be clarified. Some educators have become convinced that deaf children just need to know ASL in order to have reading taught to them. Padden and Ramsey (1998) are correct in stating that knowing signed language is not sufficient, as deaf children still need to undergo reading instruction one way or another. It is true that deaf children with access to ASL may have a cognitive and linguistic advantage for reading achievement (over deaf peers who are denied access to ASL), but they still need to perform better than is reported in the literature. Writing samples of deaf children fluent in ASL indicate serious disparities in performance when compared to second language learners who can hear (Singleton et al., 2004). Much work is evidently needed to promote English literacy among deaf children. ASL proficiency will continue to be of paramount importance, as deaf children need access to the signed language as much as any child who can hear needs access to the spoken language. Most relevant is that effective reading instruction for deaf children is contingent on their signed language knowledge.

Some of the changes in deaf education include no longer treating speech as central to the reading process or even in place of a signed language (as found with oralism). Speech can be more effectively taught to a deaf child (i.e., for the purpose of talking) based on the English language knowledge achieved through reading instruction. This would serve as another justification for the reform of deaf education. Spencer and Marschark (2003) made it clear that regardless of the advances in technology, cochlear implant surgery should not be perceived as a cure to deafness, especially when the surgery "doe[es] not change deaf people into hearing people" (p. 435). Those children who undergo cochlear implant surgery are expected to receive extensive speech therapy and auditory training. This does not constitute language acquisition in a true sense. With or without cochlear implants, deaf children are entitled to learning a signed language as a linguistic compensation for their disability. With the concept of linguistic accessibility, educators must not overvalue spoken language as it would mean discrimination against children who suffer any form of hearing impairment. With the provision of special literacy tools and instructional procedures, a research-based design for deaf education will ensure that theory and practice are combined to remove sound as a barrier to English and reading development.

NOTE

We are grateful to Cecile McKee, Laura Blackburn, and Diane Brentari for their helpful comments on a previous version of this chapter. Robin Supalla's assistance in editing the chapter's many drafts is also deeply appreciated.

REFERENCES

Battison, Robbin (1978). *Lexical Borrowing in American Sign Language*. Silver Spring, MD: Linstok Press.

Bebian, Roch-Ambroise A. (1984). Essay on the deaf and natural language, or introduction to a natural classification of ideas with their proper signs. In Harlan Lane (ed.), *The Deaf Experience: Classics in Language and Education* (pp. 126–160). Cambridge, MA: Harvard University Press.

Blackburn, Laura A., Wix, Tina R., McKee, Cecile, & Supalla, Samuel J. (2000). Making state academic standards explicit for syntax. *Syntax in the Schools*, 16(4), 1–5.

Brennan, Mary (1986). Linguistic perspectives. In Bernard Tervoort (ed.), *Signs of Life: Proceedings of the Second European Congress on Sign Language Research, Amsterdam, July 14–18, 1985* (pp. 1–16). Amsterdam: Institute of General Linguistics of the University of Amsterdam.

Brennan, Mary & Hayhurst, Allan B. (1980). The renaissance of British Sign Language. In Charlotte Baker & Robbin Battison (eds.), *Sign Language and the Deaf Community* (pp. 233–244). Silver Spring, MD: National Association of the Deaf.

Brentari, Diane (1995). Sign language phonology: ASL. In John A. Goldsmith (ed.), *A Handbook of Phonological Theory* (pp. 615–639). New York: Basil Blackwell.

Brentari, Diane (2002). Modality differences in sign language phonology and morphophonemics. In Richard P. Meier, Kearsy Cormier, & David Quinto-Pozos (eds.), *Modality and Structure in Signed and Spoken Languages* (pp. 35–64). Cambridge: Cambridge University Press.

Chamberlain, Charlene & Mayberry, Rachel I. (2000). Theorizing about the relation between American Sign Language and reading. In Charlene Chamberlain, Jill P. Morford, & Rachel I. Mayberry (eds.), *Language Acquisition by Eye* (pp. 221–259). Mahwah, NJ: Lawrence Erlbaum.

Channon, Rachel (2002). Beads on a string? Representation of repetition in spoken and signed languages. In Richard P. Meier, Kearsy Cormier, & David Quinto-Pozos (eds.), *Modality and Structure in Signed and Spoken Languages* (pp. 65–87). Cambridge: Cambridge University Press.

Conrad, Reuben (1979). *The Deaf Child*. London: Harper & Row.

Coulter, Geoffery R. (1982). On the Nature of ASL as a Monosyllabic Language. Paper presented at the annual meeting of the Linguistic Society of America, San Diego, CA.

Cripps, Jody H. & Supalla, Samuel J. (2004). Modifications to the Peabody Picture Vocabulary Test for the use with signing deaf students. *Arizona Working Papers in Second Language Acquisition and Teaching*, 11, 93–113.

Eastman, Gilbert C. (1980). From student to professional: A personal chronicle of sign language. In Charlotte Baker & Robbin Battison (eds.), *Sign Language and the Deaf Community* (pp. 9–32). Silver Spring, MD: National Association of the Deaf.

Hansen, Britta (1980). Research on Danish Sign Language and its impact on the deaf community. In Charlotte Baker & Robbin Battison (eds.), *Sign Language and the Deaf Community* (pp. 245–263). Silver Spring, MD: National Association of the Deaf.

Johnson, Robert E., Liddell, Scott K., & Erting, Carol J. (1989). *Unlocking the Curriculum: Principles for Achieving Access in Deaf Education* (Gallaudet Research Institute Working/Occasional Paper Series, No. 89–3). Washington, DC: Gallaudet Research Institute.

Karchmer, Michael A., Milone, Michael N., Jr., & Wolk, Steve (1979). Educational significance of hearing loss at three levels of severity. *American Annals of the Deaf*, 124(2), 97–109.

Klima, Edward & Bellugi, Ursula (1979). *The Signs of Language*. Cambridge, MA: Harvard University Press.

Lane, Harlan (1980). Historical: A chronology of the oppression of sign language in France and the United States. In Harlan Lane & François Grosjean (eds.), *Recent Perspectives on American Sign Language* (pp. 119–161). Hillsdale, NJ: Lawrence Erlbaum.

Lane, Harlan (1984). *When the Mind Hears*. New York: Random.

LaSasso, Carol & Metzger, Melanie (1998). An alternate route for preparing deaf children for BiBi programs: The home language L1 and Cued Speech for conveying traditionally spoken languages. *Journal of Deaf Studies and Deaf Education*, (3)4, 265–289.

MacMahon, Michael K. C. (1991). The International Phonetic Alphabet. In Kirsten Malmkjær (ed.), *The Linguistics Encyclopedia* (pp. 219–224). New York: Routlegde.

Maher, Jane (1996). *Seeing Language in Sign: The Work of William C. Stokoe*. Washington, DC: Gallaudet University Press.

Maller, Susan J., Singleton, Jenny L., Supalla, Samuel J., & Wix, Tina (1999). The development and psychometric properties of the American Sign Language Proficiency Assessment (ASL-PA). *Journal of Deaf Studies and Deaf Education*, 4(4), 249–269.

Marschark, Marc, Lang, Harry G., & Albertini, John A. (2002). *Educating Deaf Students: From Research to Practice*. New York: Oxford University Press.

Maxwell, Madeline M. (1987). The acquisition of English bound morphemes in sign form. *Sign Language Studies*, (16)57, 323–352.

Mayer, Connie & C. Akamastu, Tane (1999). Bilingual-bicultural models of literacy education for deaf students: Considering the claims. *Journal of Deaf Studies and Deaf Education*, (4)1, 1–8.

Mayer, Connie & Wells, Gordon (1996). Can the linguistic interdependence theory support a bilingual-bicultural model of literacy education for deaf students? *Journal of Deaf Studies and Deaf Education*, (1)2, 93–107.

McAnally, Patricia L., Rose, Susan, & Quigley, Stephen P. (1987). *Language Learning Practices with Deaf Children*. Boston, MA: College-Hill Press.

Meier, Richard P. (1991). Language acquisition by deaf children. *American Scientist*, 79 (January–February), 60–70.

Meier, Richard P. (2002). Why different, why the same? Explaining effects and non-effects of modality upon linguistic structure in sign and speech. In Richard P. Meier, Kearsy Cormier, & David Quinto-Pozos (eds.), *Modality and Structure in Signed and Spoken Languages*, (pp. 1–26). Cambridge: Cambridge University Press.

Meier, Richard P., Cormier, Kearsy, & Quinto-Pozos, David (eds.) (2002). *Modality and Structure in Signed and Spoken Languages*. Cambridge: Cambridge University Press.

Moores, Donald F. (1996). *Educating the Deaf: Psychology, Principles, and Practices* (4th edn.). Boston, MA: Houghton Mifflin.

Mottez, Bernard & Markowicz, Harry (1980). The social movement for the acceptance of French Sign Language. In Charlotte Baker & Robbin Battison (eds.), *Sign Language and the Deaf Community* (pp. 221–232). Silver Spring, MD: National Association of the Deaf.

Newport, Elissa & Meier, Richard P. (1985). The acquisition of American Sign Language. In Dan Slobin (ed.), *The Cross-Linguistic Study of Language Acquisition* (pp. 881–938). Hillsdale, NJ: Lawrence Erlbaum.

Padden, Carol & Ramsey, Claire (1998). Reading ability in signing deaf children. *Topics in Language Disorders* (special issue ed. Katharine G. Butler & Phillip M. Prinz), 18(4), 30–46.

Paul, Peter V. (2003). Process and components of reading. In Marc Marschark & Patricia E. Spencer (eds.), *Oxford Handbook of Deaf Studies, Language, and Education* (pp. 97–109). New York: Oxford University Press.

Paul, Peter V. & Quigley, Stephen P. (1987). Using American Sign Language to teach English. In Patricia, L. McAnally, Susan Rose, & Stephen P. Quigley (eds.), *Language Learning Practices with Deaf Children* (pp. 139–166). Boston, MA: College-Hill Press.

Petitto, Laura Ann (2000). On the biological foundations of human language. In Karen Emmorey & Harlan Lane (eds.), *The Signs of Language Revisited: An Anthology to Honor Ursula Bellugi and Edward Klima* (pp. 449–473). Mahwah, NJ: Lawrence Erlbaum.

Pinker, Stephen (1994). *The Language Instinct: How the Mind Creates Language*. New York: Harper Collins.

Quigley, Stephen P., Wilbur, Ronnie B., & Montanelli, Dale S. (1976). Complement structures in the language of deaf students. *Journal of Speech and Hearing Research*, 19(3), 448–457.

Sandler, Wendy (1990). Temporal aspects and ASL phonology. In Patricia Siple & Susan D. Fischer (eds.), *Theoretical Issues in Sign Language Research (vol. 1): Linguistics* (pp. 7–35). Chicago: The University of Chicago Press.

Singleton, Jenny L. & Supalla, Samuel J. (2003). Assessing children's proficiency in natural signed languages. In Mark Marschark & Patricia E. Spencer (eds.), *Oxford Handbook of Deaf Studies, Language, and Education* (pp. 289–302). New York: Oxford University Press.

Singleton, Jenny L., Morgan, Dianne, DiGello, Elizabeth, Wiles, Jill, & Rivers, Rachel (2004). Vocabulary use by low, moderate, and high ASL-proficient writers compared to hearing ESL and monolingual speakers. *Journal of Deaf Studies and Deaf Education*, (9)1, 86–103.

Singleton, Jenny L., Supalla, Samuel J., Litchfield, Susan, and Schley, Sara (1998). From sign to word: Considering modality constraints in ASL/English bilingual education. *Topics in Language Disorders* (special issue ed. Katharine G. Butler & Philip M. Prinz), 18(4), 16–29.

Spencer, Patricia E. & Marschark, Marc (2003). Cochlear implants: Issues and implications. In Marc Marschark & Patricia E. Spencer (eds.), *Oxford Handbook of Deaf Studies, Language, and Education* (pp. 434–448). New York: Oxford University Press.

Stokoe, William C. (1960). *Sign Language Structure: An Outline of the Visual Communication Systems of the American Deaf*, Studies in Linguistics, No. 8. Buffalo, NY: Department of Anthropology and Linguistics, University of Buffalo.

Stokoe, William C., Casterline, Dorothy C., & Croneberg, Carl G. (1965). *A Dictionary of American Sign Language on Linguistic Principles*. Washington, DC: Gallaudet College Press.

Strong, Michael (1988). A bilingual approach to the education of young deaf children: ASL and English. In Michael Strong (ed.), *Language Learning and Deafness* (pp. 113–129). Cambridge, UK; Cambridge University Press.

Strong, Michael (1995). A review of bilingual/bicultural programs for deaf children in North America. *American Annals of the Deaf*, 140, 84–94.

Supalla, Samuel J. (1990). Segmentation of Manually Coded English: Problems in the Mapping of English in the Visual/Gestural Mode. Unpublished doctoral dissertation, University of Illinois, Urbana-Champaign.

Supalla, Samuel J. (2003). English as a Second Language for Deaf Children: Building an Argument. Paper presented at the Second Language Acquisition and Teaching Colloquium Series, University of Arizona, Tucson, AZ.

Supalla, Samuel J. & Blackburn, Laura (2003). Learning how to read and bypassing sound. *Odyssey*, 5(1), 50–55.

Supalla, Samuel J. & McKee, Cecile (2002). The role of Manually Coded English in language development of deaf children. In Richard P. Meier, Kearsy Cormier, & David Quinto-Pozos (eds.), *Modality and Structure in Signed and Spoken Languages* (pp. 143–165). Cambridge: Cambridge University Press.

Supalla, Samuel J., Wix, Tina R., & McKee, Cecile (2001). Print as a primary source of English for deaf learners. In Janet Nicol & Terence Langendoen (eds.), *One Mind, Two Languages: Studies in Bilingual Language Processing* (pp. 177–190). Oxford: Blackwell.

Sutton-Spence, Rachel and Woll, Bencie (2003). *The Linguistics of British Sign language: An Introduction.* Cambridge: Cambridge University Press.

Valli, Clayton & Lucas, Ceil (2001). *Linguistics of American Sign Language: An Introduction* (3rd edn.). Washington, DC: Gallaudet University Press.

Van Cleve, John V. & Crouch, Barry A. (1989). *A Place of Their Own: Creating the Deaf Community in America.* Washington, DC: Gallaudet University Press.

Wilbur, Ronnie (1979). *American Sign Language and Sign Systems: Research and Applications.* Baltimore, MD: University Park Press.

Yoshinaga-Itano, Christine, Snyder, Lynn S., & Mayberry, Rachel (1996). How deaf and normally hearing students convey meaning within and between written sentences. *Volta Review,* 98(1), 9–38.

Zeshan, Ulrike (2002). Towards a notion of "word" in sign languages. In R. M. W. Dixon & Alexandra Y. Aikhenvald (eds.), *Word: A Cross-linguistic Typology* (pp. 153–179). Cambridge: Cambridge University Press.

14 Identity in Language and Literacy Education

CAROLYN MCKINNEY AND BONNY NORTON

The end of the twentieth and early years of the twenty-first century have witnessed a burgeoning interest in issues of learner identities in language and literacy education.[1] This interest has been accompanied by a shift in the conception of identity which foregrounds the sociocultural rather than the psychological, and conceives of identity not as static and uni-dimensional but, following poststructuralist theorists, as dynamic, multiple, and a site of struggle (Hall, 1992a; Weedon, 1997; Norton, 2000). The foregrounding of identity in language and literacy education has led to a much more sophisticated understanding of language learners that locates them in the social, historical, political, and cultural contexts in which learning takes place and explores how learners negotiate and sometimes resist the diverse positions those contexts offer them. Significantly, we would argue that this understanding has opened up the way for pedagogies that are critical and that respond to different forms of diversity in unprecedented ways.

In the context of addressing gender and English language learning, Norton and Pavlenko (2004: 509) argue that:

> EFL and ESL classrooms represent unique spaces where different linguistic and cultural worlds come into contact. Such classrooms offer unparalleled opportunities for teachers to engage with cross-cultural differences and the social construction of gender and sexuality and thus to help students develop linguistic and intercultural competence.

While this is true, many working in critical approaches to diversity in language and literacy education, including Norton and Pavlenko, would argue that the multilingual classroom is not automatically a productive site for such work. One of the greatest challenges in responding to cultural and linguistic diversity in language classrooms is to move beyond stereotyping difference or merely celebrating diversity as if it had no links to social inequality and no structural or material effects (May, 1999; Kubota, 2004). Difference and power relations must always be considered together in pedagogy that responds meaningfully to diversity, whether such diversity is structured on the grounds of gender, race, class, or other forms of difference.

In this chapter we address the question: What does the recent foregrounding of identity in language and literacy education mean for educational practice and educational change? We explore what it means to respond to diversity in language and literacy education through a range of approaches, working across different levels and contexts, from young and adolescent learners in formal schooling to older learners in higher education or adult education programs. We begin by tracing the critical and poststructuralist theoretical lenses on language, identity, and pedagogy that inform the examples of classroom practice we present. We then provide examples of practice from different regions of the world, highlighting both the possibilities and challenges of making the classroom a space that accommodates multiple identities and investments. We conclude that responding to diversity in language and literacy education requires an imaginative assessment of what is possible as well as a critical assessment of what is desirable.

Theoretical Lenses

Theorizing language

Educators interested in identity, language, and learning are interested in language as a social practice, through which relationships are defined, negotiated, and resisted. A number of theorists have been influential to such educators, most notably Mikhail Bakhtin (1981, 1963/1984) and Pierre Bourdieu (1984, 1997), whose poststructuralist theories of language foreground struggles over meaning and legitimacy. This is opposed to the structuralist view of Saussure, which conceives of signs as having idealized meanings and of linguistic communities as being relatively homogenous and consensual.

Bakhtin, a Russian philosopher, takes the position that language needs to be investigated as situated utterances in which speakers, in dialogue with others, struggle to create meanings. In this view, the notion of the individual speaker is a fiction as all speakers construct their utterances jointly on the basis of their interaction with listeners, both in historical and contemporary, actual and assumed communities. In this view, the appropriation of the words of others is a complex and conflictual process in which words are not neutral but express particular predispositions and value systems. Bourdieu, a French sociologist, focuses on the often unequal relationships between interlocutors and the importance of power in structuring speech. He suggests that the value ascribed to speech cannot be understood apart from the person who speaks, and that the person who speaks cannot be understood apart from larger networks of social relationships. To redress the inequities between what Bourdieu calls "legitimate" and "illegitimate" speakers, he argues that an expanded definition of competence should include the "right to speech" or "the power to impose reception" (1997: 648).

The fact that there is no guarantee to the right to speech for speakers follows from Bourdieu's theorizing of discourse as "a symbolic asset which can receive different values depending on the market on which it is offered." (1997: 651). Simply put, "language is worth what those who speak it are worth" (p. 651) and "the dominant usage is the usage of the dominant class" (p. 659). Bourdieu's foregrounding of power relations in language use has important implications for how language learners are positioned by others, for the opportunities they get to speak, and for the varieties of language that we teach and that they use. In the light of such theory, becoming a "good" language learner is a much more complicated process than earlier research had suggested (Norton & Toohey, 2004).

Theorizing identity

The work of Christine Weedon (1987/1997), like that of Bakhtin and Bourdieu, is centrally concerned with the conditions under which people speak, within both institutional and community contexts. Like other poststructuralist theorists who inform her work, Weedon foregrounds the central role of language in her analysis of the relationship between the individual and the social, arguing that language not only defines institutional practices, but serves to construct our sense of ourselves and our "subjectivity" (Weedon, 1987: 21). Weedon notes that the terms *subject* and *subjectivity* signify a different conception of the individual than that associated with humanist conceptions of the individual dominant in Western philosophy. While humanist conceptions of the individual presuppose that every person has an essential, unique, fixed, and coherent "core," poststructuralism depicts the individual (i.e., the subject) as diverse, contradictory, dynamic, and changing over historical time and social space. Drawing on the Foucauldian notions of discourse and historical specificity, subjectivity in poststructuralism is understood as discursively constructed, and as always socially and historically embedded. Identity is thus always in process, a site of struggle between competing discourses in which the subject plays an active role. In the exercise of such agency, learners may have differential investments in a variety of subject positions, best understood in the context of shifting relations of power.

In the field of language learning, Norton (Norton Peirce, 1995; Norton, 2000) has sought to integrate the poststructuralist conceptions of identity and human agency by developing an enriched and productive notion of "investment." Departing from current conceptions of "motivation" in the field of language learning, the concept of investment signals the socially and historically constructed relationship of learners to the target language, and their sometimes ambivalent desire to learn and practice it. Investment is best understood with reference to the economic metaphors that Bourdieu uses in his work, in particular the notion of "cultural capital." Bourdieu and Passeron (1977) use the term *cultural capital* to reference the knowledge, credentials, and modes of thought that characterize different classes and groups in relation to specific sets of social forms. They argue that cultural capital is situated, in that it has differential exchange value in different social fields. If learners "invest" in a second language, they do so with the understanding that they will acquire a wider range of symbolic and material resources, which will in turn increase the value of their cultural capital. As the value of their cultural capital increases, so learners' sense of themselves and their desires for the future are reassessed. Hence the integral relationship between investment and identity. This notion of investment has been taken up by other scholars in the field, and is proving productive for understanding the complex conditions under which language learning takes place (McKay & Wong, 1996; Angelil-Carter, 1997; Skilton-Sylvester, 2002; Pittaway, 2004; Potowski, 2004).

Poststructuralist approaches to theorizing identity have been fruitfully put to work to de-essentialize and deconstruct identity categories such as race and gender by post-colonial theorists such as Stuart Hall (1992b) and Homi Bhabha (1994). In theorizing 'cultural' identity, Stuart Hall focuses on identity as in process, 'becoming', and stresses the importance of representation following from the discursive construction of identity. In his notion of 'new ethnicities', Hall provides an alternative theorizing of race that recognizes experiences of race without homogenizing them. Hall emphasizes a multi-faceted rootedness which is not limited to ethnic minorities and which can be applied to other forms of difference. However, one of the difficulties in theorizing difference in this way is that people often wish to assert their identities as homogenous and unitary, foregrounding a particular aspect of their experience such as gender, race, or religious affiliation. We see this in the current strength of nationalisms and religious fundamentalism in different parts of the globe. Such unitary assertions of identity are often referred to as *strategic essentialism* (cf. Spivak in Fuss, 1989; Yon, 1999). The terms *identity politics* or the *politics of difference* reference this particular coalescence of identity and power relations, emphasizing the material effects of difference. Foregrounding identity and the issues that this raises are central in responding critically to diversity in language and literacy education.

Theorizing pedagogy

Critical approaches to language and literacy education can be traced back to the work of Paulo Freire (1970), who emphasized that any literacy learning worth the effort should encourage students to learn to read both the word and the world. Following Freire, theorists aligned with critical pedagogy emphasize that it aims to develop students' knowledge of the self and the social world, and the ways in which these are historically constructed in the context of frequently inequitable relations of power. In its application to the classroom, theorists of critical pedagogy often refer to the development of critical literacy (Lankshear & McLaren, 1993; Luke, 1997), which focuses on the written text, or, indeed, any other kind of representation of meaning, as a site of struggle, negotiation, and change. However, there have been critiques of critical pedagogy and critical literacy that have arisen from the attempts of practitioners to work with critical pedagogy in the classroom, where they have encountered resistance from students to dealing with social inequality (e.g., Ellsworth, 1989; Weiler, 1991; Janks, 2002; McKinney, 2004). These scholars problematize the assumption underlying critical pedagogy that revealing social inequalities to students will necessarily bring about change, whether personal, or collective. Such assumptions ignore the multiple investments that the learners bring to the classroom.

More recent work in critical pedagogy thus foregrounds issues of student identity, considering what students' investments might be, and how students are positioned both inside and outside the classroom. As the focus on investment and positioning implies, such work brings together critical theory and poststructuralist theoretical frameworks. While critical theory maintains the focus on teaching for social justice and foregrounds issues of power and inequality, poststructuralism signals multiplicity and complexity, a move away from a dogmatic approach to the deconstruction of binary oppositions such as oppressor/oppressed; masculine/feminine; advantaged/disadvantaged; white/black. The plurality in the titles of recent edited collections showcase pedagogy using such multiplicity of perspectives: *Negotiating Critical Literacies in Classrooms* (Comber & Simpson, 2001) and *Critical Pedagogies and Language Learning* (Norton & Toohey, 2004). There is now a clear recognition of the need to address issues of diversity or difference on multiple levels and to explore the intersections of different elements of difference – e.g., race, class, and gender – while also acknowledging that these intersections are not static and will differ according to subjects and specific contexts.

Critical pedagogies in practice

What then does theorizing language as sociocultural practice and identity as central to learning mean for critical classroom practice? Thesen argues that

> Although academics might embrace the concept of multiple identities in theory, in practice they often stop short of doing more than imposing their own versions of which identity categories are salient. (Thesen, 1997: 506)

Thesen may be right precisely because the multiple positionings of learners and teachers provide a significant challenge to addressing diversity in the classroom (Morgan & Ramanathan, 2005; McKinney, 2005). However, while it is useful and realistic to recognize such challenges, they do not make critical approaches invalid; the converse rather is true. Recently, scholars have developed models for critical practice that attempt to balance different and competing elements. Janks (2000) argues for a synthesis model of critical literacy education that brings together domination (recognition and analysis of power), access (to privileged forms of language and literacy), diversity (recognizing diverse social identities), and design (the ability to use multiple modes to "challenge and change existing discourses", p. 177). In a similar spirit, the New London Group (2000) have argued for a "pedagogy of multiliteracies" that combines the different elements of situated practice, overt instruction, critical framing, and transformed practice. In this section we present examples of practice across different levels of education that take seriously the diverse identities of learners, while seeking to expand the range of possibilities available to them.

Working with young learners

One might think that critical approaches, in their focus on power and social inequality, and their use of complex poststructuralist approaches to meaning making, are appropriate only for work with adolescents and adults. However some educators have worked creatively with very young learners from pre-first grade through the first few years of formal schooling in remarkable ways, showing young children's abilities to take critical perspectives on their own social worlds (O'Brien, 2001; Vasquez, 2004) and to adopt the positions of active meaning-makers despite being positioned as passive (Sahni, 2001).

Vasquez's work (2004) with very young learners (4–5 years old) takes place in a multiracial Canadian pre-school class where she aimed to help children understand the social issues around them. Reminiscent of a Freirean problem-posing approach where social issues are elicited from the lived experiences of adult learners (see Auerbach & Wallerstein, 2004), Vasquez listens carefully to her learners, believing that they will raise social and cultural issues about their everyday lives which will be fruitful for exploration in the curriculum. Vasquez discusses a successful example where children raised the issue of their exclusion at an annual school cultural event, The French Café, and shows how oral and literacy activities grew out of this issue, including the drafting of a petition.

In another part of the globe, working with 5–8-year-olds from multi-ethnic backgrounds in urban Australian schools, O'Brien's focus (2001) is on the teaching of critical reading. In particular she describes a number of success-ful activities where children worked on reading the construction of (often stereotypically) gendered identities in a range of texts including informational literature and children's literature. Through a series of classes and fun activities around Mother's Day catalogues, O'Brien takes the children through a process of critiquing gender construction and consumerism. Like Vasquez, the children are being taught to read their social worlds critically, using creative pedagogies where they get to talk about, read, and make texts of their own.

In a similar spirit, Sahni's (2001) work in a rural North Indian village concerns the empowerment of lower caste children who are not usually given a voice to "appropriate literacy" (p. 19). Such appropriation entails learners' involvement in meaning making for their own purposes, including pleasure, as well as an appropriation of a "power-commodity" such as literacy which is usually a "a set of practices controlled by dominant classes or culture" (p. 19). She calls for a conception of empowerment that allows for a focus on individual children and their learning, and shows how children moved in their writing from a position of rote copying to the development of imaginative and creative pieces. Through the invention of imagined worlds in such pieces, children were able to change their social positioning and express their aspirations, demonstrating empowerment at a micro-level. The unleashing of imagination here plays a powerful role in dramatically re-shaping the previously restricted positions and expectations of these lower caste children as learners.

Working with adolescents

Educators have used or advocated a range of critical approaches with adolescent learners, from the use of popular culture (Ibrahim, 1999; Moffat & Norton, 2005) to multimodal pedagogies (Stein, 2004; Kendrick et al., in press).

Ibrahim (1999) explores the intersections of race and gender in the differential ways in which 'continental African' immigrants to Canada learned and appropriated (American) Black Stylized English (BSE) and tapped into black hip-hop and rap genres. Since rap and hip-hop is one of the sites in which the students invested their identities, Ibrahim proposes that rap and hip-hop, as well as Black popular culture, are curriculum sites that make legitimate forms of knowledge generally regarded as illegitimate. However, considering that some of the lyrics of rap and hip-hop songs may be sexist and racist, Ibrahim cautions that the use of such texts would need to be critically framed. Such deconstruction of popular culture texts, from which young people derive pleasure, can of course be met with resistance. As Ibrahim notes, if such texts are merely deconstructed and critiqued, they will not be transformed into legitimate forms of knowledge. In their poststructuralist approach to reading gender in an Archie comic, Moffat and Norton (2005) offer one possibility for critical framing that does not necessarily 'police' young people's pleasures. In the deconstruction of binaries, a poststructuralist reading is able to examine how texts simultaneously reproduce and subvert dominant relations of power, in this case relating to gender.

In a very different context, Stein (2001) explores the way in which a South African ESL classroom in an under-resourced township school can become "an important site for the institutional reappropriation and transformation of textual, cultural and linguistic forms, which have previously either been marginalized, infantilized or undervalued by the colonial and apartheid governments" (p. 152). Stein (like Brito, Lima, & Auerbach, 2004) initially set out to design a pedagogical intervention that would value learners' previously ignored and unvalued multilingual resources; however she found learners drawing on cultural resources in their oral storytelling that were not captured within the linguistic mode. Stein's learners revelled in the opportunities they were given to produce oral counter-texts that subverted the canon, and to draw on topics sometimes considered taboo. She thus advocates the use of multi-modal pedagogies (i.e., drawing on a number of semiotic modes including linguistic, bodily, and sensory) as a way of addressing the diverse needs of disadvantaged learners. Stein (2004) does however raise the challenge of assessment in such pedagogies, which are currently linguacentric.

In another African context, Kendrick et al. (in press) note that multimodal pedagogies that include drawing, photography, and drama, while by no means new pedagogies, could be incorporated more systematically into school curricula in Uganda. Drawing on their research in two regions of the country, they argue that multimodal pedagogies offer teachers innovative ways of validating students' literacies, experiences, and cultures, and are highly effective in supporting English language learning in the classroom. They draw on Mushengyezi (2003) to make the case that communication planners in Uganda should not overlook the importance of indigenous forms of communication such as popular theatre, drumming, and storytelling for enhancing student learning at all levels (pp. 107–117). They do recognize, however, that limited resources place constraints on teachers' actions, particularly in a context in which professional development is not widely supported.

Working with post-secondary students

The higher education or college level provides many spaces that are conducive to critical language and literacy work, including the writing class, English for Academic Purposes (EAP), and academic literacy courses. Here we present Lillis's (2003) innovative recommendations for a critical approach to teaching student writing as well as McKinney and van Pletzen's (2004) experience in using critical literacy with privileged learners at a South African university.

In the United Kingdom, Lillis (2003) worked with a small group of students to develop their academic literacy. The students were all female and considered non-traditional in higher education on the basis of one or more of the following categories: age, social class, ethnicity, and religious affiliation. While it is common for students to receive written 'feedback' from their university tutors on the essays they submit, Lillis developed a methodology of 'talkback', which enabled students to make informed decisions about their writing in a dialogic engagement with the tutor. Drawing on Kress's (2000) notions of 'critique' and 'design', Lillis argues for the need to move away from the dominant model of critique in academic literacy practices to one of design, where there is a serious attempt to change institutional practices in order to validate students' knowledge. Such a practice opens up disciplinary content to external interests and influences, allowing students to explore and represent the relationships between their own lived experiences and disciplinary academic knowledge.

Working with relatively privileged students at a historically white and Afrikaans university in South Africa, McKinney and van Pletzen (2004) introduced critical reading into their first-year English studies course using two curriculum units on South African literature. In exploring representations of the apartheid past, McKinney and van Pletzen encountered significant resistance from students to the ways in which they felt uncomfortably positioned by the curriculum materials on offer. McKinney and van Pletzen attempted to create discursive spaces in which both they and the students could explore the many private and political processes through which identities are constructed. In doing so, they re-conceptualized resistance more productively as a meaning-making activity which offers powerful teaching moments. McKinney (2005) argues for the importance of recognizing the teacher's multiple identity positions and the difficulties of providing a supportive environment, while at the same time challenging investments in social inequality such as racism and sexism. Like Lillis, she emphasizes the importance of a 'design' element in critical literacy so that students are not left in the space of critical deconstruction, but are afforded opportunities to design their own texts which position them differently and enable them to produce visions of an alternative reality (McKinney, 2004).

Working with adult learners

Adult language and literacy classrooms are also sites of a range of critical interventions. While problem-posing methodology is common practice in Freirean critical pedagogy for adults (Frye, 1999), we complement discussion on this approach with critical reading (Wallace, 2003) and more recently a 'pedagogy of inquiry' that draws on Queer theory (Nelson, 1999). Frye (1999) uses a problem-posing participatory methodology in an immigrant women's only ESL class in the USA. In setting up the class, Frye responded to the particular needs of the women for a class which would not be communicatively dominated by men, which would be available during the daytime (thus safer to get to), and which had childcare facilities. Consistent with a participatory approach, Frye developed her curriculum around topics of concern elicited from the learners, such as their difficulties in relating to their children's schools and teachers, but draws our attention to inappropriate assumptions that all immigrant women from a Spanish-speaking home country will share the same needs and interests. For example, she discusses differences and animosities that arose across age and social class differences, as well as the challenge of moving from the posing of problems to taking social action.

In the United Kingdom, Wallace (2003) has worked with adult language learners on critical reading courses that address the socially embedded nature of the reading process and explore text-focused activities that address how meaning and power are encoded in texts. In doing so, she makes use of a range of popular texts, including newspaper articles, magazine articles, and advertisements. Wallace contrasts her approach with dominant EFL methodologies such as communicative language teaching (CLT) and task-based learning, arguing that such approaches are 'domesticating' for learners, teaching them only how to fit in with dominant cultures rather than to question and reshape powerful discourses. She points out that in reading texts designed for the 'native' population of a particular country, immigrant learners have an advantage in their 'outsider' status precisely because they are not the ideal reader/ audience of the text and thus find it easier to discern problematic assumptions in the texts.

In advocating a pedagogy of inquiry that draws on Queer theory, Nelson (1999) describes an example of practice that also capitalizes on the knowledge that immigrant language learners bring of the cultural contexts in their originating countries. Nelson's concern is with opportunities in language classrooms to explore the way in which "sexual identities are not universal, but are done in different ways in different cultural contexts" (p. 376). The teacher Nelson observes invites learners (themselves a diverse group in terms of gender, age, and originating country) to give different interpretations of two women walking arm-in-arm and to reflect on the possible cultural meanings of this within the United States context as well as their 'home' contexts. Nelson contrasts a pedagogy of inquiry, which asks how linguistic and cultural practices naturalize certain sexual identities, most notably heterosexuality, with a pedagogy of inclusion which aims to introduce images as well as experiences of gays and lesbians into curriculum materials. Nelson's approach can fruitfully be applied to other issues of marginalization, helping learners to question normative practices in the 'target' culture into which they have entered.

Conclusion

The examples of practice that we have discussed draw on complex notions of what it means to respond critically to linguistic and cultural diversity in the language and literacy classroom. Foregrounding learner identity, and the intersections of race, gender, class, and sexual orientation, all the examples we have examined raise different challenges in attempts to create a discursive space conducive to open dialogue and learning, which are central to critical pedagogies. Such pedagogies reveal tensions in the oft competing interests of: responding sensitively to (cultural) difference while at the same time addressing issues of social inequality; attempting to give learners access to dominant or privileged ways of knowing and doing, while at the same time validating learners' own knowledge and lived experience; using multimodality to provide learners with creative opportunities for meaning making, while at the same time taking seriously logocentric assessment practices and limited professional development opportunities; bringing youth popular culture into the official curriculum without undermining it or learners' pleasures; and finally of teachers creating a discursive space that is supportive and non-threatening, while at the same time encouraging shifts in learners' perspectives. It is in the moment by moment unfolding of classroom practice that we can assess and negotiate our achievements and disappointments. Ultimately, responding to diversity in language and literacy education requires an imaginative assessment of what is possible, as well as a critical assessment of what is desirable. Recognizing the significance of learner and teacher identities in the language and literacy classroom is at the heart of this process.

NOTE

1   Such interest is evidenced in the special journal issues devoted to the topic of identity of *Linguistics and Education* edited by Martin-Jones and Heller (1996), *Language and Education*, edited by Sarangi and Baynham (1996), *TESOL Quarterly* edited by Norton (1997), and special topic issues of *TESOL Quarterly* on gender (2004, edited by Davis & Skilton-Sylvester) and race (2006, edited by Kubota & Lin) as well as several monographs on the topic (Day, 2002; Ivanič, 1998; Kanno, 2003; Miller, 2003; Norton, 2000; Toohey, 2000).

REFERENCES

Angelil-Carter, S. (1997). Second language acquisition of spoken and written English: Acquiring the skeptron. *TESOL Quarterly*, 31(2), 263–287.

Auerbach, E. & Wallerstein, N. (2004). *Problem-Posing at Work: English for Action* (revised edn.). Edmonton, Alberta: Grass Roots Press.

Bakhtin, M. (1981). *The Dialogic Imagination: Four Essays by M. M. Bakhtin*. Austin: University of Texas Press.

Bakhtin, M. (1984/1963). *Problems of Dostoevsky's Poetics*, trans. C. Emerson. Minneapolis: University of Minnesota Press.

Bhabha, H. K. (1994). *The Location of Culture*. London/New York: Routledge.

Bourdieu, P. (1984). *Distinction: A Social Critique of the Judgement of Taste*, trans. R. Nice. London: Routledge & Kegan Paul.

Bourdieu, P. (1997). The economics of linguistic exchanges. *Social Science Information*, 16(6), 645–668.

Bourdieu, P. & Passeron, J. (1977). *Reproduction in Education, Society, and Culture*. London/Beverly Hills, CA: Sage Publications.

Brito, I., Lima, A., & Auerbach, E. (2004). The logic of non-standard teaching: A course in Cape Verdean language, culture and history. In B. Norton & K. Toohey (eds.), *Critical Pedagogies and Language Learning* (pp. 181–200). Cambridge: Cambridge University Press.

Comber, B. & Simpson, A. (eds.) (2001). *Negotiating Critical Literacies in Classrooms*. Mahwah, NJ: Lawrence Erlbaum.

Davis, K. & Skilton-Sylvester, E. (2004). Gender in TESOL. Special issue of *TESOL Quarterly*, 3(3).

Day, E. M. (2002). *Identity and the Young English Language Learner*. Clevedon, UK: Multilingual Matters.

Ellsworth, E. (1989). Why doesn't this feel empowering? Working through the repressive myths of critical pedagogy. *Harvard Educational Review*, 59(3), 297–324.

Freire, P. (1970). *Pedagogy of the Oppressed*. London: Penguin.

Frye, D. (1999). Participatory education as a critical framework for an immigrant women's ESL class, *TESOL Quarterly*, 33(3), 501–513.

Fuss, D. (1989). *Essentially Speaking: Feminism, Nature and Difference*. New York/London: Routledge.

Hall, S. (1992a). The question of cultural identity. In S. Hall, D. Held, & T. McGrew (eds.), *Modernity and Its Futures* (pp. 272–325). Cambridge: Polity Press in association with Blackwell Publishers and The Open University.

Hall, S. (1992b). New ethnicities. In J. Donald & A. Rattansi (eds.), *"Race", Culture and Difference* (pp. 252–259). London: Sage.

Ibrahim, A. (1999). Becoming Black: Rap and hip-hop, race, gender, identity, and the politics of ESL learning. *TESOL Quarterly*, 33(3), 349–369.

Ivanič, R. (1998). *Writing and Identity: The Discoursal Construction of Identity in Academic Writing*. Amsterdam: John Benjamins.

Janks, H. (2000). Domination, access, diversity and design: a synthesis for critical literacy education. *Educational Review*, 52(2), 175–186.

Janks, H. (2002). Critical literacy: Beyond reason. *The Australian Educational Researcher*, 29(1), 7–26.

Kanno, Y. (2003). *Negotiating Bilingual and Bicultural Identities: Japanese Returnees betwixt Two Worlds*. Mahwah, NJ: Lawrence Erlbaum.

Kendrick, M., Jones, S., Mutonyi, H., & Norton, B. (in press). Multimodality and English education in Ugandan schools. In *English Studies in Africa*, 49(1).

Kress, G. (2000). Design and transformation: New theories of meaning. In B. Cope & M. Kalantzis (eds.). *Multiliteracies: Literacy Learning and the Design of Social Futures* (pp. 153–161). South Yarra: Macmillan Publishers Australia.

Kubota, R. (2004). Critical multiculturalism and second language education. In B. Norton & K. Toohey (eds.), *Critical Pedagogies and Language Learning* (pp. 30–52). Cambridge: Cambridge University Press.

Kubota, R. & Lin, A. (2006). Race and TESOL. Special issue of *TESOL Quarterly*, 40(3).

Lankshear, C. & McLaren, P. (eds.) (1993). *Critical Literacy: Politics, Praxis and the Postmodern*. New York: State University of New York Press.

Lillis, T. (2003). Student writing as "academic literacies": Drawing in Bakhtin to move from Critique to Design. *Language and Education*, 17(3), 192–207.

Luke, A. (1997). Critical approaches to literacy. In V. Edwards & D. Corson (eds.), *Encyclopedia of Language and Education, vol. 2: Literacy* (pp. 143–152). Dordrecht: Kluwer Academic.

Martin-Jones, M. & Heller, M. (1996). Introduction to the special issue on Education in multilingual settings: Discourse, identities, and power. *Linguistics and Education* 8, 3–16.

May, S. (1999). Critical multiculturalism and cultural difference: Avoiding essentialism. In S. May (ed.), *Critical Multiculturalism: Rethinking Multicultural and Antiracist Education* (pp. 11–14). London/Philadelphia: Falmer Press.

McKay, S. & Wong, S. C. (1996). Multiple discourses, multiple identities: Investment and agency in second language learning among Chinese adolescent immigrant students. *Harvard Educational Review*, 66(3), 577–608.

McKinney, C. (2004). "A little hard piece of grass in your shoe": Understanding student resistance to critical literacy in post-apartheid South Africa. *Southern African Linguistics and Applied Language Studies*, 22(1&2), 63–73.

McKinney, C. (2005). A balancing act: Ethical dilemmas of democratic teaching within critical pedagogy. *Educational Action Research*, 12(3), 375–391.

McKinney, C. & van Pletzen, E. (2004). "This apartheid story . . . we've decided it's gone we've finished with it": Student responses to "politics" in a South African English Studies course. *Teaching in Higher Education*, 9(2), 159–170.

Miller, J. (2003). *Audible Difference: ESL and Social Identity in Schools*. Clevedon, UK: Multilingual Matters.

Moffat, L. & Norton, B. (2005). Popular culture and the reading teacher: A case for feminist pedagogy. *Critical Inquiry in Language Studies*, 2(1), 1–12.

Morgan, B. & Ramanathan, V. (2005). Critical literacies and language education: Global and local perspectives. *Annual Review of Applied Linguistics*, 25, 151–169.

Mushengyezi, A. (2003). Rethinking indigenous media: Rituals, "talking" drums and orality as forms of public communication in Uganda. *Journal of African Cultural Studies*, 16, 107–128.

Nelson, C. (1999). Sexual identities in ESL: Queer theory and classroom inquiry. *TESOL Quarterly*, 33(3), 371–391.

New London Group (2000). A pedagogy of multiliteracies designing social futures. In B. Cope & M. Kalantzis (eds.), *Multiliteracies: Literacy Learning and the Design of Social Futures* (pp. 9–37). South Yarra: Macmillan Publishers Australia.

Norton, B. (ed.) (1997). Language and identity. Special issue of *TESOL Quarterly*, 31(3).

Norton, B. (2000). *Identity and Language Learning: Gender, Ethnicity and Educational Change*. Harlow, UK: Pearson Education.

Norton, B. & Pavlenko, A. (2004). *Gender and English Language Learners*. Alexandria, VA: TESOL International.

Norton, B. & Toohey, K. (eds.) (2004). *Critical Pedagogies and Language Learning*. Cambridge: Cambridge University Press.

Norton Peirce, B. (1995). Social identity, investment, and language learning. *TESOL Quarterly*, 29(1), 9–31.

O'Brien, J. (2001). Children reading critically: A local history. In B. Comber & A. Simpson (eds.), *Negotiating Critical Literacies in Classrooms* (pp. 37–54). Mahwah, NJ: Lawrence Erlbaum.

Pittaway, D. (2004). Investment and second language acquisition. *Critical Inquiry in Language Studies*, 4(1), 203–218.

Potowski, K. (2004). Student Spanish use and investment in a dual immersion classroom: Implications for second language acquisition and heritage language maintenance. *The Modern Language Journal*, 88(1), 75–101.

Sahni, U. (2001). Children appropriating literacy: Empowerment pedagogy from young children's perspective. In B. Comber & A. Simpson (eds.), *Negotiating Critical Literacies in Classrooms* (pp. 19–35). Mahwah, NJ: Lawrence Erlbaum.

Sarangi, S. & Baynham, M. (1996). Special issue of *Language and Education*, 10(2&3).

Skilton-Sylvester, E. (2002). Should I stay or should I go? Investigating Cambodian women's participation and investment in adult ESL programs. *Adult Education Quarterly*, 53(1), 9–26.

Stein, P. (2001). Classrooms as sites of textual, cultural, and linguistic reappropriation. In B. Comber & A. Simpson (eds.), *Negotiating Critical Literacies in Classrooms* (pp. 151–169). Mahwah, NJ: Lawrence Erlbaum.

Stein, P. (2004). Representation, rights and resources: Multimodal pedagogies in the language and literacy classroom (pp. 95–115). In B. Norton & K. Toohey (eds.), *Critical Pedagogies and Language Learning*. Cambridge: Cambridge University Press.

Thesen, L. (1997). Voices, discourse, and transition: In search of new categories in EAP. *TESOL Quarterly*, 31(3), 487–512.

Toohey, K. (2000). *Learning English at School: Identity, Social Relations and Classroom Practice*. Clevedon, UK: Multilingual Matters.

Vasquez, V. (2004). *Negotiating Critical Literacies with Young Children*. Mahwah, NJ: Lawrence Erlbaum.

Wallace, C. (2003). *Critical Reading in Language Education*. Basingstoke: Palgrave Macmillan.

Weedon, C. (1997). *Feminist Practice and Poststructuralist Theory* (2nd edn.). Oxford: Blackwell. (1st edn. 1987.)

Weiler, K. (1991). Freire and a feminist pedagogy of difference. *Harvard Educational Review*, 61(4), 449–474.

Yon, D. A. (1999). Interview with Stuart Hall, London, England, August 1998. *Journal of Curriculum Theorising*, 15(4), 89–99.

15 Post-colonialism and Globalization in Language Education

HYUNJUNG SHIN AND RYUKO KUBOTA

Introduction

This chapter presents an overview of current discussions in language education around two important topics: post-colonialism and globalization. Supporting the view that inquiry into post-colonialism goes far beyond an analysis of the historical moment after colonialism (see Loomba, 1998), we locate post-colonialism in a past, present, and future trajectory of economic, political, and cultural processes that have produced, resisted, and transformed the relations between the colonizer and the colonized or the Self and the Other. These relations reflect a hierarchy of hegemonic power which has been persistent and yet complex, relational, and shifting. In this trajectory, globalization overlaps the neocolonial process of economic and political domination of the empire, homogenizing linguistic and cultural standards on the one hand, while heterogenizing expressions of hybrid identities on the other. Clearly, language education is embedded in sociopolitical and economic relations of power and hence plays a key role in the construction as well as transformation of inequality between the privileged and the underprivileged.

Given the current overwhelming power of English worldwide, we take the area of English language education as our focal case, although we recognize the effects of other colonial languages (e.g., Spanish, French, Portuguese, Arabic, Mandarin Chinese, and Japanese) on education and have attempted to address such issues whenever possible. In English language education, post-colonialism and globalization address questions such as how language, culture, and identity become standardized, homogenized, and imposed, while at the same time diversified, transformed, and appropriated. They also pose a question of how the cultural and linguistic images of the Self and the Other are constructed and resisted. Within the field of second language education, these topics have been discussed in the critical frameworks of the global spread of English, linguistic imperialism of English, linguistic and cultural Othering, World Englishes (WEs), advocacy of non-native speakers (NNSs) of English as English teaching professionals, adopting local languages as media of instruction, the reclamation of local knowledge, and postmethod pedagogies. Although all of these inquiries demonstrate a critical edge, there are some significant tensions and disagreements within each inquiry. This chapter synthesizes these arguments in relation to different post-colonial contestations or developments in the face of the perpetual (neo)colonial dominance of English in the current context of globalization, critically examines the strengths and limitations of these different approaches, and discusses their implications for language education in the post-colonial and globalized world. We begin with a brief overview of post-colonialism and globalization.

The Post-colonialism and Globalization Continuum: A Brief Overview

Despite their wide circulation and popularity, the notions of post-colonialism and globalization are much contested. Although presenting all differing theories of these topics is beyond the scope of this chapter, we attempt to provide a brief discussion of the relationship between the two notions in order to lay out a conceptual background for our subsequent discussions on language education.

As an intellectual movement found in such fields as literature and cultural studies, post-colonialism has created a space for resisting and writing back to the colonial domination of power, reclaiming the voices of the colonized people of color and women and revealing how colonial power has been exercised through constructing the exotic Other and making the colonized desire to speak the colonizer's language (e.g., Fanon, 1967; Said, 1979; Spivak, 1988). Central to post-colonial projects are critiquing and transforming discourses. For instance, Edward Said's pioneering work on *Orientalism* critiques the colonial discourse that has shaped knowledge and social practices in the cultural, economic, and political spheres. As Said (1979) argues, to exert power over the colonized, the colonizer has produced an essentialized knowledge of the colonized subjects as uncivilized and inferior. Although such knowledge is merely the colonizer's *representation* of the colonial subjects, it is constructed and circulated by colonial discourse as reality (see also Loomba, 1998). Resisting the colonial discourse, post-colonial writers and thinkers have created an alternative discursive space that places their histories and subjectivities at the center stage. This process involves the liberation and legitimation of subjugated voices which are reflected in language policies in education in many post-colonial societies as well as in such inquiry topics as WEs.

One misleading image of post-colonialism stems from the prefix "post," as it may imply that colonialism is over (Smith, 1999). However, effects of (neo)colonial domination and subordination persist in today's world and the post-colonial celebration of local identities often works to divert attention to the hegemony of the neocolonial empire that perpetuates unequal relations of power (Shohat, 1992; Tupas, 2004). In many post-colonial societies, the history of development and modernization has been intertwined with that of (neo)colonialism (Nkrumah, 1966). In Africa, for instance, the continuous use of the colonial language in education is closely related to the business interest of large textbook producers in France and Britain (Alidou, 2004). Under the new world order of contemporary society, the manifestations of colonialism are often disguised in the name of globalization (Smith, 1999). Furthermore, in the contemporary global politics, post-colonial subjects from the margins of the world are increasingly "being incorporated within the world's marketplace" (1999: 24). This trend requires a critical understanding of how people placed in subordinate status are continually being colonized in the contemporary world. As represented by urban ghettos in wealthy Western countries and opulent metropolises in some of what has been typically considered as the Third World, global capital renders the distinction between the colonizer and the colonized increasingly problematic (Macedo, 1999). This indicates the ubiquity of the relationship between the colonizer and the colonized in the new world system of globalization.

Conventional approaches to globalization tend to highlight global domination derived from neocolonial and neoliberal capitalism, often presenting a pessimistic representation of the world of economic and cultural homogenization such as McDonaldization. On the other hand, scholars who pay attention to the cultural dimensions of globalization (e.g., Appadurai, 1996) seek to explore how globalization is not just homogenizing, but also localizing, diversifying, and transforming societies, identities, and cultures. Indeed, globalization is not only an economic process but also about the movement of people, cultural and political processes facilitated by the global spread of ideas and information through the media, and technological advancement that connects many corners of the world (cf. the five "scapes" proposed by Appadurai, 1996). It is important to note, however, that such movements and flows are constrained by social organizations of power, notably by social categories such as race, gender, class, and ethnicity. Emerging scholarship on globalization with respect to social movements attempts to undo the binary of the global and the local and explores how the global is in fact *constructed* and thus open to contestation (Bergeron, 2001) and how the local is not merely the effects produced by but is *constitutive* of the global (Freeman, 2001).

It is clear from this brief overview that both post-colonialism and globalization are intricately connected. Language education is a particularly interesting site to examine this complex relationship, because it is manifested in the celebration of diversity, hybridity, and the reclamation of language and identity on the one hand and the persistence of colonial domination on the other.

Globalization, (Neo)Colonialism, and Language Education

In language education, globalization has stimulated scholarly inquiries into the relationship between language, nation-states, and identities (Harris, Leung, & Rampton, 2002); medium, genre, and style of communication (Cameron, 2002; Kramsch & Thorne, 2002); second/foreign language education policies (Kubota, 2002); and new ideologies of language as a commodity in the new global economy (Heller, 2003; for further discussion of globalization and English language education, see Block & Cameron, 2002; see also Block, 2006; Kumaravadivelu, 2006). Issues regarding globalization and post-colonial conditions in language education are closely related to the global hegemony of English given the status of English as a representative colonial and global language.

Global spread of English, linguistic imperialism, and discourses of colonialism

Crystal (2003) is representative of popular, celebratory accounts of the global spread of English. He argues that although English was a colonial language in the past, it is now a neutral and useful tool for anyone who wishes to use it for global travel and communication. According to Crystal, English happens to be "in the right place at the right time" (p. 120) to become an international language; other languages and cultures can thus be easily maintained along with English to keep the identities of the local people. In contrast, Phillipson's (1992) work on linguistic imperialism links the global dominance of English to the structural inequalities between the hegemonic Western (center) countries and less-developed countries in the periphery, highlighting the neocolonial economic exploitations in the contemporary world. From this perspective, the expansion of English, extended from Great Britain's colonial rule in Asia and Africa, is not accidental, but closely intertwined with both material/institutional structures such as the British Council and the ideological construction of English as a superior language. With respect to the implications for language policy and planning, this framework is connected with linguistic human rights (e.g., Skutnabb-Kangas, 2000) and language ecology (e.g., Mühlhäusler, 1996) which seek to preserve the ecology of language against English (or other killer colonial languages) through advocating the use of languages other than English as media of instruction in multilingual settings. Although preservation of minority languages and protection of linguistic human rights are vital to many post-colonial societies, arguments based on biomorphic metaphors tend to treat language as a natural static object, neglecting the dialectics of language form and human agency (Pennycook, 2004).

While Crystal's celebratory accounts of the global spread of English have been challenged because they overlook the structural conditions of the spread and thus naturalize the hegemony of English solely in relation to the globalization of economy and communication, Phillipson's political economic analysis has been criticized for its binary representation of global relations simply as center versus periphery, and for its disregard of the agency of colonized people. For example, Canagarajah (1999a) illustrates the complex ways in which post-colonial subjects take up, appropriate, and resist the hegemony of English (see also Lin & Luke, 2006).

Pennycook's (1994, 1998) cultural and historical analysis of the global spread of English is noteworthy in that it highlights the effects of the colonial *discourses* on English language education, particularly the perpetuating effects of the colonial constructions of the cultural images of superior Self and inferior Other on theories, beliefs, and practices in language education. One important consequence of such discourses in language education is the construction of the standard variety of a language (e.g., standard North American and British varieties of English) as the only legitimate medium of instruction and its speakers (so-called native speakers: NSs) as legitimate teachers of the language. Furthermore, with the discourse of globalization, (using) English is often constructed as the symbol of the global status of nation-states, as represented in the establishment of the Seoul English Village, an English immersion camp in South Korea (see Shin, 2006). Colonial storylines of Christian missionaries traveling to Africa and Asia to cultivate or civilize the Other are reproduced in the stories of NS language professionals with *global* knowledge flying to Asian/African schools to invigorate the *ineffective* educational practices in the local context. The idealized construction of the images of the Self in colonial discourses is accompanied by denigrations of other languages, cultures, and people in language education, or Othering, which we will discuss in the next section.

Othering in language education

> Why is it that Japan has 300 exams or more? These exams are being made by people who don't know what they're doing, who say they don't know what they're doing. . . . They are preparing tests that are haphazard and of unknown reliability and validity. The sad thing is that these tests are then used to make very, very important decisions about peoples' lives. All of this wouldn't bother me so much if the people making the tests were looking at them in an effort to improve. (Brown, 1998, p. 26)

Colonial constructions of the images of language and culture of the colonial subjects marked by essentialized otherness (Said, 1979) persist in language education. Kubota's analysis of the discursive construction of Japanese culture (Kubota, 1999) and the cultural images of (East-) Asian classrooms and US classrooms in language education (Kubota, 2001) provides insight into how such essentialized representations of the Other are often accompanied by constructions of the idealized images of the Self. In the North American context, colonial discourses construct ESL (English as a second language) as a pathological, stigmatizing, and racialized category (see, e.g., Goldstein, 2003), which, in turn, is materialized in curriculum and teaching practices in ESL classrooms (see, e.g., Tollefson, 1991, for a discussion of how teaching of so-called survival English is related to social reproduction in ESL classes for refugees in the United States). Rather paradoxically, recognition and affirmation of linguistic and cultural differences promoted in language education often unwittingly construct essentialized representations of the Other (Harklau, 2000; Kubota, 2001; see, e.g., Talmy, 2004, for an ethnographic analysis of such Othering observed in ESL classrooms).

No doubt most of these teachers and researchers who try to provide an account of students' cultural background are well-meaning and our analyses in no way imply that those teachers and researchers intend to essentialize the language and culture of their students. It is also important to note that not all essentialized representations of the language and culture of the Other are negative. Furthermore, the Other may use *strategic essentialism* as a means of resistance (Spivak, 1993). Yet, even well-meaning stereotypes are often used to highlight the differences of the Other and hence emphasize the superiority of the Self (Kubota, 2001). For example, some ESL practitioners of color with excellent English proficiency or NSs of color constantly receive compliments for their good English ability. Furthermore, such accounts of the language and culture of the Other are often endorsed by the Other, as represented in the case of the Japanese testing professionals in Brown's comments "who say they don't know what they're doing" (see also Kumaravadivelu, 2003 for the notion of self-marginalization and Fanon, 1967 for the colonial subject's self-condemnation). At the same time, however, resistance has emerged to challenge such colonial constructions of Self and Other, in relation to post-colonial appropriation of the colonizer's language to *write back*.

Post-colonial Appropriation and Resistance in Language Education

With the rise of post-colonial celebration of hybridity and local identities, the use of different varieties of English and the multiple identities of language teachers and students have begun to be recognized in language education. This section provides an overview of post-colonial reclamation of local languages, identities, and knowledge observed in language education. These projects attempt to go beyond the deterministic analysis of or opposition to the global dominance of English (or other colonial languages). They also challenge the fixed identity categories imposed by colonialism and instead emphasize hybridity and appropriate the language of the colonizer to rewrite colonialism from post-colonial perspectives.

Research on WEs and advocacy of NNSs

A post-colonial turn in the study of language and language teaching can be observed in the research on WEs and the advocacy of NNS teachers of English. Although these two inquiry areas, especially the latter, do not explicitly draw on post-colonialism as a theoretical framework, they signify post-colonial recognition of pluralism and local diversity, while problematizing the normative view of language that privileges the standard variety and NSs of the language.

Research on WEs has emerged out of the post-colonial recognition of linguistic diversity (B. Kachru, 1992; see also Brutt-Griffler, 2002). Advocating the legitimacy of new varieties of English in post-colonial contexts, WEs highlight linguistic diversity, hybridity, and diaspora as a result of the global spread of English, and attempt to reclaim the ownership of English. Research has been focused on the linguistic features of different varieties, language use in sociocultural and multilingual contexts, intelligibility among the varieties, attitudes toward different varieties, and implications for education (Y. Kachru, 2004). However, highlighting the validity of new varieties of English through their systematicity and creativity in their linguistic form, studies on WEs tend to overlook social power relations which perpetuate the unequal relationships between different varieties of English and run the risk of sliding into apolitical celebration of diversity and hybridity (for a critique of the WEs paradigm, see, e.g., Canagarajah, 1999b; and Pennycook, 1994). Although inquiries into WEs have challenged the colonial construction of US/British English as the only legitimate variety of English in education and other social settings, the increasing value of English as an international lingua franca in the global market constitutes great challenges to such resistance. Nonetheless, research on WEs has contributed to raising awareness of the myth of NSs as ideal language teachers and validating identities of NNS teachers of English who are often speakers of local varieties of English (Y. Kachru, 2004).

During the last decade, research on the topic of NNS teachers of English has made inroads in the field of second language education (see, e.g., Braine, 1999; Kamhi-Stein, 2004). These studies contest the construction of the NNSs as perpetual Other, who are continually striving to reach a practically unattainable linguistic standard. Problematizing the myth of NS as an ideal language teacher and the unequal access to job opportunities between NSs and NNSs, most of these studies attempt to identify the advantages and contributions of NNS teachers as bilinguals who share a mother tongue and their culture with the students, as role-models, and as privileged mediators in contact zones (see, e.g., Kramsch, 1997). Despite the contributions of these studies to hybridizing the identities of language teachers, areas of further investigation remain.

First, the emphasis on the advantages of being NNS teachers in these studies, however well intended, paradoxically further highlights their differences and contributes to constructing NNS teachers as *lacking*. Second, excessive focus on the linguistic and pedagogic aspect of the dichotomy has led to disregarding how the NS/NNS construct is intertwined with other social categories such as race and ethnicity. Third, the formation of NNSs as colonial subjects has not yet been investigated in historical contexts. Therefore, complexities within the categories of NS and NNS remain under-researched. Recent works on this topic, however, start to draw attention to the complex ways in which the NS/ NNS construct interacts with social categories such as race, gender, ethnicity, and class (see, e.g., Lin et al., 2004).

To sum up, given the persisting colonial relations in language education, validating local varieties of English and identities of language teachers who speak local varieties of English in language classrooms poses complex questions. Similarly, the increased amount of economic and cultural capital attached to English as the global lingua franca under neocolonial conditions significantly undermines post-colonial efforts to adopt the local language as the medium of instruction.

Adopting local languages as media of instruction

Post-colonial societies have taken different paths in determining the medium of instruction in educational institutions. While some societies have continued to use the former colonial language as the main medium with some bilingual instruction (e.g., Singapore, Philippines, many African countries), others have adopted a local language at least for primary education (see Tollefson & Tsui, 2004; Lin & Martin, 2005). Examples of the latter include Bahasa Melayu in Malaysia; Kiswahili in Tanzania, Kenya, and Uganda; Arabic in Morocco, Tunisia, and Algeria; Quichua in Ecuador; Quechua in Bolivia; Mäori in Aotearoa/New Zealand; and Welsh in Wales. This decolonization project signifies the affirmation of post-colonial identity and minority language rights. While there are successful minority language education initiatives, the majority face significant challenges.

One major challenge seems to have two interconnected aspects: (1) the persisting hegemony of the colonial language which has continued to privilege elites and (2) the force of globalization which has elevated the perceived importance of the colonial language, especially English. In countries such as India, Malaysia, and South Africa, the language of the empire has continued to carry cultural, economic, and symbolic capital even after decolonization. Despite the post-colonial policy to use local languages in schools and universities, institutions that provide English-medium instruction continue to produce political, economic, and academic elites, maintaining the divide between the rich and the poor. This tendency has perpetuated inequalities between bilingual elites and monolingual citizens in the local language (e.g., Wolof and French in Senegal, Johnson, 2004). One obstacle to raising the status of local languages is the limitation of linguistic capacity coupled with lack of instructional materials necessary to teach science, technology, and commerce, the fields closely linked to high-income jobs. This limitation is becoming pronounced in the neoliberal global economy. There is a growing perception that the former colonial language, especially if it is English, is the key to the economic competitiveness of the nation-state and to educational and economic opportunities for students in the global market. Malaysia, for instance, recently decided to shift the medium of instruction from Bahasa Melayu to English (Gill, 2005). In Morocco, where Arabization has been a national policy to establish Arab-Islamic identity, an option was recently created to teach science and technology in French or English. There is a general perception among students that French is more useful than Standard Modern Arabic for employment and English is more useful than French in the world (Marley, 2004).

This brief survey alone indicates a complex tension observed in the post-colonial language policies in education. A policy that has divorced the medium of instruction from the colonial language has enabled minority students to receive education in their mother tongue in some parts of the world, while in others it has served as social control by enhancing national unity and religious fundamentalism. Furthermore, the lasting hegemony of the colonial language has continued to privilege elites and the recent wave of globalization has swung the pendulum of emphasis back to the language of the empire as the medium of instruction. Despite such challenges, movements around appropriating the colonizer's language to reclaim the subordinated identity and language provide insights into the larger post-colonial project of validating local knowledge, or ways of knowing the colonial subjects.

Local knowledge and postmethod pedagogies

In globalization and (neo)colonial discourses, knowledge from the local is often particularized or culturalized (Canagarajah, 2005), while Western knowledge is often universalized. Hence, even in the claimed post-colonial world of hybridity, we tend to see a one-way flow of knowledge from the West to language classrooms in less developed countries through textbooks, theories, and teaching practices. Recent movements to reclaim local knowledge in language education (e.g., Canagarajah, 2005) take the position of *globalization from below* (see Appadurai, 2000) and attempt to pluralize the norms by legitimating local knowledge, identities, codes, and teaching practices from the perspective of the local communities. This approach is linked to a post-colonial project of postmethod pedagogies (Kumaravadivelu, 2003), a bottom-up pedagogical process situated in the local, initiated by local language teaching professionals based on their own knowledge. Kumaravadivelu (2003) conceives of current English language teaching methods as a discursively constructed colonial concept to legitimate the superiority of the Self over the Other, and proposes the concept of postmethod which signifies "a search for an alternative to method rather than an alternative method" (p. 544).

From such perspectives, the relationship between the global and the local is conceptualized in more egalitarian terms. Therefore, local language classrooms are not simply data-producing sites to support language learning theories produced in the Western academic institutions, but are equally valid spaces in developing situated language educational theories and practices. Given the global reality of ubiquitous and persisting colonial domination, however, the question of how these post-colonial contestations will gain legitimacy remains debatable. Therefore, another important post-colonial project in language education is continual problematization of post-colonial critical practices, being aware of the limitations of such contestations themselves. Ongoing critical reflection is much needed for language educators and researchers who seek to challenge the continuing colonial legacy in language classrooms in the era of globalization.

Conclusion

This chapter has discussed how language education is implicated in the discourses of colonialism and globalization in post-colonial societies and how such discourses continually legitimate constructions of Self and Other, create norms and differences, and define legitimate languages, teachers, and ways of knowing and teaching in language education. This colonial categorization process inherently privileges some while marginalizing others; thereby it contributes to the construction of social inequality. The increasing heterogeneity of the contemporary world, however, poses challenges to such colonial categorizations. The discussion also included how such constructions have been contested, appropriated, and transformed in the post-colonial and global context.

How might one envision and practice a more linguistically and culturally responsive education in the post-colonial and globalized schools of today? First, we need to work with a renewed view of language as social practice for enabling alternative expressions of post-colonial identities. Although traditional notions of language as abstract rule systems have been and still are useful to explain some aspects of language learning and teaching, they are not the most useful ones to explain the role of language and education in the construction and contestation of social inequality. For example, debates around bilingual education in the US are closely related to the social position of Spanish language speakers in the society rather than to the linguistic system of the language (see Cummins, 2000). In the increasingly heterogeneous world of globalization, it is more useful to conceptualize language use as fluid and productive, rather than constrained by rigid linguistic rules (see, for example, Pennycook, 2001, for the notion of post-colonial performativity). As illustrated in Pennycook's (2003) analysis of the language of global hip-hop used by Japanese rappers, such renewed notion of language provides insights into how global circulation of linguistic resources has created new identity options performed through language. Furthermore, from this perspective, it is more meaningful to view language learning as a process of building a linguistic repertoire (see Gumperz, 1982; Heller, 1995), rather than of acquisition of target forms, and to pay attention to how students draw on different kinds of linguistic resources available to them to move between multiple communities where they belong in the current global context (see also Canagarajah, 2005).

Next, language education can benefit from an enhanced understanding of the dialectic between the global and the local in understanding the role of language in the colonial constructions and post-colonial contestations of social inequality. For example, Park's (2004) discourse analytical approach to the ideologies of English in South Korea illustrates how the hegemony of English is not just imposed, but is in fact constructed through discourse by Koreans themselves. Local linguistic practices are thus constitutive of the global dominance of the colonial language(s). That is, the hegemony of the colonial language(s) is not a given, but is *constructed* and therefore can be challenged. This leads to the next point of identifying and particularizing the colonial norm. As Said (1979) points out, "the answer to Orientalism is not Occidentalism" (p. 328). A way to challenge and pluralize the colonial norm is to particularize the norm, not by Occidentalism, but by *provincializing Europe* (Chakrabarty, 2000). More empirical investigations to particularize the Western (Anglocentric) norm embedded in many language education theories and practices will be useful to explore how the norm is constructed and can thus be challenged. For example, although English-medium instruction in multilingual schools is often unchallenged as pedagogical norm, such school language policy entails a contradiction: It is often legitimated as a sound pedagogical choice to improve students' school performances although there is enough research evidence to support the effectiveness of mother tongue instructions for students' academic success (Cummins, 2001). While the current discussion has focused mainly on English, due to our own expertise and the global reality of English as the language of power, further studies on the impact of colonial languages other than English on education can shed light on this discussion.

The hegemony of colonial languages continues in our post-colonial classrooms. Colonialism is not finished in language education. Neither is decolonization.

REFERENCES

Alidou, H. (2004). Medium of instruction in post-colonial Africa. In J. W. Tollefson & A. B. M. Tsui (eds.), *Medium of Instruction Policies: Which Agenda? Whose Agenda?* (pp. 195–214). Mahwah, NJ: Lawrence Erlbaum.

Appadurai, A. (1996). *Modernity at Large: Cultural Dimensions of Globalization*. Minneapolis: University of Minnesota Press.

Appadurai, A. (2000). Grassroots globalization and the research imagination. *Public Culture*, 12(1), 1–19.

Bergeron, S. (2001). Political economy discourse of globalization and feminist politics. *Signs*, 26(4), 983–1006.

Block, D. (2006). *Multilingual Identities in a Global City: London Stories*. Basingstoke, UK: Palgrave.

Block, D. & Cameron, D. (eds.) (2002). *Globalization and Language Teaching*. London: Routledge.

Braine, G. (ed.) (1999). *Non-Native Educators in English Language Education*. Mahwah, NJ: Lawrence Erlbaum.

Brown, J. D. (1998). Interview with J. D. Brown. *The Language Teacher*, 22(3), 26.

Brutt-Griffler, J. (2002). *World English: A Study of its Development*. Clevedon, UK: Multilingual Matters.

Cameron, D. (2002). Globalization and the teaching of "communication skills." In D. Block & D. Cameron (eds.), *Globalization and Language Teaching* (pp. 67–82). London: Routledge.

Canagarajah, A. S. (1999a). *Resisting Linguistic Imperialism in English Teaching*. Oxford: Oxford University Press.

Canagarajah, A. S. (1999b). On EFL teachers, awareness, and agency. *ELT Journal*, 53, 207–214.

Canagarajah, A. S. (ed.) (2005). *Reclaiming the Local in Language Policy and Practice*. Mahwah, NJ: Lawrence Erlbaum.

Chakrabarty, D. (2000). *Provincializing Europe: Postcolonial Thought and Historical Difference*. Princeton, NJ: Princeton University Press.

Crystal, D. (2003). *English as a Global Language* (2nd edn.). Cambridge: Cambridge University Press.

Cummins, J. (2000). *Language, Power and Pedagogy: Bilingual Children in the Crossfire*. Clevedon, UK: Multilingual Matters.

Cummins, J. (2001). *Negotiating Identities: Education for Empowerment in a Diverse Society* (2nd edn.). Los Angeles: California Association For Bilingual Education.

Fanon, F. (1967). *Black Skin White Masks*. New York: Grove Weidenfeld.

Freeman, C. (2001). Is local: global as feminine: masculine? Rethinking the gender of globalization. *Signs*, 26(4), 1007–1037.

Gill, S. K. (2005). Language policy in Malaysia: Reversing direction. *Language Policy*, 4, 241–260.

Goldstein, T. (2003). *Teaching and Learning in a Multilingual School: Choices, Risks and Dilemmas*. Mahwah, NJ: Lawrence Erlbaum.

Gumperz, J. J. (1982). *Discourse Strategies*. Cambridge: Cambridge University Press.

Harklau, L. (2000). From the "Good kids" to the "Worst": Representations of English language learners across educational settings. *TESOL Quarterly*, 34(1), 35–67.

Harris, R., Leung, C., & Rampton, B. (2002). Globalization, diaspora and language education in England. In D. Block & D. Cameron (eds.), *Globalization and Language Teaching* (pp. 29–46). London: Routledge.

Heller, M. (1995). Code-switching and the politics of language. In L. Milroy & P. Muysken (eds.), *One Speaker, Two Languages: Cross-disciplinary Perspectives on Code-switching* (pp. 158–174). New York: Cambridge University Press.

Heller, M. (2003). Globalization, the new economy, and the commodification of language and identity. *Journal of Sociolinguistics*, 7(4), 473–492.

Johnson, N. K. (2004). Senegalese "into Frenchmen"? The French technology of nationalism in Senegal. *Nationalism and Ethnic Politics*, 10, 135–158.

Kachru, B. B. (ed.) (1992). *The Other Tongue: English Across Cultures* (2nd end.). Urbana, IL: University of Illinois Press.

Kachru, Y. (2004). Teaching and learning of World Englishes. In E. Hinkel (ed.), *Handbook of Research in Second Language Teaching and Learning* (pp. 155–173). Mahwah, NJ: Lawrence Erlbaum.

Kamhi-Stein, L. D. (ed.) (2004). *Learning and Teaching from Experience: Perspectives on Nonnative English-Speaking Professionals*. Ann Arbor, MI: University of Michigan Press.

Kramsch, C. (1997). The privilege of the nonnative speaker. *PMLA*, 112(3), 359–369.

Kramsch, C. & Thorne, S. L. (2002). Foreign language learning as global communicative practice. In D. Block & D. Cameron (eds.), *Globalization and Language Teaching* (pp. 83–100). London: Routledge.

Kubota, R. (1999). Japanese culture constructed by discourses: Implications for applied linguistics research and ELT. *TESOL Quarterly*, 33, 9–35.

Kubota, R. (2001). Discursive construction of the images of U.S. Classrooms. *TESOL Quarterly*, 35, 9–38.

Kubota, R. (2002). The impact of globalization on language teaching in Japan. In D. Block & D. Cameron (eds.), *Globalization and Language Teaching* (pp. 13–28). London: Routledge.

Kumaravadivelu, B. (2003). Critical language pedagogy: A postmethod perspective on English language teaching. *World Englishes*, 22(4), 539–550.

Kumaravadivelu, B. (2006). Dangerous liaison: Globalization, empire and TESOL. In J. Edge (ed.), *(Re)Locating TESOL in an Age of Empire* (pp. 1–26). Basingstoke, UK: Palgrave.

Lin, A. & Luke, A. (eds.) (2006). Postcolonial approaches to TESOL. Special issue of *Critical Inquiry in Language Studies*, 3(2/3).

Lin, A. & Martin, P. W. (eds.) (2005). *Decolonisation, Globalisation: Language-in-Education Policy and Practice*. Clevedon, UK: Multilingual Matters.

Lin, A., Grant, R., Kubota, R., Motha, S., Sachs, G. T., & Vandrick, S. (2004). Women faculty of color in TESOL: Theorizing our lived experiences. *TESOL Quarterly*, 38, 487–504.

Loomba, A. (1998). *Colonialism/Postcolonialism*. London: Routledge.

Macedo, D. (1999). Decolonizing indigenous knowledge. In L. M. Semali & J. L. Kincheloe (eds.), *What is Indigenous Knowledge? Voices from the Academy* (pp. xi–xvi). New York: Falmer Press.

Marley, D. (2004). Language attitudes in Morocco following recent changes in language policy. *Language Policy*, 3, 25–46.

Mühlhäusler, P. (1996). *Linguistic Ecology: Language Change and Linguistic Imperialism in the Pacific Region*. London: Routledge.

Nkrumah, K. (1966). *Neocolonialism: The Last Stage of Imperialism*. New York: International Publishers.

Park, J. S-Y. (2004). Globalization, Language, and Social Order: Ideologies of English in South Korea. Unpublished PhD dissertation, University of California, Santa Barbara.

Pennycook, A. (1994). *The Cultural Politics of English as an International Language*. London: Longman.

Pennycook, A. (1998). *English and the Discourses of Colonialism*. London: Routledge.

Pennycook, A. (2001). *Critical Applied Linguistics: A Critical Introduction*. Mahwah, NJ: Lawrence Erlbaum.

Pennycook, A. (2003). Global Englishes, Rip Slyme, and performativity. *Journal of Sociolinguistics*, 7(4), 513–533.

Pennycook, A. (2004). Language policy and the ecological turn. *Language Policy*, 3, 213–239.

Phillipson, R. (1992). *Linguistic Imperialism*. Oxford: Oxford University Press.

Said, E. (1979). *Orientalism*. New York: Vintage Books.

Shin, H. (2006). Rethinking TESOL from a SOL's perspective: Indigenous epistemology and decolonizing praxis in TESOL. *Critical Inquiry in Language Studies*, 3(2/3), 147–167.

Shohat, E. (1992). Notes on the "post-colonial." *Social Text*, 10, 99–113.

Skutnabb-Kangas, T. (2000). *Linguistic Genocide in Education – or Worldwide Diversity and Human Rights?* Mahwah, NJ: Lawrence Erlbaum.

Smith, L. T. (1999). *Decolonizing Methodologies: Research and Indigenous Peoples*. London: Zed.

Spivak, G. C. (1988). Can the subaltern speak? In C. Nelson & L. Grossberg (eds.), *Marxism and the Interpretation of Culture* (pp. 271–313). Basingstoke, UK: Macmillan Education.

Spivak, G. C. (1993). *Outside in the Teaching Machine*. New York: Routledge.

Talmy, S. (2004). Forever FOB: The cultural production of ESL in a high school. *Pragmatics*, 14(2/3), 149–172.

Tollefson, J. (1991). *Planning Language, Planning Inequality: Language Policy in the Community*. London: Longman.

Tollefson, J. W. & Tsui, A. B. M. (eds.) (2004). *Medium of Instruction Policies: Which Agenda? Whose Agenda?* Mahwah, NJ: Lawrence Erlbaum.

Tupas, T. R. F. (2004). The politics of Philippine English: Neocolonialism, global politics, and the problem of postcolonialism. *World Englishes*, 23, 47–58.

FURTHER READING

Appadurai, A. (ed.) (2001). *Globalization*. Durham, NC/London: Duke University Press.

Bigelow, B. & Peterson, B. (eds.) (2002). *Rethinking Globalization: Teaching for Justice in an Unjust World*. Milwaukee, WI: Rethinking Schools Press.

Coupland, N. (ed.) (2003). Sociolinguistics and globalization. Special issue of *Journal of Sociolinguistics*, 7(4).

Edge, J. (ed.) (2006). *(Re)Locating TESOL in an Age of Empire*. Basingstoke, UK: Palgrave.

Moore-Gilbert, B., Stanton, G., & Maley, W. (eds.) (1997). *Postcolonial Criticism*. London: Longman.

16   Levels and Goals:
   Central Frameworks
   and Local Strategies

BRIAN NORTH

Validity in Context

Since the beginning of the 1990s several national and international frameworks have appeared that seek to provide a common set of levels or reference points that can serve as standards. Perhaps the best known of these is the *Common European Framework of Reference for Languages: Learning, Teaching, Assessment* (CEFR), developed between 1993 and 1996, piloted with internal editions in 1996 and 1997, published officially in 2001 (Council of Europe, 2001), and currently available in 31 languages. This chapter explores the relationship between a central framework and local strategies with reference to the CEFR.

The CEFR aimed to establish a metalanguage common across educational sectors and national and linguistic boundaries that could be used to talk about objectives and language levels. The main ideas were (1) to encourage practitioners in the language field to reflect on their current practice, particularly in relation to learners' practical language learning needs, the setting of suitable objectives and the tracking of learner progress; and (2) to agree common reference points based on the work on objectives that had taken place in the Council of Europe's Modern Languages projects since the 1970s. The approach taken was to provide a conceptual framework made up of:

- a taxonomic *descriptive scheme*, covering such issues as domains of language use, communicative language activities and strategies, plus the competences of the learner/user;
- a set of *common reference levels*, defining proficiency in as many of these categories as possible at six levels (A1, A2, B1, B2, C1, C2) in empirically developed scales of illustrative descriptors (North, 2000a; North & Schneider, 1998).

In time, the existence of such a common reference framework would, it was hoped, help to relate courses and examinations to each other. The CEFR was not seen as a harmonization project. The aim was to provide a tool that would enable people to say where they were, not a specification telling them where they ought to be. It was intended as a compendium or thesaurus, not as a cookbook. Right at the very beginning, the authors emphasized:

> "We have NOT set out to tell practitioners what to do or how to do it. We are raising questions not answering them. It is not the function of the CEF to lay down the objectives that users should pursue or the methods they should employ." (Council of Europe, 2001: xi Note to the User)

This statement highlights the distinction between a common (national or international) framework desirable to organize education and encourage productive networking on the one hand, and the local strategies and decisions necessary to facilitate successful learning in a given context on the other hand. There is no need for there to be a conflict between these two perspectives. A central framework can, like the CEFR, be a concertina-like reference tool that provides categories and levels that educational professionals can expand/contract, elaborate/summarize, adopt/adapt according to the needs of their context. The aim is for users to adopt activities, competences and proficiency stepping-stones that are appropriate to their local context, yet can be related to the greater scheme of things and thus communicated more easily to colleagues in other educational institutions and to other stakeholders like learners, parents and employers.

One crucial question here is whether a common framework can in fact have validity both as a generic reference point and also as a specific application in a local context. A second but equally important question is the limits to such "generic" validity. Is one talking about a potentially universal tool, or is a "common framework" only another specific application in a wider (less local) context, valid only to that specific wider context for which it was originally developed? Finally, can a common framework developed for the teaching of foreign or second languages in mainstream education and the adult sector be applied in primary school to the teaching of the mother tongue or of the language of a host country?

The answer to the last question must be "No." Such a framework would surely be more interested in describing emerging abilities and competences and would have to situate the development of language competences within the overall cognitive and social development of the children concerned. Though many categories of the descriptive scheme might continue to be relevant, illustrative descriptors from a common framework designed for foreign language teaching would clearly be inappropriate to child acquisition of mother tongue or a host language. The Council of Europe's Languages Policy Division has recognized this fact and has set up a new Working Party to develop a framework for this context.

The question of the limits of validity of a "European" framework is probably a question with only a pragmatic solution. The descriptive scheme builds on the sets of objectives for specific levels developed in a European context in the 1970s–1990s in the wake of the publication of *The Threshold Level* (Van Ek, 1976; Van Ek & Trim, 1991). The research that produced the illustrative descriptors took place in the multilingual contexts of French-, German-, and Italian-speaking parts of Switzerland, with English, French, and German as the foreign languages under study (North & Schneider, 1998). A validation study that confirmed the rank order of a set of many CEFR descriptors concerned mainly Swedish-speaking learners of Finnish, a non-indo-European language (Kaftandjieva & Takala, 2002). Following a Symposium in March 2006 at which the CEFR was presented, the Osaka University of Foreign Studies is to conduct a feasibility study into the relevance of the CEFR to the Japanese context.

As regards the fundamental question of whether a common framework can have both generic and local validity, the question could be said to depend upon the way in which the framework is organized and the flexibility with which it can be used. North (2000a: 29) suggested that a framework scale ideally needs to be *context-free* in order to accommodate generalizable results from different specific contexts, yet at the same time the descriptors on the scale need to be *context-relevant*, relatable or translatable into each and every relevant context, and appropriate for the function they are used for in that context. A tall order. In practical terms, this means that the descriptive scheme of the framework needs to (1) relate to the categorization in theories of language competence, although the available theory and research is inadequate to provide a basis for it; (2) be relevant to the contexts of the learning population concerned, though these cannot be predicted with any certainty; and (3) remain user-friendly and accessible to practitioners. North (1997a, 2000a) explains how the CEFR attempts to do this.

With regard to this issue, Spolsky considered:

> A functional set of goals exists in a social context . . . Where this is consistent and common as in the Foreign Service, or in the Council of Europe notion of the Threshold Level for tourists and occasional visitors, it is not unreasonable to develop a scale that proceeds through the skills . . . If it cannot be based on a single social goal, a single set of guidelines, a single scale could only be justified if there were evidence of an empirically provable necessary learning order, and we have clearly had difficulty in showing this to be so even for structural items. (Spolsky, 1986: 154)

A common, empirically proven *learning order* can probably never be demonstrated; second language acquisition research shows no signs of confirming such an order, despite what for a time appeared promising signs (e.g., Clahsen, 1980; Meisel, Clahsen, & Pienemann, 1981; Pienemann, 1985). However, in the case of the bank of CEFR illustrative descriptors, an empirically proven interpretation of *difficulty* (i.e., the "Level" of a descriptor) can be claimed to be common across foreign languages, language regions, educational sectors (secondary, tertiary, and adult), and the learner/teacher divide. To use the technical expression the "DIF" (differential item functioning) of the CEFR illustrative descriptors was from limited to insignificant, and where it did occur it could easily be explained by not-necessarily-desirable curriculum practice (North, 2000a: 255–260).

Spolsky's point can nonetheless be interpreted as asking whether a framework can be used just to give a global "level" from a single holistic scale, even from a holistic scale for speaking (like the ACTFL scale). The problem is that the descriptor in an overall scale for "Speaking" presupposes, as Spolsky comments, that the tasks people are said to be able to do and the degree of quality to which they can do them will be the same in all the contexts that this framework scale is applied to. Right from the beginning it has been the philosophy of the CEFR to profile and 54 separate illustrative descriptor scales are provided to do so. Of those 54 scales, in addition to 2 summary scales for Overall Spoken Interaction and Overall Spoken Production respectively, 12 consider different speaking activities, 6 concern communicative strategies that can be applied to speaking, and 11 concern aspects of communicative language competence that can be applied to speaking. Thus, with regard to speaking, the CEFR provides 29 sub-scales that can be used for profiling. Of course no one would ever use all of them at once, but that is the point: there is choice. One can take some, combine others, and leave the rest – according to the needs and abilities of the learners in the context concerned.

Levels and Goals

Educational developers have to decide the level that will be set as the standard to be achieved in a particular learning context. Unfortunately, as Clark scathingly summarizes, educational standards often give the impression that they have been "plucked out of the air on the basis of intuition, which is frequently shown on closer examination to be wrongly conceived" (Clark, 1987: 44). Both Clark and Stern (1989: 214) propose developing norms of performance in real classrooms into definitions of expected performance, rather than relating standards to "some neat and tidy intuitive ideal" (Clark, 1987: 46). This posits an empirical basis to the definition of standards. The CEFR descriptors were in fact produced empirically in classroom contexts, relating learner achievement in the research context (Switzerland) to the levels on the scale. The European Language Portfolio (ELP), a reporting tool related to the CEFR which now exists in some 40 versions in different countries and sectors, provides CEFR descriptors in adapted and elaborated forms appropriate to the educational context concerned. The ELP thus provides an ideal exploratory tool to discover what level would be a realistic standard for the sector. Yet unfortunately, in many contexts a CEFR level (e.g., "B1") continues to be "plucked out of the air" without an assessment of the realism of the objective or a consideration of the investment that would be necessary to achieve it.

Furthermore, in classes organized by school year rather than by ability sets, the range of achievement can itself cover several CEFR levels. The many-faceted IRT analysis (Linacre, 1989) used in the Swiss research project produced ability estimates for the learners involved as well as difficulty estimates for the descriptors. The picture of learner proficiency produced for 1,000 learners of English showed a definite pattern (North, 2000a: 322–327). For example, in lower secondary school, after one year of English (ca.80 lessons), the median achievement was A1, but the range within 1 standard deviation extended up to A2. After two years the median was A2, but with a 1 SD range extending from A1 to B1; after three years the median was B1, with a range of 1 SD extending from A2 to B2. There is no reason to think that the Swiss context is unique in this respect and it is at least worth asking whether it makes sense to select one level as a compulsory standard unless it has significance as an educational interface (e.g., for university entrance). Also, why not define a differentiated standard, expecting a higher level at Reception than the level required for Interaction or Production? This is the approach taken in Switzerland in the Gesamtsprachenkonzept (www romsem.unibas.ch/sprachenkonzept).

Turning to the question of the formulation of descriptors, a distinction needs to be made between descriptor scales that are intended for dividing candidates into grade groups through judgments in speaking tests (descriptors = assessment criteria) and those that are intended to facilitate the development of curricula and tests (descriptors = tasks). The former have been described by Alderson (1991: 72–74) as assessor-oriented and the latter as constructor-oriented. Constructor-oriented scales should logically be exploited to create more detailed content specifications. The first scale to have such a set of content specifications was the ELTDU scale produced in 1976 for the teaching and testing of English for specific purposes. ELTDU (English Language Teaching Development Unit) was the research arm of Oxford University Press. ELTDU also produced language specifications for their scale by (1) analyzing what language functions, grammatical and vocabulary elements would be necessary to perform each of the tasks referred to in the descriptors and (2) referring to "The Threshold Level" (Van Ek, 1976). In the early 1980s, Eurocentres, with ELTDU initially used as consultants, developed the Euro-centres Scale of Language Proficiency and language specifications for it. The most recent example of this approach is the development for the Goethe Institute of "Profile Deutsch" (Glaboniat et al., 2005), by analyzing CEFR descriptor content and referring to the German equivalent of Threshold Level "Kontaktschwelle" (Baldegger, Müller, & Schneider, 1980).

The way such specifications can be exploited in practical teaching can be shown with an example from Eurocentres. In Eurocentres, weekly objectives are presented in terms of (1) communicative tasks, (2) grammar, (3) vocabulary, the latter two being the language necessary to achieve the former. At the end of each week, in a review lesson, teacher and class discuss achievement of the objectives, and do a test or revision activity. In Eurocentres France, a questionnaire lists the five or six most important communicative objectives and the five or six most important linguistic objectives. Learners are asked for each individual objective (communicative and linguistic) whether they (1) feel comfortable with their achievement of the objective, (2) feel they master it better than before, or (3) would like some more practice on the point concerned. Teachers take the feedback into account in planning the following week and in giving advice for individual work in the independent learning centre.

But content specifications for common frameworks really do raise the question Spolsky posed. In the Eurocentres case the scale and its content specifications were specifically developed for adult learners on a language learning stay abroad in an acquisition-rich learning environment, and the construction of the scale was preceded by a large-scale survey that established a common "functional set of goals." However, with content specifications for a framework applied to different sectors, it is legitimate to at least ask the question whether the same learning progression can be assumed in different contexts. Such content specifications bring great practical advantages for curriculum and syllabus design, but their main disadvantage is that up until now they have not been data-based – the content included remains expert opinion. In a new project to develop a content specification for English, Cambridge ESOL are leading a consortium that intends to consult, in addition to the CEFR descriptors and earlier Council of Europe specifications (e.g., Van Ek & Trim, 1991), a corpus of calibrated scripts drawn from the extended responses made by candidates taking the Cambridge ESOL examinations (Buckby & Saville, 2006). The resulting "English profile" will thus have an empirical base and is expected to attempt to describe the increasing complexity of language used by learners at different points on a scale of levels. The project will also control for first language transfer effects. It may therefore be able to provide evidence on the question of whether certain language features associated with complexity are acquired in a fixed order even though the order of acquisition of other features is varied according to mother tongue and other factors, as originally proposed by Clahsen (1980), Meisel et al. (1981), and Pienemann (1985).

Content specifications as discussed so far focus on the language needed for the productive skills (speaking and writing). In relation to content specifications for the receptive skills, there has been some recent criticism (Alderson et al., 2004: 7–11) that the CEFR descriptor scales do not explicitly describe in a systematic way the presence or absence of text features for each level in order to facilitate the production or classification of tests. Although the CEFR provides sub-scales for different listening situations and reading purposes, and although the way features are calibrated shows a remarkable coherence, it does not provide a systematic description of the parameters of the text concerned, nor pronounce on the relationship between such parameters – or interactions between them – and CEFR levels. The issue is complicated by the fact that the CEFR descriptors, in common with all proficiency scale descriptors, do not describe the text concerned, but the behavior of the text user. Analysis of texts used in test tasks might help to address this situation, but the very complexity of the relationship between different features and proficiency level means that in practice test providers tend to stay with restricted test formats, hence skewing the outcome of any study. Nevertheless this is another area where data-based research might again help to provide a more accurate picture.

Most curriculum objectives focus on *what* the learner should be able to do with lists of tasks, plus the language content and sometimes strategies helpful to achieve them. The style of constructor-oriented descriptors tends to be in positive "Can Do" formulation, which makes them suitable as educational objectives. But one could argue that the question of *how well* learners perform is of equal validity as an objective. The CEFR devotes one chapter to aspects of the learner's competence (chapter 5) and one could exploit the illustrative descriptors within it to include information about the *quality* of language being aimed at.

Generally the lower levels of "assessor-oriented" descriptor scales concerned with quality tend to be formulated in negative terms. The limited knowledge and operational coverage of an A2 (Waystage) performer tends to be equated with an erratic, unskilful, inaccurate performance when this may well not be the case (Trim, 1978: 6). However, there is no intrinsic reason why this should be the case and so the CEFR and the many versions of the European Language Portfolio formulate points about language quality in terms of positive objectives. For example, the following list of aspects of language quality comes in Eurocentres' self-assessment checklist for learners at A2 (presented after receptive skills, communication tasks and strategies):

- Make yourself understood using memorized phrases.
- Give short contributions, even though you may have to stop and think.
- Have a sufficient vocabulary for coping with simple everyday situations.
- Link groups of words with simple connectors like "and," "but," and "because."
- Express past, present, and future, even if you sometimes do mix up tenses.
- Pronounce English sounds so people can understand them.

Linking Local Goals to a Central Framework

The last two entries in the above list are interpretations of what is stated in the CEFR rather than formulations to be found there. Descriptors from a central framework usually need to be adapted when linking local goals to the framework. In the CEFR experience this has been done in at least three ways in countless Portfolio and curriculum reform projects. Firstly, a light editing to tweak the generic descriptor to better suit the domain in question (academic study, professional areas, primary/secondary school classroom tasks) is often undertaken. Secondly, the tightly packed descriptors more typical of the CEFR are sometimes unzipped into a more general header descriptor plus several sub-descriptors; the sub-descriptors can again take on a more specific orientation with examples appropriate to the domain. Thirdly, as in the list given above, developers often add a few points of their own, and many Portfolios contain a couple of blank lines at the end of the list of descriptors in each section in order to encourage teachers to continue this process.

The aim of a metasystem at a national or international level ought to be to facilitate reflection, communication, and networking. The aim of any local strategies ought to be to meet needs in context. The key to linking the two into a coherent system is flexibility: an expandable/contractable descriptive approach in which levels, categories, and descriptors can be merged or subdivided in a common hierarchical structure. With regard to levels, the CEFR encourages what it calls a "branching approach." For example in Finland, A1 is split into three levels to provide initial motivation. One might illustrate an approach like the Finnish one as a set of stepping stones toward independent language use, as shown in Figure 16.1.

Unlike the ALTE Framework described elsewhere in this volume (Chapter 35, Scales and Frameworks) the CEFR is a flexible descriptive tool. The ALTE Framework shares five levels with the CEFR, but does not include sublevels on the grounds that the placement of examinations is more reliable (i.e., the number of false classifications of candidates is significantly fewer) when fewer levels are used. However, the example of the treatment of the Goethe Institute's Zentrale Mittelstufenprüfung in the ALTE Framework (initially placed at B2, then at C1, and now destined to be split in two rather than classified as B2+) demonstrates (1) the difficulty of trying to force a square peg into a round hole in this way, and (2) the limitations of linking examinations to frameworks solely through expert judgment of content specifications guided by checklists.

In view of the well-established literature on linking and test equating, it is in fact surprising how long it took before European projects related to the CEFR took a principled, empirical approach to linking assessments and examinations to it (North, 2000b). In response to an increasing demand for guidance, the Council of Europe put together an authoring group, coordinated by the

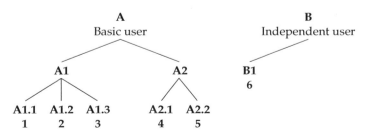

Figure 16.1 Relating local to common reference levels

current author, to produce a manual for examination providers (Council of Europe, 2003; Figueras et al., 2005). The manual, which is currently being piloted in different countries in approximately 20 case studies, proposes a linking process undertaken through three sets of procedures:

1   specification – of coverage, profiled in relation to the CEFR;
2   standardization – of interpretation, using illustrative samples of performances and test items;
3   empirical validation – checking that exam results relate to CEFR levels as intended.

This scheme was adopted (1) because these categories are a good way of grouping linking methodologies found in the literature, (2) because they reflect the classic three stages of quality management (design, implementation, evaluation) and (3) because such broad concepts could thus be applied equally to formal, high-stakes assessment situations (examinations) and to lower-stakes school and teacher assessments.

Specification: The fundamental problems in linking assessments are the facts that (1) the assessments generally test different things, and (2) that each result is reported in terms of the achievement in that particular assessment. Specification of the content of the assessment in relation to the CEFR descriptor framework (categories described at different levels) can help here. Problem (1) can be at least partially addressed by studying relevant CEFR scales, stating what is and what is not assessed, and recording how it is tested. Problem (2) can be addressed by then recording the CEFR level of proficiency that is required for each activity or each aspect of language competence.

Standardization: Discussing concrete examples of performances in relation to common criteria, supported by detailed documentation that explains why a performance is one particular level, is a very effective way of reaching an interpretation shared with colleagues in other contexts. That common interpretation can then be applied to benchmark local performance samples to the framework levels. Eurocentres has helped produce DVDs of performances illustrating the CEFR levels for the two official languages of the Council of Europe (English and French) and now, in collaboration with ALTE, the Council's Languages Policy Division is making available illustrative videos, scripts and samples of test items for a range of languages. Up-to-date information is available from www.coe.int/lang.

Empirical validation: Empirical validation involves the collection and analysis of data concerned with the quality of the test in its own right (*internal validation*) and the independent corroboration through the use of an external criterion of the linking claimed on the basis of specification and standardization (*external validation*). Internal validation is necessary to demonstrate that different forms of an assessment will be equivalent and therefore that a linking project involving one form will be valid. The outcome of an external validation process can be expressed in what is called a "Decision Table"[1] that

Table 16.1 A CEFR manual "Decision Table"

	Test (Item Bank)					
	A1 (1)	**A2 (2 & 3)**	**B1 (4 & 5)**	**B2 (6 & 7)**	**C1 (8 & 9)**	**Total**
A1 (1)	4	1				5
A2 (2 & 3)		14	4			18
B1 (4 & 5)		5	13	2		20
B2 (6 & 7)			3	16		19
C1 (8 & 9)				3	3	6
Total	4	20	20	21	3	68

Criterion (Teachers)

compares placements by the two assessments in order to count the proportion of matching classifications.

In relation to a well-defined framework, the external criterion does not necessarily need to be a scored test, it can also involve expert judgments with descriptors. Table 16.1 shows the outcome of a low-stakes study referencing an item bank to a framework scale using teacher judgments as the external criterion (North, 2000b: 561–564). Ratings by teachers were used to cross-check the provisional cut-off points between levels set for a Eurocentres item bank for testing linguistic competence in German (Jones, 1991, 1993; North, 1997b). The number of people placed at each level by the teachers (external criterion: vertical axis) is shown in the "Total" column on the extreme right above the number 68; those placed by the test (test under study: horizontal axis) are shown in the "Total" row along the bottom of the table. The numbers in brackets following the CEFR levels – e.g., A2 (2 & 3) – refer to the numbers of the Eurocentres internal scale of language proficiency subdividing CEFR levels to show progress. The table looks balanced, suggesting that the current cut-off scores work well. The correlation between the teacher ratings and levels reported by the item bank is 0.93, which is very high. The matching classifications are shown by the horizontal shading. When the highlighted classifications in the diagonal are totalled up they show that there are 50 matching classifications out of the 68, a total of 73.5 percent.

External validation with "candidate-centred" equating like this does not require complex analysis. A correlation can be established with Microsoft Excel and Table 16.1 is just a Microsoft Word table. The problem lies in the test development and in the data collection, not in the analysis. This method can also be used to equate any test to any framework, by-passing the so-called "test-centered" standard-setting procedures that are based on (very fallible) expert judgments of item difficulty.

Conclusion

Provided the descriptors in a common framework have a theoretically motivated development and provided that the framework presents a flexible structure, there is no need for a conflict between the desire to have a central framework to provide transparency and coherence and to have local strategies to provide learning goals specific to particular contexts. Methodologies exist for relating the results from local assessments to central frameworks that do not necessarily need to involve complex statistics or large-scale projects. The metalanguage about levels and language learning made available in such an approach can have a positive influence on teachers' initial training and professional development. The main danger with regard to common frameworks is a simplistic interpretation of them. The key to success is for users to appreciate that the common framework is a descriptive metasystem that is intended as a reference point, not as a tool to be implemented without further elaboration and adaptation to local circumstances.

NOTE

1   The Decision Table in this form was recommended by Nornan Verhelst (Cito, Dutch examination authority) in the Council of Europe Manual for examination authorities (Council of Europe, 2003).

REFERENCES

Alderson, J. C. (1991). Bands and scores. In J. C. Alderson & B. North (eds.), *Language Testing in the 1990s* (pp. 71–86). London: Modern English Publications/British Council/Macmillan.

Alderson, J. C., Figueras, N., Kuijper, H., Nold, G., Takala, S., & Tardieu, C. (2004). The development of specifications for item development and classification within the Common European Framework of Reference for Languages: Learning, teaching, assessment; reading and listening (Final Report of the Dutch Construct Project). Unpublished paper, July.

Baldegger, M., Müller, M., & Schneider, G. (1980). *Kontaktschwelle. Deutsch als Fremdsprache*. Strassburg: Europarat. (Also published 1981, Munich: Langenscheidt.)

Buckby, A. & Saville, N. (2006). Profiling English: A reference level description. Paper given at the EAQUALS (European Association for Quality Language Services –

www.eaquals.org) conference "Quality Initiatives in Language Education." Cambridge May 19–20.

Clahsen, H. (1980). Psycholinguistic aspects of L2 acquisition. In S.W. Felix (ed.), *Second Language Development: Trends and Issues* (pp. 57–79). Tübingen: Narr.

Clark, J. L. (1987). *Curriculum Renewal in School Foreign Language Learning*. Oxford: Oxford University Press.

Council of Europe (2001). *Common European Framework of Reference for Languages: Learning, teaching, assessment*. Cambridge, Cambridge University Press.

Council of Europe (2003). *Relating language examinations to the Common European Framework of Reference for Languages: Learning, Teaching, Assessment (CEFR)*, DGIV/EDU/LANG (2003) 5. Strasbourg: Council of Europe.

Figueras, N., North, B., Takala, S., Verhelst, N., & Van Avermaet, P. (2005). Relating examinations to the Common European Framework: A manual. *Language Testing*, 22(3), 1–19.

Glaboniat, M., Müller, M., Rusch, P., Schmitz, H., & Wertenschlag, L. (2005). *Profile deutsch A1–C2. Lernzielbestimmungen, Kannbeschreibungen, Kommunikative Mittel* [Profile Deutsch: Setting Learning Objectives, ,"Can Do" Descriptors and Communicative Aids]. Munich: Langenscheidt.

Jones, N. (1991). Test item banker: An item bank for a very small micro. In J. C. Alderson & B. North (eds.), *Language Testing in the 1990s* (pp. 247–256). London: Modern English Publications/British Council/Macmillan.

Jones, N. (1993). An item bank for testing English language proficiency: Using the Rasch model to construct an objective measure. Doctoral dissertation, University of Edinburgh.

Kaftandjieva, F. & Takala, S. (2002). Council of Europe scales of language proficiency: A validation study. In J. C. Alderson (ed.), *Case Studies in the Use of the Common European Framework* (pp. 106–129). Strasbourg: Council of Europe.

Linacre, J. M. (1989). *Multi-Faceted Measurement*. Chicago: MESA Press.

Meisel, J. M., Clahsen, H., & Pienemann, M. (1981). On determining developmental stages in second language acquisition. *Studies in Second Language Acquisition*, 3(2), 109–135.

North, B. (1997a). Perspectives on language proficiency and aspects of competence. *Language Teaching*, 30, 92–100.

North, B. (1997b). Itembanker, a computer-based objective tool for criterion-referenced proficiency and diagnostic assessment. In M. Gardenghi & M. O'Connell (eds.), *Prüfen, Testen, Bewerten im Modernen Fremdsprachenunterricht* [Examining, Testing and Assessment in the Teaching of Modern Langauges]. Frankfurt: Peter Lang.

North, B. (2000a). *The Development of a Common Framework Scale of Language Proficiency*. New York, Peter Lang.

North, B. (2000b). Linking language assessments: An example in a low-stakes context. *System*, 28, 555–577.

North, B. & Schneider, G. (1998). Scaling descriptors for language proficiency scales. *Language Testing*, 15(2), 217–262.

Pienemann, M. (1985). Learnability and syllabus construction. In K. Hyltenstam & M. Pienemann (eds.), *Modelling and Assessing Second Language Development* (pp. 23–75). Clevedon, UK: Multilingual Matters.

Spolsky, B. (1986). A multiple choice for language testers. *Language Testing*, 3, 147–158.

Spolsky, B. (1989). *Conditions for Second Language Learning: Introduction to a General Theory*. Oxford: Oxford University Press.

Stern, H. H. (1989). Seeing the wood AND the trees: Some thoughts on language teaching analysis. In R. K. Johnson (ed.), *The Second Language Curriculum* (pp. 207–221). Cambridge: Cambridge University Press.

Trim, J. L. M. (1978). *Some Possible Lines of Development of an Overall Structure for a European Unit/Credit Scheme for Foreign Language Learning By Adults*. Strasbourg: Council of Europe.

Van Ek, J. A. (1976). *The Threshold Level in a European Unit/Credit System for Modern Language Learning by Adults*. Strasbourg: Council of Europe.

Van Ek, J. A. & Trim, J. L. M. (1991). *Threshold Level 1990: A Revised and Extended Version of "The Threshold Level" by J. A. van Ek*. Strasbourg: Council of Europe.

17 Language Acquisition Management Inside and Outside the School

RICHARD B. BALDAUF, JR., MINGLIN LI, AND SHOUHUI ZHAO

Introduction

This chapter provides an overview of the issues central to language acquisition management (LAM), using examples from a range of societies that typify the problems faced both in schools and in other "educational" situations. The initial study of this topic developed from Cooper's (1989) discussion of language acquisition policy and planning, now more often known as language education policy (Spolsky, 2004) or language-in-education policy (Kaplan & Baldauf, 1997, 2003). In this chapter we first briefly define the key concepts underlying LAM, then examine patterns of strategies for LAM at various levels in schools and outside of formal education – citing brief examples before summarizing the challenges facing those working in this domain. Given the breadth of issues to be examined, the focus of the chapter is on management (i.e., policy decision making) rather than planning (for cultivation or program development; see Chapter 18, Language Cultivation in Developed Contexts, this volume; Chapter 19, Language Cultivation in Contexts of Multiple Community Languages, this volume), and we avoid detailed discussion of status planning (van Els, 2005), corpus planning (Liddicoat, 2005) or prestige planning (Ager, 2005), although these policy areas impact on LAM.

Background Issues

Before looking at the key concepts that underpin LAM, three broader issues should be addressed. First, while LAM is the responsibility of all sectors of society, it is in fact the education sector which most often is charged with its development, management, and implementation. While this may skew the types of languages, the kinds of provision, and the ways that languages are managed and provided, and therefore may not always be desirable (see Kaplan & Baldauf, 1997), it is what frequently occurs – either as a matter of policy or by default – and therefore the major focus for this chapter is on educational provision.

Second, and following on from our focus on education, are the questions of what language(s) is going to be used as the medium of instruction and what languages will be taught as second and/or foreign languages. While the medium of instruction issue can be thought of as a form of language mainten-ance, in most polities, it is not that simple. It is increasingly rare for all stu-dents to bring the same language to the classroom, and the right of students to use, study and/or learn in their own language in schools is increasingly being recognized (Spolsky, 2004). Furthermore, the matter of what second and/or foreign languages to teach is also of great concern given the multilingual nature of polities (internal considerations) and the interconnectedness of the world we live in (external forces). However, in this chapter, these matters of "which language" to teach on a broader scale are considered matters of status planning – what needs to be decided before language acquisition can be man-aged (see, van Els, 2005; Chapter 16, Levels and Goals: Central Frameworks and Local Strategies, this volume).

Finally, it needs to be recognized that LAM may be a passive process as well as a matter of active policy making. That is, management can be overt through quite specific or planned policy, but it also can be covert through implicit or unplanned policy (Baldauf, 2005). The latter can be ideologically driven, non-consultative, and top-down ideology – like the "English only" movement in the United States – or it may be more bottom-up driven and benign in intent, like the commercially driven individual demand for English in Tunisia (Daoud, 2001). Even where there is official language management support for a language (e.g., bilingual education in the Philippines), individual demand for a language (e.g., the English skills of more than six million Pilipino over-seas remittance workers, Hau & Tinio, 2003) may in fact be a more potent motivating factor. Thus, agency exists beyond official bodies, and the failure to manage a language situation or the lack of decision making also can have as significant effects on language acquisition as those decisions that are deliberately taken.

Language Acquisition Management

It has been argued (Kaplan & Baldauf, 2003; Baldauf, 2005) that language acquisition management (i.e., language-in-education policy) can be defined by decisions that are made about eight considerations, processes, or policy areas. Policy decisions in each of these areas contribute to LAM and the question of where the agency for that policy resides is important in understanding how language acquisition is managed. Each of these eight policy areas is now briefly examined in turn:

- *Access policy* asks the questions of who must study what languages at what levels for what duration. (See, e.g., Spolsky & Shohamy, 2000; van Els, 2005.)
- *Personnel policy* examines what the requirements are for teacher training, selection, and employment, and in particular whether there are language proficiency standards for teachers. This encompasses the question of whether native speakers may be preferred over non-native speakers. (See, e.g., Kaplan & Baldauf, 1997.)
- *Curriculum policy* defines what curriculum is mandated and by whom. It also asks how it is developed and who is involved. (See, e.g., the module-based Chinese mother tongue curriculum innovation that was launched in Singaporean primary schools; Tan, 2006.)
- *Methods and materials policy* describes what teaching methods and materials are prescribed. With methods, it should also examine the extent to which the method prescribed is actually implemented. (See, e.g., Kaplan & Baldauf, 2003.)
- *Resourcing policy* asks how this is going to be paid for. Where do the resources come from to support language acquisition programs? Are they adequate for the purpose? Does resourcing restrict access for certain groups? Are all languages in the polity resourced? If so by whom? (See, e.g., Cooper, 1989: 85, who examined the public's response to the Israeli Ministry of Education's attempts to remove English from the curriculum of the first three grades of primary school – probably based in part on financial constraints. Parents banded together and hired English teachers to give English in the schools, as an "extracurricular activity," although often during the regular school hours.)
- *Community policy* is about agency. To what extent is the community consulted about what languages are offered? Do students have a choice of language or are policies decided top down? (See, e.g., Cooper, 1989; D. Li, 2002. Schiffman, 2007, examines the reluctance of the Tamil community in Singapore to learn Tamil as they consider it's a language that has no "value" at all.)
- *Evaluation policy* examines the criteria that are used to measure the impact of LAM. Are students required to sit for exams? What criteria do they need to meet? Are these criteria congruent with the required methods? Are individual students' linguistic and cultural needs catered for by the criteria? Is teacher quality evaluated by student examination success? (See, e.g., Young, 2006.)
- *Teacher-led policy* asks whether teachers have agency. Are teachers given, or do they take, some agency for LAM in their classes? It has been argued that their agency or lack thereof contributes significantly to the successful management and implementation of programs (Baldauf, 2006; Li & Baldauf, submitted; Ricento & Hornberger, 1996).

Beyond the outcomes of these policy decisions, it can be argued that LAM occurs in a limited number of typical contexts, having a monolingual to multilingual dimension, and running broadly across four age-related levels: primary, secondary, and tertiary schooling (see Corson, 1999, for specific school-based policies and strategies), and in the community. In the following sections, these levels are examined using contextual examples from various polities.

LAM Inside School: Formal Primary and Secondary Education

LAM is primarily carried out by the education sectors through schooling. In most polities, language policy development and management through education are considered to play a significant role in helping to maintain national unity, to foster economic development, to provide citizens with access to social services, and as a mechanism to minimize internal conflicts between social, political, and ethnic groups. Thus, it is essential when making language-in-education policies to take into account crucial variables in the broader social-political context. Two such variables that define issues related to LAM inside school that draw on the eight previously mentioned policy areas include: (1) the choice of medium of instruction, and (2) second or foreign language selection in the forms of monolingual, bilingual, and multilingual planning.

Choice of medium of instruction

Arguably being the most important form of intergenerational transmission, medium of instruction management is a powerful means of maintaining and revitalizing a language and a culture. As medium of instruction policy, which is an integral part of educational policy, determines which social and linguistic groups have access to political and economic opportunities and which groups are disenfranchised, it is as a consequence a key means of power (re)distribution and social (re)construction (Tsui & Tollefson, 2004: 2). Tsui and Tollefson (2004: 3) point out that historically the functions of medium of instruction policies are remarkably similar in different societies, be they English-dominant countries, or former post-colonial states. No matter which language or languages were used as the medium of instruction, the goal remained the same: to subjugate the colonized. The choices of language(s) as medium of instruction and the driving forces for those choices are explored in this section by selecting a few countries that are illustrative of monolingual, bilingual, and multilingual planning.

The United States, one of the countries with the most linguistic and cultural diversity, is one of the English-dominant countries where monolingual planning characterizes its language education policies in the choice of the medium of instruction in schools. Although English has never been declared to be the official national language, it has enjoyed the highest status in political, economic, and social life in the United States. For the purpose of political subjugation of "minority groups by dominant groups and the masses by the elites, both at the intranational and the international levels" (Tsui & Tollefson, 2004: 17) and to make the nation more civilized and modernized, English was made the medium of instruction for indigenous people whatever their mother tongue had been. The "English-only" policy applied not only to indigenes, but was imposed on forced labor and immigrants including Africans, Chinese, Germans, and Japanese. Currently there are some public school districts in the State of Arizona, for example, which are required to provide foreign language instruction as part of the core K-12 curriculum, but as McCarty (2004) points out, this leads to a paradox: while requiring language study, they are expunging the non-English languages of English language learners. Kaplan and Baldauf (2007) argue that LAM and access to language policy are inherently political processes in the US context – as the interest in and funding for particular languages related to the "war on terror" has recently shown – and that little progress will be made in language study until those supporting languages become more politically astute.

Although a number of polities have bilingual education policies (e.g., Belgium and Canada), the Singaporean government, unlike that in the laissez-faire US, has instituted a deliberate multilingual and multicultural LAM system to create English-knowing bilingual education policies (Chua, 2006). With English being the main medium of instruction and the first school language in all national schools, the other official mother tongue languages of Singapore – i.e., Malay, Mandarin, and Tamil – are taught as second school languages. According to Pakir (2004: 120–121), the major aim of the government's official policy, which requires that all children in Singapore schools become bilingual and biliterate in English and one of the other three official cultural languages, is that of continuous learning for a knowledge-based economy. Different from many other countries, political stability in Singapore has been achieved through LAM by "balancing the interests of different ethnic groups and rests on the rise of the English-knowing bilingual community," where English is the main medium of instruction (Pakir, 2004: 129).

Macao provides an example of multilingual planning. Given the four centuries of Portuguese rule and its location, LAM in Macao is a complicated issue. While Chinese, Portuguese, and English are treated as the medium of instruction in schools, Cantonese is also used, but remains mainly an oral dialect (Mann & Wong, 1999; Young, 2006). Before 1994, language education policy was laissez-faire and left to market forces. Schools could make their own decision on the choice of language as medium of instruction according to their traditions, specific features and identities, their students' needs, and staff and resources available (Mann & Wong, 1999: 21). Different school systems coexist in Macao, at present including Chinese-medium schools, English-medium schools, Portuguese-medium schools, and bilingual Portuguese-Chinese-medium schools. However, in seeking some measure of uniformity, Portuguese was stipulated in the Basic Law of Macao as a secondary official language in addition to Chinese Putonghua, which implies "a plan for stable bilingualism and biculturalism" (Mann & Wong, 1999: 33).

As these examples suggest, the choice of medium of instruction – which is strongly related to access policy, and indirectly to curriculum policy and materials policy – is not only an educational issue, but closely related to the underlying social, political and economic context.

Second or foreign language selection

As in the case of choice of medium of instruction, the selection of a second or foreign language for a nation has been influenced by its broader sociopolitical context. Foreign language education policy changes in the People's Republic of China (hereafter PRC) serves as a good example of how LAM processes are influenced.

Foreign language educational policies have fluctuated with the changing sociopolitical situations since the establishment of the PRC in 1949. To support the programs of economic assistance and political solidarity from the Soviet Union, the Russian language was selected to be the first foreign language during the first few years after the establishment of the PRC. However, with the deterioration of the relationship between China and the Soviet Union and the improvement of the relationship between China and the United States in late 1950s, the first foreign language was switched from Russian to English in 1964. During the period of the Cultural Revolution (1966–76), the PRC was inward-looking and the status of foreign languages was extremely low. Ever since the end of the cultural revolution, English has returned to being the first foreign language, while other foreign languages, including French, German, Japanese, Korean, and Spanish, play important roles in school education, as they are linked to economic development and globalization (M. Li, 2007).

LAM inside school: Policy process perspective

From the perspective of policy processes, examples are given to examine LAM inside schools.

- *Access policy* is usually made by the government or the education sectors of the government, in centralized countries in particular, to meet societal, economic, or political needs. Take the PRC for example, where the government designated Russian and later English as the first foreign language in school education. In the late 1970s, foreign language study was recommended as one of the "three fundamental subjects" (*san zhu ke*) alongside Chinese and mathematics in secondary schools, which were set as compulsory subjects for entrance examinations to tertiary education (M. Li, 2007).
- *Personnel policy* differs from one country to another. In some countries, such as Japan and South Korea, admission into the teacher pool to teach English as a foreign language is achieved by formal studies either in the national normal schools or in the universities, and the criteria are fairly loose (Kaplan & Baldauf, 2003). In addition, people can be accepted to be

English teachers after finishing appropriate training programs (see, e.g., M. Li, 2007). In all cases, there is a shortage of qualified English teachers in terms of language skills. In many countries in east Asia, native English speakers (with or without training) are hired to provide oral language skills.

- *Curriculum policy* is another determinant in the implementation of LAM. In general all curriculum policy is centrally defined, and in many cases it is centrally developed and mandated (Kaplan & Baldauf, 2003) with educationists, educational linguists, and curriculum experts as policy makers. Although there have been voices supporting a bottom-up policy making involving teachers in the policy making process, the top-down curriculum policy is still dominant. This may lead to failure in curriculum implementation as in the case of English language education in the PRC (see, e.g., Li & Baldauf, submitted).

- *Methods and materials policies* are the two most closely related to the curriculum, and they are the key components in curriculum implementation process. In some polities like Japan and South Korea, methodology is often prescribed and textbooks are often centrally produced and approved. However, with some other language-in-education policies, such as the one in Indonesia, while the methods and materials are prescribed and produced centrally, training in their use may be neglected, which leads to implementation difficulty or even failure (Kaplan & Baldauf, 2003).

- *Resourcing policy* is complicated and varies in different countries with different language programs being funded at multiple levels by governments at state, regional, and/or local level, or by individuals. Undoubtedly, whether there is sufficient funding provided for a LAM program decides to a significant extent whether the goals set in the program are to be attained or not. However, there is no lack of examples where language programs have failed because of insufficient funding; for example, in Melanesia and Australia. (See, e.g., Kaplan & Baldauf, 2003.)

- *Community policy*, which is seldom put into practice where language-in-education policy is made following a top-down pattern, is gaining the increasing attention of researchers (see, e.g., van Els, 2005). To meet the various needs within a particular community when making decisions on LAM policies, it is necessary to involve people at all levels in the process, including teachers and students.

- *Evaluation policy* provides criteria to assess the extent to which students have reached the requirements of a LAM policy, and high school exit testing is a common procedure to do this in East Asian polities. (See, e.g., Kaplan & Baldauf, 2003.) In some polities, however, there are conflicting criteria employed for evaluation. Take the PRC for example, where assessment criteria are created in accordance with the prescribed methodology, but where the national entrance examination for higher education has prevented both that methodology and appropriate assessment being implemented as prescribed (Li & Baldauf, submitted). Shohamy (2006: 93) examines this issue and provides an overview of the ways that testing creates mechanisms that create covert language policies.

- *Teacher-led policy* is separate from the personnel and community policy because teachers potentially play a critical role in language policy making, particularly with the current focus on learner-centered language programs and related curricula that have made teachers (and their students) responsible for learning. While there have been examples of the role teachers may play in language program development (see, e.g., Li & Baldauf, submitted), more research needs to be conducted to examine how to successfully implement a language policy that is made from bottom-up by teachers themselves instead of by educational linguists and language curriculum experts without classroom teachers' involvement.

The ultimate purpose of language-in-education planning is to develop policy and supportive methods and materials for language teaching and learning to meet societal, institutional, or individual needs. For LAM inside schools, the eight policy processes are the key elements for successfully implementing language programs. However, as Ingram (1990: 54) points out, "language-in-education planning is more often unsystematic, incidental to other policy-making, and piecemeal than it is rational, systematic, integrated, or comprehensive." LAM, in terms of both the choice of medium of instruction and the selection of second or foreign language, has always been affected by the social, political, or economic variables in different contexts. Those eight policy processes are seldom taken into account at a time when making LAM policies, which may lead directly to the failure of the educational policy implementation.

Tertiary Study

LAM at the university level presents a different set of problems, some of which are related to language maintenance, while others are related to special language acquisition skills. Kaplan and Baldauf (1997: 256–263) suggest that such policies in Australian universities can be seen from two general perspectives: (1) from a student equity perspective, and (2) from an institutional discourse perspective. From a student equity perspective, there is a need for LAM to provide tertiary literacy skills for all students, while at the same time dealing with the language problems faced by indigenous students, mature aged students returning to study, deaf and blind students, students from culturally and linguistically different backgrounds, and overseas students.

From an institutional perspective, there are also six LAM skills that need to be dealt with: Disciplines need to (1) teach the specific literacy skills required by the discipline, (2) get students to use non-sexist (non-discriminatory) language, (3) make second languages available that are needed for study, (4) recognize the prior learning of languages useful to programs of study,

(5) develop computer literacy skills, and (6) develop electronic literacy and collaboration skills.

While universities have a number of policies in place to deal individually with most of these issues, most do not seem to have an overall comprehensive strategy for LAM. A number of examples of tertiary undergraduate language policy can be found in Rosenthal (2000).

Other Language Teaching (OLT)

The literature on LAM in additional contexts spans three major types (i.e., communal, promotional, and industrial) and predominantly falls into what can be classified as "micro" (Baldauf, 2006) or "local" (Canagarajah, 2005) LAM situations. Discussion of these types is underpinned by the far-reaching economic, social, and cultural changes that began to occur to linguistic life over the last decades of the twentieth century (Fettes, 2003: 37). From Fettes's description four parameters can be derived that have a direct influence on the role and forms of language learning and its management in this non-mainstream language teaching context. These are:

- the globalization of economic activities;
- an enlarged role for lifelong learning in educational domains and dere-gulation of education sectors;
- the increasing importance of language competence as a key professional qualification as the world goes more multilingual and multicultural;
- the impact of information technology on human life due to the explosive growth of communication and information networks in an increasingly digital society.

These parameters indicate that society and the nature of work are changing rapidly, and Egkoff (2000: 667) has identified consequential important changes in the nature of vocational education and training that relate to the need for languages that include:

- the changing character of work with its emphasis on professional development;
- an increasing number of internationally mobile workers;
- changing self-concepts of young people with new attitudes to work and the increased need for workers to remain innovative and versatile to retain high levels of employment.

These background factors emphasize the external influences that necessitate non-conventional ways of learning new knowledge. For example, as national economies have become integrated in global settings, people have become more mobile for business and tourism. Furthermore, the rapid pace of change has meant that lifelong learning is becoming one of the most important criteria for professional qualifications and quality of life in information societies. These factors make language acquisition outside the school both necessary and popular in many settings. On the other hand, with modern education being revolutionized by new concepts such as distance/correspondence education, open classes, community learning, flexible learning, and teaching through self-instruction, language learning in the digital society has also been redefined by the pervasive influence of such international communication technology as E-learning or Tele-learning.

Theoretical basis for other language planning

In contexts such as this, traditional macro language management frameworks or narrow school-based planning are inadequate, as language planning and acquisition need to occur more broadly. The theoretical grounds for non-mainstream LAM can be found in Haarmann's (1990) typology which highlights the fact that language planning programs are implemented not only through official and institutional agencies, but also by voluntary groups and enthusiastic individuals. More recently, Kaplan and Baldauf (1997, 2003) and Baldauf (2005, 2006) have emphasized that LAM can be carried out by non-traditional actors at meso and micro levels, through either overt or covert planning approaches.

Haarmann (1990) has also suggested that non-official language planning forces may affect the success of the language plan in significant ways by altering prestige. Non-mainstream language teaching, which works on market choice principles outside the mass education systems, is largely free from official intervention and political influence. Because of its politically neutral nature, the success or failure of unplanned language growth should been seen as a sensitive indicator of the prestige the public allocates to a particular language, and thus it can be argued that it serves the same role that the stock market does in economic development and planning.

Typologies of other LAM

Non-mainstream language teaching has been categorized under a range of different names and different forms (e.g., individual teaching, additional teaching, free-time language education, face-to-face language learning, alternative language learning), all of which conceptualize non-mainstream language teaching from the perspective of language learners. In the following discussion, these special forms of language teaching and learning are described under three LAM categories (i.e., communal, promotional, and industrial) derived from the objectives of service providers or the functions of learning and teaching programs. These categories are then summarized in Table 17.1 by the eight LAM policies.

Type I: Communal

Community or heritage language education is the only one of the three types of OLT that has been well researched and documented (e.g., Clyne, 1991; Hornberger, 2005). The major role of communal language teaching can be seen as language revival and maintenance in bilingual and multilingual societies and this predominantly occurs in four ways:

- *Community/heritage language schools* refer to the community sponsored language schools teaching native/ethnic/heritage languages of migrant or indigenous groups for language maintenance and intergeneration transmission. They focus on language teaching, using native language as an instructional medium. A number of such schools are not officially recognized due to political and ethnic sensitivity, and some are so-called "underground schools," e.g., Chinese teaching in Indonesia prior to 1990s. These do not include ethnically inspired native language medium education which is integrated into the national public education system, such as Chinese-medium schools in ASEAN countries.
- A number of different religions (e.g., Judaism, Greek Orthodox) run *religious schools* in languages other than the language of the host polity. Historically, and to some extent contemporaneously, mission schools spread languages like English, French, and Spanish at the expense of local languages. The need to read the Quran in Classical Arabic has led to the setting up across the Islamic world of Pesantren (Quranic schools), which in some poor areas provide the only free formal education available to children (W. Li, 2006).
- In addition to non-government *preschool programs* such as childcare centres and kindergartens that have a language focus, this group also includes *home-based learning*, and parent support for private study (e.g., Japanese *Juku*) and private tutorials, all of which are very popular in most Asian countries. Language teaching is always the main activity in these kinds of schools and tutorials which provide instruction to meet children's needs that would not otherwise be satisfied. Increasingly such schools are coming under government regulation, and in some states (e.g., Singapore) language policy regulation now is being applied to this sector.
- Communal LAM also includes *language campaigns*, such as the illiteracy weeding-out campaigns in China and North Korea in the 1950s–60s or the Speak Mandarin Campaign in Singapore beginning in 1979. Integrating/assimilating oriented programs such as Immigration English for new immigrants (Australia, Canada) and language programs offered in refugee camps also belong to this category.

Type II: Promotional

Most promotional agencies, some of which have special missions, aim to raise the status of a language in international settings, either driven by instrumental (commercial purposes) or ideological (nationalism, culture) motivations. Language promotion also occurs internally, but the highly promoted languages are usually the official languages of economically successful monolingual (or language dominant) societies, in emerging industrializing countries, which begin to promote their languages when per-capita income increases. Therefore, these are the languages with powerful political and economic bases, predominantly languages like English, French, German, Japanese, and, belatedly, Chinese (Graddol, 1997).

- The government commitments and administration of the overseas promotion of powerful languages as foreign languages have been a concurrent theme of language and cultural spread. These *language and cultural promotion agencies* have a dual role: to manage internal language use as the top state language planning organ in their home country, and to spread language overseas as a non-profit foreign organization in other countries. They are often attached to regular educational or commercial institutions, but do not operate in the way required of the regular school system. Most of such well-known international organizations originated in Europe, for example, the Alliance Française (1895) and Centre Culturel Française (1908), British Council, Instituto Cervantes (Spain, 1992), and Società Dante Alighieri (Italy, 1889). In Asia, The Japan Foundation (1972) used to be the only language spread agency in the region (Kaiser, 2003: 199), but since 2004 the Confucius Institute (Kongzi Xueyuan, China) has established 54 branches in over 30 countries. Some semi-voluntary organizations like the United States Peace Corps (1961) and Voluntary Service Overseas (UK, 1958) also largely function to support language teaching in developing countries through their worldwide networks. In some cases, the promotion is less direct, e.g., the President Mandarin Promotional Fund in Taiwan has as its objective to promote the uses of Taiwan style Mandarin among the Chinese diasporas.
- Other organizations like the World Bank and the European Union, through their contractual arrangements and/or language management policies, indirectly promote powerful languages, putting pressure on languages of lesser status and power.

Type III: Industrial

In most cases, the languages taught in this category are economically valued foreign languages from dominant monolingual societies, or a high language in a diglossia community. Three types of industrially run linguistic establishments can be identified as being involved in LAM, most of which are unregulated except by public acceptance:

- *Corporate language teaching* mainly refers to businesses that are language service providers and that take economic return as their central focus, e.g., Linguaphone International Languages, "Eikaiwa" or English Conversation schools in Japan, La Lingua and International Languages in Australia, and providers of proficiency testing (e.g., TOEFL, IELTS) and training courses. Perhaps the best-known of these is the Berlitz International Language School. These institutions also often provide other cultural activities and linguistics services, such as translating and publishing, all operating on a market philosophy. One of these, Xin Dongfang (the New East) in China, has recently listed on the American stock market. Language service brokers such as JET (Japan Exchange and Teaching), which recruits native speakers from over 30 countries for foreign language teaching and counseling positions at schools and companies in Japan, also can be included in this category.

- *In-service corporate language training and vocational schools* include the American Army Specialized Training Program (Wilkins, 1990: 524) and intensive summer language-based study programs such as language immersion programs and summer camps or tourist study groups which have become popular models for second and foreign language acquisition in elementary and secondary schools, and to a limited extent at university level as well, where language based exchange programs are common.
- The ascendance of digital technology marks a new, informal and horizontal way for LAM to occur on an unprecedented scale through *language teaching over internet*. There are increasing market-oriented applications on the internet dealing with flexible and distance learning systems across borders for large numbers of language learners. The internet provides a convenient channel for more robust language teaching that enables ordinary individuals with limited resources to access first-class facilities that were previously monopolized by elite learners. This emerging form of language teaching and learning has been developing very quickly.

Characteristics of OLT and its relationships with mainstream LAM

As this section suggests, the characteristics of OLT are quite diverse, and although managed, not subject to any centralized planning mandate. In Table 17.1 the primary features of each of the three categories as they are articulated by the eight LAM processes are set out.

There are some contradictions to be found in OLT. It is a non-governmental function, but it penetrates many sectors of society; it does not provide accreditation education, but a qualification is the main purpose for many learners; and it is not standard education, but it is marked by the normative use of methods prevailing in the formal educational spectrum. Although school and university educators may believe that most OLT is effectively no more than a matter of language teaching industrialization for a financial return, OLT is characterized by emphasizing practical language skills, including oracy rather than literacy, thus playing a supplementary and remedial role to formal

Table 17.1 Characteristics of OLT in relation to the eight policy areas of language acquisition management

	Communal	Promotional	Industrial
Examples	Saturday schools, heritage schools, religious schools, preschools, literacy campaigns	British Council, Confucius Institute, Goethe Society, Japan Foundation, Peace Corps, World Bank, European Union	Corporate training, Berlitz, Monterey Institute, Military Language Institutes
Access policy	Often attempt to revive or maintain indigenous/ancestral languages, Low language in a diglossia society	The main language (lingua franca) of a country; promote language spread policy	Dominated by English, Japanese, and other commercially valued languages, or the High language in a diglossia society
Personnel policy	From formal language teachers to amateur enthusiasts with inevitable standard variations	Certificated teachers well paid by taxpayers; or made up of volunteers	A significant number are young graduates, some are school trained teachers
Curriculum policy	Often locally customized for specific linguistic needs, heavily influenced by ethnic inclination in bi-/multi-cultural communities	Formal curricula are extensively used, but specially developed curriculum is often culturally or politically charged	Derives from the real-life situation of the learners as expressed in the themes of their reality; personally/individually tailored programs are not uncommon

Methods and materials policy	Most cases, pedagogies are very traditional and sometimes the teachers themselves have to prepare teaching materials on their own	Methods vary greatly, but most have some quality guarantee and are provided through the various agencies	Teaching approaches are normally flexible and stimulating, manifesting innovative features such as communication-oriented, student-centered, weakly framed modules, teacher as setter and facilitator, etc.
Resourcing policy	Personal support, governmental funding, or from charity foundations and ethnically inspired organizations	Through higher level institutional channels, similar to communal funding	Business investment works on market philosophy
Community policy	To convince the community that inability to speak or read a certain language is a damaging handicap; the target language learning serves to promote interethnic harmony	To enhance prestige and build image, to assure the public the language promoted is not a threat to indigenous languages; as a means of intercultural communication	Treats the community as clients; to cater to customers, it needs to get rid of its social stigma as substandard. OLT is a way to generate employment, development
Evaluation policy	Most targeted goals are very flexible; outcome evaluations are seldom conducted	Promotional impact is hard to evaluate in the short term	For some trainees, to be awarded a certificate through evaluation is essential, but otherwise evaluation is symbolic
Teacher-led policy	Teachers and grassroots agencies/partners are actively involved in both teaching and decision processes	Most officially proposed programs are highly centralized, but volunteer teachers in some circumstances play an important role	Teachers are often sidelined in well-established private/international language schools; home-based tutors working in a self-regulated maverick way

language education programs in schools. Local control and community involvement create diversity and an interdependence between what happens inside and outside school, creating parallel and powerful but less structured environments for learners. In terms of the educational consequences, there is often no clear-cut territorial separation between OLT and the public system. In many polities the role that OLT plays in LAM in the community is growing, and with the growth and spread of technology there are increasing opportunities available for niche players to offer innovative forms of language acquisition that complement and fill the gaps left by school-based programs. It can be argued that OLT practitioners act as an invisible group of language planners, impacting on the language ecology and its overall management. For this reason, in our search to understand how language acquisition is managed, micro studies of OLT need to be included, so we can better understand this unplanned and ungovernable phenomenon.

Conclusion

This examination of LAM systems in a number of polities suggests that we are dealing with a complex linguistic ecology which varies along a number of parameters (Chapter 20, Ecological Language Education Policy, this volume). In particular, eight policy processes were identified that contribute to successful LAM in primary, secondary, and tertiary education as well as in wider educational contexts. Furthermore, systems within polities vary depending on the complexity of the language situation. In the changing linguistic world in which we are living, the major challenge for LAM may be to remain open and flexible in order to deal with the evolving linguistic ecology.

REFERENCES

Ager, D. (2005). Prestige and image planning. In E. Hinkel (ed.), *Handbook of Research in Second Language Teaching and Learning* (pp. 1035–1054). Mahwah, NJ: Lawrence Erlbaum.

Baldauf, R. B., Jr. (2005). Language planning and policy research: An overview. In E. Hinkel (ed.), *Handbook of Research in Second Language Teaching and Learning* (pp. 957–970). Mahwah, NJ: Lawrence Erlbaum.

Baldauf, R. B., Jr. (2006). Rearticulating the case for micro language planning in a language ecology context. *Current Issues in Language Planning*, 7(2–3), 147–170.

Canagarajah, A. S. (2005). *Reclaiming the Local in Language Policy and Practice.* Mahwah, NJ: Lawrence Erlbaum.

Chua, S. K. C. (2006). Singaporean educational planning: Moving from the macro to the micro. *Current Issues in Language Planning*, 7(2–3), 214–229.

Clyne, M. G. (1991). *Community Languages: The Australian experience.* Cambridge/New York: Cambridge University Press.

Cooper, R. L. (1989). *Language Planning and Social Change.* Cambridge: Cambridge University Press.

Corson, D. (1999). *Language Policy in Schools: A Resource for Teachers and Administrators.* Mahwah, NJ: Lawrence Erlbaum.

Daoud, M. (2001). The language planning situation in Tunisia. *Current Issues in Language Planning*, 2, 1–52.

Egkoff, G. (2000). Vocational education and training. In M. Byram (ed.), *Routledge Encyclopedia of Language Teaching and Learning* (pp. 667–672). London/New York: Routledge.

Fettes, M. (2003). The geostrategies of interlingualism. In J. Maurais & M. A. Morris (eds.), *Languages in a Globalising World* (pp. 37–46). Cambridge: Cambridge University Press.

Graddol, D. (1997). *The Future of English?* London: The British Council.

Haarmann, H. (1990). Language planning in the light of a general theory of language: A methodological framework. *International Journal of the Sociology of Language*, 86, 103–26.

Hau, C. S. & Tinio, V. L. (2003). Language policy and ethnic relations in the Philippines. In M. E. Brown & S. Ganguly (eds.), *Fighting Words: Language Policy and Ethnic Relations in Asia* (pp. 319–352). Cambridge, MA: MIT Press.

Hornberger, N. H. (2005). Heritage/community language education: US and Australian perspectives. *International Journal of Bilingual Education and Bilingualism*, 8(2&3), 101–108.

Ingram, D. E. (1990). Language-in-education planning. In R. B. Kaplan, et al. (eds.), *Annual Review of Applied Linguistics*, 10 (pp. 53–78). New York: Cambridge University Press.

Kaiser, S. (2003). Language and script in Japan and other East Asian countries: Between insularity and technology. In J. Maurais & M. A. Morris (eds.), *Languages in a Globalising World* (pp. 188–202). Cambridge: Cambridge University Press.

Kaplan, R. B. & Baldauf, R. B., Jr. (1997). *Language Planning From Practice to Theory.* Clevedon, UK: Multilingual Matters.

Kaplan, R. B. & Baldauf, R. B., Jr. (2003). *Language and Language-in-Education Planning in the Pacific Basin.* Dordrecht: Kluwer.

Kaplan, R. B. & Baldauf, R. B., Jr. (2007). Language policy spread: Learning from health and social policy models. *Language Problems and Language Planning*, 31(2), 107–129.

Li, D. C.-S. (2002). Hong Kong parents' preference for English-medium education: Passive victims of imperialism or active agents of pragmatism? In A. Kirkpatrick (ed.), *Englishes in Asia: Communication, Identity, Power and Education* (pp. 29–62). Melbourne: Language Australia.

Li, M. (2007). Foreign language education in primary schools in the People's Republic of China. *Current Issues in Language Planning*, 8(2), 148–161.

Li, M. & Baldauf, R. B., Jr. (submitted). Implementers or policy makers: Teachers and China's national English language policy.

Li, W. (2006). Complementary schools, past, present and future. *Language and Education*, 20(1), 76–83.

Liddicoat, A. J. (2005). Corpus planning. In E. Hinkel (ed.), *Handbook of Research in Second Language Teaching and Learning* (pp. 993–1011). Mahwah, NJ: Lawrence Erlbaum.

Mann, C. & Wong, G. (1999). Issues in language planning and language education: A survey from Macao on its return to Chinese sovereignty. *Language Problems and Language Planning*, 23(1), 17–36.

McCarty, T. L. (2004). Dangerous difference: A critical-historical analysis of language education policies in the United States. In J. W. Tollefson & A. B. M. Tsui (eds.), *Medium of Instruction Policies: Which Agenda? Whose Agenda?* (pp. 71–93). Mahwah, NJ: Lawrence Erlbaum.

Pakir, A. (2004). Medium-of-instruction policy in Singapore. In J. W. Tollefson & A. B. M. Tsui (eds.), *Medium of Instruction Policies: Which Agenda? Whose Agenda?* (pp. 117–133). Mahwah, NJ: Lawrence Erlbaum.

Ricento, T. K. & Hornberger, N. H. (1996). Unpeeling the onion: Language planning and policy and the ELT professional. *TESOL Quarterly*, 30(3), 401–427.

Rosenthal, J. W. (2000). *Handbook of Undergraduate Second Language Education*. Mahwah, NJ: Lawrence Erlbaum.

Schiffman, H. F. (2007). Tamil language policy in Singapore: The role of implementation. In V. Vaish, S. Gopinathan, & Y. B. Liu (eds.), *Language, Capital, Culture: Critical Studies of Language in Education in Singapore* (pp. 209–226). Amsterdam: Sense Publishers.

Shohamy, E. (2006). *Language Policy: Hidden Agendas and New Approaches*. London/New York: Routledge.

Spolsky, B. (2004). *Language Policy*. Cambridge: Cambridge University Press.

Spolsky, B. & Shohamy, E. (2000). Language practice, language ideology, and language policy. In R. D. Lambert & E. Shohamy (eds.), *Language Policy and Pedagogy* (pp. 1–41). Philadelphia, PA: John Benjamins.

Tan, C. (2006). Change and continuity: Chinese language policy in Singapore. *Language Policy*, 5(1), 41–62.

Tsui, A. B. M. & Tollefson, J. W. (2004). The centrality of medium-of-instruction policy in sociopolitical processes. In J. W. Tollefson & A. B. M. Tsui (eds.), *Medium of Instruction Policies: Which Agenda? Whose Agenda?* (pp. 1–18). Mahwah, NJ: Lawrence Erlbaum.

van Els, T. (2005). Status planning for learning and teaching. In E. Hinkel (ed.), *Handbook of Research in Second Language Teaching and Learning* (pp. 971–991). Mahwah, NJ: Erlbaum.

Wilkins, D. (1990). Second languages: How they are learned and taught. In N. E. Collinge (ed.), *An Encyclopedia of Language* (pp. 518–551). London: Routledge.

Young, M. Y. C. (2006). Macao students' attitude toward English: A post-1999 survey. *World Englishes*, 25(3/4), 479–490.

18 Language Cultivation in Developed Contexts

JIŘÍ NEKVAPIL

The Concept of Language Cultivation

The word "cultivate" in the expression "language cultivation" means "to refine," or, put differently, "to improve something by making small changes." These "small changes" involve mainly orthography (e.g., substituting one letter for another in a particular group of words), the lexicon (e.g., introducing an appropriate term for a new phenomenon), or the style of a particular language (e.g., simplifying a certain manner of expression). However, it is not only a question of making changes in language but also of keeping it in good condition ("taking care of language"). "Language cultivation" presumes a pre-existing clarification of which variety is to be cultivated, for which language users it is to be cultivated – or, as the case may be, who is going to cultivate it – in the same way that "cultivation of soil" presumes a pre-existing clarification of, e.g., where the soil is located and to whom it belongs. It follows that dealing with a language or languages involves issues more fundamental than cultivation. These include mainly deciding which language will or will not be used in a particular community (or even in particular communication domains). This type of language treatment is often termed "status planning," while language cultivation is often referred to as "corpus planning" (or *Sprachkultur* in German, *jazyková kultura* in Czech, and similarly in Slavic languages). This chapter is devoted mainly to the latter type of language treatment.

What, however, is the object proper of "language cultivation"? A language such as French, German, or Czech is not a monolithic whole, but rather a complex of language varieties differentiated on the basis of territorial, social, functional, temporal, and other factors. Any variety of a particular language may potentially become the object of cultivation, but it is typically standard language that constitutes the main object of this treatment. As far as standard language is concerned – i.e., language with a scope not limited to a particular region, operating on the level of the whole society, and capable of fulfilling the greatest cultural and civilization needs (Havránek, 1932a; Daneš, 2006) – two stages of cultivation may be distinguished: (1) the cultivation of a particular selected variety aimed at the formation of (multifunctional) standard language, (2) the cultivation of the already formed standard language. The two stages occur during different periods in the development of a particular society (an ethnic group, a nation), and it is possible to refer to stage (2) as language cultivation in "developed contexts." On the other hand, stage (1), often called "language modernization," suggests that the language cultivation theory is closely interlinked with the theory of standard language (see below).

The cultivation of standard language pursues certain goals. While the first group of goals is tacitly or overtly tied to status planning, which means that the goals are connected with the "non-linguistic" goals of the society as a whole (e.g., the emphasis on political or cultural independence), the second group is aimed at the effectiveness of the language itself as a tool of communication. The latter group is therefore the field of linguists and teachers to a greater extent than the former.

Let us now address the first group of goals of the cultivation of standard language. According to Fishman (2006), the aims of corpus planning (or language cultivation) linked with status planning comprise (1) language purity (versus vernacularity), (2) uniqueness (versus Westernization, or more precisely, internationalization), (3) classicization (versus "panification," a word coined from the Greek form "pan" meaning "relating to the whole of," see below), (4) the departure of a particular language variety from another, structurally close to it, or the contrary, one variety approaching another ("Ausbau" and "Einbau" in Fishman's terminology). Specialists in language cultivation achieve these goals by:

1   preventing elements of certain foreign languages from entering the language (or on the contrary, sustaining a vernacular language tolerant of foreign elements);
2   advocating the characteristic features of a particular language (or vice versa – bringing the language closer to "Western" languages, or more generally, internationalizing the language);
3   incorporating elements of a classical language into the language in question, for instance, Sanskrit into Hindi (alternatively, attempting to establish a new cultural and linguistic unified formation stretching across several languages on the basis of a more or less hypothetical ancient source language, cf. the attempts to establish the Illyric language on the territory of today's southern Slavs);
4   stressing the differences between two structurally close varieties (German *Ausbau*, cf. the situation of Serbian and Croatian after the break-up of the former Yugoslavia), or vice versa – bringing the varieties closer to one another (German *Einbau*, cf. the situation of Serbian and Croatian in Yugoslavia in most of the second half of the twentieth century).

The second group of goals of the cultivation of standard language comprises stability and uniformity of the language (in other words, the limitations imposed on its variation) as well as the functional elaboration of the language, i.e., the exact differentiation of individual linguistic means according to the functions they perform (e.g., the differentiation of various nominal suffixes according to the different meanings they express), and maximization of functional scope, i.e., making it possible for the language to be used for a variety of purposes (e.g., not only as the language of liturgy, but also of schooling and science).

However, it is not merely *language* cultivation that matters but also the cultivation of the communicative process, that is, the cultivation of the way language is used (including production as well as reception). Obviously, such cultivation must involve not only the use of standard language but also, essentially, the use of all varieties of the language and, in a multilingual environment, even different languages.

The Origin of "Language Cultivation" in the Prague School of Linguistics

Following the principle "Leave your language alone" (Hall, 1950), linguistic structuralism, which developed the ideas of Ferdinand de Saussure, was not particularly interested in the cultivation of (standard) language. The linguists of the Prague School (Havránek, Mathesius, Jakobson) are exceptional in this respect: while they addressed primarily the problems of the Czech linguistic situation, in the 1930s they formulated a more general theory and principles of language cultivation (drawing on some of their predecessors as well as contemporaries, for instance, the Swedish linguist A. Noreen – see in particular Noreen & Johannson, 1892 – or the Russian G. Vinokur – see especially Vinokur, 1925). Aiming primarily at weakening the position of purism as the leading principle of corpus planning (to use present-day terminology), the theory is characterized mainly by functionalism.

The cultivation activities of the Prague School focus on contemporary standard language. Its cultivation must be based on an exact description of the state of the present standard language, the goal being to identify the "norm" of standard language. The norm is a set of linguistic means and rules considered obligatory by language users. Language cultivation should benefit the contemporary language user; therefore it is based on the norm of standard language written and spoken during the past 50 years. In practical research this means studying the way standard language is used by "good authors" (of both fiction and non-fiction) and the educated classes. The descriptive stage may then be followed by the stage of cultivation which concentrates on current or potential problems – these are always present, to a greater or lesser extent, since standard language changes together with the development of the community of its users. The aim of cultivation activities is twofold: (1) to support the stability of standard language, (2) to advance its functional differentiation and stylistic richness (Havránek, 1932b). Although achieving stability of standard language constitutes a primary goal of cultivation, it is not to be interpreted as an effort to conserve a particular state of the language. The fact that societies as well as languages develop is to be respected, the goal therefore being "flexible stability" of standard language (Mathesius, 1932). Nor does stability mean absolute uniformity – standard language serves a variety of purposes ("functions"), having various sets of linguistic means ("functional varieties") at its disposal to accommodate these demands. The following functions of standard language may be distinguished: conversational function, specialized theoretical function, specialized practical function, and aesthetic function. Systematic attention should be devoted primarily to the formation of specialized terminology, and in general "intellectualization" of language, that is, the adaptation of standard language

> to the goal of making possible precise and rigorous, if necessary, abstract statements, capable of expressing the continuity and complexity of thought, that is, to reinforce the intellectual side of speech. This intellectualization culminates in scientific (theoretical) speech, determined by the attempt to be as precise in expression as possible, to make statements which reflect the rigor of objective (scientific) thinking in which the terms approximate concepts and the sentences approximate logical judgements. (Havránek, 1932a: 45)

The stabilization of standard language is affected to a considerable extent by schooling, in which practically every member of the language community participates. The needs of schools (as well as of the general public) require that the desirable form of the standard language be codified, that is, it should be officially stated which linguistic means are correct and/or appropriate. Codification is embodied in three basic types of handbooks: dictionaries, grammars, and style manuals (Mathesius, 1932). Codification is carried out by specialists who follow three criteria when assessing the correctness or appropriateness of a particular linguistic means (Daneš, 1987):

1   compliance with the norm (Is the linguistic means well established, conventionalized, fully accepted in the language community?);
2   adequacy with respect to function (Is the linguistic means suitable, or appropriate for the performance of a particular function?);
3   systemic character (Does the linguistic means conform to the rules of the particular language system?).

The criteria constitute a hierarchy, the first being superordinate to the other two in case of a conflict among them (with the second criterion, in turn, superordinate to the third). The codification should reflect the known tendencies in the development of the norm of standard language and support them. Although codification is carried out primarily by specialists, much effort should nevertheless be devoted to the positive reception of its results by the general public. The fact that the codification is backed by a prominent institution (e.g., the Academy) is not sufficient to guarantee such reception. Language codification does not have the character of a law or directive but rather that of an "(urgent) appeal" (the failure to comply with the norm is penalized only at school). The social acceptance of the codification may only be achieved through popularization and information campaigns as well as systematic language education (for more details on the classic Prague approach and some extensions see Garvin, 1973, 1993).

Later, the Prague theory distinguished between the cultivation of language and the cultivation of the communicative process (i.e., the use of language). Language cultivation is intended to ensure that language reaches a level that allows optimum communication. This constitutes the actual purpose of language cultivation (Hausenblas, 1979). The cultivation of the communicative process, however, comprises more than the use of standard language. It is also a matter of using non-standard varieties, a combination of these varieties, or a combination of standard and non-standard linguistic phenomena, as the case may be, in a manner appropriate to the function and situation (Homoláč & Nebeská, 2000). Thus the cultivation of the communicative process is tantamount to the processes of identification, elaboration, and popularization of stylistic norms (the appropriate selection of linguistic and textual means with respect to their purpose in communication). Such norms are not as binding as linguistic norms; they are more dynamic, variable, and often not rigorously codified, although they constitute a part of language education. Norms relating to communication in a multilingual environment have been out of the range of interest of the Prague School's theory and practice.

The Current State of Language Cultivation in Two National Contexts

It will not be possible to provide a general characteristic of the countries in question here due to space limitations. I shall therefore focus on the features I consider interesting and relevant with respect to the possible applications in the context of other states.

The Czech Republic

The current state of language cultivation in the Czech Republic represents a theoretical as well as institutional continuation of the language cultivation established in the first half of the twentieth century. Prague functionalism has defeated the proponents of the historical purity of the Czech language both in theory and in practice, and codification of standard language has begun to approach the contemporary norm to a greater extent. This was welcomed especially by fiction writers, whose language also became regarded as a means of identifying the norm of standard language on the basis of the new theory. The Prague theory was implemented not only in the new dictionaries and grammars, but also in textbooks of Czech for primary and secondary schools. It is symptomatic that the textbooks were co-authored by the best linguists, the founders of the cultivation theory themselves, e.g., B. Havránek or later F. Daneš.

In the Czech Republic, like in other countries in Europe, orthography has received particular attention in schools as well as among the general public. Czech orthography has been codified since 1902 by the official handbook *The Rules of Czech Spelling* (Pravidla . . . 1902). Since its first publication, however, the handbook has not dealt merely with orthographic phenomena but also with morphology and orthoepy. Nor does it comprise rules alone. These can be found in the initial part of the handbook, with the other part providing an alphabetical list of words most difficult to use (with their forms in selected problematic cases since Czech is an inflectional language with complex morphology). Codification of Czech spelling has been dealt with by specialized committees almost continuously since the early twentieth century. The most important editions of the handbook, which brought quite fundamental changes, were published in 1902, 1913, 1941, 1957, and 1993. Since *The Rules* was co-authored by the most outstanding linguists (Gebauer, Havránek, Daneš), some of the innovations in the codification are also interesting from a theoretical point of view. For instance, the authors of *The Rules* published in 1957 adopted a novel approach to the codification of vowel length in foreign words – while the earlier codifications aimed at drawing the spelling closer to the pronunciation, the orthographic codification in 1957 attempted to influence and unify the varying pronunciation. Since the very beginning, the idea of *The Rules* has been tied to the modernization efforts of Czech society. The primary goals of the handbook comprised the rationalization of orthography, and consequently equal opportunity for all members of the society to apply the spelling rules. Since the first edition, *The Rules* has been oriented to the needs of the widest social stratum, namely people with a primary or secondary school education (codification has always catered for making it possible for the user to arrive at a relatively unambiguous decision about what is and what is not correct). However, in some areas of spelling, these goals proved to be more difficult to reach due to attempts at a codification based on the orthographic preferences of certain social groups (teachers, writers, the political elite).

The Rules is considered a basic codification manual in the Czech Republic. At schools and elsewhere, spelling is assigned excessive importance while other linguistic problems, such as the appropriate usage of words (lexical and stylistic problems) and the construction and reception of texts in general, are relegated to the background. The obligatory character of the orthographic rules is enforced particularly by the relatively centralized school system. In the first place, the use of the handbook at schools is authorized by the Ministry of Education, just like the use of textbooks of Czech. Moreover, the Ministry of Education does not authorize the use of any school textbook unless it complies with the current codification.

However extensive the authority of the Ministry of Education is, the cultivation activities proper are centered around the university departments of Czech and primarily the Czech Language Institute of the Czech Academy of Sciences. The Institute came into existence in 1947 through the transformation of the former Office of the Czech Lexicon, founded in 1911. Financed by the state, it has produced the majority of fundamental works dealing with the Czech language, including those performing the codification function (these include, in addition to orthography handbooks, especially dictionaries). The Institute publishes the journal *Naše řeč* ('Our Language', founded in 1916), devoted exclusively to the cultivation of Czech. One of the departments of the Institute, the Department of Language Cultivation, runs a linguistic consulting center for the general public. This center responds to linguistic queries over the telephone or by internet. The members of the Institute, together with university linguists, collaborate with television and radio stations on programs dealing with the problems of contemporary Czech language. They are also the authors of "language columns" in a number of newspapers and periodicals (the genre of "language column," a short article about an interesting or topical linguistic phenomenon, has become popular in the Czech Republic, not only among linguists but also among readers). Recently, the cultivation activities may also rely on a computerized corpus of the Czech language managed by Charles University in Prague, which contains more than 200 million words.

The Prague School theory of language cultivation has won recognition not only in the Czech Republic, where it is still a current issue, but also abroad. It became particularly popular in other Slavic countries but also, for instance, in Germany (see Schanhorst, 1999); its individual features are acknowledged worldwide. The theory, however, also had certain weaknesses. These include the fact that it focused exclusively on the problems of language as an effective means of communication. The relationship between language cultivation and status planning never became the object of systematic research, with status planning itself being left to the political elite. Linguists have devoted little attention to the numerous ethnic minorities, and even less to the problems of the coexistence of the Czech language and minority languages in one state. The social dimension of cultivation, performed in a number of cases for the benefit of the middle classes, was underestimated, while emphasis was placed on the technical (functional) aspects of the cultivation of standard Czech.

Sweden

There is a long tradition of institutional cultivation of the Swedish language in Sweden. Following the French model, the Swedish Academy (founded in 1786, while the French Academy was founded as early as 1635) has become the most important institution devoted to Swedish. The primary function of the Swedish Academy, like that of the French Academy, was "to give the Swedish language purity, strength and literary distinction especially as concerns the art of poetry and eloquence and as concerns the sciences . . ." (from the statute, quoted in Jernudd, 1991: 48). During the twentieth century other institutions came into existence, such as the Swedish Language Council (founded in 1944) and the Swedish Centre of Technical Terminology (1941). Generally, the Swedish cultivation institutions have pursued goals similar to those of the Czech cultivation centers mentioned above. The only marked difference consists in the greater effort devoted to the elaboration of terminology in Sweden, and the closer coordination of the cultivation of Swedish and the languages of the neighboring countries (in particular Norway and Denmark). Both the Czech and Swedish approaches to cultivation have been characterized by a strong functionalist position. Its ideological and political "neutrality," however, began to be questioned by sociologically more adequate sociolinguistic research, which won recognition in Sweden in the last third of the twentieth century (Teleman, 2005).

The language situation in Sweden at the end of the twentieth century can be characterized by three general features: (1) the increasing influence of English, (2) the growing multilingualism in Swedish society, (3) the rising demand for good knowledge of both written and spoken language. These three factors, which may certainly be found also in other developed countries, are accompanied by a number of language policy problems (Hult, 2004; Melander, 2004). As far as English is concerned, its importance for Sweden is undisputed, and the need to advance the teaching of English and its use in numerous situations is generally acknowledged. Still, to what extent, if at all, should English be allowed to exclude Swedish from certain communicative domains? Sweden is home to the speakers of five legally recognized language minorities, but the number of immigrants bringing their mother tongues along with them is on the increase (about 200 languages). In this situation, how can they be taught their respective languages at a high level while acquiring good knowledge of Swedish as a second language at the same time? Moreover, what is to be understood as good knowledge of Swedish in a multicultural society? Good knowledge of a language is indispensable in many situations typical of today's information society, both at work and in private – yet, how can all social strata be guaranteed equal opportunities to acquire such knowledge?

In pursuing a solution to the above-mentioned problems, as well as a number of other related ones, the Swedish Government set up a Parliamentary Committee in 2000, which presented its comprehensive report (735 pages) to the Minister of Culture in 2002. It provided an outline of an action program for the Swedish language (Committee on the Swedish Language, 2002).[1] The primary goals of the program include "firstly, to advance the position of Swedish, and secondly, to ensure that everyone in Sweden has equally good opportunities to acquire the Swedish language." The program (comprising 80 recommendations) focuses on the Swedish language; nevertheless, it is a complex proposal for a language policy since it does not neglect the other languages used in Sweden, dealing with Swedish in relation to these languages. It is also a prominent feature of the program that its recommendations result not only from status planning, but also from corpus and acquisition language planning, as is evident from the three primary objectives to be accomplished: "Swedish shall be a complete language, serving and uniting our society. Swedish in official and public use shall be correct and shall function well. Everyone shall have a right to language: Swedish, their mother tongue, and foreign languages."

Pursuing these goals involves vast cultivation activity. As far as the first goal is concerned, the objective of the proposed recommendations is that Swedish should or could be used alongside English in a number of areas, such as schools and universities, research, public administration, working life, the consumer area, culture, the media, which would stimulate a systematic development of the expressive potential of the Swedish language (its lexis and text patterns and genres in particular). The second goal takes into account the need for the citizens in a democratic society to be able to communicate with "their" social institutions (including the EU institutions), which requires the administrative and legal texts produced by these institutions to be highly comprehensible – the cultivation measures therefore promote the "plain language" functional variety (with specific features in syntax and style). At first glance, the third goal seems to relate only to acquisition planning. However, this is not the case: ensuring that all people have equally good opportunities to acquire a language also involves tackling to what extent the texts, the script, even the structure of the language, are "socially open" to all – and this may become a task of language cultivation. It is one of the objectives of plain language movements to make the particular texts comprehensible to everyone, irrespective of educational background. Concerning the structure of standard language, it can be variable enough to absorb features of social or regional dialects, which makes the standard language more easily accessible to the speakers of those dialects.

Finally, note the dialectical relation between corpus and status planning in the above action program. The intended cultivation activities (corpus planning) result logically from the status planning: if Swedish is to remain a complete language, a language fully functional even in such domains as education and research, much attention should be devoted to the development of terminology. And it follows logically that such a complete language, the object of deliberate permanent cultivation, may easily be planned to acquire the status of a universal means serving the whole society and unifying it.

Language Management in the Postmodern Era

Language cultivation is a type of organized language management characteristic of the era of social modernization (Neustupný, 2006). Typically, the development of language cultivation approaches is therefore tied to the formation and maintenance of standard languages. On the contrary, in today's developed societies, characterized to a varying degree by postmodern features, the processes of language destandardization may be observed (Mattheier, 1997; Spiekermann, 2005; Daneš, 2006). Destandardization means on the one hand that standard language ceases to be used in certain situations or communicative domains, and on the other that it is becoming increasingly varied as it incorporates, to a much larger extent, elements extrinsic to it until now. Language destandardization may be due to the following:

1   the need for generally accepted language standards ceases to be acknowledged in societies professing the ideology of postmodernism;
2   the awareness of the obligatory character of social norms acquired at school is in decline;
3   the codification of standards, carried out by the intellectual elites during the period of social modernization, has departed from the language used by the majority of speakers today;
4   the codification of standards has become decentralized, in Garvin's terminology (1993: 42) this may be characterized as a shift from the "academy-governed style of codification" toward the "free-enterprise style of codification."

In this situation, specialists in language cultivation may choose between two directions to take: they may either criticize the deviations from the norm, evaluating them as mistakes; or gradually adjust the standard language, increasing its variability and advancing higher tolerance toward variation in general. While cultivation usually proceeds in both directions at the same time (depending also on particular communicative domains), the latter direction seems to be preferred in postmodern societies which value plurality and diversity.

The uniformity of standard language is no longer considered obvious even in an area of language traditionally codified in the greatest detail – orthography. The reception of *The Rules of Czech Spelling* from 1993 is particularly illuminating in this respect. Though it introduced few alterations, it met with such opposition on the part of the general public that the Ministry of Education was forced to suspend its use in schools until a year later when *The Rules* was supplemented with further permitted spelling variants. On the whole, the Czech language situation has become favorable to the formation of a spelling of Czech comprising variants specific for individual functional varieties of the standard language. Specific spelling phenomena may be found in the language of fiction writers or scientists (who defend them publicly against the attempts of the codifiers at uniformity in language); specific spelling phenomena abound in e-mail communication. In other words, the following tendency seems to have begun asserting itself: the uniform spelling of the standard language is becoming decentralized and differentiated into the spelling of the language of fiction, of science, spelling for everyday use, etc. The functional differentiation of standard spelling coexists with that long established in the codification of standard pronunciation, where the categories of high, neutral, and low style are employed.

The new social situation, which stresses plurality and diversity, also restructures relations between linguistic institutions (the centers of cultivation activity) and the public (the citizens and organizations). Let us note here that the primary institution established to cater for contact between the linguists and the general public is a consulting center – an institution providing advice rather than a coercive body. The web site of the Language Consulting Centre of the Czech Language Institute presents the activity of the center to the public as follows: "We do not aim merely at providing a yes-no answer to your queries, but rather at explaining or explicating the solution to you. Nor do we proscribe, order, and 'guard'. We advise, explain, and recommend." However, the linguists answering the language queries do not only provide adequate service; they draw on the language queries themselves since they represent a valuable source of sociolinguistic information on the linguistic behavior and attitudes of the inquirers (individual members of the public, journalists, fiction writers, teachers, secretaries or institutions, civil service authorities, business organizations, etc.), which may be further used in (theoretical) linguistics research. The linguists aim to hold a *dialogue* with the public (Uhlířová, 2002). The web site of the Language Consulting Centre itself invites the readers to enter into such a dialogue in the section "We ask" with questions (and suggested answers) such as:

> "What do you think about words that have more than one inflectional suffix in a particular case? (e.g., popel*a* – popel*e* – popel*u*).
> A) It is a case of inconsistency that should be eliminated. Only one form should be prescribed in order to avoid chaos in language.
> B) It is natural and alright – it is a question of the development of the language, or a matter of choice (e.g., between a neutral and colloquial form).
> C) Another opinion or comment."

(My translation)

As mentioned above, language cultivation as a treatment of language typical of the period of social modernization barely pays any attention to the fact that the language, that is, the object of cultivation, is used in a multilingual environment; the existence of other languages is acknowledged at most as a threat to the purity of the cultivated language (cf. the ideology of purism). Minority languages are ignored, let alone made the object of cultivation. However, the situation is changing nowadays – while established languages display features of destandardization processes (as discussed above), a number of minority languages are being standardized in developed social contexts today. Yet, what should standardization in the postmodern era look like? Apparently, it can no longer be the standardization with the functions and features typical of language standardization in the period of social modernization. An example of "an undeveloped language in a developed context" is Romani, a language currently spoken, in addition to Czech (or Slovak), by approximately 100,000 people in the territory of the Czech Republic. It was not until the social changes in 1989 that the Roma ethnicity was formally recognized, and only the spelling of Romani is fully standardized in the Czech Republic nowadays. On the other hand, the social and territorial differentiation of the Romani language is being researched, a Romani–Czech dictionary has been compiled, and a detailed textbook of Romani published. Romani is employed as an auxiliary language at the first grades of primary schools, albeit to a limited extent; its standardization is therefore a pressing issue. Although the position of Romani as a minority language is specific in various respects (the Roma live in a number of European and non-European countries, none of which constitutes a natural sociocultural center for them), the extent to which the models of standardization developed on the basis of Romani are applicable to other languages as well poses a highly interesting question. One of these models, a model for the postmodern era, may be briefly characterized by the following features: "1. The standard is polycentric. 2. The standard is selectively elaborated. 3. There is no codification that is binding for participants. 4. The standard is a mixed home language. 5. The standard is a symbol of ethnic contribution to the world. 6. The standard is the property of all, not only the elites" (Hübschmannová & Neustupný, 1996: 107; see also Hübschmannová & Neustupný, 2004).

   To conclude: language cultivation is becoming a rather complex activity in the new era – it is no longer concerned only with the language (or better still, languages!) in the narrow sense of the word, but also with communication (discourse). Obviously, it is interconnected with status planning, and therefore affected, however vicariously, also by specialists in fields other than linguistics and by politicians, their interests, and ideologies; it is performed not only by linguists from governmental and non-governmental bodies but also increasingly by various groups of language users as well as by individual writers or speakers. In the new era the theory of language cultivation will therefore require a broader theoretical framework than in the period of classical and post-classical language planning. In this respect, a good option seems to be Language Management Theory (Jernudd & Neustupný, 1987; Neustupný & Nekvapil, 2003), which places less emphasis on the technical aspects of planning, focusing instead on agency. It comprises not only top-down processes, but also bottom-up ones, being "an academic response to people in power in reaction against central imposition" (Jernudd, 1993: 134). It incorporates the micro and macro dimensions of planning, while paying detailed attention to the whole "language policy cycle" (Canagarajah, 2006: 158; Nekvapil, 2006).

NOTES

Thanks are due to Viktor Elšík, Björn Melander, Petr Kaderka, Tamah Sherman, Marián Sloboda, and Jiří Zeman for helpful comments at various stages in the development of this article.

1 The Report became the basis of the Government bill Bästa språket ('The Best Language'), approved by the Swedish Parliament in 2005.

REFERENCES

Canagarajah, A. S. (2006). Ethnographic methods in language policy. In T. Ricento (ed.), *An Introduction to Language Policy* (pp. 153–169). Malden, MA: Blackwell.

Committee on the Swedish Language (2002). *Speech: Draft Action Programme for the Swedish Language. Summary* (SOU 2002: 27). Stockholm: Statens Offentliga Utredningar.

Daneš, F. (1987). Values and attitudes in language standardization. In J. Chloupek & J. Nekvapil (eds.), *Reader in Czech Sociolinguistic.* (pp. 206–245). Amsterdam: John Benjamins.

Daneš, F. (2006). Herausbildung und Reform von Standardsprachen und Destandardisierung [Development and Reform of Standard Languages and Destandardization]. In U. Ammon, N. Dittmar, K. J. Mattheier, & P. Trudgill (eds.), *Sociolinguistics: An International Handbook of the Science of Language and Society* (pp. 2197–2209). Berlin/New York: Walter de Gruyter.

Fishman, J. A. (2006). *Do Not Leave Your Language Alone.* Mahwah, NJ: Lawrence Erlbaum.

Garvin, P. (1973). Some comments on language planning. In J. Rubin & R. Shuy (eds.), *Language Planning: Current Issues and Research* (pp. 24–33). Washington, DC: Georgetown University Press.

Garvin, P. (1993). A conceptual framework for the study of language standardization. *International Journal of the Sociology of Language*, 100/101, 37–54.

Hall, R. A. (1950). *Leave Your Language Alone!* Ithaca, NY: Linguistica.

Hausenblas, K. (1979). Kultura jazykového komunikování [Cultivation of linguistic communication]. In J. Kuchař (ed.), *Aktuální otázky jazykové kultury v socialistické společnosti* [Current Problems of Language Cultivation in Socialist Countries] (pp. 122–131). Prague: Academia.

Havránek, B. (1932a). Úkoly spisovného jazyka a jeho kultura [The task of the standard language and its cultivation]. In B. Havránek & M. Weingart (eds.), *Spisovná čeština a jazyková kultura* [Standard Czech and the Cultivation of Language] (pp. 32–84). Prague: Melantrich. (Partially translated into English in P. L. Garvin (ed.) (1964). *A Prague School Reader on Esthetics, Literary Structure and Style* (pp. 3–16). Washington, DC: Georgetown University Press.

Havránek, B. (1932b). Obecné zásady pro kulturu jazyka [General principles for the cultivation of good language]. In B. Havránek & M. Weingart (eds.), *Spisovná čeština a jazyková kultura* [Standard Czech and the Cultivation of Language] (pp. 245–258). Prague: Melantrich. English translation in J. Rubin & R. Shu, (eds.) (1973). *Language Planning: Current Issues and Research* (pp. 102–111). Washington, DC: Georgetown University Press.

Homoláč, J. & Nebeská, I. (2000). Příspěvek ke kritické analýze pojmu jazyková norma [A contribution to the critical analysis of the concept language norm]. *Slovo a slovesnost* [Word and Verbal Art], 61, 102–109.

Hübschmannová, M. & Neustupný, J. V. (1996). The Slovak-and-Czech dialect of Romani and its standardization. *International Journal of the Sociology of Language*, 120, 85–109.

Hübschmannová, M. & Neustupný, J. V. (2004). "Terminological" processes in north-central Romani. *Current Issues in Language Planning*, 5, 83–108.

Hult, F. M. (2004). Planning for multilingualism and minority language rights in Sweden. *Language Policy*, 3, 181–201.

Jernudd, B. H. (1991). *Lectures on Language Problems*. Delhi: Bahri Publications.

Jernudd, B. H. (1993). Language planning from a management perspective: An interpretation of findings. In E. H. Jahr (ed.), *Language Conflict and Language Planning* (pp. 133–142). Berlin: Mouton de Gruyter.

Jernudd, B. H. & Neustupný, J. V. (1987). Language plannning: For whom? In L. Laforge (ed.), *Proceedings of the International Colloquium on Language Planning, May 25–29, 1986, Ottawa* (pp. 69–84). Québec: Les Presses de L'Université Laval.

Mathesius, V. (1932). O požadavku stability ve spisovném jazyce [On the requirement of stability for the standard language]. In B. Havránek & M. Weingart, eds. *Spisovná čeština a jazyková kultura* [Standard Czech and the Cultivation of Language] (pp. 14–31). Prague: Melantrich. French translation in É. Bédard & J. Maurais (eds.) (1983). *La norme linguistique* [The language norm] (pp. 809–813). Québec, Paris: Conseil de la langue française/Le Robert.

Mattheier, K. J. (1997). Über Destandardisierung, Umstandardisierung und Standardisierung in modernen europäischen Sprachen [On destandardization, restandardization and standardization in modern European languages]. In K. J. Mattheier & E. Radtke (eds.), *Standardisierung und Destandardisierung europäischer Sprachen* [Standardization and Destandardization of European Languages] (pp. 1–9). Frankfurt am Main: Peter Lang.

Melander, B. (2004). A Language Policy for Sweden. Paper read at the conference Small States and Minorities, Reykjavík, September 17–18.

Nekvapil, J. (2006). From language planning to language management. *Sociolinguistica*, 20, 92–104.

Neustupný, J. V. (2006). Sociolinguistic aspects of social modernization. In U. Ammon, N. Dittmar, K. J. Mattheier, & P. Trudgill (eds.), *Sociolinguistics: An International Handbook of the Science of Language and Society* (pp. 2209–2223). Berlin/New York: Walter de Gruyter.

Neustupný, J. V. & Nekvapil, J. (2003). Language management in the Czech Republic. *Current Issues in Language Planning*, 4, 181–366. Reprinted in R. B. Baldauf & R. Kaplan (eds.) (2006). *Language Planning and Policy in Europe* (vol. 2, pp. 16–201). Clevedon, UK: Multilingual Matters.

Noreen, A. & Johannson, A. (1892). Über Sprachrichtigkeit [On linguistic correctness]. *Indogermanische Forschungen. Zeitschrift für indogermanische Sprach- und Altertumskunde* [Journal of Indo-Germanic Studies], 1, 95–157.

Pravidla hledící k českému pravopisu a tvarosloví s abecedním seznamem slov a tvarů (1902). [The rules regarding Czech orthography and morphology with an alphabetical list of words and forms]. Praha: Císařský královský školní knihosklad.

Scharnhorst, J. (ed.) (1999). *Sprachkultur und Sprachgeschichte* [The Cultivation of Language and Linguistic Changes]. Frankfurt am Main: Peter Lang.

Spiekermann, H. (2005). Regionale Standardisierung, nationale Destandardisierung [Regional standardization, national destandardization]. In L. M. Eichinger & W. Kallmeyer (eds.), *Standardvariation: Wie viel Variation verträgt die deutsche Sprache?* [Variation in the Standard: How Much Variation Can the German Language Withstand?] (pp. 100–125). Berlin, New York: de Gruyter.

Teleman, U. (2005). Language cultivation and language planning II: Sweden. In O. Bandle et al. (eds.), *The Nordic Languages* (vol. 2, pp. 1970–1983). Berlin/New York: Mouton de Gruyter.

Uhlířová, L. (2002). Jazyková poradna v měnící se komunikační situaci u nás [Language consulting service in the light of recent communication changes in the Czech Republic]. *Sociologický časopis/Czech Sociological Review*, 38, 443–455.

Vinokur, G. (1925). *Kul'tura jazyka: Očerki lingvističeskoj texnologii.* [Language Cultivation: An Outline of Linguistic Technology]. Moscow: Rabotnik prosveščenija.

FURTHER READING

Chloupek, J. & Nekvapil, J. (eds.) (1993). *Studies in Functional Stylistics.* Amsterdam/Philadelphia: John Benjamins.

Cooper, R. L. (1989). *Language Planning and Social Change.* Cambridge: Cambridge University Press.

Garvin, P. (ed.) (1964). *A Prague School Reader on Esthetics, Literary Structure and Style.* Washington, DC: Georgetown University Press.

Janich, N. & Greule, A. (eds.) (2002). *Sprachkulturen in Europa: Ein internationales Handbuch* [Language Cultivation in European Countries: An International Handbook]. Tübingen: Gunter Narr.

Kaplan, R. B. & Baldauf, R. B., Jr. (1997). *Language Planning from Practice to Theory.* Clevedon, UK: Multilingual Matters.

Kondrašov, N. A. (ed.) (1988). *Teorija literaturnogo jazyka v rabotax učënyx ČSSR.* [Theory of the Standard Language in the Scholarly Works from the Former Czechoslovakia]. (= Novoe v zarubežnoj lingvistike [New trends in linguistics abroad] XX). Moscow: Progress.

Neustupný, J. V. (1978). *Post-Structural Approaches to Language.* Tokyo: University of Tokyo Press.

Scharnhorst, J. & Ising, E. (eds.) (1976/1982). *Grundlagen der Sprachkultur: Beiträge der Prager Linguistik zur Sprachtheorie und Sprachpflege* [Fundamentals of the Cultivation of Language: Prague School Contributions to the Theory of Language and Language Cultivation], vol. 1, 2. Berlin: Akademie-Verlag.

Spolsky, B. (2004). *Language Policy.* Cambridge: Cambridge University Press.

19 Language Cultivation in Contexts of Multiple Community Languages

M. PAUL LEWIS AND
BARBARA TRUDELL

Introduction

Many developing nations (described by Chumbow, 2005: 167) today are characterized by the existence of tens, even hundreds, of living languages which are spoken by and identified with particular ethnic groups within the country. These nations face particular challenges where language policy is concerned, including the choice of official language(s), the designation of particular languages as "majority" or "minority" languages within the nation, and choices regarding which languages to cultivate and which to ignore in policy formulation (Tollefson, 2002: 422).

In fact, of the thousands of languages spoken in the world today all but a handful are classified as "minority" languages. A minority language can be distinguished from a majority language by its lesser numerical *or political* importance in the country (UNESCO, 2003). The power differential between those groups with more influence though perhaps smaller numbers, and those who are more numerous but less influential, is reflected in the term "minoritized" as used in this chapter. These "minority" or "minoritized" language communities also add multiple cultural, linguistic, economic, and political dimensions to the task of formulating language policy. The effectiveness of language cultivation efforts in these contexts depends on a range of policy and implementation issues, including national political will, the availability of resources and expertise, local interpretation of national policy directions, and local readiness to participate in their implementation (cf. Bamgboṣe, 1991; Clyne, 1991; May, 2001; Mazrui & Mazrui, 1998; Ricento, 2000; Spolsky, 2004; Blommaert, 2006).

National-level policies on language cultivation in these contexts range from those which focus primarily on the diffusion of national or official languages (exoglossic policies) to those which support the development of local languages (endoglossic policies). Exoglossic policies focus on the role of official languages in developing a nationist identity, reducing inter-ethnic conflict and bringing about social and political stability. Endoglossic policies support to varying degrees the development of the local languages present in their nations. These national-level language and education policy decisions are derived from differing underlying philosophies of language diversity, discussed below.

At the other end of the spectrum of policy formation and implementation, community-supported local language cultivation initiatives are an important aspect of language cultivation (Horvath & Vaughn, 1991; Ruiz, 1995; May, 1999). Particularly in nations whose resources are limited, effective cultivation of local languages inevitably requires significant engagement by local communities. In addition, non-governmental agencies of various kinds often play a role in providing expertise and consultation. We provide two case studies (Cameroon and Papua New Guinea), which feature significant local community engagement with national-level language policy, as examples of how these diverse interests interact with each other to affect both the development of language cultivation policy and its implementation.

The Language Policy Environment

Language cultivation in contexts of multiple local languages has many dimensions; the overall policy environment in which language cultivation takes place is one of the most important of these, since this is the dimension in which the permitted sociopolitical space for language cultivation is described. Language policy in this context thus needs to respond to questions such as the following.

Question 1: Which languages?

The first major question is: "Which language or languages will be the focus of explicit national language policy?" The intended or actual roles and functions of the languages under consideration should play a significant role in how this question is answered.

In some contexts the nationist purposes of the nation-state are seen to be served best if a national or official language is cultivated and promoted (Garvin & Mathiot, 1956), performing an internally unifying and externally distinctive function. Frequently this policy choice will require many of the citizens of the nation-state to learn an additional language; however, the language chosen may over time become a potent symbol of their nationist identity. The attraction of such an exoglossic policy is its potential for enhancing national unity and providing a linguistic symbol of nationhood; however such a policy may also cause disenfranchisement of those who do not speak the selected language, or who have only limited access to its acquisition (Arthur, 2001; Goke-Pariola, 1993; Paulston, 1994; May, 2000).

In other cases, attempts are made to address these disadvantages by including additional regional or local languages within the scope of the national
language policy. In many cases, the resources available and applied to this
more endoglossic policy are few, possibly even merely rhetorical. Local
languages may be recognized in the national constitution as part of a nation's
cultural patrimony, but without any specific requirement that they be
developed or used in any particular way. Such acknowledgment does create a
degree of space for the development of local languages, however, and can
provide the basis for interest groups to lobby for the allotment of resources to
the cultivation of the minority or minoritized languages.

Question 2: Which language diversity policy?

A related question is: "What will be the policy regarding language diversity?"
While a specific official language may be identified and other languages may
also be recognized, national language policy also needs to address how all
the other languages and language varieties within the nation's boundaries
will be dealt with. Over the last decade, three distinct approaches to language
diversity have been identified (cf. Nettle, 1999; Hornberger and Skilton-
Sylvester, 2000; Hornberger, 2002), arising from three perspectives regarding
the role of language in multilingual societies.

The first perspective holds that the role of language in enhancing governance is of primary importance. Governance requires ease and efficiency in
communication; linguistic diversity is seen as a threat to the ability of the
government and other state institutions to function effectively, and is thus
a problem to be overcome or eliminated. Language policy shaped by this
perspective will tend toward the cultivation of fewer languages and, in the
extreme, the suppression of other languages and language varieties.

The second perspective views each sociolinguistic context as an ecological
system, and considers the maintenance of linguistic ecosystems as being of
primary importance. From this perspective each language variety has an
important role to play in the overall sociolinguistic system, and represents
a significant resource that must be protected and encouraged to flourish
(cf. Barton, 1995; Fishman, 2001). Linguistic diversity represents a pool of these
resources. Language policy shaped by this perspective will seek to attain
balance within the overall sociolinguistic ecosystem by encouraging tolerance
for linguistic diversity and the cultivation of as many language varieties as
possible.

The third ideological perspective views linguistic contexts in terms of
human rights (cf. Stroud, 2001; Musau, 2003). From this perspective the role
of national policy is primarily the protection of individuals' rights; thus
governments must not impinge on the rights of individuals to maintain their
identity and exercise their freedoms as members of a particular cultural group.
This includes their right to maintain and use their particular language variety.
Policy which is primarily informed by this perspective will actively protect

linguistic diversity, creating social and political space for diverse linguistic and cultural expressions.

These three perspectives are not entirely mutually exclusive. Concerns for governance, the development of linguistic resources, and the protection of individual language rights all must be considered in forming a comprehensive policy for contexts in which multiple languages exist.

Question 3: What will be the impact of language cultivation?

The ideological perspectives described above provide a way to describe the primary orientations of language policy, but policy makers may well operate without a particular ideology consciously in mind. More often, one ideological perspective or another shapes their perception of the problems to be addressed, with little attention to the implications of that approach. Nevertheless, language policy decisions are linked closely with a variety of social, political, educational, and cultural outcomes. The third major question to be addressed by policy makers, then, is: "What will be the social, political, educational, and cultural implications of these policy decisions?"

In answering this question, policy makers need to be aware of the range of options at their disposal and the benefits and costs of each option. In addition, they need an accurate assessment of the prevailing attitudes and beliefs regarding various languages and their use. Where strongly held negative attitudes exist toward any of the languages being considered for development, the cost of pursuing the cultivation of that language must be considered carefully.

In language planning terms, not only must a policy be developed but an acquisition plan – a plan for implementing the policy – must also be put into place. Building a consensus of acceptance of the proposed policy, informing the important constituencies, developing and then making the materials and resources available, are all parts of an acquisition plan (cf. Ager, 2001; Miller, 2000).

Question 4: How to resource language cultivation?

The fourth major question is: "What resources are available for the implementation of this language policy?"

Once a policy is developed and an acquisition plan prepared, adequate resources must be made available so that implementation may actually take place. This often is primarily a matter of political will; however in nations with relatively few resources, capacity for resourcing the policy in terms of both expertise and finances may pose a significant obstacle.

While it is generally assumed that national policy is resourced and implemented by the government and its agencies, in some nations the implementation of language policy may depend on assistance from international agencies, both governmental and non-governmental. In addition, the participation of local community-based development organizations becomes particularly important when the national government's capacity for resourcing policy is limited. Indeed, where resource support from the national government is not forthcoming at all, local communities may be forced to fund and equip their own language cultivation efforts.

Extra-governmental agencies and organizations are sure to have their own perspectives on what an appropriate policy should be; they may operate in line with the overall national-level policy, or work against the policy or parts of it. Some may represent and promote the particular interests of a local community (or subgroup within that community). The interplay of these different agendas can contribute significantly to the success or failure of a national policy. Ideally it is important to coordinate these diverse efforts, build a consensus among the players, and encourage collaboration among them. In practice, such coordination is not easily achieved.

Question 5: Who should participate in language cultivation?

The fifth major question related to language cultivation policy is: "Whose participation is required?" Generally, the implementation of language policy is delegated through the national formal and non-formal education system to educators at regional and local levels. However in some cases the allocation of personnel, materials, and finances for implementing language cultivation goals may be uneven and inconsistent. For example, teachers assigned to bilingual education programs may lack adequate training or language skills in the two languages to be used. Or, the pedagogical and promotional materials needed to implement the policy may not be locally available. In other cases, local educational administrators may not be aware of or in agreement with the language policy and so may obstruct its implementation.

In cases where national-level capacities for resourcing and implementation are inadequate, local capacities become essential for effective language policy implementation (Hasselbring, 2006). In these cases, local perspectives on language policy assume an especially important role. Local community leaders will need to be aware of language issues, the policy options available, and the costs and benefits of those options. In these cases consultants from organizations outside the community (whether national or international) may play a significant role in providing access to the information and expertise that these leaders need.

Summary

The wide range of possible answers to these five questions demonstrates the broad scope of language policy decisions in contexts of multiple local languages. Nevertheless, careful attention to questions such as these can help to ensure that national language policy sets a national environment in which the desired language cultivation – at both national and local levels – can successfully take place.

Implementing Language Diversity Policy

Community-based decision making

In the processes of implementing language policy, the role of local community perspective is critical. This is especially true where national-level resources for policy implementation are limited, as described above. Still, local response to any national-level language policy determines to a large extent the success of that policy, whatever its position on local language use. Given the political and social marginalization that characterizes minority language communities in general, it would be easy to assume that local decisions regarding language are of much less importance than nationally mandated policy. However, a community's language use is such a locally-sited cultural phenomenon, and so intimately bound into the identity of that community, that language use decisions made by the speakers themselves ultimately carry far more weight in the language cultivation arena than official formulations of policy – no matter how politically disenfranchised the speakers are (Adegbija, 1994).

Language use decisions in a community take place in a variety of contexts. The influence of local institutions is significant, whether they are indigenous institutions (e.g., traditional leadership, cultural associations) or nationally organized institutions with local representation (e.g., schools, government, religious institutions, national or international NGOs) (LoBianco & Rhydwen, 2001). Indeed, language cultivation initiatives cannot be sustained without adequate support from local institutions. However, this type of institutional support alone is not sufficient; the historical, sociocultural, and economic environment of a community is extremely influential, and indeed can outweigh any measure of institutional or official influence. In addition, the perspective of members of the community's elite (Prah, 1995), whether they live locally or outside of the language area, often weigh heavily with the community.

Community responses to national language policy are rarely monolithic, but trends can be tracked. Where national policy is antagonistic to cultivation of local language, its use moves entirely into informal, predominantly oral use patterns. Its speakers may deny that they speak it, even with evidence to the contrary. Explicitly supportive national policy can (but does not always) energize nationally organized institutions to engage in overt promotional activities of the local language in education, local government, and other institutional contexts. Local community institutions may or may not follow suit, and the response of community members themselves is similarly unpredictable.

National language policy that is permissive, but not accompanied by resources or implementation plans, results in the most complex mix of supportive and antagonistic perspectives at local level, as local government, non-governmental institutions, and community members take positions based on their own concerns and agendas.

Cultivation processes in local communities

Language cultivation involves both oral and written aspects; oral communication strategies are by far the most common in many minority language communities, and strengthening the utility and flexibility of a community's language must involve support for its oral use. However the cultivation of written language typically needs a great deal more support than cultivation of oral language. Often local languages lack an orthography, with no written tradition whatsoever. Yet the permanence and expanded breadth of uses made possible when a language is written are significant; indeed, we would argue that sustainable language cultivation ultimately requires its use in written form by some significant segment of the population.

Given these two necessary components, the linguistic processes involved in local language cultivation usually include linguistic analysis, orthography development, expansion of the lexicon, production of dictionaries, and other aspects of corpus planning. These processes usually require the involvement of a professional linguist, but community members should also be engaged in these processes to a significant extent. Local ownership of the orthography in particular is one of the key factors in acceptance of the written language, and so testing and consultation in local contexts is imperative.

Advocacy processes are also part of language cultivation. Negative language attitudes within the community are not immutable, and local perceptions of what the language is appropriate for can be influenced by positive example or the endorsement of locally esteemed persons or institutions. Advocacy processes targeted at community members might thus include pilot educational programs using the community language, publications in the community's language, and personal testimony from those whose opinion is respected.

Where members of the elite or institutional authorities are concerned, advocacy needs to focus particularly on the positive impact of language cultivation on their own priorities and concerns.

Pedagogical processes are also part of language cultivation: raising awareness among community members of the uses and accessibility of the written language and providing opportunities for literacy learning in both formal and non-formal educational contexts. The production of literature in the local language is also critical, for both pedagogical and attitudinal reasons. As these processes are engaged, particular issues commonly arise which pose potential obstacles to language cultivation efforts and so need to be addressed. They include local policies and beliefs regarding language and educational achievement, the sociolinguistic domains in which the local language is used in the community, and local patterns of use of written language in general for communication and learning.

Organization and planning in community-based cultivation projects

Community-based language cultivation needs to be intentional and institutionally well supported. In many cases of successful language cultivation initiatives, a local committee or commission has taken primary responsibility for the linguistic, advocacy, and pedagogical processes involved. This is not to downplay the crucial roles of non-local stakeholders, however. Universities and other national and international institutions may be crucial in providing needed technical expertise. Funding from non-local sources is also very helpful, particularly in the early stages. If *ownership* of the language cultivation efforts is not clearly local, however, sustained success of those efforts is unlikely no matter how supportive the non-local bodies are.

Summary

Not only is local community engagement a critical component of the successful implementation of a language cultivation policy in this context, but it is also a feasible one. Where local motivation for engaging with the policy is strong and adequately supported by either government or non-government institutions, community-based initiatives can make a significant contribution to language cultivation across the nation. The two case studies which follow give ample evidence of the importance of considering both local and national-level values and resourcing capacity for language cultivation.

Case Study: Cameroon

As described above, the formulation and implementation of language policy in multilingual contexts is characterized by a complex interplay between national and local perspectives. The central African country of Cameroon provides an example of this complexity. With two official languages (English and French), an English-based Pidgin, and up to 248 distinct Cameroonian languages (Breton and Fohtung, 1991) in use as well, Cameroonian national leadership has had to tread a difficult path between national unification and validation of the many unique cultures and languages which make up the country.

Upon independence in 1960 and the reunification of the British- and French-held colonies which now constitute Cameroon, national language policy was formulated to recognize both English and French as official languages. Cameroonian languages were largely ignored in early national language policy

(Gfeller, 2000), due to the potentially explosive divisiveness of promoting one community's language above the others.

However, such official neglect of Cameroonian languages has not lessened their use, particularly in the rural communities which constitute 52 percent of the population (Population Reference Bureau, 2004). Actual cultivation efforts among these languages could be seen among certain private secondary schools in the 1960s and 1970s, which included certain Cameroonian languages in their curricula (primarily as subjects). The University of Yaoundé also took a leading role in language cultivation efforts, as university linguists spearheaded the establishment of a Cameroonian national alphabet in 1979 (Tadadjeu & Sadembuo, 1979). This standardization of the alphabet was seen as a milestone in the advancement of written Cameroonian languages. In 1982, the Cameroonian government endorsed both official language bilingualism (French and English) and the promotion of minority languages as well; however, this move did not result in either resource allocation or implementation of significant language cultivation efforts among Cameroonian language communities.

Another important step in the cultivation of Cameroonian languages has taken place with the establishment of a number of local language committees from the 1980s up until the present time; these are groups of teachers and members of the local elite, whose goal is the promotion and maintenance of their own language (Trudell, 2006). These committees operate primarily by producing written materials in the language, holding literacy classes in the language, and organizing efforts to introduce the language into local primary schools as subject and/or medium of instruction. In 1995, the National Association of Cameroonian Language Committees (NACALCO) was formed, to give language committees a forum for interaction and for expressing their views to the wider Cameroonian society.

In response to the substantial efforts of such private and local stakeholders, as well as (it could be argued) in response to increasing support for local language rights on the part of international bodies such as UNESCO and the Organization of African Unity (now the African Union), the Cameroonian government took several steps toward active support of the cultivation of local languages. The National Forum on Education of May 1995 endorsed the PROPELCA (*Projet de Recherche Operationelle Pour L'Enseignement des Langues au Cameroun,* Operational Research Project for the Teaching of Cameroonian Languages), a national-level project whose goal is the development of local Cameroonian languages for use in formal mother tongue education.

This endorsement is now part of the Law of the Orientation of Cameroonian Education, passed in 1998. In a further step, the new national Constitution of January 1996 included reference to the need for maintaining and using Cameroonian languages. Official implementation of these laws and policies has been slow so far; however, in a number of communities the language committees and other local language cultivation activists are using the policies to lend official backing to their activities.

The case of Cameroon demonstrates how national language policy can both frame and restrict language cultivation efforts by local communities and non-government institutions, and also how national policy can itself be influenced by those efforts. The energy arising from local communities' desire to see their languages maintained and developed has resulted in organized, ongoing language cultivation efforts. However, it is also the case that such local cultivation efforts have only been sustainable with the active support of institutions outside the community, such as the university and language development NGOs.

Case Study: Papua New Guinea[1]

Language planning in Papua New Guinea at the national level up through independence (1975) focused on the roles of Tok Pisin and Hiri Motu, two widely used Pidgin languages, and English as languages of national identity and official functions. Local languages, of which there are more than 800 (Gordon, 2005), only came into focus for national development policy during the last decade. Previously, local language cultivation policy and implementation had been left to provincial governments. However even in this new environment, the roles for vernacular languages, Tok Pisin, and English continue to be an issue.

Up until the 1950s, Christian missions provided most basic education. As a result, various lingua francas, and in some cases local languages, were developed as "church languages" and used as vehicles for literacy and basic education. However local communities had very little influence on policy regarding their own languages (Litteral, 1999a). Beginning in the 1950s, the national government "brought the mission education systems under its control" (Ahai & Bopp, 1993; Ahai, 2005) and implemented a policy designed to Westernize the nation through the promotion of English.

However, local communities became actively engaged in advocacy on behalf of their languages. This led to the development of parallel, non-formal local-language-based primary schooling at the provincial level. These "Tok Ples" ("Talk Place," or local language) schools were developed to support the use of local languages for initial literacy and basic education. Some members of these communities remembered the local language education that had been offered in earlier years and asked that it be revived. Pilot programs in the North Solomons, Enga, and East New Britain provinces, introduced in 1980, expanded nationally to include over 250 languages by 1993. Significantly, the ideology behind the policy was "indigenous development, not westernization" (Litteral, 1999a).

In 1986 a national philosophy of education was adopted by Parliament, followed by a policy document adopted in 1989 by the Secretary of Education. The latter established the coordination and funding needed for the ongoing promotion of vernacular languages. Additional support for this effort came from the "Literacy and Awareness Program" legislation adopted by Parliament in 1989, which stated explicitly that "a child should learn to read and write in his/her own language" (Litteral, 1999a). In 1991, a review by the education sector agreed that the initial language of instruction in formal education should be the vernacular languages. This policy was adopted in 1995 with the passage of the Education (Amendment) Act. In 2000, Parliament endorsed the national literacy policy, based on the 1989 policy statement. As a result, Papua New Guinea's policies and education plans (1995–2004 and 2005–14) encourage language cultivation in both non-formal and formal education settings.

After what Litteral describes as "incremental development" over three decades, which nevertheless resulted in a "180 degree" turnaround, language policy in Papua New Guinea in the 1990s formalized the concept of indigenous development. This concept incorporates in Tok Ples education both the oral and literate uses of the language for "the whole spectrum of academic subjects and community expressed needs" (Litteral, 1999b).

The evolution of language and education policy in Papua New Guinea demonstrates the interplay of the ideological perspectives of national and regional governments (the need to govern efficiently, the desire for development and full participation in the world community) and those of the members of local communities concerned about the alienation of their young people and the loss of their languages and cultures. The development of the Tok Ples schools demonstrates that policy can be made and implemented in a way that takes into account both sets of concerns. In addition, the potential contribution that external agencies can make to language cultivation is clear. While Litteral points out that the role of NGOs in the implementation of this policy was never specified, Siegel observes that "the role of non-government organizations (NGOs) has been crucial in the promotion and development of both preschool and adult vernacular literacy programs" (Siegel, 1996).

Equally important, however, is the participation of the local community in bringing about local language education (Siegel, 1996). The government has recognized the key role of the community in this process. In East New Britain province, the provincial government assisted the community in the development of its own Tok Ples school by providing half of the teacher's salary with the community expected to provide the physical venue, give oversight through a local committee, and take responsibility for ongoing fundraising (Stephen Simpson, personal communication).

The development of Tok Ples education in Papua New Guinea provides an example of the way minority language cultivation can be facilitated through the combined efforts and resources of national and provincial governments, NGOs and local communities. The Tok Ples schools appear to have met felt needs in the local communities, and even after the program became nationalized, there is evidence that strong local participation in Tok Ples schools continues.

Conclusion

Particularly in contexts of multiple local languages, effective language cultivation policy depends upon both national and local governmental and non-governmental components. At the national level, policy decisions must be comprehensive and carefully considered in order to provide the desired policy environment. At the local level, community language cultivation processes reflect, enable, and react to national policy decisions. A well formulated national policy can help create the political, economic, and social environment in which local communities, with or without assistance from outside sources, are able to engage with implementation of the policy.

The complex interaction of national policy with local community choices also demonstrates the ways in which nationally and locally held values regarding language converge or conflict. Successful language cultivation in this context is thus the result of careful attention to both levels of decision-making, and to all of the sectors, public and private, based on an awareness of the influence of each on language policy implementation.

NOTE

1   Additional data from Robert Litteral, Chesley and Ruth Ray, Stephen Simpson, and Diane Wroge.

REFERENCES

Adegbija, Efurosibina (1994). *Language Attitudes in Sub-Saharan Africa*. Clevedon, UK: Multilingual Matters.

Ager, Dennis (2001). *Motivation in Language Planning and Language Policy*. Clevedon, UK: Multilingual Matters.

Ahai, Naihuwo (2005). Literacy in an emergent society: Papua New Guinea. http://www.sil.org/silewp/abstract.asp?ref=2005-002, accessed November 27, 2006.

Ahai, Naihuwo & Bopp, Michael (1993). *Missing links: Literacy, awareness and development in Papua New Guinea*. Papua New Guinea: National Research Institute.

Arthur, Jo (2001). Perspectives on educational language policy and its implementation in African classrooms: A comparative study of Botswana and Tanzania 2001. *Compare*, 31(3), 347–362.

Bamgboṣe, Ayọ (1991). *Language and the Nation: The Language Question in Sub-Saharan Africa*. Edinburgh: Edinburgh University Press.

Barton, David (1995). *Literacy: An Introduction to the Ecology of Written Language*. Oxford: Blackwell.

Blommaert, Jan (2006). Language policy and national identity. In Thomas Ricento (ed.), *An Introduction to Language Policy: Theory and Method* (pp. 238–254). Oxford: Blackwell.

Breton, Roland J. L. & Fohtung, Bikia (1991). *Atlas Administratif des Langues Nationales du Cameroun*. Yaoundé/Paris: CERDOTOLA and ACCT.

Chumbow, Beban Sammy (2005). The language question and national development in Africa. In Thandika Mkandawire (ed.), *African Intellectuals: Rethinking Politics, Language, Gender and Development* (pp. 165–192). Dakar/London: CODESRIA and Zed Books.

Clyne, Michael (1991). *Community Languages: The Australian Experience*. Melbourne: Cambridge University Press.

Fishman, Joshua A. (ed.) (2001). *Can Threatened Languages Be Saved? Reversing Language Shift, Revisited: A 21st Century Perspective*. Clevedon, UK: Multilingual Matters.

Garvin, Paul & Mathiot, Madeleine (1956). The urbanization of the Guarani language. In Anthony F. C. Wallace (ed.), *Men and Cultures: Selected Papers from the Fifth International Congress of Anthropological and Ethnological Sciences* (pp. 365–374). Philadelphia: University of Pennsylvania Press.

Gfeller, Elisabeth (2000). *La Société et L'Ecole Face au Multilinguisme*. Paris: KARTHALA.

Goke-Pariola, Abiodun (1993). *The Role of Language in the Struggle for Power and Legitimacy in Africa*. Lewiston, NY: The Edwin Mellen Press.

Gordon, Raymond G. (ed.) (2005). *Ethnologue: Languages of the World* (15th edn.). Dallas, TX. SIL International.

Hasselbring, Sue Ann (2006). Cross-Dialectal Acceptance of Written Standards: Two Ghanaian Case Studies. Doctoral dissertation, Department of Linguistics, University of South Africa.

Hornberger, Nancy H. (2002). Multilingual language policies and the continua of biliteracy: An ecological approach. *Language Policy*, 1, 27–51.

Hornberger, Nancy H. & Skilton-Sylvester, Ellen (2000). Revisiting the continua of biliteracy: International and critical perspectives 2000. *Language and Education*, 14:(2), 96–122.

Horvath, Barbara M. & Vaughn, Paul (1991). *Community Languages: A Handbook*. Clevedon, UK: Multilingual Matters.

Litteral, Robert (1999a). Language Development in Papua New Guinea. http://www.sil.org/silewp/1999/002/silewp1999-002.html, accessed November 27, 2006.

Litteral, Robert (1999b). Four Decades of Language Policy in Papua New Guinea: The Move Towards the Vernacular. http://www.sil.org/silewp/1999/001/silewp1999-001.html, accessed November 27, 2006.

LoBianco, Joseph & Rhydwen, Mari (2001). Is the extinction of Australia's indigenous languages inevitable? In Joshua A. Fishman (ed.), *Can Threatened Languages Be Saved?* Clevedon, UK: Multilingual Matters.

May, Stephen (ed.) (1999). *Indigenous Community-Based Education*. Clevedon, UK: Multilingual Matters.

May, Stephen (2000). Uncommon languages: The Challenges and possibilities of minority language rights 2000. *Journal of Multilingual and Multicultural Development*, 21(5), 366–385.

May, Stephen (2001). *Language and Minority Rights: Ethnicity, Nationalism and the Politics of Language*. Essex, UK: Pearson Education.

Mazrui, Ali A. & Mazrui, Alamin M. (1998). *The Power of Babel: Language and Governance in the African Experience*. Oxford/Nairobi: James Currey Ltd. and East African Educational Publishers.

Miller, Carolyn P. (2000). Modifying language beliefs: A role for mother-tongue advocates? In Gloria E. Kindell & M. Paul Lewis (eds.), *Assessing Ethnolinguistic Vitality: Theory and Practice* (pp. 167–188). Dallas: SIL International.

Musau, Paul M. (2003). Linguistic human rights in Kenya: Challenges and prospects for indigenous languages in Kenya 2003. *Language, Culture and Curriculum*, 16(2), 155–163.

Nettle, Daniel (1999). *Linguistic Diversity*. Oxford: Oxford University Press.

Paulston, Christina Bratt (1994). *Linguistic Minorities in Multilingual Settings: Implications for Language Policies*. Amsterdam: John Benjamins.

Population Reference Bureau (2004). http://www.prb.org/datafind, accessed July 19, 2004.

Prah, Kwesi Kwaa (1995). *African Languages for the Mass Education of Africans*. Bonn: DSE.

Ricento, Thomas (ed.) (2000). *Ideology, Politics and Language Policies: Focus on English*. Amsterdam: John Benjamins.

Ruiz, Richard (1995). Language planning considerations in indigenous communities. *The Bilingual Research Journal*, 19(1), 71–81.

Siegel, Jeff (1996). *Vernacular Education in the South Pacific*. Canberra: AUSAID.

Spolsky, Bernard (2004). *Language Policy*. Cambridge: Cambridge University Press.

Stroud, Christopher (2001). African mother-tongue programmes and the politics of language: linguistic citizenship versus linguistic human rights. 2001. *Journal of Multilingual and Multicultural Development*, 22:(4), 339–355.

Tadadjeu, Maurice & Sadembuo, Etienne (1979). *General Alphabet of Cameroonian Languages*. Yaoundé: University of Yaoundé.

Tollefson, James (2002). Limitations of language policy and planning. In Robert Kaplan (ed.), *The Oxford Handbook of Applied Linguistics*. Oxford: Oxford University Press.

Trudell, Barbara (2006). Local agency in the development of minority languages: Three language committees in Northwest Cameroon. *Journal of Multilingual and Multicultural Development*, 27(3), 196–210.

UNESCO (2003). *Education in a Multilingual World*. Paris: UNESCO.

FURTHER READING

Banda, Felix (2000). The dilemma of the mother tongue: prospects for bilingual education in South Africa. *Language, Culture and Curriculum*, 13(1), 51–66.

Das Gupta, Jyotindra (1970). *Language Conflict and National Development: Group Politics and National Language Policy in India*. Berkeley: University of California Press.

Hornberger, Nancy H. (1987). Bilingual education success, but policy failure. *Language in Society*, 16, 205–226.

Lodhi, Abdulaziz Y. (1993). The language situation in Africa today. *Nordic Journal of African Studies*, 2(1), 79–86.

Muthwii, Margaret Jepkirui & Nduku Kioko, Angelina (eds.) (2004). *New Language Bearings in Africa: A Fresh Quest*. Clevedon, UK: Multilingual Matters.

Ndoye, Mamadou (2003). Bilingualism, language policies and educational strategies in Africa. *IIEP Newsletter*, 21(3), 4.

Pütz, Martin (ed.) (1994). *Language Contact and Language Conflict*. Amsterdam: John Benjamins.

20 Ecological Language Education Policy

NANCY H. HORNBERGER AND FRANCIS M. HULT

The ecology of language has been a steady influence on the study of multilingualism since the late 1950s (e.g., Trim, 1959; Voegelin & Voegelin, 1964; Haugen, 1972; Arndt & Janney, 1984; Mühlhäusler, 1996; Hornberger, 2002). While the general concept of ecology can be traced back to the work of nineteenth-century naturalist Ernst Haeckel, it was theoretically refined for the study of multilingualism by Einar Haugen in the 1960s and 1970s (Hartig, 1984; Hornberger, 2002). It has since diversified to include broad, dynamic, and controversial approaches for investigating relationships between language and the (social) environment (Fill & Mühlhäusler, 2001a). Since the 1990s the ecology of language has emerged as increasingly important to language policy and planning (LPP) researchers as they seek to investigate relationships between societal multilingualism and individual language choices and, in turn, how these relationships can be managed most effectively (Ricento, 2000: 206–208).

In this chapter we focus on specific ways in which the ecology of language is fruitful for the study of multilingual educational LPP. We begin by reviewing the basic principles of the ecology of language as they were set forth by Einar Haugen and as they have been developed by researchers following in his footsteps. We then turn to a discussion of how these basic principles are applied to LPP scholarship, distilling core questions that are essential for ecologically oriented LPP research. Finally, we offer two case studies from our own research in the Andes and Sweden to illustrate the application of these core questions.

Principles of Language Ecology

Haugen (1972: 328–29) set forth the ecology of language as an approach to "[covering] a broad range of interests within which linguists can cooperate significantly with all kinds of social scientists toward an understanding of the interaction of languages and their users." He associates his approach with earlier work by Voegelin and Voegelin (1964) who state that "in linguistic ecology, one begins not with a particular language but with a particular area . . ." (cited in Haugen, 1972: 328). Since Haugen's formulation, the ecology of language has been widely taken up by language researchers:

> Pragmatics and discourse analysis, anthropological linguistics, theoretical linguistics, language teaching and research and several other branches of linguistics discovered the usefulness of ecological parameters such as interrelationships, environment and diversity . . . in the early 1990s, all the different approaches which some way link the study of language with ecology were brought together, and a unified – though still diverse – branch of linguistics was established which was called ecolinguistics. (Fill & Mühlhäusler, 2001b: 1)

The ecology of language, or ecolinguistics, now encompasses diverse, though not necessarily mutually exclusive, lines of inquiry such as environmental discourse analysis, language and biocultural diversity, social semiotics, and societal multilingualism (see Fill & Mühlhäusler, 2001a).

With respect to the investigation of societal multilingualism, the ecology of language focuses on a language's "interaction with other languages in the minds of bi- and multilingual speakers . . ." as well as "its interaction with the society in which it functions as a medium of communication" (Haugen, 1972: 325). Following this orientation, it is the overall objective of researchers to map all aspects of the language environment, from the sociological to the psychological.

The ecology of language has, thus, developed as a conceptual approach to investigating how linguistic ecologies relate to social, historical, sociolinguistic, and political forces at individual, community, and societal levels of social organization (Mühlhäusler, 1996). Conceptually, Calvet explains that

> The ecology of language assumes . . . different levels of analysis. The highest level is that of the worldwide organization of the relationship among languages . . . This world system (corresponding, in our metaphor, to the ecosphere) is constructed by a terracing of lower systems (corresponding to ecosystems). In a linguistic ecosystem, the languages in contact maintain relationships that create *ecological niches* for each of them: The "niche" of one language is constructed by its relationship with the other languages, by the place it occupies in the ecosystem, that is to say its functions, and by its place in the social environment, essentially the geography that plays a determining role in the expansion of languages. (1999: 35, translation ours)

Calvet further suggests that an ecolinguistic system can be altered by (1) the behaviors of individual speakers through, for example, population movement, learning or not learning a dominant language, and learning or not learning a subordinated language; and/or (2) government actions pertaining to, for example, language policy, education, literacy, and media (1999: 61). It becomes clear, then, that in an ecological approach, properties of societal multilingualism are viewed in tandem with individual behaviors. Linguistic ecologies shape, and are shaped by, the social interaction of individuals (Garner, 2004: 40). As Mufwene notes, ". . . it is typically the small acts of individuals, or the effects of the ecology on them, which wind up having wide-ranging effects on the overall population" (Mufwene, 2001: 14).

The crux of language ecology is that languages evolve in the context of a social environment where some languages are more equal than others, giving rise to three major themes of description and analysis: language evolution, language environment, and language endangerment. Languages, like living species, evolve, grow, change, live, and die in relation to other languages and also in relation to their sociohistorical, sociopolitical, and sociocultural environment; but it is also true that some languages, like some species and environments, may be endangered and the ecology movement is about not only studying and describing those potential losses, but also counteracting them (Hornberger, 2002: 33).

In sum, the ecology of language is an approach that is inherently both holistic and dynamic (Garner, 2004: 36–38). It is a conceptual orientation, an approach to critical thinking about multilingualism that focuses researchers on contextual interconnections in language contact situations and their wider implications for sociopolitical actions, including multilingual LPP (van Lier, 2004: 165–192). In this view, analytical emphasis is fourfold: on relationships among languages, on relationships among social contexts of language, on relationships among individual speakers and their languages, and on inter-relationships among these three dimensions.

Despite its apparent usefulness as a holistic approach to multilingualism, the ecology of language is not without its critics. Some suggest that it goes too far in relating language phenomena to natural processes (e.g., Edwards, 2002), while others suggest it does not go far enough (Garner, 2004). Some point to the many nuances that need to be critically examined and refined (Pennycook, 2004), while others still view it with cautious optimism as a useful metaphor (e.g., Spolsky, 2004: 7–8). A full review of critical viewpoints is beyond the scope of this chapter (see Pennycook, 2004 for a thorough discussion). Our focus here is on the useful application of an ecological mindset to the investigation of LPP in multilingual settings.

Contributions of Language Ecology to the Study of Educational Language Planning and Policy

It is widely accepted that language planning is divided into three major types: corpus planning relating to language form, status planning relating to language function, and acquisition planning relating to language learners and users (Cooper, 1989; Kaplan & Baldauf, 1997). While each type has its specific planning objective, Hornberger (2006) explains that all three types of planning are intimately intertwined with one another. The dynamic interplay among planning types makes the ecology of language a particularly apt conceptual approach to LPP. The analytical emphases of the ecology of language dovetail nicely with the three planning types: relationships among languages (corpus planning), relationships among social contexts of language (status planning), and relationships among individual speakers and their languages (acquisition planning). The further emphasis on inter-relationships among these dimensions pushes LPP scholars with an ecological mindset to think beyond any single planning type alone as well as beyond any one language in isolation. Such a holistic approach is valuable when investigating LPP in general and, as Kaplan and Baldauf (1997: 122–125) remark, language-in-education planning and policy in particular.

Although the ecology of language is not yet widely adopted among LPP researchers, a few scholars have put forth several useful advances that can be synthesized to form a coherent way of thinking about LPP in ecological terms. Mühlhäusler, for example, proposes an ecological approach to language planning. With respect to status planning, he states, the primary objective, in the best of all possible worlds, should be "equitable status for a maximum number of diverse languages" (Mühlhäusler, 2000: 331). As part and parcel of this objective, he points to issues that fall under what has come to be known as prestige planning, or planning related to perceptions about language (Ager, 2005). It is of central importance, Mühlhäusler notes, to attend to how linguistic diversity is socially structured, that is to say the ways in which different languages are positioned in relation to each other in the minds and hearts of speakers. Such planning involves critical examination of the circulating discourses mapped onto different languages while also trying to reframe them in equitable ways.

With respect to corpus planning, Mühlhäusler (2000: 338–339) notes that linguistic forms must be viewed in light of their social and political implications. Corpus planning in this vein would include critical reflection about the specific forms chosen during planning processes while also fostering critical awareness about different ways of speaking and their social ramifications. When attending to language form during planning, he suggests that planners would do well to focus on altering terms that are or have been used discursively to mislead or subjugate certain speakers. In all, for Mühlhäusler, ecological language planning should serve to strengthen and develop linguistic environments by fostering linguistic diversity.

Hornberger (2002) demonstrates how language education policies, specifically, might be utilized to strengthen language ecologies. Taking her continua of biliteracy framework (Hornberger, 1989; Hornberger & Skilton-Sylvester, 2000; Hornberger, 2003) as an example, she illustrates the reciprocity between policy and practice in educational LPP. Hornberger focuses on interactions among languages across contexts and the role of language education policies. She notes that decades of research on language learning reveal that power relationships in many societies have a tendency to privilege, for example, literacy rather than orality and monolingualism rather than bilingualism; national educational policies tend to focus on dominant language skills, predominantly in terms of production (Hornberger, 2002: 40). Ecological language education policy, she holds, is needed in order to achieve balance along a full range of continua of biliteracy, which include language context, development, content, and media (Hornberger, 2002: 39). Educational policies that emphasize equitable multilingualism have the potential to counteract hegemonic social processes and permit all students' languages to become valuable resources for themselves and their communities. Ultimately, Hornberger states, "multilingual language policies are essentially about opening up ideological and implementational space in the environment for as many languages as possible" (2002: 30). Often, these spaces, or niches to use Calvet's terminology, must be created in relation to dominant languages of wider communication such as English.

Building on the work of Tsuda (1994), Phillipson and Skutnabb-Kangas (1996) suggest that the relationship between language policies and the spread of English throughout the globe can be understood most usefully in terms of either a diffusion of English paradigm or an ecology of languages paradigm (cf. Tsuda, 1997). Diffusion of English is associated with factors such as capitalism; science and technology; modernization; monolingualism; ideological globalization and internationalization; Americanization and homogenization of world culture; and linguistic, cultural, and media imperialism (Phillipson & Skutnabb-Kangas, 1996: 436). In contrast, the ecology of languages paradigm, as Skutnabb-Kangas (2000: 657) further elaborates, associates English with factors that favor linguistic parity:

1   multilingualism and linguistic diversity;
2   promotion of additive foreign/second language learning;
3   equality in communication;
4   maintenance and exchange of cultures;
5   ideological localization and exchange;
6   economic democratization;
7   human rights perspective, holistic integrative values;
8   sustainability through promotion of diversity; qualitative growth;
9   protection of local production and national sovereignties;
10   redistribution of the world's material resources.

"The two paradigms," Phillipson and Skutnabb-Kangas write, "can be regarded as endpoints on a continuum. Language policy initiatives can thus be seen as attempts to shift the political or educational ground toward one end . . . or the other . . ." (1996: 436).

By using an ecology of language approach to policy analysis, a researcher focuses on, among other issues, the extent to which language policies do or do not foster linguistic diversity. In this vein, the ecologically minded LPP researcher attempts to ascertain whether or not language policies adequately take into account the complex sociolinguistic factors that are present in modern multilingual polities, an aspect that is crucial for the efficacy of language policies (Schiffman, 1996; Eggington, 1997).

It becomes evident that an ecolinguistic approach to studying societal multilingualism in general is fruitfully complemented by an ecological perspective on LPP. The former highlights the complexity of societal multilingualism and the latter allows the LPP researcher to determine the extent to which planning and/or policy address those complexities. In all, then, the ecology of language is an integrated conceptual approach to examining multilingualism in society and in LPP as well as how the two interrelate.

Taking together the work that has been done relating to ecology and LPP, several themes begin to emerge. Here, we frame these themes as overarching data-gathering and analytical questions in an attempt to provide a guide for future ecologically oriented educational LPP work. These questions, we submit, are relevant equally to those who conduct LPP research and those engaged with the practices and processes of LPP development and implementation.

An ecological orientation to (educational) LPP is a conceptual approach, not a heuristic or framework. No specific methodology is prescribed (van Lier, 2004: 205). The approach does beg certain key questions for those who seek to investigate or practice language planning and policy in any given polity. These questions are guiding questions that can be explored using a variety of research methodologies.

The first stage in ecologically oriented (educational) LPP investigation and practice is to seek out data that fully reflect the dynamic nature of the ecology of language. We propose the following as general data-gathering questions:

- How are relationships among different languages reflected in policy documents?
- How do language policies relate to individual experiences with language use and beliefs about language(s)?
- How do language policies relate to sociolinguistic circumstances 'on the ground'?

Multidimensional data gathered to address the above questions must then be analyzed in critical ways that also reflect an ecological orientation. This calls upon analysts to focus on inter-relationships among the data in an attempt to ascertain the potential for LPP efforts to foster equitable linguistic diversity. We propose the following as general guiding analytical questions:

- How do language policies at multiple levels of social organization interact?
- Do policies promote equitable multilingualism?

Each of these five questions might, of course, be fine tuned as questions specific to any particular LPP issue or context.

Examples of an Ecological Approach to Educational Language Policy

Having set forth the aforementioned general guiding questions, we turn to how we have applied the principles of the ecology of language to the investigation of educational LPP in two different settings: Sweden and the Andes. Both of these contexts share the need to manage complex multilingualism in education and society. Hult's Swedish example focuses on the representation of multi-lingualism across multiple layers of policy texts and Hornberger's Andean example highlights interculturality across individual, program, and transnational contexts. We do not here attempt to address all the above guiding questions for each case, but rather to illustrate consideration of at least one for each case.

Sweden: Multilingualism across layers of policy texts

Hult (2007) presents an ethnographic, discourse analytic study of multilingual language education policy, focusing on the impact of English language teach-ing (ELT) in Sweden. Following an ecological approach, he seeks to develop a multidimensional representation of inter-relationships among policies, speakers, and social contexts. As a whole, the study is multi-method and multi-sited. Hult uses a combination of ethnographic sociolinguistics and critical discourse analysis, exemplified in Scollon and Scollon's (2004) nexus analysis, to explore how the English language and ELT are positioned with respect to multilingualism in policy texts, among ELT practitioners, and in the wider social context of a multilingual city in the south of Sweden. For the purposes of illustrating specific aspects of an ecological approach, the focus here will be on the representation of multilingualism across policy texts and how these texts interact in the process of LPP development.

Sweden has a long LPP history, most of which has centered on cultivating and situating Swedish as the national language (Teleman, 2002, 2003). Since the 1960s the tide has been steadily changing, especially with respect to education, in favor of promoting linguistic diversity (Boyd, 2001). At present, though, there is also a resurgence of nationalism, partially in response to the increased internationalization of Europe and partially in reaction to growing immigration, which places renewed emphasis on the status of Swedish as the national language (Oakes, 2005; Milani, 2006). The latest LPP challenge for Sweden, then, has been to balance a pluralistic orientation to linguistic diversity with strengthening the status of Swedish.

A comprehensive national language policy for Sweden has been in develop-ment for over ten years. This period has seen the crafting of several key docu-ments in which multilingualism has been variously reflected. In ecological terms, it is useful to consider how multilingualism has been represented across these documents, which were developed by institutions at different levels of social organization.

Following several years of discussion among scholars and politicians about the status of the Swedish language, the Swedish Language Council (Svenska språknämnden) was charged in 1997 with drafting an action program that would serve to strengthen the position of Swedish throughout society. Much of the discussion leading up to this point had focused on the potential threat of English to the use of Swedish in certain domains (e.g., education, media, and commerce) so it is, perhaps, not surprising that this document focused heavily on Swedish and English. Accordingly, this action program was criticized for not attending sufficiently to wider linguistic diversity in Sweden (Boyd & Huss, 1999).

In 2000 a special government committee was created to follow up on the Swedish Language Council's action program. This committee was to take into account the limitations of the initial draft action program and develop recommendations that would serve to strengthen Swedish while also fostering linguistic diversity. The committee published its recommendations in 2002 in a report entitled *Speech: Draft Action Programme for the Swedish Language* (*Mål i mun: Förslag till handlingsprogram för svenska språket*).[1] Much like the Language Council's action program, this report focused heavily on the relationship between Swedish and English (Hult, 2005). Indeed, the primary recommendation of the report was for a law to codify Swedish as the official language.

The 80 recommendations set forth in the report, however, did not focus only on Swedish and English. The overall objectives, in fact, explicitly called for equitable multilingualism and invoked the notion of egalitarian language rights: "[(1)] Swedish shall be a complete language, serving and uniting our society, [(2)] Swedish in official and public use shall be correct and shall function well, and [(3)] everyone shall have a right to language: Swedish, their mother tongue, and foreign languages" (SOU, 2002: 22).[2] Multilingualism was a much stronger component of this report, though it did not appear to suggest legal codification of multilingual education beyond what existing policies already guaranteed and, in some ways, even appeared to contradict rights established in connection with the *European Charter for Regional or Minority Languages* (Boyd & Huss, 2003, 2004; Hult, 2004). Nonetheless, this report once again put multilingualism squarely on the national political agenda where it sat in limbo until 2005.

By the fall of 2005, the committee's report had finally been transformed into proposed legislation entitled *Best Language: A Concerted Language Policy for Sweden*[3] (*Bästa språket: En samlad svensk språkpolitik*) (Prop. 2005/06:2), which was later approved by Parliament in December of 2005. This new legislation echoes the committee's 2002 report, noting that the goals for national language policy shall be the following:

- Swedish is to be the main language in Sweden.
- Swedish is to be a complete language, serving and uniting society.
- Public Swedish is to be cultivated, simple, and comprehensible.

- Everyone is to have a right to language: to develop and learn Swedish, to develop and use their own mother tongue and national minority language, and to have the opportunity to learn foreign languages.

(Prop. 2005/06:2, p. 14)

Despite the similarity, the new legislation departs from the 2002 report in a major respect. While the primary recommendation of the 2002 report is that Swedish be legally codified as Sweden's official language, the new legislation specifically indicates that such a law is unnecessary. The explanatory notes point to Swedish's currently strong position as the national language de facto while also noting that Swedish and the many other languages in Sweden need to be carefully managed (Prop. 2005/2006:2, p. 15). In lieu of a law making Swedish official, the government holds that specific language planning goals (noted above) that highlight both the special status of Swedish as well as wider multilingualism are more useful (Prop. 2005/2006:2, p. 15). This move, while seemingly fair in its treatment of all languages in Sweden, proved controversial among legislators and scholars hoping for a clear language policy for Swedish; future legislative discussion on the subject was promised (Josephson, 2006).

The government took a further step toward integrated language planning in relation to the new legislation. A new umbrella agency for language planning was created to bring under one administrative unit all official bodies dealing with language issues. The Swedish Language Council (now renamed Språkrådet) was restructured to also include the Sweden Finnish Language Council and the government's clear language task force all under the auspices of the Institute for Dialectology, Onomastics and Folklore. This agency is meant to attend to the management of multilingualism not just the Swedish language.

In all, these political and administrative developments appear to be indicative of a desire by the government to manage the complex multilingualism that is part of Swedish society. Certainly the general goals set forth in the new legislation together with the new language planning agency lend themselves to LPP possibilities in Sweden. Still, it is a delicate time for Swedish LPP. The policy goals could be realized in ways that proactively strengthen and develop overall multilingualism in Sweden or they could be realized by maintaining the status quo where Swedish and English are pitted against each other for dominance of certain domains while other languages receive minimal attention. Language education, as the government points out in the new legislation, will be a major component of realizing the general language policy goals (Prop. 2005/2006:2, p. 2). Much will depend, then, on how this new legislation interacts with the national curricula for language teaching.

The Andes: Interculturality across individual, program, and transnational contexts

Bilingual intercultural education (EIB) has been an enduring educational initiative in Andean South America for several decades now, constituting as well a significant vehicle of multilingual language policy (Hornberger, 2000, 2002). Focusing here on the broad-based planning and implementation initiatives of the Program for Professional Development in Bilingual Intercultural Education for the Andean Region (PROEIB-Andes), we consider how ecological language education policies practiced and promoted by PROEIB participants relate to sociolinguistic circumstances of the multi-layered contexts in which they interact, and how these policies and practices approach the task of promoting equitable multilingualism in the Andes. We draw on Hornberger's ongoing ethnographic work on Quechua language education policy and practice in the Andes over the past 30+ years, especially her short- and longer-term visits to PROEIB beginning in 1997 and continuing to the present.

PROEIB-Andes was founded in 1996 as a six-nation consortium effort with the goal of fulfilling professional development, research, knowledge management, and cooperative network-building functions in bilingual intercultural education across the Andean countries and Latin America more generally (López, 2001, 2005a, b; Sichra, 2001; PROEIB-Andes, 2006). Among the innumerable activities carried out over the past decade has been a thriving master's program in bilingual intercultural education, the *Maestría*, established at the University of San Simón in Bolivia in 1998 and enrolling indigenous educators from Bolivia, Ecuador, Peru, Colombia, Chile, and Argentina through a selection process in each country involving their respective ministries of education, sponsoring universities, and indigenous organizations. Now in its fifth cycle, the Maestría has to date prepared approximately 150 indigenous educational leaders, most of them actively dispersed in multilingual educational endeavors throughout the Andean region. Other PROEIB-Andes activities include short courses for indigenous community leaders, international seminars and congresses, various publication series, development of an extensive library and documentation center, and collaborative projects and consultancies with national ministries of education, academic institutions in Latin America and Europe, and international organizations such as UNESCO and UNICEF.

Across these multiple layers of activity, themes of multilingualism and interculturality pervade PROEIB efforts, geared to the sociolinguistic context in which they occur. Interculturality is briefly defined as dialogue across and among ethnic or cultural groups constructed as equals (see also Hornberger, 2000). Here we cite only a few brief examples of multilingual and intercultural practice, from instances at the individual and community level, to the curriculum and classes of the Maestría itself, to national and transnational contexts.

Roberto, a Peruvian Aymara who grew up in his rural Puno community explicitly forbidden by his parents to leave for the city until he went to Normal School, and who went on from there via a trajectory through radio announcing and adult literacy work to the Maestría, remarks on the value the bilingual intercultural perspective he gained at PROEIB has for him when he returns to his Aymara communities:

This is an institution that strengthens one considerably. The best thing about here is going out to the communities and encountering them again, but now with another vision, no? in other words, with a more complete foundation, with theories that they give you here. There they ask you things, for example, no? . . . They ask you and you have to face up, respond. What is this interculturality? What is EIB? What are its principles? This is the best thing about PROEIB. (Roberto, interview, June 24, 2005)[4]

The vision, theories, and principles of interculturality Roberto refers to are pervasively instantiated in the Maestría's academic policies and practices – straight through from admission and selection processes to curriculum design, classroom interaction and social relations, and on to research and assessment activities.

Consider the language ecology of the programs' curricular organization in four obligatory academic strands, namely education, culture, language, and indigenous language, the last of which involves the students in investigating and documenting their own indigenous language, in dialogue with their peers' investigation and documentation of theirs. Oral and written interaction in this strand incorporates substantial use of the indigenous languages, whereas classroom interaction and academic writing in the first three strands is in Spanish (the lingua franca of the program and of the university). English also plays a role in this ecology as the language of access to required bibliographic and technological resources in all the strands; and the program provides the students with ongoing tutoring sessions in English to this end. Salient to the theme of interculturality here is the emphasis on managing the ecology of languages in ways that strengthen each individual participant's linguistic repertoire while simultaneously fostering multilingual (and multimodal) peer interaction and cooperative learning or *interaprendizaje* (LEL, interview, June 26, 2005; see also Luykx, Julca, & García, 2006 on strategies of interdialectal communication in Quechua within PROEIB).

Key to the success of this approach is the transnational nature of the program, with participation of educators representing a broad spectrum of both national and indigenous identities. The first cohort included some 50 students from 9 ethnolinguistic groups and 5 countries (PROEIB-Andes, 2006: 15); among the 41 enrolled in the fourth cohort, there were at least 10 indigenous ethnicities and language varieties represented, including speakers of Quechua from Bolivia, Ecuador, and Peru; Aymara from Bolivia and Peru; Asheninka, Awajún, and Huampí from Peru; Mapuche from Chile; Cofán and Wayuú from Colombia; Shwar from Ecuador; and an Argentinian Colla from Jujuy. The program has developed a rigorous and far-reaching recruitment and selection process to achieve this diversity, regarded as essential for the intercultural learning there.

Interestingly, and relevant to the underlying ecological language education policy goal of contributing to equitable multilingualism through bilingual intercultural education, this diversity was not initially foreseen in the pre-planning stages, but was rather the result of pressure brought to bear by indigenous organizations themselves, during a series of probing consultations on the curricular and institutional structure of the program, held in each of the participating countries during the two-year period leading up to PROEIB's establishment. In the words of PROEIB-Andes' founder and director, Luis Enrique López, commenting on PROEIB selection processes and criteria:

> We take the distribution of languages into account in order to have the greatest possible representation. Inevitably, though, a large contingent come from the distinct varieties of Quechua and Aymara – because of the longer contact, more individuals with the required educational background, and more demand in terms of overall numbers. There are always more Quechua and Aymara speakers. In fact, the initial program design was for Quechua and Aymara only, but in 1993, in the first big planning session we held in Lima, the indigenous organizations said – we don't want the same old story of only Quechua and Aymara. (LEL, interview, June 26, 2005)

Intercultural strengths of the program's transnational diversity are evident not only at the level of individual and community, and of curriculum and classroom interaction, but also in the consulting and mobilizing activities PROEIB undertakes at national and transnational levels. This is epitomized in the Seventh Latin American Congress on Bilingual Intercultural Education (VII-EIB), held in October 2006 in Cochabamba, Bolivia and organized by PROEIB on behalf of and in support of the Bolivian Ministry of Education, a Congress which turned out to play a strategic role at a critical juncture in Bolivia's national language education policy. From its very beginnings, PROEIB-Andes has been closely linked to Bolivia's Education Reform of 1994, a reform which included as one of its two key planks the implementation of bilingual intercultural education nationwide (Hornberger & López, 1998; López, 2005a, b, forthcoming); PROEIB faculty, students, and graduates have played ongoing consulting and staff roles in Bolivia's Ministry of Education throughout the years of the Reform.

As the time for Bolivia's legally mandated ten-year review and renewal of national educational policy drew near and was several times postponed in the context of major political upheavals in Bolivia, the future of bilingual intercultural education in Bolivia became increasingly uncertain; the more so after the watershed election of Bolivia's first indigenous president, Evo Morales, in December 2005 and his swift moves to reverse all policies associated with his predecessor's neoliberal administration (López, 2005b, forthcoming). Nevertheless, because the Ministry of Education had agreed years before to sponsor and host this seventh in a series of Latin American Congresses on EIB which began with the first hosted by Guatemala in 1995, the event became an opportunity for PROEIB-Andes, and ultimately the 700 mostly indigenous EIB Congress participants from across Latin America, to position EIB as a grassroots indigenous movement (not a neoliberal initiative) and to educate Bolivia's new leaders about interculturality and language ecology as vehicles for indigenous empowerment.

Indeed, at the conclusion of the Congress, official delegates of the 24 participating countries affirmed, among other conclusions and recommendations, that:

> EIB is the result of the struggle of indigenous peoples and has contributed to building foundations for the construction of more democratic societies in Latin America . . . EIB should be government policy. (EIB en Bolivia, 2006: 4–5)

Further, they asserted that a key challenge as EIB moves forward is the need for further analysis of the concepts of interculturality and intraculturality, a theme resonating with comments by many at the Congress, including Bolivian Minister of Education Felix Patzi who affirmed in his opening address that interculturality is not only about respect and tolerance for the other, but also about democratizing cultures and equalizing cultural conceptions, such that each learns from the other.

The overall lesson from PROEIB's decade-long practices with respect to ecological language education policy oriented toward promoting equitable multilingualism may be just that emphasis on an interculturality premised on intraculturality. In the words of PROEIB's founding director:

> interculturality, as we originally proposed it at the theoretical level in the 1970s, is not possible to implement if there is not first a prior phase of reaffirmation. As one Guatemalan indigenous leader put it: "essentialism can also be strategic." . . . Before there can be a discussion about relations among diverse peoples, cultures, identities, there is, because of the history of colonial oppression, first and foremost the necessity to reaffirm yourself as indigenous before opening yourself to the possibility of a more equitable dialogue. The Bolivian indigenous leader Froilán Condori says this very clearly. He speaks of intraculturality. There must first be a stage of intraculturality before we can move on to dialogue. We cannot speak as equals if they have always told me that mine is no good but the other's is. (LEL interview, June, 26, 2005)

Conclusion

An ecological orientation focuses on the multidimensional nature of LPP. It draws attention to the role of language planning and policy in dynamic relationships among speakers, social contexts, and languages. As reflected in the general data-gathering and analytical questions we have posited, the aim of this orientation is to approach LPP issues holistically rather than focusing on a single language, context, or set of speakers in isolation.

The two cases we have presented here illustrate briefly the application of different dimensions of an ecological approach to LPP; they also, reciprocally, illuminate the political underpinnings of LPP that an ecological approach must take into account. The Swedish case concentrated primarily on the first of our guiding data-gathering and analytical questions – relating to relationships among different languages in policies, across different levels of social organization; and illuminated the ways in which a changing European ecology of languages, including increased internationalization and the growing presence of English, may have played a role in both the call to make Swedish an official language and the reaffirmation of multilingualism. The Andean case description addressed the last of our data-gathering and analytical questions – regarding ways in which policies seek to promote equitable multilingualism within and across multilayered sociolinguistic contexts; and illuminated how a multilingual language education policy in the form of bilingual intercultural education (EIB) provided both an opening and a wedge for political mobilization and activism of indigenous language speakers within a Latin American ecology of languages that has traditionally excluded indigenous voices and decision-making.

Addressing the kinds of ecological questions we have proposed is perhaps neither straightforward nor non-controversial as an approach to educational LPP research or practice; indeed the two cases briefly presented demonstrate some of the policy contradictions and sociopolitical challenges that will most surely arise. However, the two cases also demonstrate the value of an ecological orientation for fathoming – and fashioning– the richly multilingual language education policies needed to achieve more equitable societies in today's inevitably intercultural world.

NOTES

The ideas presented here are the result of many long conversations we have had about the application of the ecology of language to language planning and policy. Many of these ideas also appear in Hult (2007).

1   The translation of the title is that of the committee which published a brief English summary of the document (Kommittén för svenska språket, 2002).
2   As translated in Kommittén för svenska språket (2002).
3   The English translations of the title and the following excerpt are taken from Ministry of Education, Research and Culture (2005).
4   All quotations in this section are translated from the Spanish by Hornberger. The original Spanish is not included here, for reasons of space.

REFERENCES

Ager, D. (2005). Image and prestige planning. *Current Issues in Language Planning* 6(1), 1–43.
Arndt, H. & Janney, R. W. (1984). The duck-rabbit phenomenon: Notes on the disambiguation of ambiguous utterances. In W. Enninger & L. M. Haynes (eds.),

Studies in Language Ecology (pp. 94–115). Weisbaden, Germany: Franz Steiner Verlag.

Boyd, S. (2001). Immigrant languages in Sweden. In G. Extra & D. Gorter (eds.), *The Other Languages of Europe* (pp. 177–192). Clevedon, UK: Multilingual Matters.

Boyd, S. & Huss, L. (1999). Det behövs en helhetssyn på språken i Sverige! [A comprehensive view of languages in Sweden is needed!] *Språkvård*, 3, 5–9.

Boyd, S. & Huss, L. (2003). *Mål i mun* och språklig mångfald [*Mål i mun* and linguistic diversity]. *Språkvård*, 1, 28–34.

Boyd, S. & Huss, L. (2004). Språkplanering för svenska i Sverige: Några kritiska synpunkter [Language planning for Swedish in Sweden: Some critical perspectives]. *Sprogforum*, 29, 42–47.

Calvet, L. (1999). *Pour une écologie des langues du monde* [Towards an Ecology of the World's Languages]. Paris: Plon.

Cooper, R. L. (1989). *Language Planning and Social Change*. Cambridge: Cambridge University Press.

Edwards, J. (2002). Old wine in new bottles: Critical remarks on language ecology. In A. Boudreau, L. Dubois, J. Maurais, & G. McConnell (eds.), *L'écologie des langues* [Ecology of Languages] (pp. 299–324). Paris: L'Harmattan.

Eggington, W. (1997). The roles and responsibilities of ESL teachers within national language policies. In W. Eggington & H. Wren (eds.), *Language Policy: Dominant English, Pluralist Challenges* (pp. 165–168). Philadelphia, PA: John Benjamins.

EIB en Bolivia (2006). *Suplemento bimensual* [Bimonthly supplement], 4(13). Cochabamba, Bolivia: Programa de Formación en Educación Intercultural Bilingüe para los Países Andinos (PROEIB Andes).

Fill, A. & Mühlhäusler, P. (eds.) (2001a). *The Ecolinguistics Reader: Language Ecology and Environment*. New York: Continuum.

Fill, A. & Mühlhäusler, P. (2001b). Introduction. In A. Fill and P. Mühlhäusler (eds.), *The Ecolinguistics Reader: Language Ecology and Environment* (pp. 1–9). New York: Continuum.

Garner, M. (2004). *Language: An Ecological View*. New York: Peter Lang.

Hartig, M. (1984). Sociolinguistics and the description of language change and language ecology or: Language splitting versus language contact. In W. Enninger & L. M. Haynes (eds.), *Studies in Language Ecology* (pp. 237–246). Weisbaden, Germany: Franz Steiner Verlag.

Haugen, E. (1972). The ecology of language. In A. Dil (ed.), *The Ecology of Language: Essays by Einar Haugen* (pp. 325–339). Stanford, CA: Stanford University Press.

Hornberger, N. H. (1989). Continua of biliteracy. *Review of Educational Research*, 59(3), 271–296.

Hornberger, N. H. (2000). Bilingual education policy and practice in the Andes: Ideological paradox and intercultural possibility. *Anthropology and Education Quarterly*, 31(2), 173–201.

Hornberger, N. H. (2002). Multilingual language policies and the continua of biliteracy: An ecological approach. *Language Policy*, 1(1), 27–51.

Hornberger, N. H. (ed.) (2003). *Continua of Biliteracy: An Ecological Framework for Educational Policy, Research, and Practice in Multilingual Settings*. Clevedon, UK: Multilingual Matters.

Hornberger, N. H. (2006). Frameworks and models in language policy and planning. In T. Ricento (ed.), *An Introduction to Language Policy: Theory and Method* (pp. 24–41). Malden, MA: Blackwell.

Hornberger, N. H. & López, L. E. (1998). Policy, possibility and paradox: Indigenous multilingualism and education in Peru and Bolivia. In J. Cenoz & F. Genesee (eds.), *Beyond Bilingualism: Multilingualism and Multilingual Education* (pp. 206–242). Clevedon, UK: Multilingual Matters.

Hornberger, N. H. & Skilton-Sylvester, E. (2000). Revisiting the continua of biliteracy: International and critical perspectives. *Language and Education*, 14(2), 96–122.

Hult, F. M. (2004). Planning for multilingualism and minority language rights in Sweden. *Language Policy*, 3, 181–201.

Hult, F. M. (2005). A case of prestige and status planning: Swedish and English in Sweden. *Current Issues in Language Planning*, 6(1), 73–79.

Hult, F. M. (2007). Multilingual Language Policy and English Language Teaching in Sweden. Unpublished doctoral dissertation. University of Pennsylvania.

Josephson, O. (2006). Lagen [The law]. *Språkvård*, 1, 3.

Kaplan, R. B. & Baldauf, R. B. (1997). *Language Planning: From Practice to Theory*. Clevedon, UK: Multilingual Matters.

Kommittén för svenska språket (2002). *Speech: Draft Action Programme for the Swedish Language: Summary*. Stockholm: Statens Offentiliga Utredningar. Available online: http://www.regeringen.se/sb/d/108/a/1443

López, L. E. (2001). Literacies and intercultural bilingual education in the Andes. In D. R. Olson & N. Torrance (eds.), *Literacy and Social Development: The Making of Literate Societies* (pp. 201–224). Malden, MA: Blackwell.

López, L. E. (2005a). Cultural diversity, multilingualism and indigenous education in Latin America. In T. Skutnabb-Kangas & O. García (eds.), *Imagining Multilingual Schools: Language in Education* (pp. 238–261). Clevedon, UK: Multilingual Matters.

López, L. E. (2005b). *De resquicios a boquerones: La educación intercultural bilingüe en bolivia* [From Fissures to Craters: Intercultural Bilingual Education in Bolovia]. La Paz: PROEIB Andes y Plural Editores.

López, L. E. (forthcoming). Top-down and bottom-up: Counterpoised visions of bilingual intercultural education in Latin America. In N. H. Hornberger (ed.), *Can Schools Save Indigenous Languages? Policy and Practice on Four Continents*. Palgrave Macmillan.

Luykx, A., Julca, F., & García, F. (2005). Estrategias de comunicación interdialectal en quechua [Strategies for interdialectal communication in Quechua]. In *Proceedings of the Conference of Indigenous Languages of Latin America-II*. Austin, Texas, October 27–29. Available online: www.ailla.utexas.org/site/cilla2_toc.html

Milani, T. M. (2006). Language planning and national identity in Sweden: A performativity approach. In C. Mar-Molinero & P. Stevenson (eds.), *Language Ideologies, Policies and Practices: Language and the Future of Europe* (pp. 104–117). Palgrave Macmillan.

Ministry of Education, Research and Culture (2005). *Summary of Government Bill 2005/06:2*. Fact Sheet U05.055.

Mufwene, S. S. (2001). *The Ecology of Language Evolution*. Cambridge: Cambridge University Press.

Mühlhäusler, P. (1996). *Linguistic Ecology: Language Change and Linguistic Imperialism in the Pacific Region*. London: Routledge.

Mühlhäusler, P. (2000). Language planning and language ecology. *Current Issues in Language Planning*, 1(3), 306–367.

Oakes, L. (2005). From internationalisation to globalisation: Language and the nationalist revival in Sweden. *Language Problems and Language Planning*, 29(2), 151–176.

Pennycook, A. (2004). Language policy and the ecological turn. *Language Policy*, 3(3), 213–239.

Phillipson, R. & Skutnabb-Kangas, T. (1996). English only worldwide or language ecology? *TESOL Quarterly*, 30(3), 429–452.

PROEIB-Andes (2006). *Interculturalidad y bilingüismo en la educación superior: Desafíos a diez años de la PROEIB Andes* [Interculturality and bilingualism in higher education: Challenges as PROEIB Andes celebrates ten years]. Cochabamba, Bolivia: Programa de Formación en Educación Intercultural Bilingüe para los Países Andinos (PROEIB Andes).

Prop. 2005/2006:2. Bästa språket: En samlad svensk språkpolitik [Best language: An integrated Swedish language policy]. Available from http://www.sweden.gov.se/sb/d/5969/a/50740

Ricento, T. (2000). Historical and theoretical perspectives in language policy and planning. *Journal of Sociolinguistics*, 4(2), 196–213.

Schiffman, H. F. (1996). *Linguistic Culture and Language Policy*. London: Routledge.

Scollon, R. & Scollon, S. W. (2004). *Nexus Analysis: Discourse and the Emerging Internet*. London: Routledge.

Sichra, I. (2001). Huellas de intraculturalidad en un ámbito intercultural de educación superior [Traces of intraculturality in an intercultural context in higher education]. In M. Heise (ed.), *Interculturalidad: Creación de un concepto y desarrollo de una actitud* [Interculturality: Creation of a concept and development of an attitude] (pp. 193–202). Lima, Peru: Programa Marco de Formación Profesional Tecnológica y Pedagógica en el Perú (FORTE-PE).

Skutnabb-Kangas, T. (2000). *Linguistic Genocide in Education or Worldwide Diversity and Human Rights?* Mahwah, NJ: Lawrence Erlbaum.

SOU (2002). *Mal i mun: Förslag till handlingsprogram för svenska språket* [Speech: Draft Action Programme for the Swedish Language] (SOU, 2002: 27). Stockholm: Statens Offentiliga Utredningar. Available online: http://www.regeringen.se/sb/d/108/a/1443

Spolsky, B. (2004). *Language Policy*. New York: Cambridge University Press.

Teleman, U. (2002). *Ära, rikedom & reda: Svensk språkvård och språkpolitik under alder nyare tid* [Glory, Wealth and Order: Swedish Language Cultivation and Politics in Early Modern Time]. Stockholm: Norstedts Ordbok.

Teleman, U. (2003). *Tradis och funkis: Svensk språkvård och språkpolitik efter 1800* [Traditionalism and Functionalism: Swedish Language Cultivation and Politics after 1800]. Norstedts Ordbok.

Trim, J. L. M. (1959). Historical, descriptive and dynamic linguistics. *Language and Speech*, 2, 9–25.

Tsuda, Y. (1994). The diffusion of English: Its impact on culture and communication. *Keio Communication Review*, 16, 49–61.

Tsuda, Y. (1997). Hegemony of English vs. ecology of language: Building equality in international communication. In L. Smith & M. Forman (eds.), *World Englishes 2000, Vol. 14* (pp. 21–31). Honolulu: University of Hawai'i Press.

van Lier, L. (2004). *The Ecology and Semiotics of Language Learning: A Sociocultural Perspective*. New York: Kluwer Academic Publishers.

Voegelin, C. & Voegelin, F. (1964). Languages of the world: Native America fascicle one. *Anthropological Linguistics*, 6(6), 2–45.

21 Education for Speakers of Endangered Languages

TERESA L. MCCARTY, TOVE SKUTNABB-KANGAS, AND OLE HENRIK MAGGA

On speech we hear many a tale unwise,
each gets judged according to size:
big peoples' language no danger will reach;
if a people is small, uncouth their speech.
(Aasen, [1996] 1863, p. 71)

A language is *endangered* "when its speakers cease to use it, use it in an increasingly reduced number of communicative domains, and cease to pass it on from one generation to the next" (UNESCO, 2003a: 2). According to Krauss (1992), *moribund* languages are those which are no longer being learned by children; *endangered* languages are those which, though still being learned by children, will, if present trends continue, cease to be learned by children during the coming century; and *safe* languages are those which are neither moribund nor endangered (pp. 5–7). UNESCO's *Red Books on Endangered Languages* use similar criteria, stressing the importance of child language learners and numbers.

Many researchers and minority groups object to the term "moribund," as it makes it seem natural that languages should disappear. Still, linguists agree that if present trends continue, many languages face extinction. "About 97% of the world's people speak about 4% of the world's languages; and conversely, about 96% of the world's *languages* are spoken by about 3% of the world's *people*. Most of the world's language heterogeneity, then, is under the stewardship of a very small number of people" (UNESCO, 2003a: 2). Optimistic estimates are that half of today's spoken languages may be extinct or seriously endangered by the end of the century (UNESCO, 2003b; www.unesco.org/endangeredlanguages). Pessimistic but realistic estimates place 90 to 95 percent of the world's languages in this category, as does UNESCO's report (2003a: 2). Not only would most languages with fewer than 10,000 speakers – over half the world's spoken languages – disappear, so too would many of those having 10,000 to 1 million speakers. If pessimistic predictions are valid, the majority of "disappeared" languages would be Indigenous languages. Most of our examples, therefore, are Indigenous languages, although the content is relevant to many minoritized languages.

Why Should We Be Concerned about Endangered Languages?

Language and culture cannot be separated . . . Our language and culture . . . tell us who we are, where we came from and where we are going.
(Task Force on Aboriginal Languages and Cultures, 2005: 58)

We are sometimes asked why we should be concerned about language endangerment; after all, these are languages with relatively few speakers and children need to master languages of wider communication (LWCs) to succeed in a global economy. The question is, given human capacities to acquire multiple languages, must acquisition of the LWC come at the price of the mother tongue? Since high-level multilinguals tend to outperform corresponding monolinguals on tests of "intelligence" and creativity, learning several languages well is an individual and a societal resource. What are the costs if these resources are forfeited and small languages disappear?

Language is our primary tool for understanding and communicating, and indeed, for creating our world. As the epigraph that begins this section powerfully illustrates, it is in and through our language that we have access to our culture and humanity. All languages have the same potential for these functions. It is therefore an enormous human impoverishment when a language, with all its collective wisdom, beauty, and richness, falls silent. The great linguist Kenneth Hale, who spoke more than 75 languages, put it this way: "When you lose a language, you lose a culture, intellectual wealth, a work of art. It's like dropping a bomb on . . . the Louvre" (*The Economist*, November 3, 2001, pp. 89, 105).

Further, linguistic and cultural diversity index biodiversity; where there are many languages, there are also many biological species (Harmon, 1995; Maffi, 2001; Skutnabb-Kangas, Maffi, & Harmon, 2003; www.terralingua.org). These diversities are mutually supportive and "an integral part of human existence, in which utilization is part of the celebration of life" (Posey, 1999: 7). "Humanity's collective knowledge of biodiversity and its use and management rests in cultural diversity; conversely conserving biodiversity often helps strengthen cultural integrity and values" (World Resources Institute et al., 1992: 21).

Viewed in this light, language loss is not an abstraction, any more than languages and cultures are substitutable "parts." "Embedded in [our] language are the lessons that guide our daily lives," Cheyenne educator Richard Littlebear (2004) writes; "we cannot leave behind the essence of our being" (p. 12). Language and culture "have spiritual links to the Creator," the Task

Force on Aboriginal Languages and Cultures points out (2005: 62). Rights to language are fundamental to collective and personal identity, and efforts to resist language loss are part of larger struggles for personal and communal well-being, self-determination, and cultural survival (Romero-Little & McCarty, 2006: 5). Language endangerment is a global crisis in which *all* the world's citizens have a stake.

Why Are Languages Endangered?

Language plays a key role in every human activity. Thus, language is affected by every effort to change power relations within or among sociopolitical systems. This is the starting point for understanding the relationship between language and society. "The fate of all languages," the World Commission on Culture and Development (1995) states, "is the result of the social and political environment, above all of power relations" (p. 179). Because minority and Indigenous languages are often viewed as obstacles to those in power, they are easily targets of attack. But even Latin, the world language of its time, was eventually affected by a change in political power relations.

The paths to language endangerment are as complex as the history of nation states and colonialism and the rise of global capitalism. Linguistic genocide (Skutnabb-Kangas, 2000) has been a prominent goal of virtually every colonial regime. Linguicidal policies went hand-in-hand with physical genocide and territorial displacement. In 1770, when the British "annexed" Australia, 300,000–600,000 Aboriginal people – speakers of some 600 Aboriginal languages – came under British rule. By the mid-1930s, only 60,000 Aboriginal people remained. Although there are now 300,000 Aboriginal people in Australia, all but 10 percent have been dispossessed of their languages; of the 90 languages still spoken, 70 are seriously threatened (May, 2001). Similarly, in Aotearoa/ New Zealand, the Māori population at the time of European contact in 1769 was 100,000. Within a century it had been decimated to 42,113, and by 1975, only 5 percent of Māori school children spoke Māori (Benton, 1988).

In the remainder of this section we focus on education as a primary cause of language endangerment, but readers should bear in mind that language survival is dependent on a complicated interplay of factors. *Societal factors* influence the relationship between minority and majority populations; *group-level factors* influence language use within speech communities; and *individual factors* influence the behavior and attitudes of individual speakers (Magga & Skutnabb-Kangas, 2003).

The role of schooling in language extinction

Language education policies for Native Americans exemplify the role of colonial schooling in eradicating Indigenous/minority languages. "Through sameness of language is produced sameness of sentiment," the US Commissioner of Indian Affairs wrote in 1887; "[s]chools should be established which children should be required to attend; their barbarous dialects should be blotted out . . ." (Crawford, 1992: 48). This mission drove four centuries of language policy, first by Christian missionaries and subsequently through the federal boarding school system established to "civilize" Native peoples. These were some of the most minutely controlled institutions ever created to transform the lives of any group of people (Lomawaima & McCarty, 2006). After cleanliness, *"No Indian Talk"* was the first rule in federal Indian schools, and infractions were brutally punished (Spack, 2002: 24).

Canadian residential schools followed the US model. As one residential school survivor describes: "The punishment for speaking Mi'kmaw began on our first day at school, but [it] has continued all our lives as we try to piece together who we are" (Grant, 1996: 191). Even in schools where children were not punished for speaking their languages, "many lost their languages as surely as they did in the more repressive schools" (Grant, 1996: 191). Australian Aboriginal peoples describe the "stolen generation" – children forcibly removed to government schools designed to dispossess them of their languages and identities (Edwards & Read, 1992). Even Quechua, spoken by 8 to 12 million people in South America, has been negatively impacted by educational policies that "have long served to repress Quechua and Quechua speakers" (Hornberger & Coronel-Molina, 2004: 28; see also King, 2001).

Similarly, the Saami, an Indigenous people in Norway, Sweden, Finland, and Russia numbering 70,000 to 100,000, spoke 11 different Finno-Ugric languages. One language is now extinct, four are considered "moribund," five are "seriously endangered," and one is "endangered." In Norway, beginning in the 1860s, a combination of Norwegian national romanticism, fear of Russian and Finnish hegemony, and racist Darwinian notions about the Saamis' intellectual capabilities led to a century-long campaign against the Saami language and culture. Financial sanctions were used to punish anyone unwilling to accept the Norwegian language and lifestyle. All social sectors – church, army, media, and administration – were involved in this "national project." Children were punished for using their language on school premises; teachers were instructed and paid extra to keep a close eye on parents' language use. Similar policies were pursued in the other countries at the time (Magga & Skutnabb-Kangas, 2003).

Submersion education of Indigenous peoples and minorities today

While schools alone cannot "save" endangered languages (Fishman, 1991), schools can extinguish them within a few generations, almost on their own. As more children have access to formal education, much of the language learning that earlier occurred in the family and community takes place in schools. If an alien dominant language is used as the primary or only medium of instruction, the language is not likely to survive because Indigenous and minority students (IMSs) educated through an alien language are not likely to pass on their mother tongue to their children and grandchildren.

In this case the educational system has, through forced assimilation, participated in what the United Nations *Genocide Convention* (1948) defines as genocide in Article II(e), "forcibly transferring children of the group to another group," and in Article II(b), "causing serious bodily *or mental* harm to members of the group" (www.hrweb.org/legal/genocide.html; emphasis added). Although many individuals may still feel that they belong to their parents'/grandparents'/ancestors' group long after their mother tongue competence has been lost (see, e.g., Sichra, 2005, for Quechua), IMSs nonetheless have been transferred to another group linguistically and often culturally. When there are no alternatives to dominant-language medium schooling and IMSs' parents do not have sufficient knowledge about the long-term consequences of "choosing" a dominant-language medium education, the transfer is forcible. Many parents are made to believe it is necessary to choose between the two languages: either a nostalgic minority identity and no economic opportunity for their child, or economic opportunity and leaving the minority language behind.

Abundant evidence exists that subtractive, submersion approaches, in which the dominant language is learned at the cost of the mother tongue, can cause serious harm and result in low school achievement, over-representation in remedial tracks, underemployment, youth and other criminality, alcoholism, suicide, and mental illness (Lomawaima & McCarty, 2006; see Magga et al., 2005 for how subtractive education violates IMSs' human rights). In contrast, in additive teaching, a dominant language is added to the child's linguistic repertoire while the mother tongue is maintained and developed.

In the last 15 to 25 years, schools have become strongholds for many Indigenous and minority languages. From there, they have taken the first steps into other domains in society. One of the most important lessons is that using the Indigenous/minority language in as many contexts as possible is the best way to promote both language maintenance and children's academic and life success.

What Is Being Done to Counter Language Endangerment?

Much has been written and said about the endangered status of Indigenous/minority languages, and much work has focused on describing and archiving these languages before they disappear (Skutnabb-Kangas, 2000: 237). Too little attention has been paid to the tenacity of these speech communities in their desire and ability to "recreate Indigenous/minority language communities" in the face of enormous pressure (McCarty & Zepeda, 2006), a topic we turn to next.

International efforts

Language rights became more central in the development of international human and minority rights law after World War II. The 1948 *Universal Declaration of Human Rights,* along with the *International Covenant on Economic, Social and Cultural Rights* and the *International Covenant on Civil and Political Rights* (both from 1966), form the *International Bill of Human Rights,* which protects individuals from language-based discrimination. The principles concerning minorities have evolved from protection from (negative) discrimination to active "positive discrimination" toward minorities ("affirmative action") for the purpose of equality. In line with this, recent international instruments obligate states to actively promote necessary conditions for the maintenance and development of minority and Indigenous languages. The International Labour Organization (ILO) *Convention 169 Concerning Indigenous and Tribal Peoples in Independent States* (1989, Article 28.3) is clear on this: "Measures shall be taken to preserve and promote the development and practice of the indigenous languages of the peoples concerned" (http://193.194.138.190/html/menu3/b/62.htm).

The *European Charter for Regional and Minority Languages* contains detailed rules on the use of minority languages within education, judicial and administrative authorities, public services, media, cultural activities and facilities, economic and social life, and contacts across national borders (http://conventions.coe.int/treaty/en/Treaties/Html/148.htm). Unfortunately, the most binding instruments and detailed regulations are limited geographically or with respect to the number of ratifying states. Still, their existence as international norms has had a strong positive impact on linguistic human rights in many countries.

International obligations can also be found in the list below (see www.ohchr.org/english/law/index.htm). It is not exhaustive, and only conventions and charters are binding, whereas declarations are not:

- *Convention for the Protection of Human Rights and Fundamental Freedoms* (European Convention on Human Rights), Council of Europe, 1950;
- *Convention against Discrimination in Education,* UNESCO, 1960;
- *International Convention on the Elimination of All Forms of Racial Discrimination,* United Nations, 1965;
- *Convention on the Rights of the Child,* UN, 1989;
- *Concluding Document of the Vienna Follow-up Meeting of the CSCE,* 1989;
- *Document of the Copenhagen Meeting of the Conference on Human Dimensions of the CSCE,* 1990;
- *Vienna Declaration and Programme of Action,* UN, 1993;
- *Declaration on the Rights of Persons Belonging to National or Ethnic, Religious and Linguistic Minorities,* UN, 1992;
- *Framework Convention for the Protection of National Minorities,* Council of Europe, 1994;

- *Charter of Fundamental Rights of the European Union*, EU, 2000;
- *Convention for the Safeguarding of the Intangible Cultural Heritage*, UNESCO, 2003.

National language policies

Language policies to promote Indigenous/minority languages exist in many states, although this is almost universally a recent development. Saami is one example. Saami was introduced in Norwegian, Swedish, and Finnish primary schools around 1970. Saami rights were strengthened in all three countries during the 1970s and 1980s; in Norway and Finland, this included constitutional reforms. In Russia, much less has been done to promote the language. It soon became evident that the maintenance and development of Saami would depend on its practical use outside the education system; for example, individuals must be able to be understood in courts and public offices, which has always been recognized as a basic human right in these countries. In Norway and Finland, the Saami Language Act entered into force in 1992 (revised in Finland in 2003), and in 2000 a similar law was passed in Sweden. In all three countries, the area of application is restricted to the northernmost communities. The legislation is designed to secure the right of Saami-speaking citizens to communicate and receive information in Saami. This creates a duty for local governments, courts, police, prisons, health and social security sectors, and the church to educate and recruit staff with proficiency in Saami. In Sweden, the right to translation is restricted to oral translation of a written decision communicated in Swedish.

Practical problems are reported in all three countries and the legislation is implemented primarily through the use of translators. Moreover, the legislation does not cover all Saami languages in Sweden and Norway, and Saami has no official status in Russia. All of this severely limits the intended effect on language development. Although Saami is co-official in the Saami homeland in Norway and Finland and the Saami have more language rights than many Indigenous peoples, the prospects for the survival of most Saami languages are rather unfavorable. The legislation has nevertheless had many positive effects for a language and speech community that has had very low status.

In the US, the 1990/1992 Native American Languages Act (NALA) reversed two centuries of federal language policy by vowing to "preserve, protect, and promote the rights . . . of Native Americans to use, practice, and develop Native American languages," including in federal Indian schools (Sec. 104[1], [5]; www.ncela.gwu.edu/pubs/stabilize/ii-policy/nala1990.htm). In some officially multilingual countries (e.g., India with 22 official languages, or South Africa with 11 official languages), even if educational provisions are quite good, there are massive implementation problems. In 2006, NALA was augmented by the Esther Martinez Native American Languages Preservation Act, which supports further language restoration efforts.

Grass roots initiatives

Two of the most impressive grass roots language revitalization efforts are Māori and Hawaiian. In both cases, by the 1970s, the Indigenous language had declined to the lowest stage of Fishman's (1991) Graded Intergenerational Disruption Scale, in which language users are socially isolated and elderly. Indigenous-language immersion programs were sparked by grass roots ethnic revival movements that led to official language status with English (for Māori, at the national level; for Hawaiian, at the state level; see Warner, 2001 and Wilson & Kamanā, 2001 for Hawaiian; May, 2005 for Māori). (In 2006, Aotearoa/ New Zealand also became the first country to make a sign language (New Zealand Sign Language) an official language.)

The Māori Kōhanga Reo and Hawaiian Pūnana Leo immersion preschools recreate environments in which Indigenous language and culture "are conveyed and developed . . . much [as] they were in the home in earlier generations" (Wilson & Kamanā, 2001: 151). The preschools are parent or community operated and aim to develop a high level of proficiency in the Indigenous language for children, teachers, and parents. Both preschool programs have followed similar trajectories, as parents successfully fought for Indigenous-language tracks and full Indigenous-language immersion in mainstream elementary and secondary schools. These efforts have dramatically increased the availability of bilingual/immersion education programs, produced significant numbers of new child speakers, and demonstrated academic gains for Indigenous students. These grass roots initiatives stand as powerful exemplars of Indigenous self-determination and language rights. Many other groups (including several Saami groups) are planning or have begun immersion programs (where the language is seriously endangered) or mother tongue-medium maintenance programs (where all generations still use the language but it has not had a place in formal education).[1]

Who is doing what to/for/with whom?

The role of states

States have for centuries been considered sovereign, with no right to interference by outside entities. So when Chief Deskaheh, spokesman for the Council of the Iroquois Confederation of Canada, traveled to Geneva in 1923 to present the case for Indigenous treaty rights, the League of Nations refused to consider it because they related it to Canada's internal affairs. This position did not change until the post-World War II development of international human rights law for minorities and Indigenous peoples. The UN opened its doors to Indigenous peoples in 1977 when the first Indigenous peoples' organization obtained consultative status with the Economic and Social Council (ECOSOC). With the establishment of the Working Group on Indigenous Populations in 1982, drafting of a universal declaration on the rights of Indigenous peoples began (it was finally adopted in September 2007).[2] In 1989, the ILO adopted the *Indigenous and Tribal Peoples Convention* (No. 169); a Decade of Indigenous Peoples (1995–2004) was then proclaimed. In 2001, a Special Rapporteur on the Situation of Human Rights and Fundamental Freedoms of Indigenous Peoples was appointed. And in 2002 the Permanent Forum on Indigenous Issues (PFII) was established, with its secretariat at the UN headquarters in New York.

The PFII is advisory to the ECOSOC, with a mandate to address Indigenous issues related to economic and social development, culture, the environment, education, health, and human rights (www.un.org/esa/socdev/unpfii/). Indigenous languages were among the themes discussed at the PFII's third session in 2004. With the creation of the PFII, Indigenous peoples established a high-level body with a mandate to address a broader range of Indigenous issues than any other body within the UN. The international community is taking a new step in recognizing the equality and rights of Indigenous peoples, of which language rights are becoming more central.

The role of (non-Indigenous/non-minority) international organizations

Non-Indigenous/non-minority, non-governmental organizations (NGOs) such as the International Work Groups for Indigenous Affairs (IWGIA), the World Council of Churches, Cultural Survival, Indigenous Peoples' Centre for Documentation (DoCip), Minority Rights Group International, Terralingua, and many others have played a central role in the development of language rights through their direct participation in international meetings and their assistance and technical support to minority and Indigenous representatives at the UN and other organizations.

The role of Indigenous peoples and Indigenous/minority organizations

Prior to World War II, states allowed little space for minorities and Indigenous peoples to organize to further their language rights. In many countries, including those with positive international images as democracies such as the Scandinavian countries, minority and Indigenous organizations were met with suspicion. In other countries, leaders of such activities were banned and persecuted. After 1945, a new era evolved as part of the new models of democracy in which civil society organizations play an important role. Through resolutions and letters to authorities, and sometimes through demonstrations and civil disobedience, these organizations, with the help of those mentioned above, have created a new understanding of the place of language and culture vis-à-vis human rights, which now extends to governments.

In 1975 the World Council for Indigenous Peoples was established as an umbrella organization for Indigenous organizations on all continents. Hundreds of minority and Indigenous organizations have initiated processes leading to education and language rights legislation, the creation of new language niches, national and international language conservation, and corpus language planning (orthographic standardization, terminology development, and so on).

The role of researchers

Without the work on Indigenous/minority languages by linguists, missionaries, priests, and teachers – often with a very high level of quality – most language revitalization and development efforts would not be possible today. Nevertheless, it is of utmost importance that the language community itself takes command over all aspects of the use and development of its own language. An old joke claims that a Saami family consists of a mother, a father, ten children, and an anthropologist (Magga & Skutnabb-Kangas, 2003: 36). This is unfortunately still true for many Indigenous peoples. Cameron et al. (1992) formulated this old dilemma in terms of outsiders doing research *on*, *for*, or *with* a (minority) group. Even in recent documents it is often envisaged that outsiders do most of the research needed not only for documenting but also for maintaining the languages. When subaltern groups have scholars of their own, academic imperialism and Western scholarly neocolonialism still have ways of marginalizing them while appropriating their knowledge. As Hountondji (2002) writes:

> We have been serving as informants . . . for a theory-building activity located overseas and entirely controlled by people there . . . And when we happened to write such books ourselves, we did everything to have them read and appreciated by them first, and only secondarily by our own people . . . These trends should be reversed. (pp. 36–37)

One useful schema for examining these issues is Bartlett's (2005) empowerment typology for governments, researchers, Indigenous peoples, and minorities, based on his discussion of Indigenous development in Guyana. The schema categorizes research and development according to four orientations: paternalism, advocacy, co-optation, and transformative empowerment. Bartlett (2005: 346) then relates these power relationships to roles of governments and Indigenous peoples as "initiators," "actors," "beneficiaries," or "patients," analyzing how these are construed in legal texts. He defines these roles in terms of the degree and quality of participation by Indigenous/minoritized peoples.

In research on endangered languages, scholars, international organizations, states, and NGOs have often been "initiators" and "actors," and have invisibilized community members in these roles. Indigenous peoples have been constructed as (the only) beneficiaries. In many cases they have not benefited much and have instead been made into "patients." Those who have benefited most from this unequal research relationship have often been researchers and their careers (Hough & Skutnabb-Kangas, 2005).

These relationships are changing in some contexts. Programs such as the American Indian Language Development Institute (AILDI) in the US are promoting genuinely collaborative relationships between Native community members and academic linguists and other researchers. Cofounded in 1978 by Hualapai educator Lucille J. Watahomigie and academic linguists, the AILDI "has prepared over 1,000 parents and school-based educators to work as researchers, curriculum developers, and advocates for the conservation and development of Indigenous languages and cultures" (McCarty et al., 2001: 372). The AILDI is a model of "transformative empowerment" for Native speakers, Native educators, communities, and children.

"From the vantage point of the colonized," Māori researcher Linda Tuhiwai Smith writes, ". . . the term 'research' is inextricably linked to European imperialism and colonialism" (1999: 1). Smith and others call for decolonizing methodologies, an approach we have sought to exemplify here, whereby Indigenous peoples are positioned as "initiators," "actors," and "co-beneficiaries." To paraphrase Māori researcher Graham Smith, such a research agenda is: (1) integrally related to "being Indigenous"; (2) connected to local Indigenous philosophy and principles; (3) grounded in Indigenous languages and cultures; and (4) concerned with "the struggle for autonomy over our own cultural well being" (L. T. Smith, 1999: 185; see also Odora Hoppers, 2002; Mutua and Swadener, 2004).

Evaluation of Present Measures: Too Little Too Late?

"There is no language for which nothing at all can be done," Joshua Fishman emphasizes (1991: 12). Even for languages with few or no native speakers, *something* can be done, as demonstrated by the inspiring work of Native American communities who are resurrecting ancestral languages from archival documents, or the master-apprentice teams of Native speakers and language learners who live, work, and communicate in everyday activities over months and years, always in the Indigenous language (Hinton, 2002). Hinton and Hale's (2001) *Green Book of Language Revitalization in Practice* (a proactive complement to UNESCO's *Red Books*), provides concrete descriptions of these and other innovative language revitalization efforts under way, including Indigenous-language immersion, Indigenous literacy programs, new uses of media and technology, and teacher preparation. To these we would add the PFII initiatives, the annual international Stabilizing Indigenous Languages Conference, the Working Group for Indigenous Populations, the NGOs previously discussed, the Canadian Task Force on Aboriginal Languages and Cultures, the Advocates for Indigenous California Language Survival, the new Nunavut plans, and the Kosrae Micronesian Traditional Ecological Knowledge curriculum project, among others.

The most promising pedagogical approach for reversing language shift is Indigenous/minority-language immersion, which promotes both (re)acquisition of mother tongues and IMS academic achievement. In some cases schools have become allies in immersion teaching, particularly when they are under Indigenous community control. Some school-based programs are being supplemented or replaced by Native-language immersion programs developed and operated by tribes, as exemplified by the Pueblos of the US Southwest (Romero-Little & McCarty, 2006). And in Alaska, a statewide Indigenous initiative has created language and cultural standards to support such school- and community-based efforts, "predicated on the belief that a firm grounding in the heritage language and culture . . . is . . . fundamental . . . for . . . culturally-healthy students and communities" (Assembly of Alaska Native Educators, 1998). These and similar initiatives reinforce the the right of *choice*. As language educator and activist Wayne Holm (2006) puts it:

> Children whose parents or schools deny them access to their language deprive children of choice . . . By the time a teenager or young adult might choose to speak the language, for most, it is already too late. (cited in McCarty & Zepeda, 2006: 41–42)

What Does the Future Hold for Endangered Languages?

As most people feel that more should be done in order to stop physical genocide in wars, it is equally important to stop linguistic genocide. They are two sides of (the same) humanity. Both can be done. Evidence from research and life experience point in the same direction: all languages have the same potential and are therefore equal, the mother tongue is central to all learning processes, and everyone should have the right and opportunity to learn to read and write her/his own language as well as at least one national and one international language.

Whatever we do, our efforts in education, research, teaching, and policy making will not save *all* the endangered languages in the world. On the other hand, if there is a strong determination to maintain and develop a language, there is ample evidence that there are no limitations or laws of nature to make this unrealistic. This places responsibility on everyone – governments at all levels, education and research institutions, media, NGOs, and individuals – to ensure that individual and collective human rights are protected and that the world's cultural and linguistic wealth continues to flourish.

NOTES

1   In Nepal, a pilot project at six community sites is planning materials development and teacher training with the long-term aim of teaching all Nepal's IMSs through

their mother tongues during the first school years (there are at least 100 languages). In Orissa, India, 200 schools have begun teaching tribal children in their mother tongues (10 languages). A similar project is underway in Assam, with plans for extending mother tongue teaching to other Indian states with tribal peoples.

2   For further information on the status of the Declaration; see online: www.un.org/esa/socdev/unpfii/en/declaration.html.

REFERENCES

Aasen, Ivar (1996 [1863]). *Symra* [translation by Tove Skutnabb-Kangas]. Oslo: Det Norske Samlaget.

Assembly of Alaska Native Educators (1998). *Alaska Standards for Culturally Responsive Schools*. Anchorage: Alaska Native Knowledge Network.

Bartlett, Tom (2005). Amerindian development in Guyana: Legal documents as background to discourse practice. *Discourse and Society*, 16(3), 341–364.

Benton, Robert (1988). The Māori language in New Zealand education. *Language, Culture and Curriculum*, 1, 75–83.

Cameron, Deborah, Frazer, Elizabeth, Harvey, Penelope, Rampton, M. B. H., & Richardson, Kay (1992). *Researching Language: Issues of Power and Method*. London/New York: Routledge.

Crawford, James (1992). *Language Loyalties: A Source Book on the Official English Controversy*. Chicago: University of Chicago Press.

Edwards, Coral & Read, Peer (eds.) (1992). *The Lost Children: Thirteen Australians Taken from their Aboriginal Families Tell of the Struggle to Find Their Natural Parents*. Sydney: Doubleday.

Fishman, Joshua A. (1991). *Reversing Language Shift: Theoretical and Empirical Foundations of Assistance to Threatened Languages*. Clevedon, UK: Multilingual Matters.

Grant, Agnes (1996). *No End of Grief: Indian Residential Schools in Canada*. Winnipeg, Manitoba: Pemmican Publications.

Harmon, David (1995). The status of the world's languages as reported in the Ethnologue. *Southwest Journal of Linguistics*, 14(1&2), 1–28.

Hinton, Leanne (with Matt Vera and Nancy Steel and the Advocates for Indigenous California Language Survival) (2002). *How to Keep Your Language Alive: A Commonsense Approach to One-on-One Language Learning*. Berkeley, CA: Heyday Books.

Hinton, Leanne & Hale, Ken (eds.) (2001). *The Green Book of Language Revitalization in Practice*. San Diego, CA: Academic Press.

Hornberger, Nancy H. & Coronel-Molina, Serafin M. (2004). Quechua language shift, maintenance, and revitalization in the Andes: The case for language planning. *International Journal of the Sociology of Language*, 167, 9–67.

Hough, David A. & Skutnabb-Kangas, Tove (2005). Beyond good intentions: Combating linguistic genocide in education. *Alternative: An International Journal of Indigenous Scholarship*, 1(1), 114–135.

Hountondji, Paulin J. (2002). Knowledge appropriation in a post-colonial context. In Catherine A. Odora Hoppers (ed.), *Indigenous Knowledge and the Integration of Knowledge Systems: Towards a Philosophy of Articulation* (pp. 23–38). Claremont, South Africa: New Africa Books.

King, Kendall A. (2001). *Language Revitalization Processes and Prospects: Quichua in the Ecuadorian Andes*. Clevedon, UK: Multilingual Matters.

Krauss, Michael (1992). The world's languages in crisis. *Language*, 68(1), 4–10.

Littlebear, Richard (2004). One man, two languages: Confessions of freedom-loving bilingual. *Tribal College Journal*, 15(3), 11–12.

Lomawaima, K. Tsianina & McCarty, Teresa L. (2006). *"To Remain an Indian": Lessons in Democracy from a Century of Native American Education*. New York: Teachers College Press.

Maffi, Luisa (ed.) (2001). *On Biocultural Diversity: Linking Language, Knowledge and the Environment*. Washington, DC: The Smithsonian Institute Press.

Magga, Ole Henrik & Skutnabb-Kangas, Tove (2003). Life or death for languages and human beings: Experiences from Saamiland. In Leena Huss, Antoinette Camilleri Grima, & Kendall A. King (eds.), *Transcending Monolingualism: Linguistic Revitalisation in Education* (pp. 35–52). Lisse: Swets and Zeitlinger.

Magga, Ole Henrik, Nicolaisen, Ida, Trask, Mililani, Dunbar, Robert, & Skutnabb-Kangas, Tove (2005). *Indigenous Children's Education and Indigenous Languages*. Expert paper written for the United Nations Permanent Forum on Indigenous Issues. New York: United Nations.

May, Stephen (2001). *Language and Minority Rights: Ethnicity, Nationalism and the Politics of Language*. Essex, UK: Longman/Pearson Education.

May, Stephen (ed.) (2005). Bilingual/Immersion Education in Aotearoa/New Zealand. Special issue of *International Journal of the Sociology of Language*, 8(5).

McCarty, Teresa L. & Zepeda, Ofelia (eds.) (2006). *One Voice, Many Voices: Recreating Indigenous Language Communities*. Tempe: Arizona State University Center for Indian Education.

McCarty, Teresa L., Watahomigie, Lucille J., Yamamoto, Akira Y., & Zepeda, Ofelia (2001). Indigenous educators as change agents: Case studies of two language institutes. In Leanne Hinton & Ken Hale (eds.), *The Green Book of Language Revitalization in Practice* (pp. 371–383). San Diego, CA: Academic Press.

Mutua, Kagendo & Swadener, Beth Blue (eds.) (2004). *Decolonizing Research in Cross-Cultural Contexts: Critical Personal Narratives*. Albany, NY: State University of New York Press.

Odora Hoppers, Catherine A. (ed.) (2002). *Indigenous Knowledge and the Integration of Knowledge Systems: Towards a Philosophy of Articulation*. Claremont, South Africa: New Africa Books.

Posey, Darrell (ed.) (1999). *Cultural and Spiritual Values of Biodiversity: A Complementary Contribution to the Global Biodiversity Assessment*. New York: United Nations Environmental Programme; and Leiden: Intermediate Technologies, Leiden University.

Romero-Little, Mary Eunice & McCarty, Teresa L. (2006). *Language Planning Challenges and Prospects in Native American Communities and Schools*. Tempe: Arizona State University Education Policy Studies Laboratory. Available online at www.asu.edu/educ/epsl/EPRU/documents/EPSL-0602-105-LPRU.pdf

Sichra, Inge (2005). Transcending or strengthening Quechua's emblematic value: Language identity in Cochabamba. *Working Papers in Educational Linguistics*, 21(1), 37–59.

Skutnabb-Kangas, Tove (2000). *Linguistic Genocide in Education – Or Worldwide Diversity and Human Rights?* Mahwah, NJ: Lawrence Erlbaum.

Skutnabb-Kangas, Tove, Maffi, Luisa, & Harmon, David (2003). *Sharing a World of Difference: The Earth's Linguistic, Cultural, and Biological Diversity*. Paris: UNESCO,

Terralingua, and World Wide Fund for Nature. Available online at www.terralingua. org/RecPublications.htm

Smith, Linda Tuhiwai (1999). *Decolonizing Methodologies: Research and Indigenous Peoples.* London/New York: Zed Books.

Spack, Ruth (2002). *America's Second Tongue: American Indian Education and the Ownership of English, 1860–1900.* Lincoln: University of Nebraska Press.

Task Force on Aboriginal Languages and Cultures (2005). *Towards a New Beginning: A Foundational Report for a Strategy to Revitalize First Nation, Inuit and Métis Languages and Cultures.* Report to the Minister of Canadian Heritage (June). Ottawa: Aboriginal Languages Directorate. Available online at www.aboriginallanguagestaskforce.ca

UNESCO (2003a). *Language Vitality and Endangerment.* Paris: UNESCO. Available online at http://portal.unesco.org/culture/en/file_download.php/947ee963052abf0293b22 e0bfba319cclanguagevitalityendangerment.pdf

UNESCO (2003b). *Education in a Multilingual World.* Paris: UNESCO. Available online at http://unesdoc.unesco.org/images/0012/001297/129728e.pdf

Warner, Sam L. No'eau (2001). The movement to revitalize Hawaiian language and culture. In Leanne Hinton & Ken Hale (eds.), *The Green Book of Language Revitalization in Practice* (pp. 133–144). San Diego, CA: Academic Press.

Wilson, William H. & Kamanā, Kauanoe (2001). "*Mai loko mai o ka 'i'ini*: Proceeding from a Dream": The 'Aha Pūnana Leo connection in Hawaiian language revitalization. In Leanne Hinton & Ken Hale (eds.), *The Green Book of Language Revitalization in Practice* (pp. 147–176). San Diego, CA: Academic Press.

World Commission on Culture and Development (1995). *Our Creative Diversity: A Report of the World Commission for Culture and Development.* Paris: UNESCO.

World Resources Institute, World Conservation Union, and United Nations Environment Programme (1992). *Global Biodiversity Strategy: Guidelines for Actions to Save, Study, and Use Earth's Biotic Wealth Sustainably and Equitably.* Available online at http://biodiv.wri.org/pubs_pdf.cfm?PubID=2550

FURTHER READING

Aikio-Puoskari, Ulla & Pentikäinen, Merja (2001). *The Language Rights of the Indigenous Saami in Finland under Domestic and International Law* (Juridica Lapponica 26). Rovaniemi: University of Lapland.

Cantoni, Gina (ed.) (1996). *Stabilizing Indigenous Languages.* Flagstaff, AZ: Northern Arizona University Center for Excellence in Education.

Crystal, David (2000). *Language Death.* Cambridge: Cambridge University Press.

Fishman, Joshua A. (ed.) (2001). *Can Threatened Languages Be Saved? Reversing Language Shift, Revisited: A 21st Century Perspective.* Clevedon, UK: Multilingual Matters.

Fishman, Joshua A. (2006). *DO NOT Leave Your Language Alone: The Hidden Status Agendas within Corpus Planning in Language Policy.* Mahwah, NJ: Lawrence Erlbaum.

Grenoble, Lenore A. & Whaley, Lindsay J. (eds.) (1998). *Endangered Languages: Language Loss and Community Response.* Cambridge: Cambridge University Press.

Hornberger, Nancy H. (ed.) (1996). *Indigenous Literacies in the Americas: Language Planning from the Bottom Up.* Berlin: Mouton de Gruyter.

Hornberger, Nancy H. (ed.) (2008). *Can Schools Save Indigenous Languages? Policy and Practice on Four Continents.* Basingstoke, UK: Palgrave/Macmillan.

Hyltenstam, Kenneth & Stroud, Christopher (1991). *Språkbyte och språkbevarande. Om samiskan och andra minoritetsspråk* [Language Shift and Language Maintenance: On Saami and Other Minority Languages]. Lund: Studentlitteratur.

Journal of Linguistic Anthropology (2002). Examining the language of language endangerment: An exchange. Special focus, *Journal of Linguistic Anthropology*, 12(2), 119–156.

Kouritzin, Sandra G. (1999). *Face[t]s of First Language Loss*. Mahwah, NJ: Lawrence Erlbaum.

Loh, Jonathan & Harmon, David (2005). A global index of biocultural diversity. *Ecological Indicators*, 5, 231–241. Available online at www.elsevier.com/locate/ecolind

McCarty, Teresa L. & Zepeda, Ofelia (eds.) (1998). Indigenous Language Use and Change in the Americas. Special issue of *International Journal of the Sociology of Language*, 132.

McCarty, Teresa L., Watahomigie, Lucille J., & Yamamoto, Akira Y. (eds.) (1999). Reversing Language Shift in Indigenous America: Collaborations and Views from the Field. Special issue of *Practicing Anthropology*, 20(2), 1–47.

Phillipson, Robert (ed.) (2000). *Rights to Language: Equity, Power, and Education*. Mahwah, NJ: Lawrence Erlbaum.

Tsunoda, Tasaku (2006). *Language Endangerment and Language Revitalization: An Introduction*. Berlin: Mouton de Gruyter.

Wong Fillmore, Lily (1991). When learning a second language means losing the first. *Early Childhood Research Quarterly*, 6, 323–346.

22 The Impact of English on the School Curriculum

YUN-KYUNG CHA AND SEUNG-HWAN HAM

Up until the beginning of the twentieth century, English was seldom represented as a legitimate curricular subject in schools. Few independent countries incorporated any modern foreign languages into the primary school curriculum by the turn of the twentieth century. Although many countries began to teach modern foreign languages in secondary school before the twentieth century, the propensity to adopt German or French rather than English spread across countries until the mid-twentieth century. However, the situation has dramatically changed. English has emerged as the first "global language" in history, which is "now a factor that needs to be taken into account in its language policy by any nation-state" (Spolsky, 2004: 91). English is currently the dominant or official language in over 75 territories, and it is widely taught as de facto the most important foreign language in primary and secondary schools across diverse countries (Cha, 1991; Crystal, 2003). The number of people who speak English as a native language is estimated at about three or four hundred million. Other English speakers, estimated at about four or six hundred million, are those who learn English as a second or foreign language.[1] In this situation, many national societies around the world have pursued steadfast educational reforms to provide English instruction for schoolchildren in the last few decades. A certain high level of ability to communicate in English seems to be becoming in many countries a new kind of basic literacy that no longer conveys Western ideological connotations just as computer or information literacy is considered as a basic requirement for today's world citizens (Cha & Ham, 2005). Why, then, are so many people and societies so enthusiastic for English education?

This chapter tries to scrutinize the transnational character of English and its impact on the school curricula of diverse countries. Many current versions of the functionalist idea attempt to understand whether or not English is incorporated into the school curriculum of a country as the result of a deliberate policy decision contingent upon the concrete local conditions in which the country is situated. Although how to define the concept of "function" varies depending on the ideological orientations of different forms of functionalist thought, we may reasonably speculate from the functionalist perspective that English is expected to be taught in schools according to its "functional" fitness to the economic, political, and cultural conditions of a given country. However, we argue that there are two limitations in such views. The first is that they do not question whether or not a specific body of school knowledge, now English, really functions to meet certain substantive societal needs at hand. It is very interesting that we generally take for granted such a positive causal relationship, especially when it comes to issues on education, despite the paucity of empirical evidence that supports such a connection. The second is that although such conventional views convey useful insight on the diversity dimension in school curricula across countries, they generally miss the influences from the wider environment that provides a world-cultural basis for social actors such as national governments, schools, and educational professionals. By analyzing comprehensive historical and comparative data on school curricula, this chapter empirically describes the patterns of the institutionalization of English as a legitimate school subject over time and place in order to see how English has had an impact on the school curriculum.

Data

Historical and comparative data on primary and secondary curricula analyzed in this chapter were gathered from various sources. Data sources for the post-World War II period include various official documents and reports of education-related organizations such as UNESCO, International Bureau of Education (IBE), National Institute for Educational Research (NIER), and Eurydice (UNESCO, 1958; IBE and UNESCO, 1958, 1984, 1986, 1992, 2003, 2004b; UNESCO Regional Office for Education in Asia, 1966; UNESCO and NIER, 1970; Eurydice, 2005). Also, studies by Sasnett and Sepmeyer (1966) and Fishman, Conrad, and Rubal-Lopez (1996) provided valuable information. Data for the inter-war period were mostly from the country reports in the *Educational Yearbook* edited by Kandel (1924–44) and the reports of IBE (1937). Data before World War I were collected from a series of special educational reports of the British Education Department and the Board of Education (1897–1914) and a series of educational reports of the US Bureau of Education (1873–1915).

As for the coding scheme of the data, we first divided historical time into several periods (i.e., 1850–74, 1875–99, 1900–19, 1920–44, 1945–69, 1970–89, and 1990–2005), and then we coded 1 for a given country in a certain period of time if English was incorporated into the official school curriculum as the first foreign language[2] during that period of time in the country. Otherwise, we coded 0 for a given country in a certain period of time. If English was an official language in a country and at the same time the first language of more than 50 percent of the population,[3] we regarded the country as having English as the first language (i.e., mother tongue) of the biggest ethno-linguistic group and thus excluded it from the sample in order to examine the institutionaliza-tion of English instruction in non-English-speaking countries. In addition, unless English was used as the first language by more than 50 percent of the population in a country, we regarded it as de facto a foreign language in this study, even if it had an official status in the country. Many ex-colonies of English-speaking countries, for example, are classified in this category.

Overall Trends

Figure 22.1 shows the percentage of countries teaching English as the first foreign language in primary and secondary schools over the period from the mid-nineteenth century to the present. Our historical data indicate that Eng-lish as the first foreign language was given little attention as a regular school subject before the twentieth century. During the 1875–99 period, the percent-age of countries where English was incorporated as the first foreign language in the school curriculum was less than 6 percent (N = 18) at the secondary level. Moreover, during the same period, no country in the sample (N = 25) was observed to provide English instruction as the first foreign language in primary schools. During the 1990–2005 period, however, the percentage dramatically increased to nearly 70 percent (N = 151) at the primary level and more than 80 percent (N = 154) at the secondary level.

Table 22.1(a) shows the percentage of countries teaching one of the five world languages – English, French, German, Spanish, or Russian – as the first foreign language in schools over time. It is notable that German and French were the most dominant modern foreign languages taught in the secondary school until the 1920–44 period. It was only from the 1945–69 period that English emerged as the most widely taught foreign language across countries. Table 22.1(b), which reports the same data for constant panels of countries at two successive points in time, reveals basically the same trends reported in Table 22.1(a). A sudden increase in the percentage of countries incorporating English into school curricula as the first foreign language during the 1920–69 period is especially noticeable (11.9% and 25.4% (N = 59) at the primary level and 35.4% and 62.5% (N = 48) at the secondary level respectively in the 1920–44 and 1945–69 periods). It seems that English was consolidated as the predominant world language especially after 1945 when the United States rose as the unchallenged hegemonic power at the end of World War II.

Some might plausibly argue that the rapid expansion of English instruction is largely due to the addition of newly independent former British or US colonies in the sample. However, the results in Table 22.1(b) once again imply that the argument is not adequately supported by empirical data from the constant panels of countries. Additional analyses of the data reveal that among the countries which have not been colonies of English-speaking colonizers, the percentage having English as the first foreign language taught in schools has also increased rapidly (16.8% (N = 101), 23.4% (N = 94), and 51.5% (N = 103)

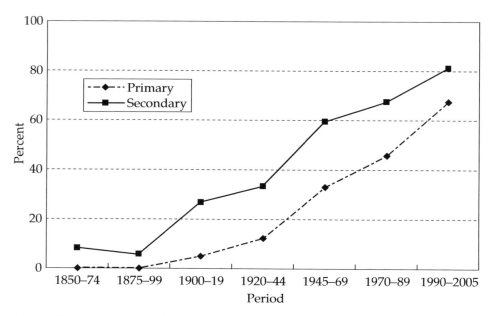

Figure 22.1   Percentages of countries teaching English as the first foreign language in primary and secondary schools, 1850–2005

Note: For the number of countries included for analysis for each period of time, see Table 22.1(a). The countries included for analysis for the most recent period, 1990–2005, are: Afghanistan, Algeria, Angola, Argentina, Austria, Bahrain, Bangladesh, Belarus, Belgium-Flemish Community, Belgium-French Community, Benin, Bolivia, Botswana, Brazil, Brunei, Bulgaria, Burkina Faso, Burundi, Cambodia, Cameroon, Cape Verde, Central African Republic, Chad, Chile, China, Colombia, Comoros, Congo-Democratic Republic of, Congo-Republic of, Cook Islands, Costa Rica (S), Cuba, Cyprus, Czech Republic, Denmark, Djibouti, Dominica, Dominican Republic, Ecuador, Egypt-Arab Republic of, El Salvador, Eritrea, Estonia, Ethiopia, Finland, France, Gambia, Georgia, Germany, Ghana, Greece, Guadeloupe, Guam, Guatemala, Guinea, Honduras, Hong Kong, Hungary, Iceland, India, Indonesia, Iran, Iraq, Israel, Italy, Japan, Jordan, Kazakhstan, Kenya, Kiribati, Korea-Republic of, Kuwait, Kyrgyz Republic, Laos, Latvia, Lebanon, Lesotho, Liberia, Libya, Liechtenstein (S), Lithuania, Luxembourg, Macau, Macedonia, Madagascar, Malawi, Malaysia, Maldives, Malta, Mauritania, Mauritius, Mexico, Monaco (S), Mongolia, Morocco, Mozambique, Myanmar, Namibia, Nepal, Netherlands, Nicaragua, Niger, Nigeria, Norway, Oman, Pakistan, Panama, Papua New Guinea, Peru, Philippines, Poland, Portugal, Puerto Rico, Qatar, Romania, Russia, Rwanda, Samoa, Saudi Arabia, Senegal, Seychelles, Sierra Leone, Singapore, Slovak Republic, Slovenia, Solomon Islands, South Africa, Spain, Sri Lanka, St. Lucia, Sudan, Suriname, Swaziland, Sweden, Switzerland (S), Syrian Arab Republic, Taiwan, Tanzania, Thailand, Togo, Tonga (P), Tunisia, Turkey, Turkmenistan, Uganda, Ukraine, United Arab Emirates, Uruguay, Venezuela, Vietnam, West Bank and Gaza, Yemen, Yugoslavia, Zambia, and Zimbabwe. (P = Data at the primary level only available for this period; S = Data at the secondary level only available for this period.) Other countries included for analysis for at least one of the earlier periods are: Albania, Cote d'Ivoire, Gabon, Germany-Eastern, Greenland, Haiti, Italian Somalia, Mali, Northern Ireland, Paraguay, Russian Federation, Ryukyu Islands, San Marino, Sao Tome and Principe, Scotland, Somalia, Spanish North Africa, Saint Pierre and Miquelon, Vanuatu, Vietnam-South, and Zanzibar and Pemba.

Table 22.1 Percentages of countries teaching English, French, German, Spanish, or Russian as the first foreign language in schools, 1850–2005

(a) All cases

Primary level

	1850–74 (N = 15)	1875–99 (N = 25)	1900–19 (N = 40)	1920–44 (N = 65)	1945–69 (N = 134)	1970–89 (N = 140)	1990–2005 (N = 151)
English	0.0	0.0	5.0	12.3	32.8	45.7	67.5
French	0.0	0.0	5.0	1.5	17.2	16.4	13.2
German	0.0	0.0	0.0	3.1	0.0	0.0	0.7
Spanish	0.0	0.0	0.0	0.0	0.0	0.0	0.0
Russian	0.0	0.0	0.0	0.0	7.5	5.7	3.3

Secondary level

	1850–74 (N = 12)	1875–99 (N = 18)	1900–19 (N = 37)	1920–44 (N = 54)	1945–69 (N = 128)	1970–89 (N = 135)	1990–2005 (N = 154)
English	8.3	5.6	27.0	33.3	59.4	67.4	81.2
French	33.3	38.9	45.9	35.2	28.1	17.0	13.6
German	50.0	44.4	24.3	14.8	0.0	0.0	0.6
Spanish	0.0	0.0	0.0	0.0	0.0	0.0	0.0
Russian	0.0	0.0	0.0	0.0	7.8	5.9	3.2

Table 22.1 (cont'd)

(b) Constant panels of countries

Primary level

	1850–99 (N = 15)		1875–1919 (N = 23)		1900–44 (N = 40)		1920–69 (N = 59)		1945–89 (N = 121)		1970–2005 (N = 129)	
	1850–74	1875–99	1875–99	1900–19	1900–19	1920–44	1920–44	1945–69	1945–69	1970–89	1970–89	1990–2005
English	0.0	0.0	0.0	0.0	5.0	10.0	11.9	25.4	34.7	40.5	48.1	69.0
French	0.0	0.0	0.0	4.3	5.0	2.5	1.7	5.1	16.5	16.5	17.1	13.2
German	0.0	0.0	0.0	0.0	0.0	0.0	0.0	0.0	0.0	0.0	0.0	0.8
Spanish	0.0	0.0	0.0	0.0	0.0	0.0	0.0	0.0	0.0	0.0	0.0	0.0
Russian	0.0	0.0	0.0	0.0	0.0	0.0	0.0	8.5	7.4	6.6	3.9	0.0

Secondary level

	1850–99 (N = 12)		1875–1919 (N = 18)		1900–44 (N = 36)		1920–69 (N = 48)		1945–89 (N = 112)		1970–2005 (N = 127)	
	1850–74	1875–99	1875–99	1900–19	1900–19	1920–44	1920–44	1945–69	1945–69	1970–89	1970–89	1990–2005
English	8.3	0.0	5.6	11.1	25.0	36.1	35.4	62.5	64.3	65.2	70.1	84.3
French	33.3	41.7	38.9	38.9	47.2	44.4	39.6	18.8	25.9	19.6	17.3	13.4
German	50.0	50.0	44.4	44.4	25.0	13.9	8.3	0.0	0.0	0.0	0.0	0.8
Spanish	0.0	0.0	0.0	0.0	0.0	0.0	0.0	0.0	0.0	0.0	0.0	0.0
Russian	0.0	0.0	0.0	0.0	0.0	0.0	0.0	10.4	7.1	7.1	3.9	0.0

at the primary level and 49.0% (N = 98), 56.7% (N = 90), and 72.0% (N = 107) at the secondary level respectively in the 1945–69, 1970–89, and 1990–2005 periods). Further analyses of the data show that such an increasing trend is also observed among the countries that had once been French colonies. Although it is obviously true that there has been a tendency to choose French rather than English as the first foreign language among those countries, it is notable that French has been increasingly substituted by English after World War II. Among the former French colonies, the percentage of countries teaching English instead of French as the first foreign language has notably increased (9.1% (N = 22), 9.5% (N = 21), and 18.2% (N = 22) in the primary level and 16.7% (N = 24), 25.0% (N = 20), and 30.4% (N = 23) in the secondary level respectively in the 1945–69, 1970–89, and 1990–2005 periods). This means that the reluctance to incorporate English into school curricula as the first foreign language has been diminishing over time. In sum, the implication of the empirical data analyzed above is quite clear: the legitimacy of English as a regular school subject is unquestionable, and English has been incorporated into school curricula by an increasing number of countries.

Regional Variations

A further breakdown of the data by region in Table 22.2 confirms the previous findings and provides additional information on the regional and cultural variation in incorporating English as a legitimate school subject. Due to the limited number of cases, data before 1945 were excluded from analysis. The overall results reported in Table 22.2 once again clearly show an increasing tendency of the worldwide commitment to English instruction in schools over time and across regions. The dramatic increase in the number of Western countries teaching English as the first foreign language in primary schools is especially noticeable. The rapid spread of English in the West seems primarily due to the recent consolidation of the European Union as a supranational political, economic, and cultural entity whereby learning foreign languages is strongly encouraged.

Another noticeable fact is that most of the former Soviet Union countries and also a few other central European countries incorporated English into their primary and secondary curricula as the first foreign language during the 1990–2005 period when the United States became de facto the single unchallengeable superpower in the world with the fall of the Soviet Union. Considering the fact that "all countries in central and eastern Europe in which Russian was a mandatory [foreign] language [in the school curriculum at a particular stage of compulsory education] in 1982/83 abandoned this policy from the beginning of the 1990s" (Eurydice, 2005: 37), it seems clear that this sudden increase in the percentage of countries teaching English as the first foreign language in this region was not entirely due to the addition of newly independent former Soviet Union countries in the sample.

Table 22.2 Percentages of countries teaching English as the first foreign language in schools, by region, 1945–2005

Primary level

	1945–69		1970–89		1990–2005	
Sub-Saharan Africa	50.0	(N = 42)	45.9	(N = 37)	53.7	(N = 41)
Middle East and North Africa	43.8	(N = 16)	50.0	(N = 18)	65.0	(N = 20)
Asia	33.3	(N = 21)	54.2	(N = 24)	83.3	(N = 24)
Latin America and Caribbean	19.0	(N = 21)	25.0	(N = 20)	44.4	(N = 18)
Central Europe and Former Soviet Union	18.2	(N = 11)	20.0	(N = 10)	68.4	(N = 19)
Western Europe and North America	9.5	(N = 21)	45.0	(N = 20)	83.3	(N = 18)
Oceania	50.0	(N = 2)	81.8	(N = 11)	100.0	(N = 11)

Secondary level

	1945–69		1970–89		1990–2005	
Sub-Saharan Africa	50.0	(N = 38)	54.1	(N = 37)	58.5	(N = 41)
Middle East and North Africa	68.8	(N = 16)	73.7	(N = 19)	85.0	(N = 20)
Asia	65.0	(N = 20)	76.2	(N = 21)	100.0	(N = 24)
Latin America and Caribbean	85.0	(N = 20)	89.5	(N = 19)	100.0	(N = 19)
Central Europe and Former Soviet Union	18.2	(N = 11)	20.0	(N = 10)	68.4	(N = 19)
Western Europe and North America	59.1	(N = 22)	71.4	(N = 21)	85.0	(N = 20)
Oceania	100.0	(N = 1)	87.5	(N = 8)	100.0	(N = 10)

Sub-Saharan Africa, which shows a relatively moderate increase in the number of countries incorporating English as the first foreign language into the school curriculum, is the only exception. This phenomenon is probably due to the fact that countries in this region are marked by a high degree of ethno-linguistic fragmentation (i.e., more than 0.6 on average in Greenberg's diversity index)[4] and thus inherited, upon independence, the metropolitan languages of the former colonizers (i.e., French, Portuguese, and Spanish as well as English) as "neutral" official languages. Since these languages are de facto foreign languages for the speakers of local languages, they may have difficulties accommodating an additional foreign language in the school curriculum. Nevertheless, it is important to note that a lot of such countries also teach English as a required foreign language in schools in addition to the metropolitan languages inherited from their former colonizers. Former French colonies in this region such as Central African Republic, Congo, Madagascar, Mauritania, Niger, and Togo, for example, teach English as well as French as a compulsory subject in secondary schools, although slightly less curricular emphasis is devoted to English compared with French.

English Education as an Institution

Our primary concern now becomes: Through what process does English become a legitimate body of educational knowledge in school curricula? Most conventional answers to this question follow the logic of functionalism. A widely shared assumption among different forms of functionalist thought is that whether or not a specific field of study makes its way into the official school curriculum is determined by its "functional" fitness to the concrete local conditions. Following the functionalist assumption of the close linkage between concrete local conditions and the curricular contents of a given country, English instruction would not be incorporated into school curricula of a country without substantive societal needs for the English language for a certain practical reason. Institutional theory, however, provides an alternative explanation with regard to the rise and institution-alization of English as a legitimate school subject. In this line of thought, the school curriculum is understood as largely influenced by the institutional dynamics of a world-cultural system (Meyer et al., 1992; Schissler & Soysal, 2005; Benavot & Braslavsky, 2006). In the modern world system, which con-sists of not merely economic networks, but also transnational cultural rules and values, national educational systems are by and large built on the basis of highly rationalized world education models (Meyer et al., 1997; Baker & LeTendre, 2005). The school curriculum, an integral component of the modern educational system, is expected to share the same quality: the legitimacy of a body of school knowledge that is "isomorphic" with the world curriculum model is mostly taken for granted, regardless of its immediate utility.

Table 22.3 Numbers of countries teaching English as the first foreign language in schools (FFL), by the first export partner's national language (FENL), 1945–2005 (expected counts in parentheses)

Primary level

	FENL, 1945–69			FENL, 1970–89			FENL, 1990–2005		
	English	Other lang.	Total	English	Other lang.	Total	English	Other lang.	Total
English as FFL	24 (16)	10 (18)	34	21 (20)	34 (35)	55	35 (34)	62 (63)	97
Other lang. as FFL	26 (34)	47 (39)	73	23 (24)	45 (44)	68	16 (17)	32 (31)	48
Total	50	57	107	44	79	123	51	94	145
Chi-square test	$\chi^2 = 11.397$, d.f. = 1, sig. = 0.001			$\chi^2 = 0.251$, d.f. = 1, sig. = 0.616			$\chi^2 = 0.106$, d.f. = 1, sig. = 0.744		

Secondary level

	FENL, 1945–69			FENL, 1970–89			FENL, 1990–2005		
	English	Other lang.	Total	English	Other lang.	Total	English	Other lang.	Total
English as FFL	40 (30)	25 (35)	65	33 (31)	49 (51)	82	49 (42)	71 (78)	120
Other lang. as FFL	8 (18)	30 (20)	38	12 (14)	25 (23)	37	3 (10)	25 (18)	28
Total	48	55	103	45	74	119	52	96	148
Chi-square test	$\chi^2 = 15.796$, d.f. = 1, sig. = 0.000			$\chi^2 = 0.662$, d.f. = 1, sig. = 0.416			$\chi^2 = 9.037$, d.f. = 1, sig. = 0.003		

An important implication of the institutional perspective is that there may be a "loose coupling" between specific curricular categories and immediate practical concerns (Weick, 1976; Meyer & Rowan, 1977). This implies that the legitimacy of a specific school subject keenly reflects changes in global structure and shifts in world discourse which might be quite extraneous to a given country. Hence, it is quite reasonable to expect that the wider environment external to a given society, such as "the structural transformation and hierarchical rearrangement of hegemonic powers in the international system" (Cha, 1991: 31) and associated "changes in the complex ecology of the world's language system" (Spolsky, 2004: 90), exerts a powerful influence in defining a legitimate body of knowledge to be taught in schools. Based on the institutional argument, we thus expect to see an increasing number of countries incorporate English into the school curriculum regardless of its immediate utility. Specific local conditions or unique historical trajectories of individual countries may have little to do with incorporating English into the school curriculum.

The chi-square tests in Table 22.3, for example, examine if there is any relationship between whether or not English is incorporated as the first foreign language into school curricula of a country and whether or not English is the national language of the country's first export partner. Considering the prevailing assumption of a close relationship between curricular contents and country-specific conditions, the results reported in Table 22.3 are quite suggestive. The chi-square values for the 1945–69 period are indeed statistically significant ($\chi^2 = 11.397$, d.f. = 1, p $\leq$ 0.001 at the primary level and $\chi^2 = 15.796$, d.f. = 1, p $\leq$ 0.001 at the secondary level), meaning that a country with the first export partner using English as the national language was more likely to incorporate English as the first foreign language into its school curricula during the 1945–69 period. However, the chi-square values for the succeeding periods are only slightly significant in terms of the statistical significance level (all χ^2 values are below 1 except for the secondary level in the 1990–2005 period), implying that the relationship between the institutionalization of English instruction in school curricula and the national language of the first export partner has been diminishing or at least inconsistent over time. In other words, the results in Table 22.3 are not compatible with the conventional argument that English education in schools reflects substantive functional requirements or concrete local conditions of a given country.

It is important to stress that English is more than just a foreign language in the sense that the institutional impact of English on the educational sector is witnessed virtually everywhere in the world. As shown in Table 22.3, the degree of our social attention given to English education often exceeds the functional requirements of individual national societies. South Korea is a good example in this respect. Although the first export partner of Korea is China (19.7 percent in 2004) and the first import partner is Japan (20.6 percent in 2004), English is the only compulsory foreign language taught in schools. Considering the fact that China and Japan are the two closest neighbors of

Korea in terms of both geography and history, it is very interesting that Chinese and Japanese are receiving relatively very limited social attention in Korea.

On the contrary, English is now taught in virtually every school in Korea as a compulsory subject for ten years of formal schooling from the third year of primary education to the end of the upper secondary school. The Korean government is seriously considering teaching English from the very beginning of primary education in the near future, and some pilot primary schools are providing English instruction for schoolchildren in the first and second years as well. Moreover, English proficiency has long been one of the most decisive factors in gaining a high score in Korea's Scholastic Aptitude Test, the nation-wide university entrance examination administered annually by the Ministry of Education of Korea. Korea's recent education policies at both governmental and provincial levels stipulate many ambitious strategies to enhance the quality of English education for schoolchildren. Some examples of such policy items include: giving opportunities for English teachers to study abroad in native English-speaking countries; introducing native English speakers into public schools as assistant English teachers; and even setting up English-only villages exclusively for educational purposes.

Another very important and noticeable worldwide phenomenon is that English is no longer likely to be seen as an embodiment of Western ideologies. The English language is becoming neutralized as an efficient medium of inter-national communication and English education is consolidating its status as a world institution. In Russia, for example, English is very popular nowadays. Children in Russia usually begin to learn English in schools at a very early age, and some even engage private tutors who teach English at home. Native speakers of English participate in developing English textbooks for Russian schoolchildren. Meanwhile, the educational aim of teaching the Russian language is now being focused on developing children's communicative ability and practical skills for linguistic competence (IBE and UNESCO, 2004a). These trends in Russia epitomize the fact that language education in both the national language and foreign languages in Russia is shifting toward a new phase in which communicative functions are considered of the utmost import-ance, while ideological or nationalistic concerns are giving way to a broader perspective. English would not be so deeply integrated into the school curricula of Russia if English were understood as de facto the "national" language of the United States, once the major ideological counterforce against the Soviet Union. As far as English education for schoolchildren is concerned, it seems that national boundaries are largely blurred in the contemporary structural context where national societies are deeply embedded in the institu-tional environment of the larger "imagined community" (Anderson, 1991) or the "world polity" (Meyer et al., 1997).

Discussion and Conclusion

The major purpose of this chapter was to describe and explain the rise and expansion of English as a legitimate school subject during the last 150 years. Extensive historical and comparative data analyzed in the chapter show that English instruction has been incorporated into school curricula by an increasing number of countries over time. Distinct country-specific conditions seem to play rather insignificant roles in the worldwide expansion of English in school curricula. This phenomenon is not expected from the assumptions of the most current theoretical perspectives that emphasize a tight linkage between concrete local conditions of a given country and the school curriculum.

In order to understand the strikingly rapid diffusion of English in school curricula around the world, we need to see modern mass education and the school curriculum from an alternative perspective which provides more comprehensive insights into the dialectic relationship between the larger institutional surroundings and education. We argue that modern mass education is a highly rationalized "secular religion," a standardized system of rites giving institutional legitimacy to both knowledge and personnel, organized around elaborate rationales and theories carrying worldwide connotations (Meyer, 1977). This accounts for why national educational systems and their curricular contents are more keenly responsive to the cultural conditions of the wider institutional environment rather than to specific local conditions. The worldwide expansion of English education during the recent period symbolically reflects the wider institutional dynamics of the modern international system where the increasingly consolidated world society has formulated various rationales and theories, both in "scientific" fashion, that function as legitimating accounts of the importance of English as a core component of curricular contents. Also, the rise of the United States as an unchallengeable superpower after World War II has also consolidated the legitimate status of English as the most predominant language for international communication. With these world-cultural influences combined, the effects of English education extend not merely to its contribution to substantive local or national needs, but rather to its institutional impact on our cognition by which English is conceived as a "taken-for-granted" component of world curriculum models.

NOTES

1   Estimating the exact number of English speakers in the world is practically an impossible task. However, one of the most reliable sources of the current language statistics is Ethnologue: Languages of the World (Gordon, 2005).
2   "The first foreign language" in this study is technically defined as the most widely taught foreign language that has a "regular" status in the school curriculum. A "regular" school subject here denotes an independent school subject that is officially

stipulated as a legitimate one in national documents such as national curricular recommendations or guidelines and national educational reports to international organizations. A compulsory subject or a compulsory elective subject taught in primary schools and general secondary schools was taken into account as a "regular" one. An optional subject was excluded from analysis unless it was taught in almost all schools (approximately more than 90 percent) in a given country.

3   Such countries are: Antigua and Gibraltar, Australia, Bahamas, Barbados, Barbuda, Belize, Bermuda, British Virgin Islands, Canada, Cayman Islands, Ireland, Guyana, Grenada, Jamaica, New Zealand, St. Kitts-Nevis, St. Vincent and the Grenadines, Trinidad and Tobago, the United Kingdom, the United States, and US Virgin Islands.

4   This index denotes the probability that any two persons picked at random in a country will speak different mother tongues, ranging from 0.00 for no diversity to near 1.00 for high diversity (Lieberson, 1981).

REFERENCES

Anderson, Benedict (1991). *Imagined Communities* (2nd edn.). London: Verso.

Baker, David P. & LeTendre, Gerald K. (2005). *National Differences, Global Similarities: World Culture and the Future of Schooling.* Stanford, CA: Stanford University Press.

Benavot, Aaron & Braslavsky, Cecilia (eds.) (2006). *School Knowledge in Comparative and Historical Perspective: Changing Curricula in Primary and Secondary Education.* Hong Kong: Hong Kong University Press.

Board of Education (England and Wales) (1897–1914). *Special Reports on Educational Subjects* (vols. 1–28). London: Eyre & Spottiswoode.

Cha, Yun-Kyung (1991). Effect of the global system on language instruction, 1850–1986, *Sociology of Education,* 64(1), 19–32.

Cha, Yun-Kyung & Ham, Seung-Hwan (2005). The global institutionalization of information science education: A cross-national study. *Korean Journal of Comparative Education,* 15(1), 167–190.

Crystal, David (2003). *The Cambridge Encyclopedia of the English Language* (2nd edn.). Cambridge: Cambridge University Press.

Eurydice (2005). *Key Data on Teaching Languages at School in Europe.* Brussels: Eurydice.

Fishman, Joshua A., Conrad, Andrew W., & Rubal-Lopez, Alma (1996). *Post-Imperial English: Status Change in Former British and American Colonies, 1940–1990.* Berlin: Mouton de Gruyter.

Gordon, Raymond G., Jr. (ed.) (2005). *Ethnologue: Languages of the World* (15th edn.). Dallas, TX: SIL International.

IBE (International Bureau of Education) (1937). *L'enseignement des Langues Vivantes.* Geneve: IBE.

IBE (International Bureau of Education) and UNESCO (1958). *Preparation and Issuing of the Primary School Curriculum.* Paris: IBE and UNESCO.

IBE (International Bureau of Education) and UNESCO (1984, 1986, 1992, 2004a). *National Reports to International Conference on Education.* Geneva: IBE and UNESCO.

IBE (International Bureau of Education) and UNESCO (2003). *World Data on Education* (5th edn., CD-ROM). Geneva: IBE and UNESCO.

IBE (International Bureau of Education) and UNESCO (2004b). *A Guide to the Organization of Teaching Subjects and Curricular Time in National Educational Systems*, Geneva: IBE and UNESCO.

Kandel, Isaac L. (ed.) (1924–44). *Educational Yearbook*. New York: Bureau of Publications, Teachers College, Columbia University.

Lieberson, Stanley (1981). *Language Diversity and Language Contact*. Stanford, CA: Stanford University Press.

Meyer, John W. (1977). The effects of education as an institution. *American Journal of Sociology*, 83(1), 55–77.

Meyer, John W. & Brian Rowan (1977). Institutionalized organizations: Formal Structure as myth and ceremony. *American Journal of Sociology*, 83(2), 340–363.

Meyer, John W., Kamens, David H., Benavot, Aaron, Cha, Yun-Kyung, & Wong, Suk-Ying (1992). *School Knowledge for the Masses: World Models and National Primary Curricular Categories in the Twentieth Century*. Washington, DC: Falmer Press.

Meyer, John W., Boli, John, Thomas, George M., & Ramirez, Francisco O. (1997). World society and the nation-state. *American Journal of Sociology*, 103(1), 144–181.

Sasnett, Martena & Sepmeyer, Inez (1966). *Educational Systems of Africa*. Berkeley: University of California Press.

Schissler, Hanna & Soysal, Yasemin N. (eds.) (2005). *The Nation, Europe, and the World: Textbooks and Curricula in Transition*. Oxford: Berghahn Books.

Spolsky, Bernard (2004). *Language Policy*. Cambridge: Cambridge University Press.

UNESCO (1958). *World Survey of Education* (vol. 2). Paris: UNESCO.

UNESCO and National Institute for Educational Research (NIER) (1970). *Asian Study of Curriculum* (vols. 1–3). Tokyo: NIER.

UNESCO Regional Office for Education in Asia (1966). *Curriculum, Methods of Teaching, Evaluation and Textbooks in Primary Schools in Asia*. Bangkok: UNESCO Regional Office for Education in Asia.

US Bureau of Education (1873–1915). *Report of the Commissioner of Education*. Washington, DC: US Government Printing Office.

Weick, Karl E. (1976). Educational organizations as loosely coupled systems. *Administrative Science Quarterly*, 21(1), 1–19.

FURTHER READING

Cenoz, Jasone & Genesee, Fred (eds.) (1998). *Beyond Bilingualism: Multilingualism and Multilingual Education*. Clevedon, UK: Multilingual Matters.

Fishman, Joshua A., Cooper, Robert L., & Conrad, Andrew W. (eds.) (1977). *The Spread of English: The Sociology of English as an Additional Language*. Rowley, MA: Newbury House.

Kachru, Braj B. (2005). *Asian Englishes: Beyond the Canon*. Hong Kong: Hong Kong University Press.

23 Literacy

GLYNDA A. HULL AND
GREGORIO HERNANDEZ

Foundations

Introduction

The topic of literacy has attracted great interest and inspired serious debate among researchers in a number of fields, including linguistics, anthropology, sociology, and psychology, as well as among teachers and other practitioners. Long assumed foundational for schooling and the mark of an educated person, a facility with written language has also been variously promoted as a human right, a precursor to economic development, and a path to critical consciousness. Scribner (1988) helpfully captured such multiple meanings and purposes by examining literacy from the vantage point of three metaphors, each of which suggests particular affordances, constraints, and contradictions: literacy as "adaptation," literacy as "liberation," and literacy as a "state of grace." As implied by these terms, some understandings of literacy have privileged its practical function as a necessary everyday tool; others have looked to its emancipatory potential, linking it to heightened political awareness and collective movements; others still have focused on literacy's promise to elevate the individual through the access it promises to literature and knowledge and the entry point it provides to religions of the book. Perhaps the single most important conceptual advance in the study of literacy over the last 30 years has been just this: an appreciation of its definitional impermanence, its fluidity, and its multiplicity. Indeed, it has become commonplace within certain bodies of scholarship to speak of "literacies," and further to argue that literacy should be considered a social practice, as embedded within culture and as depending for its meaning and practice upon social institutions and conditions, including the technological tools at hand. What will become apparent in this chapter, however, is that such understandings of literacy have often conflicted not only with competing academic strains, but with the customary ways in which literacy is defined and regulated within schools and other institutions. The field of literacy studies is most definitely a contested one.

Below we briefly review some of the hallmark research that led, if by somewhat circuitous routes, to the eventual conceptualization of literacy as a situated social practice. By focusing on this particular theoretical orientation, we of necessity omit numerous studies that have examined literacy from other disciplinary points of view, including important work in psycholinguistics and cognitive psychology on reading comprehension, reading and writing processes, language development in writing, and spelling. For such perspectives, we refer readers to Williams' (2004) recent review, which divides literacy studies into "narrow" and "broad" camps and then concerns itself primarily with the former, highlighting research that privileges individual capacities and offers reading and writing as separate domains. By contrast, we review the scholarship that Williams characterizes as taking a "broad" interpretation of literacy. It focuses on literacy use in a range of contexts, including but not limited to school; it takes as its unit of analysis, not an individual psycholinguistic act, but the broader historical, cultural, and social contexts that lend literacy its meanings within purposeful human activities; it connects the production and reception of written texts with oral language and increasingly with other modes of signification, such as images; and it remains alert to the insight that literacy, though commonly offered unselfconsciously as a neutral tool, does not operate in a decontextualized manner outside fields of power, and can itself be implicated in the maintenance of social and political inequalities as well as turned toward the egalitarian.

To be sure, the above description is dauntingly broad and interdisciplinary, but both the genius and the Achilles heel of the emergent field called the New Literacy Studies (Street, 1993; Gee, 1996) is its determination to capture the multiplex human activity of meaning making through textual artifacts and other modalities in all of its complexity and constraints and potential. This hybrid field is thereby an exciting enterprise, welcoming all comers and making room for new research conceptualizations. With technical advances in digital communication and digital media; with new theoretical insights from related fields such as semiotics, cultural geography, and social and cultural studies; and let it be said clearly, with our ever increasing global economic disparities and senses of religious, cultural, and ethnic difference and division, now more than ever there is the need to understand the nature and purposes of texts and their related compositional tools, and to advocate, foster, and design their more equitable distribution and their more just and critical use.

A brief history

It is a commonplace to note that an interest in written language came late to linguistics. In the same way that oral language took pride of place for decades, the assumption being that the spoken word is primary and writing just a means of representing speech, reading dominated academic studies of literacy for much of the twentieth century and was in fact more often than not solely equated with literacy among academics and the wider public. The beginning of literacy studies proper is often linked with Goody and Watt's (1968) provocative essay, "The Consequences of Literacy," which argued for literacy's pivotal role in cognitive, social, and economic development. Placing great stock in the invention of the Greek alphabet as a prime mover – it led, they surmised, to different understandings of space and time, to the development of history or a sense of the "pastness of the past," and even to the development of logic and the spread of democracy – Goody and Watt singled out literacy as a primary explanation for Greek and thereby Western achievements. This essay, and related bodies of work that adopted a similar strong and causal view (Ong, 1982; McLuhan, [1964] 1995), collectively came to be known as "Great Divide" theories. These were quickly challenged by a range of scholars who reined in such claims by providing their own persuasive counterexamples from other cultures and times. The alphabet isn't the sine qua non of logical thinking, anthropologists and linguists were quick to point out, and indeed, Goody himself soon offered qualifications to his and Watt's claims. Literacy has implications, it came to be said, rather than consequences. Yet the view of literacy as a dividing line, as signaling in ways that mere speech has not, important differences in habits of mind and human and societal capacity, is a powerful trope, one that continues to wield influence in policy, practice, and scholarship the world over.

Subsequent to Goody and Watt's essay, the scholarship on literacy flowered, much of it seeking to understand more precisely and accurately the power that literacy could be legitimately said to wield and under what circumstances. One monumental study that was led by psychologists, and that ultimately took the conceptualization of literacy in fundamentally new directions, was Scribner and Cole's (1981) work with the Vai of North Africa, a people who have the distinction of inventing an original writing system for the Vai language as well as employing the scripts for English and Arabic. Pushing the boundaries of psychology's accepted methods and concepts for cross-cultural studies of thinking and development, Scribner and Cole set out to investigate some of the grand claims that had been made about literacy. They were especially interested in testing empirically the theorizing of the influential Soviet thinker, Vygotsky (1978), who had assigned special import to writing as a psychological tool that structures mental activity. What they discovered, combining ethnographic field work with surveys and experiments to determine the cognitive benefits that accrued from literacy in the three languages, was that literacy does indeed have consequences for mental life. However, those effects are particular to specialized literacy practices, so the impacts of literacy can be more or less powerful, depending on the varied social and cultural contexts that afford and constrain them. The term "practice" is important here; though commonplace in literacy studies now, Scribner and Cole were to our knowledge the first to introduce it. They defined a practice as "a recurrent, goal-directed sequence of activities using a particular technology and particular systems of knowledge" (p. 236), and literacy as a socially organized practice: "not simply knowing how to read and write a particular script but applying this knowledge for specific purposes in specific contexts of use" (p. 237).

This shift was huge, implying as it did different assumptions about the nature of literacy as a human activity, and different starting places for research agendas that would investigate its acquisition and effects. It turned out, happily, that these insights were paralleled and multiplied by compatible research done in roughly the same time period but from different disciplinary starting places. Bringing together perspectives from linguistics and anthropology, Hymes (1964) urged the study of language in context and the inclusion of language in the study of cultures. He proposed that an "ethnography of communication" would usefully reveal the communicative patterns of a community and contrastively the range of patterns across communities. And so it did, perhaps most brilliantly for literacy studies, via Shirley Brice Heath's (1983) long-term ethnography of three contiguous US communities over a decade in the 1960s and 70s. Her juxtaposition of the "ways with words" that characterized a black working-class, a white working-class, and a racially mixed middle-class community revealed the interdependence of language use with habits and values and ways of participating in local social worlds. Far from being a neutral skill with governable cognitive or social consequence, or even a monolithic concept, literacy was variably conceptualized and experienced, and of course, offered differential rewards, depending on the distance that certain ways of using language maintained from the middle-class standard. Heath's research demonstrated, as did numerous likeminded accounts following hers (Taylor & Dorsey-Gaines, 1988; Cushman, 1998), that while communities had developed functional uses of written language, schools were not in the habit of viewing them as such, and as a matter of fact, were mostly unaware of the sociolinguistic and cultural differences that characterize and separate children when they enter and progress through schooling. Being unaware of such differences, many scholars have noted, can blind educators to children's resources and abilities.

It remained for literacy studies to engage front and center with the expression and maintenance of power. Rather than assume that literacy is invariably an empowering tool, researchers and theorists have attempted both to characterize empowering versions of literacy and to delineate the ways in which literacy can be implicated in relations of power. This strand of work is indebted first to Freire ([1970] 1997) and his contribution to an understanding of literacy as a coming to consciousness regarding sociopolitical circumstances and positionings, including the conception of self as an agent capable of remaking one's relation to history. Although Freire's work is sometimes taken to task because his "causal" view of literacy's potential power can be likened to work within the "Great Divide" tradition, and also because his political critique, at least early on, was turned primarily toward a class-based analysis, few doubt his contribution to power-sensitive treatments of literacy and education. More recent analyses have grown from work at the crossroads of sociolinguistic and anthropological theories of language and schooling and ethnographic and discourse analytic methodologies, often under the banner of the New Literacy Studies (NLS) (Street, 1993; Gee, 1996). NLS built on the ethnography of communication tradition, continuing to document literacy practices in local communities, but it began to provide more explicitly an analysis of the interplay between the meanings of local events and the role of literacy within them, and a sensitivity to the structural dimensions of institutions and economic and political relationships.

Gee's (1996) important contribution to this enterprise was to situate the study of literacy within an understanding of discourse, drawing on a range of social theorists to trace connections between social practice, or ways of behaving, interacting, valuing, and believing, and uses of language and literacy. Interestingly, his focus on discourse de-centered literacy, making us aware of the ways in which failures to become literate may be seen as rejections of particular social roles and affiliations with others. Street's similarly pivotal research pushed at the long-accepted view of literacy as just a technical skill. Carrying out an ethnography of village life in Iran during the 1970s, Street provided an influential analytic framework for viewing literacy as an ideological practice rather than an "autonomous" skill (1984). He further argued that school-based literacy is simply one type of literacy practice, often a very limited and circumscribed one. He called for the documentation of literacy practices cross-culturally, and subsequent to his study, researchers gathered examples of literacy practices in local communities across the world (Street, 1993; Moss, 1994; Barton, Hamilton, & Ivanic, 2000).

Core Themes

Historicizing literacy

One of the helpful early turns in literacy research that continues to this day is taking an historical view, often in order to gain purchase on contemporary literacy issues. Early work focused on charting the landscape of readers and nonreaders through an examination of wills, marriage records, and other documents, while later work looked into how literacy was distributed across socioeconomic classes and what advantages accrued from being literate. It was through such historical studies as Graff's (1979) examination of nineteenth-century Canada and his characterization of "the literacy myth" that certain claims about the consequences of literacy were qualified and rethought, and that we have come to consider the development of literacy practices over time as containing both "continuities and contradictions." One major contradiction, for example, was uncovered by Cook-Gumperz (1986) through her examination of how and where a facility with literacy was acquired in nineteenth-century England. Reversing the usual equation of literacy with schooling,

Cook-Gumperz revealed that literacy was largely acquired in informal, out-of-school settings for portions of the British population, and it was in fact partly the desire to gain some control over literacy acquisition that motivated the establishment of schools. Resnick and Resnick (1977), by tracing the shifting of what has counted as literacy over time, helpfully called attention to the way the ante has continuously been raised, from considering the ability to sign one's name as evidence of sufficient literacy, to reading rates calibrated according to what is required to read at particular grade levels, to the capacity to comprehend unfamiliar texts and write academic essays.

Most recently, work on literacy that has taken a historical turn has increasingly tended to examine in finer detail particular historical contexts, illustrating the range of literacy practices associated with local scenes and attempting to capture their variability and richness. This work has tended to challenge commonplaces in the field. To wit, McHenry and Heath's (1994) look at African American middle class in the nineteenth century, whose deep involvement in literacy practices partly through the abolitionist movement and other political activism makes clear that the literacy legacy of this group is deep and wide, contrary to most portraits in the literature. Other historical work has characterized everyday literacy practices in ways that complicate old categories, including the assumed division between orality and literacy, such as Chartier's (1989) depiction of the conviviality associated with reading aloud in early modern Europe. Other historically sensitive work has offered new categories that enliven contemporary analyses, such as Brandt's (2001) conceptualization of the "sponsors" of literacy – agents who "enable, support, teach, and model, as well as recruit, regulate, suppress, or withhold literacy" (p. 19) – and who provide a connection between literacy as seen as individual development and literacy as economic development.

Technologizing the word

Another recurrent theme in literacy studies treats the material tools associated with literacy: books, writing implements, and of course now digital technologies. In point of fact, scripts such as the alphabet can in themselves be viewed as technologies, as Ong (1982) noted when he coined the phrase "the technologizing of the word." In effect, whatever it is that transforms spoken language into other modalities acts upon it in ways that have long held the interest of researchers. There have been major studies of broad shifts that have resulted from new ways of producing and distributing the printed word, such as Eisenstein's (1979) examination of the influence of the printing press, and provocative if controversial accounts that argue the transformative effect of technologies on cognition and culture, McLuhan's ([1964] 1995) work being the most famous of these. With such claims have come more balanced views of the power of new technologies, including complex understandings of the ways in which new technologies exist side-by-side with old ones, assuming for a period of time their customary functions.

Much of the work around technologies and literacy currently focuses on the promise of digital tools for communication and for representation, including an interest in how the internet and multiple audiences and spaces for authorship aid the construction of new identities. Lam (2000), for example, provided a telling case study of a Chinese American adolescent who found a productive context for learning English and building an identity, not in the English as a Second Language classroom, but in electronic chat rooms and email communication. An important branch of this scholarship is interested in characterizing what counts as literacy in a digital multimodal world. That is, now that images, sounds, and motion are almost as easily incorporated into a digital artifact as are words, then semiotics, the science of signs, must inform our understanding of literacy (Kress, 2003; Hull & Nelson, 2005). Indeed, there have been attemps of late to join studies of multimodality with the NLS movement (Pahl & Rowsell, 2006). Another compatible line of theorizing comes from those who attempt to capture the nature and effects of globalization. Appadurai (1996), for example, has powerfully claimed that the primary characteristic of our global world is the movement of both texts and populations. Understanding literacy in a textually mobile world, including the implications for those who don't have access to digital technologies, will surely occupy researchers for some time.

Literacies across languages and cultures

With Street's call for the documentation of social practices across cultures came and still continue to arrive a wealth of studies depicting the variation and nuance of reading, writing, and speaking practices in a range of cross-cultural and cross-national contexts (Street, 1993). A hallmark of these studies is "close descriptions of the actual uses and conceptions of literacy in specific cultural contexts" (Street, 1993: 2). And thus, researchers documented how villagers in Papua New Guinea applied literacy for religious and personal purposes; how immigrant women in Los Angeles experienced literacy as threat and desire; how, for Hmong refugees, reading and writing practices intertwined with kinship networks. These are but a few examples from an impressive nuanced literature. An extension to work in this tradition has recently focused explicitly on bilingual or multilingual literacies. If literacy in one language can be considered a multiple construct, then the addition of different languages, language varieties, and scripts increases this diversity and complexity exponentially. Despite a monolingual ethos in countries such as the US and Great Britain, it is of course the case that many people in the world have more than one spoken or written language as part of their communicative repertoire.

With globalization and the cross-national spread of popular cultural forms among youth, such as rap and hip-hop (Pennycook, 2003; Mahiri, 2004), it becomes ever more important to understand how people make meaning by drawing on multiple language and literacy resources. Hornberger first offered a helpful and much-cited framework for understanding the dimensions of biliteracy (1989), but most research on biliteracy and multilingual literacies is more recent. As Martin-Jones and Jones (2000) note in their edited volume that assembles research on multilingual literacies, to study multilingual language and literacy practices has meant more often than not to be engaged with people from linguistic minority groups. Hence, such practices likely also index unequal power relationships among social, linguistic, and ethnic groups, calling attention to the need to be alert to these relationships in analyses of literacy practices, including school-based studies. The contributors to Martin-Jones and Jones' book note the lack of awareness among many teachers of the richness of the linguistic and cultural resources that children bring to classrooms. However, Kenner's (2004) work provides a window onto the kinds of learning opportunities that accrue when multiple scripts and languages are valued in a nursery school classroom.

Literacy and development

The study of literacy has long coincided with studies of development broadly conceived – both as an individual's participation in changing literacy practices across the life span, and more traditionally, the role of literacy in the growth of communities and societies. From the sociocultural perspective that motivates the work reviewed in this chapter, and drawing on the foundational thinking of Vygotsky (1978) about the social nature of learning and of Bakhtin (1986) about the tensions that thereby thread through it, researchers of children's literacy learning have also been interested in how children build upon their social worlds – their families and peers as well as society's ideologies and institutions – for form, content, and motive as they learn to read and write in classrooms (Dyson, 2003). While much thinking about children's language development and literacy learning has been based on white middle-class norms, increasingly researchers seek to be informed by the study of diverse cultures, ethnicities, and social classes, and to be attentive to gender influences as well. Newkirk (2002), for example, has illustrated how the predilection of particular young North American boys for certain topics, genres, and styles influences their classroom literacy success and participation. Interest in particular age groups also surfaces as part of developmentally attuned research. And thus, the subfield of "adolescent literacy" has gained prominence over the last 10 years, attracting the interest of policy makers and funders in the US (Greenleaf et al., 2001).

With the pressures of transnational economic competition, the literacy levels of adults regularly receive attention and scrutiny as well, as employers call for workers able to manage increasingly complex symbolic systems and textually saturated workplaces (Gee, Hull, & Lankshear, 1996). Researchers have continued to challenge what seem to be too facile correlations between literacy rates and economic productivity, noting that opportunities to become literate are themselves fostered or limited by the broader economic and political context

(Hernandez, 2004). Yet, demands for improved literacy among adults are regularly and loudly voiced, along with governmental and NGO-sponsored programs that answer the call, and these are often joined to a need for knowledge of how to use computers and the internet.

Research/Practice

To date, perhaps the most provocative and comprehensive application of theory and research from NLS to conceptions of practice was offered by the New London Group (1996), an interdisciplinary team of scholars meeting in 1994 in New London, New Hampshire; their ambitious aim was to conceptualize a pedagogy for literacy, one fit for current and future times. Their manifesto called for literacy pedagogy to take into account "the context of our culturally and linguistically diverse and increasingly globalised societies"; "the multifarious cultures that interrelate and the plurality of texts that circulate"; and "the burgeoning variety of text forms associated with information and multimedia technologies" (New London Group, 1996: 60). At the center of their argument was the concept of semiotic activity, which they termed "design." In the view of the New London Group, it is through an informed, intentional process of design on the part of individuals – making creative use of available preexisting designs and resources that one has to hand – that meanings, selves, and communities are powerfully made and remade.

There are fine cross-national examples in the literature of how perspectives from NLS have positively and durably impacted practice, including work derived directly from the New London framework (Cope & Kalantzis, 2000). Stein (2004), for example, writing about her work in South Africa, powerfully captured the range of modalities that were used by students to represent their experiences in addition to reading and writing – song, oral story, even silence – and called for a multimodal pedagogy. Yet, as Stein made clear, it will do little good to value multiple literacies and multiple modalities in classrooms, unless assessment and evaluation methods also take new definitions of literacy and learning into account. And here is the rub. We currently know more about literacy learning than has ever been the case before, as research within the NLS framework has offered theoretically sound, pedagogically powerful, and politically alert principles for conceptualizing and teaching literacy as a situated social practice. It is indeed an irony, then, that literacy continues to be viewed and experienced by many as a problem, much worried over by schools, governments, and assorted others.

Indeed, within many "developed" countries, big gaps persist between the performance of social classes and ethnic/racial groups. In the US, blacks and Latinos consistently fall below Asians and whites on literacy-based achievement tests, and poorer children do worse than their economically advantaged peers. The last 15 years' response in the US and Great Britain, and to an increasing extent in New Zealand and Australia as well, has been to regulate the curriculum, teachers, and schools through accountability measures: scripted curricula for teachers; high-stakes testing for students; performance measures for schools; and punitive consequences for not making the grade, as a child or an educational institution (Allington, 2002). Programs for adults have also been included in these reforms, as work-related curricula and testing mandates have proliferated. The definitions of literacy that predominate are what Street has termed "autonomous" – as decontextualized neutral skills. Indeed, in the latest round of what have come to be called in the US context the "reading wars" (Pearson, 2004), those who currently dominate the debate have placed instructional emphasis on heavy doses of skills practice in phonemic awareness and phonics, in effect marginalizing literature-based, "meaning-making" approaches to the teaching of reading and writing.

Thus, as definitions of literacy continue to be debated, pendulum swings in public policy have shifted the attention of schools and teachers to what some consider increasingly narrow understandings of literacy. This narrowing has occurred even as a great deal of research has simultaneously documented the considerable intellectual accomplishments of children, youth, and adults in out-of-school settings, accomplishments that often contrast their poor school-based performance and suggest a different view of their potential as capable learners and doers in the world (Hull & Schultz, 2001). In literacy research, studies have highlighted the kinds of writing that adults do as part of everyday life; others have highlighted the literacy-related activities that many adolescents do on their own, especially in relation to the internet, as well as the literacies that accompany engagement in sports and hobbies. Yet, as most literacy researchers would likely agree, the task for future research is not only to find ways to bridge the successes in literacy and learning that can be demonstrated out of school with school-based literacy practices, but to once again rethink perspectives on literacy and educational policy. Heath (2000) calls for an ecology of learning environments, rather than a sole reliance on schools, as well as new forms of assessment and the display of learning in multiple modes. Luke (2003) proposes "a rigorous sociological, demographic, and economic analysis of how literacy makes a difference in communities and institutions in relation to other forms of available economic and social capital" (p. 134). Thus, signs point to a new turn in literacy studies, one of equal import to the shift from the "Great Divide" accounts to social practice perspectives, but the nature of that shift is not yet clear.

REFERENCES

Allington, Richard L. (2002). *Big Brother and the National Reading Curriculum*. Portsmouth, NH: Heinemann.

Appadurai, Arjun (1996). *Modernity at Large: Cultural Dimensions of Globalization*. Minneapolis: University of Minnesota Press.

Bakhtin, Mikhail M. (1986). *Speech Genres and Other Late Essays*, trans. Vern W. McGee, ed. Caryl Emerson & Michael Holquist. Austin: University of Texas Press.

Barton, David, Hamilton, Mary, & Ivanic, Roz (eds.) (2000). *Situated Literacies: Reading and Writing in Context*. London: Routledge.

Brandt, Deborah (2001). *Literacy in American Lives*. Cambridge: Cambridge University Press.

Chartier, Roger (1989). Leisure and sociability: Reading aloud in Early Modern Europe. In Susan Zimmerman & Ronald F. E. Weissman (eds.), *Urban Life in the Renaissance* (pp. 103–120). Newark: University of Delaware Press.

Cook-Gumperz, Jenny (1986). Literacy and schooling: An unchanging equation? In Jenny Cook-Gumperz (ed.), *The Social Construction of Literacy* (pp. 16–44). Cambridge: Cambridge University Press.

Cope, Bill & Kalantzis, Mary (eds.) (2000). *Multiliteracies: Literacy Learning and the Design of Social Futures*. London: Routledge.

Cushman, Ellen (1998). *The Struggle and the Tools: Oral and Literate Strategies in an Inner City Community*. Albany, NY: State University of New York Press.

Dyson, Anne Haas (2003). *The Brothers and Sisters Learning to Write: Popular Literacies in Childhood and School Cultures*. New York: Teachers College Press.

Eisenstein, Elizabeth L. (1979). *The Printing Press as an Agent of Change: Communications and Cultural Transformations in Early Modern Europe*. New York: Cambridge University Press.

Freire, Paulo ([1970] 1997). *Pedagogy of the Oppressed* (20th anniversary edn.), trans. Myra Bergman Ramos. New York: Continuum Publishing.

Gee, James Paul (1996). *Social Linguistics and Literacies: Ideology in Discourses* (2nd edn.). London: Taylor & Francis.

Gee, James Paul, Hull, Glynda, & Lankshear, Colin (1996). *The New Work Order: Behind the Language of the New Capitalism*. Boulder, CO: Allen & Unwin.

Goody, Jack & Watt, Ian (1968). The consequences of literacy. In Jack Goody (ed.), *Literacy in Traditional Societies* (pp. 27–68). Cambridge: Cambridge University Press.

Graff, Harvey (1979). *The Literacy Myth: Literacy and Social Structure in the Nineteenth-Century City*. New York: Academic Press.

Greenleaf, Cynthia L., Schoenbach, Ruth, Cziko, Christine, & Mueller, F. L. (2001). Apprenticing adolescent readers to academic literacy. *Harvard Educational Review*, 71(1), 79–129.

Heath, Shirley Brice (1983). *Ways with Words: Language, Life, and Work in Communities and Classrooms*. Cambridge: Cambridge University Press.

Heath, Shirley Brice (2000). Seeing our way into learning. *Cambridge Journal of Education*, 30(1), 121–32.

Hernandez, Gregorio (2004). Identity and Literacy Development: Life Histories of Marginal Adults in Mexico City. Unpublished doctoral dissertation. University of California, Berkeley.

Hornberger, Nancy (1989). Creating successful learning contexts for bilingual literacy. *Teachers College Record*, 92(2), 212–229.

Hull, Glynda & Nelson, Mark (2005). Locating the semiotic power of multimodality. *Written Communication*, 22(2), 224–62.

Hull, Glynda & Schultz, Katherine (2001). Literacy and learning out of school: A Review of theory and research. *Review of Educational Research*, 71(4), 575–611.

Hymes, Dell (1964). Introduction: Toward ethnographies of communication. In John J. Gumperz & Dell Hymes (eds.), *The Ethnography of Communication* (pp. 1–34). Washington, DC: American Anthropological Association.

Kenner, Charmian (2004). *Becoming Biliterate: Young Children Learning Different Writing Systems*. London: Trentham Books.

Kress, Gunther (2003). *Literacy in the New Media Age*. London: Routledge.

Lam, Wan Shun Eva (2000). L2 Literacy and the design of self: A case study of a teenager writing on the internet. *TESOL Quarterly*, 34(3), 457–82.

Luke, Allan (2003). Literacy and the Other: A sociological approach to literacy policy and research in multilingual societies. *Reading Research Quarterly*, 38(1), 134–41.

Mahiri, Jabari (ed.) (2004). *What They Don't Learn in School: Literacy in the Lives of Urban Youth*. New York: Peter Lang.

Martin-Jones, Marilyn & Jones, Kathryn (eds.) (2000). *Multilingual Literacies: Reading and Writing Different Worlds*. Amsterdam: John Benjamins.

McHenry, Elizabeth & Heath, Shirley Brice (1994). The literate and the literary: African Americans as writers and readers – 1830–1940. *Written Communication*, 11, 419–444.

McLuhan, Marshall ([1964] 1995). *Understanding Media: The Extensions of Man* (3rd printing). Cambridge, MA: MIT Press.

Moss, Beverly (ed.) (1994). *Literacy across Communities*. Cresskill, NJ: Hampton Press.

New London Group (1996). A pedagogy of multiliteracies: Designing social futures. *Harvard Educational Review*, 66(1), 60–92.

Newkirk, Tom (2002). *Misreading Masculinity: Boys, Literacy, and Popular Culture*. Portsmouth, NH: Heinemann.

Ong, Walter J. (1982). *Orality and Literacy: The Technologizing of the Word*. New York: Routledge.

Pahl, Kate & Rowsell, Jennifer (eds.) (2006). *Travel Notes from the New Literacy Studies: Instances of Practice*. Clevedon, UK: Multilingual Matters.

Pearson, P. David (2004). The reading wars. *Educational Policy*, 18(1), 216–252.

Pennycook, Alastair (2003). Global Englishes, *Rip Slyme*, and performativity. *Journal of Sociolinguistics*, 7(4), 513–533.

Resnick, Daniel P. & Resnick, Lauren (1977). The nature of literacy: A historical explanation. *Harvard Educational Review*, 47, 370–385.

Scribner, Sylvia (1988). Literacy in three metaphors. In Eugene R. Kintgen, Barry M. Kroll, & Mike Rose (eds.), *Perspectives on Literacy* (pp. 71–81). Carbondale, IL: Southern Illinois University Press.

Scribner, Sylvia & Cole, Michael (1981). *The Psychology of Literacy*. Cambridge, MA: Harvard University Press.

Stein, Pippa (2004). Representation, rights, and resources: Multimodal pedagogies in the language and literacy classroom. In Bonny Norton & Kelleen Toohey (eds.), *Critical Pedagogies and Language Learning* (pp. 95–115). Cambridge: Cambridge University Press.

Street, Brian (1984). *Literacy in Theory and Practice*. Cambridge: Cambridge University Press.

Street, Brian (ed.) (1993). *Cross-Cultural Approaches to Literacy*. Cambridge: Cambridge University Press.

Taylor, Denny & Dorsey-Gaines, Catherine (1988). *Growing Up Literate: Learning from Inner-City Familes*. Portsmouth, NH: Heinemann.

Vygotsky, Lev (1978). *Mind in Society*, ed. M. Cole, V. John-Steiner, S. Scribner, & E. Souberman. Cambridge, MA: Harvard University Press.

Williams, Eddie (2004). Literacy studies. In Alan Davies & Catherine Elder (eds.), *The Handbook of Applied Linguistics* (pp. 576–603). Oxford: Blackwell Publishing.

FURTHER READING

Ball, Arnetha F. & Warshauer Freedman, Sarah (eds.) (2004). *Bakhtinian Perspectives on Language, Literacy, and Learning*. Cambridge: Cambridge University Press.

Collins, James & Blot, Richard K. (2003). *Literacy and Literacies: Texts, Power, and Identity*. Cambridge: Cambridge University Press.

Cushman, Ellen, Kintgen, Eugene R., Kroll, Barry M., & Rose, Mike (eds.) (2001). *Literacy: A Critical Sourcebook*. Boston: Bedford/St. Martin's.

Finnegan, Ruth (2002). *Communicating: The Multiple Modes of Human Interconnection*. London: Routledge.

Kern, Richard (2000). *Literacy and Language Teaching*. New York: Oxford University Press.

Kintgen, Eugene, Kroll, Barry M., & Rose, Mike (eds.) (1988). *Perspectives on Literacy*. Carbondale, IL: Southern Illinois University Press.

Leander, Kevin M. & Sheehy, Margaret (eds.) (2004). *Spatializing Literacy Research and Practice*. New York: Peter Lang.

McKenna, Michael C., Labbo, Linda D., Kieffer, Ronald D., & Reinking, David (eds.) (2006). *International Handbook of Literacy and Technology*, vol. 2. Mahwah, NJ: Lawrence Erlbaum.

Wagner, Daniel A., Venezky, Richard L., & Street, Brian V. (eds.) (1999). *Literacy: An International Handbook*. Boulder, CO: Westview Press.

24 Vernacular and Indigenous Literacies

KENDALL A. KING AND
CAROL BENSON

There are approximately 300–350 million indigenous people in the world; together they speak 4,000–5,000 languages and reside in more than 70 countries (UNESCO, 2006). Despite these numbers, there is a significant disparity between indigenous and non-indigenous peoples when it comes to basic literacy skills. In Ecuador, for example, the country-wide literacy rate is 91 percent while for indigenous people it is only 72 percent; in Vietnam, the national literacy rate is 87 percent, but as low as 4 percent for some linguistic minorities (UNESCO, 2006). While limited access to formal education is clearly a factor in low literacy rates for many indigenous groups, so too is the language of instruction once students arrive at school.

Extensive empirical international research affirms the efficacy of providing initial literacy instruction in learners' first languages. A corresponding series of international policy statements over the last five decades asserts the importance of vernacular and indigenous literacies in cultivating individual self-actualization, greater social equality, and political democratization. Many international agreements further stress that failure to provide instruction in people's own languages constitutes a violation of human rights as well as a threat to worldwide linguistic and cultural diversity. Given the number and strength of these research findings and policy recommendations, why is it that so many people in the world still do not have the opportunity to learn in their own language(s)? This chapter briefly reviews the field of indigenous and vernacular literacies and addresses this critical question. We first overview how terminology, theory, and research have evolved in recent decades. From this vantage point, we then explore why so few enjoy the benefits of learning to read and write in the language they understand best.

In many contexts, promotion of vernacular or indigenous literacies involves work with languages that have not yet been standardized in written form. Such language planning efforts are often associated with development in former colonial countries. Yet in many areas, writing systems, or sets "of visible or tactile signs used to represent units of language in a systematic way" (Coulmas,

1989: 560), thrived independently of and prior to European writing systems (see, e.g., Gough, 1988, in Wiley, 2006). Although colonization is often linked with the spread of literacy, it often meant not the development of indigenous literacy practices but rather their contraction (Wiley, 2006). In Mesoamerica, for example, scripts for Mayan languages date from 200 BCE and consisted of glyphs as well as phonetic signs representing all possible sounds (Lo, 2006). Indigenous writing systems were forced out of use with the arrival of the Spanish, who viewed them as 'the devil's work' and institutionalized Spanish as the *lingua franca* and language of literacy throughout much of Latin America (for exceptions, see King & Hornberger, 2006). Similar patterns of domination shaped the underdevelopment of indigenous African scripts; as Alexander (2003) points out, indigenous African languages seem poorly suited for formal education only because they have been systematically ignored or devalued since colonial times.

Because discussion of indigenous and vernacular literacies is often linked to national development in post-colonial contexts, we draw many of our examples from such countries. Where relevant, we also include examples from Asian contexts where many so-called 'linguistic minority' groups are still excluded from educational programs, as well as examples from economically developed countries with indigenous groups.

Terms and (Re)definitions

Each of this chapter's title terms – *vernacular*, *indigenous*, and *literacy* – has been challenged and redefined as paradigms of research, theory and practice have evolved over the past 50 years. Here we briefly discuss each term and provide an overview of some of the major paradigmatic shifts. Our aim is to highlight potential problems and ambiguities rather than to definitively resolve them.

Vernacular generally describes 'a language which is the mother tongue of a group which is socially or politically dominated by another group speaking a different language' (UNESCO, 1968 [1953]: 689), but this term can be demeaning to language communities that lack power, status, or formal education. More recent formulations have contested the low-status aspect of the definition; for instance, in his introduction to an edited volume that re-evaluates vernacular literacy, LePage (1997: 6) explains:

> The use of the term "vernacular" is certainly not for us synonymous with "minority" or even "dominated" language. We use it in this book to mean "the everyday spoken language or languages of a community," as contrasted with a standard or official language.

Nevertheless, this formulation, like many others (e.g., Richards, Platt, & Weber, 1989), defines the vernacular in opposition to a higher-status standard, formal, or literary variety. Thus, vernacular is a linguistically imprecise term because it can be applied not only to language varieties that differ from the standard in relatively minor ways, such as African American Vernacular English (now more commonly African American English) in the US, but also to languages that are not linguistically related in any way to the so-called standard, such as xiChangana in Mozambique, where the official language is Portuguese. Thus, 'vernacular' tells us very little about the linguistic relationship between that language and the standard, but a great deal about the economic, social, and political status of the language and its speakers.

In part due to the negative and vague connotations of vernacular, and in an attempt to emphasize linguistic autonomy, the term *indigenous* has been preferred in recent years. An early definition of indigenous language was "the language of the people considered to be original inhabitants of an area" (UNESCO, 1968 [1953]: 689–690). Within some socially conscious circles, the term Indigenous is now capitalized to mark it as a nationality parallel, for instance, to 'Irish' or 'Mexican'. Yet like vernacular, the term indigenous has been used pejoratively, especially in the Americas, where there have been efforts to replace it with *original* (as in original peoples, original languages) to emphasize the long-standing geographic presence of groups marginalized through centuries of 'othering' (Ricento, 2005). In Africa, the generally preferred term is *ethnic groups*, though indigenous is still used to contrast people of African ancestry from the descendents of European colonizers or Asian settlers. From the point of view of the UN Working Group on Indigenous Populations, indigenous groups are pastoralists or hunter-gatherers with distinct cultural and territorial identities like the Maasai or Tuareg in Africa (ILO, 1999, in Eversole, 2005); yet these groups are not the only ones who are indigenous to these territories, nor are they the only ones who have been marginalized. In Asia, the preferred term is *ethnic minority*, which is ambiguous in terms of (1) how language and ethnicity intersect and (2) how minority is defined – by relative size or by power (see Spolsky, 2004).

Finally, we come to *literacy*, traditionally defined as the basic skills of reading and writing, and operationalized by UNESCO as "the ability to read and write, with understanding, a short simple sentence about one's everyday life" (2006, Part II). Though in some parts of the world this skill-based perspective has been expanded to include notions of functionality and critical thinking, a relatively narrow and simplistic formulation still holds in most policy arenas. For example, for India's national census, a literate person is defined as one who is at least seven years old and can read and write with understanding in any language (DPEP, 2003). In contrast, Australia's policy is that "effective literacy is intrinsically purposeful, flexible and dynamic, [and] involves the integration of speaking, listening, and critical thinking, and reading and writing" (DEET, 1991: 5, in Hammond, 2001). Even within these expanded definitions, measurement is problematic, usually limited to self-reports (and thus to respondents' own definitions of literacy) or extrapolated from total years of formal schooling. A further complication is whether literacy is defined in terms of any language or a particular (official) one (Rassool, 1999).

From a policy perspective, literacy has been credited, since the 1950s, with a strong human capital effect and viewed as critical for individual and national economic development (Auerbach, 1989; Lo Bianco, 2001). Further, "literacy is variously said to cultivate values, norms of behaviour and codes of conduct, to create benign citizens, develop powers of thinking and reasoning, enculturate, emancipate and empower, provide enjoyment and emotional development, develop critical awareness, foster religious devotion, community development and not the least to be central to academic success across the curriculum" (Baker, 2003: 78). Such claims have propelled the widespread view of literacy as a basic individual and societal need, and supported many mass literacy campaigns. Within development agencies, literacy (especially for women) is seen to contribute to general health and well-being, lowered child and maternal mortality, improved family nutrition, better economic conditions, and democratic decision-making (UNESCO, 2006). There is research support for many of these claims; for example, one analysis concluded that differences in average literacy skill levels across countries explained 55 percent of the disparity in economic growth between 1960 and 1994 (UNESCO, 2006).

While few question the importance and usefulness that reading, writing and other school-related skills have for many aspects of modern life, some claimed benefits have been contested. Stromquist (2002), among others (see Rassool, 1999), questions the simplistic economic and social causality of many such claims, demonstrating that access to literacy does not directly relieve poverty, nor does formal schooling guarantee upward social mobility. Psychologists, in turn, have long questioned the very definition and assumptions behind what it means to be literate. For example, Scribner and Cole's groundbreaking (1981) work on literacy and cognitive skills among the Vai of Liberia challenged the presumed 'great cognitive divide' between literates and illiterates. Their study demonstrated that literacy alone made little difference in the cognitive performance of the trilingual Vai, though specific types of literacy tended to promote particular types of cognitive skills.

New Literacy Studies (NLS) scholars have further challenged the treatment of literacy as a skill-set, arguing that such an approach "obscures literacy's connections to power, to social identity, and to ideologies" by "privileging certain types of literacies and certain types of people" (Gee, 1996: 46). These NLS scholars have focused on understanding literacy as a social and cultural activity, where literacy is seen as consisting of fluid, purposeful social practices which are embedded in broader social goals, cultural activities, power relationships, and historical contexts (Street, 2002). This perspective allows literacy to be understood and defined from the vantage point of its users, thus encompassing activities ranging from recognizing a product label to interaction with technology to expressing words, feelings, and history simultaneously (see, e.g., Menezes de Souza, 2005, on multimodal Kashinaw communication that combines alphabetic and multiple forms of visual representation). Many now use the term *literacies* (plural) to underline this range of possible communicative forms and representations that make up the repertoire to which an educational program is expected to contribute.

In light of the above, we adopt the term 'literacies' here to stress the range of practices potentially involved. We use 'Indigenous' (with a capital I as a reminder of its contestation) and 'vernacular' interchangeably, along with terms such as mother tongue and local language, with the understanding that these terms refer to people's first languages (or language varieties) which have traditionally been excluded from formal educational programs for Indigenous groups.

International Policy and Research Supporting Indigenous and Vernacular Literacies

The importance of teaching in Indigenous and vernacular languages surfaced in the 1950s in the context of international efforts to promote mass basic education. Higher literacy rates and greater access to formal education were viewed as precursors to national development, a perspective that remained dominant throughout the 1960s and 1970s as dozens of nation-states gained independence. Early language planning efforts in post-colonial contexts tended to treat linguistic diversity as an obstacle to national development and unity, and (post-)colonial languages remained prominent in formal education (Wiley, 2006). As Obanya (2002) observes, the clear need across Africa to transform colonial education at independence did *not* result in any serious contestation of foreign (European) languages in formal schooling (with rare exceptions like Guinea under Sekou Touré).

Within this rapidly changing context, UNESCO released a policy paper in 1953 recommending that every pupil should begin formal education in his or her mother tongue (see UNESCO, 1968 [1953]). In this extensively cited document, UNESCO supported initial reading, writing, and learning in the language of the learner on psychological and pedagogical grounds. This position has since been strengthened by abundant empirical evidence that students learn to read and write most efficiently and effectively when instruction takes place through the medium of their mother tongue (see, e.g., Ramirez, Yuen, & Ramey, 1991; Dutcher, 1995, 2004; Thomas & Collier, 2002; Alidou et al., 2006; Daniel & Baxter, 2006). In brief, there is overwhelming evidence that (1) students learn to read more quickly when taught in their mother tongue, (2) students who learn to read in their mother tongue also learn to read in a second/foreign language more quickly than do those who initially are taught to read in a second/foreign language, and (3) students taught to read in their mother tongue acquire academic content and skills more quickly (Mehrotra, 1998).

These research findings have been paralleled by a large number of international agreements supporting the human rights principles behind the original UNESCO report. These include the 1966 International Covenant on Civil and Political Rights (recognizing the right of minority persons to "use their own language in communication with the other members of their group," Article

27); the 1989 ILO Convention 169 concerning Indigenous and Tribal Peoples in Independent Countries (requiring that "children belonging to the peoples concerned shall, *wherever practicable,* be taught to read and write in their own Indigenous language or in the language most commonly used by the group to which they belong," Article 28, emphasis added); the 1989 Convention on the Rights of the Child (confirming that the child's education "shall be directed to the development of respect for the child's cultural identity, language and values", Article 29); and the 1992 Declaration on the Rights of Persons belonging to National or Ethnic, Religious and Linguistic Minorities (noting that "states should take appropriate measures so that, *wherever possible,* persons belonging to minorities have adequate opportunities to learn their mother tongue or to have instruction in their mother tongue," Article 4, emphasis added) (see UNESCO, 2003: 21–22). While these recommendations and mandates are in keeping with the intent of the 1953 UNESCO document, they often contain 'opt out' provisions (in italics above) so that they are not binding (Skutnabb-Kangas, 2000).

Arguments for use of Indigenous literacies in education have ranged from psychological and pedagogical to sociocultural and human rights-based. UNESCO has been a major voice in defending both the human rights basis and the pedagogical effectiveness of mother tongue literacy in formal educa-tion. This stance was affirmed in UNESCO's 2003 follow-up report, which takes up a third argument in favor of promotion of Indigenous literacies: the protec-tion of endangered languages, emphasizing that "safeguarding this diversity today is one of the most urgent challenges facing our world" (p. 11). This sense of urgency is in response to warnings that about half of the world's current languages are in danger of extinction by 2100 (Krauss, 1992; Wurm, 2001).

As demonstrated here, there is a substantial body of policy recommenda-tions, formed on the basis of extensive research, stressing the efficacy of mother tongue use in education and the concomitant importance of development of Indigenous literacies. Yet many of the world's children continue to have their first formal exposure to literacy in a language that is not their mother tongue (Walter, 2003), and approximately 771 million adults, or 18 percent of total world population, lack even minimal literacy skills (UNESCO, 2006). In the following section we address some of the reasons why Indigenous literacy instruction has not been embraced fully, as well as some major debates in the field and practical challenges on the ground.

Why Monolingualism and Monoliteracy?

Given the above, why are there not more sound programs in place? One potential explanation is that such policies are directly undermined by what Dorian (1998: 11) describes as "Western language ideologies," including an "ideology of contempt" for non-standard languages and a belief that "bilin-gualism (and by extension multilingualism, all the more so) is onerous" at both individual and societal levels. Despite the fact that most of the world is bilingual or multilingual – and people with such competencies reap numerous benefits (Skutnabb-Kangas, 2000) – monolingual ideologies continue to undergird decision-making in much of the world. Shohamy (2006) argues that five specific mechanisms result in this de facto monolingualism: (1) rules and regulations, (2) educational language policies, (3) language testing, (4) public language use, and (5) ideology, myths, propaganda, and coercion. She maintains that these mechanisms work together both covertly and overtly to violate democratic principles and personal rights. Below, we discuss how such mechanisms abet the promotion of moniliteracy (i.e., literacy in only one language) and the concomitant denial of access to Indigenous literacy.

Declared language policies

Meaningful use of Indigenous literacies usually entails well crafted and supported language policies in three areas (Cooper, 1989): (1) *status planning* (about the uses of the language); (2) *corpus planning* (about the language itself); and (3) *acquisition planning* (about the users of the language). As widely noted, language planning goals are most likely to be attained if work is undertaken across these areas simultaneously (Fishman, 1979). For instance, declaration of Quechua as a co-official language in Peru in 1975 (status planning) spurred extensive Quechua linguistic work, including dictionary and grammar writing (corpus planning), together with bilingual education experimentation and Quechua literacy instruction (acquisition planning) (Hornberger, 1988). Progress in each of these areas was linked, and Quechua would not otherwise have gained such widespread use as a language of literacy instruction.

Unfortunately, this sort of pro-active, multi-pronged policy and implementation approach supporting Indigenous literacies is the exception rather than the rule. Indeed, few countries give full official recognition to Indigenous languages. With some notable exceptions like South Africa's post-apartheid recognition of 11 official languages (Alexander, 2003), many of the world's 193 countries have declared only one or two of their many languages official. Cameroon, for instance, is home to 25 African language groups, but officially recognizes only English and French. While official recognition does not guarantee the acceptance and development of Indigenous literacies, without it, their widespread expansion and use remains unlikely (see Hornberger & King, 1996).

Language education policies

Even when vernacular languages have some sort of official status, there is no guarantee that effective language education policies will be put into place. One reason is the perceived cost; it is often claimed that implementing mother tongue-based programs would be too expensive, especially when multiple languages are involved. Until recently, advocates have counter-argued that higher costs constitute a necessary and worthwhile investment (e.g., UNESCO, 2006). However, economic analyses of primary bilingual programs (see Alidou et al., 2006) have demonstrated that, while new bilingual programs appear to raise per-pupil expenditure (due to inputs of teacher education and materials, especially for previously lesser developed languages), costs are actually *lower* when balanced against the benefits of lower dropout and failure rates (Patrinos, 1996; Vaillancourt & Grin, 2000; Grin, 2005). Using data from Guatemala and Senegal, Vawda and Patrinos (1998) report that the cost of publishing in local languages represents only a fraction of a percent of the recurring education budget (0.13% for Guatemala), and startup costs are recoverable within three years.

Piloting of bilingual programs can support or hinder use of vernacular literacies. In the case of Niger (Hovens, 2002), bilingual school 'experimentation' has gone on since 1975 without substantially influencing language and education policy. In other countries like Bolivia (Albó & Anaya, 2003) and Mozambique (Benson, 2004), lessons learned through experimentation have fed into establishment of national policies and far-reaching reforms, beginning in 1994 and 2002 respectively. Yet even once appropriate policies are in place, there is often another hurdle: chronic under-resourcing. This may represent true lack of funds or staff, but it more likely indicates that Indigenous literacy programs are given low priority, or worse yet, that 'lip service' policies are passed with no intention to implement them (King & Benson, 2004). Taking the two cases just mentioned, implementation of the Bolivian program has been successful due to regional and donor cooperation, but is ironically now being dismantled by the country's first Indigenous president; in the case of Mozambique, public demand greatly outweighs the resources allocated thus far to 'bilingualizing' schools (Bazilashe, Dhorsan, & Tembe, 2004).

Language tests

Language tests are covert but powerful mechanisms, "capable of manipulating language realities by redefining, standardizing and perpetuating language knowledge and correctness [and] maintaining and promoting the status of a particular (often national) language(s)" (Shohamy, 2006: 109). In many countries, high-stakes testing has become an increasingly pervasive and powerful mechanism promoting de facto monolingualism – and monoliteracy.

East Timor, with two official languages (Tetum and Portuguese) and sixteen Indigenous ones, provides a current example. Fewer than 5 percent of the population is literate in Portuguese (UNDP, 2006), although governmental institutions maintain it is spoken by nearly 25 percent of Timorese. Since independence from Indonesia in 2002, Portuguese has gained status and power. Many high-stakes tests, including those required for teaching and administrative positions, have been offered *only* in Portuguese (J. Sarmento, June 2006, personal communication). This effectively excludes most of the population from these jobs, exacerbating inequalities and undermining the position of Indigenous languages and literacies. Another example comes from the US, where the 2001 No Child Left Behind Act requires all public schools to demonstrate 'annual yearly progress' as measured through student test scores in reading, math, and science, all in English. Schools are thus under intense pressure to de-emphasize Indigenous language instruction, for instance Navajo language and literacy, and focus on English-based testing skills (Leonard, 2004).

Language in the public space

The question of which languages are used for which written purposes is an often-overlooked mechanism promoting de facto language policy and reinforcing de facto monoliteracy. "Those in authority use language in the public space to deliver symbolic messages about the importance, power, significance and relevance of certain languages or the irrelevance of others" (Shohamy, 2006: 112). Indeed, what happens in public spaces often matters as much or more than official policy. For example, most Peruvians know little about the policy change that made Quechua co-official with Spanish in the mid-1970s; yet nearly everyone of a certain age recalls their first impressions upon seeing national news (in print and on television) delivered in both Quechua and Spanish.

Globalization has meant the increasing domination of public space by European languages, and English in particular. This visible penetration of 'world languages' into local spaces potentially undermines the utility and symbolic importance of Indigenous languages. Further, domination of such languages fuels the desire and demand for them; yet as Markee (2002: 272) argues, "the younger or the more disadvantaged the participants are, the more likely it is that [Indigenous language] will provide the most viable means of access to development," which she defines as a reduction in vulnerability. As Bruthiaux (2002) and others have long suggested, in former colonial countries, English and other world languages often exacerbate rather than reduce inequality.

Ideology, myths, propaganda and coercion

Ideology is increasingly recognized as central to the study of language policy and education (Spolsky, 2004). The promotion of Indigenous literacies in formal education is often undermined by general ideologies surrounding language and bilingualism (such as those discussed at the start of this section), as well as challenged by commonplace (mis)understandings of literacy and pedagogy. We offer as examples two commonplace myths.

One pervasive myth that undermines many programs (in particular, those for adults) is that literacy is a set of skills that can be acquired quickly and easily with the proper instruction and degree of learner effort. As a result, many literacy programs aim to achieve literacy (or even biliteracy) in very short periods of time (e.g., several months). Not only are such programs often ineffective in transmitting basic skills, but as Stromquist (2002) points out, the secondary benefits of literacy are acquired only over a much longer period of time. A second and more pernicious myth is that use of the mother tongue in education should be minimized in order to maximize exposure to the higher-status second/foreign language (Skutnabb-Kangas, 2000). In fact, research demonstrates that the opposite is true: investing time and effort into developing literacy and learning through the first language tends to result in higher levels of second language mastery. While this point seems counterintuitive to many, studies from different parts of the world show how parents become active supporters of Indigenous literacy programs once they see how effectively their children are learning (Hovens, 2002; Benson, 2004).

Moving Beyond Monoliteracy?

Language ideologies – those of Indigenous language speakers *and* majority language speakers – are critical for both the creation and the resolution of many of the challenges we have discussed here. There are too many documented cases of well designed Indigenous literacy programs not fully succeeding because learners reject use of their own language(s) in formal education (Hornberger, 1988; Menezes de Souza, 2006). Many Indigenous people quite logically do so because they recognize the low status and utility of their language(s) across wider society. As Indigenous languages are typically ignored or stigmatized in official policy on the one hand, and marginalizing and stigmatizing in many public domains of use on the other, we should hardly be surprised when Indigenous parents are eager for their children to acquire the standard variety as soon and as well as possible. Why should they value literacy in the vernacular if no one else does?

As we consider the way forward, it is useful to keep in mind that the same mechanisms – official policy, education policy, language testing, public language use, and myths and propaganda – can also be used to support vernacular and Indigenous literacies. Indeed, it is through these very same mechanisms that monolingual and monoliterate policies can be resisted because day-to-day, local practices and interactions can in turn influence ideology (Shohamy, 2006). For instance, grassroots, small-scale Indigenous literacy efforts among the Shuar in the Ecuadorian Amazon in the 1970s and 1980s were instrumental in challenging the ideology that the Shuar language could not be written or used as a language of literacy and learning, and this change of attitude paved the way for experimentation and eventually, widespread implementation of bilingual education (King, 2001).

More broadly, an important step in challenging such ideologies is to continue to work toward expanding local participation in designing and implementing Indigenous language programs. Central to this issue would be the establishment of bilingualism and biliteracy (Ouane, 2003) as a goal of *all* formal and non-formal education. Not only would such a goal symbolically demonstrate the value of Indigenous languages across the wider society, but it would also directly benefit all members of society in pedagogical terms. For monolingual speakers of majority languages, programs designed to meet this goal would introduce them to bilingualism and biliteracy from a young age and add locally useful languages to their repertoires (Albó & Anaya, 2003; López, 2006). For speakers from threatened language communities, education designed toward this goal would signal societal support for their languages and cultures. And for vernacular language speakers, the goal of bilingualism and biliteracy would help to ensure that education is meaningful and effective, both short- and long-term.

REFERENCES

Albó, Xavier & Anaya, Amalia (2003). *Niños Alegres, Libres, Expresivos: La Audacia de la Educación Intercultural Bilingüe en Bolivia* [Happy, Free, and Expressive Children: The Audacity of Intercultural Bilingual Education in Bolivia] (Investigation Notebooks 58). La Paz: UNICEF/CIPCA.

Alexander, Neville (2003). The African renaissance and the use of African languages in tertiary education. *PRAESA Occasional Papers No. 13*. Cape Town: PRAESA.

Alidou, Hassana, Boly, Aliou, Brock-Utne, Brigit, Diallo, Yaya Satina, Heugh, Kathleen, & Wolff, Ekkehard H. (2006). *Optimizing Learning and Education in Africa: The Language Factor. A Stock-Taking Research on Mother Tongue and Bilingual Education in Sub-Saharan Africa*. Paris: Association for the Development of Education in Africa (ADEA). www.adeanet.org/biennial-2006/doc/document/B3_1_MTBLE_en.pdf

Auerbach, Elsa (1989). Toward a social-contextual approach to family literacy. *Harvard Educational Review*, 59(2), 165–181.

Baker, Colin (2003). *Foundations of Bilingual Education and Bilingualism*. Clevedon, UK: Multilingual Matters.

Bazilashe, Juvenal, Dhorsan, Adelaide, & Tembe, Cristina (2004). Curriculum reform, political change, and reinforcement of national identity in Mozambique. In Sobhi Tawil and Alexandra Harley (eds.), *Education, Conflict and Social Cohesion* (pp. 207–253). Geneva: UNESCO International Bureau of Education.

Benson, Carol (2004). Bilingual schooling in Mozambique and Bolivia: From experimentation to implementation. *Language Policy*, 3(1), 47–66.

Bruthiaux, Paul (2002). Hold your courses: Language education, language choice, and economic development. *TESOL Quarterly*, 3(3), 275–296.

Cooper, Robert (1989). *Language Planning and Social Change*. New York: Cambridge University Press.

Coulmas, Florian (1989). *The Writing Systems of the World*. Malden, MA: Blackwell.

Daniel, Louise & Baxter, Sandra (eds.) (2006). Mother tongue first: Children's right to learn in their own languages. *id21 Insights Education no. 5*. http://www.id21.org/insights/insights-ed05/insightsEdn5.pdf

DEET (Department of Employment, Education, and Training) (1991). *Australia's Language: The Australian Language and Literacy Policy*. Canberra: DEET.

Dorian, Nancy (1998). Western language ideologies and small-language prospects. In Lenore A. Grenoble & Lindsay Whaley (eds.), *Endangered Languages: Current Issues and Future Prospects* (pp. 3–21). Cambridge: Cambridge University Press.

DPEP (District Primary Education Program) (2003). Concepts and definitions in educational planning: Educational attainment. http://www.dpepmis.org

Dutcher, Nadine (1995). *The Use of First and Second Languages in Education: A Review of International Experience*. Pacific Island Discussion Paper Series No. 1. Washington DC: World Bank.

Dutcher, Nadine (2004). *Expanding Educational Opportunity in Linguistically Diverse Societies* (2nd edn.). Washington, DC: Center for Applied Linguistics. http://www.cal.org/pubs/ford/eeolds.html

Eversole, Robyn (2005). Overview: Patterns of indigenous disadvantage worldwide. In Robyn Eversole, John McNeish, & Alberto Cimadamore (eds.), *Indigenous Peoples and Poverty: An International Perspective* (pp. 29–37). CROP International Studies in Poverty Research. New York: Zed Books.

Fishman, Joshua (1979). Bilingual education, language planning, and English. *English World-Wide*, 1(1), 11–24.

Gee, James P. (1996). *Social Linguistics and Literacies: Ideology in Discourses* (2nd edn.). London: Taylor & Francis.

Gough, Kathleen (1988). Implications of literacy in traditional China and India. In Eugene R. Kintgen, Barry M. Kroll, & Mike Rose (eds.), *Perspectives on Literacy* (pp. 3–27). Carbondale, IL: Southern Illinois University Press.

Grin, François (2005). The economics of language policy implementation: Identifying and measuring costs. In Neville Alexander (ed.), *Mother Tongue-Based Bilingual Education in Southern Africa: The Dynamics of Implementation* (pp. 11–25). Cape Town: PRAESA.

Hammond, Jenny (2001). Literacies in school education in Australia: Disjunctions between policy and research. *Language and Education*, 15(2&3), 162–177.

Hornberger, Nancy (1988). *Bilingual Education and Language Maintenance: A Southern Peruvian Quechua Case*. Dordrecht, Holland: Foris.

Hornberger, Nancy & King, Kendall (1996). Language revitalization in the Andes: Can the schools reverse language shift? *Journal of Multilingual and Multicultural Development*, 17(6), 427–441.

Hovens, Mart (2002). Bilingual education in West Africa: Does it work? *International Journal of Bilingual Education and Bilingualism*, 5(5), 249–266.

ILO (1999). *Indigenous peoples of South Africa: Current trends. Report of the Project for the Rights of Indigenous and Tribal Peoples*. Geneva: International Labour Office.

King, Kendall (2001). *Language Revitalization Processes and Prospects: Quichua in the Ecuadorian Andes*. Clevedon, UK: Multilingual Matters.

King, Kendall & Benson, Carol (2004). Indigenous language education in Bolivia and Ecuador: Contexts, changes, and challenges. In James Tollefson & A. B. M. Tsui (eds.), *Medium of Instruction Policies: Whose Agenda? Which Agenda?* (pp. 241–261). Mahwah, NJ: Lawrence Erlbaum.

King, Kendall & Hornberger, Nancy H. (2006). Quechua as a lingua franca. *Annual Review of Applied Linguistics*, 26, 177–194.

Krauss, Michael (1992). The world's languages in crisis. *Language*, 68(1), 4–10.

Leonard, Leland (2004). Navajo nation testimony regarding the implementation of the No Child Left Behind Act of 2001 to the Senate Committee on Indian Affairs. http://www.senate.gov/~scia/2004hrgs/061604amhrg/leonard.pdf

LePage, Robert (1997). Introduction. In Andrée Tabouret-Keller, Robert B. LePage, Penelope Gardner-Chloros, & Gabrielle Varro (eds.), *Vernacular Literacy: A Re-Evaluation* (pp. 1–19). Oxford: Clarendon Press.

Lo, Lawrence (2006). *Mesoamerican Writing Systems.* www.ancientscripts.com/ma_ws.html

Lo Bianco, Joseph (2001). Policy literacy. *Language and Education,* 15(2&3), 212–227.

López, Luis Enrique (2006). *De Resquicios a Boquerones: La Educación Intercultural Bilingüe en Bolivia.* La Paz: PROEIB Andes.

Markee, Numa (2002). Language in development: Questions of theory, questions of practice. *TESOL Quarterly,* 36(3), 265–274.

Mehrotra, Santosh (1998). *Education for All: Policy Lessons From High-Achieving Countries.* New York: UNICEF.

Menezes de Souza, Lynn Mario (2005). The ecology of writing among the Kashinawá: Indigenous multimodality in Brazil. In Suresh Canagarajah (ed.), *Reclaiming the Local in Language Policy and Practice* (pp. 73–95). Mahwah NJ: Lawrence Erlbaum.

Menezes de Souza, Lynn Mario (2006). Writing by right: Indigenous writing in Brazil as resistance to assimilation. Paper presented at AAAL/CAAL, Montreal, June.

Obanya, Pai (2002). *Revitalising Education in Africa.* Ibadan: Stirling-Horden.

OECD (2000). Literacy in the Information Age: Final Report of the International Adult Literacy Survey. http://www1.oecd.org/publications/e-book/8100051e.pdf

Ouane, Adama (ed.) (2003). *Towards a Multilingual Culture of Education.* www.unesco.org/education/uie/publications/uiestud41.shtml

Patrinos, Harry A. (1996). Bilingual education: Costs and benefits. In Wolfgang Küper (ed.), *Mother Tongue Education: A Reader* (2nd edn.). Eschborn: GTZ.

Ramirez, John David, Yuen, Sandra D., & Ramey, Dina R. (1991). *Final Report: Longitudinal Study of Structured English Immersion Strategy, Early-Exit and Late-Exit Transitional Bilingual Education Programs for Language-Minority Children.* Report for United States Department of Education. San Mateo, CA: Aguirre International. No. 300-87-0156. www.nabe.org/documents/research/Ramirez.pdf

Rassool, Naz (1999). *Literacy for Sustainable Development in the Age of Information.* Clevedon, UK: Multilingual Matters.

Ricento, Thomas (2005). Language rights and language resources in the United States: Limitations and false hopes in the promotion of linguistic diversity. *Journal of Sociolinguistics,* 9(3), 348–368.

Richards, Jack, Platt, John, & Weber, Heidi (1989). *Longman Dictionary of Applied Linguistics.* Harlow, UK: Essex.

Scribner, Silvia & Cole, Michael (1981). *The Psychology of Literacy.* Cambridge, MA: Harvard University Press.

Shohamy, Elana (2006). *Language Policy: Hidden Agendas and New Approaches.* New York: Routledge.

Skutnabb-Kangas, Tove (2000). *Linguistic Genocide in Education – Or Worldwide Diversity and Human Rights?* Mahwah NJ: Lawrence Erlbaum.

Spolsky, Bernard (2004). *Language Policy.* Cambridge: Cambridge University Press.

Street, Brian (2002). Literacy events and literacy practices: Theory and practice in the New Literacy Studies. In Marilyn Martin-Jones & Kathryn E. Jones (eds.), *Multilingual Literacies: Comparative Perspectives on Research and Practice* (pp. 17–30). Amsterdam: John Benjamins.

Stromquist, Nelly (2002). Literacy and gender: When research and policy collide. In Mia Melin (ed.), *Education: A Way Out of Poverty?* (pp. 24–42). New Education Division Documents No. 12. Stockholm: Sida.

Thomas, Wayne & Collier, Virginia (2002). *A National Study of School Effectiveness for Language Minority Students' Long-Term Academic Achievement.* Santa Cruz, CA: Center for Research on Education, Diversity and Excellence. http://www.crede.ucsc.edu/research/llaa/1.1_final.html

UNDP (2006). United Nations Development Program: East Timor. http://www.undp.east-timor.org/

UNESCO (1968 [1953]). The use of vernacular languages in education. In Joshua Fishman (ed.), *Readings in the Sociology of Language* (pp. 688–716). The Hague: Mouton.

UNESCO (2003). *Education in a Multilingual World*. Hamburg: UNESCO. http://unesdoc.unesco.org/images/0012/001297/129728e.pdf

UNESCO (2006). *Education for All Global Monitoring Report. Literacy for Life*. Paris: UNESCO. http://portal.unesco.org/education/en/ev.php-URL_ID=43009&URL_DO=DO_TOPIC&URL_SECTION=201.html

Vaillancourt, François & Grin, François (2000). The choice of a language of instruction: The economic aspects. Distance Learning Course on Language Instruction in Basic Education. Washington, DC: World Bank Institute.

Vawda, Ayesha Y. & Patrinos, Harry A. (1998). Cost of producing educational materials in local languages. Washington, DC: World Bank.

Walter, Stephen L. (2003). Does language of instruction matter in education? In Mary Ruth Wise, Thomas N. Headland, & Ruth M. Brend (eds.), *Language and Life: Essays in Memory of Kenneth L. Pike* (pp. 611–635). Dallas, TX: SIL International and the University of Texas at Arlington.

Wiley, Terrence G. (2006). The lessons of historical investigation: Implications for the study of language policy and planning. In Thomas Ricento (ed.), *An Introduction to Language Policy: Theory and Method* (pp. 135–152). Malden, MA: Blackwell Publishing.

Wurm, Stephen A. (ed.) (2001). *Atlas of the World's Languages in Danger of Disappearing* (revised edn.). Paris: UNESCO.

25 Religious and Sacred Literacies

JONATHAN M. WATT AND
SARAH L. FAIRFIELD

The field of *educational linguistics* applies a scientific study of language to many practical issues related to learning. It forms a bridge between abstract conceptions of human language and the application concerns that arise with the acquisition and use of a particular language. Its subfield of *religious literacy* specifically relates the teaching and acquisition of language to the performance of religious acts, broadly understood, especially when sacred texts and written traditions are integral to these acts.

Religions almost invariably posit the existence of transcendence and deity for, traditionally, religion has been described as something "founded on the subjective experience of an invisible presence" (Keane, 1997: 47). Not surprisingly, then, religions often ascribe a vital role to divine speech, as does Jewish sacred literature with its attribution of the creation of the world to God's very words (Genesis 1:1–2, 4) followed by a solemnizing of the new creation with a blessing. Similarly, one Christian Gospel titles Jesus "the Word of God" (John 1:1–3), while Islam's Qur'an has been described as the Word of God "inlibriate." Religions that link divine revelation with comprehensible language encode in their sacred literature representations of divine dialogue, thus it can be expected that a highly specific ideology of language will emerge amongst religious practitioners. Furthermore, religions almost invariably offer ways in which their practitioners may communicate with the objects of their devotion. Keane observes (1997: 48) that "Religious observance tends to demand highly marked and self-conscious uses of linguistic resources." He adds on the one hand that "Language is one medium by which the presence and activity of beings that are otherwise unavailable to the senses can be made presupposable, even compelling, in ways that are publically [*sic*] yet also subjectively available to people as members of social groups." On the other, he notes (pp. 64–5) that "some language practices seem designed to permit people to carry on without demanding an explanation of what is happening." However, religion can be defined quite broadly, involving not only an interaction with a transcendent deity but also with the humanity of past and present. Even remembrance of a great human tragedy could be considered a "sacred task" (Wollaston in Davies & Wollaston, 1993: 37). In either case, the language of sacred texts significantly frames and prescribes the kinds of language used in private and public religious practices, however religion may be defined.

Inasmuch as writing is "the technology of the intellect" (Goody, 1968: 1), religious literacy can offer access to the defining concepts of a faith, promising its adherents windows not only into present truths but also to transcendent reality. Ong (1982: 105) states that text "makes possible the great introspective religious traditions such as Buddhism, Judaism, Christianity and Islam," for religious literacy facilitates a communal homogeneity by orienting diverse believers around a central body of common tenets. As Goody observes, writing creates a new medium of communication, objectifying speech and providing a set of visible signs as a "material correlative" to the spoken forms. Yet its potentials extend still further. For whereas a conversion is guided by the words of language – the prominent fourth-century churchman Augustine related that his conversion occurred in a garden as was directed by a child's voice to "Take up and read, take up and read," thereby pointing him to the sacred text – writing becomes "a central phenomenon both in language policy and in religion" (Spolsky, 2003: 83). Viewed on the whole, writing facilitates greater complexity in the storage and retrieval of knowledge and thereby advances potentials for understanding and bureaucratization (Stubbs, 1986: 209).

The enormous power of language, sacred or secular, lies partly in the fact that words originating in one context can be preserved and relayed across vast expanses of geography, time, and culture, echoing in a form of natural human language the very transcendence of the deity from whom they originated. John Davies, for example, notes (Davies & Wollaston, 1993: 26) that "War memorials are a refusal by the living to let the dead die," and they constitute a kind of vernacular religion centered about the memorization of themes such as sacrifice, death, and redemption. Literacy, then, becomes both process and goal: it can gather adherents into clearly defined boundaries, and thereby it classifies more effectively the insider from the outsider, the believer from the unbeliever, the participant from all others. Therefore, to the degree that developed societies consider education essential to their maintenance and improvement, religious groups within such societies are likely to be intensely devoted to a set of priorities and means for promoting religious literacy. When such sacred text becomes foundational to a religious community, literacy in the sacred becomes a necessity.

Recent Scholarship on Religious Literacy

The historically close connection between religion and literacy is hardly surprising, given that a preponderance of the world's ancient texts are religious in nature. Studies of religious language are numerous (e.g., Keane, 1997), though the secularization of the academy appears to have delayed investigation into the nature of the connection between language and religion, making this "an area relatively little explored to date" (Spolsky, 2003: 81). Sawyer and Simpson's *Concise Encyclopedia of Language and Religion* (2001) is the most extensive and systematic study of the relationship. The approach falls under six primary headings followed by a major biographic section: Language in the Context of Particular Religions; Sacred Texts and Translations; Religious Languages and Scripts; Special Language Uses; Beliefs About Language; and Religion and the Study of Language.

Religious language has had various effects upon societies, but these may appear in works that are not specifically identifiable as linguistic. For example, explorations of the effects of colonialism (e.g., Vail, 1989) may reference the impact of Western European languages – usually English – upon developing nations. Missionaries acquainted with the presence of biblical themes, imagery, and idiom in writers from Chaucer to Shakespeare to Bunyan would, in turn, bring a religious worldview ensconced in their native language into all the communal activities of the societies they evangelized. Their influence was both direct and indirect: as the tenets and experiences of the religion arrived, so did a legacy of mission schools and social agencies that operated long after their founders were gone, which placed in harmony or rivalry many sets of ideas and values. They often set in motion a need for language planning with a significant literary influence, for this involves (per Einar Haugen, cited in Cooper, 1989: 29) "the activity of preparing a normative orthography, grammar and dictionary for the guidance of writers and speakers in a non-homogeneous speech community."

Religious literacy thereby holds enormous potentials that supersede and exceed the original practitioners of the religion for, as Samuel Huntington (1993) shows, complex civilizations – which are facilitated by literacy – are typically animated by a religious core. Whether or not a culture is inextricably connected to one language in particular (popular perception may conflict with scholarly opinion, yet it becomes real because it is perceived to be true), the language of a civilization – or a local community – becomes the tool of its self-extension. By association, religion becomes intertwined with language and society, and a faith can hardly be separated from code and country, at least in the popular mind. When juxtaposed with a dominant community, religion is undeniably forceful when it comes to language spread and the subsequent shift that often takes place in a receptor community. The force for change is multi-valenced, for it may be more the society and its resources rather than the religion per se which provides the impetus for any language changes being experienced within a community. An ideology of language favoring religious development can promote the outward extension of an entire society, and form the inward perceptions that society holds toward itself. And conversely, as Sawyer notes, "Religion has had an enormous influence on the history of the study of language" (Sawyer & Simpson, 2001: 321).

Insofar as *life is religion*, the implications of language choices are enormous when it comes to religious affairs. By adding a literacy parameter, one may consider even more particularly how self-defined, literate religious communities concern themselves with a plethora of related issues.

Languages of Sacred Texts

Examination of the role of language in religion almost invariably raises issues related to that faith's sacred texts. What forms of that religion's sacred texts are regarded as trustworthy and reliable? Although sacred texts almost necessarily must be accessible to a religion's adherents at the time of their development, the inevitabilities of history have often led to a chasm of understanding between text and practitioner. The Sanskrit of the Vedas has not been a native language for countless centuries. The use of the Hebrew of the Jewish *Tanak* was waning amongst the general Jewish population in the face of the Hellenist surge within a century of the religion's last canonical prophet, while the presence of Egyptian hieratic and Greek below the hieroglyphs of the Rosetta Stone attest to the highly restricted usage of Egyptian hieroglyphics by the late second century BCE. Only a minority of the world's billion Moslems speak some form of Arabic as their first language even though Islam widely regards the Qur'an to be the truly divine word only in its variety of Classical Arabic. A similar veneration is reported for Avestan texts in Zoroastrian worship.

Sawyer (1999: 24) observes that retention of a sacred language often leads to the rise of "a class of priests or other experts who are the only people who can translate and interpret, and this gives them a unique status and power over the rest of the community." Specialists are expected to facilitate the connection between the dead or moribund languages of their sacred texts and the believer who lacks competency in the sacred autographa. For "even a literate [person] needs to be guided through the learning to be won from books; an independent approach to the written word is fraught with mystical dangers" (Goody, 1968: 13). Their ability faithfully to transmit this written text is also proverbial. He cites (p. 48) the "special emphasis on the writing down of their sacred texts and on the special power and sanctity of their script" as proverbial among the medieval Masoretes who conveyed the Hebrew texts, for study of central texts is almost synonymous with study of the religion. Sawyer notes (Sawyer & Simpson, 2001: 321f.) that competence in Hebrew and Aramaic have traditionally been expected of rabbinic students, not only to interpret the TANAK but also the Talmudic literature. The same can be said for patristic Christianity as well, with its love for reliable written texts becoming a vital factor in the popularization of the codex (a transitional form between scrolls and books), and a widespread (though by no means universal) expectation that seminarians must be able to access the original Hellenistic Greek of the New Testament.

Judaism is proverbially famous for its respect for the very fabric of the sacred text. Over the centuries, new editions of the Hebrew Scriptures were traditionally copied letter by letter from an already recognized text, while

copies too worn for continued usage traditionally have been buried respect-
fully. Copyists (scribes) were trained in various techniques designed to ensure
accuracy.

Religious Codes in Religious Acts

What language(s), dialect(s) or style(s) are practitioners of a religion expected
to use in order to be genuinely involved with it? "Religious observance tends
to demand highly marked and self-conscious uses of linguistic resources"
(Keane, 1997: 48; see also Samarin, 1972). The connection of religious materials
with religious communities occurs under three distinct rubrics. The base
rubric involves canonization, i.e., the decision to include certain texts and
exclude others, in an authoritative book. A secondary level occurs in the area
of translation. It can happen that a translated text comes to be treated almost
as sacred canon itself. A third level involves decisions pertaining to the performance (including spontaneous verbal translation) of religious acts.

Canonization has many historical and theological components that are not
essentially dependent upon language issues, though questions about origin-
ality are a necessity (as shown already). But at the second level, to what
degree does the language of a text then become the language of daily use?
The answer differs between religions and even, to some extent, between their
subgroups or sects. "Common to many religions is the tradition that rituals
must be performed in a particular language, frequently a language clearly
distinguished from the language of everyday use" (Sawyer, 1999: 23). The Old
Order Amish of North America traditionally use a German translation of the
Bible for reading which is translated into Pennsylvania German dialect for
the sake of the listener. These kinds of arrangements often lead to diglossic
situations; in this case, the text is in the "high" form while the sermon given
in a worship service constitutes the "low" form, which may be the same as
the code of common daily interaction. Emigration and other geopolitical developments often promote these situations and, with the passage of enough
time, the living code of a community can become distinct from its linguistic
ancestor, as, for example, Italians today will experience when attending a
Latin mass.

Islam is perhaps the most widely recognized world religion to demand that
certain religious acts take place in the language of the ancient text. The reading
of the Qur'an may occur only in its Classical (variety of) Arabic in order to be
considered truly divine revelation, and formulary prayers – especially the
Shahadah (the general profession of faith) and the Fatiha (the first surah of the
Qur'an recited at regular prayer intervals) – are to be memorized and uttered
in their original code. During interviews with this writer, some North
American Jews have reported a preference for synagogue services that give
prominence to Scripture readings in Hebrew, even when they have to be trans-
literated into English lettering, as authenticity tolls loudest when rung out by

ancient syllables. Some Protestants, likewise, report that their conversion to a branch of Orthodoxy was prompted by the substantial presence of ancient Greek in the liturgy. However, spontaneous, ecstatic religious language known as glossolalia (or xenoglossia), familar to Pentecostal Christians (e.g., see Samarin, 1972), is purely a spoken form and falls outside of the field of literacy even when a community comes to expect it of its adherents.

However, another development can be the emergence of a translation tradition which gains exceptional status. The Septuagint (translated during the third and second centuries BCE) appears to have enjoyed such a standing even amidst Levantine Jews of the late Second Temple period (i.e., fifth century BCE through first century CE). The same happened with the Latin Vulgate within the medieval and modern western church, the King James Version of the Bible amongst Christian Evangelicals, and the Revised Standard Version amongst Neo-Orthodox Protestants.

How do translated texts gain recognition and acceptance in the religious communities for which they were prepared? How do various editions (with their distinguishing dialects and styles) become more authoritative than others? For original texts, the process of canonization is complex, involving a variety of factors both internal and situational, including: affinity with an already prestigious code; alignment with an established literary tradition; a philosophy of translation and its compatibility with the hermeneutics of a group within the religious tradition; and even ideological factors relating to, but not necessarily integral with, a religion's key values. For example, the King James Version of the Bible (in more recent editions, with emended and updated wording) seems to have become firmly ensconced for different reasons at various points in its four centuries of existence. Its initial impetus was, obviously, its royal benefactor, alongside its scholarly support due to its textual approach (producing what is called the *Textus Receptus*, or Received Text). Despite origins associated closely with Roman Catholicism, many Protestants would come to embrace the King James Version because its poetic archaisms seems to accord with the general social conservatism – something that often goes hand-in-hand with traditional biblical ethics.

Language in Religious Education

Religious education necessarily requires some dimension of *language planning*, a term introduced generally to the field of linguistics by Uriel Weinreich and specifically into the literature by Einar Haugen (Cooper, 1989: 29). Cooper (1982) notes that various factors contribute to language spread, including banking, and even the mere presence of orthographic systems. Among these factors is religion, and one of the most basic arenas of religious education is the mission field. The already strong bond between religion and language is a powerful mechanism for animating missionary outreach. This became apparent in the spread of Buddhism beyond its original Chinese setting, in the extension of Orthodox Christianity into Eastern Europe during the middle ages, in the entrance of Catholicism into Asia in the seventeenth century, and in the expansive reach of Protestantism into India and Asia since the late eighteenth century.

The interaction of religious literacy with Christian missionary activity and the post-colonial world has been another major area of study in religious literacy. Anything that requires planning will, of necessity, bear the marks of its designers' intentionality and ideology. Canagarajah (1999: 15–17) claims that traditional mainstream pedagogical orientations perceive learning to be a detached cognitive activity which is transcendental, universal, value free, and pre-constructed, as opposed to critical pedagogical approaches that are personal, situated, culturally connected, ideological, and negotiated. It is hardly surprising, therefore, that some scholars (see, e.g., various discussions in Cooper, 1982; Davies & Wollaston, 1993; and Canagarajah, 1999) have been critical of religious missions that established one language or regional dialect over others in a given region.

However, it should be noted that the reason for giving linguistic preeminence to a code may relate to practical necessity (i.e., reaching for a language of wider communication) or to the fact that nationals who have acquired an ecclesiastical language have found it to be their "ticket to their world." Ideology resides in the minds of receivers as much as in those of senders. Mission efforts undeniably have been instrumental in the establishing of certain regional codes, in part because some missionaries have been the first to commit those codes to writing particularly for the purpose of Bible translation. Education of *any* kind forces language choices (Davies & Wollaston, 1993; Vail, 1989). The effect may be the raising of the status of one language, or the extension of a code into new regions. The latter, called language spread, involves "an increase, over time, in the proportion of a communication network that adopts a given language or language variety for a given communicative function" (Cooper, 1982: 6), or more simply (p. 16) "as a geographical phenomenon . . . language spread represents an increase, over time, in the area over which a language has been adopted."

Study of the linkage between a religion's sacred texts and the adherents of that religion who are to become literate in those texts falls under two rubrics: the epistemological/philosophical, and the methodological/pedagogical. Learning and knowledge (in religion, or any other topic) inevitably shape a culture, but that culture simultaneously shapes its processes. To investigate language in religious education is to study a cyclical process, theoretically or practically, and the literature on the topic is substantial.

So what are the means by which participants in a religion may be effectively educated, especially when a particular form of education may be deemed essential for the shaping of their religious perceptions? Sawyer (1999: 24) observes that "where the people are permitted or encouraged to learn the sacred language and participate more fully in the religion, education is inevitably dominated from an early age by language-learning." Blomberg (1982: 190) likewise notes that "It is only when we use language creatively, when we have risen above the conventional and the ordinary, to search not just for the acceptable way of saying something, but for the most appropriate way, that lingual insight is displayed."

Education and Faith Development in Relation to Religious Literacy

Consideration of the interaction of religion, educational literacy, and the performance of religious acts inevitably leads to issues of belief and faith, for religion typically implies the presence of transcendence – the otherwise unseen and unknown. But can religious literacy be connected with the *experience* of faith as well as the *acts* of faith? Furthermore, can that connection truly bridge the cross-cultural barriers as most religions claim they can? For religious traditions and texts are influenced by the culture in which they reside and by the operating worldviews of those who wrote, as well as those who read, their texts. Conversely, religions exert an influence on the very societies which cradle and clarify them. This influence often comes directly from the sacred texts themselves, though not surprisingly it also comes through the official representatives of the religions (i.e., trained theologians, clergy, and holy men) as they offer extensive constructions on their religion.

Perceptions of reality abound at both formal/written and informal/oral cultural levels, though they may not always agree with each other (and, as Davies & Wollaston observe, understanding the religion of "everyday life" is an "extraordinarily difficult cultural task," 1993: 60). Nevertheless, most religious traditions assume that religious literacy must be connected to faith development and religious growth, and it assumes some kind of understanding of the dominant language in use, for language is the primary means by which people come to know anything.

Given that language is the essential means of learning and development, it is easy to see that faith, language, and society become powerfully intertwined. Inevitably, then, the linkage between communication and religion raises that "basic linguistic question to be answered by the agent of cultural change: What language shall be chosen as the principle means of communication . . . in the process of change," and subsequently, "the nature of the writing system to be introduced" for the benefit of previously non-literate societies (Ferguson, 1968: 255, 258). Language, then, constitutes a form of normative knowing, and provides a link between education and language. Faith, in turn, will be framed and in some way influenced by the language selected as its medium.

Measuring how religious literacy influences faith is surely difficult, though faith development theory attempts just that. Faith is measured in a person's ability to understand and deal with life's greater complexities, though how one knows what is known is the concern of epistemology. Saint Augustine once mused on the enigma of knowing in a way suitable also to this complex connection: "If I don't think about it, I know what it is, but when you ask me to define it, I can't." Education, language, and religious faith are surely interconnected, so one must necessarily consider the field – epistemology – which touches upon all of them, for it raises questions about how a person comes to know and make meaning of any kind.

Now, as previously noted, the word "religion" bears a wide range of meanings to different people and societies. Roy Clouser, in *The Myth of Religious Neutrality* (1991), stresses that religious belief (a concern with a divine authority that everything else in life is dependent on) unavoidably plays a role in theory making. Thus, by linking religion and knowledge there are implications for educating people in religious literacy. In order to understand the role of education in religious development, one must attempt to understand faith development. James Fowler proposes that there are six stages of faith development that people undergo from childhood to adulthood. The stages are: intuitive-projective faith, mythic-literal faith, synthetic-conventional faith, individual-reflective faith, conjunctive faith, and universalizing faith. These stages operate sequentially, from the first to the last, as people grow in age and maturity. They represent a process, such that faith development can occur no matter what age a person is. Movement from one stage to the next occurs when one experiences cognitive disequilibrium. Thus, the style of learning is an important factor in putting people into a phase of disequilibrium. The more a person is faced with disequilibrium, the more that person integrates concepts and principles of their sacred text into daily life. Thus, the way one reads a text will influence the measurement of religious growth as well. Even non-traditional religious traditions may operate from these presumptions.

Faith development and education therefore begin to intersect with developmental psychology, a field pioneered by Erik Erikson and Jean Piaget, among others. Even the etymology of the word *psychology* points toward the study of the soul. The soul is determined by the cause of an individual's life, and development of this cause is often sought out through faith (Parks, 1986). Erikson's work is relevant here. He proposed that people progress through eight stages during life: "basic trust vs. mistrust, autonomy vs. shame and doubt, initiative vs. guilt, industry vs. inferiority, identity vs. role confusion, intimacy vs. isolation, generativity vs. stagnation, ego integrity vs. despair" (Parks, 1986: 32). Piaget, on the other hand, was a genetic epistemologist who focused on development in relation to age and biology. He theorized that the life process is typified by four stages: sensorimotor, preoperational, concrete operational, and formal operational. Few adults, however, enter the formal operational stage.

Experiences of assimilation and accommodation play significant roles in moving people through life stages, so disequilibrium acts as the catalyst for those two experiences, and perhaps for prompting people to transition through Erikson's stages as well. As people encounter something new, they can either assimilate or accommodate it into their working framework. Assimilation allows a person to understand something because of previously composed structures of knowing. The new element gets assimilated into a person's knowing framework and, in turn, it promotes further development. However, if a person's present knowing structures are inadequate for receiving and making sense of something new, then that person must accommodate the new element into their thinking patterns and reshape their structures. For a person to assimilate or accommodate, ownership of thought and mind must be present, thus rendering the role of language and education vital to their development of faith.

Issues of choice and the making of meaning promptly come into play, so a connection between processes of development and culture can be made too. The culture and community that surround a person deeply impact one's developmental process. Thus, it is necessary to consider both how to impact someone and the outcomes of influencing such a process. Religious communities influence a person's development in significant ways. The primary ways a religious community influences people are through personal contact, norms, and structures of its particular institution, and any sacred text that directs the institution. For example, devout Moslems live a disciplined life, involving rituals such as praying five times a day. Formal Islamic prayers must be said in Arabic, which is telling: it shows a commitment to the faith with its sacred language and text, the Qur'an. Therefore, the issue of how a person develops faith will vary according to each faith tradition. The means of educating a person in faith development will also differ, of necessity, with each faith tradition.

Examples of practical religious education include, but are not limited to, attending worship services, taking religious classes, study of a sacred text, and general interaction with one's community of faith. Naturally, such education may be directed by clergy trained in the reading and interpretation of sacred texts in their original language since, in many religious traditions (such as Christianity), the majority of the religion's followers are unfamiliar with the original languages of the sacred texts because of cross-cultural or diachronic gaps. This factor raises a curious issue with regard to the influence of text upon faith development, for while many adherents would claim that the sacred text they follow is critical, few are able to read it in its original language. Nevertheless, many religious persons are quite dogmatic about which translated text they use, despite their lack of training in the original languages – an irony that eludes many of them.

The authors of this chapter designed a focused survey of traditional undergraduate students at a small Christian liberal arts college in North America (Watt & Fairfield, 2006). When asked which translation of the Bible they preferred, most indicated the New International Version, a dynamic equivalence translation of the Bible. Over 70 percent of students identified their preferred translation based on its literal accessibility; that is, they reported it was easy to read and understand. This rationale differs, however, from what many trained clergymen report. Only 30 percent of students indicated that accuracy of translation played a primary role in their choice of translation, while more than 50 percent reported choosing a translation merely because their church used it. This shows that scholars and trained clergy can influence adherents via a kind of trickle-down effect. When students were shown unfamiliar quotations from three different translations to identify as their preferred reading, without the translation source being identified, the results consistently pointed back to the same translation they had reported as their preference.

Thus, religious literacy and the educating of religious literacy play a significant role in developing committed adherents in a religious tradition. Religious literacy is a part of faith development. The promotion of religious literacy falls into educative methods which transcend individual faith traditions. Even though trained clergymen and adherents may not be on the same intellectual level of religious literacy, it remains a vital enterprise in the promulgation of religions. It is vital to the growth and development of religious communities which influence their culture, and religious literacy will profoundly shape the world. In most ways, religious literacy is no different than other types of literacy, for it uses similar interpretive skills and learning styles. However, it is no simple task to measure how religious literacy influences religious growth due to the factor of individual experiences. The precise nature and mechanisms of its influence – while broadly assumed – are starting to be explored under the rubric of educational linguistics.

REFERENCES

Blomberg, Doug (1982). Toward a Christian theory of knowledge. In Jack Michielson (ed.), *No Icing on the Cake: Christian Foundations for Education* (pp. 186–195). Melbourne: Brooks-Hall Publishing Foundation.

Canagarajah, A. Suresh (1999). *Resisting Linguistic Imperialism in English Teaching.* Oxford: Oxford University Press.

Clouser, Roy A. (1991). *The Myth of Religious Neutrality: An Essay on the Hidden Role of Religious Belief in Theories.* Notre Dame, IN: University of Notre Dame Press.

Cooper, Robert L. (ed.) (1982). *Language Spread: Studies in Diffusion and Social Change.* Bloomington: Indiana University Press.

Cooper, Robert L. (1989). *Language Planning and Social Change.* Cambridge: Cambridge University Press.

Davies, Jon & Wollaston, Isabel (eds.) (1993). *The Sociology of Sacred Texts.* Sheffield: Academic Press.

Ferguson, Charles A. (1968). St. Stefan of Perm and applied linguistics. In Joshua Fishman, Charles A. Ferguson, & Jyotirindra Das Gupta (eds.), *Language Problems of Developing Nations* (pp. 253–265). New York: John Wiley.

Goody, Jack (ed.) (1968). *Literacy in Traditional Societies.* Cambridge: Cambridge University Press.

Huntington, Samuel P. (1993). The clash of civilizations. *Foreign Affairs,* 72(3), 22–49.

Keane, Webb (1997). Religious language. *Annual Review of Anthropology*, 26, 47–71.

Ong, Walter J. (1982). *Orality and Literacy: The Technologizing of the Word*. London: Methuen.

Parks, Sharon (1986). *The Critical Years: The Young Adult Search for a Faith to Live By*. San Francisco: Harper & Row.

Samarin, William J. (1972). *Tongues of Men and Angels*. New York: The Macmillan Company.

Sawyer, John F. A. (1999). *Sacred Languages and Sacred Texts*. London/New York: Routledge.

Sawyer, John F. A. & Simpson, J. M. Y. (eds.) (2001). *Concise Encyclopedia of Language and Religion*. Amsterdam: Elsevier.

Spolsky, Bernard D. (2003). Religion as a site of language contact. *Annual Review of Applied Linguistics*, 23, 81–94.

Stubbs, Michael (1986). *Educational Linguistics*. Oxford: Basil Blackwell.

Vail, Leroy (1989). *The Creation of Tribalism in Southern Africa*. London: James Currey.

Watt, Jonathan M. & Fairfield, Sarah L. (2006). Religious inclinations. Unpublished results of survey administered to 157 current students, aged 17–22, at Geneva College, Beaver Falls, Pennsylvania.

FURTHER READING

Cooper, Robert L. et al. (eds.) (2001). *New Perspectives and Issues in Educational Language Policy*. Amsterdam/Philadelphia: John Benjamins.

Moran, Gabriel (1989). *Religious Education as a Second Language*. Birmingham, AL: Religious Education Press.

Samarin, William J. (ed.) (1976). *Language in Religious Practice*. Rowley, MA: Newbury House.

Spolsky, Bernard D. (1991). Control and democratization of sacred literacy. In: Samuel Rodin (ed.), *Encounters with Judaism: Jewish Studies in a Non-Jewish World* (pp. 37–53). Hamilton, New Zealand: Waikato University and Colcom Press.

Spolsky, Bernard D. (ed.) (1999). *Concise Encyclopedia of Educational Linguistics*. Amsterdam: Elsevier.

26 Genre and Register in Multiliteracies

MARY MACKEN-HORARIK
AND MISTY ADONIOU

Introduction

Engaging with the world of "multiliteracies" entails two kinds of recognition – acknowledgment of the sociocultural diversity of our learners' worlds, and awareness of the impact of new communication technologies that combine linguistic modes of meaning with visual, gestural, spatial, and audio modes. There is no doubt that young people inhabit a vastly different communication environment to that of their parents. They interact with video games, internet sites, and text messaging systems as "digital natives," whilst those from previous generations are, at best, digital immigrants (Prensky, 2001). Multimodality is increasingly on the agenda in classrooms and some educators are endeavoring to bridge the digital divide. In a unit of work on fairytales, students will watch the movie, *Shrek*, as well as read traditional fairytales. They will discuss the humorous intertextual play that characterizes the popular feature film and they will themselves innovate on these traditional tales in their own responses – perhaps developing fractured fairytales in storyboard, animation or written mode.

The authors of the New London Group have coined the word "Multiliteracies" to bring out the contrast between these possibilities and more traditional notions of literacy.

> The notion of Multiliteracies supplements traditional literacy pedagogy by addressing these two related aspects of textual multiplicity. What we might term "mere literacy" remains centred on language only, and usually on a singular national form of language at that, being conceived as a stable system based on rules such as mastering sound–letter correspondence . . . A pedagogy of Multiliteracies, by contrast, focusses on modes of representation much broader than language alone. These differ according to culture and context, and have specific cognitive, cultural and social effects. In some cultural contexts – in an Aboriginal community or in a multimedia environment, for instance – the visual mode of representation may be much more powerful and closely related

to language than "mere literacy" would ever be able to allow. (Cope & Kalantzis, 2000: 5)

To put social and semiotic "difference" at the centre of literacy education is both pedagogically challenging and unavoidable if we are to make connections with our students' lives. It invites us to bring marginal discourses into dialogue with mainstream ones and to talk about these in new ways. That is what this chapter is about – talk about language and other modes of communication – *meta*language. We focus on a metalanguage for talking productively about linguistic and multimodal texts – a functional metalanguage drawing on Halliday's systemic functional linguistics. The concept of multiliteracies draws extensively on the flexible tool kit of this grammar.

> A metalanguage needs to be quite flexible and open-ended. It should be seen as a tool kit for working on semiotic activities, not a formalism to be applied to them. We should be comfortable with fuzzy-edged, overlapping concepts. Teachers and learners should be able to pick and choose from the tools offered. They should also feel free to fashion their own tools. Flexibility is critical because the relationship between descriptive and analytical categories and actual events is, by its nature, shifting, provisional, unsure and relative to the contexts and purposes of analysis. Furthermore, the primary purpose of the metalanguage should be to identify and explain differences between texts and relate these to the contexts of culture and situation in which they seem to work. (Cope & Kalantzis, 2000: 24)

Exploring "differences between texts" and "relating these to the contexts of culture and situation in which they seem to work" can only be achieved if we can move systematically between context and text. It was Michael Halliday who first proposed a systematic connection between social context and text meanings. In the late 1970's, he observed that the internal organization of language corresponded to the external organization of the social environment:

> The context of situation, the context in which the text unfolds, is encapsulated in the text, not in a kind of piecemeal fashion, not at the other extreme in any mechanical way, but through a systematic relationship between the social environment on the one hand, and the functional organization of language on the other. If we treat both text and context as semiotic phenomena, as modes of meaning, so to speak, we can get from one to the other in a revealing way. (Halliday, in Halliday & Hasan, 1985: 11–12)

Halliday represents the immediate social environment in terms of *context of situation*. This construct comprises three crucial variables: *field, tenor,* and *mode*. The *field* refers to the social action occurring, *tenor* to the interactive roles of participants, and *mode* to the channel of communication – whether spoken or written (Halliday, in Halliday & Hasan, 1985: 12). In recent applications of register theory, educators have expanded the scope of mode to include visual, gestural, dynamic, and other channels of communication (see, for example, Unsworth, 2001). Collectively, these three contextual variables determine the pattern of meanings dispersed through a text – its *register*.

Educational linguists such as Jim Martin, Joan Rothery, and others, known as the "Sydney School" (Macken et al., 1989; Martin, 1993; Hyon, 1996; Johns, 2002) have added another layer to the functional model of context. In addition to the notion of register variation, they propose that texts vary in their overall gestalt as a result of the purposes they have evolved to serve in the culture. Getting things done in the culture is achieved through genres which Martin defines as "staged, goal-oriented, social processes" (Martin, 1984, 1992; Rothery, 1989). In this formulation, *generic structure* is used to describe the sequence of communicative acts in a text (e.g., explaining, describing, evaluating) which together contribute to a larger scale communicative purpose such as telling a story, providing instruction for a task, arguing a case, and so on. However, as van Leeuwen points out, "the concept of genre is a multimodal concept" (2005: 129). Telling a story, for example, can be realized (or expressed) linguistically or in a combination of linguistic and visual modes, as in a storyboard, an animation, or a film. If we combine categories of genre and register, we are able to "fill out" the picture of semiotic variation using four lenses on choices for meaning in texts (semiosis).

In the remaining sections of this chapter, we look more closely at narrative semiosis from the point of view of *genre, field, tenor,* and *mode.* We use these to analyze children's narratives in different modes: a traditional fairytale (verbal mode), a cartoon version of the same narrative (visual and verbal), a "still" from the narrative (visual), and a series of "stills" from a computer animation (multimodal). We aim to show how the metalanguage generated by genre and register theory can be applied to texts and linked to the ways of knowing (epistemologies) powerful in school English.

Genre in Narrative

Semiotic variation is not simple when it comes to complex "macro genres" such as narrative. However, we need to start somewhere and Labov's metalanguage has provided a useful "way in" to narrative structure. Labov (1972) described oral narratives of personal experience as a sequence of functional stages based on the functional contribution of each stage to the whole. Each successful story featured an *Orientation* stage, establishing the situation of the story participants, a *Complication* (or problem), and a *Resolution*, providing closure of some kind. Sprinkled throughout the event sequence were *Evaluations* that pointed out the significance of events. The evaluation is a vital stage in a narrative in part because it fends off the "so what?" question that threatens the validity of the tale and its teller.

Table 26.1   Teachers' notes for helping students with narrative writing

Narrative as genre	Notes for teachers on purposes and stages
Social function (purpose)	Narratives "project" a possible world in which unexpected things happen to individual characters and problems which they need to confront and resolve. Narratives explore human experience in order to entertain, move, and instruct their readers/viewers.
Overall pattern of stages of genre	**(Western) narratives innovate on these stages:** **Orientation**: setting up the "possible world" of the characters and their situation; **Complication(s)**: introducing problem(s) to be resolved by (one or more) character(s); this can be an internal or external problem for the characters; **Evaluation(s)**: pointing up the significance of what happens in the narrative by narrator or characters; **Resolution(s)**: providing some closure on the events for characters – resolving problems, posing new questions; **Coda**: (optional stage) bridging between events of the story and the present, often pointing out moral of the story.

Linking the social purpose of a genre like narrative ("to entertain and inform readers") to its unfolding pattern of stages makes intuitive sense to teachers (Rothery, 1989, 1994; Martin, 1993). Furthermore, it gives students "something to shoot for" when they are asked to produce a text in an unfamiliar genre (Macken-Horarik, 2002). If all texts innovate on the genres they draw on, they nevertheless "trade" on their predictable patterns of structure. Table 26.1 displays curriculum information about the social function and stages of narrative genre.

The text below exemplifies the work produced during a genre-based literacy project in Sydney (Macken et al., 1989). *The Dragon's Tooth* was produced by a Year 5 girl and regarded as successful by teacher and students. It is reproduced as Figure 26.1 with the generic stages indicated in the left-hand column. Annotating her text in this way highlights the author's control of narrative structure – the functional contribution of each stage to its unfolding gestalt.

A knowledge of the prototypical structure of a genre gives teachers a handle on the beginning-middle-end structure of a text. As van Leeuwen expresses this, the category of genre gives us a "template for doing communicative things" (van Leeuwen, 2005: 128). Genre awareness facilitates a holistic approach to text structure. In a multimodal narrative, however, the "same

Generic stages	The Dragon's Tooth
Orientation	Many years ago when the world was full of magic there lived a princess who was more beautiful than you can imagine.
Complication (1)	One day she was walking through the woods smelling wild flowers and listening to the animals and birds, when suddenly a witch jumped out in front of her and screamed "Aha!" The witch pull(ed) a tube containing some green liquid out of her pocket and drank it, then instantly turned into a beautiful lady looking just like the princess.
	The witch dropped a piece of paper and the princess picked it up, it read:
	The Cure "The princess Agather must kill a dragon and pull out its tooth to regain her beauty (without help or weapons)."
Evaluation	Agather wondered what it meant by "regain her beauty". Presently she came across a shining clear lake! She couldn't help going over to the lake and just letting her hands glide through the water. As she leant over to pick up a lily, Agather looked at her reflection she saw the face of a witch. She frantically ran around weeping and imagining herself as an old spinster.
Complication (2) *Evaluation*	Presently she came across a cave with the words "Beware A Dragon" written above it. It reminded her of the instructions on the paper. Agather walked in bravely, looking around cautiously, when she came to a halt. There in front of her was some stairs and below that – low and behold was the dragon!!!
Complication (2) continues **Evaluation** *Resolution begins* *Resolution (dragon is killed)*	She grabbed a stick for protection. The dragon turned its gigantic head, breathing fire, the princess held the stick out for protection and closed her eyes, when she opened them again and realised the top of the branch had caught alight. She worked up some courage, and with a running jump aimed for the dragons back. Agather was usually a frisky sporty girl but had put on a lot of weight when the witch changed her. She didn't jump far enough and landed with a bump but was too frightened to feel a thing. She ran stumbling over her own feet. Luckily as Agather ran she didn't drop the stick and the flame didn't go out. Agather clambered up the dragon's tail, burning him as she went. Just as she got to the top the dragon jolted and she slipped off. She burnt the dragon to death!! Agather pulled out a tooth and the blood oozed out of the dragon's mouth. The princess sank down into the hard soil.
Resolution continues **(arrival of knight)** *Evaluation* *Coda*	Just as the dragon gave his last wail a knight passed by and went into the cave. He found the princess beautiful again, exhausted holding the tooth. The knight carried both the princess and the tooth back to the castle. When they got there the princess had miraculously recovered and screamed "Never again". The princess had a pimple on her nose because she used a weapon but the knight and princess married and lived happily ever after. Nicole Year 5

Figure 26.1 *The Dragon's Tooth*

Figure 26.2   Storyboard of narrative in Figure 26.1

stage" will be realized differently. Figure 26.2 is a visual image produced by a child in the same grade as Nicole, albeit at a different time. Dimitri was asked to create a storyboard version of Nicole's narrative, rendering the events in words and pictures. If we consider one still from his work, we can see how differently *Evaluation* is realized in his multimodal narrative.

Dimitri communicates Agather's evaluation of her transformation visually. Her eyes are wide with horror as she gazes into the pool. The effect is both vivid and economical. In Nicole's text, on the other hand, the evaluation stage is realized through behavioral and perceptual processes: "As she leant over to pick up a lily, Agather *looked* at her reflection (and) she *saw* the face of a witch. She frantically *ran around weeping* and *imagining* herself as an old spinster." Dimitri applies (perhaps unconsciously) a resource common to both television soaps and art-house movies, technically called a "shot-reverse shot." The camera cuts from the scene observed (object of the gaze) to the observer (subject's reaction). In this technique, the viewer is visually "stitched in" to the character's viewpoint – seeing things through his or her eyes. The implications for genre teaching are clear. Once we move beyond verbal texts, we need to become aware of other resources for evaluating experience.

Register in Narrative

The category of genre will take us only so far. Though they share family resemblances, detective narratives differ from romances and both differ from fables. Assuming that every narrative begins with an *Orientation* will be unproductive when it comes to producing a gripping detective story which usually begins with the *Complication* (a crime). Awareness of the global structure of a prototypical text needs to be supplemented with register theory. As will be observed, what is entailed here is the creation of a *field* of experience, adopting a particular *tenor* of interaction and deciding on a *mode* of communication. We can adapt Halliday's notion of register to this challenge, differentiating each variable as follows:

1 *Field*: While its topics are potentially limitless, every narrative creates a *"possible world,"* peopled by characters and their actions and reactions. Students need to learn to create and resolve a world of (problematic) experience for one or more characters.
2 *Tenor*: We *animate the relationships* of these characters and their world and *evaluate the significance* of what happens for them (and for readers). Students need to learn how to evaluate experience and to position their readers to respond with feelings such as empathy, suspense, judgment, and humor.
3 *Mode*: We *compose a text that coheres with itself* and with its context. Students need to learn to produce texts that create and sustain the conditions for their interpretation. In written narratives, the reader needs to build the context for interpretation by means of language alone. In multimodal texts, this is achieved through different mechanisms, such as layout and editing.

In an educational environment register needs to be co-articulated with the "ways of knowing" relevant to particular disciplines. With narrative, for example, the three register variables can be productively connected to both narrative and film theory. These theories increasingly shape the epistemologies of school English. In the case of narrative, understandings about fields of experience should take young learners into new understandings of "plot," "characterization," and "setting"; tenor should enable them to work with "point of view" (often called "focalization"); and mode should introduce them to the semiotic organization of written, spoken, and multimodal narratives. In short, a discipline-specific model of register allows us to connect text production and discussion about text to the epistemological demands of schooling. We are now in a position to turn our attention to a more detailed exploration of what register offers the study of narrative semiosis.

The *field* dimension of any narrative focuses our attention on "what happens." Technically, activity (or event) sequences are realized through choices for participants, processes, and circumstances of experience and their temporal sequencing. When it comes to narrative, students need to learn to control event sequences relevant to a "plot," to individualize participants in some way ("characterization"), and to situate events in relevant circumstances of time and place ("setting"). In verbal narratives control of tense and of evocative vocabulary are also important. Table 26.2 exemplifies the *field* challenge of narrative, using Nicole's text.

Table 26.2   The field challenge of written narrative

Field challenge	**Creating activity sequences** relevant to the plot
Creating a "possible world" peopled by characters and their actions and reactions.	(not too many or too few) *(see below for examples of this)*

• Introduction of **individualized participants**:
A princess who was more beautiful than you can imagine; Princess Agather – an old spinster – a frisky sporty girl.

• Situating events through **circumstances of time and place**:
Time: *Many years ago – one day – suddenly – instantly;*
Space: *through the woods – over to the lake – through the water – on the paper – in front of her – into the hard soil,* etc.

• Use of **tenses** relevant to the timing of the events:
Was – lived – was walking – smelling – listening (**past**)
(princess) must kill . . . and pull out . . . to regain (**future**)

• Use of discriminating and evocative **lexis**:
Agather walked in bravely, looking around
cautiously . . .

When we move to an exploration of the field of narratives in other modes, the participants and processes of its "possible world" are created with different semiotic tools. Figure 26.3 shows six stills from a computer animation by a young adult. It is perhaps ironic in academia we are still locked into monomodal (re)presentations of this work even when we are talking about multimodal texts. It is a short animation of a pink bunny transforming into a black witch against a muted purple/brown-washed background.

The participants in this sequence are individualized here, not via evocative noun groups but through tools from the Photoshop paintbox. The bunny was created using a large paintbrush so that he appears soft and fluffy, whilst the witch was outlined with a thin paintbrush to give her clean, sharp lines. Ria, the author, has made choices about how she will use these tools. The bunny, for example, has been painted from the center to the outside so that there are no hard outlines to the shape. Texture, line, and color become her discriminating and evocative lexis. The bunny in baby pink, with a soft fluffy texture, is in stark contrast to the black witch with her smooth lines and sharp angles. In the final moment of the animation the gestural mode is used to further characterize the witch as she closes the sequence with a sly wink to the viewer (though this cannot be brought out in the stills). Circumstances of time and place are realized through the spatial and gestural modes inherent in an animation, whilst the visual mode has been used to create the setting through

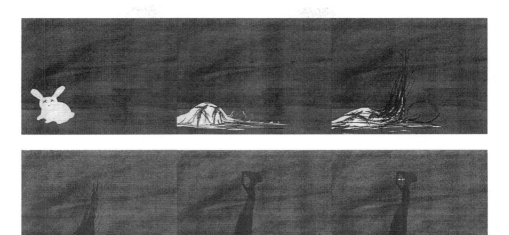

Figure 26.3   Six stills from a computer animation

the use of a painted watercolor scanned into the text. The muted background works as a neutral setting for a fluffy bunny, but morphs into a more sinister setting when used as the backdrop for the witch. The creation of a setting that situates the "possible world" of characters and their actions is equally important in verbal, and multimodal texts.

The *field* of a narrative can be conceived quite narrowly in terms of subject matter or topic (e.g., a princess confronting a dragon in an effort to regain her beauty or a bunny turning into a witch) or more abstractly (e.g., the possibility of transformation through a character's confrontation with the dark material of the unconscious). Fairytale worlds are related to real experience, but they depart from this in imaginative ways. Participants can begin as princesses and turn into witches and return to the prior identity (albeit marked by the experience). The dynamics of these experiences can be represented materially as a sequence of activities (or events). The activities occurring early in Nicole's narrative include the following:

1   Princess Agather is introduced walking through the woods;
2   a witch jumps out and drinks some liquid and then screams;
3   the witch turns into a beautiful lady like the princess and drops a note for her to read;
4   the (real) princess picks up the note that informs her about what she has to do to regain her beauty;
5   Princess Agather looks into a lake and finds herself looking at the face of a witch.

At an abstract level, however, narrative experience is a field of transformation and this can be realized verbally or visually (or multimodally, as in a movie). In Figure 26.3, the bunny transmogrifies into a witch through movement from one still to another. Transformation can be realized visually as well as verbally but we can help our students "get traction" on this by creating activity sequences or by identifying visual motifs that create both change and continuity over the course of a narrative.

The *tenor* dimension of narrative offers a view of text–audience relations – how experience is evaluated by narrator, characters, and, more covertly, by the text as a whole. This takes us within narrative theory into the territory of "point of view." For young learners, the tenor challenge entails exploring human motives through evaluative language – getting inside characters' heads and hearts. Agather's curiosity about her appearance is rendered in Nicole's narrative through mental processes such as "Agather *wondered* what it meant by 'regain her beauty'" and "it *reminded* her of the instructions on the paper." Management of internal point of view is typically rendered through direct and indirect thought whereas external viewpoints are often projected in direct or indirect speech as in "The princess *screamed*, 'Never again'." Table 26.3 summarizes the tenor challenge of written narrative.

Table 26.3   The tenor challenge of narrative

Tenor challenge *Animating relationships between characters and evaluating significance of what happens for them (and for readers).*	• Exploring human motives, etc., through **evaluative language** Agather *wondered what it meant by* "regain her beauty." "Presently she came across *a shining, clear lake! She couldn't help* going over to the lake and *just letting* her hands *glide through the water. As she leant over to pick . . ."*
	• Presenting different points of view via **direct/ indirect speech and thought** It *read*: "The princess must kill a dragon . . ." Presently she came across a cave with the words "Beware a dragon" written above it. It *reminded* her of . . ." When they got there, the princess had miraculously recovered and *screamed* "Never again".
	• Experimenting with literary devices (e.g., **exclamations**) to build atmosphere, suspense or humor. There in front of her was some stairs and below that – *low and behold was the dragon!*

Figure 26.4   Dimitri's picture of Agather's confrontation with the dragon

Tenor creates drama in narrative. This can be realized in writing through punctuation and exclamatives, as in, "Low and behold was the dragon!" But the interpersonal resources available differ in other modes. In Figure 26.4, Dimitri represents the dragon very differently from the way Nicole does in her story. His tenor is visual – enacted through the size and redness of the dragon which literally looms over the tiny witch-princess. Nicole and Dimitri have different interests. As Figure 26.4 indicates, Dimitri has made the dragon dominant in his image, using visual tools of space and color. He chooses red for the dragon, a color associated in the West with power and danger. Another interpersonal feature is the diagonal gaze-line from the dragon's eye through his flames down to the diminutive Agather. Given that Dimitri knows the outcome of this story – that Agather will overcome the dragon – this image is evaluative, revealing the enormity of the task Agather faces in her confrontation with the dragon.

Nicole is far more interested in the agency displayed by her heroine than in the dominance of the dragon. After a difficult moment, she works up some courage, "and with a running jump aimed for the dragon's back." In fact, for this heroine, and by implication for Nicole, it is not an unfettered victory. Agather's recent weight gain makes it hard for her to jump on the dragon's back. She stumbles over her own feet and eventually "clambered up the dragon's tail, burning him as she went." Nicole is clearly playing with tenor possibilities here, as is Dimitri, in a different way. The representations are surely gendered, though exploring these is not within the scope of our chapter.

The *mode* dimension offers a view of the semiotic organization of a genre – how it is put together to create a communicative whole. Mode provides resources for integration such as cohesion in written texts, layout in magazines and newspapers, and editing and continuity for moving images and sound.

In linguistic narratives, time phrases allow authors to signpost the temporal organization of their text. These often occur at crucial changes in the staging of the event sequence and punctuate its flow powerfully. In English, what we place first in the sentence takes on a thematic prominence. What are technically called *Themes* are crucial to the signposting necessary in a well-structured written narrative. Nicole uses time clauses, phrases, and conjunctions in Theme position to give temporal coherence to her narrative. For example:

Many years ago when the world was full of magic
One day
Presently
Just as ..
When . . .

Table 26.4 summarizes the mode challenge of producing a coherent written narrative.

Texturing principles vary from one mode to another. One relevant resource is what Martin calls *participant identification* (Martin, 1992). This enables storytellers to introduce and keep track of participants throughout a text. In Nicole's narrative, we are introduced to "*A princess* who was more beautiful than you can imagine" and then this participant is referred back to as "*the princess*", or "*she*" in later mentions. Computer animators also face the challenge of creating both change and continuity in a participant's identity. Figure 26.5 shows six stills from the five-second animation featured earlier. The stills have been chosen to highlight continuity in the eyes of the central participant. In this case we can track transformations in the major participant by means of cohesive devices such as shape and color.

As can be seen, continuity and transformation is important to both linguistic and visual narratives. The cohesive devices used by the writer are related to but different from those used by the animator. Nevertheless, choices have to be made if the artist is to create a coherent text. Teachers and students need a metalanguage for exploring these and the resources of mode have proved

Table 26.4   The mode challenge of narrative

Mode challenge Composing a text that coheres with itself and can "stand alone" for the reader to interpret.	• Using first position in sentences (**Themes to do with setting in time**) to signpost development of the text *Many years ago . . .* *One day . . .* *The witch* *The Princess Agather* *Agather* *Presently she*
	• Combining clauses in **compound and complex sentences** to produce logical development of events *One day she was walking through the woods// smelling wild flowers// and listening to the animals and birds// when suddenly a witch jumped out in front of her// and screamed "Aha!"*
	• Using a range of range of connectives to link messages appropriately (focus on **conjunction**) Agather was usually a frisky sporty girl *but* had put on a lot of weight *when* the witch changed her. She didn't jump far enough *and* landed with a bump *but* was too frightened to . . .
	• Presenting and tracking participants consistently throughout the text (focus on **reference**) *A princess* *a witch* *She* *the witch* *The princess* *a beautiful lady* *The princess Agather* *the witch*

productive (see Unsworth, 2006; and van Leeuwen, 2005 for recent applications of cohesion to analysis of multimodal texts).

Conclusion

The educational implications of reckoning with social and textual difference are far reaching. However, alongside the diverse modes of communication (multiple ways of making meaning), perhaps intruding on them, are the realities of social and institutional power. The educational experiences of students

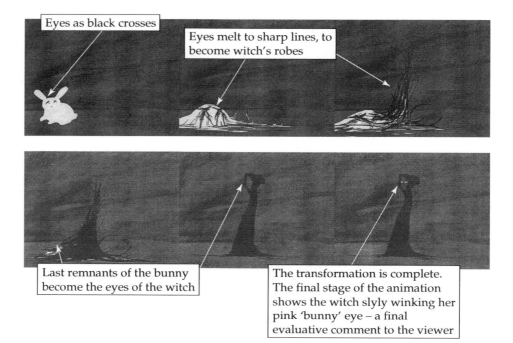

Eyes as black crosses

Eyes melt to sharp lines, to become witch's robes

Last remnants of the bunny become the eyes of the witch

The transformation is complete. The final stage of the animation shows the witch slyly winking her pink 'bunny' eye – a final evaluative comment to the viewer

Figure 26.5   Annotated computer animation

are not equal; nor are the educational outcomes. Some students simply have access to and control over meaning potentials as a result of class position, ethnicity, and other accidents of birth and social location. In addition to this, there is the downward pressure on schools to demonstrate improved outcomes on relatively narrow indicators of literacy achievement. The interests of the latter group are overwhelmingly monomodal.

In this chapter, we have explored the potential of metalinguistic tools of genre and register for exploring multimodal and monomodal communication in narrative. Both aspects of the multiliteracies environment must be engaged with effectively if we are not to "short change" our students. They need "ways in" to their complex textual environment if they are to manage it effectively and ways of tackling the textual demands of particular disciplines within the school environment. Genre and register provide powerful lenses on the design principles of texts and ways of exploring at least four dimensions of these. Moving across the expanding range of texts and modes requires that we make use of tools that highlight commonalities across apparently unlike texts and tools that unearth the unique qualities of texts in their particularity. Both are important if educators are to help young learners "get traction" on their increasingly complex communicative environment. They not only live in a changing digital world in their everyday lives, this world is making its way inside the classroom. Our talk about the texts of this changing world – our metalanguages – needs to enable students to move beyond the pleasures available to consumers so that they can understand better the source of their enjoyment of a video game, a feature film, an animation, or a traditional literary tale, in short, so they can understand the semiotics of this enjoyment. Our chapter opens up one path to such possibilities.

NOTE

The authors would like to thank Nicole, Ria, and Dimitri for permission to reproduce their texts for our paper.

REFERENCES

Cope, B. & Kalantzis, M. (eds.) (2000). *Multiliteracies: Literacy Learning and the Design of Social Futures*. London/New York: Routledge.

Halliday, M. A. K. (1978). *Language as Social Semiotic: The Social Interpretation of Language and Meaning*, London: Edward Arnold.

Halliday, M. A. K. & Hasan, R. (1985). *Language, Context and Text: Aspects of Language in a Social-Semiotic Perspective*. Geelong, Victoria: Deakin University Press.

Hyon, S. (1996). Genre in three traditions: Implications for ESL. *TESOL Quarterly*, 30(4), 693–721.

Johns, A. (ed.) (2002). *Genre in the Classroom: Multiple Perspectives*. Mahwah, NJ: Lawrence Erlbaum.

Labov, W. (1972). The transformation of experience in narrative structure. *Language in the Inner City* (pp. 354–396). Philadelphia: University of Pennsylvania Press.

Macken, M., Kalantzis, M., Kress, G., Martin, J. R., Cope, B., & Rothery, J. (1989). *An Approach to Writing K-12: The Theory and Practice of Genre-Based Writing, Years 3–6*. Sydney: Literacy and Education Research Network (LERN) in conjunction with NSW Department of Education.

Macken-Horarik, M. (2002). "Something to shoot for": A systemic functional approach to teaching genre in secondary school science. In A. Johns (ed.), *Genre in the Classroom: Multiple Perspectives* (pp. 17–42). Mahwah, NJ: Erlbaum.

Martin, J. R. (1984). Language, register and genre. In F. Christie (ed.), *Language Studies: Children Writing Reader* (pp. 21–30). Geelong, Victoria: Deakin University Press.

Martin, J. R. (1992). *English Text: System and Structure*. Philadelphia/Amsterdam: Benjamins.

Martin, J. R. (1993). Genre and literacy: Modelling context in educational linguistics. *Annual Review of Applied Linguistics*, 13, 141–172.

Prensky, M. (2001). Digital natives digital immigrants. *On the Horizon*, (9)5, 1–6.

Rothery, J. (1989). Learning about language. In R. Hasan & J. R. Martin (eds.), *Language Development: Learning Language, Learning Culture. Meaning and Choice in Language:*

Studies for Michael Halliday, vol. 27 Advances in Discourse Processes (pp. 199–256). Norwood, NJ: Ablex.

Rothery, J. (1994). *Exploring Literacy in School English. Write it Right: Resources for Literacy and Learning.* Sydney: Disadvantaged Schools Program Metropolitan East Region, NSW Department of School Education.

Unsworth, L. (2001). *Teaching Multiliteracies Across the Curriculum: Changing Contexts of Text and Image in Classroom Practice.* Buckingham, UK: Open University Press.

Unsworth, L. (2006). Towards a metalanguage for multiliteracies education: Describing the meaning making resources of language-image interaction. *English Teaching: Practice and Critique*, 5(1), 55–76. http://education.waikato.ac.nz/research/files/etpc/2006v5nart4.pdf

van Leeuwen, T. (2005). *Introducing Social Semiotics.* London/New York: Routledge.

27 Order of Acquisition and Developmental Readiness

KATHLEEN BARDOVI-HARLIG
AND LLORENÇ COMAJOAN

Order of Acquisition in L1 and L2 Language Acquisition

Description and explanation

The process of learning a language for children (L1 acquisition) and adults (L2 acquisition) is not haphazard but systematic. How such systematicity is described and explained in the linguistic disciplines is sometimes controversial. Researchers agree upon some of the facts regarding language development, but disagree on the answers to theoretical and practical questions related to the facts (Table 27.1).

Of the questions in Table 27.1, this chapter focuses on the one regarding the systematic nature of language learning, which is related to the concept of *acquisitional stage*. Ingram (1989) provided eight possible definitions of *stage* depending on their stable or dynamic characteristics. An example of a stable definition of *stage* is the "point on a continuum"; that is, "a continuous stage is one where a single dimension of behavior is being observed" (p. 33). For instance, researchers talk of the two-year stage versus the three-year stage, but this definition of *stage* is of little use for the study of language development, because it situates linguistic facts along a continuum of development without taking into account the overlap of stages. In contrast, a dynamic definition takes into account not only the succession of language elements, but also an initial state, developmental stages, and an end state. In a dynamic view a stage is a "period of rapid acceleration in the development of linguistic development that will end in a plateau, i.e., a steady rate of use (possibly final acquisition) afterwards" (Ingram, 1989: 34). In this chapter, we adopt a dynamic definition of stage and examine it focusing on the acquisition of tense-aspect morphology.

Table 27.1   Common themes in language acquisition research

Common themes	*Common questions: different answers*
(a) The development of language learning is a window to the nature of the human language faculty.	(a) Is learning a language like learning other skills or it is a special type of learning?
(b) Language learners go through systematic development. Language development can be divided into stages.	(b) What type of evidence is needed to define a system and a stage? How are the stages explained?
(c) Language is made up of form and function, and learning a language involves learning both.	(c) How do learners relate form and function? Is one a prerequisite for the other? Do children and adults process them differently?
(d) Language and the individual are situated within a social space.	(d) What is the role of the linguistic input that children and adults receive when learning a language? Is language acquired through interaction?

Development in L1 and L2 acquisition

Children develop language at the same time as other skills (motor, cognition, socialization, and communication). In contrast, adults come to L2 acquisition with cognitive skills already developed, although some other skills, such as specific communicative and socialization routines in the L2, may develop simultaneously. The research design of L1 and L2 acquisition research also varies.

L1 acquisition studies tend to be longitudinal, studying the development of language over a period of time. The length of study varies depending on the resources and the availability of the participants. Longitudinal studies have shown, for instance, that between 0 and 12 months, children are in a pregrammatical stage in which no language is produced, but language is comprehended. Once words, morphology, and syntax begin to develop, there are roughly four main stages (Tomasello & Brooks, 1999; Serra et al., 2000: 285), shown in Table 27.2.

The stages in Table 27.2 outline how language develops structurally in L1 acquisition, but they do not say much about what accounts for such development. Another way to examine the different stages is to ask what rules govern the child's linguistic development. In the pregrammatical stage, the child's

Table 27.2 Four main stages of development in morphology and syntax

Age in months	Stage	Type of construction
12–18	Single-word utterances	Single linguistic symbols
18–24	First word combinations	More than one symbol in combination. Single intonation line.
24–36	Simple sentences, partial productivity	Use of morphological and syntactic markers. No overgeneralization of the markers.
36+	Complex sentences, adult competence	Coordination and subordination

language is tied to context, in the grammatical stage to structure and rules, and in the postgrammatical stage to discourse (Serra et al., 2000). Context and discourse also play a role in adult L2 acquisition, as we will discuss later.

A pioneering longitudinal study of L1 acquisition was conducted by Brown (1973). He studied the early stages of morpheme acquisition of English by three children (at the start of the study, Eve was 18 months, and Adam and Sarah were 27 months old). Eve was studied for about one year, and Adam and Sarah for four years. The length of the study allowed Brown to posit an acquisition order for L1 English morphemes (Table 27.3).

Table 27.3 Order of acquisition of 14 morphemes for English L1 (Brown, 1973: 278)

Morpheme		Example	
1.	Present progressive	1	+ing
2–3	Prepositions	2–3	in/on
4	Plural	4	noun + s
5	Past irregular	5	went, swam
6	Possessive	6	hers
7	Uncontractible copula	7	she was good
8	Articles	8	the, a
9	Past regular	9	looked, talked
10	Third person regular	10	she has
11	Third person irregular	11	she talks
12	Uncontractible auxiliary	12	she was talking
13	Contractible copula	13	she's good
14	Contractible auxiliary	14	she's talking

Note. The criterion for acquisition was generally 90% occurrence in obligatory contexts in approximately 6 hours of transcription.

Table 27.4   Sequence of L1 acquisition of Catalan and Spanish

	Morpheme	Catalan	Spanish
1	First and third person singular, verb	X	X
2	Third person plural		X
3	Gender	X	X
4	Plural	X	X
5	Article	X	X
6	Infinitive, present and present perfect	X	X
7	*a* (locative preposition)	X	X
8	Reflexive pronoun	X	X
9	First person weak pronoun		
10	First person singular possessive	X	

Note. X means that a morpheme was acquired in the language by at least two of the three children studied.

Later research in L1 acquisition attempted to replicate Brown's (1973) findings for other languages. Table 27.4 displays the order of acquisition of L1 Spanish and Catalan morphemes (Aparici, Díaz, & Cortés, 1996; Serra et al., 2000: 323), and it shows that the order of acquisition coincides in general for closely related languages like Catalan and Spanish, but it differs from that of English.

L2 acquisition studies can be either cross-sectional or longitudinal. Cross-sectional studies investigate acquisition by groups of learners at different proficiency levels and assume that what is observed mirrors the development of language across time. For the study of language development, L2 longitudinal studies are more informative than L2 cross-sectional studies, but for practical reasons (e.g., learners leave the language program) most L2 acquisition studies are cross-sectional.

The L1 morpheme studies prompted L2 studies that investigated the acquisition of morphology by L2 learners cross-sectionally. The resulting *morpheme studies* described accuracy orders of morphemes in L2 English for learners with different L1s (Table 27.5). A remarkable result from these studies was that the order of acquisition did not depend on the learners' L1.

Later studies of L2 morphemes revealed variation depending on the method of data collection or analysis: Rank order studies found that the regular past preceded the irregular past for children and adults (Dulay & Burt, 1974). In contrast, hierarchical ordering of morphemes (Dulay, Burt, & Krashen, 1982) placed irregular past before regular past. Longitudinal studies of adults also reported that irregular precedes regular (Klein, Dietrich, & Noyau, 1995).

The morpheme studies became landmarks for the study of language acquisition because they showed a degree of systematicity of language learning that did not depend exclusively on the input. However, the morpheme studies were

Table 27.5 Adult and child L2 morpheme order (Bailey, Madden, & Krashen, 1974; Dulay, Burt, & Krashen, 1982)

Morpheme

---

1   Pronoun case nominative (*I*)/accusative (*me*)
2   Progressive (V + *ing*)
3   Contractible copula
4   Plural (*-s*)
5   Article (*the*, *a*)
6   Contractible auxiliary (*she's talking*)
7   Past irregular (*went*, *swam*)
8   Possessive ('*s*, *girl's*)
9   Third person (*s*, *runs*)
10 Long plural (syllabic, *-es*, *runs*)

---

not devoid of problems. Later research criticized them on the grounds of their design (accuracy as an indicator of acquisition) and the underlying learning theory (learning a language as a cumulative process, one morpheme at a time).

The chief flaw of morpheme studies was their focus on the endpoint of acquisition. Dittmar (1981) observed that "the criterion approach" (used in the morpheme order studies) treats a feature of acquisition as if the morpheme and its meaning were "indissolubly wedded; or at least, shows no interest in either form or meaning until they reach 80% or 90% appropriate use" (p. 146). Studies that focus on high rates of both well-formedness and appropriate use focus on the result of acquisition, and not the arguably more interesting process of acquisition, thus ignoring most of a learner's developmental history. Later studies supported Dittmar's claim that form and meaning should be considered separately in acquisition. For instance, form was considerably more accurate than use in essays, cloze passages, and oral production (Bardovi-Harlig, 1992; Klein et al., 1995).

Acquisition of Tense and Aspect

Whereas early morpheme studies examined acquisition in a variety of grammatical systems, more recent research has investigated the development of morphology and the relevant form–meaning relationships in a single linguistic domain. Here we focus on the acquisition of a tense-aspect system, because it provides a window to how language is acquired from several vantage points: the early marking of temporal and aspectual information, the relationship between the acquisition of form and function, and the comparison between L1 and L2 acquisition (Bardovi-Harlig, 2000; Weist, 2002).

An L2 learner must master how tense and aspect are marked in the L2 in order to be able to express temporal reference in that language. Tense and aspect are part of temporal expression, which includes all linguistic means of reference to time, such as adverbials (*yesterday, when I was a child*), tense-aspect morphology (simple past *I went* vs. progressive *I was going* in English), and chronological order. Both concepts are concerned with time, but in different ways: tense locates events or situations in time with respect to a reference point and the moment of speaking, whereas aspect refers to the internal temporal make-up (temporal constituency) of a situation (Comrie, 1976). In English, *John sings* and *John sang* differ in tense, and *John sang* and *John was singing* differ in grammatical aspect, although both are in the past tense.

Investigating temporal expression as a system led to the identification of three general L2 stages: the pragmatic, lexical, and morphological. In the pragmatic stage, the earliest resource that learners have is their interlocutors' turns, which may provide a time frame on which learners can build (this is called *scaffolding*), and on universal principles such as chronological order by which listeners assume that events in narratives are told in the same order in which they happened. Next, in the lexical stage, learners use temporal and locative adverbials as well as connectives (e.g., *and then*) to indicate time. Finally, learners may move to the morphological stage, in which tense indicates temporal relations.

The morphological stage is itself composed of several stages. Before past forms emerge, learners use base forms. In English, the morphology to express the past appears in a sequence of past > past progressive > present perfect > pluperfect, and in the expression of future the sequence is: *will* > *going to* > present progressive or simple present. As for the acquisition of Romance past morphology (e.g., Spanish, French, Italian, and Catalan), the so-called preterite (perfective) forms precede the imperfect (imperfective). No sequence is completely rigid, and learners often exhibit earlier and later forms and meanings in the same stage. Nevertheless, the characteristic use of a single stage can still be captured.

Another way to view acquisition sequences is to investigate the development of a single morpheme as it emerges and spreads across a system. The acquisition of perfective and imperfective morphology in several Romance languages has been examined from this perspective. Without principled investigation, we might think that once learners encounter the past tense, they should be able to use it with all verbs. However, observation shows that is not the case. Across languages, learners apparently associate verbal morphology with predicates that encode compatible (aspectual) meanings. For instance, verb phrases with inherent endpoints like *die, notice, read a book*, and *paint a picture* attract the simple past tense in English or the preterite in Romance languages, whereas predicates that encode ongoing activities attract progressive or imperfect morphology. Categorizing predicates this way, according to the type of event or activity, draws on *lexical aspect*, and these divisions are often referred to as *lexical (aspectual) categories*. The role such lexical categories play in the acquisition of L2 past morphology is captured by the *aspect hypothesis.*

Predicates with inherent endpoints that can be thought of as happening in a single moment are called *achievements*; predicates with some duration and an endpoint, such as *read a book* and *paint a picture*, are called *accomplishments*; and those that describe ongoing activities are called *activities*. These classes make up the dynamic (or *action*) verbs or verb phrases. In contrast to the dynamic verbs are the *states*, which encode situations that continue without additional energy. Predicates in this class include *be* and *have* and their equivalents (for example *ser, estar*, and *tener* in Spanish; *être* and *avoir* in French). Aspectual classes form a continuum from most to least stative (or least to most dynamic) across which L2 verbal morphology spreads. These sequences were first identified by Andersen (1991) and have been corroborated by a number of studies of the aspect hypothesis in various languages (Andersen & Shirai, 1996).

The sequences predicted by the aspect hypothesis indicate that the past appears first in achievements and accomplishments.

1 Past/preterite moves from   Achievements > Accomplishments >Activities > States.
2 Imperfect moves from   States > Activities > Accomplishments > Achievements.
3 Progressive moves from   Activities > Accomplishments > Achievements.

In languages that have an imperfect form (e.g., Romance languages and Japanese), the imperfect generally begins in states. The morphology then spreads from the most prototypical associations, where predicates and morphology have similar semantics, to increasingly less semantically compatible predicates. As the morphology spreads, the system becomes more targetlike, and the morphology takes on more targetlike functions, such as indicating previous events rather than echoing the aspectual meaning of the verb. The emergence and spread of verbal morphology is also ordered, as discussed earlier, and the imperfect emerges and begins to spread throughout the system well after the preterite appears.

Not all researchers agree that the aspect hypothesis is the best interpretation of the data. One counterexample was raised by Salaberry (2000), who suggested that in the earliest stages of learning the past in Spanish, English speakers may use the preterite as a default past with all types of verbs, and only later begin to distinguish among verb classes as the aspect hypothesis predicts. Klein et al. (1995) also concluded that tense precedes aspect. Finally, Comajoan (2005, 2006) reviewed several studies on the early acquisition of tense-aspect morphology of Romance languages (Spanish, French, and Catalan) by L1 English learners and concluded that lexical aspect was one variable in the acquisition of tense-aspect morphology, arguing that tense marking, discourse grounding, and input should also be considered.

Explanations of the Order of Acquisition

In trying to explain the acquisition of language, research has traditionally isolated specific factors that could account for the development of language depending on the theoretical framework adopted. Here, we focus on the following factors: the initial state of the learner (linguistic universals and the L1), input, readiness, instruction, and multiple factors.

The initial state (universals and L1)

Language universals and the L1 represent the initial state of the language learner in the sense that they are part of the knowledge with which the (adult) learner begins the task of learning a language. A number of universal principles have been proposed to account for the orders and sequences observed in L1 and L2 acquisition. This section focuses on some principles separately, namely, the relevance, congruence, and one-to-one principles (see under "Multiple factors" below for the interaction of several factors).

Andersen and Shirai (1994) argued that the affinity of certain tense-aspect morphology for predicates of particular aspectual classes can be explained by three principles (relevance, congruence, and the one-to-one) and by distributional bias which applies to input (see below). The relevance principle predicts that learners first use a grammatical morpheme depending on how relevant it is to the meaning of the verb; that is, learners may first use verbal morphemes as aspect markers because aspect is more relevant to the meaning of the verb than tense, mood, or agreement. The congruence principle states that learners select from the various aspectual morphemes in the input the morpheme that is most congruent with the aspectual meaning of the verb (Giacalone Ramat, 1997). By the one-to-one principle, learners expect each new morpheme to have only one meaning and function. In a prototype account, learners infer a prototypical meaning for each inflection from the input, such as "'action in progress at that moment' for progressives" (Andersen & Shirai, 1994: 148), and the prototypical meaning is the first one to emerge. In sum, learners are constrained by the one-to-one principle to first associate an inflection with its prototypical meaning and by relevance and congruence to use the inflection with predicates that most closely share its meaning.

Morphosyntactic complexity has also been implicated in acquisition orders, for example, as one reason for the order of past before present perfect in L1 acquisition (Gathercole, 1986). Although complexity accounts for the acquisition of the simple past before the present perfect in L1 and L2 (e.g., *wrote* before *have written*), it is a less satisfying explanation if the pluperfect is taken into account in L2 acquisition. Although both emerge after the simple past, morphosyntactically the present perfect and the pluperfect (e.g., *had written*) are equally complex, differing only in the formal tense marker. Nevertheless, pluperfect emerges after the present perfect in L2 acquisition. Thus, complexity does not account for the difference between them, only between the perfects and the simple past.

Within the larger stages of development, there are multiple discrete stages. The morphological stage, for example, exhibits many substages, in which different morphemes emerge and enter into meaning–form associations. One explanation for the order of acquisition of morphemes within the same subsystem is functional load. Every linguistic device, whether a structure, morpheme, or word, has a function. For example, if an adverb such as *yesterday* is the only indicator that an event happened in the past (*yesterday I go*), then it has high functional load. If the past tense also indicates the time frame (*yesterday I went*), the functional load of both the adverb and the verbal morphology is less than for either one occurring alone. Meanings that can be expressed grammatically and comprehensibly are less likely than others to promote acquisition of a new form. Take as an example the present perfect (*have gone*) and the pluperfect (*had gone*). They are equally complex structurally, having both a tensed form of *have* plus a past participle; yet, longitudinally the present perfect emerges noticeably earlier in adult L2 acquisition, even when both are taught simultaneously (Bardovi-Harlig, 2000). The difference between them is that the present perfect has no functional equivalent. In contrast, the meaning of the pluperfect can be expressed by the simple past plus an adverbial. This helps explain the order of emergence: an emergent interlanguage system puts greater store in range of expression than in redundancy.

In addition to universal principles, the specific L1 being learned plays an important role in language acquisition. Although languages display universal characteristics, on the surface they also display differences which can influence language acquisition (see Tables 27.3 and 27.4). For instance, languages grammaticalize tempo-aspectual meanings in different ways (Dahl, 1985), and how each meaning–form association is represented in the input will be a factor in acquisition. Spanish grammaticalizes progressive meaning with perfective (1) and imperfective (2) forms, whereas English does not. Furthermore, the imperfective progressive in (2) is compatible with the imperfective in (3). In addition, imperfective forms in Spanish can be used as markers of politeness (4), similar to the way conditional forms are used in English. Thus, Spanish imperfective forms carry more functions than English imperfective forms, which is likely to play a role in the acquisition of L2 Spanish imperfective morphology.

(1)   Estuvo   jugando toda la tarde.
      He be-perf. playing all afternoon

(2)   Cuando estaba   jugando, empezó a llover.
      When   he be-impf. playing it started to rain

(3)   Cuando jugaba,   empezó a llover.
      When   he play-impf. it started to rain

(4)   Quería   dos barras de pan.
      I like-impf. two loaves of bread

The role of the L1 is a major topic of SLA research, with multiple lines of argumentation depending on the theoretical framework adopted. Regarding the acquisition of tense-aspect morphology, studies in different theoretical frameworks assign different weights to the role of L1 (and universal tendencies through L1). For instance, within a Minimalist framework, Slabakova and Montrul (2002) argued that L2 learners of Spanish (L1 English) were sensitive to the perfective-imperfective Spanish distinction and that Universal Grammar was accessible to L2 learners. From a functionalist framework, Bardovi-Harlig (2000) argued that no specific patterns could be attributed to the learners' L1 in a corpus of L2 English from four L1s. Overall, universal trends can account for the general picture (perfectivity before imperfectivity), but a role for the L1 may also be warranted for the specific nuances of the target language. For example, Shirai (2002) found that Chinese L1 learners of L2 Japanese trans-ferred progressive markers from their L1 to the L2. Salaberry (2005) studied the acquisition of L3 Portuguese by speakers of L1 English and L2 Spanish and found that the learners could transfer their knowledge of L2 Spanish to tense-aspect in L3 Portuguese except for the category of states, suggesting that although transfer occurs, some universal tendencies (difficulties marking states) may persist even at high levels of proficiency. In sum, L1 plays a role in language acquisition but is not the only factor that affects it.

Input

While some researchers argue that universals are at the heart of acquisition, others claim that target language input explains certain acquisition sequences and relative rates of acquisition among different L2s. For instance, Klein et al. (1995) argued that L2 acquisition is "inductive and heavily input oriented" (p. 271).

Ease of acquisition may be due to good form–meaning correspondences, where the form–meaning correspondence is clear (cf. Slobin's operating principles, 1973). Giacalone Ramat (1995: 132) observed that "a higher degree of iconicity between form and function" in Italian leads L2 learners of Italian (from various L1 backgrounds) to earlier morphological sensitivity than in languages where the match is not as good, such as in French, English, and German. In Swedish, tense-aspect morphology is realized as an invariable suffix with no person agreement and seems to result in the early use of tense-aspect morphology in L2 Swedish (Noyau et al., 1995). However, the association of form with mean-ing takes place much later. In other words, invariance may help morphology get noticed, but may not lead to early form–meaning associations.

Input has also been proposed as an explanation for the observed effects of the aspect hypothesis. The distributional bias hypothesis argues that "native speakers in normal interaction with other native speakers tend to use each verb morpheme with a specific class of verbs, also following the aspect hypothesis" (Andersen & Shirai, 1994: 137), which may account for the L2 learners' order of acquisition of the tense-aspect system. Not surprisingly, native speakers are also able to separate the use of tense-aspect morphology from prototypical uses.

It is tempting to conclude that if prototypical combinations are found in the input, learners could copy those combinations and incorporate them into their emerging systems. However, input by itself cannot account for what learners do. Studies that compare child-directed speech and child's speech have found that there is a distributional bias toward prototypical combinations in adult speech, but the prototypical associations are stronger in the speech produced by children than in the input produced by the adults (Aksu-Koç, 1998; Shirai, 1998). In L2 acquisition, comparison data between native and non-native speakers on the same tasks show that non-native speakers produce more prototypical combinations than native speakers (Salaberry, 2000).

Readiness

Readiness in language development refers to the processing constraints that act as prerequisites for the acquisition of language. Pienemann's multidimensional model and teachability hypothesis (Pienemann, 1998) have incorporated readiness as the central construct for L1 and L2 acquisition in a theoretical framework that has strong implications for educational linguists teaching L2s. The teachability hypothesis states that (1) developmental sequences are motivated by processing constraints, (2) the learners' linguistic behavior may vary according to socio-psychological factors, and (3) the acquisition of specific forms via formal instruction will only be effective if the learner is ready for it (i.e., if some formal prerequisites have been met).

In this view, developmental stages are related to the specific language processing strategies used by the learners as they acquire a language. There are three main strategies: canonical order (at the beginning, always produce language in the same order; use other cues to provide meaning, such as intonation and information focus); initialization/finalization (move things from the beginning to the end or from the end to the beginning); and subordinate clause (move syntactic blocks within clauses). For instruction, the model suggests that processing constraints act as prerequisites for the instruction of language; that is, teaching a structure that involves the subordinate clause strategy will not be effective until the other strategies are in use. For instance, teaching the Spanish subjunctive (which occurs in subordinate clauses), will not be effective until learners have acquired the other strategies.

Instruction

Instruction can be a positive influence on L2 acquisition, and the domain of the tense-aspect system is no exception. Instructional method influences the success of instruction and so does the method of evaluation (Bardovi-Harlig, 2000; Norris & Ortega, 2001). In general, instruction that links form and meaning generally facilitates targetlike use of tense-aspect morphology. Studies that evaluate the effect of instruction based on development or moving one step ahead in an acquisitional sequence, rather than relying exclusively on targetlike or "correct" use, show more positive results for instruction.

Yet, instruction does not change acquisitional sequences nor does it seem to help learners skip stages. Although classroom instruction often focuses on tense-aspect morphology, learners still exhibit the pragmatic and lexical stages of temporal expression. Within the morphological stage, the steps are also ordered. For example, the pluperfect emerges after the present perfect even when they are taught together. Learners must satisfy the acquisitional prerequisites for a form to appear, even with the help of instruction. In sum, sequences seem to be so strong that they are maintained even when teaching orders and input are the opposite. For example, the *going to* future in English emerges well after the *will* future even when *going to* is taught several weeks before *will* and is used widely by teachers in conversations with the learners (Bardovi-Harlig, 2004).

Multiple factors

In identifying the factors that account for patterns of language acquisition, one must consider whether it is not one, but several factors together that influence developmental paths. For example, both lexical aspect and discourse structure interact to influence the acquisition and use of tense-aspect morphology. Certain types of predicates, namely achievements and accomplishments, attract the use of past, but these same predicates generally form the main storyline of a narrative (called the *foreground*), which itself encourages the use of past. The interaction of several factors in L2 acquisition was investigated by Goldschneider and DeKeyser (2001), who conducted a meta-analysis study that took into account the following five factors in the acquisition of L2 English morphemes: perceptual salience, semantic complexity, morphophonological regularity, syntactic category, and frequency. The results of the study showed that no single factor accounted for the morpheme order, but rather it was all five factors. Goldschneider and DeKeyser argued that what all the factors had in common was salience, concluding that the order of acquisition of morphemes was input-driven rather than based on innate syntactic properties. Unfortunately, the studies that Goldschneider and DeKeyser reviewed did not provide specific data on L1 influence, a fact that weakens the claim that salience in the input is the predictor of the order of acquisition since L1 transfer was excluded.

Researchers have also argued that just one variable cannot account for the tense-aspect system due to the multidimensionality of tense-aspect systems (Andersen, 2002). For instance, studies of the aspect hypothesis have argued that lexical characteristics of predicates are not the only facilitators of acquisition of tense-aspect, because discourse structure (foreground vs. background) also guides acquisition of the tense-aspect system. In other words, lexical aspect and discourse structure conspire in the acquisition of past tense and progressive in English (Bardovi-Harlig, 2000): learners use simple past more with achievements and accomplishments than with activities, and they use simple past more in the foreground than in the background. And the same interaction between discourse and lexical aspect is found when we consider activities, for example: activities in the foreground carry the simple past before activities in the background, and activities in both the foreground and background show lower rates of use of past than achievements and accomplishments.

Conclusion

In this chapter we have argued for an approach that examines developmental stages in L1 and L2 acquisition as a dynamic process that takes learners from the initial state to a final stage of acquisition through several stages. We have characterized the stages as systematic in the sense that at any point in time certain regularities are observed when taking into account factors such as order of acquisition, input, instruction, and readiness. In the end, the evidence from the studies reviewed, and more specifically the evidence from tense-aspect studies, shows that multiple factors intervene in the acquisition of language.

REFERENCES

Aksu-Koç, Ayhan (1998). Input and tense aspect in Turkish. *First Language*, 18, 255–280.

Andersen, Roger W. (1991). Developmental sequences: The emergence of aspect marking in second language acquisition. In Thom Huebner & Charles A. Ferguson (eds.), *Crosscurrents in Second Language Acquisition and Linguistic Theories* (pp. 305–324). Amsterdam: Benjamins.

Andersen, Roger W. (2002). The dimensions of pastness. In Rafael Salaberry & Yasuhiro Shirai (eds.), *The L2 Acquisition of Tense-Aspect Morphology* (pp. 79–106). Philadelphia: Benjamins.

Andersen, Roger W. & Shirai, Yasuhiro (1994). Discourse motivations for some cognitive acquisition principles. *Studies in Second Language Acquisition*, 16, 133–156.

Andersen, Roger W. & Shirai, Yasuhiro (1996). The primacy of aspect in first and second language acquisition: The pidgin–creole connection. In William C. Ritchie & Tej K. Bhatia (eds.), *Handbook of Second Language Acquisition* (pp. 527–570). San Diego, CA: Academic Press.

Aparici, Melina, Díaz, Gloria, & Cortés, Montserrat (1996). El orden de adquisición en catalán y castellano [The order of acquisition in Catalan and Spanish]. In Miguel Pérez-Pereira (ed.), *Estudios sobre la adquisición del castellano, catalán, eusquera y gallego* [Studies on the Acquisition of Spanish, Catalan, Basque, and Galician] (pp. 165–174). Santiago, Spain: Universidade de Santigago de Compostela.

Bailey, Nathalie, Madden, Carolyn, & Krashen, Stephen D. (1974). Is there a "natural sequence" in adult second language learning? *Language Learning*, 21, 235–243.

Bardovi-Harlig, Kathleen (1992). The relationship of form and meaning: A cross-sectional study of tense and aspect in the interlanguage of learners of English as a second language. *Applied Psycholinguistics*, 13, 253–278.

Bardovi-Harlig, Kathleen (2000). *Tense and Aspect in Second Language Acquisition: Form, Meaning, and Use*. Oxford: Blackwell.

Bardovi-Harlig, Kathleen (2004). The emergence of grammaticalized future expression in longitudinal production data. In Mark Overstreet, Susanne Rott, Bill VanPatten, & Jessica Williams (eds.), *Form and Meaning in Second Language Acquisition* (pp. 115–137). Mahwah, NJ: Lawrence Erlbaum.

Brown, Roger (1973). *A First Language: The Early Stages*. Cambridge, MA: Harvard University Press.

Comajoan, Llorenç (2005). The acquisition of perfective and imperfective morphology and the marking of discourse grounding in Catalan. In Dalila Ayoun & Rafael Salaberry (eds.), *Tense and Aspect in Romance Languages* (pp. 35–78). Philadelphia: Benjamins.

Comajoan, Llorenç (2006). The aspect hypothesis: Development of morphology and appropriateness of use. *Language Learning*, 56, 201–268.

Comrie, Bernard (1976). *Aspect*. Cambridge: Cambridge University Press.

Dahl, Östen (1985). *Tense and Aspect Systems*. New York: Blackwell.

Dittmar, Norbert (1981). On the verbal organization of L2 tense marking in an elicited translation task by Spanish immigrants in Germany. *Studies in Second Language Acquisition*, 3, 136–164.

Dulay, Heidi & Burt, Marina (1974). Natural sequence in child second language acquisition. *Language Learning*, 24, 37–53.

Dulay, Heidi, Burt, Marina, & Krashen, Stephen (1982). *Language Two*. Oxford: Oxford University Press.

Gathercole, Virginia C. (1986). The acquisition of the present perfect: Explaining differences in the speech of Scottish and American children. *Journal of Child Language*, 13, 537–560.

Giacalone Ramat, Anna (1995). Iconicity in grammaticalization processes. In Raffaele Simone (ed.), *Iconicity in Language* (pp. 119–139). Amsterdam: Benjamins.

Giacalone Ramat, Anna (1997). Progressive periphrases, markedness and second language data. In Stig Eliasson & Ernst H. Jahr (eds.), *Language and its Ecology: Essays in Memory of Einar Haugen* (pp. 261–285). Berlin: Mouton.

Goldschneider, Jennifer M. & DeKeyser, Robert M. (2001). Explaining the "natural order of L2 morpheme acquisition" in English: A meta-analysis of multiple determinants. *Language Learning*, 51, 1–50.

Ingram, David (1989). *First Language Acquisition: Method, Description and Explanation*. New York: Cambridge University Press.

Klein, Wolfgang, Dietrich, Rainer, & Noyau, Colette (1995). Conclusions. In Rainer Dietrich, Wolfgang Klein, & Colette Noyau (eds.), *The Acquisition of Temporality in a Second Language* (pp. 261–280). Amsterdam: Benjamins.

Norris, John M. & Ortega, Lourdes (2001). Does type of instruction make a difference? Substantive findings from a meta-analytic review. *Language Learning*, 51, supplement 1, 157–213.

Noyau, Colette, Dorriots, Beatriz Sjöström, Sören, & Voionmaa, Kaarlo (1995). The acquisition of Swedish. In Rainer Dietrich, Wolfgang Klein, & Colette Noyau (eds.), *The Acquisition of Temporality in a Second Language* (pp. 211–259). Amsterdam: Benjamins.

Pienemann, Manfred (1998). Developmental dynamics in L1 and L2 acquisition: Processability theory and generative entrenchment. *Bilingualism: Language and Cognition*, 1, 1–20.

Salaberry, Rafael (2000). *The Development of Past Tense Morphology in L2 Spanish.* Philadelphia: Benjamins.

Salaberry, Rafael (2005). Evidence for transfer of knowledge of aspect from L2 Spanish. In Dalila Ayoun & Rafael Salaberry (eds.), *Tense and Aspect in Romance Languages* (pp. 179–210). Philadelphia: Benjamins.

Serra, Miguel, Serrat, Elisabet, Solé, Rosa, Bel, Aurora, & Aparici, Melina (2000). *La adquisición del lenguaje* [Language Acquisition]. Barcelona: Ariel.

Shirai, Yasuhiro (1998). Tense-aspect morphology in Japanese. *First Language*, 18, 281–309.

Shirai, Yasuhiro (2002). The prototype hypothesis of tense-aspect acquisition in second language. In Rafael Salaberry & Yasuhiro Shirai (eds.), *The L2 Acquisition of Tense-Aspect Morphology* (pp. 455–478). Philadelphia: Benjamins.

Slabakova, R. & Montrul, S. (2002). On viewpoint aspect and its L2 acquisition: A UG perspective. In Rafael Salaberry & Yasuhiro Shirai (eds.), *The L2 Acquisition of Tense-Aspect Morphology* (pp. 363–395). Amsterdam: John Benjamins.

Slobin, Dan I. (1973). Cognitive prerequisites for the development grammar. In Charles A. Ferguson & Dan I. Slobin (eds.), *Studies of Child Language Development* (pp. 175–208). New York: Holt, Rinehart & Winston.

Tomasello, Michael & Brooks, Patricia (1999). Early syntactic development: A construction grammar approach. In Martyn Barrett (ed.), *The Development of Language* (pp. 161–190). London: Psychology Press.

Weist, Richard (2002). The first language acquisition of tense and aspect: A review. In Rafael Salaberry & Yasuhiro Shirai (eds.), *The L2 Acquisition of Tense-Aspect Morphology* (pp. 21–78). Philadelphia: Benjamins.

28 Language Socialization

KATHLEEN C. RILEY

Introduction

Elinor Ochs and Bambi B. Schieffelin developed the concept of *language socialization* in the early 1980s to refer to the two intertwined processes by which humans learn to become competent members of their speech communities – i.e., "socialization through the use of language and socialization to use language" (Schieffelin & Ochs, 1986: 163). The first half of this formulation expresses the notion that individuals acquire sociocultural knowledge, skills, and values by witnessing and participating in verbal interactions and speech routines. The second half is shorthand for the idea that through engagement in social interaction individuals acquire not only the phonology, morphology, and syntax of their linguistic code(s) needed for communicating thoughts and information (i.e., what Chomsky (1965) refers to as *linguistic competence*) but also many more subtle conversational resources for signaling who they are, how they feel, and what they want to accomplish (i.e., what Hymes (1971) termed *communicative competence*). This chapter looks first at the development of the paradigm and its methodology and then moves on to examine some of the key axiomatic issues of language socialization studies.

Evolution of a Theoretical Approach and Its Methodologies

As articulated by Ochs and Schieffelin in a series of jointly authored publications (e.g., 1984, 2007), the foci, theoretical frameworks, and methodologies of the language socialization approach have been developed out of cross-fertilization between psycho- and sociolinguistic studies of language acquisition and anthropological studies of socialization and the use of language in context.

The psycholinguistic program for studying child language acquisition was inspired in large measure by the Chomskyan structuralist tenet of linguistic universality (Brown, 1973). However, some of these researchers (e.g., Slobin, 1985–97) insisted on studying language acquisition cross-linguistically, attending not only to universal regularities but also to sociolinguistic variation in order to understand how children learn to pick out particular linguistic forms and map them onto the particular social meanings and practices to which they are being simultaneously exposed.

Initially, Ochs and Schieffelin (1979) applied the term *developmental pragmatics* to this study of how competent members of a society learn not only the phonological and morpho-syntactic structures of a language (i.e., Chomsky's linguistic competence), but also how to use it in contextually appropriate ways (i.e., Hymes' communicative competence). However, soon after, Ochs and Schieffelin (1984) saw the theoretical need to highlight the fact that children acquire not only linguistic resources and the ability to use them, but also a host of cultural knowledge that on the one hand facilitates the former but on the other hand is itself also learned via discourse. They posited then that the acquisition of linguistic and communicative competence is not wholly determined by an innate language organ, but also influenced by culture-specific socialization practices.

This theoretical development rested heavily on earlier anthropological studies of *socialization* (e.g., Mead, 1961 [1929]), yet the problem with these earlier studies was that they had never looked at the acquisition of sociocultural knowledge and practices in sufficiently situated or micro-interactive detail. Instead, for the formulation of their new paradigm of language socialization, Ochs and Schieffelin borrowed from recent developments in *linguistic anthropology* (see Chapter 7, Linguistic Anthropology, this volume) in order to merge in theory (as was already the case in developmental practice) these two processes: socialization as a dynamic and language-rich process, and acquisition of communicative competence as a culturally coded experience.

Language socialization shares with linguistic anthropology its commitment to analyzing the relationship between linguistic practice, cultural knowledge, and societal structure within both Western and non-Western settings. Intrinsic to this framework is the notion that language both encodes culture and is employed by culture in contextually sensitive ways – what Silverstein (2004) refers to as the *language–culture nexus*. Couched within this broader framework, a methodology was developed for examining the interaction between forces of linguistic and sociocultural reproduction and change within the locus of everyday verbal interactions among children and their caregivers (Garrett, 2007).

This methodology is derived partly from psycholinguistics, partly from the *ethnography of speaking* (Gumperz & Hymes, 1972), and partly from *conversational analysis* (Sacks, Schegloff, & Jefferson, 1974). What is borrowed directly from psycholinguistic studies is the longitudinal approach in which a novice's development is studied by recording and analyzing their talk over a significant period of time. The ethnography-of-speaking approach lends to language socialization studies a methodology that emphasizes the ethnographic analysis of sociocultural factors governing who engages how in socially significant types of speech activities. From conversational analysis, language socialization takes its focus on the micro details of how, turn by turn, conversation accomplishes various social ends. By contrast with psycholinguistic studies that rely on experimentation or elicitation, the latter two methodologies depend on the analysis of discourse in its naturally occurring contexts, an approach that has informed the methodology formulated by Ochs and Schieffelin.

Thus, language socialization studies begin with long-term ethnographic engagement in the community in order to establish the macro and micro sociocultural contexts for immediately observed interactions. Secondly, language socialization studies analyze data culled from interactions recorded in their natural contexts regularly over an extended period of time. Third, researchers use participants as assistants in the transcription process, eliciting their commentary not only about what was said and what it means, but also about all the social background information implicit in the interactions. Researchers are looking here for consultants' patterned expressions of *metapragmatic awareness* – i.e., their consciousness of how members of their speech community are communicating – as well as of *language ideology* – i.e., their beliefs about the value and functioning of language in general and specific linguistic forms in particular (Schieffelin, Woolard, & Kroskrity, 1998). These data are then also analyzed as part of the socializing context. To summarize, researchers observe the linguistic input and participant structures of situated conversations over developmental time as well as tease out the sorts of cultural presuppositions that shape the socializing process, such as local expectations about developmental stages.

Not all those that claim to be studying language socialization use an ethnographic methodology and the longitudinal analysis of naturalistic discourse (e.g., Bayley & Schechter, 2003); nonetheless, citing the paradigm implies an understanding that language socialization is the result of culturally contextualized linguistic interactions that might be studied in this way. For instance, Williams and Riley's work (2001) with Franco-Americans in northern Vermont relies on interviewing family members about childhood domestic interactions in order to reconstruct the socialization patterns that resulted in variable French-English bilingualism and eventually language shift. This methodology was indicated here because the context of acquisition was no longer available for study. However, most of the studies discussed in this chapter have conducted language socialization research over developmental time using discourse analysis and the ethnographic method.

Axiomatic Issues of the Language Socialization Paradigm

As discussed above, the language socialization paradigm has made a definitive contribution to the psycholinguistic study of language acquisition as well as to the anthropological study of the transmission of the language–culture nexus by showing that individuals learn language and culture in linguistically and culturally specific and interrelated ways. In addition to looking more closely at this interrelationship, this section also illustrates a number of other key issues and variables that influence our understanding of how exactly language socialization is accomplished.

Socialization through and into language

Because social interactions are organized and mediated by way of cultural semiotics, the socialization of language and the socialization of culture are inextricably intertwined over interactive, psychosocial, and historical time. Nonetheless, these two processes may be and sometimes are separated for analytic purposes as some studies focus primarily on the transmission of communicative knowledge and behavior while others target the reproduction of sociocultural structures and values.

When the acquisition of communicative resources is highlighted, research may focus on indexically loaded grammatical forms, socially organized speech acts, culturally significant speech genres, or entire identity-marking codes. For example, Ochs (1988) examines how Samoan children acquire ergative markers and affect features as a result of specific interactive routines. By contrast, Garrett (2005) analyzes how children develop some degree of competence in Kwéyòl in order to engage in curses and other self-asserting genres in St. Lucia. Other studies have focused on the acquisition of an expanded set of communicative forms ranging from body language (Haviland, 1998) to literacy (Heath, 1983). However, research of this genre also addresses the cultural values that fashion the functions and appropriateness of these forms of speaking. For example, in an analysis of the socialization of specific Japanese communicative forms (e.g., indirect directives and expressions of empathy), Clancy (1986) examines the cultural values such as conformity associated with these forms as well as the close-knit social structures made possible by these forms.

By contrast, other language socialization studies focus primarily on the acquisition of sociocultural structures, knowledge, practices, values, and identities. For example, Paugh (2005b) looks at how American children in dual-earner households are engaged through dinner-time conversation in an understanding of how and what it means to "work." And in her research with Navajo children, Field (2001) examines the maintenance of traditional notions of authority and community as these are invested in indigenous triadic participant structures. While they highlight the transmission of culture, these studies are, nonetheless, also sensitive to language and interaction at a number of levels: the lexicon associated with cultural beliefs and practices, the speech genres or narrative forms used, and the speaking roles allocated to participants. For example, Baquadeno-Lopèz (1997) reveals how Latino identity is effectively socialized as a consequence of language choice (Spanish vs. English) and the collaborative engagement of children in narratives of Our Lady of Guadalupe in *doctrina* classes in a Los Angeles parish.

Schieffelin's (1990) work with the Kaluli in Papua New Guinea demonstrates very clearly how processes of cultural and linguistic socialization cannot be disentangled. According to Kaluli language ideology, children's babbling and language-play is considered 'soft' and purposeless and is symbolically associated with death and decay via the sounds of certain birds, who are thought to be spirits of the dead. Thus, adults believe that children's language must be intentionally 'hardened' and that use of a baby-talk register would be detrimental to this project. Instead, once children have demonstrated their readiness to learn *to halaido* 'hard language' by producing the words for 'breast' and 'milk', adults instruct them to say culturally appropriate things to others in socially appropriate ways using well-formed syntactic constructions. These ideologically loaded socialization routines not only expose children to the forms, meanings, and functions of the language but also engage them in emotionally charged, socially organized interactions that teach them local values and behaviors.

The ways and means and models of language socialization

Three closely related principles govern our assumptions about how exactly language socialization occurs: when, to whom, by whom, in what contexts, under what constraints, and toward what ends. First is the notion that language socialization must be studied as a form of apprenticeship across the lifespan rather than as a form of computer programming that occurs only in early childhood. Secondly, language socialization is understood to be an interactive or dialogic process that nonetheless operates within structural constraints. Third, the language socialization paradigm assumes that language and culture are multiple, heterogeneous, and ever-transforming targets being acquired over a range of variable social and cultural contexts.

Apprenticeship across the lifespan

First of all, language socialization research rests on the assumption that language, culture, and social membership are acquired by unique agents (i.e., as apprentices not computers) across the lifespan (i.e., not merely as young children) and as a result of the socializing practices of others of varying ages and competencies. Thus, many researchers actively eschew an ageist and normative perspective which focuses only on mature community members as the ideally competent socializers of developmentally "normal" children.

The traditional psycholinguistic model of *learner-as-computer* highlights young children's cognitive processing of linguistic input provided by adult speakers whereas the language socialization model of the *learner-as-apprentice* foregrounds cultural influences on the use and acquisition of interactive forms by novices of all ages through interaction with initiates of all ages (Kramsch, 2002). For instance, early work by Schieffelin (1990) with the Kaluli and by Ochs (1988) in

Samoa highlights the important roles played by older siblings in the socialization of their younger siblings as well as the ways in which older siblings continue to learn communicative practices appropriate to their new statuses. More recently, Dunn's (1999) work with university-aged Japanese students' acquisition of polite registers demonstrates how the socialization of communicative competence may continue well into adulthood.

Additionally, the computer model takes off from the assumption that most healthy individuals will inevitably succeed at acquiring competence in the language of their speech community. By contrast, an apprentice model allows for the study of individuals who do not achieve the norm with respect to linguistic, communicative, or cultural competence (i.e., may be considered "failures" by the standards of their speech community). For instance, Kulick and Schieffelin (2004: 352) have examined the ways in which the introduction of new social standards into a community (as happened in the case of Christian missionizing among the Kaluli) may result in the variable socialization of "different kinds of culturally intelligible subjectivities" – i.e., some adults become "good subjects" and some are reformulated as "bad." In a similar vein, Wortham (2005) looks at how a ninth-grade student was discursively transformed from a "good student" into a "disruptive student" over the course of the school year in a US high school science class.

Children may be similarly mis-socialized in variable ways, not only by adults but also by other children, i.e., through peer socialization. For example, Ochs (2002) takes "abnormal" learners as her subjects – two autistic children – whose engagement in and apprehension of the world is shaped by their social interactions with other "normal" children and adults. Paugh's (2005a) study of code choice in Dominica similarly highlights the ways in which the discourse of children among themselves proves to be an important site for examining the processes by which codes are maintained (in this case Patwa) in ways that are specifically disapproved by adults in the speech community (who say they want their children to speak only English).

Thus, while much of the early language socialization research focused on normal children acquiring language and culture from normal adults, a growing number of studies look at the socialization of adults by other adults as well as the socialization of children by their peers in ways that do not necessarily produce fully ratified speaking members of a culture.

Dialogic socialization within structural constraints

Language socialization studies have from the beginning addressed tensions between structural domination and strategic agency. While language socialization is clearly sensitive to authority, whether informal or institutional, language socialization is also understood to be a dialogic process of co-construction (i.e., a two-way interaction between apprentices and their "masters"). In either case, researchers refrain from taking an egocentric perspective that privileges individual intention (of either the novice or the teacher). Here we look briefly at the impact of power structures on how learners learn and then survey the interactionist approaches that challenge these notions of structural constraint.

Early sociolinguistic discussions of the effects of macro-political-economic phenomena on socialization include Bernstein's analysis of how the "restricted code" of the British working class results in reducing their *educability* (1971). In a similar vein, Bourdieu (1991) elaborated the notion that certain distinctive semiotic practices or *habitus* are valued on the symbolic market place due to their association with those who occupy socially powerful positions, and that access to this symbolic capital will be restricted to the few who are socialized early on to occupy these positions.

Linguistic anthropologists also began to study how communicative restraint takes shape at the interactive level. For instance, Philips (1970) examined how the communicative styles learned by Warm Springs Indian children in the home affected the ways they interacted and therefore achieved at school. And Heath (1983) focused on how differences in the way white and black, working-class and middle-class American children are exposed to literacy practices in the home have a huge impact on their success in learning to read at school.

When put together with Ochs and Schieffelin's theoretical and methodological tools, these enquiries have made it possible to ask how exactly hegemonic ideologies and practices are produced and reproduced at the local level. For example, colonial power relations can be seen to have real-world consequences in northern Canada where Crago et al. (1993) have examined the influence of mainstream North American beliefs on language socialization within Inuit homes. And in Corsica, Jaffe (2001) has examined the impact of interpolating French language ideologies and pedagogical practices into Corsican classrooms, even when teaching the Corsican language.

Similarly, in the domain of gender relations, Farris (1991) explores how, in Taiwan school yards, boys and girls voice dominant ideologies of how and about what men and women ought to communicate, thus reproducing a long tradition of Chinese gender inequality. Fader's (2006) study of the language socialization of "faith" among the Hasidic community in Brooklyn identifies the everyday practices through which mothers engage their daughters in the reproduction of gender inequality.

Important in all of this work is the endeavor to look not only at the macro structures of inequality, but also at micro structures of authority as they are interactively constructed – whether in the home between parents and children, at school between students and teachers, or in the street and at work among peers. For instance, some researchers (e.g., Field, 2001; Wortham, 2005) demonstrate how the authoritative voice of the teacher can be traced to their possession of the dominant code as well as to their age, ethnicity, institutional status, and/or assigned role in the participant structure. This instantiated authority as "expert" provides their socialization moves with a force they might otherwise lack. However, the teachings of an "expert" are not necessarily incorporated by a novice. How is that?

Kramsch's (2002) *ecological* model makes explicit the notion that socializing practices and authorities are determined by social forces that must be deconstructed rather than accepted as willful acts and conscious agents. Similarly while individuals variably acquire the linguistic and cultural knowledge and practices to which they are exposed, they need not be treated as strategic actors "choosing" to "accept" or "resist" the resources being offered to them. Instead, socialization is interactively achieved, mediated sometimes by communicated intentions but more frequently by unconscious preconceptions. As Kulick and Schieffelin (2004) articulate it, subjectivities are dialogically produced as a compromise between authoritative transmission and creative (but not necessarily conscious) agency.

Explicitly interactive or dialogic approaches have been undertaken by researchers in a number of contexts and with a variety of goals. Zentella's (1997) work with New York Puerto Ricans focuses an *anthropolitical lens* on the tension between dominant communicative norms and local community practices resulting in the interactive socialization of Spanglish, a code-switching code which effectively expresses a synthetic Nuyorican identity. Similarly, Riley (2001) examines how children in the Marquesas are socialized to code-switch (between French and 'Enana) in ways that may on the one hand re-frame the immediate interaction or may on the other express their dialogic identity as both French and Polynesian. And in his work with Indian, Pakistani, Jamaican, and Anglo youth in England, Rampton (1995) has formulated his notion of *crossing* as the dialogic trying on of ethnicities that are not one's own.

With more of a focus on the micro-interactional participant structures, He (2004) investigates how novices contribute (or not) to their own socialization via the negotiation of speech roles in Chinese heritage language classrooms. Field (2001) explores the ways in which Navajo children engaged in triadic participant directives learn not only what to say in ways appropriate to their speech community, but also how these forms may be used to assert their own positional needs. And de León's (1998) work with Mayan children contributes to the literature on how infants emerge as conversational participants due to their immersion in polyadic interactions.

Work along these lines supports the point made in the previous section that not all language socialization "succeeds" in the construction of normative members of a speech community. Instead, this lack of success underscores the final point to be outlined in the next section, which is that definitive speech community norms do not exist at all except as ideological reifications.

Language and culture as multiple, moving targets

Patterns of language socialization vary across a wide array of linguistic, cultural, and social contexts; additionally, the communicative resources, cultural knowledge, and social competencies being acquired are multiple, heterogeneous, and constantly transforming objectives (i.e., more like moving targets than set skills to be definitively mastered). Thus, researchers seek a specifically non-ethnocentric perspective, examining both the dynamic effects of micro and macro structures on specific patterns of socialization as well as the impact of socialization on its encompassing structures.

Given its emergence out of the disciplines of anthropology and sociolinguistics, language socialization research has always highlighted the diversity of cultural contexts, socializing situations, and forms of interactional input (Schieffelin & Ochs, 1986; Garrett and Baquedano-López, 2002; Bayley & Schecter, 2003). Studies have been conducted in societies ranging from small-scale and homogeneous (e.g., Schieffelin's, 1990 analysis of the Kaluli of PNG just after first contact with European missionaries) to large-scale and heterogeneous (e.g., Miller's, 1982 work with working-class American families) as well as in societies resulting from the collision of small-scale and complex in a globalizing world (e.g., work by Crago et al., 1993 with Inuit families).

And although early language socialization research (e.g., Ochs, 1988) tended to focus on the domestic sphere, since the beginning studies have also been conducted in a wide range of formal to informal contexts, including high schools (Wortham, 2005), heritage language classrooms (He, 2004), and religious training classrooms (e.g., Baquedeno-López, 1997). Some research spans elementary school and home contexts (e.g., Heath, 1983; Field, 2001). Other informal venues include the street and the playground (e.g., Farris, 1991; Zentella, 1997). Workplaces are a sphere attracting more recent attention (e.g., Bayley & Schecter, 2003).

In all of these studies, the heteroglossic nature of languages, ideologies, and speech communities is a given. Even in the smallest scale societies, researchers examine the socializing effects of contrasts in the speech styles and belief systems between men and women or upper- and lower-rank members of the community (e.g., Ochs, 1988; Schieffelin, 1990). These contrasts become far more complex as soon as new ecologies are formed out of colonial contact, globalization, immigration, and urbanization (e.g., Kulick & Schieffelin, 2004). Additionally, in some of this work, even the notion of "context" is problemetized. For instance, in Moore and Moritz's (2005) research on the acquisition of Arabic literacy by Fulbe children, non-verbal aspects of the context and the socialization process are highlighted. And when studying classroom identity formation, Wortham (2005) looks not only at recurrent speech events within static social contexts but also at semiotic events that transform along a continuum of timescales: from social-historical transformations across millenia to microgenetic interactions lasting several seconds. This diversity of socializing contexts and linguistic input has contributed to theoretical examination of the universals and cross-cultural differences involved in communicative acquisition as well as the role of language in the development of sociocultural knowledge and identities.

Finally, just as language socialization is sensitive to the heterogeneous contexts (both micro and macro) within which it unfolds, so does it also have an impact on those contexts. That is, language socialization represents a dynamic link in the dialectical transmission and transformation of language and culture. First of all, novices have the capacity to dramatically alter linguistic usage within a heteroglossic economy, contributing to the production of creoles, to new patterns of code-switching, and to language shift and maintenance (Kulick, 1992; Zentella, 1997; Garrett, 2005; Paugh, 2005a; Howard, 2007). Secondly, through their playful constructions of new linguistic forms, communicative practices, and interactional contexts and relationships, apprentices have the potential to transform the cultural concepts, emotional values, and social identities enacted through linguistic exchanges (e.g., Cook-Gumperz, Corsara, & Streeck, 1986; Rampton, 1995; Riley, 2001). Such heteroglossic, interactivist approaches are the only way to comprehend how structurally sensible transformation rather than inevitable reproduction occurs.

Conclusion

The study of language socialization is the study of two interconnected processes. On the one hand, verbal interaction allows for the transmission of sociocultural beliefs, structures, and practices. Simultaneously, cultural belief systems and social contexts affect the ways in which individuals acquire the communicative competence needed to interact successfully within a speech community. While it is taken as axiomatic that socialization contributes to a consensual understanding of a shared set of communicative values, it is also understood that (1) no unified community or body of values can be assumed; (2) consensus must be considered more of a temporary and contextually dependent interactive achievement; and (3) rather than being imposed by older experts onto younger novices, socialization is an interactive sharing that may happen at any point in the life cycle.

The result of these fine points is that language socialization becomes a powerful yet fluid paradigm for understanding how the culture–language nexus is both produced and transformed over interactive, developmental, and historical time. That is, just as variable contexts have an impact on the socialization of individuals, so does the socialization of individuals through developmental time have a cumulative effect over historical time on the larger aggregates of language, culture, and society. Given this interplay between macro and micro structures (i.e., the impact of economics, politics, religion, and education on domestic language socialization issues and vice versa), many studies (e.g., Heath, 1983; Zentella, 1997) have been conducted with an eye toward the potential applicability of their findings to real-world practices, policies, institutions, and values.

REFERENCES

Baquedano-López, Patricia (1997). Creating social identities through doctrina narratives. *Issues in Applied Linguistics*, 8(1), 27–45.

Bayley, Robert & Schecter, Sandra R. (eds.) (2003). *Language Socialization in Bilingual and Multilingual Societies.* Clevedon, UK: Multilingual Matters.

Bernstein, Basil B. (1971). *Class Codes and Control: Theoretical Studies towards a Sociology of Language.* London: Routledge.

Bourdieu, Pierre (1991). *Language and Symbolic Power*, trans. Gino Raymond & Matthew Adamson. Cambridge, MA: Harvard University Press. (Original work published 1982.)

Brown, R. (1973). *A First Language: The Early Stages.* Cambridge, MA: Harvard University Press.

Chomsky, Noam (1965). *Aspects of the Theory of Syntax.* Cambridge, MA: MIT Press.

Clancy, Patricia M. (1986). The acquisition of communicative style in Japanese. In Bambi B. Schieffelin & Elinor Ochs (eds.), *Language Socialization across Cultures* (pp. 213–250). Cambridge: Cambridge University Press.

Cook-Gumperz, Jenny, Corsaro, William A., & Streeck, Jürgen (eds.) (1986). *Children's Worlds and Children's Language.* Berlin: Mouton de Gruyter.

Crago, Martha B., Annahatak, Betsy, & Ningiuruvik, Lizzie (1993). Changing patterns of language socialization in Inuit homes. *Anthropology and Education Quarterly*, 24, 205–223.

de León, Lourdes (1998). The emergent participant: Interactive patterns in the socialization of Tzotzil (Mayan) infants. *Journal of Linguistic Anthropology*, 8(2), 131–161.

Dunn, Cynthia D. (1999). Reflections on the future work of anthropology and education: Toward the study of communicative development as a lifespan process. *Anthropology and Education Quarterly*, 30(4), 451–454.

Fader, Ayala (2006). Learning faith: Language socialization in a Hasidic community. *Language in Society*, 35(2), 207–229.

Farris, Katherine S. (1991). The gender of child discourse: Same-sex peer socialization through language use in a Taiwanese preschool. *Journal of Linguistic Anthropology*, 1(2), 198–224.

Field, Margaret (2001). Triadic directives in Navajo language socialization. *Language in Society*, 30(2), 249–263.

Garrett, Paul (2005). What a language is good for: Language socialization, language shift, and the persistence of code-specific genres in St. Lucia. *Language in Society* 34(3), 327–361.

Garrett, Paul (2007). Researching language socialization. In Patricia Duff & Nancy Hornberger (eds.), *Encyclopedia of Language and Education, (vol. 10): Research Methods and Methodology* (pp. 189–201). Dordrecht: Kluwer Academic Publishers.

Garrett, Paul & Baquedano-López, Patricia (2002). Language socialization: Reproduction and continuity, transformation and change. *Annual Review of Anthropology*, 31, 339–361.

Gumperz, John J. & Hymes, Dell (eds.) (1972). *Directions in Sociolinguistics: The Ethnography of Communication.* Oxford: Basil Blackwell.

Haviland, John B. (1998). Early pointing gestures in Zincantán. *Journal of Linguistic Anthropology*, 8(2), 162–196.

He, Agnes (2004). Novices and their speech roles in Chinese heritage language classes. In Robert Bayley & Sandra R. Checter (eds.), *Language Socialization in Bilingual and Multilingual Societies* (pp. 128–146). Clevedon, UK: Multilingual Matters.

Heath, Shirley B. (1983). *Ways with Words: Language, Life, and Work in Communities and Classrooms.* Cambridge: Cambridge University Press.

Howard, Kathryn M. (2007). Language socialization and language shift among school-aged children. In Patricia Duff & Nancy Hornberger (eds.), *Encyclopedia of*

Language and Education, (vol. 8): Language Socialization (pp. 187–199). Dordrecht: Kluwer Academic Publishers.

Hymes, Dell (1971). *On Communicative Competence.* Philadelphia: University of Pennsylvania Press.

Jaffe, Alexandra (2001). Authority and authenticity: Corsican discourse on bilingual education. In Monica Heller & M. Martin-Jones (eds.), *Voices of Authority: Education and Linguistic Difference* (pp. 269–296). Westport, CT: Ablex.

Kramsch, Claire (ed.) (2002). *Language Acquisition and Language Socialization: Ecological Perspectives.* London: Continuum.

Kulick, Don (1992). *Language Shift and Cultural Reproduction: Socialization, Self and Syncretism in a Papua New Guinean Village.* New York: Cambridge University Press.

Kulick, Don & Schieffelin, Bambi B. (2004). Language socialization. In Alessandro Duranti (ed.), *A Companion to Linguistic Anthropology* (pp. 349–368). Malden, MA: Blackwell.

Mead, Margaret (1961 [1929]). *Coming of Age in Samoa.* London: Cape. First published (1929), New York: William Morrow & Co.

Miller, Peggy (1982). *Amy, Wendy and Beth: Language Learning in South Baltimore.* Austin: University of Texas Press.

Moore, Leslie & Moritz, Mark (2005). Dimensions of context in Koranic literacy socialization. Ninth International Pragmatics Conference. Riva del Garda Congressi, Riva del Garda, Italy.

Ochs, Elinor (1988). *Culture and Language Development: Language Acquisition and Language Socialization in a Samoan Village.* New York: Cambridge University Press.

Ochs, Elinor (2002). Becoming a speaker of culture. In Claire Kramsch (ed.), *Language Acquisition and Language Socialization* (pp. 99–120). London: Continuum.

Ochs, Elinor & Schieffelin, Bambi B. (eds.) (1979). *Developmental Pragmatics.* New York: Academic Press.

Ochs, Elinor & Schieffelin, Bambi B. (1984). Language acquisition and socialization: Three developmental stories and their implications. In R. A. Shweder & R. A. LeVine (eds.), *Culture Theory: Essays on Mind, Self, and Emotion* (pp. 276–320). New York: Cambridge University Press.

Ochs, Elinor & Schieffelin, Bambi B. (2007). Language socialization: An historical overview. In Patricia Duff & Nancy Hornberger (eds.), *Encyclopedia of Language and Education, (vol. 8): Language Socialization* (pp. 1–13). Dordrecht: Kluwer Academic Publishers.

Paugh, Amy (2005a). Multilingual play: Children's code-switching, role play and agency in Dominica, West Indies. *Language in Society*, 34(1), 63–86.

Paugh, Amy (2005b). Learning about work at dinnertime: Language socialization in dual-earner American families. *Discourse and Society*, 16(1), 55–78.

Philips, Susan (1970). Participant structure and communicative competence: Warm Springs children in community and classroom. In J. E. Alatis (ed.), *Bilingualism and Language Contact: Anthropological, Linguistic, Psychological, and Social Aspects* (pp. 370–394). Washington, DC: Georgetown University Press.

Rampton, Ben (1995). Language crossing and the problematisation of ethnicity and socialization. *Pragmatics*, 5, 485–513.

Riley, Kathleen C. (2001). The Emergence of Dialogic Identities: Transforming Heteroglossia in the Marquesas, F.P. Doctoral dissertation, CUNY Graduate Faculty.

Sacks, Harvey, Schegloff, Emanuel A., & Jefferson, Gail (1974). A simplest systematics for the organization of turn-taking in conversation. *Language*, 50, 696–735.

Schieffelin, Bambi B. (1990). *The Give and Take of Everyday Life: Language Socialization of Kaluli Children*. Cambridge: Cambridge University Press.

Schieffelin, Bambi B. & Ochs, Elinor (1986). Language socialization. *Annual Review of Anthropology*, 15, 163–191.

Schieffelin, Bambi B., Woolard, Kathryn A., & Kroskrity, Paul V. (eds.) (1998). *Language Ideologies: Practice and Theory*. New York: Oxford University Press.

Silverstein, Michael (2004). "Culture" concepts and the language–culture nexus. *Current Anthropology*, 45(5), 621–652.

Slobin, Dan Isaac (ed.) (1985–97). *The Crosslinguistic Study of Language Acquisition* (5 vols.). Mahwah, NJ: Lawrence Erlbaum.

Williams, Robert S. & Riley, Kathleen C. (2001). Acquiring a slice of Anglo-American pie: A portrait of language shift in a Franco-American family. In R. D. González (ed.), *Language Ideologies: Critical Perspectives on the Official English Movement, (vol. 2): History, Theory, and Policy* (pp. 63–90). Mahwah, NJ: Lawrence Erlbaum.

Wortham, Stanton E. F. (2005). Socialization beyond the speech event. *Journal of Linguistic Anthropology*, 15(1), 95–112.

Zentella, Ana Celia (1997). *Growing Up Bilingual: Puerto Rican Children in New York*. Malden, MA: Blackwell.

FURTHER READING

Boggs, Stephen T. (1985). *Speaking, Relating, and Learning: A Study of Hawaiian Children at Home and at School*. Norwood, NJ: Ablex.

Briggs, Jean (1995). The study of Inuit emotions: Lessons from a personal retrospective. In J. A. Russell, J-M. Ferndez-Dols, A. S. R. Manstead, & J. C. Wellenkamp (eds.), *Everyday Conceptions of Emotion* (pp. 203–220). Dordrecht: Kluwer Academic.

Doucet, Rachelle (2003). Language Ideology, Socialization, and Pedagogy in Haitian Schools and Society. Doctoral dissertation, New York University.

Goodwin, Marjorie Harness (1990). *He-Said She-Said: Talk as Social Organization among Black Children*. Bloomington: Indiana University Press.

Ochs, Elinor (1991). Misunderstanding children. In Nikolas Coupland, Howard Giles, & John M. Wiemann (eds.), *"Miscommunication" and Problematic Talk* (pp. 44–60). Newbury Park, CA: Sage Publications.

Ochs, Elinor & Schieffelin, Bambi B. (1983). *Acquiring Conversational Competence*. London: Routledge.

Riley, Kathleen C. (2007). To tangle or not to tangle: Shifting language ideologies and the socialization of charabia in the Marquesas, French Polynesia. In Miki Makihara & Bambi B. Schieffelin (eds.), *Consequences of Contact: Language Ideologies and Sociocultural Transformations in Pacific Societies* (pp. 70–95). New York: Oxford University Press.

Schieffelin, Bambi B. (1994). Code-switching and language socialization: Some probable relationships. In J. F. Duchan, L. E. Hewitt, & R. M. Sonnenmeier (eds.), *Pragmatics: From Theory to Practice* (pp. 20–42). Englewood Cliffs, NJ: Prentice-Hall.

Schieffelin, Bambi B. & Gilmore, Perry (eds.) (1986). *The Acquisition of Literacy: Ethnographic Perspectives*. Westport CT: Praeger.

Scollon, Ron & Scollon, Suzanne B. K. (1981). *Narrative, Literacy, and Face in Interethnic Communication*. Norwood NJ, Ablex.

29 Interlanguage and Language Transfer

PETER SKEHAN

The study of interlanguage and language transfer have been long-standing issues in applied linguistics, as evidenced by Weinreich's (1953) classic analysis of cross-linguistic influence and Selinker's (1972) introduction of the term *interlanguage*. Both have been of interest at a number of levels. First of all, atheoretically, it has been fascinating descriptively, as researchers have tried to identify and categorize the different sorts of interlanguage and cross-linguistic influences which exist. Second, they have considerable theoretical interest – *any* significant theory of second language acquisition (SLA) has to account for transfer, and for transitional stages. Third, they have been of huge importance to the pedagogic domain also, with widespread assumptions that transfer, both negative and positive, has a major impact on second language learning and should therefore inform teaching decisions, and that developmental stages need to be incorporated in any SLA-informed account of syllabus design.

Definitions, Terminology, and Scope

Definitions are helpful at the outset. For language transfer, this is taken from the major book-length treatment of the subject, Odlin (1989):

> Transfer is the influence resulting from the similarities and differences between the target language and any other language that has been previously (and perhaps imperfectly) acquired. (p. 27)

The definition brings out a number of features. First, the neutral term *influence* enables us to consider that positive and negative impact may arise. Second, the source of these impacts is the similarities and differences between the language systems. Third, the definition is consistent with multiple language learning, so that L2–L3 influences (and so on) are also covered by transfer. In passing, it should also be noted that other terms are possible in this area. For example, *cross-linguistic influence* may be more appropriate since it has a greater neutrality than the more active-sounding *transfer* (Cook, 2000). However, transfer is the term which is widely used, and has become accepted by convention.

Regarding interlanguage, Ellis (1994: 710) suggests that:

> The term has come to be used with different but related meanings (i) to refer to the series of interlocking systems which characterize acquisition, (ii) to refer to the system that is observed at a single stage of development ("an interlanguage"), and (iii) to refer to particular L1/L2 combinations (for example, L1 French/L2 English vs. L1 Japanese/L2 English).

As we will see, the two areas, transfer and interlanguage, are considerably intertwined, and can be considered together most of the time, with L1 influences (transfer) having a strong influence on interlanguage. Bardovi-Harlig and Comajoan (Chapter 27, Order of Acquisition and Developmental Readiness, this volume) also discuss the developmental readiness and order of acquisition issues that are more prominent in the first two meanings in Ellis' characterization.

Fundamental Issues and Early Developments

Weinreich's (1953) exploration was of cross-linguistic influences between languages more generally. Later investigators, such as Lado (1957) and Stockwell, Bowen, and Martin (1965) focused more narrowly on transfer. Issues which then become important were the relative importance of positive *and* negative transfer, with the former seen as facilitating language learning through language similarity and the latter creating a range of difficulties. Most investigators, including Weinreich (1953), regarded negative transfer as the more significant effect, but others, e.g., Ringbom (1987), argued strongly for the centrality of positive transfer effects. Certainly during the 1950s and 1960s, the study of transfer was linked with Contrastive Analysis (CA), and attempts were made to establish a hierarchy of difficulty for different language combinations (a sort of scale of language distance), as well as methods of predicting where learning difficulties would occur (Stockwell et al., 1965).

Initial approaches to conceptualizing second language development and transfer generally had connections to behaviorist and associationistic approaches to psychology. Hence the naturalness of terms like positive and negative. Even before the development of SLA studies in the 1970s, though, there were doubts expressed about the relevance and scale of transfer. Ellis (1994), for example, describes the 'minimalist' position, which emphasizes the similarities between L2 and L1 acquisition. Newmark and Reibel (1968), for example, see the effects of transfer as following from communication problems, rather than an underlying interlanguage, saying: ". . . from the learner's point of view, all he is doing is the best he can: to fill in his gaps of training he refers for help to what he already knows." In other words, the L1 is a temporary support, but not the reflection of an underlying L2 system.

The contrastive viewpoint was also challenged by early SLA, since this was strongly influenced by developments in first language acquisition research. This emphasized the independence of the learner from input material, and the child's capacity to formulate hypotheses regarding the language being learned. A hypothesis testing approach was applied in the second language domain also (Corder, 1967), and so an early question concerned the origin of L2 learners' hypotheses. At the outset a distinction was made between interlingual and intralingual hypotheses, with the first being essentially transfer-based, and the second linked to the structure of the language being learned. Selinker (1972) extended the sources of hypotheses and the influences upon interlanguage to include teaching, communication strategies, and simplification. Essentially, then, the L1 was seen as one of the sources of hypotheses which would influence the path of language development, although perhaps a particularly important source. Selinker (1972) also introduced the term *fossilization* to refer to the situation where learning stops, in a manner consistent with an incomplete rule-generated system, prior to a native-like level.

Interestingly, and very soon, this view of hypothesis generation was rejected. Dulay and Burt (1974), in their formulation of the Creative Construction Hypothesis, claimed that the vast majority of errors are *intra*-lingual, and reflect a second language being learned in the same ways as the first. For them, transfer was of only minor importance, since the development of an L2 is essentially the result of the direct interaction between the learner's acquisitional capacities and the data to which the learner is exposed (the L2). This viewpoint was very significant theoretically and also practically, for example through publications such as *Language 2* (Dulay, Burt, & Krashen, 1982), not least in the way it was associated with Krashen's Input Hypothesis (Krashen, 1985).

Constraints on Interlanguage Development and Transfer

By the 1980s these early approaches to interlanguage and transfer had been superseded by a range of alternative accounts which can be viewed through the notion of constraint. The six constraints to be covered fall into two main types. The first three – language level, sociolinguistic influences and task, and language distance and psychotypology – function more at a descriptive level. The second three – linguistic influences, psycholinguistic influences, and developmental factors – are more theoretically motivated accounts of what occurs in language change and transfer. It is interesting that these different, more theoretical accounts are not directly built to explain interlanguage or transfer, but rather provide an explanatory framework for transfer and inter-language development. The section which follows emphasizes transfer slightly. (See Chapter 27, Order of Acquisition and Developmental Readiness, for order of acquisition and developmental readiness as these reflect L1-independent influences on interlanguage development.)

Language level

One influence on transfer is the different area of the language system which is concerned. Ellis (1994) and Hansen (2006) argue for strong effects of transfer on phonology, with the sound systems of a first language being particularly deep seated and difficult to change. It has been argued that word order is not so strongly affected by L1 influences (but see Odlin,1990 for counter-evidence), although syntax too is generally the site for many claims of transfer influence, particularly where language parameters are concerned (see below, on Universal Grammar). Ellis (1994) proposes that syntax is slightly less affected by transfer than other areas because metalinguistic factors can have a dampening influence. The potential availability of clear feedback, as well as a clear focus on the area within teaching, may also reduce the amount of transfer at this level. But if these two areas are regarded as central, that does not mean that transfer influences have not been proposed elsewhere. Lexis is affected (Kellerman, 1978), and interacts in interesting ways with learner perceptions of difficulty and plausible transferability (see below). There is also the area of discourse, which is possibly more difficult to study, as discourse violations may not always be so evident. But Olshtain (1983) was able to show interesting over-use effects with apologies used by US English speakers learning Hebrew. These English L1 learners transferred their direct apology expressions into Hebrew in ways which were not native-like.

Sociolinguistic and task effects

In one sense these comments could appear in the methodology section, in that the point to consider here is that performance may be partly a function of elicitation task or language context. As a result, transfer may manifest itself differently in different contexts, and indeed transfer may not always occur in categorical fashion. Ellis (1994), for example, argues that if pedagogic norms are more prominent, in what he terms focused communities, then transfer will be less evident. This may be a reflection of the more general point that now it is clear that the accuracy level of performance varies as a function of different conditions. Skehan (2001) reports, in the context of task research, that monologic tasks, or tasks requiring more transformations, or based on unfamiliar or abstract information, are associated with higher levels of error. Tarone (1985) similarly reports different patterns of task effect on low meaning forms, e.g., third person -s; high meaning forms, e.g., plural -s; and discourse salient forms, e.g., pronouns, articles. Such findings would be consistent with the view that transfer is, at least in part, a performance phenomenon, and second language speakers have to resort to the L1 when they are dealing with greater communicative problems (cf. Newmark & Riebel, above).

Language distance and psychotypology

Languages vary considerably in how close they are to one another, and this has been of interest in two ways. First, greater language distance may have effects on the nature of transfer. Second, language effects may have influences on *perceptions* of transferability where these are linked to psychological factors which impact on performance. Taking the first of these, there are, of course, a wide range of studies of transfer based on different language combinations (see Odlin, 1989, 2003 for review). The difficulty is in finding controlled situations where language distance can be presumed to be the only (or at least main) factor which is operative. In this respect, a case which has been explored is the learning of English by Swedish and Finnish speakers, given Swedish's much closer Indo-European position to English, relative to the Finno-Ungric, yet with both groups being broadly similar culturally (Jarvis & Odlin, 2000). Jarvis (2000), for example, in a study exploring the retelling of Chaplin's *Modern Times*, reports the Swedish narrators as using verb-particle combinations, e.g., *run on*, which is a clear transfer from Swedish, while the Finnish narrators never did this. Ringbom (1987) showed that two groups of learners (with Finnish and Swedish backgrounds), both fluent in Swedish and Finnish, transferred word morphology from Swedish but not Finnish.

This leads naturally to the issue of psychotypology. It seems to be the case that the students whose home and cultural background was Finnish nonetheless transferred from Swedish more readily. Of course, there may be psycholinguistic processes which underlie this transfer choice. But it is also possible that the students themselves had perceptions of relatedness which meant that, when the need for an L1 form materialized, it was Swedish that was seen to be more relevant because of the greater language relatedness. A study by Kellerman (1978) extends this view of learner *perceptions* as having a major influence. He explored Dutch learners' views on the translatability of the Dutch *breken* by the English *break*. In fact, the two words are very readily translatable, but Kellerman found that the learners themselves did not see things as being so easy. Instead, they were much more willing to translate 'prototypical' uses, such as "break one's leg" rather than uses such as "to break a strike." The source of the psychological approach is different from the Ringbom study, but the underlying issue is the same: learners have perceptions of similarity which may be independent of the real state of affairs.

Linguistic factors

Perhaps the most well-known theoretically-motivated account of transfer derives from Universal Grammar (UG). More properly, one should say that there are, in fact, a range of positions on transfer, since there are a range of positions on the role of UG in L2 learning (see White, 2003a for a comprehensive account). White (2003b) summarizes five: (1) full transfer/partial access; (2) no transfer/partial access; (3) full transfer/full access; (4) partial transfer/full access; (5) partial transfer/partial access. Essentially, the different positions reflect whether UG is still active in the second language case; whether the results of UG from first language acquisition, i.e., parameter settings, are available as a starting point or an influence on second language learning; and how completely the different positions operate. In principle, there may still be partial access directly to UG (e.g., Vainikka & Young-Scholten, 1998) through what is called the minimal trees hypothesis, or alternatively there may still be complete access, so that second language learners interact with data in the same way as first language learners do (Schwartz & Sprouse, 1996). Similarly, some domains may actually be transferred but others not, in a selective manner. In this case, the key issue would be the determination of which language domains are most affected and which least. It certainly is interesting here to see the extent of the contrast with Pienemann (2005). UG researchers are assuming that the end state of the process of first language acquisition is where the second language learner starts, so that whether from direct access and complete transfer, or from some diluted version of these, the learner is equipped at the starting point with whatever has been learned before. In contrast, Pienemann argues that the learner, effectively, starts again, and can only operate within the constraints of processing. This will be developed more fully below.

Psycholinguistic accounts: The Competition Model

The Competition Model exemplifies modern empiricism (Bates & MacWhinney, 1982; MacWhinney, 1997, 2001). It does not regard language as a special domain, but instead portrays the human brain as a general purpose learning device, strongly influenced by frequency of occurrence, cue reliability and availability. The model uses a connectionist approach to second language development which emphasizes communicative functions, as these are encoded in the surface elements of language. For example, the model focuses on the agent identification in a sentence. This role is seen as identifiable through surface cues such as pre-verbal positioning, agreement marking, use of article, animacy, presence of *by* and other cues of this nature. So, in a sentence such as "The boy is annoying the parrots" (MacWhinney, 2001) the cues combine to make it most likely that the sentence agent is *boy*, through positive factors such as the use of the definite article, agreement, pre-verbal positioning, word order more generally, and absence of *by*, for example. Such surface level cues are weighted to make the best *probabilistic* decision. The Competition Model has been evaluated through computer simulation (Ellis & Schmidt, 1997) and also through a range of empirical studies of actual language learners (MacWhinney, 1997, 2001).

Regarding transfer, the key point with the Competition Model is that different surface cues are linked with decisions on e.g., agency, in different ways in different languages. In English, for example, the role of actor is strongly associated with pre-verbal positioning. However, in other languages, e.g., German or Italian, other cues may be more important in learning to assign the actor role (Bates & MacWhinney, 1982), e.g., agreement. The central issue for transfer then is what the learner of an L2 does regarding the cues that have been learned to be important in the L1. As MacWhinney (2001: 80) says: "Initially, the learning of the L2 is highly parasitic on the structures of the L1 in both lexicon . . . and phonology . . ." Later he says: "This means that initially the L2 system has no separate conceptual structure and that its formal structure relies on the structure of the L1. The learner's goal is to build up L2 representations as a separate system." Data is reported consistent with this claim. For example, McDonald (1987) studied English learners of Dutch (for which case inflection is important) and Dutch learners of English (for which word order is important). The research shows that as proficiency level increases, the English learners move from relying on word order information to relying on case inflection, while the Dutch learners of English pay less attention to case inflection and much more to word order.

Processing accounts

This approach emphasises the consequences of processing constraints for second language development. An early example of such an approach is represented in the work of Roger Andersen (1983). He proposes, following Slobin's (1973) work in first language acquisition, that there are processing constraints which mean that:

- learners may need to reach a certain stage of development before transfer becomes possible (Zobl, 1980);
- language development is delayed when an L1 structure coincides with a developmental structure.

More generally, Andersen (1983) proposes his 'Transfer to Somewhere Principle', at a very general level: "Transfer can only function in conjunction with the operating principles that guide language learners and users in their choice of linguistic forms to express the intended meaning." The principles, with children, are meant to reflect general cognitive operations, but linked to how children are able to process language. Andersen then applies them to the second language case, arguing that when they apply transparently in particular language combinations, transfer is more likely to occur. Comparing a Spanish-speaking and Japanese-speaking child, he uses principles like frequency, transparency, and congruence to account for greater transfer and greater success for the Spanish-speaking child.

A more recent and extensive processing viewpoint is associated with the work of Manfred Pienemann. Drawing on Lexical-Functional Grammar (Bresnan, 1982) and also Levelt's Speech Production Model (1989, 1999), he offers an incremental (i.e., cumulative) account of language development. This moves:

- from the lemma,
- to the category procedure (i.e., involving the lexical category of the lemma),
- to the phrasal procedure (which presupposes knowledge of the category of the head of the phrase),
- to the S-procedure and target language word order rules,
- ending with the subordinate clause procedure.

The order is the consequence of what information needs to be exchanged in order to achieve successful performance at each level, and as such, reflects the increasing development of the L2 system, and also the constraints introduced by limited capacity memory systems. In other words, each of the stages is a pre-requisite for more complex stages, and more complex stages cannot be used unless the earlier stages have been achieved. Pienemann (2005) contains a number of articles which apply Processability Theory to a range of different L1–L2 combinations, including Japanese, Chinese, Arabic, and so on.

Processability Theory (PT) is important for transfer. Pienemann et al. (2005) write: "The theoretical assumptions underlying our approach . . . include the following two hypotheses: (1) that L1 transfer is contrained by the processability of the given structure and (2) that the initial state of the L2 does not necessarily equal the final state of the L1 . . . because there is no guarantee that the given L1 structure is processable by the under-developed L2 parser." In other words, for transfer to be possible, *two* conditions have to be met: (1) there is something which could be transferred, and (2) the L2 learner has to be sufficiently advanced to be able to process that something effectively. This stands in strong contrast to the sort of claim made by the Competition Model, such as "the early second language learner should experience a massive amount of transfer from L1 to L2 . . . connectionist models . . . predict that all aspects of the first language that can possibly transfer to L2 will transfer" (MacWhinney, 1997: 119). Pienemann (1998) characterizes this position as 'bulk transfer' and argues that it will lead to problems if underlying processing conditions are not met, and also lead to the proliferation of unwieldy hypotheses. Pienemann et al. (2005) suggest: "it is hypothesized that such cases of L1 transfer occur as part of the overall reconstruction process. This means that L1 transfer is *developmentally moderated* and will occur when the structure to be transferred is processable within the developing L2 system." Pienemann et al. (2005) cite studies by Haberzettl (2000), showing the way in which advantages occur through typological similarity after a processing condition is met, and Kawaguchi (1999), showing how typological dissimilarity is not a disadvantage, for similar reasons.

Methodology

The central problem for methodology with interlanguage and transfer is to establish convincing explanations of data, where particular interpretations are shown not only to account for data, but also to be the best or only account of that data. Regarding cross-linguistic influences, any language learner is likely to have the conviction that they can point to examples of transfer, especially the more salient negative transfer. However, the introspective and anecdotal conviction that transfer is operative is not sufficient. Most fundamentally, there is the issue of data. In practice, naturally-occurring data is most commonly used, and attention drawn to the transfer that is seen to underlie learner productions, as reflected in linguistic analyses of the L1 and L2. This data has considerable positive features: naturalism, spontaneity, etc. However, there are also a number of difficulties. First there is the issue of frequency of occurrence. Forms which might reflect transfer may occur only rarely, so that waiting for relevant data can take a long time, and as a result, transfer could be underestimated. Second, there is the problem of avoidance (Schachter, 1974), where L2 speakers may know enough to know they have a problem, and so may find ways of expressing an idea differently. Again, the extent of transfer can be underestimated. Similarly, there is the issue of over-use of positively transferred forms. These may be correct in the L2 but not naturally used so frequently. In this case, transfer will again be underestimated, since its extent will go unnoticed.

A deeper problem, though, is the difficulties that arise from multiple determination. In an attempt to address this range of issues, Jarvis (2000) proposes three criteria that need to be met for transfer to be established:

1 *Similarities between native and L2 performance:* This is the most basic and most widely applied criterion, and requires that L2 performance look as if it is connected to the L1 system.
2 *Inter-group heterogeneity:* This means that L2 learners of a particular language who have different L1s should show differences in performance from one another, e.g., French and Japanese learners of English (say) should make (some) different errors. Meeting this criterion is important to rule out simplification or developmental explanations of an error.
3 *Intra-group homogeneity:* This focuses on the consistency of L2 performance of a group of learners who do share an L1, e.g., there should be some consistency in the Mandarin errors (say) of L1 Spanish learners of this language.

In some ways, these joint conditions may seem restrictive. However, they have the considerable virtue that they make it more likely that particular claims of transfer are sustainable and not accounted for by alternative explanations. Perhaps allied to these more strictly expressed criteria, there is also value in calling for multiple sources of data and converging evidence for the establishment of transfer, including spoken and written data, comprehension-based data, intuition, and even perception-based data, e.g., Kellerman (1978).

Regarding interlanguage studies, methodology has a slightly different role. Earlier studies were data driven, and the focus was on finding systematicity and progression in interlanguage development. This line of inquiry has continued to some degree, but now broader theoretical accounts have, as we have seen, assumed greater importance. As a result, theory and prediction have become more prominent, and simply identifying patterns in data is less central. One area which does have specific importance here is the role of longitudinal studies. Long (2003), for example, argues that such studies are essential if fossilization, one of the key concepts in interlanguage, is to be established, rather than simply assumed.

Interlanguage, Transfer, and Performance Models

An interesting development in recent years has been the more widespread adoption within SLA studies of psycholinguistic models of first language speech production. The most influential of these has been Levelt's (1989, 1999) Speech Production Model, and its direct adaptations to the second language case by, for example, De Bot (1992) and Kormos (2006). The models provide a general framework for speech production, especially with Levelt's stages of Conceptualization, Formulation, and Articulation. This may not currently explain very much about interlanguage or transfer, but it enables different effects to be located in a more satisfying manner, and linked to underlying knowledge systems. We can, in this way, perhaps relate pre-emptive avoidance to the Conceptualizer stage, and most transfer and interlanguage stages to the Formulator and Articulator stages. It is also possible, in this way, to re-interpret, slightly, performance accounts of transfer, in that the Conceptualizer may deliver to the Formulator communicative requirements which the Formulator cannot handle and so therefore the improvisation that the Formulator has to achieve draws on L1 sources, and transfer is the consequence. De Bot (1992) also makes proposals about common lexical stores which are drawn on in performance, and also that parallel speech plans may be produced by the bilingual, and so when difficulties in one plan are encountered the parallel L1 plan may be drawn on. Proposals such as these have not been elaborated into specific hypotheses about transfer, but it would seem likely that this approach will have increasing importance in the future, with the two areas being integrated in a more satisfactory manner.

Pedagogy

Earlier sections have covered theoretical and empirical aspects of interlanguage and language transfer, and considered the wider significance of learner errors.

But a central point with such research is that it can be used to inform pedagogic decisions. This may be at a general level, for example language distance may correlate with length of time different L1 speakers will take to reach designated levels of L2 proficiency. A concern for issues at this level may enable more effective macro decision making, which may impact upon national educational systems. This might include national coursebook series which are attuned to local knowledge about particular L1–L2 transfer problems.

But there are also micro issues. The point is that individual learners may be having difficulty and it may help a teacher to have resources to analyze error more effectively. This would be a particularly acute problem in contexts where learners do not share an L1, so that although the teacher will be dealing with a common L2, the range of L1s and therefore different potential transfer errors can be very large. There are publications available for this situation, at least for the learning of English, which provide resources on the difficulties which can be expected from speakers of different L1s. Swan and Smith (2001), for example, provide information for teachers of English outlining transfer difficulties for a wide range of different L1s. The assumption is that errors which are made by particular learners may have their origin in the L1, and therefore can only be intelligently handled if the teacher has knowledge of what is presumed to be the source of the error.

REFERENCES

Andersen, R. (1983). Transfer to somewhere. In S. Gass & L. Selinker (eds.), *Language Transfer in Language Learning*, (pp. 177–201). Rowley, MA: Newbury House.

Bates, E. & MacWhinney, B. (1982). Functionalist approaches to grammar. In E. Wanner & L. Gleitman (eds.), *Language Acquisition: The State of the Art*. New York: Cambridge University Press.

Bates, E. & MacWhinney, B. (1989). Functionalism and the competition model. In B. Macwhinney & E. Bates (eds.), *The Cross-Linguistic Study of Sentence Processing*. Cambridge: Cambridge University Press.

Bresnan, J. (1982). *The Mental Representation of Grammatical Relations*. Cambridge, MA: MIT Press.

Cook, V. (2000). Is *transfer* the right word? Paper presented at the International Pragmatics Association, Budapest, July 11.

Corder, S. Pit (1967). The significance of learners' errors. *International Review of Applied Linguistics*, 5, 161–169.

De Bot, K. (1992). A bilingual production model: Levelt's "Speaking" model adapted. *Applied Linguistics*, 13, 1–24.

Dulay, H. & Burt, M. (1974). Natural sequences in child second language acquisition. *Language Learning*, 24, 37–53.

Dulay, H., Burt, M., & Krashen, S. (1982). *Language Two*. New York: Oxford University Press.

Ellis, R. (1994). *The Study of Second Language Acquisition*. Oxford: Oxford University Press.

Ellis, N. & Schmidt, D. (1997). Morphology and longer-distance dependencies. *Studies in Second Language Acquisition*, 2, 145–171.

Haberzettl, S. (2000). Der Erwerb der Verbstellung in der Zweitsprache Deutsch durch Kinder mit typologisch verschiedenen Muttersprachen: Eine Auseinandersetzung mit Theorien zum Syntaxerwerb anhand von vier Fallstudien [The acquisition of verbs in German as a second language by children with typologically different mother tongues: An analysis of theories regarding syntax acquisition using four case studies]. Doctoral dissertation, Potsdam University.

Hansen, J. (2006). *Acquiring a Non-Native Phonology: Linguistic Constraints and Social Barriers*. New York: Continuum.

Jarvis, S. (2000). Methodological rigor in the study of transfer: Identifying L1 influence in the interlanguage lexicon. *Language Learning*, 50, 245–309.

Jarvis, S. & Odlin, T. (2000). Morphological type, spatial reference, and language transfer. *Studies in Second Language Acquisition*, 24, 387–418.

Kawaguchi, S. (1999). The acquisition of syntax and nominal ellipsis in JSL discourse. In P. Robinson (ed.), *Representation and Process: Proceedings of the Third Pacific Second Language Research Forum* (vol. 1, pp. 85–93). Tokyo: Aoyama Gakuin University.

Kellerman, E. (1978). Giving learners a break: Native language intuitions about transferability. *Working Papers in Bilingualism*, 15, 59–92.

Kormos, J. (2006). *Speech Production and Second Language Acquisition*. Mahwah, NJ: Lawrence Erlbaum.

Krashen, S. (1985). *The Input Hypothesis*. London: Longman.

Lado, R. (1957). *Linguistics across Cultures*. Ann Arbor: University of Michigan Press.

Levelt, W. (1989). *Speaking: From Intention to Articulation*. Cambridge, MA: MIT Press.

Levelt, W. (1999). Language production: A blueprint of the speaker. In C. Brown & P. Hagoort (eds.), *Neurocognition of Language* (pp. 83–122). Oxford: Oxford University Press.

Long, M. H. (2003). Stabilisation and fossilization in interlanguage development. In C. Doughty & M. H. Long (eds.), *Handbook of Second Language Acquisition* (pp. 487–536,). Oxford: Blackwell.

MacWhinney, B. (1997). Second language acquisition and the competition model. In A. De Groot & J. Kroll (eds.), *Tutorials in Bilingualism: Psycholinguistic Perspectives* (pp. 113–142). Mahwah, NJ: Lawrence Erlbaum.

MacWhinney, B. (2001). The competition model: The input, the context, and the brain. In P. Robinson (ed.), *Cognition and Second Language Instruction* (pp. 69–90). Cambridge: Cambridge University Press.

McDonald, J. L. (1987). Sentence interpretation in bilingual speakers of English and Dutch. *Applied Psycholinguistics*, 8, 379–413.

Newmark, L. & Reibel, D. (1968). Necessity and sufficiency in language learning. *International Review of Applied Linguistics in Language Teaching*, 6, 145–164.

Odlin, T. (1989). *Language Transfer*. Cambridge: Cambridge University Press.

Odlin, T. (1990). Word order, metalinguistic awareness, and constraints on foreign language learning. In B. Van Patten & J. Lee (eds.), *Second Language Acquisition and Foreign Language Learning* (pp. 95–117). Clevedon, UK: Multilingual Matters.

Odlin, T. (2003). Cross-linguistic influence. In C. Doughty & M. H. Long (eds.), *Handbook of Second Language Acquisition* (pp. 436–486). Oxford: Blackwell.

Olshtain, E. (1983). Sociocultural competence and language transfer: The case of apology. In S. Gass & L. Selinker (eds.), *Language Transfer in Language Learning* (pp. 232–249). Rowley, MA: Newbury House.

Pienemann, M. (1998). *Language Processing and Second Language Development: Processability Theory.*

Pienemann, M. (ed.) (2005). *Cross-Linguistic Aspects of Processability Theory.* Amsterdam: John Benjamins.

Pienemann M., Di Biase B., Kawaguchi, S., & Hakansson, G. (2005). Processability, typological distance, and L1 transfer. In M. Pienemann (ed.), *Cross-Linguistic Aspects of L2 Processability* (pp. 85–116). Amsterdam: John Benjamins.

Ringbom, H. (1987). *The Role of the First Language in Foreign Language Learning.* Clevedon, UK: Multilingual Matters.

Schachter, J. (1974). An error in error analysis. *Language Learning, 27,* 205–214.

Schwarz, B. & Sprouse, R. (1996). L2 cognitive states and the Full Transfer/ Full Access model. *Second Language Research, 12,* 40–72.

Selinker, L. (1972). Interlanguage. *International Review of Applied Linguistics, 10,* 209–231.

Skehan, P. (2001). Tasks and language performance. In M. Bygate, P. Skehan, & M. Swain (eds.), *Researching Pedagogic Tasks: Second Language Learning, Teaching, and Testing* (pp. 167–185). London: Longman.

Slobin, D. (1973). Cognitive prerequisites for the development of grammar. In C. Ferguson & D. Slobin (eds.), *Studies in Child Language Development* (pp. 175–208). New York: Holt, Rinehart & Winston.

Stockwell, R., Bowen, J., & Martin, J. (1965). *The Grammatical Structure of English and Spanish.* Chicago: Chicago University Press.

Swan, M. & Smith, B. (2001). *Learner English: A Teacher's Guide to Interference and Other Problems* (2nd edn.). Cambridge: Cambridge University Press. (1st edn. 1987.)

Tarone, E. (1985). Variability in interlanguage use: A study of style-shifting in morphology and syntax. *Language Learning, 35,* 373–403.

Vainikka, A. & Young-Scholten, M. (1998). The initial state in the L2 acquisition of phrase structure. In S. Flynn, G. Martohardjono, & W. O'Neil (eds.), *The Generative Study of Second Language Acquisition* (pp. 17–34). Mahwah, NJ: Lawrence Erlbaum.

Weinreich, U. (1953). *Languages in Contact.* The Hague: Mouton.

White, L. (2003a). *Second Language Acquisition and Universal Grammar.* Cambridge: Cambridge University Press.

White, L. (2003b). On the nature of interlanguage representation: Universal grammar in the second language. In C. Doughty & M. H. Long (eds.), *Handbook of Second Language Acquisition* (pp. 19–42). Oxford: Blackwell.

Zobl, H. (1980). The formal and developmental selectivity of L1 influence on L2 acquisition. *Language Learning, 30,* 43–57.

30 Second Language Acquisition and Ultimate Attainment

DAVID BIRDSONG AND JEE PAIK

Though sometimes confused with nativelikeness, the term "ultimate attainment" is properly used in a neutral sense in reference to the outcome of second language acquisition (L2A), irrespective of whether this outcome is similar to or different from nativelikeness. In the literature, ultimate attainment, end state attainment, and asymptotic attainment are often freely substituted.

Researchers often speak of varying levels of observed ultimate attainment, ranging upwards toward, and sometimes including, nativelikeness. When L2 ultimate attainment reaches a level that is inferior to nativelikeness, it is viewed as incomplete vis à vis the L2. For example, in a study of the acquisition of modal past unaccusative structures in Italian, Sorace (1993) found that highly proficient Anglophone learners of Italian could not decide between the auxiliary *avere* ('Mario non <u>ha</u> potuto venire') and the auxiliary *essere* ('Mario non é potuto venire'). The Anglophones' grammaticality judgments appeared indeterminate: there was no clear pattern in their responses. (The grammar of Italian permits both auxiliaries in such constructions, and native Italian controls in the Sorace study decisively accepted both auxiliaries.) The Anglophone data suggest an absence of representation for the L2 property in question. Thus the acquisition of the target grammar is considered to be incomplete.

In the same study, highly proficient Francophone learners of L2 Italian systematically selected *avere* as the only possible auxiliary in the same unaccusatives. Unlike the Anglophones' judgments, the Francophones' judgments were not equivocal, but determinate. The Francophones' representation is considered divergent since, as mentioned, both *essere* and *avere* auxiliaries are licensed in such contexts.

With respect to underlying representations, there are potentially several ways that L2 end-state grammars may diverge from those of natives: for example, they may instantiate non-compliance with constraints of Universal Grammar, configurational properties found in the L1 but not in the L2, configurational properties common to neither the L1 nor the L2, or non-nativelike optionality (Sorace, 2003).

Long (1990) was among the first to make a case for the relevance of ultimate attainment data to L2A theory. A central concern of L2A research is to identify, characterize, and understand putative constraints on L2 learning. Neither data relating to the pace of acquisition (e.g., numbers of contact hours required to reach a proficiency criterion) nor data relating to stages or developmental sequences in L2A speak directly to the acquisitional potential of the L2 learner. Without a clear mapping-out of the upper limits of attainment, researchers are deprived of key points of reference in their exploration of constraints on learning. Accordingly, in recent years, studies of ultimate attainment have become increasingly prevalent.

The study of ultimate attainment is not uncontroversial, however. Larsen-Freeman (2005: 196) argues that the "static view of finite linguistic competence" implied by the notion of ultimate attainment is conceptually and empirically at odds with the view that an individual's language (the L1 as well as the L2) is a dynamic system. However dynamic the outcomes of L1A and L2A may be, it is potentially very instructive to compare these outcomes. Indeed, as a complement to the notion of initial state (a construct of undeniable utility, to which few take exception) the idea of an acquisitional end state has considerable heuristic value. Beyond the initial state, what types and degrees of progress are typical, and what kinds and degrees of progress are possible? By sampling L2 learners at end state, one can get a sense of the range of ultimate outcomes. Comparisons with adult natives reveal convergences, divergences, and shortcomings – findings that contribute to the overall picture of attainment potential in L2A. This knowledge has driven research into L2 learning mechanisms, experiential and biological factors, and inter-individual differences in L2 learning style and ability. This knowledge also serves as the empirical basis of L2A theory. In comparing L2A with L1A – the most basic enterprise in L2A research – facts about outcomes simply cannot be ignored.

Empirical investigation of L2 ultimate attainment implies a determination that a learner has reached the end state of L2 learning. Although there is no universally accepted way of operationalizing the end state, researchers usually stipulate a minimum length of residency requirement in the L2 context. In the literature, the criterion is commonly five or more years' continuous or cumulative residence, with ranges to 15 years or more not unheard of. Needless to say, residency by itself is no guarantee of contact with the L2. Commonsensically, a given individual does not approach the end state of L2A without long-term immersion in the L2 and extensive interaction with native speakers.

Nativelike Ultimate Attainment

There is a negative and generally linear correlation between age of acquisition (AoA) – usually understood as age of immersion in the L2 context – and ultimate level of L2 attainment. By virtue of this relationship, the likelihood of nativelike ultimate attainment in subject groups with advancing AoA decreases (for discussion of the nature of the AoA-attainment function, see Birdsong, 2005a).

Some researchers claim that nativelike attainment for post-pubertal AoA is impossible, or is so rare as to be irrelevant (Bley-Vroman, 1989). However, in more than 20 behavioral studies conducted over the past 15 years, nativelike attainment has been observed at incidences ranging from 3 percent to 45 percent of the subjects sampled. In some of these studies, subjects were pre-screened to ensure high levels of L2 proficiency, resulting in an artificially inflated rate of nativelikeness, relative to the population of L2 learners at large. In most end-state studies, however, the subject sample is more representative of L2 learner populations. Consequently, the relatively modest rates of nativelikeness observed in these unbiased samples (typically, 10–15 percent) lend themselves more readily to generalization.

Low rates of authentic (unaccented) pronunciation are common in studies of late L2 learners at end state. For example, Flege, Munro, and MacKay (1995) studied 120 Italian natives with post-pubertal immersion in English; of these subjects, only 6 percent had no detectable accent, and none had begun speaking English after age 16. However, impressive rates of nativelike pronunciation among late learners (AoA > 12 years) were found by Bongaerts for Dutch natives learning English and French (Bongaerts, 1999). Subjects in the Bongaerts studies were required to read aloud sentences and lists of words in the L2. Their recorded samples, intermixed with those of natives and lower-achieving learners, were blindly rated by natives. To cite the most relevant result, three of nine highly proficient L2 French learners were found to have unaccented French pronunciation, this despite the fact that none of the learners had spent significant time in a Francophone context. Birdsong (2003) studied speech samples of 22 Anglophone late learners (AoA > 12 years) of French, along with samples from 17 native controls. From word-list reading tasks, acoustic measurements for Voice Onset Time (VOT) and vowel length were taken. For recordings of subjects reading aloud paragraphs in French, global ratings were given by three judges. Two of the Anglophone late learners performed like French natives on the acoustic measures and in global accent ratings.

Long (1990), Scovel (1988), and Hyltenstam and Abrahamsson (2000, 2003) have claimed that nativelikeness is observed in restricted domains of the target language. For example, a learner may display nativelike accuracy in certain areas of the grammar but not others; or the learner may have mastered surface morphosyntactic features of the language but have accented pronunciation. This contention is not upheld by the results of Marinova-Todd (2003). This study involved 30 late learners (AoA > 16 years) of English, with a minimum of five years of residence in an Anglophone environment. All had been informally screened for high proficiency in English. They and the 30 native controls were college educated. Subjects performed nine tasks, which tested both spontaneous and read-aloud pronunciation, morphosyntactic knowledge in both off-line and on-line tasks, lexical knowledge, and language use in narratives and discourse. Across all nine tasks, three late learners performed like natives and six others were nativelike on seven of the tasks. Adding to the significance of these results is the fact that some of the tasks involved spontaneous production, with no time allowed for reflection or metalinguistic analysis.

Certain types and domains of processing in the L2 appear to be resistant to nativelike attainment. Recent studies comparing highly proficient late L2 learners with monolingual natives have found non-nativelike lexical retrieval, structural ambiguity resolution, and perception of acoustic features such as consonant voicing and syllable stress (see references in Birdsong, 2005b). Researchers have observed quantitative differences involving speed and accuracy. Learners and natives appear also to diverge qualitatively. Clahsen and Felser (2006) argue that L2 learner grammars may represent non-nativelike syntactic configurations, which lead learners to perform shallow parses of sentence structure. Other processing differences between natives and proficient late learners have been revealed in eye-tracking studies (Frenck-Mestre, 2005).

To date, the majority of investigations of L2A have employed behavioral data. However, the past ten years have witnessed increasing numbers of studies – many of them targeting L2 learners at high degrees of proficiency and at the L2A end state – that employ brain-based data. With ERP methodology, researchers look at the temporal characteristics of language processing (the *when* question), especially the N400 and P600 electrophysiological components of semantic processing and syntactic processing, respectively. Imaging techniques, particularly fMRI, are able to identify the location of brain activity during various types of language processing (the *where* question). Both these major strands of investigation have tended to focus on two factors as potential predictors of degree of L1-like processing of the L2: AoA and level of proficiency. In the context of the present contribution, the most relevant generalization emerging from these studies is that both the temporal patterns as well as the regional brain activity patterns of highly proficient late L2 learners are largely congruent with those of early bilinguals or with the same subjects' patterns when processing their L1 (Green, 2005).

Tempering somewhat the findings relating to L2–L1 similarities in locus of processing, Stowe and Sabourin (2005) note that L2 processing tends to involve greater neural activity in a given brain region than L1 processing. This finding has been observed among both early and late highly proficient bilinguals. We also note that the degree of similarity in regional brain activity among L2 high-proficients varies considerably from study to study, as a function of task, sampling, and methodological differences between studies (Birdsong, 2006b). In ERP studies, the degree of congruence between highly proficient L2 users and native speakers often varies between the electrophysiological components (N400, P600 and Left Anterior Negativity (LAN), which may reflect sensitivity to ungrammaticality). Stowe and Sabourin (2005) note that different L1s may be associated with differences in some ERP signal components, as may be varying amounts of L2 input over the lifespan. They also point out that, even among L2 high-proficients, the amplitudes of ERP components tend to be greater than those of natives, suggesting more effortful processing in the L2.

Factors in Ultimate Attainment

To account for the generally discrepant outcomes of L1A and L2A, researchers have suggested a variety of factors. Among these are loss of neural plasticity (Penfield & Roberts, 1959); lateralization of cognitive neurofunction (Lenneberg, 1967); cognitive-developmental factors such as decline of implicit learning ability (DeKeyser, 2003); and affective-motivational factors such as psycho-social identification and acculturation with the L2 population (Moyer, 2004). Some of these are explored in more depth below. However, at this point it is important to mention two further types of explanation.

First, it must be recognized that, among users of multiple languages, not only does the L1 influence the L2 but the L2 also influences the L1. Reflexes of the L2 in the L1 can be found in VOT, collocations, grammaticality judgments, and syntactic processing (Cook, 2003). In these and other respects, the L1 performance of a bilingual may not be identical to a monolingual's performance in the same language. One would never ascribe such differences to deficient learning of the L1. By the same token, we can expect at least some L1 effects in the L2 (and thus departures from the performance of monolinguals) to be reflections of processes inherent in multiple language use, and not necessarily indicative of declines in language learning ability.

Secondly, experiential factors relating to L2 use and interaction with L2 speakers may be implicated in the ultimate attainment of learners. For example, Flege and Liu (2001) demonstrated that, other factors such as length of residence in the target language environment being equal, Chinese learners of L2 English with relatively high proportions of contact with English natives outperform lower-contact peers on tests relating to listening comprehension, grammatical knowledge, and perception of word-final English consonants. In general, however, the literature suggests that L2 input and/or use accounts for a small percentage of the variance in L2 ultimate attainment: around 10 percent, as opposed to 50 percent and more accounted for by AoA. As Flege (in press) points out, however, the apparently small role of L2 input and use may in part be an artifact of comparisons of this factor with the "macro-variable" of AoA. AoA is a proxy for several variables that have been hypothesized to affect ultimate L2 attainment, such as state of neural development; state of cognitive development; state of L1 phonetic category development; level of L1 proficiency; level of L1 representational entrenchment; and proportion of contact with native-speaker versus non-native L2 users. Were L2 use/input to be compared to these variables singly, we could more accurately quantify the relative contribution of use/input to L2 ultimate attainment.

The Age Function and Ultimate Attainment

The nature of the relationship between AoA and ultimate level of L2 attainment has been the subject of considerable study and vigorous debate.

Proponents of a critical period for L2A argue that nativelike ultimate attainment is possible only within a limited temporal span, or more precisely, across a limited range of AoA. The duration of this period has been variously put at (birth to) 3 years to more than 20 years. This duration may depend on what domain of language attainment is being assessed. It may also vary as a function of what biological and developmental factors are put forward as being responsible for, on the one hand, assuring nativelike ultimate attainment, and, on the other hand, compromising the acquisitional process. Thus, for example, it is widely believed that the critical period for nativelike attainment in pronunciation is shorter than that for morphosyntax.

A critical period for L2A implicates specific temporal and geometric features of the function that relates AoA to attainment. A period wherein nativelike attainment is possible would be represented by a flat segment at ceiling, on the left side (beginning) of the age function. This would be followed by a downward slope extending rightward. Some proponents of the critical period (Johnson & Newport, 1989; Pinker, 1994) posit an end to this decline, at the point where neurocognitive maturation is complete. The decline would thus be followed by a leveling off of the function, which would be represented by a second flat segment at the right side. The idea behind positing such a floor effect is that, once maturation is complete, there are no longer any neurological developments that would cause the L2 attainment function to depart from a horizontal trajectory.

A review of the behavioral literature in L2A end-state studies (Birdsong, 2005a) reveals some evidence that is consistent with the flat segment at the beginning of the AoA function, but little if any support for the second segment. Instead, from these studies the most reliable feature of the AoA function is an ongoing, indefinite decline in ultimate attainment over increasing AoA. In other words, age-related declines in L2 attainment appear not to be bounded or confined to a period.

Additional problems relate to timing. The ages at which declines in attainment are purported to start varies considerably from researcher to researcher, as do the ages at which declines are thought to end. Curiously, in the literature there is no unanimity as to whether maturation is thought to condition the beginning of age effects, the end of the effects, or both.

Cognitive Aging and Biological Aging

As suggested above, it is important to distinguish temporally-bounded age effects that are putatively maturational in nature from effects that persist across the lifespan. The latter type of effect is observed in both the cognitive literature and in the biological literature on aging.

Birdsong (2006b) examines the linkage of these declines with declines in L2 processing and acquisition over age. Three general areas of cognitive aging are identified: decreases in processing speed, decreases in the ability to suppress irrelevant information, and declines in working memory capacity. Each of these capacities is implicated in language acquisition and use. (Because much of L1 processing is automatized, the effects of these declines in L1 use are likely to be less pronounced than in the L2 case.) Cognitive declines are not observed to the same degree across the board. Significant declines beginning in young adulthood are seen in working memory, associative memory, episodic memory, and incremental learning. In contrast, relatively mild declines are found in tasks involving priming, implicit memory, procedural memory, recent memory, and semantic memory. When processing new information, and under demands of speed and accuracy, performance declines begin in the early twenties and the decline over the remainder of the lifespan is continuous and typically linear. A range of inter-individual differences is observed. In general, these facts are compatible with behavioral evidence in L2 use and acquisition.

In the biological aging literature, researchers have identified changes in neurochemical and hormonal levels that are associated with declines in cognitive performance. Acetylcholine molecules mediate a variety of neural functions, including learning, memory, and attention. In normal aging, declines of acetylcholine and cholinergic receptors start in about the fourth decade of life and progress thereafter. With age and stress, abnormally high levels of cortisol are created in the brain. These increases have been explicitly linked to hippocampal atrophy, resulting in declines in ability to lay down new memories, particularly declarative memories. Age-related changes in estrogen levels have been associated with functional declines in verbal processing and production. Of particular note are declines over age in dopamine receptors, starting in the early twenties. Dopamine is known to mediate a number of motoric and higher-order cognitive functions, some of which are involved in language learning and processing (Bäckman & Farde, 2005). Schumann et al. (2004) argue that dopamine may be involved in motivation to learn a second language and in reinforcement of learning. It is also thought to be necessary for "defossilization," the process by which automated non-targetlike performance is undone, thus removing a barrier to nativelike attainment.

Birdsong (2006b) also considers the question of age-related declines in regional brain volume and the possible effects of such shrinkages on cognitive processes underlying L2 acquisition and use. Longitudinal in vivo studies using MRI reveal four brain regions particularly susceptible to volumetric declines: the entorhinal cortex, hippocampus, frontal lobe, and caudate nucleus (Raz, 2005). Declines are observed to be linear. The onset of decline varies from region to region, with declines in the caudate, cerebellum, and cortical structures beginning in adolescence. Once begun, the declines appear to be linear and unbounded, and thereby consistent with L2 behavioral evidence. However, the relationship between brain volume decreases and observed cognitive declines may not be straightforward in all cases. Raz (2000: 65) suggests that the expression of cognitive deficits begins only after structural deterioration has reached a certain threshold, and thereafter the decline is linear. Obviously, this precludes direct inferencing from regional brain volume decreases to specific cognitive deficits that plausibly underlie difficulties in L2 learning and processing.

Psycho-Social Variables and Nativelikeness

Different levels of L2 ultimate attainment have been linked to individual differences along psycho-social and sociocultural dimensions. People vary in their experiences of society and culture, their ideologies of the L1 and the L2, and in their reasons for learning the L2. Individuals' goals for the outcome of learning vary as well. To a certain degree, therefore, the level of attainment and the way L2 knowledge is implemented in L2 use are determined by the learner (Gillette, 1994). In such instances it would be pointless to speak of deficiencies in learning ability.

Conversely, the desire to assimilate is often associated with high L2 proficiency, near-nativelikeness, and nativelikeness. Piller (2002) looked at L2 speakers who desire to *pass for* native speakers of the L2. Conversations with natives involve psychologically motivated "identity play"; those who are most eager to be identified as natives, and who in some sense take on an identity associated with the L2, are often able to fool their native interlocutors. In her sociolinguistic study of the linguistic practices of bilingual couples, Piller (2002) found that some 40 percent of the individual subjects (with AoAs between 15 and 29) claimed to have attained high-level proficiency and were able to pass for natives on certain occasions. The degree to which L2 learners emulate the performance of natives when speaking with them can vary from one interactional context to the next. Nativelikeness also depends on whether the L2 speaker wishes to be dealt with as a foreigner (which sometimes provokes stereotypical attitudes from interlocutors). Many L2 users seem to weigh, consciously or not, the benefits and disadvantages of the passing-for-native act; this calculus plays out in their L2 speech, with resulting variations in perceived nativelikeness.

Future Directions

Moving forward, psychological, linguistic, and neuro-cognitive investigations of ultimate attainment in L2A will undoubtedly bring clarity, and perhaps some degree of resolution, to the issues raised thus far. Additional concerns that may figure in future research include the following:

L2 dominance

In both the behavioral and brain-based literature, studies of L2–L1 attainment differences have often dealt with samples of highly proficient learners. For example, earlier we considered processing studies that showed qualitative and quantitative differences between highly proficient L2 users and native speakers. Birdsong (2006a) suggests that such results should not necessarily be construed as meaning that L2–L1 processing differences are inevitable, because it is not clear that L2 high-proficients, as a group, represent the upper limits of L2 attainment. Under-represented in L2A research are individuals whose L2, particularly if learned late, is their dominant language. For a given individual, dominance can be operationalized psycholinguistically, for example by comparing recall or recognition of words heard under noise in the L1 with this performance in the L2. Until processing studies focus on individuals who are strongly L2-dominant, it is premature to conclude that the upper limits of processing in late L2A are inferior to those in L1A. (To round out the picture, it would be instructive to have comparisons of late L2-dominants with early bilinguals – both L1- and L2-dominants.) The same line of evidentiary logic could be applied to individuals who rarely use their L1 – frequency of use being another way to operationalize dominance – as well as to L1-attriters, whose L2 processing may be less impacted by influence of the L1 than, say, balanced bilinguals or high-L2-proficients.

Approximating the L1 learning context

If one were interested in determining the upper bounds of L2 attainment, it would be important to study L2 learners under conditions of immersion and interaction with natives that are known to favor learning. One candidate approach would be to approximate, within the limits of practicality, the external conditions of the L1 learner: full immersion in the L2, linguistic interactions solely with L2 speakers, and no contact whatsoever with the L1.

As an extreme illustration of such an approach, consider the study of Pallier et al. (2003). Eight children, born in Korea and raised speaking Korean, were adopted and moved to the Paris area at ages ranging from 3 to 8 years. As the adoptees were completely deprived of contact with their L1, French replaced Korean as their everyday language. Behavioral tests on the subjects, now in their adult years, revealed no evidence of knowledge of Korean. Similarly, fMRI imagery revealed no brain activation when listening to Korean. To the extent measurable by these methods, it appeared that their first language had been "lost." Most notable in the context of upper limits of L2 attainment is the fact that the adoptees performed like L1 French controls on formal and informal measures of French knowledge and use (Ventureyra, 2005). This finding leads one to wonder what levels of L2 ultimate attainment could be reached if one could somehow "subtract" the influences of representational entrenchment of the L1 (MacWhinney, 2005), along with the influences of routine use and maintenance of the L1.

Ultimate understanding of ultimate attainment

The preceding discussion points to the desirability of isolating the limits on L2A that might be artifacts of increasingly entrenched L1. More generally, it is by teasing apart – conceptually at least, and empirically to the degree that our methods permit – the candidate constraining factors in L2A that we can begin to paint the picture of L2A in its full richness and complexity. As we have seen in this contribution, the candidate factors may relate to the neurobiology of the species, cognitive aging, socio-psychological orientations toward learning, and experiential variables such as amount of L2 use.

Future inquiry will not, of course, be limited to these factors. For example, it will be useful to further specify the components of L2-learning aptitude and the role of each component in determining L2 ultimate attainment (Robinson, 2002). In addition, we expect continued interest in the possibility that training can contribute to nativelikeness in low-level processes such as auditory discrimination (McClelland, Fiez, & McCandliss, 2002) and imitation ability (Bongaerts, 1999). If for no other reason, the range of ultimate outcomes in L2A compels examination of such factors which by their nature vary quantitatively or qualitatively from one individual to the next.

REFERENCES

Bäckman, Lars & Farde, Lars (2005). The role of dopamine systems in cognitive aging. In Roberto Cabeza, Lars Nyberg, & Denise Park (eds.), *Cognitive Neuroscience of Aging: Linking Cognitive and Cerebral Aging* (pp. 58–84). New York: Oxford University Press.

Birdsong, David (2003). Authenticité de prononciation en français L2 chez les apprenants tardifs anglophones: analyses segmentales et globales [Nativelike pronunciation in L2 French among Anglophone late learners: Segmental and global analyses]. *Acquisition et Interaction en Langue Etrangère* [Acquisition and Interaction in Foreign Language], 18, 17–36.

Birdsong, David (2005a). Interpreting age effects in second language acquisition. In Judith F. Kroll & Annette M. B. DeGroot (eds.), *Handbook of Bilingualism: Psycholinguistic Perspectives* (pp. 109–127). New York: Oxford University Press.

Birdsong, David (2005b). Why not fossilization. In ZhaoHong Han & Terence Odlin (eds.), *Studies of Fossilization in Second Language Acquisition* (pp. 173–188). Clevedon, UK: Multilingual Matters.

Birdsong, David (2006a). Dominance, proficiency, and second language grammatical processing. *Applied Psycholinguistics*, 27, 46–49.

Birdsong, David (2006b). Age and second language acquisition and processing: A selective overview. *Language Learning*, 56, 9–49.

Bley-Vroman, Robert (1989). What is the logical problem of foreign language learning? In Susan Gass & Jacqueline Schachter (eds.), *Linguistic Perspectives on Second Language Acquisition* (pp. 41–68). Cambridge: Cambridge University Press.

Bongaerts, Theo (1999). Ultimate attainment in L2 pronunciation: The case of very advanced late learners. In David Birdsong (ed.), *Second Language Acquisition and the Critical Period Hypothesis* (pp. 133–159). Mahwah, NJ: Lawrence Erlbaum.

Clahsen, Harald & Felser, Claudia (2006). Grammatical processing in language learners. *Applied Psycholinguistics, 27*, 3–42.

Cook, Vivian (ed.) (2003). *Effects of the Second Language on the First*. Clevedon, UK: Multilingual Matters.

Dekeyser, Robert M. (2003). Implicit and explicit learning. In Catherine Doughty & Michael H. Long (eds.), *The Handbook of Second Language Acquisition* (pp. 313–348). Malden, MA: Blackwell.

Flege, James E. (in press). Give input a chance! In Thorsten Piske & Martha Young-Scholten (eds.), *Input Matters*. Clevedon, UK: Multilingual Matters.

Flege, James E. & Liu, Serena (2001). The effect of experience on adult's acquisition of a second language. *Studies in Second Language Acquisition, 23*, 527–552.

Flege, James E., Munro, Murray, & MacKay, Ian (1995). Factors affecting the degree of perceived foreign accent in a second language. *Journal of the Acoustical Society of America, 97*, 3125–3134.

Frenck-Mestre, Cheryl (2005). Ambiguities and anomalies: What can eye movements and event-related potentials reveal about second language sentence processing? In Judith F. Kroll & Annette M. B. DeGroot (eds.), *Handbook of Bilingualism: Psycholinguistic Perspectives* (pp. 268–281). New York: Oxford University Press.

Gillette, Barbara (1994). The role of learner goals in L2 success. In James P. Lantolf & Gabriela Appel (eds.), *Vygotskian Approaches to Second Language Research* (pp. 195–214). Norwood, NJ: Ablex.

Green, David W. (2005). The neurocognition of recovery patterns in bilingual aphasics. In Judith F. Kroll & Annette M. B. DeGroot (eds.), *Handbook of Bilingualism: Psycholinguistic Perspectives* (pp. 516–530). New York: Oxford University Press.

Hyltenstam, Kenneth & Abrahamsson, Niclas (2000). Who can become native-like in a second language? All, some, or none? On the maturational constraints controversy on second language acquisition. *Studia Linguistica, 54*, 150–166.

Hyltenstam, Kenneth & Abrahamsson, Niclas (2003). Maturational constraints in SLA. In Catherine J. Doughty & Michael H. Long (eds.), *The Handbook of Second Language Acquisition* (pp. 539–588). Malden, MA: Blackwell.

Johnson, Jacqueline & Newport, Elissa (1989). Critical period effects in second language learning: The influence of maturational state on the acquisition of English as a second language. *Cognitive Psychology, 21*, 60–90.

Larsen-Freeman, Diane (2005). Second language acquisition and the issue of fossilization: There is no end, and there is no state. In ZhaoHong Han & Terence Odlin (eds.), *Studies of Fossilization in Second Language Acquisition* (pp. 189–200). Clevedon, UK: Multilingual Matters.

Lenneberg, Eric H. (1967). *Biological Foundations of Language*. New York: Wiley.

Long, Michael H. (1990). Maturational constraints on language development. *Studies in Second Language Acquisition, 12*, 251–285.

MacWhinney, Brian (2005). Emergent fossilization. In ZhaoHong Han & Terence Odlin (eds.), *Studies of Fossilization in Second Language Acquisition* (pp. 134–156). Clevedon, UK: Multilingual Matters.

Marinova-Todd, Stefka H. (2003). Comprehensive analysis of ultimate attainment in adult second language acquisition. Unpublished doctoral dissertation, Harvard University.

McClelland, James L., Fiez, Julie A., & McCandliss, Bruce D. (2002). Teaching the /r/-/l/ discrimination to Japanese adults: Behavioral and neural aspects. *Physiology and Behavior*, 77, 657–662.

Moyer, Alene (2004). *Age, Accent and Experience in Second Language Acquisition.* Clevedon, UK: Multilingual Matters.

Pallier, Christophe, Dehaene, Stanislas, Poline, Jean-Baptiste, LeBihan, Denis, Argenti, Anthony M., Dupoux, Emmanuel, & Mehler, Jacques (2003). Brain imaging of language plasticity in adopted adults: Can a second language replace the first? *Cerebral Cortex*, 13, 155–161.

Penfield, Wilder & Roberts, Lamar (1959). *Speech and Brain Mechanisms.* Princeton, NJ: Princeton University Press.

Piller, Ingrid (2002). Passing for a native speaker: Identity and success in second language learning. *Journal of Sociolinguistics*, 6, 179–206.

Pinker, Steven (1994). *The Language Instinct: How the Mind Creates Language.* New York: William Morrow.

Raz, Naftali (2000). Aging of the brain and its impact on cognitive performance: Integration of structural and functional findings. In Fergus I. M. Craik & Timothy A. Salthouse (eds.), *The Handbook of Aging and Cognition* (pp. 1–90). Mahwah, NJ: Erlbaum.

Raz, Naftali (2005). The aging brain observed in vivo: differential changes and their modifiers. In Roberto Cabeza, Lars Nyberg, & Denise Park (eds.), *Cognitive Neuroscience of Aging: Linking Cognitive and Cerebral Aging* (pp. 19–57). New York: Oxford University Press.

Robinson, Peter (2002). Effects of individual differences in intelligence, aptitude and working memory on adult incidental SLA: A replication and extension of Reber, Walkenfield and Hernstadt, 1991. In Peter Robinson (ed.), *Individual Differences and Instructed Language Learning* (pp. 211–266). Amsterdam: John Benjamins.

Schumann, John H., Crowell, Sheila, Jones, Nancy E., Lee, Namhee, Schuchert, Sara A., & Wood, Lee A. (2004). *The Neurobiology of Learning: Perspectives from Second Language Acquisition.* Mahwah, NJ: Lawrence Erlbaum.

Scovel, Thomas (1988). *A Time to Speak: A Psycholinguistic Inquiry into the Critical Period for Human Speech.* Rowley, MA: Newbury House.

Sorace, Antonella (1993). Incomplete vs divergent representations of unaccusativity in non-native grammars of Italian. *Second Language Research*, 9, 22–47.

Sorace, Antonella (2003). Near-nativeness. In Catherine J. Doughty & Michael H. Long (eds.), *The Handbook of Second Language Acquisition* (pp. 130–1–51). Malden, MA: Blackwell.

Stowe, Laurie A. & Sabourin, Laura (2005). Imaging the processing of a second language: Effects of maturation and proficiency on the neural processes involved. *International Review of Applied Linguistics in Language Teaching*, 43, 329–353.

Ventureyra, Valerie A. (2005). À la recherche de la langue perdue: étude de l'attrition de la première langue chez des coréens adoptés en France [In search of lost language: A psycholinguistic study of first language attrition among Korean adoptees in France]. Unpublished doctoral dissertation, École des Hautes Études en Sciences Sociales, Paris.

FURTHER READING

Bialystok, Ellen & Hakuta, Kenji (1999). Confounded age: Linguistic and cognitive factors in age differences for second language acquisition. In David Birdsong (ed.), *Second Language Acquisition and the Critical Period Hypothesis* (pp. 161–181). Mahwah, NJ: Lawrence Erlbaum.

Davies, Alan (2003). *The Native Speaker: Myth and Reality*. Clevedon, UK: Multilingual Matters.

Lantolf, James P. & Pavlenko, Aneta (2001). (S)econd (L)anguage (A)ctivity Theory: Understanding language learners as people. In M. Phyllis Breen (ed.), *Learner Contributions to Language Learning* (pp. 141–158). Harlow, UK: Longman.

Park, Denise C. (2000). The basic mechanisms accounting for age-related decline in cognitive function. In Denise C. Park & Norbert Schwarz (eds.), *Cognitive Aging: A Primer* (pp. 3–21). Philadelphia: Psychology Press.

Singleton, David & Ryan, Lisa (2004). *Language Acquisition: The Age Factor*. Clevedon, UK: Multilingual Matters.

31 Explicit Form-Focused Instruction and Second Language Acquisition

ROD ELLIS

Introduction

There are two good reasons for examining the effect that explicit form-focused instruction (FFI) has on second language (L2) acquisition. The first is *pedagogical*. Language instruction has traditionally been of the explicit kind, based on linguistic syllabuses. There is an obvious need, however, to ascertain whether explicit FFI is effective. The second reason is *theoretical*. Current theories of L2 acquisition (e.g., N. Ellis, 2002, 2005) distinguish two types of linguistic knowledge – implicit and explicit knowledge. Theoretical differences exist with regard to the potential for explicit instruction to affect these two types of knowledge. DeKeyser (1998), for example, adopts a strong interface position, arguing that instruction consisting of explicit rule-presentation followed by communicative practice can guide the learner from a declarative representation of a linguistic feature to a procedural one. In contrast, Doughty (2003a) claims that explicit instruction only aids the development of metalinguistic knowledge (i.e., explicit knowledge) and does not contribute to the acquisition of implicit knowledge.

Definitions

The term *instruction* will be used narrowly to refer to attempts to intervene in the process of interlanguage development. I will not concern myself with instruction directed at skill development (i.e., listening, reading, speaking, or writing). In Ellis (1997), I distinguish two kinds of instruction: Communication-Focused Instruction and Form-Focused Instruction (FFI). The former involves the use of tasks that focus learners' attention on meaning. The latter refers to "any pedagogical effort used to draw the learner's attention to language form" (Spada, 1997: 73). Our concern here is with one type of FFI, explicit FFI.

Table 31.1   Implicit and explicit forms of form-focused instruction (Housen & Pierrard, 2006)

Implicit FFI	*Explicit FFI*
• *attracts* attention to target form	• directs attention to target form
• is delivered *spontaneously* (e.g., in an otherwise communication-oriented activity)	• is *predetermined* and *planned* (e.g., as the main focus and goal of a teaching activity)
• is unobtrusive (minimal interruption of communication of meaning)	• is obtrusive (interruption of communicative meaning)
• presents target forms in context	• presents target forms in isolation
• makes no use of metalanguage	• uses metalinguistic terminology (e.g., rule explanation)
• encourages free use of the target form	• involves controlled practice of target form

Following DeKeyser (2003), I will distinguish explicit/implicit instruction and deductive/inductive instruction. Explicit FFI involves "some sort of rule being thought about during the learning process" (DeKeyser, 1995). In other words, learners are encouraged to develop metalinguistic awareness of the rule. This can be achieved deductively, as when a rule is given to the learners, or inductively, as when the learners are asked to work out a rule for themselves from an array of data illustrating the rule. Implicit instruction is directed at enabling learners to infer rules without awareness. Thus it contrasts with explicit instruction in that there is an absence of awareness of what is being learned. Housen and Pierrard (2006) differentiate implicit and explicit FFI in terms of a number of characteristics, as shown in Table 31.1.

The distinction between explicit and implicit FFI needs to be considered in relation to another common distinction. Long (1991) distinguished "focus on forms" and "focus on form" instruction. Focus-on-forms is evident in the traditional approach to grammar teaching based on a synthetic syllabus. The underlying assumption is that language learning is a process of accumulating distinct entities. In such an approach, learners are required to treat language primarily as an "object" to be studied and practised bit by bit and to function as "students" rather than as "users" of the language. In contrast, focus-on-form "draws students' attention to linguistic elements as they arise incidentally in lessons whose overriding focus is on meaning or communication" (Long, 1991: 45–46). Such an approach, according to Long and Robinson (1998), is to be distinguished not only from focus-on-forms but also from focus-on-meaning, where there is no attempt to induce attention to linguistic form at all. It is clear that, as defined, focus-on-forms entails explicit language teaching of the deductive or inductive kind. But what of focus-on-form instruction? Does this correspond to implicit instruction? The answer would seem to lie in how learners' attention to linguistic elements takes place. If the means used are implicit types of corrective feedback (such as unobtrusive reformulations of learners' erroneous utterances), then the instruction can be considered implicit in terms of the definition given above. On the other hand, if the means involve the provision of more explicit types of corrective feedback (for example, overt correction or metalinguistic explanation) then focus-on-form can be considered explicit. To sum up, whereas focus-on-forms involves explicit instruction, focus-on-form can involve both implicit and explicit instruction.

The terms explicit and implicit instruction can only be defined from a perspective external to the learner. That is, it is the teacher, materials writer, or course designer who determines whether the instruction is explicit or implicit (or, more likely, a mixture of the two). In contrast, the terms implicit/explicit learning and intentional/incidental learning can only be considered in relation to the learner's perspective. Thus, implicit learning takes place when the learner has internalized a linguistic feature without awareness of having done so while explicit learning involves awareness. Schmidt (2001), however, has pointed out that there are two types of awareness: awareness as noticing and awareness as understanding. The former involves conscious attention to "surface elements" (Schmidt, 2001). This would suggest that there is no such thing as complete implicit learning, as some degree of awareness (at the level of noticing) is required. Thus, for Schmidt a better definition of implicit learning might be "learning without any metalinguistic awareness." Other researchers (e.g., Williams, 2005), however, have argued that learning without awareness is possible. N. Ellis (2005: 306) claims that "the vast majority of our cognitive processing is unconscious." Thus there is no consensual definition of implicit learning. Explicit learning is less problematic: it is learning that involves metalinguistic awareness. The intentional/incidental distinction is also less problematic. Learners learn intentionally when they elect to focus their conscious attention on some specific property of the L2 that they want to learn. An obvious example would be the attempt to memorize the conjugation of an L2 verb. Learners learn incidentally when they internalize L2 features without intending to do so (but not necessarily without awareness). A good example would be the acquisition of vocabulary as a result of reading a novel for pleasure.

What then is the relationship between explicit/implicit instruction and these other distinctions? Self-evidently explicit instruction is directed at intentional, explicit learning while implicit instruction is aimed at implicit, incidental learning. However, these correlations are not exact ones as the external, instructional perspective may not match the internal, learner's perspective (Batstone, 2002). For example, the teacher may provide the learners with an explicit explanation of the use of the English definite and indefinite articles but, assuming that this explanation is provided through the medium of the L2 and that the learner is not motivated to attend to the teacher's explanation, the learner may end up acquiring implicitly and incidentally a number of lexical items that happen to figure in the teacher's explanation. In other words, a learner can always elect to respond to what the teacher says as "input" rather than as "information." In such a case, explicit instruction can result in implicit learning as a result of the incidental noticing of instances of language. This is an important point to consider when evaluating the results of research that has investigated the effects of explicit instruction. We cannot expect explicit instruction to be effective in achieving its goals unless we are sure that the instructional perspective matches the learner's perspective. Also, we need to recognize that explicit instruction, like implicit instruction, affords opportunities for implicit, incidental learning.

Finally, we will consider definitions of explicit and implicit L2 knowledge. In Ellis (2004), I characterized explicit knowledge as conscious, declarative, accessible only through controlled processing, verbalizable, learnable (in the sense that any piece of factual information is learnable), and typically employed when learners experience some kind of linguistic problem. Implicit knowledge, in contrast, is unconscious (i.e., we are not aware of what we know implicitly), procedural, accessible for automatic processing, not verbalizable (except as an explicit representation), "acquirable" (i.e., can be internalized implicitly), and typically employed in unproblematic, free-flowing communication. Disagreement exists as to whether these two types of knowledge are distinct and separate (as Paradis, 1994 claims) or whether they comprise poles on a continuum (i.e., there are degrees of explicitness and implicitness). Along with N. Ellis (2005), I have argued for the former position. Disagreement also exists as to whether there is any interaction between these two knowledge sources. Krashen (1981) adopted a non-interface position (i.e., argued they did not interact) whereas other researchers, such as myself and N. Ellis, have argued for an interface position. The nature of this interface is a point of further controversy. Whereas supporters of a "skill-learning theory" of L2 acquisition (e.g., DeKeyser, 1998) have argued for a strong interface (i.e., explicit knowledge can convert into implicit knowledge through communicative practice), supporters of a "consciousness-raising theory" (e.g., R. Ellis, 1993; N. Ellis, 2005) have staked out the case for a weak interface position (i.e., explicit knowledge does not convert directly into explicit knowledge but rather facilitates its development indirectly by inducing attention to form).

Again, no straightforward correlation can be expected between explicit/implicit instruction and the development of these two types of knowledge. The goal of explicit instruction is not just explicit knowledge but rather implicit knowledge, with explicit knowledge seen just as a starting point. In other words explicit instruction is premised on either a strong or a weak version of the interface hypothesis. It is also possible that implicit instruction will result in explicit knowledge. This might occur if learners are not developmentally ready to incorporate the target of instruction into their interlanguage systems and thus temporarily store information about the target as explicit knowledge (see Gass, 1997). It should also be noted that the effects of instruction on learners' ability to use the target structure in unplanned language use may not be immediately evident; they may only emerge later when explicit knowledge is put to work as "pattern recognizers for linguistic constructions" (N. Ellis, 2005).

It is clearly crucial to distinguish the effects of instruction in terms of the explicit/implicit knowledge distinction. Drawing on a meta-analysis of FFI studies by Norris and Ortega (2000), which showed that the bulk of the instruments used in studies to date involved metalinguistic judgments (e.g., grammaticality judgment tests), selected responses (e.g., multiple choice items), or constrained constructed responses (e.g., sentence combining exercises), Doughty (2003b) argued that such assessment instruments do not measure linguistic competence (i.e., implicit knowledge) but rather "they merely require knowledge of language as an object" (i.e., explicit knowledge; p. 273). She claimed that the use of such measures favors explicit instruction and that the true test of the effect of any kind of instruction is whether it results in implicit knowledge. To achieve this, a different kind of assessment instrument is needed – what Norris and Ortega call "freely constructed responses" (e.g., a written composition or an oral narrative). In Ellis (2005) I presented the results of a study of a battery of measures of L2 acquisition, which indicated that an elicited oral imitation test could also serve as a measure of implicit knowledge.

Types of Explicit Instruction

Types of explicit instruction can be distinguished by juxtaposing two dimensions, as shown in Table 31.2. The deductive/inductive dimension has already been considered. Proactive FFI consists of interventions directed at preventing error; reactive FFI is found in interventions that address an error when it has been committed.

Table 31.2   Types of explicit form-focused instruction

	Deductive	*Inductive*
Proactive	Metalinguistic explanation	Consciousness-raising tasks Practice activities • production based • comprehension based
Reactive	Explicit correction Metalinguistic feedback	Repetition Corrective recasts

Proactive/deductive explicit FFI

This type of explicit FFI is realized by means of metalinguistic explanations. These typically consist of information about a specific linguistic property supported by examples. Metalinguistic explanations can be provided orally by the teacher or in written form in a textbook or reference grammar.

Proactive/inductive explicit FFI

Proactive/inductive explicit FFI involves either consciousness-raising (CR) tasks or practice exercises. In Ellis (1991) I defined a CR task as "a pedagogic activity where the learners are provided with L2 data in some form and required to perform some operation on or with it, the purpose of which is to arrive at an explicit understanding of some regularity in the data" (p. 239). Thus, CR tasks constitute a form of discovery learning.

Practice activities constitute a proactive/inductive type of explicit FFI only when the students are either told or implicitly expected to derive meta-linguistic awareness of the target feature. That is, they invite intentional rather than incidental learning. Practice activities can involve production, in which case they can be "text-manipulating" (i.e., involve what Norris and Ortega (2000) called "constrained constructed response") or "text-creating" (i.e., involve the use of tasks that require learners to employ their own linguistic resources). Production activities can also be error-avoiding (most commonly) or error-inducing, as in Tomsello and Herron's (1988) study. In the latter case, learners are led into making overgeneralization errors and then receive corrective feed-back. Practice activities can also be comprehension based. In this case they take the form of "interpretation tasks" (Ellis, 1995) consisting of structured input (i.e., input that has been seeded with the target structure) and some form of operation (e.g., carrying out an action or pointing at an object in a picture) to demonstrate comprehension.

Reactive/deductive explicit FFI

Two types of FFI are reactive/deductive in nature: explicit correction and metalinguistic feedback. Lyster and Ranta (1997) define explicit correction "as the explicit provision of the correct form" (p. 46) accompanied by a clear indication that what the learner said was incorrect. They define metalinguistic feedback as follows:

> Metalinguistic feedback contains either comments, information, or questions related to the well-formedness of the student's utterance, without explicitly providing the correct form. (p. 47)

Reactive/inductive explicit FFI

The key characteristic of this type of explicit FFI is that learners are provided with feedback that is unambiguously corrective in force by indicating that an error has been committed. Two kinds of corrective feedback manifest this characteristic: repetition and corrective recasts. The former involves the repetition of the student's erroneous utterance with the location of the error signaled by means of emphatic stress. A corrective recast reformulates the learner's erroneous utterance with the correct form highlighted intonationally, as in this example from Doughty and Varela (1998):

> L: I think that the worm will go under the soil.
> T: I *think* that the worm *will* go under the soil?
> L: (no response)
> T: I *thought* that the worm *would* go under the soil.
> L: I *thought* that the worm *would* go under the soil.

Such feedback can be considered inductive because learners are required to carry out a cognitive comparison of their original and reformulated utterances. I have chosen to consider repetition and corrective recasts as explicit (see Ellis & Sheen, 2006). However, other researchers (e.g., Long, 2006) view them as implicit.

A Review of Explicit FFFI Studies

In this review, I will distinguish between explicit proactive and reactive FFI.

Proactive explicit FFI studies

The review will be organized in terms of the different research questions which the studies have addressed.

Question 1: What is the effect of different ways of providing metalinguistic information on L2 learning?

In an important article, Sharwood Smith (1981) proposes that explicit teaching techniques can vary in terms of the degree of elaboration or conciseness with which the explicit information is presented and the degree of explicitness or intensity of the information. He distinguished four types, as shown in Table 31.3. However, little effort has been made to investigate the specific effect of different types of instruction in metalinguistic knowledge.

Question 2: What are the relative effects of deductive and inductive FFI on L2 acquisition?

Several studies have compared proactive deductive and inductive FFI where both included practice activities. Unfortunately, these two types of instruction have been operationalized very differently, making comparison of their results difficult. In a review of such studies, Erlam (2003), not surprisingly, found conflicting results, with some studies favoring deductive instruction, others inductive, and some finding no difference. Erlam's own study investigated the effects of these two types of instruction on the acquisition of direct object pronouns in French as a foreign language. She reported a distinct advantage

Table 31.3   Types of metalinguistic explanation (based on Sharwood Smith, 1981: 161)

Elaboration

10

Type A	Type B
Covert but elaborate guidance (e.g., through the use of "summarizers")	Elaborated and explicit guidance (e.g., in the form of an algorithm)
Type C	Type D
Brief indirect "clues" that hint at a regularity	Concise prescriptions using simple metalanguage

0   10

Explicitness

for the deductive instruction in both comprehension and production tests but she also noted that there was much greater individual variation in the deductive group.

Other studies have examined the relative effects of metalinguistic explanations provided by the teacher (i.e., deductive FFI) and CR tasks where learners discover rules for themselves (i.e., inductive FFI). Fotos and Ellis (1991) found that both teacher-provided metalinguistic explanation and a CR task resulted in significant gains in understanding of the target structure (dative alternation), although the former seemed to produce the more durable gains. However, Fotos (1994) found no statistically significant difference between these two types in a follow-up study that investigated three different grammatical structures (adverb placement, dative alternation, and relative clauses). Mohamed (2001) found that a CR task was more effective than metalinguistic explanation with groups of high intermediate ESL learners from mixed L1 backgrounds, but not with a group of low-intermediate learners. This study suggests that the effectiveness of CR tasks may depend on the proficiency of learners. Leow (1997) asked learners to think aloud while they completed a crossword puzzle designed to develop awareness of Spanish irregular third person singular and plural preterite forms of stem-changing -*ir* verbs such as *repetir*. He found that increased levels of meta-awareness correlated with greater "conceptually driven processing" such as hypothesis-testing and morphological rule formation. Furthermore discrete-item post-tests showed that those learners who demonstrated high levels of meta-awareness were better able to both recognize and produce the correct target forms.

However, none of these studies produced convincing evidence that proactive/ deductive FFI resulted in L2 implicit knowledge as the tests they used to measure learning were of the kind that were likely to tap explicit knowledge. Fotos (1993) was able to show that the explicit knowledge the learners gained from her CR tasks may have aided the processes believed to be involved in the acquisition of implicit knowledge. She was able to show that completing the CR tasks aided subsequent noticing of the targeted features.

Question 3: Does explicit deductive instruction result in the acquisition of L2 implicit knowledge?

This is the key question. Doughty (2003b), it will be recalled, queried Norris and Ortega's (2000) general finding that such instruction was effective (and, in fact, more effective than implicit FFI) on the grounds that the measures of acquisition employed measured explicit rather than implicit knowledge. Therefore, the six studies I will now consider all employed measures of either free oral or free written production. These are summarized in Table 31.4. It is clear that these studies produced mixed results. Three of them (Lyster, 1994; Spada, Lightbown, & White, 2006; Housen, Pierrard, & Vandaele, 2006) found that the experimental groups performed significantly better than the control groups in the free production tests and the two studies that included delayed tests showed that this superiority was maintained over time. However, the other three studies (VanPatten & Sanz, 1995; Salaberry, 1997; Williams & Evans, 1998) failed to demonstrate that the explicit instruction had any effect on learners' accuracy in free production. What might explain these different findings? It is noticeable that in all the studies where a positive effect was found the instruction was prolonged (i.e., the learners continued to receive both metalinguistic information and practice activities over a period of several weeks). In contrast, in two of the studies where no effect was observed the explicit instruction was of a much shorter duration. In the other study where no effect was found (Williams & Evans, 1998) the explicit instruction was integrated into a writing course and for this reason may not have been especially salient to the learners. Williams and Evans' own explanation for the lack of effect was the difficulty of their target structure (English passive constructions), but it is worth noting that Housen, Pierrard, and Vandaele (2006) found that their explicit instruction was equally effective for their complex structure (French passive constructions) and their simple structure (sentence negation). A tentative conclusion, therefore, is that explicit instruction involving metalinguistic information and practice activities is effective if it is substantial. What is not at all clear at the moment is the relative contributions of the metalinguistic explanations and the practice to the efficacy of the instruction.

Question 4: Do practice activities work best with or without accompanying metalinguistic information?

This question has been addressed by studies based on VanPatten's theory of Input Processing Instruction, which VanPatten (1996: 2) defines as follows:

Table 31.4 Proactive/deductive FFI studies involving measures of acquisition based on free production

Study	Subjects	Target structure	Treatment	Measure of acquisition	Results
Lyster (1994)	106 Grade 8 early French immersion students	Various sociolinguistic expressions of politeness (especially *vous*)	Explicit explanation; input highlighting in written texts; contextualized production practice	(1) Oral production – role-played responses to slides depicting formal and informal situations (2) Written composition – formal letter	(1) Differences between experimental and control group significant on written composition (p < 0.00001) and oral production (p < 0.0001) (2) Similar results on delayed PT Results on OP largely due to increased use of *vous*
VanPatten and Sanz (1995)	44 3rd semester university students of L2 Spanish	Pre-verbal object pronouns; word order	2 days of input processing instruction consisting of explicit explanation and structured input activities	Oral story telling task – subjects watched videos twice and then told the story. Oral and written production.	No statistically significant differences on oral version of story; experimental group significantly better on written version.
Salaberry (1997)	65 3rd semester university students of L2 Spanish	Pre-verbal object pronouns; word order	1.5 hrs of input processing instruction/production based instruction consisting of explicit explanation and structured input activities/production practice	Oral narrative based on one-minute silent video clips. Both immediate and delayed PT.	No significant differences between either experimental group and control group. Number of tokens of target structure very low.

Study	Participants	Target structure	Instruction	Task	Results
Williams and Evans (1998)	11 intermediate adult ESL students enrolled in writing classes	Passive verb forms	FFI occurred in the context of 2 hours of writing instruction per week for 15 weeks. One group received input flooding, and the other explicit instruction + input flooding in context of survey task about cultural values.	Short written essay based on a series of five or six pictures designed to elicit use of the passive 2 weeks after completion of instruction. Dictogloss task.	None of the groups showed any significant improvement in use of the passive in the written essays or dictogloss task.
Spada, Lightbown, & White (2006)	90 French-speaking 11–12-year-old learners of L2 English	(1) the possessive pronouns *his* and *her* (2) inversion in questions	4 weeks of instruction (4 hrs per day) involving opportunities to hear and produce the target structures in a variety of activities + explicit instruction (rule of thumb)	Possessive pronouns; oral production task based on describing a cartoon. Questions: written production task requiring students to write questions based on an imaginary situation and oral communicative task	Possessive pronouns: both experimental and control group showed development over time but with much stronger gains for the experimental group. Questions: no difference on written test between experimental and control groups on progress through acquisitional stages but clearer differences in oral production task in favor of experimental group.
Housen, Pierrard, & Vandaele (2006)	69 14–15-year-old Dutch-speaking learners of L2 French	(1) French sentence negation (simple structure) (2) French passive constructions (complex structure)	Four weeks of instruction consisting of: (1) metalinguistic pedagogical rule; (2) reading text, (3) identification of exemplars in the text; (4) description of these examples; (5) controlled practice exercises (sentence-transformation and answering semi-open questions)	An unplanned written production task consisting of an oral interview with open questions about pictures and objects which they had to answer instantly.	No difference between experimental and control groups on absolute number of tokens of target structure produced on the immediate post-test but experimental groups significantly outperformed the control group in accuracy of production. Same pattern for delayed post-test. The complexity of the target structure did not effect the results.

Processing instruction is a type of grammar instruction whose purpose is to affect the ways in which learners attend to input data. It is input-based rather than output-based.

VanPatten and Oikennon (1996) compared three groups: (1) received explicit information about the target structure followed by structured input activities, (2) received only explicit information, and (3) just completed the structured input activities. Acquisition was measured by means of both comprehension and production tests. In the comprehension test, significant gains were evident in groups (1) and (3) but not (2). In the production test, group (1) did better than group (2). VanPatten and Oikennon interpreted these results as showing that it was the structured input rather than the explicit information that was important for acquisition. Other studies (e.g., Sanz & Morgan Short, 2004; and Benati, 2005) have since replicated these results. Benati concluded that explicit information does not play a major role in comprehension-based instruction.

Question 5: Do input-based and production-based practice have differential effects on L2 acquisition?

VanPatten's theory of input processing predicts that input-based practice that draws attention to form–meaning mappings will prove more effective than traditional, production practice. VanPatten and others have tested this claim in a series of studies that compared the relative effects of practice involving structured input activities and controlled production activities on learners' acquisition as measured by both interpretation and production tests. Two points need to be noted about these studies. The first is that the instructional treatments generally included metalinguistic explanations. The second is that, with a few exceptions, the tests measuring acquisition did not measure learners' ability to process the target structures in unplanned language use.

By and large the studies support VanPatten's prediction. That is, they show that input-based instruction results in superior performance to controlled output-based instruction when acquisition is measured by means of interpretation tests and in equal performance in discrete item production tests (see, for example, studies by VanPatten & Cadierno, 1993; and Benati, 2005). However, some studies have produced different results (e.g., DeKeyser & Sokalski, 1996), where no difference between the experimental groups was found. Also, in some studies (e.g., Allen, 2000) production-based practice was shown to result in higher scores in the production tests. Two explanations for these non-predicted findings have been offered. VanPatten (2002a) has argued that input-processing instruction is only effective for those target structures that involve learners overcoming default processing strategies (e.g., assigning the role of agent to the first noun phrase in a sentence) and that studies where no advantage was found for input-based practice had selected inappropriate target structures. The second explanation is that some studies (e.g., Erlam, 2003) compared input-based practice with *meaning-based* production practice rather than with traditional production practice and that such instruction, like input-processing instruction, enables learners to map meaning onto form. Input-processing instruction continues to attract the attention of researchers (see, for example, the collection of studies in VanPatten, 2004 and also debate (see, for example, DeKeyser et al.'s (2002) commentary on VanPatten's (2002b) defence of input-processing instruction).

Question 6: Is there a relationship between the quantity of practice opportunities and L2 acquisition?

In Ellis (1988), I reviewed a number of early studies that investigated the effects of practice activities where there was no metalinguistic explanation of the target form. The studies were all correlational in nature (i.e., they examined whether there was any relationship between the amount of practice engaged in by individual learners and measures of either general proficiency or the acquisition of specific forms) and were problematic for that reason. Correlation statistics do not address cause and effect. Thus, even if a strong correlation was found between practice and some measure of acquisition it cannot be interpreted as practice leading to acquisition, for it is just as likely that acquisition determines the amount of practice individual learners receive in a classroom (i.e., learners who know a form are more likely to volunteer or be chosen by the teacher to practice it). I also made the point that "practice" cannot be considered a monolithic phenomenon. It is, in fact, highly varied, subject to a whole host of social and personal factors.

Reactive explicit FFI studies

A number of studies (see Table 31.5) examined the effects of explicit forms of corrective feedback on learners' acquisition of specific linguistic features by comparing the relative effects of implicit and explicit types of feedback. The implicit feedback typically took the form of recasts or requests for clarification while the explicit feedback consisted of explicit rejection, explicit correction, metalinguistic information, or some combination of these. There is evidence from these studies that implicit feedback results in acquisition (e.g., Carroll & Swain, 1993; Sanz, 2003; Lyster, 2004; Rosa & Leow, 2004). However, there is stronger evidence that explicit feedback is effective; all the studies in Table 31.5 found that explicit feedback resulted in gains in accuracy. Also, several of the studies (e.g., Carroll & Swain, 1993; Carroll, 2001; Ellis, Loewen, & Erlam, 2006) reported that the explicit feedback was more effective than the implicit feedback. However, only one of the studies (Ellis et al., 2006) included a measure of implicit knowledge (an oral imitation test).

Further evidence of the efficacy of explicit attention to form in the context of performing communicative tasks can be found in Griggs (2006). Griggs conducted a longitudinal study of French learners of English by asking them to perform communicative tasks in pairs, record them, and then listen to the recordings to note down and correct their mistakes. Griggs divided the

Table 31.5 Studies comparing the effects of implicit and explicit corrective feedback

Study	Participants	Target structure	Design	Tests	Results
Carroll & Swain (1993)	100 Spanish adult ESL learners (low-intermediate)	Dative verbs.	Five groups; (A) direct Metalinguistic feedback, (B) explicit rejection, (C) recast, (D) indirect Metalinguistic feedback, (E) control. Treatment consisted of two feedback sessions, each followed by recall (i.e., production without feedback).	Recall production tasks following each feedback session.	All the treatment groups performed better than the control group on both recall tasks. Group A (direct Metalinguistic feedback) outperformed the other groups.
Carroll (2001)	100 adult low-intermediate ESL learners	Forming nouns from verbs (e.g., "help" (V) → "help/helping" (N)) and distinguishing THING and EVENT nouns.	Five groups as in Carroll and Swain (1993).	Elicited verb-noun conversions in a sentence format.	All types of feedback helped learners to learn the targeted items but only explicit metalinguistic information and indirect prompting enabled learners to form a generalisation. Modelling / correction (i.e., recasts) did not facilitate generalization.
Sanz (2003)	28 first-year university learners of Spanish	Position of clitic pronouns between object and verb.	Computer-delivered input processing instruction without prior explicit instruction. Three groups: (A) explicit metalinguistic feedback, (B) implicit feedback (e.g., "Sorry, try again."), (C) control.	(1) interpretation tests; (2) production tests, (a) sentence completion and (b) written video retelling.	Both groups significantly increased ability to interpret and accurately produce the target structure with no difference between the groups on any measure.

Study	Participants	Target feature	Treatment	Tests	Results
Lyster (2004)	148 (grade 5) 10–11-year-olds in a French immersion programme	French grammatical gender (articles + nouns).	Group (A) received FFI + recasts; Group (B) FFI + prompts (including explicit feedback); Group (C) FFI only; Group (D) control.	Four tests: (1) binary choice test, (2) text completion test, (oral production tasks), (3) object identification test, (4) picture description test. Two post-tests (PT) with PT 2 administered eight weeks after PT1.	FFI-prompt group was only group to outperform control group on all 8 measures (PT1 and PT2). FFI-recast group outperformed control group on 5 out of 8 measures. FFI-only group outperformed control group on 4 out of 8 measures. Statistically significant differences between FFI-prompt and FFI-only groups but not between FFI-recast and FFI-prompt.
Rosa & Leow (2004)	100 adult university learners of L2 Spanish enrolled in advanced courses.	Contrary to the fact conditional sentences in the past.	Computer-based exposure to input-based jigsaw task. Three groups: (A) explicit feedback to both correct and incorrect responses involving metalinguistic explanation + opportunity to try again if incorrect; (B) implicit feedback indicating whether the answer was right or wrong; (C) control group.	Three multiple-choice recognition tests and three written controlled production tests; immediate and delayed post-tests.	Results presented in terms of "old" and "new" items. For the recognition tests a statistically significant difference evident between (A) and (B) for new but not old items. For the production tests a statistically significant difference was evident for the old but not the new items. Both groups outperformed the control group.
Ellis, Loewen, & Erlam (2006)	34 adult ESL learners with mixed L1s	Regular past tense -ed	Three experimental groups completed one hour of communicative tasks. Feedback consisted of (A) recasts and (B) metalinguistic feedback (without correction). (C) control group.	An oral elicited imitation test (OEIT); an untimed grammaticality judgment test (GJT); a metalinguistic knowledge test.	No group differences on immediate post-test; on delayed post-test the metalinguistic group outperformed both the recasts and the control group on the OIET and on the grammatical items in the untimed GJT.

learners into two groups according to the rate of repair work, which he deemed a measure of their metalinguistic activity. The high metalinguistic activity group demonstrated significantly greater progress than the low group in measures of accuracy derived from the communicative tasks and also, to a lesser extent, in fluency. This study provides convincing evidence that reactive metalinguistic activity assists development.

Conclusion

In this chapter, I have shown that there is ample evidence that both proactive and reactive explicit FFI assist acquisition and I have also produced some evidence to show that this assistance can be seen even in measures of un-planned language use, which are hypothesized to tap L2 implicit knowledge. I have also suggested some of the characteristics of explicit FFI that appear to be especially facilitative. In this respect, the characteristic that emerges as especially noteworthy is metalinguistic activity involving such instructional strategies as providing learners with metalinguistic information (proactively or reactively), inviting them to discover grammatical rules for themselves, and encouraging reflection on and self-repair of their errors. However, there is no evidence that such strategies work in isolation; rather, the evidence indicates that they work when learners are either subsequently or concurrently engaged in practice activities, which in many of the studies were communicative in nature.

Why is metalinguistic activity on the part of learners apparently so valu-able? One reason can be found in Schmidt's (2001) claim that while awareness at the level of noticing is necessary for learning, awareness at the level of understanding will foster deeper and more rapid learning. Clearly, meta-linguistic activity entails both awareness at the level of noticing and under-standing and in so doing fosters the development of not just L2 explicit knowledge but also implicit knowledge. It should be noted, however, that this is not to deny the existence and value of implicit learning (which may be of special importance for younger learners), nor does it constitute an argument against task-based teaching, which claims that learning is best fostered when learners attend to form in the context of communicative activity (i.e., "focus on form").

REFERENCES

Allen, L. (2000). Form-meaning connections and the French causative: An experiment in input processing. *Studies in Second Language Acquisition*, 22, 69–84.

Batstone, R. (2002). Contexts of engagement: A discourse perspective on "intake" and "pushed output." *System*, 30, 1-1-4.

Benati, A. (2005). The effects of processing instruction, traditional instruction and meaning-output instruction on the acquisition of the English past simple tense. *Language Teaching Research*, 9, 67–93.

Carroll, S. (2001). *Input and Evidence: The Raw Material of Second Language Acquisition.* Amsterdam: John Benjamins.

Carroll, S. & Swain, M. (1993). Explicit and implicit negative feedback: An empirical study of the learning of linguistic generalizations. *Studies in Second Language Acquisition*, 15, 357–366.

DeKeyser, R. (1995). Learning second language grammar rules: An experiment with a miniature linguistic system. *Studies in Second Language Acquisition*, 17, 379–410.

DeKeyser, R. (1998). Beyond focus on form: Cognitive perspectives on learning and practicing second language grammar. In C. Doughty & J. Williams (eds.), *Focus on Form in Classroom Second Language Acquisition* (pp. 42–63). Cambridge: Cambridge University Press.

DeKeyser, R. (2003). Implicit and explicit learning. In C. Doughty & M. Long (eds.), *The Handbook of Second Language Acquisition* (pp. 313–348). Malden, MA: Blackwell Publishing.

DeKeyser, R. & Sokalski, K. (1996). The differential role of comprehension and production practice. *Language Learning*, 46, 613–642.

DeKeyser, R., Salaberry, R., Robinson, P., & Harrington, M. (2002). What gets processed in processing instruction? A commentary on Bill VanPatten's "Processing instruction: an update." *Language Learning*, 52(4), 805–823.

Doughty, C. (2003a). Instructed SLA: Constraints, compensation and enhancement. In C. Doughty & M. Long (eds.). *The Handbook of Second Language Acquisition* (pp. 256–310). Malden, MA: Blackwell Publishing.

Doughty, C. (2003b). Effects of instruction on learning a second language: A critique of instructed SLA research. In B. VanPatten, J. Williams, & S. Rott (eds.), *Form-Meaning Connections in Second Language Acquisition* (pp. 181–202) Mahwah, NJ: Lawrence Erlbaum.

Doughty, C. & Varela, E. (1998). Communicative focus on form. In C. Doughty & J. Williams (eds.), *Focus on Form in Classroom Second Language Acquisition* (pp. 114–138). Cambridge: Cambridge University Press.

Ellis, N. (2002). Frequency effects in language processing: A review with implications for theories of implicit and explicit language acquisition. *Studies in Second Language Acquisition*, 24, 143–188.

Ellis, N. (2005). At the interface: Dynamic interactions of explicit and implicit knowledge. *Studies in Second Language Acquisition*, 27, 305–352.

Ellis, R. (1988). The role of practice in classroom language learning. *AILA Review*, 5, 20–39.

Ellis, R. (1991). *Second Language Acquisition and Language Pedagogy.* Clevedon, UK: Multilingual Matters.

Ellis, R. (1993). Second language acquisition and the structural syllabus. *TESOL Quarterly*, 27, 91–113.

Ellis, R. (1995). Interpretation tasks for grammar teaching. *TESOL Quarterly*, 29, 87–105.

Ellis, R. (1997). *SLA Research and Language Teaching.* Oxford: Oxford University Press.

Ellis, R. (2004). The definition and measurement of L2 explicit knowledge. *Language Learning*, 54, 227–275.

Ellis, R. (2005). Measuring implicit and explicit knowledge of a second language: A psychometric study. *Studies in Second Language Acquisition*, 27, 141–172.

Ellis, R. & Sheen, Y. (2006). Re-examining the role of recasts in L2 acquisition. *Studies in Second Language Acquisition*, 28, 575–600.

Ellis, R., Loewen, S., & Erlam, R. (2006). Implicit and explicit corrective feedback and the acquisition of L2 grammar. *Studies in Second Language Acquisition*, 29, 339–368.

Erlam, R. (2003). The effects of deductive and inductive instruction on the acquisition of direct object pronouns in French as a second language. *The Modern Language Journal*, 87, 242–260.

Fotos, S. (1993). Consciousness-raising and noticing through focus on form: Grammar task performance vs. formal instruction. *Applied Linguistics*, 14, 385–407.

Fotos, S. (1994). Integrating grammar instruction and communicative language use through grammar consciousness-raising tasks. *TESOL Quarterly*, 28, 323–351.

Fotos, S. & Ellis, R. (1991). Communicating about grammar: A task-based approach. *TESOL Quarterly*, 25, 605–628.

Gass, S. (1997). *Input, Interaction and the Second Language Learner*. Mahwah, NJ: Lawrence Erlbaum.

Griggs, P. (2006). Assessment of the role of communicative tasks in the development of second language oral production skills. In A. Housen & M. Pierrard (eds.), *Investigations in Instructed Second Language Acquisition* (pp. 407–432). Berlin: Mouton de Gruyter.

Housen, A. & Pierrard, M. (2006). Investigating instructed second language acquisition. In A. Housen & P. Pierrard (eds.), *Investigations in Instructed Second Language Acquisition* (pp. 1–27). Berlin: Mouton de Gruyter.

Housen, A., Pierrard, M., & Vandaele, S. (2006). Structure complexity and the efficacy of explicit grammar instruction. In A. Housen & M. Pierrard (eds.), *Investigations in Instructed Second Language Acquisition* (pp. 199–234). Berlin: Mouton de Gruyter.

Krashen, S. (1981). *Second Language Acquisition and Second Language Learning*. Oxford: Pergamon.

Leow, R. (1997). Attention, awareness, and foreign language behaviour. *Language Learning*, 47, 467–505.

Long, M. (1991). Focus on form: A design feature in language teaching methodology. In K. de Bot, R. Ginsberg, & C. Kramsch (eds.), *Foreign Language Research in Cross-Cultural Perspective* (pp. 39–52). Amsterdam: John Benjamins.

Long, M. (2006). Recasts in SLA: The story so far. In M. Long, *Problems in SLA*. Mahwah, NJ: Lawrence Erlbaum.

Long, M. & Robinson, P. (1998). Focus on form: Theory, research and practice. In C. Doughty & J. Williams (eds.), *Focus on Form in Classroom Second Language Acquisition* (pp. 15–41). Cambridge: Cambridge University Press.

Lyster, R. (1994). The effect of functional-analytic teaching on aspects of French immersion students' sociolinguistic competence. *Applied Linguistics*, 15, 263–287.

Lyster, R. (2004). Differential effects of prompts and recasts in form-focused instruction. *Studies in Second Language Acquisition*, 26, 399–432.

Lyster, R. & Ranta, L. (1997). Corrective feedback and learner uptake: Negotiation of form in communicative classrooms. *Studies in Second Language Acquisition*, 19, 37–66.

Mohamed, N. (2001). Teaching grammar through consciousness-raising tasks. Unpublished MA Thesis, Auckland, University of Auckland.

Norris, J. & Ortega, L. (2000). Effectiveness of L2 instruction: A research synthesis and quantitative meta-analysis. *Language Learning*, 50, 417–528.

Paradis, M. (1994). Neurolinguistic aspects of implicit and explicit memory: Implications for bilingualism and SLA. In N. Ellis (ed.), *Implicit and Explicit Learning of Languages* (pp. 393–419). San Diego: Academic Press.

Rosa, E. & Leow, R. (2004). Computerized task-based exposure, explicitness, type of feedback, and Spanish L2 development. *The Modern Language Journal*, 88, 192–216.

Salaberry, M. (1997). The role of input and output practice in second language acquisition. *Canadian Modern Language Review*, 53, 422–451.

Sanz, C. (2003). Computer delivered implicit vs. explicit feedback in processing instruction. In B. VanPatten (ed.), *Processing Instruction: Theory, Research, and Commentary*. Mahwah, NJ: Lawrence Erlbaum.

Sanz, C. & Morgan-Short, K. (2004). Positive evidence versus explicit rule presentation and explicit negative feedback: A computer-assisted study. *Language Learning*, 54, 35–78.

Schmidt, R. (2001). Attention. In P. Robinson (ed.), *Cognition and Second Language Instruction* (pp. 3–30). Cambridge: Cambridge University Press.

Sharwood Smith, M. (1981). Consciousness-raising and the second language learner. *Applied Linguistics*, 2, 159–169.

Spada, N. (1997). Form-focused instruction and second language acquisition: A review of classroom and laboratory research. *Language Teacher*, 30, 73–87.

Spada, N., Lightbown, P., & White, J. (2006). The importance of form/meaning mappings in explicit form-focused instruction. In A. Housen & M. Pierrard (eds.), *Investigations in Instructed Second Language Acquisition* (pp. 235–269). Berlin: Mouton de Gruyter.

Tomosello, M. & Herron, C. (1988). Down the garden path: Inducing and correcting overgeneralization errors. *Applied Psycholinguistics*, 9, 237–246.

VanPatten, B. (1996). *Input Processing and Grammar Instruction in Second Language Acquisition*. Norwood, NJ: Ablex.

VanPatten, B. (2002a). Processing instruction: An update. *Language Learning*, 52, 755–803.

VanPatten, B. (2002b). Processing the content of input processing and processing instruction research: A response to DeKeyser, Salaberry, Robinson, and Harrington. *Language Learning*, 52, 825–831.

VanPatten, B. (2004). Input-processing in second language acquisition. In B. VanPatten (ed.), *Processing Instruction: Theory, Research, and Commentary*, (pp. 5–31). Mahwah, NJ: Lawrence Erlbaum.

VanPatten, B. & Cadierno, T. (1993). Explicit instruction and input processing. *Studies in Second Language Acquisition*, 15, 225–241.

VanPatten, B. & Oikennon, S. (1996). Explanation versus structured input in processing instruction. *Studies in Second Language Acquisition*, 18, 495–510.

VanPatten, B. & Sanz, C. (1995). From input to output: Processing instruction and communicative tasks. In F. Eckman et al. (eds.), *Second Language Acquisition Theory and Language Pedagogy*. Mahwah. NJ: Lawrence Erlbaum.

Williams, J. (2005). Learning with awareness. *Studies in Second Language Acquisition*, 27, 269–304.

Williams, J. & Evans, J. (1998). What kind of focus and on which forms? In C. Doughty & J. Williams (eds.), *Focus on Form in Classroom Second Language Acquisition* (pp. 139–155). Cambridge: Cambridge University Press.

32 Language Assessments: Gate-Keepers or Door-Openers?

LYLE F. BACHMAN AND JAMES E. PURPURA

Introduction

It has long been recognized that tests in general, and language assessments in particular, are intended to provide a valuable service to society, in that they yield information that can help decision makers allocate resources on the basis of merit, rather than lineage or patronage. At the same time, many researchers have pointed out the potential for language assessments to be used for purposes other than those for which they were designed, often with unintended negative consequences to various groups of test takers (e.g., Spolsky, 1981; Shohamy, 2001). Irrespective of whether language assessments are used appropriately or inappropriately, they serve as both door-openers and gate-keepers. That is, the decisions that are made on the basis of language assessments will involve allocating resources, opportunities, or rewards to some while denying these to others.

Language assessments are used in the service of a variety of decisions, including student selection, certification, classification, tracking, promotion or retention in educational programs, and allocating resources to schools. In order to assure that the decisions that are made, at least in part on the basis of language assessments, are fair and equitable, we must consider the specific uses or decisions for which the test is intended and designed, and the consequences of these decisions for different groups of individuals. Equally important, we need to consider the quality (i.e., reliability, validity) of the information provided by the assessment, and the relevance of that information to the decision to be made. This inevitably leads to questions about what a particular language test measures and how useful the results are for informing the intended decision.[1]

The decisions that are made on the basis of scores from language tests can be classified as *relative* or *absolute*, according to both the number of individuals who can be given the reward and the level of ability or proficiency needed to obtain it. In some situations, the number of individuals who can be given the reward is limited by the availability of the reward. In such situations, the cut-score corresponding to the level of ability that is required for allocating the reward is relative to the number of individuals who take the test. An example of a *relative decision*, in which the decision to give the reward to a particular individual depends on his or her relative standing in the group of test takers, is a college or university entrance decision. Some colleges and universities are highly selective, while others may have limited resources for instruction and mentoring. Such institutions can admit only a small percentage of applicants, and will thus typically admit only those students whose test scores, among other criteria, are in the very top percentage of all the test takers. If the numbers of applicants, or their test scores, vary greatly from one year to the next, then the criterion score used for deciding whom to admit may also vary.

In other situations, the number of individuals who can be given the award is essentially limitless, but the cut-score corresponding to level of ability required for allocating the reward is based on an absolute level of competence or mastery that has been specified before the test is administered by the test user or test developer. A certification decision is an example of an *absolute decision*, in which the decision to give the reward to a particular individual depends on a previously specified level of mastery. In many countries, for example, individuals who are not native speakers of the dominant language want to obtain professional certification (e.g., for practicing medicine or law, or for teaching). As part of their professional certification, such individuals typically have to pass a language test to insure that their level of language proficiency is sufficient for them to perform their professional duties and responsibilities. In such cases, there is no limit on how many doctors, nurses, lawyers, or teachers can be certified. However, their test scores must be at or above the criterion level of language proficiency required by that particular profession. In such situations, the criterion for certification does not vary from one time to the next, but the numbers of individuals who achieve certification may vary.

There are two ways in which we can interpret scores from language tests that are relevant to the type of decision to be made. For relative decisions, we need a test that will spread individuals out across a broad range of scores, so that it is possible to make fine distinctions among individuals at a wide ability level. Tests designed to do this provide scores that can be interpreted with reference to the performance of a particular group of test-takers. Scores from a *norm-referenced* test thus indicate an individual's relative standing with reference to a group of test takers, and are most appropriate for making relative decisions. The *Internet-Based Test of English as a Foreign Language* (iBTOEFL) is an example of a norm-referenced language test (www.toefl.org). For *absolute decisions*, we need a test that adequately represents the criterion, whether this refers to a domain of content as in an achievement test (see below) or a specified level of language proficiency. Scores from a *criterion-referenced* test thus indicate which test takers have attained the criterion level of mastery or proficiency and which ones have not, and are most appropriate for making absolute decisions. The *Oral Proficiency Interview* of the American Council for the Teaching of Foreign Languages (ACTFL) is an example of a criterion-referenced language test (www.languagetesting.com).

In this chapter we will first discuss a variety of purposes for which language assessments are designed and used, and the consequences of the decisions that are made. We will then discuss what language assessments typically measure, and the relevance of these abilities to different types of decisions.

Intended Uses of Language Tests

The primary purpose of giving a language test is to generate scores that can be interpreted as indicators of what test takers know or can do with the language for some intended purpose. These score-based interpretations can then be used as a source of information for making merit-based decisions about test takers within some assessment context. The interpretation of test scores is always linked to how the test scores will be used, and the decisions that will ensue from those inferences. As the examples below illustrate, the score-based information from language assessments can be used to make a wide range of decisions, which may open doors for some candidates and close them for others.

One common use of language assessment results is to inform decisions about whether or not students are academically prepared, or ready to pursue studies. These *selection* decisions are usually made in conjunction with other measures of ability such as a student's grades or letters of recommendation. For example, the *Internet-Based Test of English as a Foreign Language* (iBTOEFL) is designed to measure "the ability of a nonnative speaker to use and understand English as it is spoken, written, and heard in college and university settings" (retrieved June 12, 2006 from www.toefl.org). Scores from this test can be interpreted as evidence that a prospective student has the English language skills needed to pursue studies successfully in an English medium academic setting. Therefore, based on this assessment (and other selection criteria), students who have the requisite English language skills in conjunction with other qualifications (e.g., grades) are provided with the opportunity to study at the university, whereas those who lack the minimum English language skills (and/or other qualifications) are denied this opportunity. Given that the university can accommodate only a limited number of students, the merit-based selection decisions from university applications can be viewed as relative rather than absolute.

Another common use of language assessments is to provide score-based information for classifying and tracking students so that decisions can be made about differentiated instruction for those of varying needs and ability levels. For example, scores from language placement tests allow educators to classify students according to their level of language ability (i.e., beginning or advanced), so that they can receive level-appropriate instruction. These *placement*, or *readiness* decisions provide score-based information for tracking students into homogeneous groups according to ability level or their readiness to engage in a specific level of instruction. Similarly, scores from language tests, together with other assessments, have been used in US schools to classify students as English language learners (ELLs) and to determine if students have an appropriate level of proficiency to "participate meaningfully and equitably" in English-medium classrooms (Heubert & Hauser, 1999: 212).[2] Scores from these assessments are used as a basis for deciding whether students may have access to a range of services to help them transition from their native language to English-medium instruction (August & Hakuta, 1997). These language test scores can also be used to track low-ability students in slower-paced classrooms, to exclude them from grade-level math and science instruction, or to reclassify students from ESL to mainstream English-medium instruction (Berman et al., 1992).

A third use of language assessments is to provide score-based information on student progress or the effectiveness of learning. Interpretations about "progress" or "achievement" are used to provide stakeholders with information for making summative and formative decisions. *Summative* decisions about retention, promotion to the next course level, or the assignment of grades can be made on the basis of assessments of student attainment. *Formative* or improvement-oriented decisions for guiding instruction and learning, on the other hand, can be based on diagnostic assessments of students' strengths and weaknesses. For example, the achievement tests to accompany the ESL textbook *On Target 1* (Purpura et al., 2001) were designed to measure the students' mastery of the grammar, pronunciation, reading, and writing content in each chapter. Score-based interpretations from these tests are used to provide information to help students make formative decisions for focusing their learning on the areas in which they need to improve, and for teachers to monitor students' areas of strength, weakness, and progress in the course so as to make decisions about further learning and instruction. These tests can also be used to assign grades to students at the end of the course. As any number of students could receive high grades based on the criteria, these decisions can be characterized as absolute.

A fourth use of language assessments is to provide score-based information for certifying that an individual has achieved an acceptable level of English-language knowledge and skills or has mastered a set of predetermined English-language standards for some intended purpose. These *certification decisions* are based on the assumptions that the test measures test takers' language knowledge and their ability to use this knowledge in some target language use domain and that the cut-scores used to differentiate mastery from non-mastery constitute accurate or reliable measures of the required competencies. Certification decisions often carry an implicit predictive interpretation, where high language test scores reflect both mastery of the language competencies being measured and the ability to use these competencies to communicate successfully at some level. An example is the *Occupational*

English Test (OET) (www.cae.edu.au/OET) – a test of English language competency designed for overseas-trained medical and health professionals whose native language is not English and who wish to gain provisional registration to practice their profession in Australia. Scores from this test are used to certify that medical and health professionals have acquired an adequate level of English language ability to listen, read, write, and speak competently in a professional context. Those who achieve the grade required by their profession are assumed to be prepared to function successfully in their relevant professional contexts, and are, therefore, granted permission to practice their profession. Those who do not achieve the grade are prevented from practicing their profession until such standards are met. The decisions used to determine certification can be characterized as absolute.

Still another common use of language assessments is to provide score-based information so that the long-term effectiveness of language instruction in a program can be monitored. This *accountability* information can then be used to ascertain the extent to which the expected program objectives are being met, as well as to indicate areas of deficiency. This information can also be used by the program to make school-level allocations of resources or to justify the need for and use of these resources (Brindley, 1998). For example, in cases where performance levels have been met, administrators might decide to allocate the same level of resources, whereas in cases where performance levels are below standard, they might decide to allocate more resources to the program or, conversely, to sanction the program in some way.

In summary, assessments are intended to provide information for making decisions. These assessments cannot be fully understood or evaluated without consideration of the specific use(s) for which they are intended, as well as the potential consequences of these uses.

Consequences and Fairness of Decisions

According to Messick (1989), decisions that are based on test scores will necessarily have consequences – both intended and unintended. Consider, for example, scores from an oral skills test, in which we expect students who have achieved a high level of speaking ability within the domain to get high scores, and those who have not attained the standard to get low scores. Suppose that these scores are used to determine if international teaching assistants (ITAs) have acquired sufficient command of the target language to teach a course (e.g., chemistry lab) at a university. The stated purpose of this test is to measure the test takers' speaking ability in order to decide which ones can be hired as ITAs and which ones cannot. The intended consequences of this use of the test scores would be to serve the needs of the educational system by ensuring that ITAs are capable of making themselves understood in class. In this high-stakes example, several stakeholder groups (e.g., students, program faculty, program directors, school and university officials) may be seriously affected in one way or another by the use of the test results. These stakeholders would surely be interested in knowing that the scores used to classify ITAs as linguistically competent are accurate predictors of who does and does not have sufficient speaking ability in English to be teaching.

In making such classification decisions (mastery, non-mastery), we expect that a mastery level score indicates minimum competence for some ability and that a non-mastery level score reflects less than minimum competence. However, we must also consider the possibility of classification errors, the consequences of those errors, and the relative costs of making classification or decision errors, given the relative stakes of the test. In the *high-stakes* assessment example above for ITAs, one type of mastery/non-mastery decision error would occur if an ITA were incorrectly classified as a "master" when in fact his actual ability was *below* the cut-score level (i.e., a false positive). Another type of decision error would arise if an ITA were incorrectly labeled as a "non-master" when in fact his true ability was *above* the cut-score level (i.e., a false negative). Such decision errors in the context of high-stakes assessments may carry unintended consequences that could incur major costs to the stakeholders. In other words, a false-positive decision could impede learning in a content course, thereby frustrating students and depriving them of their right to learn. A false-negative decision could harm the individual ITA by denying him or her the funding needed to pursue studies and it would deny students the opportunity to learn from a competent teacher. In high-stakes situations, the effects of these decision errors are difficult to reverse. Given the seriousness of the score-based decisions in high-stakes situations, test developers and test users must insure that the decisions based on test scores are as accurate as possible.

Intended consequences, or benefits

The use of language tests in making merit-based decisions is generally based on a claim that some benefit will ensue from the intended use of the scores. In other words, tests will be used to open and close doors when deemed appropriate for educational, social, and political purposes. The use of tests is also based on the claim that if properly designed and monitored, and if used as intended, tests will maximize the chances for fair and equitable treatment of individuals and groups in terms of their access to opportunities based on merit. Some examples of intended beneficial consequences of test use involve claims about preventing linguistically unprepared students from pursing costly academic studies in a program where they are likely to fail (selection decisions) or the assurance that students are placed into classes appropriate to their ability level (placement decisions). Other examples include the appointment of workers such as healthcare providers or ITAs to jobs where they will have the linguistic skills needed to contribute meaningfully to their mission, and indirectly to society (certification decisions), or the setting of high achievement standards and the opportunity to receive feedback for further learning (achievement and diagnostic decisions). Still another example of intended benefits is the claim that tests will transform the educational culture to "leave no child behind" or to change the quality of classroom instruction by imposing accountability sanctions and rewards.

Unintended consequences

While the use of language tests is generally intended to have positive educational, social, and political consequences, language test use can conceivably incur unintended negative consequences. For example, if deficiencies in the test as a measurement instrument, such as unreliable scores or invalid interpretations, are detected, then concerns about the use of this instrument in decision-making would obviously be called into question. In other words, test users should seriously consider not using scores from a test for making decisions if questions about score reliability or the validity of interpretations are raised, or if the test scores are systematically higher or lower due to group membership (American Educational Research Association et al., 1999). Such might be the case when an ELL's scores on "story problems" in math are significantly lower due to limited English language proficiency. Concerns about fairness of test use might also arise if there is evidence that test takers are not given equitable treatment in the administration and scoring of the test. For example, if the test administration conditions are inappropriate or if the quality of ELLs' language in their answers to math problems is a factor in the scoring, this would surely raise questions of fairness with respect to equitable treatment in the testing process. Finally, test score use would be questioned on the grounds of fairness if test takers have not had the opportunity to learn the material tested, especially if scores were used to require the test taker to repeat a course or to deny the test taker a certificate of graduation (Darling-Hammond, 1997; American Educational Research Association et al., 1999). In other words, the test score might provide an accurate reflection of what test takers know and can do, but their low scores may derive from not having had the opportunity to learn, rather than from having failed to learn when provided the opportunity.

Darling-Hammond (1997) describes two New York City schools. In an international high school 450 ELLs from more than five countries are taught to engage in challenging content through an activity-based curriculum. The pedagogy in this school encourages students "to practice English as they also learn to examine ideas through social sciences and literature, think mathematically and scientifically, and test their view against reason, evidence and alternative perspectives" (p. 3). In contrast, a traditional suburban high school a few miles away has an enrollment of 2,500 students. In this high school, teachers are expected to follow a traditional lock-step curriculum based on a transmission model of pedagogy, and instruction is teacher-directed with little time for engaging group work. For example, in a remedial English class, consisting mostly of African American, Latino, and recent immigrant students, students are expected to listen, copy, memorize and respond, without much questioning. Unsurprisingly, the international school has had ten years of success not only in graduating virtually every student, but also in enabling students to pass both the New York State (NYS) competency exams and the more challenging school-developed performance assessments. The traditional school, on the other hand, saw an extremely high dropout rate by twelfth grade with few passing the NYS competency exams. Scores on these exams for the traditional school students were more a reflection of the their lack of opportunity to learn than a failure to learn. While the NYS competency exams may have produced consistent and meaningful test score interpretations of the abilities they were intended to measure for the general population, their use with the traditional school students as indicators of ability for the purposes of awarding a high school diploma raises serious concerns about equity and fairness.

Defining the Aspects of Language Ability to be Assessed

If decisions about allocating the resources of educational systems and society are to be made at least in part on the basis of individuals' language ability, then we must assure that the language ability to be assessed is, in fact, relevant to the decision to be made. For example, it may be clear that individuals' academic reading ability would be relevant to decisions about admitting students to a college or university, but that such information would not be relevant if we wanted to hire someone to perform simultaneous translation orally from one language to another. We thus need to consider how we define the ability to be assessed with respect to the decision to be made. For example, if we wanted to know, for purposes of promotion to the next grade, how well students have mastered the reading skills that have been taught in early elementary school, we would most likely define the ability to be assessed in terms of how this has been taught, and perhaps what level of reading will be expected of them in the succeeding grades. If we were interested in knowing if students have the pre-literacy skills needed to benefit from instruction in reading, we would most likely define the ability to be assessed in terms of a theory of early literacy and reading development. Or if we wanted to know, for possible employment, if a person is capable of reading marketing reports, then we would most likely define the ability to be assessed in terms of the knowledge and skills needed to read such reports. Thus, the way we define the ability to be assessed must be considered with reference to the decision(s) to be made.

Test developers also need to assure test users and other stakeholders that the interpretations of ability to be inferred from the assessments generalize to the target language use (TLU) domain, which is the domain that defines the context in which the decisions will be made. Bachman and Palmer (forthcoming) define a TLU domain "as a set of specific language use tasks that the test taker is likely to encounter outside of the assessment itself, and to which we want our inferences or interpretations about language ability to generalize." For example, interpretations of writing ability based on an assessment that requires test takers to write on a variety of general topics and in a range of general genres might generalize to a TLU domain which is very broad. However, the assessment results might not generalize to a TLU domain in which the writing tasks consisted entirely of written genres that follow very specific organizational formats, such as writing marketing reports or grant proposals. Thus, the kinds of assessment tasks we present test takers must be considered with reference to the TLU domain.

In defining the language ability to be assessed, test developers need to consider several issues. One issue that has been discussed in the language testing literature is the distinction between proficiency and achievement tests (e.g., Davies, 1968, 1990; Bachman, 1990; Alderson, Clapham, & Wall, 1995). Bachman (1990) focuses on the *content* upon which these two types of tests are based: achievement tests are based on the content of a specific curriculum or course of instruction, while proficiency tests are based on a general theory of language ability, or proficiency. Davies (1968, 1990), on the other hand, focuses on the *uses* for which language tests are intended. For Davies, achievement tests are intended to inform test users about how much language an individual has learned during a course of instruction; proficiency tests, on the other hand, are used to predict performance in the language on some future activity. Bachman's and Davies' definitions clearly suggest that test developers should consider both the content upon which the test is based and the decision for which it is intended (cf., Brown, 1996). The examples in the section on "Intended Uses of Language tests" above, of using language tests to make decisions about readiness, progress, diagnosis, and accountability, would most likely involve defining the ability to be assessed in terms of a specific course of instruction. Other examples given above, of using language tests for college selection, classifying students as ELLs, and certification, would most likely involve defining the ability to be assessed in terms of either a general theory of language proficiency or an analysis of the areas of language ability that will be needed to perform specific tasks in the TLU domain.

A second issue is whether to define the ability to be assessed in terms of language ability alone, or to define it as language ability plus some area of background knowledge. Bachman and Palmer (forthcoming) discuss these two options, along with the situations in which each option is likely to be appropriate, and some of the potential problems with each. They argue that the choice will depend upon the decision to be made. If, for example, we want to know how well test takers can use the language accurately and appropriately, we would define the construct in terms of the relevant components of language ability. If, on the other hand, we wanted to predict test takers' future performance on tasks that involve language use, as well as other areas of knowledge, then we would define the construct more broadly to include both language ability and skills and knowledge related to the task to be performed.

McNamara (1996) has discussed this issue from a slightly different perspective in terms of what he has called "strong" and "weak" senses of language performance assessment. In the "strong" sense, test takers' performance is judged in terms of task completion, which may require knowledge and skills other than language proficiency. In the "weak" sense, however, performance is judged in terms of the quality of the language that is produced, and score interpretations are likely to be about various aspects of the test takers' language, or about their overall language proficiency. While McNamara argues that "strong" performance assessments are not really language tests, his primary point is that language test developers and test users need to specify more clearly what it is that they intend to measure, and not simply assume that background knowledge is or is not part of what their tests measure.

Douglas (2000) considers this issue from the perspective of language for specific purposes (LSP). He argues that tests of LSP entail McNamara's "strong" sense of performance assessment, and defines what he calls "specific purpose language ability" as including both language knowledge and specific purpose background knowledge. Douglas' view is particularly relevant to situations in which the purpose is to assess individuals' capacity for using language to perform tasks or jobs in particular settings. We see this, for example, when assessing "academic" language of second language learners in elementary schools for the purposes of making decisions about categorization, tracking, promotion, and retention or when assessing special purpose professional language, for making decisions about employment or professional certification.

In summary, the way we define the ability to be assessed needs to be relevant to both the decision that is to be made, and to the domain of language use to which we want our score-based interpretations to generalize.

Are Language assessments Gate-Keepers or Door-Openers?

We have argued in this chapter that language tests are used to provide score-based information for making a wide range of decisions, such as the selection, categorization and tracking of students, the assignment of grades, professional certification, and the allocation of resources. As a consequence of these decisions, some people are rewarded and some are not. In other words, language tests serve as gate-keepers for some and door-openers for others.

The nature of the test – as gate-keeper or door-opener – will be perceived differently by different stakeholders. Test takers who do well on a test are likely to see it as a door-opener to the rewards entailed by the decision, while those who do poorly will see it as a gate-keeper, excluding them from these rewards. Similarly, teachers and school programs that are rewarded because of their students' high test scores are likely to see the test as beneficial, while those who are penalized or sanctioned because of low scores may feel that the test is unfair. Test developers who have designed and developed the test and test users who have decided to use the test are likely to see the test as beneficial, viewing it as an effective means for fairly and appropriately allocating the rewards at their disposal. Thus, they would see rewarding students who do poorly or denying rewards to students who do well as unfair, uneconomical, and perhaps unethical.

Finally, there is the issue of who decides. Who decides that the rewards should be allocated according to merit, rather than according to lineage or patronage? Who decides to use a language assessment, as opposed to other types of information, for allocating these rewards? Who decides where to set the cut-score that divides those who will receive the rewards from those who will not? This issue has been discussed extensively in the language assessment literature (e.g., McNamara, 1998, 2001; Shohamy, 2001; McNamara & Roever, 2006), and there appears to be little consensus among researchers on how language testers should address this. Ultimately, the issue of who decides is, in our view, one that involves societal, cultural, and community values that are beyond the control of the language test developer. Nevertheless, these values need to be carefully considered as we design, develop, and use language assessments.

NOTES

1   Since reliability and validity are discussed elsewhere in this volume, we will not discuss them here.
2   Different terms have been and are used for learners in schools whose native language or mother tongue is not the same as the language which is the medium of instruction. In the US, the term "Limited English Proficient" (LEP) has generally been replaced by the term "English Language Learner" (ELL), which is the term we will use throughout.

REFERENCES

Alderson, J. C., Clapham, C., & Wall, D. (1995). *Language Test Construction and Evaluation.* Cambridge: Cambridge University Press.

American Educational Research Association, American Psychological Association, & National Council on Measurement in Education (1999). *Standards for Educational and Psychological Testing.* Washington, DC: American Educational Research Association.

August, D. & Hakuta, K. (eds.) (1997). *Improving Schooling for Language-Minority Children: A Research Agenda.* Washington, DC: National Academy Press.

Bachman, L. F. (1990). *Fundamental Considerations in Language Testing*. Oxford: Oxford University Press.

Bachman, L. F. & Palmer, A. S. (forthcoming). *Language Assessment in Practice* (2nd edn.). Oxford: Oxford University Press.

Berman, P., Chambers, J., Gandara, P., McLaughlin, B., Minicucci, C., Nelson, B., et al. (1992). *Meeting the Challenge of Language Diversity: An Evaluation of Programs for Pupils with Limited Proficiency in English*. Berkeley, CA: B. W. Associates.

Brindley, G. (1998). Outcomes-based assessment and reporting in language learning programmes. *Language Testing*, 15, 45–85.

Brown, J. D. (1996). *Testing in Language Programs*. Upper Saddle River, NJ: Prentice-Hall Regents.

Darling-Hammond, L. (1997). *The Right to Learn: A Blueprint for Creating Schools that Work*. San Francisco, CA: Jossey-Bass.

Davies, A. (1968). Introduction. In A. Davies (ed.), *Language Testing Symposium* (pp. 1–18). Oxford: Oxford University Press.

Davies, A. (1990). *Principles of Language Testing*. Oxford: Blackwell.

Douglas, D. (2000). *Assessing Language for Specific Purposes: Theory and Practice*. Cambridge: Cambridge University Press.

Heubert, J. P. & Hauser, R. M. (eds.) (1999). *High Stakes: Testing for Tracking, Promotion and Graduation*. Washington, DC: National Academy Press.

McNamara, T. (1996). *Measuring Second Language Performance*. London: Longman.

McNamara, T. (1998). Policy and social considerations in language assessment. *Annual Review of Applied Linguistics*, 18, 304–319.

McNamara, T. (2001). Language assessment as social practice: Challenges for research. *Language Testing*, 18(4), 333–349.

McNamara, T. & Roever, K. (2006). *Language Testing: The Social Dimension*. Malden, MA: Blackwell.

Messick, S. (1989). Validity. In R. L. Linn (ed.), *Educational Measurement* (3rd edn., pp. 13–103). New York: American Council on Education and Macmillan Publishing Company.

Purpura, J., Bino, A., Gallagher, J., Ingram, M., Kim, H., Kim, J.-H., et al. (2001). *Achievement Tests for On Target 1*. White Plains, NY: Pearson Publishers.

Shohamy, E. (2001). *The Power of Tests: A Critical Perspective on the Uses of Language Tests*. London: Pearson.

Spolsky, B. (1981). Some ethical questions about language testing. In C. Klein-Braley & D. K. Stevenson (eds.), *Practice and Problems in Language Testing* (pp. 5–21). Frankfurt: Peter D. Lang.

FURTHER READING

Bachman, L. F. (2002). Alternative interpretations of alternative assessments: Some validity issues in educational performance assessments. *Educational Measurement: Issues and Practice*, 21(3), 5–18.

Bachman, L. F. (2005). Building and supporting a case for test use. *Language Assessment Quarterly*, 2(1), 1–34.

Brindley, G. (1989). *Assessing Achievement in the Learner-Centred Curriculum*. Sydney: National Centre for English Language Teaching and Research, Macquarie University.

Chapelle, C. (1999). Validity in language assessment. *Annual Review of Applied Linguistics*, 19, 254–272.

Davies, A. (2004). The ethics of language assessment. Special issue of *Language Assessment Quarterly*, 1(2&3).

Kunnan, A. J. (2000). Fairness and justice for all. In A. J. Kunnan (ed.), *Fairness and Validation in Language Assessment* (pp. 1–14). Cambridge: Cambridge University Press.

Kunnan, A. J. (2004). Test fairness. In M. Milanovic & C. Weir (eds.), *European Language Testing in A Global Context* (pp. 27–48). Cambridge: Cambridge University Press.

Spolsky, B. (1997). The ethics of gatekeeping tests: What have we learned in a hundred years? *Language Testing*, 14, 242–247.

33 Diagnostic and Formative Assessment

ARI HUHTA

This chapter presents an overview of diagnostic and formative assessment, which share the same purpose: improvement of learning. The focus is on assessing second and foreign languages, although relevant work in the first language (L1) and in non-language subjects is also considered. First, several definitions of diagnostic and formative assessment are presented, followed by an attempt to analyze their differences and similarities. Some central themes of research into these types of assessment are then described. In the chapter, the term *assessment* will be used to refer to all kinds of procedures used to assess individuals (e.g., informal observations, self-assessments, quizzes, interviews, tests), whereas *tests* denote a particular type of formal, often carefully designed instruments.

Applied linguistics abounds in terms that have multiple, even conflicting meanings. *Diagnostic* assessment must be one of most problematic terms in this sense, and distinguishing between diagnostic (DA) and formative (FA) assessment appears particularly difficult. Accordingly, this chapter covers both forms of assessment and occasionally also refers to other learning-related assessments (e.g., dynamic, placement, and summative assessment).

Defining Diagnostic and Formative Assessment

There is little research on DA in second/foreign language education, and there are few diagnostic tests. This observation was made by Spolsky in the early 1980s (see Spolsky, 1992 for details) but the situation has not changed in the past 25 years (Alderson, 2005). In contrast, diagnosis is well established in many other fields such as mathematics, science, and L1 (Nitko, 1993). FA, however, must have existed as long as there has been teaching, although the term itself was coined only in the late 1960s by Scriven (1967). Compared with practicing FA, research into it is obviously more recent and can be traced to assessment for mastery learning (where feedback, incidentally, is often referred to as *diagnostic* feedback) in the 1960s (Black & Wiliam, 1998). FA research in foreign language education is even more recent and one can only find a substantial number of articles on the topic in the past ten years.

What exactly do diagnostic and formative assessment mean? A number of definitions from both educational measurement and language testing literature will be reviewed next.

Diagnostic and Formative Assessment in General Education

The International Encyclopedia of Educational Evaluation analyzes DA at some length: Delandshere (1990: 340) distinguishes diagnostic procedures that focus on specific learning disabilities from those used in classrooms for assessing learning difficulties. He divides the classroom procedures into three types. (1) DA involves examining an individual's profile of strengths and weaknesses, and comparing them against certain norms or criteria. (2) Diagnostic tests do the same but tend to focus specifically on students' learning *problems*. (3) Mastery tests measure attainment of specific objectives, and are diagnostic because "they describe the teaching/learning process and student performance." Interestingly, Delandshere equates mastery and formative tests (p. 342).

In defining FA, the same encyclopedia (Lewy, 1990) admits that there is no full consensus on the precise meaning of the term. Typically FA takes place during learning, focuses on details, and aims at improving learning. According to some authors reviewed by Lewy, FA also seeks causes for assessment results. It is contrasted with summative assessment, which occurs at the end of learning, is less detailed, and aims at finding out the outcomes of instructional programs or individual learners.

Although diagnostic and formative assessment have different roots, the meanings of the two terms began to approach each other soon after the latter was coined. Scriven (1967) used FA only for curriculum evaluation, but Bloom, Hastings, and Madaus (1971) extended it to the assessment of individuals and stated that it is closely related to DA. They stated that the purposes of diagnosis were:

> either to place the student properly at the outset of instruction or to discover the underlying causes of deficiencies in student learning as instruction unfolds ... Diagnostic evaluation performed while instruction is underway has its primary function determining the underlying circumstances or causes of repeated deficiencies in a student's learning that have not responded to the usual form of remedial instruction. (1971: 87)

For Bloom et al. (1971: 117–118), FA is "the use of systematic evaluation in the process of curriculum construction, teaching and learning for the purpose of improving any of these three processes ... in (FA) one must strive to develop the kinds of evidence that will be most useful in the process, [and] seek the most useful method for reporting the evidence."

For Nitko (1993), diagnostic testing purports "to recognize psychological, physical, or environmental symptoms manifested by students with extraordinary or recurrent learning and/or classroom problems" (p. 451). He adds (p. 455) that:

> no other area of testing has been viewed as more closely linked to instruction than diagnostic testing. The two major purposes of such testing are to identify which learning goal(s) a learner has not acquired and to point to the probable cause(s) of a learner's failure to acquire them. The first purpose focuses on the content to be learned: manifested behaviors, covert knowledge structures, and covert mental processes. The second purpose focuses on providing specific information needed to identify the instructional procedure to be used with a particular learner to remediate his or her deficit.

However, Nitko recognizes the vagueness of terminology: "for many educators, diagnosis, behavioral objectives, and criterion referencing are inseparable concepts" (p. 458)

According to Nitko (1993: 451), FA aims "to provide on-going feedback to the teacher for the purposes of 1. choosing or modifying subsequent learning experiences, 2. prescribing remediation of group or individual deficiencies." FA also provides continuous feedback to the students "for the purpose of directing advanced or remedial study."

Experts on FA, Black and Wiliam (1998), state that FA does not have a well-defined and widely accepted meaning. They define it as all activities that teachers and students engage in to provide feedback that modifies teaching and learning. A key requirement for assessment to be formative is that the feedback is *used* in some way to address individual learners' needs.

Diagnostic and Formative Assessment in Second/Foreign Language Assessment

Alderson's (2005) review of definitions of diagnosis in language testing concludes that there is little agreement on the meaning of the term, and that diagnostic testing is often equated with placement testing (e.g., by Bachman & Palmer, 1996; and Davies et al., 1999). This may show the influence of Bloom et al. (1971).

The Association of Language Testers in Europe defines diagnostic tests (ALTE, 1998: 142) as tests which are "used for the purpose of discovering a learner's specific strengths or weaknesses. The results may be used in making decisions on future training, learning or teachings," and FA as "(t)esting which takes place during, rather than at the end of, a course or programme of instruction. The results may enable the teacher to give remedial help at an early stage, or change the emphasis of a course if required. Results may also help a student to identify and focus on areas of weakness" (p. 146).

Alderson (2005) analyzes diagnostic testing of second/foreign language proficiency with reference to the new DIALANG assessment system. According to him (pp. 256–7):

> Diagnostic tests are designed to identify both strengths and weaknesses in a learner's knowledge and use of language. Focusing on strengths will enable the identification of the level a learner has reached, and focusing on weaknesses or possible areas for improvement should lead to remediation or further instruction. Moreover, diagnostic tests should enable a detailed analysis and report of responses to tasks, and must give detailed feedback which can be acted upon. Test results and feedback should be provided as soon as possible after the test . . . The content of diagnostic tests may be based on material which has been covered in instruction, or which will be covered shortly. Alternatively, it may be based on a detailed theory of language proficiency.

Dynamic Assessment and Other Close Relatives

What makes defining DA and FA even more difficult is the existence of several other approaches whose aims and definitions resemble them. One such approach is "alternative assessment" which comprises a range of perspectives that share the same purpose with FA and DA. To give an example, Wiggins' (1998: 12) educative assessment is "deliberately designed to teach (not just measure) by revealing to the students what worthy adult work looks like . . . Such assessment improves performance and requires tasks, criteria and standards that are shared by teachers and students." Rich feedback that enables students to self-assess and self-adjust their performance is essential.

Dynamic assessment is an approach that has the same purpose as FA and DA. However, it is argued to differ fundamentally from FA (Poehner & Lantolf, 2005), because it is based on a specific theory of cognitive development and on the concept of the zone of proximal development (Sternberg & Grigorenko, 2002; Lantolf & Poehner, 2004). The central aim of assessment is to find out how well the learner can perform when assisted by, for example, the teacher, because only mediated performance informs us about a person's learning potential. Independent performance tells only half the story and may not indicate future learning.

Comparing Diagnostic, Formative, and Other Assessments

Figure 33.1 compares formative and diagnostic assessment with some other types of assessment in terms of two continua: (1) level of detail of assessment

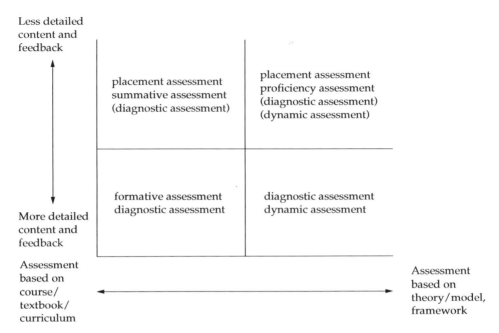

Less detailed
content and
feedback

| | placement assessment summative assessment (diagnostic assessment) | placement assessment proficiency assessment (diagnostic assessment) (dynamic assessment) |
| | formative assessment diagnostic assessment | diagnostic assessment dynamic assessment |

More detailed
content and
feedback

Assessment
based on
course/
textbook/
curriculum

Assessment
based on
theory/model,
framework

Figure 33.1 Comparison of diagnostic and formative assessment with some other types/purposes of assessment

and feedback, and (2) basis of assessment (course/curriculum vs. theory). It is not suggested that purposes of assessment could be unambiguously classified in this way; rather the chart may help one to perceive certain key similarities and differences between DA and FA.

FA is easier to locate on the two continua: FA is firmly based on some specific course or curriculum and it tends to focus on details of content and performance – it also provides detailed feedback. As the definitions reviewed above suggested, DA is more difficult to pin down in Figure 33.1. Usually, DA focuses on details, but it can relate either to a course or theory. According to some definitions, diagnosis can also be less detailed and relate to placement (Bloom et al., 1971; Bachman & Palmer, 1996). An example of broader diagnosis grounded on a theory or framework is DIALANG (Alderson, 2005; Alderson & Huhta, 2005), which is based on the Common European Framework. The fact that non-detailed DA is somewhat atypical is indicated by the brackets around it in Figure 33.1.

Dynamic assessment is close to both FA and DA: it usually focuses on details and it is firmly based on a specific theory. Lantolf and Poehner (2004) argue that dynamic assessment can be conducted also at group level, which implies that feedback may sometimes be broader.

Going beyond Figure 33.1, one distinguishing feature of DA is that it seeks to find underlying reasons for learning problems or even disorders; this is rare in the definitions of FA. However, the overlap between DA and FA is extensive, and many testers consider them very closely related, almost synonymous (e.g., Bloom et al., 1971; Spolsky, 1992). Both types of assessment focus on finding out learners' strengths and weaknesses, and both can be based on a curriculum.

Some important themes of research into DA and FA are considered next.

Effects of Assessment on Learning

All definitions reviewed above agree that diagnostic and FA are closely linked with instruction – dynamic assessment goes as far as to erase the distinction between instruction and assessment (Poehner & Lantolf, 2005). Not surprisingly, researchers have been interested in the effects of FA (and DA, when not distinguishable from FA) on the participants, processes, and products of learning.

Research that has compared the use of ongoing FA to other types of assessment shows that FA can lead to significant learning gains, as reported in the review by Black and Wiliam (1998) of studies on FA in different contexts (from kindergarten to university) and subjects (mathematics, language skills, science). Research (Fuchs & Fuchs, 1986; Black & Wiliam, 1998) indicates that the effect of FA is significantly increased when it leads to changes in instruction. Secondly, when teachers had to perform regular, systematic FA, results were better than in instruction with irregular, haphazardly executed FA. Thirdly, displaying FA data (results) graphically instead of through numbers improved learning; presumably, graphs help both teachers and students to analyze their performance. Some research also indicates that ongoing FA is more beneficial than placement type diagnostic testing.

Diagnostic testing of first language skills is certainly effective as testified by the many diagnostic approaches and instruments that lead to remedial instruction and, thus, to improvement in L1 skills (cf. Alderson, 2005).

There appear to be no published studies on the effects of DA or FA on learning a second or foreign language. However, two studies in interactionist dynamic assessment illustrate that mediated assessment can help gain a more accurate picture of learners than traditional assessment based on solo performance. Consequently, teaching of these learners could be adjusted more accurately, which presumably should improve learning. An unpublished study reviewed by Lantolf and Poehner (2004), used dynamic assessment to place students to advanced Spanish courses; it showed how a mediated narrative task could discover how two students who displayed the same linguistic problem in their independent task turned out to differ significantly in how they controlled certain morphology. That is, their developmental levels differed and, thus, they needed different types of instruction. Another study (Gibbons, 2003) demonstrated how traditional assessment would have resulted in an underestimation of students' ability to use scientific terminology in content–

language integrated teaching. Their progress was only revealed by the use of dynamic assessment procedures.

Leung and Mohan (2004) suggested that FA that takes place via reasoned decision-making discussion can be beneficial for any subject matter (language as a medium of learning across curriculum), even if it takes place in a language classroom, and may even prepare students for academic written discourse. This claim has not apparently been studied yet.

In conclusion, it should be pointed out that FA alone is not enough to bring about positive results. It needs to be part of wider innovation in instruction and classroom practices that entail more feedback between teachers and students, an active involvement of the learners (e.g., through self-assessment), and – as noted above – the use of FA information to adjust teaching and learning (Black et al., 2003). In language testing, similar arguments have been presented by, for example, Shohamy (1992) about using tests to create change.

Ability to Diagnose Performance

As any other assessment, FA and DA can also be carried out by using test-like instruments or by making human judgments about performance. Both require some sound basis for deciding on the content and procedures for assessment. The latter also requires that the human judge (teacher or learner) be able to notice crucial features in the performance and to interpret them appropriately. He/she also needs to decide which learning activities to engage in next.

Sadler's (1989: 121) analysis of FA suggests what diagnostic competence requires. According to Sadler, effective FA has three necessary conditions. First, the assessors (teachers or students) must have a clear understanding of what constitutes quality in performance, on a specific task or overall; secondly, they need to be able to compare the learner's current performance with the target; and thirdly, they need to be able to choose which activities would move the learner closer to the target.

Edelenbos and Kubanek-German (2004) specifically addressed language teachers' "diagnostic competence," which they define as "the ability to interpret students' foreign language growth, to skilfully deal with assessment material and to provide students with appropriate help in response to this diagnosis" (p. 260). The researchers identified a dozen behavioral features that they combined into a six-level scale of diagnostic competence. Level 4 illustrates their definitions (p. 278):

> Ability to write a report with many prefabricated formulas; emerging ability of the teacher to create a narrative about an individual learner; ability to understand categories of diagnosis; ability to compare children using these categories; ability to judge a child's silence; ability to situate in terms of her/his own language learning trajectory; mental ongoing diagnosis leading to expansion, code-switching, etc.

At the highest level of diagnostic competence, a teacher can "promote optimum student learning" and "give a rich hermeneutic interpretation of the learning situation" (p. 279).

Rea-Dickins and Gardner (2000) touched on diagnostic competence by studying the reliability and validity of FA. They compared teachers' notes of learners' performances in classroom activities with the transcriptions of what the learners actually said, and found that teachers often failed to notice key features of performance and made mistakes in writing down students' utterances. This raises concern about the accuracy of what teachers can notice (or make notes of) and illustrates the need to train teachers in FA.

Nature and Practices of Formative Assessment

General education has an extensive body of research on the nature and quality of FA. The review of practices in several countries and subject areas by Black and Wiliam (1998) paints a rather bleak picture. It concludes that FA is not well understood by teachers and is weak in practice – for, example, classroom assessment often encourages superficial and rote learning – and that the demands for certification and accountability have a strong effect on FA. Poehner and Lantolf (2005: 254) argue that FA "seems to be a hit-or-miss process that varies from teacher to teacher and presumably even for the same teacher from episode to episode." They argue that unless assessors have a theory-based understanding of how the subject matter develops and relate the learner to that, they cannot make systematic assessment that benefits learning.

Again, there is less research on second/foreign language assessment, but in recent years, interest in studying FA has increased.

Teasdale and Leung (2000) were concerned about the compatibility of alternative (formative) and summative assessment because of their different theoretical underpinnings. They concluded that an uninformed mixture of the two approaches can indeed cause problems and that research is needed on the applicability of traditional criteria of quality of the psychometric measurement to formative classroom assessment. Rea-Dickins and Gardner (2000) argued that reliability and validity may indeed be important in FA. The reason was that, contrary to common belief, the FA that they studied turned out to be quite high-stakes: the learners could, for example, be denied access to remedial instruction on the basis of FA.

Rea-Dickins (2001) described the assessment practices of the teaching staff working with young learners for whom the language of instruction was not their L1. She used the practices to build a framework for understanding and analyzing classroom assessment strategies and processes. The framework has four stages, two of which are central to FA. The implementation stage involves introducing the assessment to the learning situation, scaffolding during assessment, monitoring by the learners, and the provision of immediate feedback. The monitoring stage comprises recording and interpreting evidence from assessment activities, which may be followed by the revision of teaching and learning plans.

To illustrate what might be involved in FA practices in a specific activity, some features identified by Leung and Mohan (2004) are listed below. They used systemic linguistics to analyse the decision-making discourse of teachers and learners who were completing a reading comprehension task as a group.

- Learners were encouraged to decide on their answers rather than guess, and to provide reasons for their answers.
- The teacher clarified the criteria for deciding on the answers and repeated them if necessary.
- The teacher treated learners' answers as provisional rather than final; learners were allowed (even encouraged) to revise them.
- The teacher scaffolded the process by questions and comments, which led the learners to evaluate the correctness of their answers and to think about reasons for the decisions.

Diagnosis of Comprehension Skills

In L1 education, the diagnosis of reading is particularly advanced, especially when compared with the situation in second/foreign languages (Alderson, 2005). However, studies on foreign language comprehension items at the Educational Testing Service, in particular, have diagnostic implications, although their main aim was to improve item writing.

Freedle and Kostin (1996) studied three types of listening items: main idea, explicit statement, and inference. They discovered that different attributes (e.g., rhetorical structure of passage, location of information) were related to difficulty in the different item types.

Buck and Tatsuoka (1998) applied rule-space methodology to analyzing second language listening items. They specifically tried "to provide diagnosis and help with remediation" (p. 149) and argued that learners would benefit from information about their mastery of such attributes. Examples of the significant cognitive and linguistic attributes identified in the study (p. 141) include the ability to:

- scan fast spoken text, automatically and in real-time;
- process dense information;
- identify relevant information without any explicit marker to indicate it;
- understand and utilize heavy stress.

A total of 15 attributes and 14 interactions between the attributes proved significant – more than in other cognitive domains (e.g., mathematics). According to the authors, this indicates how complex linguistic processing is.

This also suggests that we should not expect the diagnosis of second/ foreign language comprehension to be simple and straightforward.

Another promising approach to the analysis of item characteristics is the neural net technique that has been used in predictive studies in many fields. Boldt and Freedle (1996) applied the technique to the analysis of the TOEFL reading items and managed to improve the prediction of item difficulty in comparison with the traditional linear prediction studies. A challenge for the widespread use of both the rule-space and neural net techniques is that they require a very high level of specialist knowledge.

Building on previous research on the TOEFL reading and listening tests (e.g., Nissan, DeVincenzi, & Tang, 1996; Freedle and Kostin, 1999), Kostin (2004) explored the dialogue items used in the TOEFL listening tests. She analyzed 49 item characteristics categorized into word-level, sentence-level, discourse-level, and task-processing factors.

Kostin (2004) identified factors that have diagnostic potential. These include presence of infrequent words and idioms (word-level), presence of two or more negatives in the dialogue (sentence-level), content related to academic campus life (discourse-level), need for inference, and inconsistency between the dialogue and the question (item included, e.g., sarcasm). Correlations were low, which is consistent with theoretical views of comprehension processes being influenced by many different factors (Freedle & Kostin, 1999) – again, a reason not to expect an easy diagnosis of comprehension.

Recently, subskills have been implemented and studied in DIALANG, in which feedback on reading and listening includes a breakdown of correct and incorrect responses into three subskills (main idea, inference, specific detail). Alderson (2005) concluded that performance on subskills did not relate to learners' level of proficiency. That is, users at different levels did not display different patterns of performance on the three types of items. It is, however, possible that individuals may benefit from the information that they have problems in a particular subskill. Such feedback may also raise the learners' awareness that comprehension can be multi-faceted. Research in progress by the author shows that DIALANG users perceive feedback on subskills as useful but more research is needed into how learners actually benefit from such information.

Content and Construct of Assessment

FA and DA based on specific curricula obviously draw on the content speci-fications and materials for their content. Materials and specifications may or may not be based on developmental theories. In the light of Alderson's (2005) conclusion that we lack detailed theories on how second/foreign languages develop, most language curricula and materials are likely to be based on intui-tion, tradition, or, at most, (specific-purpose) needs analyses. If the content of

FA/DA adequately represents curriculum content, and if assessment is of high quality, the results probably give a fairly good picture of the learner's ability to, for example, use specific demonstrative pronouns or describe his/her hobbies. However, without reference to a theory of development it is difficult say how weaknesses in specific content should be addressed. It would also be difficult to decide, in a principled way, how best to integrate the instruction of, say, these particular pronouns into other grammatical features or into wider communicative context. What should precede them in instruction? What should come after?

The above problems can best be addressed by means of research into language development and with reference to theories based on the findings of such research, as argued by Alderson (2005, 2007). We need to know more about how the abilities or components of abilities contribute to second/foreign language development and, in particular, how the lack of such abilities is related to weaknesses. Diagnosis of L1 reading often focuses on discrete components of reading ability (e.g., visual word discrimination, recognizing sound–symbol relations). Alderson argues further that discrete-point tests of specific language elements and "low-level" language skills rather than more integrated, higher-order skills, are likely to be useful for diagnosis also in foreign languages. According to Nitko (1993: 460) a general limitation of diagnostic testing is that it often focuses only on the surface features of the subject matter (i.e., content) and does not provide specific information that leads to remedial action. For him, more complete diagnosis would entail finding out how learners perceive the structure and organization of the content (e.g., which of the links are incorrect or missing), and how they process information.

Although it is evident that teacher-based assessment can be a haphazard, "hit-and-miss" activity (see Black et al., 2003), it is nevertheless worth using teachers' and learners' insights to inform us about what DAs should contain (Alderson, 2007). This ties in well with the recommendation in general education that assessment helps learning best when it involves everybody concerned (Black et al., 2003). Dynamic assessment offers an interesting, broader theoretical framework of development in which to carry out FA and DA (cf. Poehner & Lantolf, 2005), but it does not remove the need to develop more specific theories of second/foreign language development.

Conclusions

Assessment that aims at improving learning is not a unitary concept, rather it divides into several interrelated strands, two of which are analyzed here: diagnostic and formative assessment. Space allows the treatment of only some themes addressed in the literature: effects of assessment, assessment practices, ability to diagnose, diagnosis of comprehension, and the content/construct of assessment.

Other themes in DA/FA deserving attention include at least:

- the theory of development/ability that underlies assessment (e.g., positivism vs. socio-constructivism);
- computerized assessment (several authors mention the potential of ICT for DA/FA, and several innovative systems are referred to);
- differences between assessing comprehension and production (only implied in the literature; see however Alderson, 2007);
- tests vs. other assessment procedures: the test method does not appear to be an essential concern (cf. Spolsky, 1992); however, Delandshere (1990), Ebel and Frisbie (1991), Alderson (2007) suggest that tests often focus on problems. In dynamic assessment, the procedure itself is crucial.

Both DA and FA have been under-researched in language assessment. Recently, it has been argued that we need more research into how second/ foreign language proficiency develops if DA is to improve (Alderson, 2005). Ideally, this would be studied jointly by second language acquisition and language testing researchers (cf. Bachman & Cohen, 1998); in fact, such research is emerging in Europe, in particular, because of increasing interest in the validity of the Common European Framework. Such studies hopefully help design truly DA instruments and also instructional materials and curricula that reflect actual development more accurately.

Although complex in itself, developing accurate diagnosis will only be half the story. Additional obstacles will have to be overcome when diagnosis is applied, as Ebel and Frisbie (1991: 309) point out:

> One reason for the lack of success in educational diagnosis in most fields other than elementary reading and arithmetic is that most learning difficulties are not attributable to specific or easily correctable disorders. Instead, they usually result from accumulations of incomplete learning and of distaste for learning. Neither of these causes is hard to recognize; neither is easy to cure. Diagnosis is not the real problem, and diagnostic testing can do little to solve that problem. Another reason . . . is that effective diagnosis and remediation take a great deal more time than most teachers have or most students would be willing to devote.

We should not expect the availability of diagnostic information to solve language learning problems, for example, on its own: how the information is used is also crucial. It has been shown that (formative) assessment can indeed improve learning – but only if instruction is reorganized to make use of the assessments (Black & Wiliam, 1998). To fully benefit from research into the development of proficiency, we should pay careful attention to how new diagnostic tools and the information they provide can be integrated meaningfully into teaching and learning.

REFERENCES

Alderson, J. Charles (2005). *Diagnosing Foreign Language Proficiency: The Interface between Learning and Assessment*. New York: Continuum.

Alderson, J. Charles (2007). The challenge of (diagnostic) testing: Do we know what we are measuring? In Janna Fox, Mari Wesche, Doreen Bayliss, Liyang Cheng, Carolyn Turner, & Christine Doe (eds.), *Language Testing Reconsidered* (pp. 21–39). Ottawa: Actexpress and University of Ottawa Press.

Alderson, J. Charles & Huhta, Ari (2005). The development of a suite of computer-based diagnostic tests based on the Common European Framework. *Language Testing*, 22(3), 301–320.

ALTE (1998). *Multilingual Glossary of Language Testing Terms*. Cambridge: Cambridge University Press.

Bachman, Lyle F. & Cohen, Andrew D. (eds.) (1998). *Interfaces between Second Language Acquisition and Language Testing Research*. Cambridge: Cambridge University Press.

Bachman, Lyle F. & Palmer, Adrian S. (1996). *Language Testing in Practice*. Oxford: Oxford University Press.

Black, Paul & Wiliam, Dylan (1998). Assessment and classroom learning. *Assessment in Education*, 5(1), 7–71.

Black, Paul, Harrison, Christine, Lee, Clare, Marshall, Bethan, & Wiliam, Dylan (2003). *Assessment for Learning: Putting It into Practice*. Maidenhead, UK: Open University Press.

Bloom, Benjamin S., Hastings, J. Thomas, & Madaus, George F. (1971). *Handbook on Formative and Summative Evaluation of Student Learning*. New York: McGraw-Hill.

Boldt, Robert & Freedle, Roy (1996). *Using a Neural Net to Predict Difficulty* (Technical Report 11). Princeton: Educational Testing Service.

Buck, Gary & Tatsuoka, Kikumi (1998). Application of the rule-space procedure to language testing: examining attributes of a free response listening test. *Language Testing*, 15(2), 119–157.

Davies, Alan, Brown, Annie, Elder, Catherine, Hill, Kathryn, Lumley, Tom, & McNamara, Tim (1999). *Dictionary of Language Testing*. Cambridge: Cambridge University Press.

Delandshere, G. (1990). Diagnostic assessment procedures. In Herbert Walberg & Geneva Haertel (eds.), *The International Encyclopedia of Educational Evaluation* (pp. 340–343). Oxford: Pergamon Press.

Ebel, Robert L. & Frisbie, David A. (1991). *Essentials of Educational Measurement*. Englewood Cliffs, NJ: Prentice-Hall.

Edelenbos, Peter & Kubanek-German, Angelika (2004). Teacher assessment: The concept of "diagnostic competence." *Language Testing*, 21(3), 259–283.

Freedle, Roy & Kostin, Irene (1996). *The Prediction of TOEFL Listening Comprehension Item Difficulty for Minitalk Passages: Implications for Construct Validity* (Research Report 56). Princeton: Educational Testing Service.

Freedle, Roy & Kostin, Irene (1999). Does the text matter in a multiple-choice test of comprehension? The case for the construct validity of TOEFL's minitalks. *Language Testing*, 16(1), 2–35.

Fuchs, Lynn & Fuchs, Douglas (1986). Effects of systematic formative evaluation: A meta-analysis. *Exceptional Children*, 53(3), 199–208.

Gibbons, Pauline (2003). Mediating language learning: Teacher interactions with ESL students in a content-based classroom. *TESOL Quarterly*, 37(2), 247–273.

Kostin, Irene (2004). *Exploring Item Characteristics that Are Related to the Difficulty of TOEFL Dialogue Items* (Research Report 79). Princeton: Educational Testing Service.

Lantolf, James P. & Poehner, Matthew E. (2004). Dynamic assessment of L2 development: Bringing the past into the future. *Journal of Applied Linguistics*, 1(1), 49–72.

Leung, Constant & Mohan, Bernard (2004). Teacher formative assessment and talk in classroom contexts: Assessment as discourse and assessment of discourse. *Language Testing*, 21(3), 335–359.

Lewy, A. (1990). Formative and summative evaluation. In Herbert Walberg & Geneva Haertel (eds.), *The International Encyclopedia of Educational Evaluation* (pp. 26–28). Oxford: Pergamon Press.

Nissan, Susan, DeVincenzi, Felicia, & Tang, K. Linda (1996). *An Analysis of Factors Affecting the Difficulty of Dialogue Items in TOEFL Listening Comprehension* (Research Report 51). Princeton: Educational Testing Service.

Nitko, Anthony J. (1993). Designing tests that are integrated with instruction. In Robert L. Linn (ed.), *Educational Measurement* (pp. 447–474). Phoenix, AZ: Oryx Press.

Poehner, Matthew E. & Lantolf, James P. (2005). Dynamic assessment in the language classroom. *Language Teaching Research*, 9(3), 233–265.

Rea-Dickins, Pauline (2001). Mirror, mirror on the wall: Identifying processes of classroom assessment. *Language Testing*, 18(4), 429–462.

Rea-Dickins, Pauline & Gardner, Sheena (2000). Snares and silver bullets: Disentangling the construct of formative assessment. *Language Testing*, 17(2), 215–243.

Sadler, D. Royce (1989). Formative assessment and the design of instructional systems. *Instructional Science*, 18, 119–144.

Scriven, Michael (1967). The methodology of evaluation. In Robert W. Tyler, Robert M. Gagné, & Michael Scriven (eds.), *Perspectives of Curriculum Evaluation* (pp. 39–83). Chicago: Rand McNally.

Shohamy, Elana (1992). Beyond proficiency testing: A diagnostic feedback testing model for assessing foreign language learning. *Modern Language Journal*, 76(4), 513–521.

Spolsky, Bernard (1992). The gentle art of diagnostic testing revisited. In Elana Shohamy & A. Roland Walton (eds.), *Language Assessment for Feedback: Testing and Other Strategies* (pp. 29–41). Dubuque, IA: Kendall/Hunt Publishing Company & National Foreign Language Center.

Sternberg, Robert J. & Grigorenko, Elena L. (2002). *Dynamic Testing: The Nature and Measurement of Learning Potential*. Cambridge: Cambridge University Press.

Teasdale, Alex & Leung, Constant (2000). Teacher assessment and psychometric theory: A case of paradigm crossing? *Language Testing*, 17(2), 163–184.

Wiggins, Grant (1998). *Educative Assessment: Designing Assessments to Inform and Improve Student Performance*. San Francisco: Jossey-Bass.

34   Accountability and Standards

ALAN DAVIES

Accountability has become a watchword in public sector enterprises. It is one of several themes . . . that are symptomatic of the late twentieth century loss of confidence in the state as a provider of services. Nowhere have demands for accountability become more strident than in education.

(Moore, 2001: 177)

Introduction

Accountability is introduced as a required means of reporting on the accountable. The canonical example of accountability is the law which serves as the model for all professions, instantiated in their rules and their codes of ethics and practice. The current pervasive drive to accountability which imposes uniform ways of being accountable appears to be less effective than local initiatives. The demands of accountability typically involve the establishing of standards both in statements of principle such as the No Child Left Behind legislation in the USA (Bailey & Butler, 2004) and in the form of test protocols such as the very widely used PISA reading tests. Tests such as PISA (2003) embody standards and provide what are regarded as necessary information to satisfy the demand of accountability. Standards may be considered in three ways: the skills required to meet a goal; the publication of a set of principled statements regarding the agreed standards, such as the ILTA Code of Ethics; and combination of the first two ways. Large-scale requirements for accountability through standards, such as the Common European Framework, appear problematic, both in terms of reliability and in terms of the tension between the local and the global. Overall frameworks, such as professional statements, often embodied in a Code of Ethics, may offer coherence but they may also permit differential use of those statements. Nevertheless, the examination of the accountable and reporting on it through accountability may help us to reevaluate our view of language and of language use.

What is Accountability?

Giving an account is, Goffman writes, (1997 [1967]: 122) a form of remedial work, like apologies and requests. This suggests that an account is a way of explaining that what has been done is appropriate and necessary. The canonical example of an accountability domain is the law, which has to do with the issues of charges and defences, pleas, the mitigation of offences, and the defensibility of claims. Accountability, therefore, is a process or set of procedures for measuring some activity or behavior against a blueprint or rule book. The blueprint for behavior found in the law may be paralleled in the rules of a profession, its standards, or even its code(s) of ethics and of practice. What the actor (in our case, the language tester) is saying, therefore, to the stakeholder (e.g., the test user) is "evaluate my practice against these statements of principle (standards, codes, etc.) and then determine how far I have met these goals." That openness to judgment by stakeholders is what accountability is about. One area of dispute concerns who the relevant stakeholders are, who should be the judges of accountability: Should they be insiders, members of the firm, school, company, profession that is being held to account; or should they be outsiders, whose careers and futures are not bound up with the judgments brought through the accountability referral? Accountability, then, requires standards, to which we come later.

For Garfinkel, "the policy is recommended that any social setting (should) be viewed as self-organizing with respect to the intelligible character of its own appearances as either representations of or as evidence-of-a-social-order. Any setting organizes its activities to make its properties as an organised environment detectable, countable, recordable, tell-a-story-aboutable, analyzable, in short *accountable*" (Garfinkel, 1984 [1967]: 33).

The current drive for accountability may explain the pervasiveness and ubiquity of standards and therefore delude us into the naive view that the standards concept is new and original. It is not. The concept of and the concern for standards have a long tradition, sometimes under different names, the most common probably being norms, but there are other familiar terms too such as rules and conventions. What they all indicate is that there are social goals and that there are agreed ways of reaching toward those goals.

Accountability and Standards

In language studies, one of the most common uses of standard is bracketed with (a) language, thus Standard Language (Standard English, French, and so on). What is meant here seems to be that there is one (or more) dialect(s) of a language to which is attached social prestige and which is therefore accorded official status in education, publishing, teaching foreigners, and so on. Because of its official uses, descriptions of the standard written language are likely to be readily available in published grammars, books of usage, dictionaries, and style and punctuation manuals. What are unlikely to be so readily available are manuals on how to *speak* the standard language, since no one accent is accorded the status of a standard.

Standards, then, are ways of behaving, like conventions, but within institutions they have more authority since they can be used as non-negotiable goals (Elder, 2000a). Brindley places standards under the broad heading of outcome statements: these, he considers, can refer to standards themselves and to benchmarks, attainment targets, bandscales, profiles, and competencies, all of which are "broadly speaking, standards of performance against which learners' progress and achievement can be compared" (Brindley, 1998: 48).

From this point of view, accountability is the method used by participants ("members" in Garfinkel's terminology) to demonstrate that the activity they are engaged in and the social setting in which that activity takes place are 'normal' that they are not random, and that they are analyzable – and accountable – in terms of accepted norms and standards.

Of course, *being accountable*, in the sense Garfinkel intends, is inherent in all settings. *Accountability* requires that the potential be turned into the actual, that the actors be held to account.

Educational Standards

Educational standards have figured prominently in recent debates over educational policy (Goldstein & Heath, 2000). What these debates conclude is that (1) the very notion of "standard" has to be viewed in its historical and social context – there is no universally agreed meaning of standards; (2) there is no objective definition of educational standard. All standards are determined subjectively, and, ironically, the efforts made to reach agreement among, for example judges, raters, etc. lead not to an objective standard but to an enforced homogenization. As Torrance (2002), writing about the UK experience, points out: "it is important to try to summarise the costs and benefits of a national curriculum and assessment programme. The positives can be summarised in terms of clarity, direction and organization" (p. 11). But there are costs too: "policy has not been able to avoid the enduring threat of any narrowly-based testing programme – that of coaching for the test or concomitantly narrowing the curriculum to the small number of objectives that are answerable to large-scale paper-and-pencil testing" (p. 16). "Furthermore," he continues "England now uses such tests at more ages and stages than any other country" (p. 16). To redress these problems, Torrance advocates local uses of central test item banks and the development of teachers' formative assessment skills at classroom level.

Researchers in the USA have come to a similar conclusion. West and Peterson (2006) report that: "Targeted stigma and school voucher threats under a revised 2002 Florida accountability law have positive impacts on school performance as measured by the test score gains of their students. In contrast, stigma and public school choice threats under the US federal accountability law, No Child Left Behind, do not have similar effects in Florida" (p. C46). This conclusion is similar to that of Torrance in that it is in favor of local control in place of federal or national control.

A Californian study of educational standards, focusing on the Academic Performance Index (API), considers the issue of the No Child Left Behind (NCLB) project, referred to above, in Bailey and Butler's (2004) NCLB study. Bailey and Butler point out that there was inherent bias in the NCLB approach since no account was taken of non-native speakers of English. Since their study was carried out, some flexibility has been introduced: it was "decided that both subgroups under discussion (English learners and students with disabilities) will be required to demonstrate comparable improvement in the same way as other subgroups . . . each numerically significant subgroup, including English learners and students with disabilities, must achieve an API growth of at least 80% of the school-wide API range in order to meet comparable improvement" (Academic Performance Index, 2005: 7).

This may not satisfy the TESOL profession, where the view is strongly held that English as a Second Language (ESL) should be treated not as dependent on English but as a separate language. However, it does go some way to meeting the concerns that the profession has expressed.

More generally in the USA there have been serious attempts to impose standards nationally on language teaching. Spolsky (1999) comments: "Language teaching in the US has for the last decade been under the influence of the Standards Movement" (p. 390). No doubt, as in the UK, this tendency may be regarded as part of the centralization which is surely one aspect of the concern for national accountability. Spolsky notes that in foreign language teaching "there has been criticism of the standards . . . but there are signs of major influence in the way that the Foreign Language profession sees its tasks" (p. 391). With regard to ESL, the TESOL organization has collaborated with the Center for Applied Linguistics to develop the ESL Standards document. This "sets out the language competencies that students in elementary and secondary schools need to become fully proficient in English, to have unrestricted access to grade-appropriate instruction in challenging academic subjects, and ultimately to lead rich and productive lives" (p. 391).

Centralized control, no doubt of a fairly loose sort, is ensured by the development of scales, "whether in the form of proficiency guidelines or standards or in the form of Key Stages – as in the UK National Curriculum Modern Foreign Languages Common Requirements" (Spolsky, 1999: 391, 2). These, as Torrance points out, provide goals but need not impose instructions on how to reach them.

The PISA Project

An influential approach to delineating standards or goals has been taken by the Organisation for Economic Cooperation and Development/Programme for International Student Assessment (OECD/PISA), created as a continuing project in 1997 (PISA, 2003).

> PISA is a collaboration effort on the part of the Member countries of the OECD to measure how well students at age 15, and therefore approaching the end of compulsory schooling, are prepared to meet the challenge of today's societies. The OECD/PISA assessment takes a broad approach to assessing knowledge and skills that reflect the current changes in curricula, moving beyond the school based approach towards the use of knowledge in everyday tasks and challenges.' (PISA, 2003: 9)

The overarching term PISA uses for these knowledges and skills is *literacy*, literacy very broadly understood and intended to represent the PISA construct of "the use of knowledge in everyday tasks and challenges." There are now four literacy areas investigated at three-year intervals: these are reading, mathematics, science, and problem solving. Forty-two countries took part in the second cycle in 2003, with between 4,500 and 10,000 students tested in each country. PISA is not the first such comparative study of school systems. In the last 40 years surveys such as those conducted by the International Association for the Evaluation of Educational Achievement (IEA) and by Educational Testing Service's International Assessment of Educational Progress (IAEP) have been carried out, but always concentrating on curriculum outcomes. What above all distinguishes PISA in terms of the standards it establishes is that the knowledge and skills it assesses "are defined not primarily in terms of a common denominator of national school curricula but in terms of what skills are deemed to be essential for future life" (PISA, 2003: 14). Participating countries use their own official language as the assessment medium: comparability is controlled by translation and back translation.

Reading literacy is defined as "an individual's capacity to understand, use and reflect on written texts in order to achieve one's goals, to develop one's knowledge and potential and to participate in society" (p. 15). Both continuous texts (e.g., narrative, expository, argumentative) and non-continuous texts (e.g., charts and graphs, tables, advertisements) are included in the Reading battery, the aim being to cover these five processes: retrieving information, forming a broad general understanding, developing an interpretation, reflecting on and evaluating the content of a text, and reflecting on and evaluating the form of a text. PISA uses five levels of reading literacy. Each level provides elaborate descriptors in terms of both subscales and text format/type. Thus for continuous texts at Level 5 we read that students can "negotiate texts whose discourse structure is not obvious or clearly marked, in order to discern the relationship of specific parts of the text to implicit theme or intention" (p. 126).

One of the attractive features of PISA, a feature which distinguishes it from earlier surveys, is its regularity. The commitment to cover multiple assessment domains with updates every three years makes regular monitoring possible, providing data which countries can use to determine their progress in meeting learning objectives. The overall goals of the assessment are instantiated by test items and tasks which for example require students to:

- hypothesize about an unexpected phenomenon by taking account of outside knowledge along with all relevant information in a complex table on a relatively unfamiliar topic;
- locate information in a tree diagram using information in a footnote;
- connect evidence from a long narrative to personal concepts in order to justify opposing points of view.

(p. 123)

About half the test items in the 2003 cycle were open construct-response items which required judgment on the part of the marker. Overall there was in 2003 a high correlation across the five subscales:

- Retrieve information
- Form a broad understanding
- Develop an interpretation
- Reflect on and evaluate content of text
- Reflect on and evaluate form of text

but country by country results differ in terms of their interactions. Such differences lead to interesting questions: "In some countries, the important question may be how to teach the current curriculum better. In others, the question may not only be how to teach but also what to teach" (p. 120).

Standards in Assessment

In language assessment, standards have two senses. I note them here and then discuss each in turn:

1   The skills and/or knowledge required in order to achieve mastery and the proficiency levels leading to mastery, along with the measures that operationalize these skills and/or knowledge and the grades indicative of mastery at each level.
2   The full set of procedures followed by test constructors which provide evidence to stakeholders that the test/assessment/examination/evaluation is serious and can be trusted, demonstrating, often through a code of ethics, that the test constructors are operating professionally.

Standards as goals

In the first sense, standards are the goal, the level of performance required or explained, thus "the standard required for entry to the university is an A in

English"; "English standards are rising" (Davies et al., 1999: 185). Stakeholders, of course, rightly wish to know what is meant by such statements, how they are arrived at, and what is the evidence for making them. For this, there are three requirements: description, measurement, and reporting. The first is that the levels of performance (the "standards'") need to be made explicit. Such description is not easy (McNamara, 1997) and in second language learning becomes less and less easy as the learner progresses. In the initial stages we might say: "You must master these 50 vocabulary items." At later stages we say, for example: "You must demonstrate understanding of texts taken from given newspapers, facility to initiate and maintain a conversation with a native speaking peer, the capacity to write a letter of complaint and so on." These types of achievement are more difficult to delineate and to circumscribe. And even the initial level (50 vocabulary items) may, depending on our view of language learning, be absorbed into more complex uses of those items. But the three-stage process remains: there needs to be a description of the standard or level, an explicit provision of the measure that will indicate that the level has or has not been reached, and a means of reporting that decision, through grades, scores, impressions, profiles, and so on.

Description, measure, report – these three stages are essential, although there may be blurring of stages 2 and 3, such that the report is included within the measure. Where classical objective tests such as the Test of English as a Foreign Language (TOEFL) and the International English Language Testing System (IELTS) differ from the scale approaches of the Inter-Agency Round Table (IAR), the American Council on the Teaching of Foreign Languages (ACTFL) and the International Second Language Proficiency Ratings (ISLPR) is in their unequal implementation of the three stages. The tests offer measures and reports, but may be light on the first stage, description. The scales provide description and reports but may lack a measuring instrument. Proponents of the two methods (tests and scales) do not readily accept such criticism, maintaining that, in the case of the testing approach, the description is incorporated into the test and its supporting manuals; and in the case of the scaling approach, that the scale itself (which we consider to be a description) incorporates its own measuring instrument. *Quot homines, tot sententiae.* Ideally, scales require the support of a test instrument to provide reliable assignment to a level (or band) on a scale, in other words to offer an objective cut-off rather than leave the designation of a level to the subjective judgments of the interviewer/judge/rater (Davies, 1995). However, it is not only scalar systems that are open to such claims of unreliability (Leung & Teasdale, 1997): tests such as IELTS incorporate components of scalar judgments in their Speaking and Writing sub-tests where performance is judged by only one rater, effectively offering a scalar outcome (and leaving themselves open to questions about reliability).

The move away in recent times from the objective test to the subjective scale is no doubt part of the widespread rejection in the social sciences of positivism, fueled by the sociocultural turn (Lantolf, 1994) and concern for critical language testing (Shohamy, 2001). But it also has a more practical explanation. In large-scale operations common standards may be more readily acceptable if they are imposed by a scale which is open to local interpretations (much the same may be said of an international code of practice). A contemporary example of this is found in the Council of Europe's Common European Framework (CEFR) of Reference for Languages: Learning, Teaching, Assessment (CEFR, 2003). The CEFR claims to be the "basis for a coherent and transparent structure for effective teaching/learning and assessment relevant to the needs of learners as well as society, and that can facilitate personal mobility" (p. ix). Building on the earlier Threshold level and the Common Reference Levels (A1–C2), "the CEFR is now . . . inspiring a new generation of sets of objectives for curriculum developers . . . This current Manual, with its emphasis on relating assessments to one another through the mediation of the CEFR, is a logical complement to the developments on levels and objectives" (p. ix). The CEFR, then, is not a measure. For measuring purposes the CEFR operates as a common reference to which local and national assessment instruments can relate (Taylor, 2004). This makes good sense, but there is undoubtedly the danger of the tail wagging the dog: that, in order to enable mediation through the CEFR, local systems will massage their own measures so as to secure accord with the CEFR. In other words, the apparent freedom offered by the CEFR to local systems could be an illusion and, as Fulcher (2004) insists, established without proper research.

Large-scale operations like the CEFR may be manipulated unthinkingly (rather than, as we have suggested, deviously) by juggernaut-like centralizing institutions. Mitchell describes the misconceived imposition of the Attainment Targets and Level Descriptors of the UK's National Curriculum for Modern Foreign Languages, asserting that the longer-term impact of these standards "will certainly be to reduce diversity and experimentation . . . we are likely to lose the more ambitious and more experiential interpretations of communicative language teaching, which has . . . historically been found at local level' (Mitchell, 2001: 174). Elder reports a similar case of inappropriate standards for LOTE (Languages other than English) in Australia (Elder, 2000b). Bailey and Butler, discussing the No Child Left Behind (NCLB) program in the USA, complain that, because of recent changes to the federal law, no distinction is made between English learners and native speakers. The law now requires "the inclusion of English Language Learner students in future mandated assessment systems. The NCLB Act of 2001 increases school accountability . . .' (Bailey & Butler, 2004: 183). Such mismatches are not wholly unlike the possible CEFR massaging of local measures, to which I have referred, since in all cases what is in train is the imposition of one overall set of standards nationally, regionally, or even universally, the macdonaldization of language standards. However, our scepticism may be misjudged and out of place, since by their very nature standards are properly ambitious for wider and wider acceptance. There really is little point, after all, in establishing standards just for me if they have no meaning or application to you or anyone else: similarly with standards for a class, school, city, and so on. What then is wrong about the cases discussed by Mitchell, Elder, and Bailey and Butler is not that they were attempts at expanding the range and distribution of standards, but that they were, for the populations discussed, the wrong standards, cavalierly taking for granted that, for example, there is no difference between what is required of young L1 and L2 learners.

Standard setting and ethics

If "standards" in our first sense refers to a level of performance required or experienced, the emphasis being on the language user or test taker, a second sense refers to a set of principles which can be used as a basis for evaluating what language testers do, such as carrying out the appropriate procedures. When a school principal maintains that his/her school is "maintaining standards" the implication is that achievement levels over time are constant. When an examination body such as Educational Testing Service (ETS) or the University of Cambridge Local Examinations Syndicate (UCLES) claims that they are "maintaining standards" what they seem to mean is that they are carrying out the appropriate procedures, such as standard-setting (Griffin, 2001). Standard-setting is a technical exercise, involving, as it does, the determining of cut-scores for a test, either for pass/fail or for each level in a band system. But it is worth remembering, as Lumley, Lynch & McNamara conclude, that standard-setting remains a substantially political and ethical issue: "there can be no purely technical solution to the problem of standard setting in this context" (of an English test for ESL health professionals), the decision "remains intrinsically ethical and political; no amount of technical sophistication will remove the necessity for such decisions" (Lumley et al., 1994: 39). Seeking to be ethical, behaving as responsible professionals, means that examination bodies must ensure that their products are reliable and valid, that they are properly maintained and renewed over time, that appropriate research is in place and that the needs of all stakeholders are being addressed. It seems also necessary to demonstrate publicly that their claimed standards are being maintained. Hence the professional statements embodied in a Code of Ethics (ILTA, 2000; ALTE, 2001). Sceptics may object that language testing was professional before testers felt the need to claim a professional status in a Code of Ethics. But there is another interpretation, that just as the reach of grammar expands into the area of discourse, so what we are seeing in the professionalizing and ethicalizing of language testing is a wider and wider understanding of validity.

To an extent, this is where Messick's theorizing (1989) has taken us in his attempt to provide one overall coherent framework for the description, the measurement, and the reporting of standards and the systematic effects they have on all stakeholders. The term that has come to be associated with his conceptualization is that of consequential validity, but it does seem that impact may be an alternative name for it. Impact (Hawkey, 2006) studies the effects that a test has when put to use: this is more than the generally used term washback precisely because it is concerned not with just how a test works in one situation but with its systemic influences. As such, impact can investigate fundamental issues about standards: Are they the right ones for the purposes intended, are they fully and openly described, are they attached to reliable and valid measures and is the reporting clear and precise and does the test produce desirable outcomes in the form of more appropriate and useful teaching? What impact studies, then, can do is to enable us to re-evaluate and make explicit not just the standards we promote but the very view of language we take for granted.

Conclusion

Goffman, it will be remembered, considers accounts to be a form of remedial work. Remedial work is necessary when something has not been done properly. Hence the need for pro-active accountability which makes very clear through the public standards it sets itself its openness to accountability, accountability now not at a later date. Or, as Garfinkel points out, the properties of a setting are always accountable. What accountability provides is a report on the accountable.

REFERENCES

Academic Performance Index Base Report (2005). Pasadena: California Department of Education.

ALTE (2001). The Association of Language Testers of Europe Code of Practice. www.alte.org

Bailey, Alison L. & Butler, Frances A. (2004). Ethical considerations in the assessment of the language and content knowledge of English language learners K-12. *Language Assessment Quarterly*, 1(2&3), 177–193.

Brindley, Geoff (1998). Outcomes-based assessment and reporting in language learning programmes: A review of the issues. *Language Testing*, 15(1), 45–85.

CEFR (2003). Relating language examinations to the Common European Framework of Reference for Languages: Learning, Teaching, Assessment (CEFR). Manual: Pilot Preliminary Version. Council of Europe, Strasbourg: Language Policy Division.

Davies, Alan (1995). Introduction: Measures and reports. *Melbourne Papers in Language Testing*, 4(2). 1–11.

Davies, Alan, Brown, Annie, Elder, Catherine, Hill, Kathryn, Lumley, Tom, & McNamara, Tim (1999). *Dictionary of Language Testing*. Cambridge: University of Cambridge Local Examinations Syndicate and University of Cambridge.

Elder, Catherine (2000a). Preface. In Catherine Elder (ed.), Defining Standards and Monitoring Progress in Languages other than English. Guest edited issue of the *Australian Review of Applied Linguistics*, 23(2), 1–5.

Elder, Catherine (2000b). Learner diversity and its implications for outcomes-based assessment'. In Catherine Elder (ed.), Defining Standards and Monitoring Progress in Languages other than English. Guest edited issue of the *Australian Review of Applied Linguistics*, 23(2), 36–61.

Fulcher, Glenn (2004). Are Europe's tests being built on an unsafe framework? An article for the *Guardian Weekly TEFL Supplement*, in Association with the BBC World Service, 18 March.

Garfinkel, Harold (1984 [1967]). What is ethnomethodology? In *Studies in Ethno-methodology* (pp. 1–34). Cambridge: Polity Press. Originally published 1967, Englewood Cliffs, NJ: Prentice-Hall 1967.

Goffman, Erving (1997 [1967]). Social life as ritual. In Charles Lemert & Anne Branaman (eds), *The Goffman Reader* (pp. 109–127). Oxford: Blackwell. Previously published (1967) in *Interaction Ritual: Essays on Face-to-Face Behavior* (pp. 42–45), New York: Random House.

Goldstein, Harvey & Heath, Anthony (eds.) (2000). *Educational Standards*. Oxford: The British Academy and Oxford University Press.

Griffin, Patrick (2001). Establishing meaningful language test scores for selection and placement. In C. Elder, A. Brown, K. Grove, E. Hill, N. Iwashita, T. Lumley, T. McNamara, & K. O'Loughlin (eds.), *Experimenting with Uncertainty: Essays in Honour of Alan Davies* (pp. 97–107). Cambridge: Cambridge University Press.

Hawkey, Roger (2006). *Impact Theory and Practice: Studies of the IELTS test and Progetto Lingue 2000* (Studies of Language Testing, 24). Cambridge: Cambridge University Press and UCLES.

ILTA (2000). International Language Testing Association Code of Ethics. Available on line at: http://www.iltaonline.com/code.pdf (accessed September 2006).

Lantolf, James P. (ed.) (1994). Sociocultural theory and second language learning. Special issue of *The Modern Language Journal*, 78.

Leung, Constant & Teasdale, Alex (1997). Raters' understanding of rating scales as abstracted concept and as instruments for decision making. *Melbourne Papers in Language Testing*, 6(2), 45–71.

Lumley, Tom, Lynch, Brian, & McNamara, Tim (1994). Are raters' judgements of language teacher effectiveness wholly language based? *Melbourne Papers in Language Testing*, 3(2), 40–59.

McNamara, Tim (1997). Wording the criterion statement: What's in a name? Plenary Address National Working Forum on Assessment and Reporting in English Language and Literacy Programs: Trends and Issues. NCELTR: Macquarie University.

Messick, Samuel (1989). Validity. In Robert L. Linn (ed.), *Educational Measurement* (3rd edn., pp. 13–103). New York: American Council on Education/Macmillan.

Mitchell, Rosamond (2001). Prescribed language standards and foreign language classroom practice: relationships and consequences. In C. Elder, A. Brown, E. Grove, K. Hill, N. Iwashita, T. Lumley, T. McNamara, & K. O'Loughlin (eds.), *Experimenting with Uncertainty: Essays in Honour of Alan Davies* (pp. 163–176). Cambridge: Cambridge University Press.

Moore, Helen (2001). Rendering ESL accountable: Educational and bureaucratic technologies in the Australian context. In C. Elder, A. Brown, K. Grove, K. Hill, N. Iwashita, T. Lumley, T. McNamara, & K. O'Loughlin (eds.), *Experimenting with Uncertainty: Essays in Honour of Alan Davies* (pp. 177–190). Cambridge: Cambridge University Press.

PISA (2003). *The PISA 2003 Assessment Framework: Mathematics, Reading, Science, Problem Solving – Knowledge and Skills*. Paris: OECD.

Shohamy, Elana (2001). *The Power of Tests: A Critical Perspective on the Uses of Language Tests*. London: Pearson.

Spolsky, Bernard (1999). Standards, scales and guidelines. In B. Spolsky (ed.), *Concise Encyclopedia of Educational Linguistics* (pp. 390–392). Oxford: Elsevier.

Taylor, Lynda (2004). Introduction: Issues of test comparability. *Research Notes*, 15 Cambridge UCLES: 2–5.

Torrance, Harry (2002). Can testing really raise educational standards? Professorial lecture delivered at the University of Sussex, 11 June.

West, Martin R. & Peterson, Paul E. (2006). The efficacy of choice threats within school accountability systems: Evidence from legislatively induced experiments. *The Economic Journal*, 116(510), C46–62.

35 Scales and Frameworks

NEIL JONES AND NICK SAVILLE

Overview

Scales and frameworks are familiar metaphors for representing language proficiency. Scales represent language proficiency as a vertical progression from lower to higher, perhaps divided into step-like levels with salient features that can be characterized. Frameworks align different scales horizontally or vertically, implying some comparability between them, and perhaps offering a wider, unifying interpretation of the progression which the scales describe. Like all metaphors these are accessible representations of a more complex reality. Language assessment deals with the reality defined by particular learner groups and testing purposes, to provide interpretations of test performance which are as valid and useful as the particular context allows. Sometimes interpreting performance is simple and direct, because the test mirrors real-life tasks in which the candidate must be competent – for example, waiting on tables in a café. Either the candidate demonstrates the required skills or fails to; no further interpretation is necessary. But such situations are the exception: mostly we wish to generalize beyond specific instances of performance to candidates' language abilities in broader terms, necessarily *less* directly related to the details of test performance, but consequently *more* useful as indicators of ability to manage in a wider range of situations. Validity relates to how performance in a test supports inference to performance in some more or less defined target language use situation (hereinafter referred to as the 'real world', in inverted commas because many learners' world of language use may not extend beyond the classroom). The wider the range of valid inference, the more useful the test result should be found to be.

Proficiency scales extend inference by implication: an advanced learner can do everything an intermediate one can, and more. Frameworks extend inference from a specific context to the more context-neutral – not an absolute distinction, but a case of less and more.

What language proficiency is has been much discussed. We think the term is best used in relation to a potential or actual act of measurement. Seeing proficiency as a measure necessarily places it in a context (of *who, what,* and *why*) and allows us to distinguish it clearly from other terms such as *communicative competence,* or other models of cognition or learning, which may be important concepts to incorporate in our approach to *generating* the measurement – that is, in our *construct* of language proficiency. In latent trait theory, as presented below, measures arise from the *interaction* of features of learners and test tasks, and this captures well the relationship of proficiency to underlying competence as one of the features constituting a testing situation. 'Context-neutral' proficiency frameworks are further discussed in Chapter 16, Levels and Goals: Central Frameworks and Local Strategies.

Our focus is on relating the general and the specific: on developing language tests and arguments for their validity which take into account both the similarities and the differences between contexts. Our interest is in scales and frameworks as communicative devices – as interpretations of language proficiency. Following through the inferential chain which leads from test design to interpretations we will touch on some mechanics of scaling and measurement, but this is not our primary concern. Further, we exclude interpretations based purely on *norm-referenced* statistical devices such as percentile ranks, normal-curve equivalents, or stanines. Recommendations for further reading are provided.

Spolsky (1995: 5) asserts that assessment traditionally has stressed description at the expense of measurement, or measurement at the expense of meaningful description. Thus the tradition characterized as 'psychometric' has focused on reliably ranking learners on a continuum rather than explaining how that relates to useful outcomes. If this was ever the case, we believe it is no longer so. Firstly, there is a general, continuing movement in education towards criterion-based goals and interpretations. The US has seen the rise of 'standards-based education', including in foreign languages (National Standards in Foreign Language Project, 1996). In European language learning the most striking development of recent years has been the rise to prominence of the Common European Framework of Reference (CEFR) (Council of Europe, 2001).

Secondly, we point to developments in recent thinking on the concept of validity in language assessment. The work of Sam Messick in the 1980s and early 1990s has been influential, particularly in addressing the issue of how inferences should be made from test scores and by drawing attention to the social values and consequences associated with this (Messick, 1989: 20). Lyle Bachman has set out Messick's approach in terms of language testing theory and practice (Bachman, 1990; Bachman & Palmer, 1996), and in educational measurement Mislevy, Kane and colleagues have picked up and developed Messick's thinking. Mislevy has argued for an approach to validation referred to as *evidence centred test design* (Mislevy, 1996; Mislevy, Steinberg, & Almond, 2002, 2003), which provides an 'abstract blueprint' for the design of tests and for building evidence of test validity through validation studies. Similarly, Kane has described a process setting out stages in the development of a *validation argument* to support inferences about a candidate's abilities from evidence provided by test performance (Kane, 1992, 2004; Kane, Crooks, & Cohen, 1999; see also Weir, 2005). Our presentation in this chapter is coherent with these lines of thinking.

Scales

Origins of proficiency scales

Language proficiency scales have arisen in three contexts (North, 2000: 13):

1   as *rating scales* – most influentially, that of the US Foreign Service Institute (FSI), dating from the 1950s;
2   as *examination levels*, for example, the development over time of the Cambridge ESOL exams. This five-level system was extended within the Association of Language Testers in Europe to become the ALTE Framework, which subsequently aligned with the CEFR;
3   as *stages of attainment*, associated with the objectives of an educational system or course of instruction, for example, as expressed by the UK's national curriculum and more recently in the USA in response to the No Child Left Behind Act.

In assessment, descriptive proficiency scales serve different purposes (Alderson, 1991: 72–74: Pollitt & Murray, 1996):

1   *user-oriented*, with the function of describing typical behaviors of learners at a given level;
2   *assessor-oriented*, with the function of guiding raters, typically with respect to salient aspects of performance quality;
3   *constructor-oriented*, with the function of guiding item writing and test construction;
4   *diagnosis-oriented*, with the function of providing detailed feedback on performance to learners.

Proficiency scales are thus heterogeneous in context and purpose.

Subjective judgment or intuition necessarily plays an important part in the construction of descriptive proficiency scales; yet as North (2000: 23) comments, language proficiency scales have mostly arisen without reference to *measurement scales* or scaling theory. The validity of subjectively constructed scales has been challenged; for example, Lantolf and Frawley (1992: 35) consider the ACTFL Guidelines to be "groundless, made up – arbitrarily." But scales, however constructed, should be seen as simplifying, heuristic models of reality, rather than claims about the nature of reality itself. Moreover, areas of applied linguistics such as second language acquisition have not provided much concrete assistance.

While a sound theoretical basis for scale development is surely desirable, language assessment cannot wait for better theories, and does not need to. Its goal should be rather to incorporate what is useful in current theory into a comprehensive test validity model which underpins practical test development processes. The next sections outline such a model.

Scales in a test validity model

Figure 35.1 presents a model for test validation as a five-step process from test construction through to 'real-world' interpretation. The steps make up the chain of inference through which interpretations are supported: each step asks a question and indicates the kind of evidence needed to answer it (Kane et al., 1999; Mislevy et al., 2002; Weir, 2005). Two major stages are identified: *scale construction* and *standard setting*. The first stage concerns developing

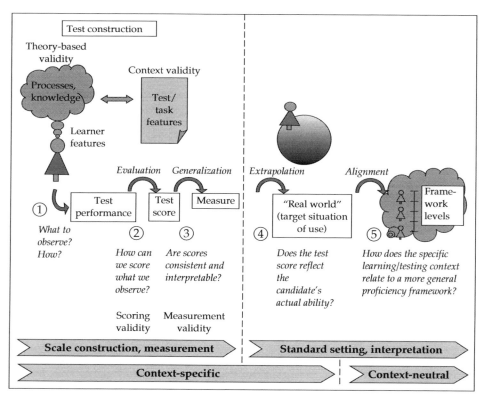

Figure 35.1   A five-step model for test validation

a valid measuring instrument; the second characterizes what it is we have measured.

Scale construction

Step 1 concerns test design, which begins with the learners who are potential candidates: who they are, their purposes in seeking accreditation, their context of learning, and so on. Learner groups may be more or less well defined; in any case the test should be relevant, while also reflecting a theory-based construct of language proficiency. Weir (2005) proposes a socio-cognitive validation framework which considers the interaction of learners and test tasks in terms of *context validity* – the purpose and format of tasks, their linguistic demands – and *theory-based validity* – a model of the processes the learner engages in and the knowledge mobilized in order to respond to tasks.

A learner's test performance must then be scored (step 2 – the inference of *evaluation*). Scoring is critical to how the proficiency construct is implemented, particularly for skills which are subjectively marked by expert raters (speaking and writing): which features of performance are attended to; which are rewarded or penalized.

Scores on tests are numbers which, depending on the success of step 1, should convey information about learners, but they depend entirely for their meaning on the particular testing context. Step 3, the inference of *generalization*, is critical in two respects. First, an observed score relates to a single event. Would the candidate get the same result on a different occasion, on a different test version? This question concerns *reliability*. A second, even more important aspect of generalization concerns linking to a wider proficiency scale, which may be seen as the process of transforming *scores* into *measures*.

How scores are assigned differs by skill: listening and reading are generally objectively marked, often by machine, while speaking and writing are subjectively rated by experts. These approaches have been characterized as *counting* and *judging* (Pollitt, 1991), using a sporting metaphor: track events or the high jump involve counting; diving or skating involve judgment. Judging links performance to interpretation fairly directly. With counting this is not so, firstly because test tasks (multiple-choice questions, for example) bear little resemblance to real world tasks, and secondly because scores may require transformation before they can be interpreted.

Types of measurement scale

A categorization of scales representing increasing degrees of measurement was proposed by Stevens (1946). A *nominal* scale is an unordered set of categories, (e.g., gender or first language). An *ordinal* scale is a ranking (e.g., of learners by test score). An *interval* scale captures the distance between learners in units that can be treated as equal. A *ratio* scale (e.g., centimeters) has a true zero point as well as equal intervals. The increasing amount of information conveyed by each scale is reflected in the statistical transformations that they support.

Although widely used, this classification has been criticized, because the status of real-life data is often not clear-cut. Raw test scores have shortcomings as a scale, but they may hold the necessary information to construct meaningful measurement scales.

Scales for objectively-marked tests: Item response theory and item banking

One evident limitation of raw test scores is that they are bounded by 0% and 100%. To measure language proficiency over a wide range of levels we need a scale that can be extended indefinitely – hence a different kind of number.

The concepts familiar to everyone who has ever taken tests are shown in italics in Figure 35.2. These are *facility* ("Nobody got more than half marks"), the *pass mark* ("the pass mark was 60%") and the *pass rate* ("so we all failed"). But as Figure 35.2 shows, these numbers only express interactions between more fundamental values: the *ability* of learners, the *difficulty* of tests, and the *standard* which is set. For example, if the test were made harder, then, other things being equal, the facility would decrease and the pass mark would need to be lowered in order to pass the same proportion of learners. So what interest us are not scores as such, but the underlying features of learners and test items which lead to those scores being observed. We view the language proficiency continuum as a *latent trait* upon which learners, items, and criterion levels of ability (standards) can all be located.

Although Figure 35.2 seems to represent ability and difficulty as different things, they are really different aspects of the same thing – language proficiency as measured in a particular testing context. Ability and difficulty are

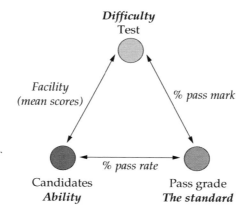

Figure 35.2   Classical item statistics and the underlying trait

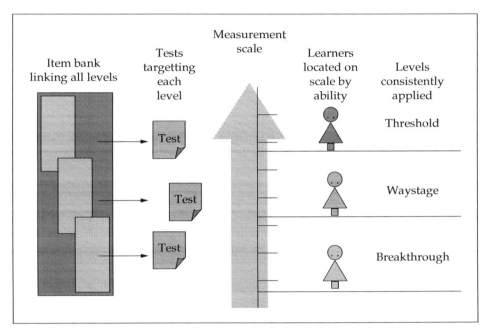

Figure 35.3 Item banking approach to scale construction

mutually defining: they arise in the *interaction* of learners and tasks. However, learners have features (their age, learning experience, competences, etc.) as do tasks (topic, testing focus, linguistic complexity, etc.). These should explain the outcome of particular interactions.

Statistical approaches use *item response theory (IRT)* or *Rasch modeling* (Hambleton, Swaminthanan, & Rogers, 1991; Wright & Stone, 1979; Bond & Fox, 2001); the associated test construction methodology is called *item banking*. Item banking involves assembling a bank of *calibrated* items – that is, items of known difficulty. Designs for collecting response data ensure a link across items at all levels. Thus a single measurement scale can be constructed. This scale has useful features akin to the direct measurement of physical properties such as weight or temperature: it is linear and extensible; intervals on it can be meaningfully compared. It relates different testing events within a single frame of reference, greatly facilitating the development and consistent application of standards (Figure 35.3).

IRT is the best available way to construct a measurement scale from object-ively marked item response data. While classical test theory addresses some of the same issues, e.g., providing a range of techniques to equate test versions by transforming raw scores, we do not discuss these here.

Construct and measurement issues

We should consider the adequacy of a trait model for the purposes of educational assessment. An item banking model for British educational assessment was proposed and rejected as long ago as the 1970s, as offering too narrow a conception of learning and progression (Lacey & Lawton, 1981). As Mislevy (1992: 15) states, "contemporary conceptions of learning do not describe developing competence in terms of increasing trait values, but in terms of alternative constructs." That is, we should be interested in how learners differ in the *nature* of their ability, particularly if the purpose of testing is to inform further learning. This is doubtless true, but it assumes strong theories of cognition or learning which applied linguistics have not yet provided. Currently it seems that language proficiency can be adequately assessed through a traditional model of skills and competences – reading, writing, listening, speaking, language knowledge – with learners represented as progressing steadily, if unevenly, in each of these traits.

This does not mean that we need only one language proficiency construct; as indicated above proficiency tests arise in a context, for some purpose. Neither does it mean that we neglect differences between individual learners. A benefit of the trait model is that it provides a baseline against which individual profiles of performance can be drawn.

Moreover, we can use a trait model without thinking of language proficiency as something uniform and homogeneous. Classical test theory has taught us to view reliability as an aspect of construct validity reflected in measures of *internal consistency* – that is, the extent to which all items test the same thing. However, in a single scale covering a wide range of proficiency levels the notion of internal consistency becomes meaningless, because it is inaccessible to study: no tasks enable direct comparison of learners widely separated on the scale. The term *vertical equating* used of linking tests across several levels is inappropriate to the extent that *equating* is strictly only possible when tests are matched in content. In fact we recognize that language proficiency changes as learners progress. It has been described as an 'upside-down pyramid', growing in range as well as level, or more formally, as becoming increasingly multidimensional. Traits observable at higher levels are irrelevant at lower levels. Constructing and interpreting a scale should thus focus more on what distinguishes levels than on what they have in common, and this is as true for objectively constructed scales as for subjective ones.

Scales for subjectively rated skills (writing and speaking)

Language proficiency can be described in terms of *what* things people can do and *how well* they can do them. Different aspects of 'can do' can be identified: functional, in relation to real-world tasks; linguistic, in relation to features of accuracy, range, etc.; impact on reader or interlocutor, in relation to salient features of a level. A scale for subjectively rated skills can be constructed by selecting appropriately challenging tasks to elicit performance that can be rated with respect to each level. In practice the factors of task difficulty and performance quality (the *what* and the *how well*) are hard to disentangle in performance assessment (for example, the statement *I can write a short text on a range of familiar topics* requires us to define *short, familiar,* and what features of linguistic range, accuracy, etc., are expected). This is why proficiency scales expressed in such user-oriented, can-do terms do not translate simply into rating instruments. Matching a performance to the description of a level entails finding some best fit across a range of features. In this situation exemplars, and training and standardization centered on these, are essential to consistent rating.

To define levels in terms of tasks and expected performance features, and then place learners at levels according to their performance, is potentially circular. However, the illustrative scales of the CEFR exemplify an approach to escaping this circularity: the descriptors have been calibrated and assigned to levels on the basis of extensive response data from raters using descriptors to rate learners. These scales can be considered to have objectivity to the extent that they summarize the perceptions of many practitioners focusing on concrete samples of performance, rather than the judgment of an individual or a committee.

Standard setting

This brings us to step 4 – the inference of *extrapolation* from test performance to 'real-world' interpretation. This step clearly depends on decisions made earlier at the design stage. For subjectively rated skills, the meaning of levels is an intrinsic part of scale construction and the rating procedure. Thus a score (after any adjustments, particularly to compensate for rater severity) relates directly to its interpretation. For objectively marked skills, however, step 4 presents quite a challenge. The steps taken so far should ensure that a learner's score locates them consistently at a point on a scale. The question is how to interpret that point, given the indirect relation of objective test tasks to real world performance.

Standard setting has become an increasingly important issue in assessment, reflected in the space devoted to it in the *Standards for Educational and Psychological Testing* (AERA, APA, NCME, 1999). In consequence a canon of theory and techniques has developed. Zieky (2001) identifies four stages in the history of this development: innocence, awakening, disillusionment, and realistic acceptance. The disillusionment and subsequent realism relate to a recognition that standards are essentially judgmental. Judgments may be valid if based on well-defined and defensible procedures, but not 'correct', because finally they rest on unquantifiable notions of social worth, or consequences.

Language testing too has become increasingly concerned with standard setting. An example is the development of a methodology for relating language assessments to the CEFR (Council of Europe, 2003). Techniques have been borrowed from the above-mentioned canon. However, this is problematic. Aligning different languages to a common proficiency framework implies some degree of comparability between them. Even taking into account the specific contexts of assessments, it seems reasonable that there should be a 'correct' or at least a best-fit answer to the question first posed by Alderson: "is my B1 your B1?"

The view that standards are wholly judgmental follows from an emphasis in the literature and in practice on *task-centered* approaches, where experts study the content of tests and make judgments about how scores relate to levels of competence. But if we focus standard setting on the real-world language skills of learners, then it is clearly *learner-centered* techniques that are needed. These can potentially find 'correct' answers, if we accept that functional language ability provides a basis for comparison, through which standards set for one language can be validated against others.

The CEFR pilot manual (Council of Europe, 2003, ch. 6) discusses three such approaches under the heading *external validation*:

1   linking test performance to performance on another test taken as a criterion measure;
2   teacher ratings or learners' self-assessments, using can-do rating instruments;
3   qualitative studies e.g., of the processes learners employ when engaging with test or real-world tasks.

The problem of circularity is evident in the first approach: how can one judge if another test is a good criterion? The can-do approach is a promising one which has been successfully employed in the construction of the CEFR descriptor scales, and in the ALTE Can Do project (Jones, 2002) which related exam performance to candidates' self ratings of ability. Qualitative studies have also produced valuable insights.

Frameworks

By separating the validity of proficiency tests as measures, which is addressed at the design stage using theoretical and empirical arguments and evidence, from standard setting, which is an empirical process focusing on the real-world skills of learners, we find a reasonable approach to defining interpretable levels for a specific testing context. But step 5 shows a further step in which the specific context is aligned to a wider proficiency framework, serving as a more neutral point of reference.

Kinds of framework

When does a scale become a framework? The term is used of a system which brings together different purposes (e.g., teaching and assessment), users (e.g., exam providers), or qualifications. Thus the elements aligned within a framework vary. Within language education, frameworks may:

1   be programs for change or instruments for regulation and harmonization;
2   have international, national, or local scope;
3   encompass the whole of teaching and assessment or just one of these;
4   relate more or less clearly to language proficiency.

The US *Standards for Foreign Language Learning* (National Standards in Foreign Language Learning Project, 1996) exemplify an aspirational program for change – "a gauge against which to measure improvement in the years to come." The standards identify as broad goals the "five C's of foreign language education" – communication, cultures, connections, comparisons, communities. This framework seeks ambitiously to align content and performance standards to assessment, instruction, and learning.

The Canadian Language Benchmarks (CLB) (Centre for Canadian Language Benchmarks, 2002) exemplify a framework operated with a specific mandate. The benchmarks provide a standard framework for planning teaching and assessment in Canadian adult ESL programs. The body operating them is funded by federal and provincial governments, and has the authority to approve assessments for CLB use. The authors of the CEFR, on the other hand, carefully stress its neutrality – their intention is not to impose methodologies or harmonize language policies (see too Chapter 16 Levels, and Goals: Central Frameworks and Local Strategies).

The UK's National Qualifications Framework exemplifies a different purpose: to organize a wide range of qualifications in terms of their formal value. Within this framework language qualifications may align differently to the way they would within a purely proficiency framework.

The utility of frameworks

Relating performance to a proficiency framework is a tradeoff: specificity is lost, but the framework levels may be better known and have wider currency, hence utility. An example is Asset Languages, a multilingual framework development by Cambridge Assessment, in which the authors of this chapter are engaged. The assessments implement the Languages Ladder, a proficiency framework emerging from the UK's national languages strategy (DfES, 2002), and constitute a voluntary accreditation system supporting lifelong learning. Tests are available for three age groups from primary to adult, at all levels and in a wide range of languages. Clearly these learning contexts vary widely, and require differentiated tests. But it is evidently useful to relate these differ-ent groups to the same framework, as validly as possible.

The argument of utility however does not justify any kind of claim. The worldwide impact of the CEFR, for example, makes test providers want to advance claims of alignment to it, or educational planners to take it as a reference point. But the CEFR is an action-oriented, functional proficiency framework, and this has implications for both tests and teaching which cannot be ignored. If the goals and methods of either happen to be at odds with the basic func-tional approach, then any alignment is meaningless – a purely paper exercise.

Linking educational assessments

Mislevy (1992) discusses the feasibility of aligning local and national learning goals and assessments, in the US context of implementing 'standards-based education'. Purely statistical techniques have very limited application: differ-ences in the construct of *what* is tested and *how* it is tested seriously limit the power of purely statistical inference. Mislevy describes four levels of linking.

1   *Equating* is the strongest link, possible if two tests have been constructed from the same test specification to the same blueprint. Equating such tests allows them to be used interchangeably.
2   *Calibration* can link two tests constructed from the same specification but to a different blueprint, thus giving them different measurement characteristics.
3   *Projection* is an option where constructs are differently specified – tests do not measure 'the same thing'. It aims at predicting learners' scores on one test from another; predictive power naturally depends on the degree of similarity.
4   *Moderation* links tests where performance on one does not predict perform-ance on the other for an individual learner, e.g., tests of French and German. The tests are unrelated, but some comparison is desired. Moderation is thus based on some measure not of equivalence but of comparable *worth*. Figure 35.4 illustrates the hierarchical relation of these links.

Linking tests through alignment to a framework is an instance of modera-tion in this scheme: clearly a judgmental process, but one which, as we have argued above, can be empirically informed and replicable across languages.

Alignment to a proficiency framework depends on finding a basis of com-parison, identifying salient features of level descriptors which can be matched to salient features of the performance of specific groups. Re-interpreting or modifying descriptors may be necessary. For example, the scales illustrating the CEFR reference levels relate most clearly to an adult context. However, many projects connected with adapting the CEFR to young learners have suc-ceeded in constructing a link; and the learning objectives *Threshold* and *Waystage*, (van Ek & Trim, 1990a, 1990b), now subsumed as levels within the CEFR, have been successfully adapted for learners of all ages. Through such detailed and

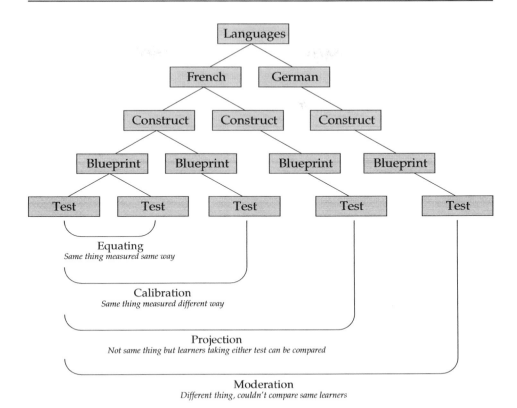

Figure 35.4 Hierarchy of links between assessments (after Mislevy, 1992)

concrete work the net of links between the framework and specific contexts is strengthened, and the meaning of the framework itself enriched.

The comparisons made within proficiency frameworks are, finally, not of assessments but of people. In this assessment-related chapter we have referred to these people as *learners* rather than *candidates* or *testees*, because learning is a fundamental factor deciding why most people take exams, the skills they bring to them, and the appropriate approach to assessing them. Proficiency frameworks are always, as importantly, learning ladders. Engaging more closely with learning, while providing valid interpretation of outcomes, is the next major challenge and goal for language assessment.

REFERENCES

AERA, APA, NCME (1999). *Standards for Educational and Psychological Testing.* American Psychological Association, National Council on Measurement in Education, American Educational Research Association.

Alderson, J. C. (1991). Bands and scores. In J. C. Alderson & B. North (eds.), *Language Testing in the 1990s: The Communicative Legacy* (vol. 1, no. 1, pp. 71–86). London: Macmillan.

Bachman, L. F. (1990). *Fundamental Considerations in Language Testing*. Oxford: Oxford University Press.

Bachman, L. F. & Palmer, A. S. (1996). *Language Testing in Practice: Designing and Developing Useful Language Tests*. Oxford: Oxford University Press.

Bond, T. G. & Fox, C. M. (2001). *Applying the Rasch Model*. Mahwah, NJ: Lawrence Erlbaum.

Centre for Canadian Language Benchmarks (2002). *Canadian Language Benchmarks 2000: Theoretical Framework*. Retrieved June 1 2007 from http://www.language.ca/

Council of Europe (2001). *Common European Framework of Reference for Languages*. Cambridge: Cambridge University Press.

Council of Europe (2003). Relating language examinations to the CEFR. Manual; Preliminary Pilot Version. Retrieved June 1 2007 from http://www.coe.int/T/DG4/Linguistic/Manuel1_EN.asp

DfES (2002). Languages for all: Languages for life. Retrieved June 1 2007 from http://www.dfes.gov.uk/languagesstrategy/

Hambleton, R. K., Swaminathan, H., & Rogers, H. J. (1991). *Fundamentals of Item Response Theory*, vol. 2. Newbury Park, CA: Sage.

Jones, N. (2002). Relating the ALTE Framework to the Common European Framework of Reference. In Council of Europe, *Common European Framework of Reference for Languages: Learning, Teaching, Assessment: Case Studies* (pp. 167–183). Strasbourg: Council of Europe Publishing.

Kane, M. T. (1992). An argument-based approach to validity. *Psychological Bulletin*, 12, 527–535.

Kane, M. T. (2004). Certification testing as an illustration of argument-based validation. *Measurement: Interdisciplinary Research and Perspectives*, 2(3), 135–170.

Kane, M. T., Crooks, T., & Cohen, A. (1999). Validating measures of performance. *Educational Measurement: Issues and Practice*, 18(2), 5–17.

Lacey, C. & Lawton, D. (1981). *Issues in Evaluation and Accountability*. London: Methuen.

Lantolf, J. P. & Frawley, W. (1992). Rejecting the OPI – Again: A response to Hagen. *ADFL Bulletin*, 23(2), 34–37.

Messick, S. (1989). Validity. In R. L. Linn (ed.), *Educational Measurement* (3rd edn., pp. 1–103). New York: American Council on Education/Macmillan.

Mislevy, R. J. (1992). *Linking Educational Assessments: Concepts, Issues, Methods, and Prospects*. Princeton: ETS.

Mislevy, R. J. (1996). Test theory reconceived. *Journal of Educational Measurement*, 33(4), 379–416.

Mislevy, R. J., Steinberg, L. S., & Almond, R. G. (2002). Design and analysis in task-based language assessment. *Language Testing*, 19(4) 477–496.

Mislevy, R. J., Steinberg, L. S., & Almond, R. G. (2003). On the Structure of Educational Assessments. *Measurement: Interdisciplinary Research and Perspectives*, 1(1), 3–62.

National Standards in Foreign Language Project (1996). *Standards for Foreign Language Learning: Preparing for the 21st Century*. Yonkers, NY: The National Standards in Foreign Language Project.

North, B. (2000). *The Development of a Common Framework Scale of Language Proficiency*. New York: Peter Lang.

Pollitt, A. (1991). Giving students a sporting chance: assessment by counting and by judging. In J. C. Alderson & B. North (eds.), *Language Testing in the 1990s* (pp. 46–59). London: Macmillan.

Pollitt, A. & Murray, N. L. (1996). What raters really pay attention to. In M. Milanovic & N. Saville (eds.), *Performance Testing, Cognition and Assessment* (Studies in Language Testing 3, pp. 74–91). Cambridge: University of Cambridge Local Examinations Syndicate.

Spolsky, B. (1995). *Measured Words: Development of Objective Language Testing*. Oxford: Oxford University Press.

Stevens, S. S. (1946). On the theory of scales of measurement. *Science*, 103, 677–680.

Van Ek, J. A. & Trim, J. L. M. (1990a). *Threshold 1990*. Cambridge: Cambridge University Press.

Van Ek, J. A. & Trim, J. L. M. (1990b). *Waystage 1990*. Cambridge: Cambridge University Press.

Weir, C. (2005). *Language Testing and Validation*. Basingstoke, UK: Palgrave Macmillan.

Wright, B. D. & Stone, M. H. (1979). *Best Test Design*. Chicago, IL: MESA Press.

Zieky, M. J. (2001). So much has changed: How the setting of cutscores has evolved since 1980. In G. J. Cizek (ed.), *Setting Performance Standards: Concepts, Methods and Perspectives* (pp. 19–52). Mahwah: NJ: Lawrence Erlbaum.

FURTHER READING

Alderson, J. C., Clapham, C., & Wall, D. (1995). *Language Test Construction and Evaluation*. Cambridge: Cambridge University Press.

Hughes, A. (2003). *Testing for Language Teachers*. Cambridge: Cambridge University Press.

Kolen, M. J. & Brennan, R. L. (2004). *Test Equating, Scaling, and Linking: Methods and Practices*. New York: Springer.

McNamara, T. (1996). *Measuring Second Language Performance*. New York: Longman.

Pellegrino, J. W., Chudowsky, N., & Glaser, R. (2001). *Knowing What Students Know: The Science and Design of Educational Assessment*. Washington, DC: National Academy Press.

Peterson, N. S., Kolen, M. J., & Hoover, H. D. (1989). Scaling, norming and equating. In R. L. Linn (ed.), *Educational Measurement* (3rd edn., pp. 221–262). New York: American Council on Education/Macmillan.

Weir, C. J. & Milanovic, M. (2003). *Continuity and Innovation: Revising the Cambridge Proficiency in English Examination 1913–2002*. Cambridge: Cambridge University Press/UCLES.

36 Nationally Mandated Testing for Accountability: English Language Learners in the US

MICHELINE CHALHOUB-DEVILLE AND CRAIG DEVILLE

Introduction

Educational reform is primarily an expression of concern with how well schools are functioning and with the quality of educational outcomes and/or student learning. This concern is expressed in many countries around the world. For example, educational reform is widely discussed in the UK (Broadfoot, 1996), Australia (Brindley, 2001), Israel (Shohamy, 2001), and the USA (Wixson, Dutro, & Athan, 2003). The call for educational reform is propelled by political rhetoric emphasizing that education lies at the heart of economic development, international competitiveness, and social harmony (Haertel & Herman, 2005). Advocating education as a significant vehicle that propels society to achieve such goals and improve people's quality of life is not new. What is new, however, is the push for accountability, its scope, and its implications. Accountability is increasingly operationalized as testing systems that include all students and that reward/punish schools and teachers based on students' performance.

The present chapter addresses educational reform that has affected English language learners (ELLs) in the US. The chapter opens with an overview of recent policies in the US that culminated in the No Child Left Behind Act (PL 107-110, 2001), referred to as NCLB, which includes Title III requirements to test all ELLs. Next, challenges encountered when developing assessment batteries that meet NCLB's Title III requirements are discussed. Finally, the chapter provides a critical analysis of some of the realities of testing the ELL student population.

Federal/National Intervention and Mandated Testing

The expanded involvement of the US federal government in education can be traced back to the enactment of the Elementary and Secondary Education Act, or ESEA (PL 89-10, 1965). Public schools that seek funds from the federal government are required to abide by ESEA regulations. Over the years, these regulations have increasingly been mandating tests, enlarging the scope of who is held accountable for test results, and expanding the system of rewards or sanctions associated with those results. "In the 1960s . . . attempts to use tests for school accountability generally failed to be approved . . . In the following two decades, states moved toward statewide testing programs that had higher stakes initially for students and later for schools and educators" (Linn, 2005: 2). In the past, test scores were typically used to monitor student achievement and growth in school, and students were often held accountable for their performance. A shift happened in the 1980s in terms of who is accountable. At that time, states and the federal government began holding educators and schools accountable, and this shift has taken more concrete forms under the last three presidents and has occurred across both Republican and Democratic administrations, i.e., both political parties have taken up the banner of accountability and testing.

In recent decades, the push for educational reform and for raising expectations of students' performance was given a huge boost when President Bush (I) convened the 1989 Education Summit, which all 50 state governors attended, including then-Governor Clinton. The governors agreed to a number of far-reaching goals for education that were to be achieved by the year 2000. The Educate America Act (PL 103-227, 2000), or Goals 2000 as it is known, focused attention on the need for rigorous standards together with assessment systems related to those standards. Later, President Clinton also embraced Goals 2000 and made them the centerpiece of his educational agenda. President Clinton, however, tied educational reform to accountability demands by requiring states seeking federal funds to implement national standards and a national test to ensure the realization of Goals 2000. His efforts to institute standards and tests were fiercely blocked by Republican leaders in office. Nevertheless, as Wixson et al. (2003) write:

> although the *national* standards and assessments movement had been forced "underground" in the mid-1990s, it quickly took root and blossomed through different venues. Ironically, it would be the conservative Republican leaders who wanted to reduce the power of the federal government in education during the mid-1990s who orchestrated the new tools of national and federal education reform in the late 1990s and early 2000s. (pp. 79–80, emphasis in original)

Essentially, when President George W. Bush (II) came into office, he revived Clinton's ideas in the form of mandated state-based standards and assessments tied to a federal system of rewards and corrective measures. These efforts were formalized in the NCLB Act.

NCLB

NCLB attempts to influence educational practices in each state by holding public schools accountable for the test scores of all students and by applying sanctions to schools whose students do not exhibit adequate yearly progress (AYP). In terms of the substance of the Act, NCLB emphasizes content standards focusing on rigorous educational goals in reading, math, and science; calls for external testing to measure student achievement in grades 3–8, and one high school grade; requires documentation of growth and progress from year to year, i.e., AYP; mandates the testing of every population subgroup (racial groups, students with disabilities, ELLs, among others); sets the goal that all students will achieve proficiency by 2014; and finally, institutes a system of sanctions to induce educational reform. If schools fail on any of the criteria over a period of time, they are designated as "in need of improvement" and actions are taken to restructure/reconstitute the school. Relevant to the present chapter is NCLB's stipulation that all students be tested, including subgroups, such as ELL students, whom schools have often excluded from testing in the past.

Starting in the 1990s, teachers and administrations were increasingly being asked to assess students who are non-native speakers of English (LaCelle-Peterson & Rivera, 1994; August & Hakuta, 1997). As Abedi et al. (2000) write, the reauthorization of the ESEA, the Improving America's Schools Act (PL 103–302, 1994), dictates that "all children should be given educational experiences to assist them in achieving high standards. It follows that children previously excluded from large-scale assessments because of . . . limited proficiency in English must have the opportunity to participate" (p. 16). As such, the ESEA of 1994 required ELL students to take subject area tests, from which they had before been exempted. This stipulation, however, was a cause of trepidation. Educators (Council of Chief State School Officers, 2001) expressed concern that the language of these assessments is entirely in English, a language the ELLs are still learning. ELLs' performances on accountability tests are thus confounded with their English language proficiency, which compromises the construct validity of the ensuing scores and negatively impacts the demonstration and interpretation of ELLs' level of knowledge and skills in the content areas.

While educators were concerned about the likely misinterpretation and use of ELLs' scores on accountability tests, they were also cautious about calling for the exclusion of these students from such tests. Bailey and Butler (2003) state that: "if ELL students are not tested, information on their achievement is, in effect, absent from any decision-making that impacts their school careers" (p. 3). In accommodating such concerns, NCLB specifies that students whose English language proficiency precludes them from obtaining meaningful test scores on content area tests must be administered an academic English language proficiency test. The regulations that guide the academic language assessment of ELLs are presented in Title III of the NCLB Act.

NCLB Title III

The substance of NCLB Title III requirements reflects the conclusions and recommendations from numerous researchers. For example, Bailey (2000) examines the language present in already existing tests at the eleventh grade level, including mathematics, science, and reading comprehension, and raises concerns that the English language demands of these tests are beyond most beginning ELLs. She recommends that ELL students be administered an "assessment of academic language proficiency itself to determine whether ELLs are indeed linguistically equipped to succeed on standardized content assessments independent of their content area knowledge" (p. 99). Implicit and critical in the quote from Bailey (2000) is that the field, at the time, lacked measures of *academic* language proficiency.

Butler and Castellon-Wellington (2000) also argue that general language proficiency tests commonly used before NCLB were inadequate to document ELL students' academic language proficiency. After studying ELLs' test scores on one such general measure, the Language Assessment Scales (LAS), and their relationship to scores on a state-mandated achievement test, the researchers conclude that "the LAS criterion for competent performance may not be adequate for determining whether ELLs can handle the type of language found on content assessments" (p. 52). As a result, the researchers call for measures that specifically assess academic language use.

NCLB's Title III formalized the call for appropriate measures of ELLs' academic language proficiency. The Act requires reporting scores that document ELLs' academic language abilities in the four modalities of listening, speaking, reading, and writing, plus comprehension. Typically, comprehension has been operationalized as some combination of reading and listening scores. NCLB states that ELLs must demonstrate AYP on this assessment battery with the objective that they soon have the requisite language skills to be able to take the state's subject area tests (in English).

While the law is specific in terms of assessing the four modalities with regard to academic language proficiency, it understandably lacks information and guidance with regard to the specific features involved in testing academic language use. Test developers have had to grapple with fundamental design issues when creating Title III instruments, including how to operationalize the construct and how to ground the assessment frameworks across grade levels using published standards.

Operationalization of Academic Language Use

NCLB's Title III requires schools to assess the academic English language proficiency of ELL students, with the assumption that there exists a difference between academic and non-academic, i.e., social, language use. In the second language (L2) field, this differentiation in language proficiency has long been advanced as a functional approach to represent the L2 construct (Cummins, 1981). Cummins differentiates between everyday communicative language skills and more abstract, academic language ability. He calls these two types of language use cognitive/academic language proficiency (C/ALP) and basic interpersonal and communicative skills (BICS). Cummins holds that C/ALP pertains to the language needed to perform in academic situations and that BICS encompasses language used in situations outside formal learning contexts.

Because students sound proficient in everyday communication does not mean they are proficient in using the language to perform more cognitively demanding and abstract tasks, i.e., to use appropriate language in the school and classroom environment. As Cummins (2001) states:

> classroom instruction should focus not only on developing students' conversational fluency in English but also on their academic proficiency. Students must gain access to the language of literature, science, math, and other content areas . . . academic language entails vocabulary that is much less frequent than typically found in interpersonal conversation, grammatical constructions that are unique to text and considerably more complex than those found in conversation, and significant cognitive processing demands that derive from the fact that meanings expressed paralinguistically in conversation (e.g., gestures, facial expressions, intonation, etc.) must be expressed linguistically in text. (pp. 123–124)

The quote articulates fundamental differences between everyday and academic language use in terms of grammar, vocabulary, discourse, and cognitive demands. It also provides some guidance toward the domains of language use, e.g., subject areas from which to sample for academic language instruction and testing. The literature in general, however, does not provide any detailed operationalization of the construct of academic language proficiency in these different subject areas, making test development exceedingly difficult.

Butler and Stevens (2001) and Bailey and Butler (2003) make the same argument. They contend that very little information is available about the language employed in textbooks, classrooms, schools, and achievement tests at various grade levels. Butler and Stevens write: "[t]here is an urgent need to systematically operationalize academic language across content areas by describing the language used in mainstream classrooms and on content tests and then translating that information into academic assessments and guidelines for teachers" (p. 26). A plausible and actually mandated place for test developers to look for guidance to help delineate the academic language use domain is the published language and content standards. As will be shown below, however, standards-based test development presents its own challenges.

Standards

The alignment between standards and what is assessed lies at the heart of NCLB accountability testing. Those engaged in the development of Title III ELL academic language tests are required to incorporate in their test construction efforts those standards promulgated by both subject area and English as a second language (ESL) professional organizations. These various sets of standards articulate in their respective documents the content knowledge and skills, along with the academic language, students need in order to function in school settings.

Starting in the 1990s and escalating with NCLB, educators have witnessed a proliferation of standards. Professional organizations such as the National Council of Teachers of Mathematics (NCTM), as well as those for English language arts, science, etc., have published standards and benchmarks that guide curriculum developers, textbook authors, and test constructors. These standards are more like compendia than systematic prescriptions as to what should be taught (and tested) at different grade levels, meaning that no sensible educator would attempt to cover the entire compendium of standards and expectations. States typically create modified versions of these standards, which are then employed by schools for instructional and assessment purposes. In spite of the standards' widespread backing and use, their theoretical underpinnings have been questioned (Wixson et al., 2003), a phenomenon also observed with the ESL standards.

In terms of ELL language instruction and assessment, states have for the most part aligned their own standards to the *ESL Standards for Pre-K-12 Students* (TESOL, 1997). The *ESL Standards* organize language use pedagogical information within three goals, covering social, academic, and diverse cultural settings, referred to as Goals 1–3 respectively. The *ESL Standards* represent a functional approach to language use, and are essentially task- and behavior-oriented, not so much construct-driven. In this regard, the *ESL Standards* resemble popular language assessment frameworks, which define proficiency according to a hierarchy of tasks, often with little theoretical support.

Apart from these concerns, a serious challenge that developers have to contend with when designing their Title III test frameworks is identifying the language and task demands underlying the subject area standards. Trying to extract the language demands embodied in the content standards is quite unwieldy for a variety of reasons, including the reality that the standards were developed with an eye toward delineating their subject area content and not the ELL language demands associated with that content. As for the *ESL Standards*, analysis by Bailey and Butler (2003) reveals considerable overlap in terms of language and task expectations for the social and academic Goals 1 and 2. Such overlap of essentially C/ALP and BICS language use adds to the difficulty of defining and designing differentiated item/task specifications for measuring academic language.

Another difficulty facing those developing Title III assessments is the need to reconcile the information in the varying subject area standards as well as that from the *ESL Standards*. Until very recently, this critical issue has not been addressed. Researchers such as Bailey, Butler, and Sato (2005) have been actively exploring and making headway developing standard-to-standards linkages, i.e., alignment frameworks incorporating both content and language demands. Already their framework has proved informative by demonstrating where there is good correspondence between the *ESL Standards* and the content language underlying instructional tasks. Their work has also pointed out where gaps between the sets of standards exist, a problem which can then be addressed by responsive instructors and test developers alike. This important work will go a long way in helping professionals construct better tests of academic language proficiency for ELLs.

Content aside, still another matter to consider is the sticky issue of performance standards. The lack of consistency and uniformity in the specific content standards, commented on above, is also observed with regard to performance standards across states. States have set, with approval from the US Department of Education, very different performance standards, i.e., proficiency thresholds, to meet the NCLB requirements (Linn, 2005). Linn shows that the state averages of the percentage of students attaining proficiency using state-defined standards bears little relationship to the percentage of proficient students as found in scores from national tests. Some states that appear at the bottom of rankings on the national tests will rank very high with respect to the percentage of their students deemed proficient on their own state tests.

In summary, content, language, and performance standards provide a rather shaky foundation upon which to build solid curricular and assessment frameworks. As Linn (2005) argues, standards vary too much in their quality, with respect to both rigor and specificity, to be truly useful. He goes on to say that some states' standards are so wanting that they do not even specify what is to be learned at different grade levels. Thus, if the standards and performance levels, which are supposed to undergird tests, are confusing and weak, then tests are quite unlikely to have the desired impact in terms of educational reform and defensible accountability. On the other hand, if tests are based on rigorous content/language and challenging performance standards, then tests have a chance to serve as one strategy for educational reform. Serious consideration, therefore, should be given to evaluating and strengthening the quality of the available standards. Until then, test developers have to work with what is available and essentially use the present-day content and language standards as a starting point to initiate the process of operationalizing the academic language use construct.

ELL Proficiency and Grade Level

A consternating challenge when conceptualizing, developing, and implementing an assessment system for ELLs is the need to create tests that take into
account a full range of proficiency – minimal to advanced proficiency – at each
grade level. Additionally, students' cognitive development, maturity, and
interests dictate that different language features must accommodate different
age groups. An immediate question arises as to whether a separate academic
language test would need to be developed for each grade or whether a span of
school grades could be administered the same test. In this regard, different
considerations come into play, including the ELLs' language, academic, and
cognitive development across grades.

Researchers such as Collier (1989) and Cummins (1981) provide evidence
that length of time in school is an important variable in determining how long
students need to attain BICS (about two years) and C/ALP (at least seven
years). Fradd, McGee, and Wilen (1994) argue that in addition to time in
school, the different subject areas should also be considered: "There are differences in the length of time required to learn different aspects of the curriculum. These differences are based on the subject areas being tested" (p. 66).
In short, the language development literature argues that – unlike knowledge
in subject areas such as math and science – school grade level is not indicative
of proficiency level in English but depends on the number of years in school
and just as importantly on the subject area. Academic language test developers,
therefore, must accommodate the increasingly complex language that students
learn and need in each subject area, and they must capture the key linguistic
growth that occurs at different grade junctures.

Content and language and standards incorporate different grade spans to
signify shifts in the nature of the subject area and language curricula at those
junctures. For example, the standards in mathematics, the *Principles and Standards for School Mathematics* (NCTM, 2000) segment their standards into grades
K–2, 3–5, 6–8, and 9–12. The *National Science Education Standards* (National
Research Council, 1996) include the following divisions: K–4, 5–8, 9–12. The
ESL Standards for Pre-K-12 Students (TESOL, 1997) partition the standards into:
K–3, 4–8, 9–12. Interesting to note is the consensus on these junctures at the
upper grade levels but not at the lower grades.

In line with the standards cited above, NCLB Title III instruments have
adopted similar grade spans at the upper grade levels. For example, the
revised LAS and ELDA (English Language Development Assessment) agree in
their grouping of grades 6–8 and 9–12. However, LAS divides the lower-
grade testing into K–1, 2–3, and 4–5 groupings, while ELDA tests grade groups
K–2 and 3–5. A plausible reason for the lack of conformity in the formation of
grades spans at the lower levels is that pupils in the primary grades learn and
develop so quickly. Learners move from pre-literacy to literacy at different
rates, both curriculum and instruction are more learner- than group-centered,

and these factors lead to how the variations in school and grade configurations, and hence test administration policies, are established. So, as sometimes
happens, the realities and exigencies of testing can determine both test construction and administration practices. Yet, until sound theory and research
are available, these testing practices are reasonable and functional.

The Realities of NCLB Standardized Testing

It is difficult to categorize strengths and weaknesses of critical NCLB Title III
issues, since each exhibits both advantages and disadvantages. Below are some
important realities of this legislation with both their positive and negative
aspects presented.

Mandate of 100 percent proficiency for all

Performance improvement and proficiency attainment are emphasized for all
students under NCLB. Such rhetoric is hard to argue with, but Linn (2005)
contends that the NCLB expectation that all students achieve proficiency
is unrealistic. Based on comparisons to performance trends found on the
NAEP, a widely used national test designed specifically to monitor student
achievement, Linn maintains that "the rate of improvement in student achievement would have to be many times faster for the next decade than it has been
for any comparable period of time in the last 40 years" (p. 15). While this
reality may not detract from the utility of an overly optimistic goal, it does call
into question sanctions imposed on schools when unrealistic goals have not
been attained.

Item type and cost

Many bemoan the fact that accountability measures, like NCLB, continue
to rely heavily on selected response item types, like multiple-choice, when
many educators have been calling for performance-based assessments (e.g.,
Madaus, 1993). The rationale for more complex measures is that performance-
based assessments are thought to better evoke and engage the more multi-
faceted abilities involving higher order thinking and problem solving. Yet,
what test developers and state users must also consider are issues of cost.
For example, the "U.S. General Accounting Office (2003) recently estimated
the cost to states of implementing NCLB using only multiple-choice tests is
approximately $1.9 billion, whereas the cost if states were also to include a
small number of hand-scored open-response items such as essays would be
about $5.3 billion" (Hamilton, 2003: 31). As such, states are faced with tough
decisions when they try to balance matters of content and cost.

Disaggregation of scores by subgroups

The NCLB requirement to report scores for ELL students separately has been viewed positively by many educators. The potential downside of this, however, is that schools with sizable ELL subgroups also tend to have sizable subgroups of other students (e.g., those on free and reduced lunch, i.e., from poor income families, students with disabilities, etc.). Additionally, a relatively high number of ELL students qualify for these other subgroups. The more the subgroups a school has, the greater the probability that such schools will fail to show AYP, and thus face sanctions.

Redesignation of ELL students

As ELL students gain English language proficiency, they are moved out of the ELL subgroup and are no longer designated as part of the ELL subgroup for testing purposes. This seemingly positive occurrence has negative implications, however. The predicament is that the redesignation of the proficient students presents problems for a school having to exhibit AYP for the ELL subgroup. Simply put, the high-performing students are removed from the subgroup of ELLs and schools are then asked to report how well the less proficient ELL students perform on the subject matter tests. The US Department of Education has become aware of this paradox that prevents the ELL subgroup from demonstrating progress. The government now allows states, for score reporting purposes, to include the performance of the ELL-proficient students for up to two years after their redesignation. This amendment will only partially solve the problem because new ELLs are continuously and in greater numbers being added into the subgroup.

ELL related state policies

The policies affecting the testing of ELLs in the 50 states are far from uniform. According to a survey of state policies conducted by Rivera et al. (2000), numerous states have mandated that ELLs be included in statewide assessment after the students have been in the schools a specified length of time, anywhere from one to three years. That is, ELLs in one state may be required to sit for subject matter tests after just one year in school, while those elsewhere may experience a longer wait time before having to take the state's content area assessments. This prescribed readiness based on time in school neglects that fact that ELL students vary greatly in terms of cognitive abilities, language development, academic history, literacy background, length of time in the US, among other variables (as discussed above). ELLs are a relatively heterogeneous group. Decisions as to a student's capability to take a standardized subject matter achievement test in English (where the test scores reflect meaningful representations of what the student knows and can do) should ideally be made for each student individually, not for the group as a whole. The challenge is to create a system that systematically integrates these variables to help make the appropriate decisions for the differentiated ELL students.

Conclusion

NCLB represents the federal government's most far-reaching attempt to influence educational practices and engender reform. Both parties, Democrats and Republicans, have championed reform driven by accountability testing. As such, it is reasonable to conclude that NCLB may, in the future, change some of its provisions, but is not likely go away, irrespective of the party affiliation of the administration in power. Accountability testing will likely remain a mainstay of the US educational system.

The accountability push under NCLB requires the testing of all students, including ELLs, to ensure that no students are excluded from efforts to raise educational achievement. While this practice has been lauded by most in the professional community, serious concerns continue to be raised regarding the efficacy and fairness of testing for accountability, especially given how inconsistently the law has been interpreted and implemented.

On a broader note, some educators express concerns that tests intended for accountability differ markedly from tests for learning. As Haertel and Herman (2005) state, this difference is "not so much in source – external versus classroom – but more importantly in design impetus and use. Assessments designed to serve learning purposes provide feedback for students and teachers that can be used to modify teaching and learning activities in which they are engaged" (p. 26). Somewhat cynically, Haertel and Herman go on to say that: "perhaps accountability testing merely offers the public some hollow assurance as to elected officials' commitment to education. After all, those who propose new testing programs are likely to see achievement gains in 2 or 3 years, right on schedule for the next election" (p. 2). In other words, testing and accountability seem to be the most expedient approach used by politicians to show the electorate their dedication to education.

Past experience indicates that test-driven educational reform has repeatedly fallen short in delivering the desired educational change. By implementing testing legislation, policy makers put too much faith into test scores as accurate and appropriate single measures of student progress and indicators of the general health of educational affairs. Educational reform has to consider other change agents and indices of improvement besides testing. Significant factors such as the professional preparation of teachers (not just language teachers, but also content teachers, staff, and administrators), availability and quality of instructional materials and other resources, and community and parental support have to be targeted in a systematic manner as well. No shortage of valuable educational indicators exists, and an accountability system that ignores these and focuses exclusively on test scores will never adequately address real reform.

REFERENCES

Abedi, Jamal, Lord, Carol, Hofstetter Carolyn, & Baker, Eva (2000). Impact of accommodation strategies on English language learners' test performance. *Educational Measurement: Issues and Practice*, 19(3), 16–26.

August, Diane & Hakuta, Kenji (eds.) (1997). *Improving Schooling for Language-Minority Children*. Washington, DC: National Academy Press.

Bailey, Alison L. (2000). Language analysis of standardized achievement tests: Considerations in the assessment of English Language Learners. In *The Validity of Administering Large-Scale Content Assessments to English Language Learners: An Investigation From Three Perspectives* (Final Deliverable to OERI/OBEMLA; pp. 85–115). Los Angeles: University of California, National Center for Research on Evaluation, Standards, and Student Testing (CRESST).

Bailey, Alison L. & Butler, Frances A. (2003). *An Evidentiary Framework for Operationalizing Academic Language for Broad Application to K-12 Education: A Design Document* (CSE Report 611). Los Angeles, CA: University of California, National Center for Research on Evaluation, Standards, and Student Testing (CRESST).

Bailey, Alison L., Butler, Frances A., & Sato, Edynn (2005). *Standards-to-Standards Linkage under Title III: Exploring Common Language Demands in ELD and Science Standards* (CSE Report 667). Los Angeles, CA: University of California, National Center for Research on Evaluation, Standards, and Student Testing (CRESST).

Brindley, Geoff (2001). Outcomes-based assessment in practice: Some examples and emerging insights. *Language Testing*, 18, 393–407.

Broadfoot, Patricia (1996). *Education, Assessment and Society: A Sociological Analysis*. Buckingham, UK: Open University Press.

Butler, Frances A. & Stevens, Robin (2001). Standardized assessment of the content knowledge of English language learners K-12: Current trends and old dilemmas. *Language Testing*, 18, 409–427.

Butler, Frances A. & Castellon-Wellington, Martha (2000). Students' concurrent performance on tests of English language proficiency and academic achievement. In *The Validity of Administering Large-Scale Content Assessments to English Language Learners: An Investigation from Three Perspectives* (Final Deliverable to OERI/OBEMLA; pp. 51–83). Los Angeles, CA: University of California, National Center for Research on Evaluation, Standards, and Student Testing (CRESST).

Collier, Virginia P. (1989). How long? A synthesis of research on academic achievement in a second language. *TESOL Quarterly*, 23, 509–531.

Council of Chief State School Officers (2001). *Summary of State Responses to Informal Survey: State Development of English Language Development Standards and Aligned ELD Assessment*. Washington, DC: Council of Chief State School Officers.

Cummins, James (1981). Age on arrival and immigrant second language learning in Canada: A reassessment. *Applied Linguistics*, 2, 132–149.

Cummins, James (2001). Assessment options for bilingual learners. In Josefina V. Tinajero & Sandra Rollins Hurley (eds.), *Literacy Assessment of Bilingual Learners* (pp. 115–129). Boston: Allyn & Bacon.

Elementary and Secondary Education Act (ESEA) of 1965, Public Law No. 89-10.

Fradd, Sandra H., McGee, Patricia L., & Wilen, Diane K. (1994). *Instructional Assessment: An Integrative Approach to Evaluating Student Performance*. Reading, MA: Addison Wesley.

Goals (2000). Educate America Act, Public Law No. 103-227.

Haertel, Edward & Herman, Joan (2005). *A Historical Perspective for Validity Arguments for Accountability Testing* (CSE Technical Report No. 654). Los Angeles: University of California, National Center for Research on Evaluation, Standards, and Student Testing (CRESST).

Hamilton, Laura (2003). Assessment as a policy tool. In Robert E. Floden (ed.), *Review of Research in Education* 27, 25–68.

Improving America's Schools Act of 1994, Public Law No. 103-382.

LaCelle-Peterson, Mark W. & Rivera, Charlene (1994). Is it real for all kids? A framework for equitable assessment policies for English language learners. *Harvard Educational Review*, 64(1), 55–75.

Linn, Robert L. (2005). *Test-Based Educational Accountability in the Era of No Child Left Behind* (CSE Tech. Report No. 651). Los Angeles: University of California, National Center for Research on Evaluation, Standards, and Student Testing (CRESST).

Madaus, George F. (1993). A national testing system: Manna from above? An historical/technological perspective. *Educational Assessment*, 1(1), 9–26.

National Council of Teachers of Mathematics (NCTM) (2000). *Principles and Standards for School Mathematics*. Reston, VA: National Council of Teachers of Mathematics.

National Research Council (1996). *National Science Education Standards*. Washington, DC: National Academy Press.

No Child Left Behind Act (NCLB) of 2001, Public Law No. 107-110.

Rivera, Charlene, Stansfield, Charles W., Scialdone, Lewis, & Sharkey, Margaret (2000). *An Analysis of State Policies for the Inclusion and Accommodation of English Language Learners in State Assessment Programs During 1998–1999*. Arlington, VA: The George Washington University Center for Equity and Excellence in Education.

Shohamy, Elana (2001). *The Power of Tests: A Critical Perspective on the Uses of Language Tests*. London: Longman.

TESOL (1997). *ESL Standards for Pre-K-12 Students*. Alexandria, VA: TESOL.

Wixson, Karen K., Dutro, Elizabeth, & Athan, Ruth G. (2003). The challenge of developing content standards. *Review of Educational Research*, 27, 69–107.

FURTHER READING

Brindley, Geoff (1998). Outcomes-based assessment and reporting in language learning programmes: A review of the issues. *Language Testing*, 15, 45–85.

Collier, Virginia P. (1987). Age and rate of acquisition of second language for academic purposes. *TESOL Quarterly*, 21, 617–641.

Cummins, James (1979). Cognitive/academic language proficiency, linguistic interdependence, the optimal age question, and some other matters. *Working Papers on Bilingualism*, 19, 197–205.

Heck, Ronald H. (2004). *Studying Educational and Social Policy: Theoretical Concepts and Research Methods*. Mahwah, NJ: Lawrence Erlbaum.

Part III   Research–Practice Relationships

37 Task-Based Teaching and Learning

TERESA PICA

Research and Practice Relationships

Since its inception, the field of educational linguistics has challenged teachers and researchers to define their roles, extend their responsibilities, and make a difference in the education of language learners. "Tasks," the focus of this chapter, provide an opportunity for teachers and researchers to respond to the challenges of their field in complementary and productive ways.

For teachers, challenges have arisen at both academic and professional levels, seen most recently in a broadening of their responsibilities as teachers of language to those of "teachers of language learners." They are expected to guide their students' acquisition of social rules, learning strategies, and linguistic features, and to foster their appreciation of cultural diversity and identity. Teachers assigned to immersion programs or subject content and theme based classrooms find themselves charting unfamiliar academic disciplines and teaching new material in a language that their students are struggling to learn. As illustrated in this chapter, tasks can serve as productive, instructional tools in these circumstances.

Language researchers, too, are challenged in their academic and professional pursuits. They are expected to maintain a robust research agenda and a solid record of publication, conference participation, and community service. Many are asked to prepare teachers and researchers in the expanding disciplinary and methodological content of their field, and to write grant proposals to fund these efforts. Their course assignments range from theoretical and sociolinguistics to second language acquisition (SLA), to methods of teaching, testing, and research. For an increasing number of researchers, tasks have come to serve as a focus of their research questions, a tool in their research methodology, a topic that cuts across their courses, and an instructional approach that piques their interest.

Both teachers and researchers find the methodological options made available by their field among the most challenging, yet gratifying, aspects of their work. Nowadays, it is not unusual for teachers and researchers to dip into the same store of materials and activities as they make decisions about classroom instruction or data collection. Until recently, however, they seldom looked to each other to inform their decisions and concerns. When questions arose in their everyday practice, teachers would select activities and materials from course textbooks and turn to standards and criteria set by program administrators and policy makers. Although relevant information could be extracted from research on SLA (as reviewed in Pica, 1994), most SLA studies were not designed to address specific classroom issues. Teachers found them remote from their experiences and irrelevant to their students' needs. Often studies whose findings could have been of value to teachers went without their notice, as they were featured in publications and conferences that were not readily accessible or affordable.

Because early SLA research needed first to tackle theoretical questions about learning processes and developmental sequences, carefully controlled, laboratory-like conditions were required. These conditions bore little resemblance to the linguistically diverse classroom settings where teachers and their students convened. Researchers were well aware of questions about the classroom as a site for SLA, but were not yet prepared methodologically to address them. (Tarone, Swain, & Fathman, 1976; Hatch, 1978).

In recent years, these issues of access and preparation have eased. New outlets, forged through online journals, email correspondence, organizational websites, and listservs have opened opportunities for contact and exchange of materials and ideas. Much teacher education at pre-service and in-service levels now includes research focused courses, assignments, and readings. Teachers have become savvy research consumers and researchers, as they carry out studies on their classrooms (Allwright & Bailey, 1991) and engage in reflective and exploratory practice (Allwright, 2005). Groundbreaking studies on classroom discourse have provided a foundation for researchers to work in schools and classrooms. Their publications on the processes and practices of teaching and learning have helped to dispel the view of the classroom as a "black box", whose interactions, relationships, and activities could be neither studied nor understood (see Pica, 1997; Lightbown, 2000; Chaudron, 2005).

Whereas earlier studies examined L2 communication, input, and interlocutor relationships in lab-like settings, and applied their findings to classroom practice, newer research has looked at these features within classroom contexts, and made instructional recommendations on that basis. The teaching–research relationship has also become bi-directional, as instructional practice has influenced theory driven research. This is especially apparent in the growing interest in tasks, long a staple of the communicative classroom (Ur, 1988), as instruments for data collection on learning strategies and outcomes, as well as treatments that activate underlying cognitive and social processes.

Tasks have been used to gather data in research on input comprehensibility (Doughty & Pica, 1986) and L2 development (Mackey, 1999), and have themselves been studied as to their suitability for generating modified input and output for SLA (Mackey & McDonough, 2000). With their multiplicity of uses and flexibility of roles, tasks have made it possible to address educational issues that arise in the everyday lives of teachers, and to offer an approach to the contexts, processes, and outcomes of L2 learning.

Tasks in Teaching and Research

Many attributes have been applied to tasks as activities for language teaching and research. Foremost among them are an emphasis on communication and completion. Task participants must communicate information in order to make decisions, solve problems, and reach outcomes. They must be accurate and comprehensible in their communication, letting each other know when they are unclear, and giving each other opportunities to adjust their L2 sounds, syntax, and lexicon accordingly. A task is considered completed if decisions are made, problems solved, and outcomes attained.

These design features have made tasks suitable as instructional units (Willis, 1996), course activities (Prabhu, 1987), and enhancements to the language curriculum (Nunan, 1989; Crookes & Gass, 1993). Task features have also made them effective research treatments for learners to receive modified input and feedback, produce modified output, and advance developmental outcomes (Pica et al., 1996; Iwashita, 2003). Tasks can serve as instruments for collecting samples of interlanguage from learners as they exchange information and respond to corrections and clarification questions (Mackey & Oliver, 2002; Gass & Alvarez-Torres, 2005). Tasks can also provide data on specific grammatical features. Interview tasks, for example, are well suited to research on question formation (Mackey, 1999) and comparison tasks, for the study of English morphemes *-er* and *-est* (Loschky & Bley-Vroman, 1993).

Tasks can be implemented by teachers and researchers for independent or joint purposes. A problem-solving task, for example, can originate in either a student textbook or professional resource guide (e.g., Ur, 1988). A teacher might assign the task to a group of students, making sure the information needed to solve the problem was distributed evenly, so that they all might engage in collaborative planning and practice. The same task might be adopted by the researcher, and used with the same student group in order to study the linguistic features of their planning and practice as sources of modified, comprehensible input and output. A single task can be implemented jointly when teachers and researchers share identical concerns, for example, on task sufficiency for language acquisition or on task integration within an already existing curriculum. With planning and cooperation, they should be able to implement a single task, at the same time, and in the same classroom, without interfering with each other's work.

As instructional activities, tasks have long been at home in the classroom. In serving a role as research instruments, tasks have gradually taken their place in the classroom as well. In so doing, tasks have given the classroom increasing prominence as a site for research. Despite the popular perception of the classroom as a source of "messy data" which have little external validity, the classroom has become a context for addressing contemporary questions on SLA. Many of these questions relate to L2 features that take a long time for learners to notice, internalize, and retain. Data must be collected over many months, so many, in fact, that it is often not possible for researchers to secure the commitment of learners to assemble in specially constructed, controlled settings over a sufficient stretch of time. Access to classroom learners enrolled in semester or year-long classes can offset these difficulties considerably.

As classroom ethnographies have clearly demonstrated, however, researchers must translate access into actuality if they are to gain the acceptance of their research participants. Students and teachers must feel a sense of involvement in their learning if they are to be reliable candidates for research. Researchers themselves must be ready to participate in classroom life in ways that are compatible with their interests and goals, but supportive to teachers and students. It is in this context that tasks can play a dual and vital role.

Research tasks can be constructed from communication games, topic centered discussion activities, and content focused readings, all of which are employed extensively as instructional tools across a growing number of classrooms. This has been shown by several studies to date in which researchers devised tasks from materials already in classroom use. A teacher then implemented the tasks to assist L2 learning as the researcher addressed matters of practical consequence for classroom SLA, e.g., social interaction and cognitive processes (Pica, Kang, & Sauro, 2006), collaborative learning (Swain & Lapkin, 2001), and L2 features that take a long time to master (Doughty & Varela, 1998; Harley, 1998).

These studies reveal the dual roles of tasks in promoting, as well as understanding, the SLA process. The studies are especially relevant to teachers at this time because they were carried out in classrooms where students study subject content in a language for which they have yet to gain sufficient knowledge and control, and where teachers have taken on the responsibility of helping them learn the language for content access, linguistic accuracy, and communicative proficiency. Efficient and effective approaches to both research and instruction are needed as the range and frequency of these classrooms have been steadily growing, in elementary and secondary schools, community colleges, and university departments. Although these learning environments are widely held as successful sites for SLA, this judgment has been based largely on theoretical assumptions, anecdotal evidence, and data from studies with limitations of design (Pica, 2002). The encouraging results of this new group of task-based studies provides an impetus for the further development of tasks.

What these studies also reveal is that the design and implementation of effective tasks require teamwork and planning. They further suggest that attention be paid to four basic features: tasks must be authentic to teachers and students; easy to produce, adjust, and implement throughout the curriculum; focused on areas where students need extra assistance; and able to effect successful L2 outcomes. Tasks, in themselves, are not endowed with these features, but these studies have revealed ways in which they can be designed and implemented to do so.

Features of Effective Tasks for Teaching and Research

Authentic to classroom participants

To be authentic for students at work in their classrooms, tasks must comply with their purposes for taking a course or coming to a class. Tasks cannot be perceived as tests or research instruments. A test-like format might be tolerated for a single class or a few brief meetings. However, if tasks are to help students notice L2 forms and features embedded in content, the tasks need to be able to engage their interest and do so over the long term. A variety of tasks must be used to avoid the effects of monotony that a single task type might have on students' interest and attention. Tasks must also be integrated into the curriculum content, thereby perceived as compatible with students' goals and interests and their teacher's allegiance to school policy and practice.

Noted in the previous section, information gap tasks, which have begun to establish a solid track record in teaching and research, provide a good example of authenticity. Participants hold unique information, which must be shared in order to complete the task. Examples have appeared in popular student texts and professional resource books (e.g., Ur, 1988), and in widely read research publications (e.g., *Studies in Second Language Acquisition*, *The Modern Language Journal*, *TESOL Quarterly*). Those most familiar to students and teachers are *Spot the Difference* (e.g., Long, 1981; Crookes & Rulon, 1988; Pica et al., 2006), *Jigsaw* (e.g., Doughty & Pica, 1986; Pica et al., 1996; Swain & Lapkin, 2001; Pica et al., 2006), and *Grammar Communication* (e.g., Fotos & Ellis, 1991; Fotos, 1994; Pica et al., 2006).

In *Spot the Difference* tasks, students are given slightly different pictures or texts and asked to identify a given number of ways in which these items differ, e.g., students might have pictures of public places, with many people in them. In one student's picture, a woman is wearing a hat with a feather; in the other student's picture, the same woman is wearing a hat with a flower. Other people in the pictures have slight clothing differences as well. *Jigsaw* tasks often take the form of "strip stories," in which the sentences from a text are distributed among students who must reassemble them into the original story. *Grammar Communication* tasks resemble multiple choice exercises. However, unlike exercises, which do not qualify as tasks, *Grammar Communication* task directions require students to choose one answer, justify it to their partners, and reach a conclusion; hence their task orientation.

Tasks designed from written texts are authentic to a content-based curriculum, course, or classroom, as reading and writing assignments are typically given to students in these contexts. In an Educational Linguistics course, for example, students might read and discuss a text passage, such as that shown in the brief excerpt in Figure 37.1. The task would ask the students to compare different versions of the passage, then choose "the better, or best sounding" sentences of these versions, justify their choices, and use them to reconstruct the original passage they read. Portions of *Spot the Difference, Jigsaw,* and *Grammar Communication* tasks are shown in Figures 37.2–4. Each shows two versions of the original passage from Figure 37.1, with sentences numbered and differences underlined for purposes of illustration.

To further advance task authenticity, students can be encouraged to see the link between carrying out a task and reaching their larger academic, professional, or occupational goals. For example, academic and professional students can be told that the *Spot the Difference* task can help them become more accurate in proofreading and editing their papers; that the *Jigsaw* task can help them organize information effectively; and the *Grammar Communication* task can help them select and use words with precision.

A language policy is made of a number of components. It may be defined by language, by function or role, by segment of the population to whom it applies, and by the action involved.
A policy statement, typically, takes a paradigmatic form. The process of making a language policy is complex.

Figure 37.1   Portion of a passage from Spolsky and Shohamy (1997: 94)

Version to Student A	Version to Student B
1. A language policy is made of a number of components. 2. It may be defined by language, by function or role, by segment of <u>the population</u> to whom it applies, and by the action involved. 3. A policy statement, typically, takes <u>paradigmatic form</u>. 4. <u>The process</u> of making a language policy is complex. . . .	1. A language policy is made of a number of components. 2. It may be defined by language, by function or role, by segment of <u>population</u> to whom it applies, and by the action involved. 3. A policy statement, typically, takes <u>a paradigmatic form</u>. 4. <u>A process</u> of making a language policy is complex. . . .

Figure 37.2   Portion of versions for a *Spot the Difference* task

Version to Student A	Version to Student B
1. A language policy is made of a number of components.	1. A language policy is made of a number of components.
Sentence ____. The process of making a language policy is complex.	Sentence ____. A process of making a language policy is complex.
Sentence ____. A policy statement, typically, takes paradigmatic form.	Sentence ____. A policy statement, typically, takes a paradigmatic form.
Sentence ____. It may be defined by language, by function or role, by segment of the population to whom it applies, and by the action involved.	Sentence ____. It may be defined by language, by function or role, by segment of population to whom it applies, and by the action involved.

Figure 37.3 Portion of versions for a *Jigsaw* task

Version to Student A	Version to Student B
1. A language policy is made of a number of components. 2. It may be defined by language, by function or role, by segment of the population of a population to whom it applies, and by the action involved. 3. A policy statement, typically, takes paradigmatic form one paradigmatic form. 4. The process, one process of making a language policy is complex.	1. A language policy is made of a number of components. 2. It may be defined by language, by function or role, by segment of population, of its population to whom it applies, and by the action involved. 3. A policy statement, typically, takes a paradigmatic form, the paradigmatic form. 4. A process, their process of making a language policy is complex.

Figure 37.4 Portion of versions for a *Grammar Communication* task

Easy to produce and implement

Teachers are busy meeting numerous responsibilities and preparing for their classes. Researchers have multiple obligations that can stifle their attempts at frequent engagement with them. Classroom tasks must be designed with these conditions in mind. They must be easy to produce and implement, with directions that are easy to follow. Their format must be adaptable to new task production, so that once a successful task design is accomplished, it can serve as a template for future tasks to accommodate new passages and emphasize new forms.

Spot the Difference, Jigsaw, Grammar Communication tasks can be designed to meet these criteria. Across all three tasks, learners proceed through the same five steps and directions. In Step 1, they both read the same passage, an

---

1. A language policy is made of a number of components. 2. It may be defined by language, by function or role, by segment of _____ to whom it applies, and by the action involved.
3. A policy statement, typically, takes _____. 4. _____ of making a language policy is complex.

Figure 37.5   Portion of cloze version of passage

example of which is displayed in Figure 37.1. Next, in Step 2, they each read a slightly different version of the passage, as is shown in Figures 37.2–4. In Step 3, they compare their passages and identify the forms, phrases, and sentences that are different. They are asked to choose which ones they think 'sound better' and to justify their choices. Next, they proceed to Step 4, where, without looking back at their choices or the passages they have read, they work together to write their choices in a single cloze version of the original passage, shown in Figure 37.5. Finally, in Step 5 they re-read the original passage, with the correct answers underlined. They compare it with their cloze version, identify any discrepancies, and pose explanations for them.

Focused on areas in need of assistance

Tasks should be focused on forms and features of language and communication that students find difficult to learn on their own. A major reason for their difficulty is that these elements are not perceptually salient and therefore go unnoticed. In designing tasks from subject content, selecting such elements is quite straightforward, as the forms that learners tend not to notice, for example, articles, pronouns, connectors, modal verbs, and verb endings are abundant in the phrases and sentences of most content passages. A fundamental rule of language learning is that learners can internalize only the forms and features that they are developmentally ready to learn. However, these hard to notice items do not develop in sequences and stages, as is the case for items that comprise question development. Instead, contexts for their use arise early in the learner's development. Typically, the forms are often omitted or substituted with more transparent items before they are supplied with accuracy. Articles, for example, might occur as numerals, or be left off completely from noun phrase contexts. Base forms of verbs might appear without tense marking morphemes, but accompanied by adverbs of time. According to Pienemann (1989), learners are ready to attend to such features as soon as they begin to produce them, however slightly or occasionally that may be.

When teachers and researchers are in doubt, their decisions about difficult to learn forms can be based on markedness principles drawn from linguistic theory and based on findings from SLA research. Harley (1989) and Long

(1996) are helpful resources. Again, these would be the forms that are low in perceptual saliency. Thus, third singular *-s* and regular past *-ed* would be more strategic choices for task construction than progressive *-ing* or irregular past. The more infrequent a feature, the greater the difficulty it poses for learners. Hence a text with contexts for past perfect would be a better candidate for a task than one that emphasized the more widely available simple past. The less semantically transparent a form in relation to its function and meaning, the more limited its saliency. Thus, the bound morpheme plural *-s* would be more difficult to notice than free morpheme quantifiers such as *few* or *many*. Modals of probability would be more difficult to grasp than those of ability. Pronouns that refer to multiple items would be more difficult to trace than those that refer to the same item. Although these features are available in learners' input, tasks can be an effective way of making them more noticeable for their L2 development.

Research has also begun to reveal ways in which task implementation can activate processes claimed theoretically to support successful SLA. Inter-action processes of negotiation, instruction, and correction over difficult forms can occur throughout task implementation. Cognitive processes of attention and awareness can be activated as well. The excerpts below illustrate these processes as students carried out tasks designed to enhance a content focused course entitled "Language and Film." The first excerpt illustrates how a *Jigsaw* task provided students with opportunities to attend to difficult to learn verb forms as they speculated about the career choices of the central character in *Stand and Deliver* while they were reading new versions of an earlier passage. They discussed and negotiated whether *could do, does, did,* and *could have done* would make one of the sentences sound better. The form that had appeared in the original passage was *could do.*

Student A	**Student B**
And did.	*Wasn't doing.* Yes, *wasn't doing.*
Yeah, all of them we need past tense in this sentence.	And *wasn't doing* everything he possibly
Could do?	*Did. Could do.* I think it's *could do.*
Why?	Yes.
Oh . . . possibly-uh, huh	*Could do* is . . . is possibly *could do.*
You mean it's not certain it's so it is kind of possibility? In the near future or . . . ?	It's not *did.* He didn't do it so
	I think it's . . .
Oh, he possibly *could do.*	Not definitely do . . . yeah so . . .

(*Grammar Communication* task, based on review of
Stand and Deliver, Ebert, 1990: 699–700)

When the students justified their choices, they often provided form-focused instruction and corrective feedback that drew connections between difficult forms, their functions, and meanings. This is shown in students' deliberations over *one day* and *some day*, regarding a review of the film, *Philadelphia*, as shown in the following excerpt:

Student A	Student B
Kind of future, you know. *One day* is something like, un . . . day in the past, like it happened already, or . . .	Yeah, certain day, but it already happened . . . it already happened, or in the previous day . . . the past
Just this. Um, and *some day some day* is	*One day* just mention uh, on certain day, or
Yeah . . . the previous yeah. If we use *some day* this means perhaps this will be happen in the future. In the one day or future.	

(*Spot the Difference* task, based on review of *Philadelphia*,
Ebert, 1997: 593–594)

As the students reached Step 3, and filled in the cloze version of the task passage, they recalled forms they had chosen from the two different versions. In so doing, they often asked for clarification and provided each other with feedback. This allowed the students to focus on the L2 forms they needed to learn, and for the researcher to study the students' growing awareness of these items as they analyzed their function and meaning. This is shown in the following:

Student A	Student B
Now I got it. This sentence is any lawyer *will not risk*. Right. So it means, I don't want to take that risk so. This is the future	Before we used *would risk*. It's a supposing sentence. Usually we use *would*
	Yeah. We know the difference use. Any lawyer *would not* listen. *Would not*. It's supposing, supposing sentence, right. If you *would* . . .

(*Jigsaw* task, based on review of *Philadelphia*, Ebert, 1997: 593–594)

Able to effect learning outcomes

Activating learning processes has been a noble goal of teachers and researchers. Tasks provide an important opportunity for students to experience such processes in a classroom setting. However, achieving learning outcomes is really what students, teachers, and researchers want and deserve. Longitudinal studies in long-term courses can reveal the extent to which successful L2 outcomes are possible in the classroom, and whether tasks can play a defining role. This work can also provide answers to questions that arise after more typical, one- or two-week studies, as to why students all too often fail to retain the very features they had been able to use during the studies. Was an intervention withdrawn too early? Had it been poorly designed? Were the students simply not ready to internalize the feature? Such questions require close, protracted observation, and the solid participation of students, their teacher, and the researcher.

Long-term studies are not easy to carry out, however, as they require extensive commitment of time and sustained expression of interest among participants. Many teachers and their students are eager to join in, even though their involvement is limited by a curriculum preset by policy and tradition. As teachers and researchers become more informed, more professionalized, and more visible and relevant to each other, so too will opportunities arise for their greater collaboration and dialogue. As long as teachers and researchers find ways to work together in the classroom, and remain committed to long-term relationships with language learners and with each other, tasks provide them with direction and hope.

Conclusions

This chapter began by describing the challenges that confront teachers and researchers, as they define their roles and build relationships within the field of educational linguistics. Some of the most fruitful relationships have been built by teachers and researchers who work with language learners. Teachers have seen their concerns about language classroom strategies become the basis for researchers' questions on language learning processes. Materials that originated in the classroom have been adopted for use as research instruments and activities that were designed as research interventions have been adapted for teaching practice. Teachers have begun to approach researchers for source material to inform their classroom practice, while researchers have turned to teachers for classroom sites to study the language learning process. In almost every case, the relationship, however collaborative and complementary in spirit, has been independent in its origin, and the outcomes of this collaboration have been one-way in their application.

This chapter has also looked at the collaborative and complementary dimensions of the research–practice relationship that are evident in task-based learning and teaching. It has revealed ways in which teachers and researchers can work together to develop tasks that suit the needs and styles of students and teachers, and at the same time insure the collection of valid and reliable data on their learning and teaching processes. Working with the learners' needs and learning goals in mind, teachers and researchers can co-design form-focusing tasks from the subject content curriculum. Together, they can choose grammatical items whose perceptual features make them pedagogically and theoretically difficult for students to grasp on their own. They can also compose directions that are authentic to classroom practice and consistent with reliability standards. The outcomes of such collaboration are bi-directional in application and far-reaching in their impact on the learner, teacher, and researcher alike. Through their work on tasks, teachers and researchers can build relationships that assist language development, inform teaching practice, contribute to language acquisition theory, and advance the research enterprise.

REFERENCES

Allwright, Dick (2005). Developing principles for practitioner research: The case of exploratory practice. *The Modern Language Journal*, 89(3), 353–366.

Allwright, Dick & Bailey, Kathleen M. (1991). *Focus on the Language Classroom*. New York: Cambridge University Press.

Chaudron, Craig (2005). Progress in language classroom research: Evidence from *The Modern Language Journal*, 1916–2000. *The Modern Language Journal*, 85(1), 57–76.

Crookes, Graham & Gass, Susan M. (eds.) (1993). *Tasks and Language Learning: Integrating Theory and Practice*. Clevedon, UK: Multilingual Matters.

Crookes, Graham & Rulon, Kathryn A. (1988). Topic and feedback in native speaker/ non-native speaker conversation. *TESOL Quarterly*, 22(4), 675–681.

Doughty, Catherine & Pica, Teresa (1986). "Information gap tasks": An aid to second language acquisition? *TESOL Quarterly*, 20(3), 305–325.

Doughty, Catherine & Varela, Elizabeth (1998). Communicative focus on form. In Catherine Doughty & Jessica Williams (eds.), *Focus on Form in Classroom Second Language Acquisition* (pp. 114–138). Cambridge: Cambridge University Press.

Ebert, Roger (1990). *Roger Ebert's Movie Home Companion*. Kansas City, MO: Andrews & McMeel.

Ebert, Roger (1997). *Roger Ebert's Video Companion*. Kansas City, MO: Andrews & McMeel.

Fotos, Sandra (1994). Integrating grammar instruction and communicative language use through grammar consciousness-raising tasks. *TESOL Quarterly*, 28(3), 323–351.

Fotos, Sandra & Ellis, Rod (1991). Communicating about grammar: A task-based approach. *TESOL Quarterly*, 2(4), 605–628.

Gass, Susan M. & Alvarez-Torres, Maria José (2005). *Studies in Second Language Acquisition*, 27(1), 1–31.

Harley, Birgit (1998). The role of focus on form tasks in promoting child L2 acquisition. In Catherine Doughty & Jessica Williams (eds.), *Focus on Form in Classroom Second Language Acquisition* (pp. 156–174). Cambridge: Cambridge University Press.

Hatch, Evelyn (1978). Apply with caution. *Studies in Second Language Acquisition*, 2(2), 123–143.

Iwashita, Noriko (2003). Negative feedback and positive evidence in task-based interaction. *Studies in Second Language Acquisition*, 25(1), 1–36.

Lightbown, Patsy (2000). Classroom SLA research and second language teaching. *Applied Linguistics*, 21(4), 431–462.

Lightbown, Patsy & Spada, Nina (1999). *How Languages are Learned* (2nd edn.). Oxford: Oxford University Press.

Long, Michael H. (1981). Input, interaction, and second language acquisition. In Harris Winitz (ed.), *Native and Foreign Language Acquisition: Annals of the New York Academy of Sciences*, 379, 259–278.

Long, Michael H. (1996). The role of the linguistic environment in second language acquisition. In William C. Ritchie & Tej K. Bhatia (eds.), *Handbook of Language Acquisition, vol. 2: Second Language Acquisition* (pp. 413–468). New York: Academic Press.

Loschky, Lester & Bley-Vroman, Robert (1993). Grammar and task-based methodology. In Graham Crookes & Susan M. Gass (eds.), *Tasks and Language Learning* (vol. 1, pp. 123–167). Clevedon, UK: Multilingual Matters.

Mackey, Alison (1999). Input, interaction, and second language development. *Studies in Second Language Acquisition*, 21(4), 557–588.

Mackey, Alison & McDonough, Kim (2000). Communicative tasks, conversational interaction and linguistic form: An empirical study of Thai. *Foreign Language Annals*, 33(1), 82–91.

Mackey, Alison & Oliver, Rhonda (2002). Interactional feedback and children's L2 development. *System*, 30(4), 459–477.

Nunan, David (1989). *Designing Tasks for the Communicative Classroom*. Cambridge: Cambridge University Press.

Pica, Teresa (1994). Questions from the language classroom: Research perspectives. *TESOL Quarterly*, 28(1), 49–79.

Pica, Teresa (1997). Second language research and language pedagogy: A relationship in process. *Language Teaching Research*, 1(1), 48–72.

Pica, Teresa (2002). Subject matter content: How does it assist the interactional and linguistic needs of classroom language learners? *The Modern Language Journal*, 86(1), 1–19.

Pica, Teresa (2005). Classroom learning, teaching, and research: A task-based perspective. *The Modern Language Journal*, 89(3), 339–352.

Pica, Teresa, Kang, Hyun Sook, & Sauro, Shannon (2006). Information gap tasks: Their multiple roles and contributions to interaction research methodology. *Studies in Second Language Acquisition*, 28(2), 301–338.

Pica, Teresa, Lincoln-Porter, Felicia, Paninos, Diana, & Linnell, Julian (1996). Language learner interaction: How does it address the input, output, and feedback needs of second language learners? *TESOL Quarterly*, 30(1), 59–84.

Pienemann, Manfred (1989). Is language teachable? Psycholinguistic experiments and hypotheses. *Applied Linguistics*, 10(1), 52–79.

Prabhu, N. S. (1987). *Second Language Pedagogy*. Oxford: Oxford University Press.

Spolsky, Bernard & Shohamy, Elana (1997). Language in Israeli Society and Education. *The International Journal of the Sociology of Language* (special issue, ed. Jacob Landau), 137, 93–114.

Swain, Merrill & Lapkin, Sharon (2001). Focus on form through collaborative dialogue: Exploring task effects. In Martin Bygate, Peter Skehan, & Merrill Swain (eds.), *Researching Pedagogic Tasks* (pp. 99–118). Harlow: Longman.

Tarone, Elaine, Swain, Merrill, & Fathman, Ann (1976). Some limitations to the classroom applications of current second language acquisition research. *TESOL Quarterly*, 35(2), 19–31.

Ur, Penny (1988). *Grammar Practice Activities*. Cambridge: Cambridge University Press.
Willis, Jane (1996). *A Framework for Task-Based Learning*. Harlow: Longman.

FURTHER READING

Ellis, Rod (2003). *Task Based Language Teaching and Learning*. Oxford: Oxford University Press.
Long, Michael H. & Crookes, Graham (1992). Three approaches to task-based syllabus design. *TESOL Quarterly*, 26(1), 27–56.
Samuda, Virginia (2001). Guiding relationships between form and meaning during task performance: The role of the teacher. In Martin Bygate, Peter Skehan, & Merrill Swain (eds.), *Researching Pedagogic Tasks* (pp. 119–134). Harlow: Longman.
Skehan, Peter (1988). Task-based instruction. *Annual Review of Applied Linguistics*, 18, 268–286.

38 Corpus Linguistics and Second Language Instruction

SUSAN M. CONRAD AND KIMBERLY R. LEVELLE

Corpus linguistics is an approach for investigating the use of language. It employs computer-assisted techniques to analyze large collections of writing or transcribed speech in order to describe the typical – or unusual – language choices that speakers and writers make in particular circumstances. In this chapter, we provide an overview of this relatively new approach to applied linguistics, emphasizing its applications in second language instruction. We begin with a review of the characteristics of work in corpus linguistics. We then discuss its connections to instruction from three perspectives: studies to better understand learners, commercially available teaching materials, and teachers' use of corpus linguistics for course design and classroom activities. We conclude by reviewing some issues crucial to the further development of corpus linguistics in teaching.

Throughout the chapter we provide examples of work in English and other languages, but far more has been published about English corpus linguistics than any other language and our references reflect that dominance. Nevertheless, all the issues covered in the chapter are applicable to any language.

Characteristics of Corpus Linguistics

We have said that corpus linguistics is "an approach" because it encompasses a variety of specific techniques. However, all corpus linguistics work shares certain traits. We summarize four important characteristics below; more details can be found in book-length introductions to corpus linguistics (McEnery & Wilson, 1996; Biber, Conrad, & Reppen, 1998; Kennedy, 1998; Partington, 1998; Tognini-Bonelli, 2001; Hunston, 2002; Meyer, 2002).

Emphasis on empirical analysis of patterns in language use

Although some consider corpus linguistics "essentially a technology" (Simpson & Swales, 2001: 1), an identifiable philosophy lies beneath its use of technology. The philosophy follows from a Firthian tradition in language study (Firth, 1957; Palmer, 1968; Stubbs, 1993). Central to the philosophy is that language study is primarily an empirical endeavor. That is, descriptions of language and theories of language are developed from systematic observations of language behavior. The contributions that corpus linguistics makes to language instruction stem largely from this emphasis on empirical analysis, in order to see what is typical and what is unusual. Intuition and casual observations are important in corpus linguistics for leading to research questions, and interpretation of corpus-based findings include subjective impressions about language choices, but the empirical analysis of a large amount of language is at the heart of corpus linguistics.

Use of a corpus

For its empirical analysis, all corpus linguistics work uses a corpus – a large, principled collection of naturally occurring texts that are stored electronically (generally on a server, hard drive, or CD-ROM). "Naturally occurring" refers to the fact that the texts were produced by language users in real communication situations. That is, they were not based on intuition or anecdotal evidence about how language is likely to be used. The language may be completely spontaneous (e.g., casual conversation) or, especially in the case of language learners, part of a specific task (e.g., essays written for a class assignment). Corpora can include written texts, transcribed spoken texts, or both. Many spoken corpora are now including sound files in addition to transcription, so that features of intonation and pronunciation can also be heard (see, e.g., the Santa Barbara Corpus of Spoken American English available at http://www.ldc.upenn.edu/).

A corpus is meant to represent a variety or varieties of language. The varieties can be very general, such as Australian English conversation, or very specific, such as abstracts of medical research articles. Although large compilation projects such as the British National Corpus (BNC, Aston & Burnard, 1998) and the American National Corpus (Reppen & Ide, 2004) are widely known, a host of other languages and varieties have been covered in corpus projects in recent years. Even a few examples give a sense of the variety: Arabic (Al-Sulaiti & Atwell, 2005), Czech (Čermák, 1997; Kučera, 2002), written Estonian (Hennoste et al., 1998), spoken Hebrew (Izre'el & Hary, 2001), Thai (Isahara & Ma, 2000), Xhosa English (de Klerk, 2006). Other varieties of English are also included in the International Corpus of English, which will include 20 varieties of English from around the world, and in more specialized corpora, such as the Michigan Corpus of Spoken Academic English (Simpson, Lucka, & Ovens, 2000).

The design of a corpus is extremely important for reliable and generalizable results, whether the corpus is being used for large research projects or for small investigations by learners in a classroom. Advances in computer technology have made much larger corpora possible over the past few decades. In the 1970s, 1-million-word corpora were considered large (e.g., the London/Oslo-Bergen or LOB corpus, see Johansson, Leech, & Goodluck, 1978), but today the Bank of English consists of about 450 million words and is still growing (see current information at www.titania.bham.ac.uk). Many factors other than overall size are important in corpus design, however. The types of texts that are included, the number of different types of texts, the number of different samples of each type of text, the sampling procedures, and the size of each sample are all important considerations.

Unfortunately, investigations into the best ways to represent varieties of language have not kept pace with advances in storage capacity. In the early 1990s, Biber (1990, 1993) found 1,000 word samples were reliable for representing many grammatical features, and 10 texts reliable for representing genre categories in the LOB (e.g., official documents, academic prose), although much larger samples and texts are necessary for rare grammatical features and lexicographic work. Since then, too few studies have empirically investigated the most efficient and effective sampling and sizing procedures (but see Kilgarriff, 2001, for lexical work). Generally, corpus development projects seek to make corpora as representative as possible by collecting texts based on certain characteristics of speakers and contexts (e.g., purpose, production circumstances, named genres, etc.). The exchange between Lee (2001) and Aston (2001b) discusses the categories in the British National Corpus (BNC), and provides different perspectives on their usefulness.

Computer-assisted analysis techniques

In order to handle the large quantity of data in a corpus, analysts rely on computer-assisted techniques. In classroom instruction and for most teachers, the most common type of software that is used is a concordancer. A concordancing program will display all the occurrences of a word with surrounding context (called "concordance lines" or a Key Word in Context "KWIC" display, as in Table 38.1). It will typically also calculate frequencies of words, analyze collocates (words that occur near each other in the texts), and often calculate statistical measures of the strength of word association (that is, the likelihood of two words occurring near each other).

Concordance lines can be sorted in a variety of ways and often reveal patterns in how words are used. Often these patterns are obvious in the concordance lines, but do not come to mind spontaneously. For instance, an ESL teacher recently reported that she did not know how to answer when a student asked her the difference between the verbs *reject* and *refuse*. Even a

Table 38.1   Concordance lines comparing *refuse* and *reject*

. . . it difficult for eligible companies to	refuse	to join. "It also opens the door to sim . . .
. . . for the rest of Latin America. They	refuse	to recognize the government that took . . .
. . . l key sections. Bush said he would	refuse	to obey a requirement that the admini . . .
. . . Census forms stating either that they	refuse	to cooperate, are doing so under threat . . .
. . . d when he resigned, Arpino said, "I	refuse	to participate in an organization which . . .
. . . e-year budget deal has forced him to	reject	bigger tax cuts for children and for ca . . .
. . . sibility that the full commission will	reject	it because of opposition with it to wh . . .
. . . n voted unanimously Wednesday to	reject	the company's final contract offer, on . . .
. . . es subscribers go out of their way to	reject	the change. In some cases customers . . .
. . . m entrepreneurs turn to when banks	reject	their loan applications. Typically, mo . . .

traditional dictionary may not be helpful, explaining *reject* as "to refuse to have, take, recognize, etc." (*Webster's Encyclopedic Unabridged Dictionary of the English Language*, 1989). However, Table 38.1 displays some of the concordance lines comparing *reject* and *refuse* in a corpus of American newspapers, sorting by the first word to the right (the word immediately following *refuse* or *reject*). Immediately it is apparent that one of the differences in these words concerns their grammatical patterns: *refuse* is often used with a *to*-clause following it.

Many areas of interest in language do not lend themselves to analysis with concordancers. For example, Conrad (1999) describes an analysis of linking adverbials (transition words such as *in contrast* and *therefore*) that includes associations among several variables: register (conversation, newspaper writing, and academic prose), semantic category (e.g., result, contrast), position in the clause, grammatical structure (e.g., single adverb, prepositional phrase, clause), and the exact choice of the adverbial. Such analyses are possible with computer programs written specifically for the analysis, including interactive programs that ask the user to check analyses that the computer has made based on programmed algorithms. In addition, computer techniques can be combined with more discourse-level analyses; L. Flowerdew (2003, 2005) and Upton and Connor (2001) incorporate corpus techniques with genre-based or textlinguistic approaches. (See also Conrad, 2002, for a review of discourse-level corpus techniques.) Nevertheless, most corpus-based instruction today revolves around concordancing and frequency lists.

Use of quantitative analysis and qualitative/ interpretive techniques

Within corpus linguistics, there is variation in how much emphasis is given to quantitative analysis and how much to descriptions and interpretations without presenting counts of features (see contrasting views by Biber & Conrad, 2001; and McCarthy & Carter, 2001). However, all work includes both aspects of analysis to some extent. Recognizing patterns in how language is used necessarily entails making a quantitative assessment; merely saying something is "typical" or "common" means that it is occurring more frequently than other choices. However, counts alone explain little about language use. Even the most complex quantitative analyses must be tied to functional interpretations of the language patterns. For example, many ESL textbooks cover verb + gerund and verb + infinitive structures extensively (e.g., *I stopped trying, I wanted to go*). Corpus work can tell not only which verbs are most common with gerunds and infinitives, but also meanings expressed by the most common verbs (see Biber et al., 1999: ch. 9).

Corpus Linguistics' Contributions to Language Instruction

By examining patterns in language use, particularly on a wider scale than was previously feasible, corpus linguistics has begun to make valuable contributions to the field of second and foreign language teaching and learning. We summarize below the use of corpus linguistics for studying learner language and the process of language learning; for improving materials development, especially commercially available textbooks; and for developing class activities and improving course design.

Understanding learners: Corpus linguistics and work in second language acquisition

An important foundation for second language instruction concerns understanding the process of second language acquisition (SLA), including issues such as orders of acquisition (see Chapter 27, Order of Acquisition and Developmental Readiness, this volume) and the influence of the first language (see Chapter 29, Interlanguage and Language Transfer, this volume). The study of learners' interlanguage has always relied on empirical analysis and thus shares a characteristic with corpus linguistics work. However, a corpus approach for interlanguage analysis has some distinct strengths and limitations. The strengths include the ability for studies to include more data and more participants and to examine the interaction of more variables than has generally been feasible with previous approaches. At the same time, however, corpus-based work is limited in the amount of context provided for the analysis. Corpus studies provide "big picture" patterns that are a complementary perspective to more intensive analyses from case studies and ethnographies. (For additional details on advantages of corpus work in SLA see Granger, 2004; Myles & Mitchell, 2004; Nesselhauf, 2004; Barlow, 2005).

Corpus studies that contribute to our understanding of second language acquisition depend on learner corpora, that is, corpora composed of language produced by learners. Most widely known is the International Corpus of Learner English (ICLE, Granger, 1998, 2003), which consists of essays written by intermediate and advanced EFL students, with 14 nationalities represented on the currently available CD-ROM. A variety of corpora from other contexts have been developed in recent years. They include a number of different ESL/EFL situations besides those in ICLE – e.g., a corpus of spoken interactions of advanced non-native speakers and native speakers of English in Hong Kong (Cheng & Warren, 2000). They also include corpora of learners of languages other than English, such as corpora of learners of French that include oral texts by children and young adults (Myles & Mitchell, 2004; http://www.flloc.soton.ac.uk/); and corpora of electronic communication, such as Belz's (2004) corpus of computer mediated interactions between learners of German as a foreign language and learners of English as a foreign language. (For additional learner corpora sources, see Pravec, 2002.)

Studies with learner corpora have a variety of applications to language teaching. One approach has been to compare learner language to native speaker language, in order to identify areas of difficulty and omission by students. This approach has been used in widely differing contexts – for example, by L. Flowerdew (1998) for teaching cause/effect markers in EAP writing, by Cheng and Warren (2000) for identifying confusing use of tag questions and discourse markers by non-native speakers in spoken interactions with native speakers, and by Hasselgren (2002) for evaluating fluency in the speech of non-native speakers. A number of other writers have questioned the appropriateness of comparing native speaker and learner corpora (see discussion in Barlow, 2005; and Seidlhofer, 2002); we discuss this point further in the conclusion.

Another perspective included in many studies of learner corpora is comparisons of learners from different first languages, investigating first language influences versus universal patterns of development in SLA. For example, Aijmer (2002) compares Swedish L1 writers of English with French and German L1 writers of English, comparing use of modal auxiliaries and other devices for modality. She finds some consistent tendencies across the groups – such as more frequent use of modals overall when compared with a native speaker corpus – but also much higher use of particular items by certain L1 groups (such as *indeed* and *certainly* for the French group). Her analyses include useful discussion not only of possible L1 influences, but of a variety of factors that still need further study, including cultural groups' preconceptions about how direct academic writing should be, and the influence of spoken forms on all the groups' writing.

Corpus studies can also provide a means of expanding on SLA studies that were conducted earlier with smaller data sets or shorter language samples. Housen (2002), for example, investigates the development of forms and functions of the English verb system for 46 children learning English as a foreign language, finding similarities with previous, smaller studies and studies of adults. Tono (2000) analyzes the morpheme accuracy in a 300,000-word corpus of texts written by Japanese L1 ESL learners. He compares the results to Dulay and Burt's (1974) study of Chinese and Spanish L1 learners that used the Bilingual Syntax Measure (BSM). He finds that articles and plural -s appear to be later acquired and possessive -s earlier acquired than in the previous study. As with Aijmer's study above, Tono notes a number of variables that need to be examined more fully in order to interpret the differences between his results and Dulay and Burt's – including the difference in spoken versus written orders of acquisition and the impact of the BSM versus the composition task, in addition to the effect of the L1.

Given the new perspectives that corpus linguistics could bring to SLA work, it is somewhat surprising that it still tends to be little known in the field of SLA generally. It is uncommon to find a corpus-based methodology in an article in major journals such as *Studies in Second Language Acquisition* or *Language Learning*, for example. One reason may be because learner language is often difficult to interpret outside of its context of production – especially at low levels and especially in speech, where nonverbals contribute to meaning. The lack of context with most corpora can thus limit their usefulness for SLA studies. However, Reder, Harris, and Setzler (2003) describe a project that could keep a transcribed corpus linked to more contextual information. They explain the Multimedia Adult ESOL Language Corpus – a five-year project that involves videotaping four low-level classrooms each year, conducting in-home interviews with some students, and storing the audio and visual data digitally. Conrad (2006) describes the process needed to develop this multimedia database into a corpus for corpus-based second language acquisition research, with transcriptions available for analysis but also linked to the video of the classroom so that the learner language can be disambiguated when necessary.

Commercially available corpus-based teaching materials

Numerous studies in English corpus linguistics have compared language used in corpora to the language taught to learners in textbooks, and suggested that publishers would do well to consider more corpus findings when producing textbooks. For example, McCarthy, Carter, and their associates working with the CANCODE corpus of spoken English have long noted that typical grammars neglect to cover many features important in spoken interactions (Carter & McCarthy, 1995; McCarthy & Carter, 1995, 2001; Carter, 1998; Carter, Hughes, & McCarthy, 1998). Römer (2004, 2006) finds that several popular German EFL books misrepresent common uses of modals. Conrad (2004) finds that a sample lecture from a lecture practice textbook misrepresents certain language features typical of lectures in US universities, making the lecture more like written prose than speech. Biber and Reppen (2002) question the decision by several books to cover the present progressive before simple present tense, when simple present is far more common in English conversations. Such studies do not argue that only language found in a corpus should be taught to learners or that native-speaker frequency information alone is all that matters for designing a language syllabus. Rather, they argue that when pedagogical decisions are made, they should consider information about frequencies in different contexts, lexico-grammatical associations, and collocations, as well as other factors such as difficulty, teachability/learnability, and usefulness for learners. As Aston (2000) and Gavioli and Aston (2001) note, if a syllabus includes a language item that is rare, while excluding or delaying a more frequent item, it is reasonable to ask what other pedagogical considerations make this sequencing appropriate.

Corpus-based dictionaries for English learners began to become popular with the *Collins Cobuild English Language Dictionary* (described in Sinclair, 1987), and most major English language training publishers now have one (e.g., *Longman Dictionary of Contemporary English, Cambridge Learner's Dictionary*). Textbooks have been slower in development, however. Some earlier books for learners were quite different in approach from traditional books, and hard to use in a classroom. For example, Carter and McCarthy's (1997) *Exploring Spoken English* had long, transcribed excerpts of spoken interactions with line-by-line commentary. For example, an utterance such as *"Biscuit?"* was explained "This is a heavily ellipted version of 'Do you want/Would you like a biscuit?' and is thus a repetition of [line] 1.14. It is likely that the biscuit is physically offered . . ." (p. 68). Other than a few preliminary questions and predictions before each transcript, there were no specific exercises for students.

More recently, corpus-based textbooks have begun to look more like other textbooks. Examples extracted from a corpus may be modified for pedagogical purposes – for example, to make highly contextualized language in conversation easier for students to understand (see discussion in Carter, Hughes, & McCarthy, 1998). The books cover items common in naturally occurring language that other books do not cover, but users of some books may not even be aware they are corpus-based. Cambridge's *Touchstone* series, for example, looks like a traditional coursebook, but includes points for spoken interaction based on analysis of corpora; for example, students work on restating ideas with *I mean* (McCarthy, McCarten, & Sandiford, 2005: 49) and using discourse markers such as *all right* and *ok* to move a conversation along (McCarthy, McCarten, & Sandiford, 2006: 103). Schmitt and Schmitt's *Focus on Vocabulary* (2005) appears in many ways like other vocabulary books for English for Academic Purposes (EAP), with highlighted words in readings, and some fill-in and matching exercises. However, the words come from the Academic Word List, a list of vocabulary found in Coxhead's (2000) corpus-based study to be used across a wide variety of academic disciplines. The book also includes practice with common collocates of these words.

Since many teachers lack preparation time even if they are trained in corpus linguistics, commercially available corpus-based textbooks are likely to have the most widespread pedagogical impact of all corpus work. As these textbooks become increasingly available, issues related to corpus appropriateness and the need for empirical studies of effectiveness become increasingly important – two issues we return to in the conclusion.

Using corpus linguistics for course design and class activities

Besides using a corpus-based textbook, there are a variety of ways for teachers to integrate corpus linguistics into instruction. One approach is to use corpus-based research in making decisions about course content and supplementary exercises for students. A large number of corpus-based research publications now exist. They range from extensive reference grammars, such as the *Longman Grammar of Spoken and Written English* (Biber et al., 1999) and *Cambridge Grammar of English* (Carter & McCarthy, 2006), to papers describing more specific topics, such as modal particles in spoken German (Möllering, 2001) and collocations in Singaporean-Malaysian English (Ooi, 2000). Although the amount of work has increased tremendously in the last decade, it is still difficult to track just how much impact it has had on instruction since many classroom language teachers never write about their decisions and experiences. An interesting exception is Scovel's (2000) explanation of changes made to the topics covered in an advanced grammar class based on information from the *Longman Grammar of Spoken and Written English* (see also the reply by Mills, 2001).

Some teachers also compile and analyze their own corpora specifically for course development purposes. As early as 1993, J. Flowerdew described the usefulness of compiling a corpus of biology lectures to use as a basis for syllabus design for his language-support course (Flowerdew, 1993). Teachers have used their own learner corpora to determine features causing difficulty to their learners so that these areas can be incorporated into coursework (e.g., L. Flowerdew, 1998, 2003).

Throughout the literature in corpus linguistics, there are also many descriptions of concordancing activities that teachers have used effectively with their students. Even a small sample shows the variety of contexts in which concordancing has been used: Zorzi (2001) discusses the teaching of spoken discourse markers with an Italian corpus; Jones (1997) describes sensitizing German L2 learners to variation through the use of a spoken German corpus; St John (2001) describes the use of parallel corpora in German and English by a beginning-level German user; working in EAP, Donley and Reppen (2001) develop students' vocabulary skills through concordancing activities; O'Sullivan and Chambers (2006) have intermediate level students use a concordancer for writing essays in French as a second language. Numerous other examples of classroom activities can be found in collections about corpus linguistics (see, e.g., Burnard & McEnery, 2000; Aston, 2001a; Ketteman & Marko, 2002; Connor & Upton, 2004; Sinclair, 2004).

Corpus-based activities that students are asked to do in classrooms can vary widely – from exercises with concordance lines that the teacher has carefully edited to their own concordancing with a large corpus. In all cases, students are led through an inductive process of looking at the corpus samples and making generalizations about how the language is used – sometimes called "discovery learning" or "data-driven learning" (e.g., see Johns, 1994, and www.eisu.bham.ac.uk/johnstf/timconc.htm). For many years corpus linguists have pointed out that such activities are consistent with several principles currently popular in language teaching (see, e.g., Johns, 1994; Aston, 1995; Leech, 1997; Willis, 1998; Bernardini, 2001; Gavioli, 2001; Gavioli & Aston, 2001). Learner autonomy is increased as students are taught how to observe language and make generalizations, rather than depending on a teacher who states rules for them. In addition, the process of coming to generalizations with one corpus and then checking the generalizations with another corpus is a process of hypothesis generating and testing, much like the process with which interlanguage is thought to progress generally. Furthermore, corpus analysis activities can easily be designed to promote noticing and consciousness-raising by calling attention to particular aspects of structure and use. Finally, since the work follows an inductive approach and most grammar teaching has traditionally been deductive, concordancing work may well appeal to learners whose learning style preference has previously been overlooked.

Positive experiences with classroom concordancing abound in descriptions from teachers (although training for learners is crucial, see discussions in, e.g., Gavioli, 1997, 2001; Seidlhofer, 2000; Bernardini, 2001; Kennedy & Miceli, 2001). Nevertheless, there is no question that more empirical investigation is needed into the effectiveness of concordancing and other corpus activities for students. Yoon and Hirvela (2004) investigate attitudes of EAP students toward concordancing as a tool for improving their writing, and find a generally positive response. Few studies set out to measure student improvement, however. An exception is work by Cobb (1997, 1999). In examining vocabulary instruction with concordancing, he finds small but consistent gains for students with concordancing over other techniques, and finds definitional and transfer knowledge better for students who used a concordancer in addition to word lists and dictionaries for vocabulary study, rather than only word lists and dictionaries. In another study, Gaskell and Cobb (2004) find that learners are generally successful in using concordancers to correct vocabulary errors in their writing.

The Future of Corpus Linguistics in Language Instruction

In a chapter of this size it is impossible to do justice to all aspects of corpus linguistics and language instruction. Much more could be said, for instance, about the more specialized uses of corpora, such as parallel corpora and the teaching of translation (e.g., Botley, McEnery & Wilson, 2000; Bernardini, 2003) and other special purpose applications (see Bowker & Pearson, 2002). In closing, however, we want to raise two areas that we find of particular concern in considering the future of corpus linguistics in any language instruction context.

The first issue concerns corpora. Criticism of the use of English native speaker corpora with learners of English whose goal is not to interact with native speakers (e.g., Widdowson, 1991, 1996; Prodromou, 1996a, 1996b; Cook, 1997, 1998) has highlighted the importance of English as a lingua franca and projects to develop corpora of English as a lingua franca are now underway (Mauranen, 2003; Prodromou, 2003; Seidlhofer, 2004, 2005). This development will certainly extend the usefulness of corpus linguistics for English learners. Equally heartening is the increase in corpora in languages other than English (e.g., see links at calper.la.psu.edu/corpus.php) and varieties of English other than British and American – including the International Corpus of English which will include 20 varieties of English (Meyer, 2001). Alarming, however, is the small amount of empirical study of principles of corpus design, especially corpora most applicable to language instruction (as opposed to computational linguistic applications). To reliably represent a category of discourse, how many samples are needed for a text? How long must the samples be? How many samples are needed? The answers to such questions will differ, of course, for different categories of texts (that is, a very general category is likely to have more variation and require more samples). Since corpus compilation can be extremely time-consuming and expensive, knowing how much is enough is important for most projects. In addition, with increased interest in the web as a corpus, issues concerning how to represent categories become increasingly complex (Fletcher, 2004; Hundt, Biewer, & Nesselhauf, 2006). It is only through studying the representation in current corpora that we can improve future corpora, but too few studies are conducted with a goal of improving corpus design.

A second issue for the future of corpus linguistics concerns the lack of empirical study of the effects of using corpus-based techniques in instruction. Most of the published work on corpus linguistics in the classroom has relied on teachers' impressions of effectiveness or has examined only short-term use of concordancing. While these experiences are not to be disregarded, empirical investigations of the effectiveness of different kinds of corpus-based instruction are needed, along with investigations of the impact of corpus-based instruction over time. Corpus linguistics has generated excitement among many teachers and students; further investigating and refining its effectiveness for instruction is an important step in the maturation of the field.

REFERENCES

Aijmer, Karin (2002). Modality in advanced Swedish learners' written interlanguage. In Sylviane Granger, Joseph Hung, & Stephanie Petch-Tyson (eds.), *Computer Learner*

Corpora, Second Language Acquisition and Foreign Language Teaching (pp. 55–76). Amsterdam: Benjamins.

Al-Sulaiti, Latifa & Atwell, Eric (2005). Extending the corpus of contemporary Arabic. In Pernilla Danielsson & Martijn Wagenmakers (eds.), *Proceedings from the Corpus Linguistics Conference Series* 1(1), www.corpus.bham.ac.uk/PCLC.

Aston, Guy (1995). Corpora in language pedagogy: Matching theory and practice. In Guy Cook & Barbara Seidlhofer (eds.), *Principles and Practice in Applied Linguistics* (pp. 257–270). Oxford: Oxford University Press.

Aston, Guy (2000). Corpora and language teaching. In Lou Burnard & Tony McEnery (eds.), *Rethinking Language Pedagogy from a Corpus Perspective* (pp. 7–17). Frankfurt: Lang.

Aston, Guy (ed.) (2001a). *Learning with Corpora*. Houston, TX: Athelstan.

Aston, Guy (2001b). Text categories and corpus users: A response to David Lee. *Language Learning and Technology*, 5, 73–76.

Aston, Guy & Lou Burnard (1998). *The BNC Handbook: Exploring the British National Corpus with SARA*. Edinburgh: Edinburgh University Press.

Barlow, Michael (2005). Computer-based analyses of learner language. In Rod Ellis & Gary Barkhuizen (eds.), *Analyzing Learner Language* (pp. 335–357). Oxford: Oxford University Press.

Belz, Julie A. (2004). Learner corpus analysis and the development of foreign language proficiency. *System*, 32, 577–591.

Bernardini, Silvia (2001). "Spoilt for choice": A learner explores general language corpora. In Guy Aston (ed.), *Learning with Corpora* (pp. 220–249). Houston, TX: Athelstan.

Bernardini, Silvia (2003). Designing a corpus for translation and language teaching: The CEXI experience. *TESOL Quarterly*, 37, 528–537.

Biber, Douglas (1990). Methodological issues regarding corpus-based analyses of linguistic variation. *Literary and Linguistic Computing*, 5, 257–269.

Biber, Douglas (1993). Representativeness in corpus design. *Literary and Linguistic Computing*, 8, 243–257.

Biber, Douglas & Conrad, Susan (2001). Quantitative corpus-based research: Much more than bean counting. *TESOL Quarterly*, 35, 331–336.

Biber, Douglas & Reppen, Randi (2002). What does frequency have to do with grammar teaching? *Studies in Second Language Acquisition*, 24, 199–208.

Biber, Douglas, Conrad, Susan, & Reppen, Randi (1998). *Corpus Linguistics: Investigating Language Structure and Use*. Cambridge: Cambridge University Press.

Biber, Douglas, Johansson, Stig, Leech, Geoffrey, Conrad, Susan, & Finegan, Edward (1999). *The Longman Grammar of Spoken and Written English*. Harlow: Pearson Education.

Botley, Simon, McEnery, Anthony, & Wilson, Andrew (eds.) (2000). *Multilingual Corpora in Teaching and Research*. Amsterdam: Rodopi.

Bowker, Lynne & Pearson, Jennifer (2002). *Working with Specialized Language: A Practical Guide to Using Corpora*. London: Routledge.

Burnard, Lou & McEnery, Anthony (eds.) (2000). *Rethinking Language Pedagogy from a Corpus Perspective*. Frankfurt: Lang.

Carter, Ronald (1998). Orders of reality: CANCODE, communication, and culture. *ELT Journal*, 52, 43–56.

Carter, Ronald & McCarthy, Michael (1995). Grammar and the spoken language. *Applied Linguistics*, 16, 141–158.

Carter, Ronald & McCarthy, Michael (1997). *Exploring Spoken English*. Cambridge: Cambridge University Press.

Carter, Ronald & McCarthy, Michael (2006). *Cambridge Grammar of English*. Cambridge: Cambridge University Press.

Carter, Ronald, Hughes, Rebecca, & McCarthy, Michael (1998). Telling tails: Grammar, the spoken language, and materials development. In Brian Tomlinson (ed.), *Materials Development in Language Teaching* (pp. 67–86). Cambridge: Cambridge University Press.

Čermák, Frantiaek (1997). Czech National Corpus: A case in many contexts. *International Journal of Corpus Linguistics*, 2, 181–197.

Cheng, Winnie & Warren, Martin (2000). The Hong Kong Corpus of Spoken English: Language learning through language description. In Lou Burnard & Anthony McEnery (eds.), *Rethinking Language Pedagogy from a Corpus Perspective* (pp. 133–144). Frankfurt: Peter Lang.

Cobb, Tom (1997). Is there any measurable learning from hands-on concordancing? *System*, 25, 301–315.

Cobb, Tom (1999). Breadth and depth of lexical acquisition with hands-on concordancing. *Computer Assisted Language Learning*, 12, 345–360.

Connor, Ulla & Upton, Thomas (2004). *Applied Corpus Linguistics: A Multi-Dimensional Perspective*. Amsterdam: Rodopi.

Conrad, Susan (1999). The importance of corpus-based research for language teachers. *System*, 27, 1–18.

Conrad, Susan (2002). Corpus linguistic approaches for discourse analysis. *Annual Review of Applied Linguistics*, 22, 75–95.

Conrad, Susan (2004). Corpus linguistics, language variation, and language teaching. In John Sinclair (ed.), *How to Use Corpora in Language Teaching* (pp. 67–85). Amsterdam: Benjamins.

Conrad, Susan (2006). Challenges for English corpus linguistics in second language acquisition research. In Yuji Kawaguchi, Susumu Zaima, & Toshihiro Takagaki (eds.), *Linguistic Informatics and Spoken Language Corpora: Contributions of Linguistics, Applied Linguistics and Computer Science* (pp. 67–88). Amsterdam: Benjamins.

Cook, Guy (1997). Language play, language learning. *ELT Journal*, 51, 224–231.

Cook, Guy (1998). The uses of reality: A reply to Ronald Carter. *ELT Journal*, 52, 57–63.

Coxhead, Averil (2000). A new academic word list. *TESOL Quarterly*, 34, 213–238.

De Klerk, Vivian (2006). *Corpus Linguistics and World Englishes: An Analysis of Xhosa English*. London: Continuum.

Donley, Kate & Reppen, Randi (2001). Using corpus tools to highlight academic vocabulary in SCLT. *TESOL Journal*, 10(2/3), 7–12.

Dulay, Heidi & Burt, Marina (1974). Natural sequences in child second language acquisition. *Language Learning*, 24, 37–53,

Firth, J. R. (1957). *Papers in Linguistics*. Oxford: Oxford University Press.

Fletcher, William H. (2004). Making the web more useful as a source for linguistic corpora. In Ulla Connor & Thomas Upton (eds.), *Applied Corpus Linguistics: A Multidimensional Perspective* (pp. 191–205). Amsterdam: Rodopi.

Flowerdew, John (1993). Concordancing as a tool in course design. *System*, 21, 231–244.

Flowerdew, Lynne (1998). Integrating "expert" and "interlanguage" computer corpora findings on causality: Discoveries for teachers and students. *English for Specific Purposes*, 17, 329–345.

Flowerdew, Lynne (2003). A combined corpus and systemic-functional analysis of the problem-solution pattern in a student and professional corpus of technical writing. *TESOL Quarterly*, 37, 489–511.

Flowerdew, Lynne (2005). An integration of corpus-based and genre-based approaches to text analysis in EAP/ESP: Countering criticisms against corpus-based methodologies. *English for Specific Purposes*, 24, 321–332.

Gaskell, Delian & Thomas Cobb (2004). Can learners use concordancer feedback for writing errors? *System*, 32, 301–319.

Gavioli, Laura (1997). Exploring texts through the concordancer: Guiding the learner. In Anne Wichmann, Steven Fligelstone, Tony McEnery, & Gerry Knowles (eds.), *Teaching and Language Corpora* (pp. 83–99). London: Longman.

Gavioli, Laura (2001). The learner as researcher: Introducing corpus concordancing in the classroom. In Guy Aston (ed.), *Learning with Corpora* (pp. 108–137). Houston, TX: Athelstan.

Gavioli, Laura & Aston, Guy (2001). Enriching reality: Language corpora in language pedagogy. *ELT Journal*, 55, 238–246.

Granger, Sylviane (ed.) (1998). *Learner English on Computer*. London: Longman.

Granger, Sylviane (2003). The International Corpus of Learner English: A new resource for foreign language learning and teaching and second language acquisition research. *TESOL Quarterly*, 37, 538–546.

Granger, Sylviane (2004). Computer learner corpus research: Current status and future prospects. In Ulla Connor & Thomas Upton (eds.), *Applied Corpus Linguistics: A Multidimensional Perspective* (pp. 123–145). Amsterdam: Rodopi.

Hasselgren, Angela (2002). Learner corpora and language testing: Small words as markers of learner fluency. In Sylviane Granger, Joseph Hung, & Stephanie Petch-Tyson (eds.), *Computer Learner Corpora, Second Language Acquisition and Foreign Language Teaching* (pp. 143–173). Amsterdam: Benjamins.

Hennoste, Tiit, Koit, Mare, Roosmaa, Tiit, & Saluveer, Madis (1998). Structure and usage of the Tartu University corpus of written Estonian. *International Journal of Corpus Linguistics*, 3, 279–304.

Housen, Alex (2002). A corpus-based study of the L2-acquisition of the English verb system. In Sylviane Granger, Joseph Hung, & Stephanie Petch-Tyson (eds.), *Computer Learner Corpora, Second Language Acquisition and Foreign Language Teaching* (pp. 77–116). Amsterdam: Benjamins.

Hundt, Marianne, Nesselhauf, Nadja, & Biewer, Carolin (eds.) (2006). *Corpus Linguistics and the Web*. Amsterdam: Rodopi.

Hunston, Susan (2002). *Corpora in Applied Linguistics*. Cambridge: Cambridge University Press.

Isahara, Hitoshi & Ma, Qing (2000). ORCHID: Building linguistic resources in Thai. *Literary and Linguistic Computing*, 15, 465–478.

Izre'el, Shlomo & Hary, Benjamin (2001). Designing CoSIH: The corpus of spoken Hebrew. *International Journal of Corpus Linguistics*, 6, 171–197.

Johansson, Stig, Leech, Geoffrey, & Goodluck, H. (1978). *Manual of Information to Accompany the Lancaster-Oslo/Bergen corpus of British English, for Use with Digital Computers*. Oslo, Norway: Department of English, University of Oslo.

Johns, Tim (1994). From printout to handout: Grammar and vocabulary teaching in the context of data-driven learning. In Terence Odlin (ed.), *Perspectives on Pedagogical Grammar* (pp. 293–313). Cambridge: Cambridge University Press.

Jones, Randall (1997). Creating and using a corpus of spoken German. In Anne Wichmann, Steven Fligelstone, Tony McEnery, & Gerry Knowles (eds.), *Teaching and Language Corpora* (pp. 146–156). London: Longman.

Kennedy, Claire & Miceli, Tiziana (2001). An evaluation of intermediate students' approaches to corpus investigation. *Language Learning and Technology*, 5, 77–90.

Kennedy, Graeme (1998). *An Introduction to Corpus Linguistics*. London: Longman.

Ketteman, Bernard & Marko, Georg (eds.) (2002). *Teaching and Learning by Doing Corpus Analysis*. Amsterdam: Rodopi.

Kilgarriff, Adam (2001). Comparing corpora. *International Journal of Corpus Linguistics*, 6, 1–37.

Kučera, Karel (2002). The Czech National Corpus: Principles, design, and results. *Literary and Linguistic Computing*, 17, 245–257.

Lee, David (2001). Genres, registers, text types, domains, and styles: Clarifying the concepts and navigating a path through the BNC jungle. *Language Learning and Technology*, 5, 37–72.

Leech, Geoffrey (1997). Teaching and language corpora: A convergence. In Anne Wichmann, Steven Fligelstone, Tony McEnery, & Geoffrey Knowles (eds.), *Teaching and Language Corpora* (pp. 1–23). London: Longman.

Mauranen, Anna (2003). The corpus of English as lingua franca in academic settings. *TESOL Quarterly*, 37, 513–527.

McCarthy, Michael & Carter, Ronald (1995). Spoken grammar: What is it and how can we teach it? *ELT Journal*, 49, 207–218.

McCarthy, Michael & Carter, Ronald (2001). Size isn't everything: Spoken English, corpus, and the classroom. *TESOL Quarterly*, 35, 337–340.

McCarthy, Michael, McCarten, Jeanne, & Sandiford, Helen (2005). *Touchstone 1*. Cambridge: Cambridge University Press.

McCarthy, Michael, McCarten, Jeanne, & Sandiford, Helen (2006). *Touchstone 3*. Cambridge: Cambridge University Press.

McEnery, Tony & Wilson, Andrew (1996). *Corpus Linguistics*. Edinburgh: Edinburgh University Press.

Meyer, Charles (2001). The International Corpus of English: Progress and prospects. In Rita Simpson & John Swales (eds.), *Corpus Linguistics in North America* (pp. 17–31). Ann Arbor, MI: University of Michigan Press.

Meyer, Charles (2002). *English Corpus Linguistics: An Introduction*. Cambridge: Cambridge University Press.

Mills, Don (2001). Open letter to Tom Scovel. *CATESOL News*, 33(1), 20–21.

Möllering, Martina (2001). Teaching German modal particles: A corpus-based approach. *Language Learning and Technology*, 5, 130–151.

Myles, Florence & Mitchell, Rosamond (2004). Using information technology to support empirical SLA research. *Journal of Applied Linguistics*, 1, 169–196.

Nesselhauf, Nadja (2004). Learner corpora: Learner corpora and their potential for language teaching. In John Sinclair (ed.), *How to Use Corpora in Language Teaching* (pp. 125–152). Amsterdam: Benjamins.

Ooi, Vincent (2000). Asian or Western Realities? Collocations in Singaporean-Malaysian English. In John M. Kirk (ed.), *Corpora Galore: Analysis and Techniques in Describing English* (pp. 73–89). Amsterdam: Rodopi.

O'Sullivan, Íde & Chambers, Angela (2006). Learners writing skills in French: Corpus consultation and learner evaluation. *Journal of Second Language Writing*, 15, 49–68.

Palmer, Frank R. (ed.) (1968). *Selected papers of J. R. Firth 1952–59*. London: Longman.

Partington, Alan (1998). *Patterns and Meanings: Using Corpora for English Language Research and Teaching*. Amsterdam: Benjamins.

Pravec, Norma A. (2002). Survey of learner corpora. *ICAME Journal*, 26, 81–114.

Prodromou, Luke (1996a). Correspondence. *ELT Journal*, 50, 88–89.

Prodromou, Luke (1996b). From Luke Prodromou. *ELT Journal*, 50, 369–371.

Prodromou, Luke (2003). In search of the successful user of English. *Modern English Teacher*, 12(2), 5–14.

Reder, Stephen, Harris, Kathryn, & Setzler, Kristen (2003). The Multimedia Adult Learner Corpus. *TESOL Quarterly*, 37, 546–557.

Reppen, Randi & Ide, Nancy (2004). The American National Corpus: Overall goals and the first release. *Journal of English Linguistics*, 32, 105–113.

Römer, Ute (2004). A corpus-driven approach to modal auxiliaries and their didactics. In John Sinclair (ed.), *How to Use Corpora in Language Teaching* (pp. 185–199). Amsterdam: Benjamins.

Römer, Ute (2006). Looking at *looking*: Functions and contexts of progressives in spoken English and "school" English. In Antoinette Renouf & Andrew Kehoe (eds.), *The Changing Face of Corpus Linguistics: Papers from the 24th International Conference on English Language Research on Computerized Corpora (ICAME 24)* (pp. 231–242). Amsterdam: Rodopi.

Schmitt, Diane & Schmitt, Norbert (2005). *Focus on Vocabulary: Mastering the Academic Word List*. White Plains, NY: Longman.

Scovel, Tom (2000). What I learned from the New Longman Grammar. *CATESOL News*, 32(3), 12–16.

Seidlhofer, Barbara (2000). Operationalizing intertextuality: Using learner corpora for learning. In Lou Burnard & Tony McEnery (eds.), *Rethinking Language Pedagogy from a Corpus Perspective* (pp. 207–223). Frankfurt: Lang.

Seidlhofer, Barbara (2002). Pedagogy and local learner corpora. In Sylviane Granger, Joseph Hung, & Stephanie Petch-Tyson (eds.), *Computer Learner Corpora, Second Language Acquisition and Foreign Language Teaching* (pp. 213–234). Amsterdam: Benjamins.

Seidlhofer, Barbara (2004). Research perspectives on teaching English as a Lingua Franca. *Annual Review of Applied Linguistics*, 24, 209–239.

Seidlhofer, Barbara (2005). English as a lingua franca. *ELT Journal*, 59, 339–341.

Simpson, Rita & Swales, John (eds.) (2001). *Corpus Linguistics in North America: Selections from the 1999 Symposium*. Ann Arbor: University of Michigan Press.

Simpson, Rita, Lucka, Bret, & Ovens, Janine (2000). Methodological challenges of planning a spoken corpus with pedagogical outcomes. In Lou Burnard & Tony McEnery (eds.), *Rethinking Language Pedagogy from a Corpus Perspective* (pp. 43–49). Frankfurt: Peter Lang.

Sinclair, John (ed.) (1987). *Looking Up*. London: Collins.

Sinclair, John (ed.) (2004). *How to Use Corpora in Language Teaching*. Amsterdam: Benjamins.

St John, Elke (2001). A case for using a parallel corpus and concordancers for beginners of a foreign language. *Language Learning and Technology*, 5, 185–203.

Stubbs, Michael (1993). British traditions in text analysis: From Firth to Sinclair. In Mona Baker, Gill Francis, & Elena Tognini-Bonelli (eds.), *Text and Technology* (pp. 1–33). Philadelphia: Benjamins.

Tognini-Bonelli, Elena (2001). *Corpus Linguistics at Work*. Amsterdam: Benjamins.

Tono, Yorio (2000). A computer learner corpus based analysis of the acquisition order of English grammatical morphemes. In Lou Burnard & Tony McEnery (eds.), *Rethinking Language Pedagogy from a Corpus Perspective* (pp. 123–132). Frankfurt: Peter Lang.

Upton, Thomas & Connor, Ulla (2001). Using computerized corpus analysis to investigate the textlinguistic discourse moves of a genre. *ESP Journal*, 20, 313–329.

Webster's Encyclopedic Unabridged Dictionary of the English Language (1989). New York: Random House.

Widdowson, Henry (1991). The description and prescription of language. In James Alatis (ed.), *Georgetown University Roundtable on Language and Linguistics, 1991. Linguistics and Language Pedagogy: The State of the Art* (pp. 11–24). Washington, DC: Georgetown University Press.

Widdowson, Henry (1996). Comment: Authenticity and autonomy in ELT. *ELT Journal*, 50, 67–68.

Willis, Jane (1998). Concordances in the classroom without a computer: Assembling and exploiting concordances of common words. In Brian Tomlinson (ed.), *Materials Development in Language Teaching* (pp. 44–66). Cambridge: Cambridge University Press.

Yoon, Hyunsook & Hirvela, Alan (2004). ESL student attitudes toward corpus use in L2 writing. *Journal of Second Language Writing*, 13, 257–283.

Zorzi, Daniela (2001). The pedagogic use of spoken corpora: Learning discourse markers in Italian. In Guy Aston (ed.), *Learning with Corpora* (pp. 85–107). Houston, TX: Athelstan.

Corpus linguistics websites

Numerous websites about corpus linguistics now exist, and a short list cannot do them justice. The five sites recommended below were chosen to provide hands-on practice using a corpus and links for pursuing particular interests in more detail. The first three sites allow free corpus searches on the web with very different types of corpora. The fourth site provides a further look at language teaching materials based on corpus analysis. The fifth site is the most comprehensive source for links to other corpus linguistics-related sites.

1 http://view.byu.edu/

Mark Davies' website *Variation in English Words and Phrases* allows searches for words and phrases in the 100 million word British National Corpus (BNC). Word and phrase frequencies can be compared across the categories in the BNC (such as spoken vs. newspapers vs. fiction writing), as well as viewed in the Key Word in Context (KWIC) displays. Searches for combinations of grammatical tags are also possible.

2 http://www.lsa.umich.edu/eli/micase/index.htm

The *Michigan Corpus of Academic English* (MICASE) consists of over 1,800,000 words of spoken academic discourse spoken by faculty, students, and staff. The web interface allows searches of words or phrases along with selection for certain speaker attributes (such as age range, gender, academic role, first language) and the type of speech event (e.g., large lectures, seminars, office hours, study groups). The site also includes sound files for some transcripts in the corpus. Some examples of ESL/EAP teaching materials based on MICASE are also available for download.

3   http://www.fflch.usp.br/dlm/comet/consulta_cortec.html

The *CorTec* website provides an example of working with comparable corpora in two languages, in this case English and Portuguese. Sub-corpora cover five subjects: the environment, information technology, hypertension, contract law, and cooking (recipes). Concordance searches, frequency lists, and lists of word sequences are available so that word choices can be compared in the two languages.

4   http://www.lextutor.ca/

Tom Cobb's *Compleat Lexical Tutor* describes itself as "for data driven language learning on the web." Many different kinds of activities that use concordance lines, vocabulary profiles, and phrase extractors are included. Teachers will also find tools for making exercises or quizzes from a text. A number of the activities are available in both French and English.

5   http://devoted.to/corpora

David Lee's website, *Bookmarks for Corpus-Based Linguists*, contains almost 1,000 annotated links to other corpus websites. The site includes links to corpora of all sorts, software tools, corpus linguistics courses, individuals' and conference websites, and much more. With its easy-to-follow organization, this site is an excellent place to start finding other sites that fit specific interests – or just to get a sense of the range of corpus information that is now available.

39 Interaction, Output, and Communicative Language Learning

MERRILL SWAIN AND WATARU SUZUKI

Introduction

Most researchers and theoreticians in the field of second language acquisition (SLA) assume that participation in communicative interaction is one way in which a second language (L2) is acquired by learners. Activities that occur during interaction (e.g., the provision of corrective feedback, noticing, the production of modified output, the negotiation of meaning) are considered to play an integral role in the learning processes. In this chapter, we begin with a brief discussion of the question of *whether* interaction actually does promote L2 acquisition. This is followed by a section of *how* interaction facilitates L2 learning by focusing on key concepts that have been discussed widely in the last decade. We end by indicating how these concepts are important for pedagogical practice.

Whether Interaction Promotes L2 Learning

Research into the role of interaction in L2 learning originated in the early 1980s. For example, Krashen (1985) claimed that comprehensible input was a necessary and sufficient condition for L2 acquisition to occur. Long (1983) investigated and proposed various conversational modifications (e.g., clarification requests, confirmation checks) through which input could become comprehensible to learners. Throughout the 1980s and early 1990s, researchers focused on the patterns in conversational modifications between learners and their interlocutors during communication. The overall results from these many studies indicated that conversational modifications were linked to improved comprehension on the part of the learner (see Long, 1996 for a review).

In the mid-1990s, SLA research began to examine *whether* L2 learning is facilitated through different kinds of conversational patterns, particularly those which include the provision of corrective feedback (e.g., Mackey & Philp, 1998) and production of modified output (e.g., Swain & Lapkin, 1995). Although a few studies reported no effects of interaction on L2 learning (e.g., Loschky, 1994) there is now ample evidence that interaction promotes L2 acquisition (see Mackey, 2007; Mackey & Goo, 2007 for a review).

How Interaction Facilitates L2 Learning

Since the mid-1990s, the mechanisms (e.g., noticing, attention) that mediate between communication and acquisition have been a primary focus in SLA research (Gass & Mackey, 2006). Long (1996) claims that interaction facilitates L2 acquisition because it connects input, attention, and output in productive ways. The focus in the present decade is to explain *how* interaction facilitates L2 acquisition, especially, how corrective feedback and output promote L2 learning and development (see Gass & Mackey, 2006 for a review). To do this, SLA researchers have continued to borrow and extend various concepts discussed in other disciplines such as cognitive psychology (see Robinson, 2003), cultural psychology (see Lantolf, 2006), and psycholinguistics (see Chapter 4, Psycholinguistics, this volume). In the rest of this section, we will address the question of how interaction facilitates L2 acquisition. To do so, we will select key recent studies from these three disciplinary backgrounds and describe them in detail.

Attention, awareness, and noticing

Most researchers stress the important role of attention, awareness, and noticing in L2 learning (e.g., Long, 1996; Swain, 2005; Gass & Mackey, 2006). Long (1996) argues for the role of selective attention during interaction in L2 acquisition. Swain (2005) claims that producing language plays a role in stimulating learners' awareness of linguistic forms, encouraging learners to pay attention to L2 grammar. Then, what and how are attention, awareness, and noticing defined in SLA research? Simply put, attention is a limited capacity system and is the process of selecting information for further processing, while awareness is the subjective experience of noticing. Although most researchers claim that attention is necessary for L2 acquisition to take place, there is disagreement on the role of awareness in L2 acquisition. For example, Tomlin and Villa (1994) argue that there is no association between awareness and L2 acquisition, while Schmidt (2001) assumes that some level of awareness is crucial for L2 acquisition. Further theoretical discussion is beyond the scope of this chapter. What is more important here is the general consensus within the SLA literature that noticing with some level of awareness plays a facilitative role in L2 acquisition (see also Robinson, 2003).

The relationship between noticing of corrective feedback and L2 development has been the object of intensive empirical inquiry in SLA research (e.g., Mackey, Gass, & McDonough, 2000; Philp, 2003; Mackey, 2006). For example, Mackey (2006) examined whether learners' noticing of corrective feedback during classroom interactions impacts their L2 development. She employed a pretest–treatment–post-test research design. The participants were 28 ESL learners, 15 in the experimental group and 13 in the comparison group. Both groups participated in three 50-minute classroom activities. During the activities, the experimental participants received corrective feedback (i.e., recasts or negotiation of meaning) in response to their production problems with questions, plurals, and past tense forms while the comparison group participants did not. Noticing was operationalized as "incidences of noticing of form were identified when learners' reports indicated that they were aware of the fact that their production or comprehension of form was problematic or that the form was new to them (p. 417)." The noticing data were obtained from a combination of the following sources. During the class periods, the experimental participants filled out the learning journals that asked about what they noticed during classroom interactions. Four days after the classroom activities, stimulated recall interviews were conducted using the videotaped classroom interactions. At the end of the stimulated recall session, the participants were asked to report, in whatever language they preferred, whether they had noticed anything in particular about the classroom activities. Finally, participants were asked to fill out the final L2 questionnaires designed to elicit information about what they noticed during the experimental period. The results show that there was a positive relationship between noticing and an increase in the production of correct question forms. However, no such relationship was found between noticing and the development of plurals and past tense forms. The main reason given for the different results between question forms and plurals/past tense forms was the counting and coding of what did or did not constitute evidence of noticing (i.e., the operationalization of noticing). The noticing episodes were small and unequal for each form. Therefore, results should be interpreted cautiously. However, Mackey concludes that the fact that a positive relationship between noticing and development was found for one of the three forms indicates an important role of noticing in L2 development (see also Mackey et al., 2002; Philp, 2003).

The relationship among noticing of corrective feedback, uptake (i.e., modified output), and L2 development has also been explored in recent years (e.g., Loewen, 2005; McDonough, 2005). "Uptake," or modified output in response to corrective feedback, is believed to indicate that learners have noticed the feedback. If learners repair their original erroneous utterances by incorporating the target forms from corrective feedback, they must have noticed these forms with some level of awareness. Lyster and Mori (2006) and Sheen (2004) have examined the immediate effect of corrective feedback (i.e., uptake) in various instructional contexts, but have not explored the relationship between uptake and L2 development. A few studies (e.g., Loewen, 2005; McDonough,

2005; McDonough & Mackey, 2006), however, have examined the link between modified output and L2 development.

Loewen (2005) showed that modified output in response to corrective feedback (i.e., uptake) best predicted L2 development. He was interested in the effectiveness of "incidental focus on form" in promoting L2 development. Incidental focus on form "overtly draws learner's attention to linguistic items as they arise spontaneously – without prior planning – in meaning-focused interaction" (Loewen, 2005: 361). In general, teachers draw learners' attention to linguistic items through corrective feedback such as recasts and clarification requests. In response to corrective feedback, learners may produce uptake. Loewen observed 17 hours of communicatively oriented L2 lessons in a private language school in New Zealand. He identified focus on form episodes (FFEs), defined as "the discourse from the point where the attention to linguistic form starts to the point where it ends, due to a change in topic back to message or sometimes another focus on form" (Ellis, Basturkmen, & Loewen, 2001: 294). He then used FFEs to construct individualized test items for the students who participated in specific FFEs. Statistical analysis showed that modified output was the most significant predictor of correct test scores among the characteristics of FFEs (e.g., complexity, explicitness, and timing) that he studied. In other words, Loewen showed that modifying their output in response to corrective feedback best predicts L2 development (see also McDonough, 2005, discussed below).

Working memory

Working memory is the ability to store and manipulate information simultaneously for various complex cognitive tasks. A number of SLA studies suggest that working memory plays a crucial role in L2 acquisition (see Robinson, 2003 for a review). Therefore, working memory capacities help to explain how L2 learners benefit from corrective feedback during communicative interaction. If attention is limited by working memory capacities, there must be relationships among working memory capacities, noticing, and L2 development. However, SLA research is just beginning to examine such complex interactions (e.g., Mackey et al., 2002).

Mackey et al. (2002) examined the relationship between working memory, noticing of interactional feedback, and L2 development. They employed a research design which included a pretest, treatment, immediate post-test, and delayed post-test. In their study, 30 adult Japanese learners of English took three working memory tests (i.e., a nonword recall test, a listening span test in English and in Japanese). An indication of noticing was obtained through stimulated recalls and questionnaires. Mackey et al. operationalized noticing as "the learners' articulation of response to the input, without distinguishing the degree of understanding involved, or the focus of noticing" (p. 188). They operationalized L2 development as "advances through the developmental stages of English question formation" (p. 188). Participants received recasts following their non-targetlike production of question forms during three 30-minute sessions of dyadic interaction (treatment). Their results were mixed. First, participants who reported more noticing episodes tended to have higher working memory capacities than those who reported fewer noticing episodes. Second, participants at a lower developmental level indicated more noticing than those at a higher developmental level. Finally, the participants with higher working memory capacities tended to demonstrate L2 development in the delayed post-test, while those with low working memory capacities seemed to show L2 development in the immediate post-test. These results suggest complex relationships among working memory capacities, noticing of corrective feedback, and L2 acquisition. Certainly, these complex interactions will be more closely examined in further research.

Explicit knowledge and implicit knowledge

According to Hulstijn (2005), "explicit and implicit knowledge differ in the extent to which one has or has not (respectively) an awareness of the regularities underlying the information one has knowledge of, and to what extent one can or cannot (respectively) verbalize these regularities" (p. 130). In SLA research it is generally recognized that explicit knowledge plays a role in facilitating the acquisition of implicit knowledge (Ellis, 2005, Chapter 31 this volume). However, the relationship between the two types of knowledge still remains controversial. Research has recently begun to examine the effectiveness of corrective feedback in the acquisition of explicit and implicit knowledge (e.g., Lyster, 2004; Ammar & Spada, 2006; Ellis, Loewen, & Erlam, 2006).

Lyster (2004) examined the differential effects of "prompts" (i.e., clarification requests, repetitions, metalinguistic clues, and elicitation) and recasts during form-focused instruction activities. He employed a pretest–treatment–post-test research design. The study was implemented in the context of regular subject-matter instruction during which 179 fifth-grade French immersion students receive either prompts or recasts over five weeks. Lyster found that those receiving prompts resulted in statistically greater gains on written tasks eliciting explicit knowledge than those receiving recasts. Furthermore, Lyster found that, although to a much lesser degree, prompts resulted in more gains on the oral tasks eliciting implicit knowledge than recasts. In a similar vein, Ammar and Spada (2006) examined the relative effectiveness of prompts and recasts for ESL learners. In their research design, clarification requests were excluded because they are sometimes interpreted as providing feedback on meaning. Therefore, Ammar and Spada (2006) considered prompts and recasts as explicit and implicit feedback techniques, respectively. They found overall effectiveness of prompts over recasts on both a controlled written task eliciting explicit knowledge and an oral task eliciting implicit knowledge. Taken together with Lyster (2004), the general findings of superiority of prompts over recasts may indicate that certain corrective feedback types (e.g., prompts) facilitate the acquisition of both explicit and implicit knowledge more effectively than others (e.g., recasts).

Recently Ellis et al. (2006) investigated the relative effectiveness of explicit and implicit corrective feedback on the acquisition of explicit and implicit knowledge. They employed a pretest–treatment–post-test research design. In the treatment session, low-intermediate ESL learners performed two communicative tasks during which they received either recasts (implicit feedback) or metalinguistic explanation (explicit feedback) in response to utterances containing errors in regular past tense *-ed*. Untimed grammaticality judgment and metalinguistic tests were designed to measure explicit knowledge, while an oral imitation test was intended to measure implicit knowledge (see Ellis, 2005; Erlam, 2006). Metalinguistic explanation was found to contribute to the internalization of the target feature more than recasts. In other words, explicit feedback benefited both explicit and implicit knowledge. This finding suggests that to examine the effects of corrective feedback in L2 acquisition, measures eliciting both explicit and implicit knowledge should be incorporated in further studies (Ellis, Chapter 31 this volume).

Negative evidence and positive evidence

Corrective feedback can provide learners with positive evidence and/or negative evidence. Positive and negative evidence refers to information about what is or what is not (respectively) possible in the target language (Long, 2006). It is generally recognized that the negative evidence that corrective feedback provides facilitates the acquisition of implicit knowledge (Ellis & Sheen, 2006; Long, 2006). Here, we consider whether corrective feedback constitutes a source of negative or/and positive evidence. In SLA research, corrective feedback techniques (e.g., recasts, clarification requests) have been examined in order to understand the role of positive and negative evidence in L2 acquisition (see Ellis & Sheen, 2006; Long, 2006 for a review).

Recasts are believed to provide two important pieces of information for L2 learners. First, recasts may inform the learners that their own form is ungrammatical (i.e., negative evidence). Second, recasts may reveal the information of what is grammatical (i.e., positive evidence). Leeman (2003) addressed this issue, examining the relative effectiveness of the negative and positive evidence contained in the recasts for L2 acquisition. She employed a pretest–treatment–post-test research design to examine the effects of recasts on the acquisition of Spanish gender and number agreement on nouns and adjectives. The participants performed a series of communicative tasks during which they received (1) recasts (i.e., negative evidence and enhanced salience of positive evidence), (2) negative evidence (indicating the source of a problem but without correcting), (3) enhanced positive evidence (using stress and intonation to make the target form salient), or (4) unenhanced positive evidence. Only the recast and enhanced positive evidence groups outperformed the comparison group on the post-tests. Based upon her finding, Leeman concluded that recasts facilitate acquisition because they provide enhanced salience to positive evidence, not because they constitute negative evidence.

Whether recasts offer negative evidence or/and positive evidence has been explored through the examination of how learners interpret recasts (e.g., Mackey et al., 2000; Carpenter et al., 2006). Carpenter et al. (2006) addressed this issue, examining how and what learners perceive when presented with recasts provided in communicative interaction. They showed clips of recasts and repetitions to their ESL participants. One group saw clips in which the learners' initial non-targetlike utterances were removed. In contrast, another group saw the same video clips with the initial problematic utterances retained. After watching each clip, both groups were asked to indicate whether they were hearing a recast, a repetition, or something else. Carpenter et al. reported that learners who did not see the initial non-targetlike utterances were significantly less successful in terms of distinguishing recasts from repetitions. Carpenter et al. interpret their results as showing that recasts may be effective because they provide learners with the immediate contrast between learners' non-targetlike utterance and interlocutors' targetlike utterance. Recasts may also constitute a source of negative evidence because recasts provide learners with opportunity to interpret recasts as corrective (Ellis & Sheen, 2006; Long, 2006). Whether learners perceive recasts as corrective or not has been examined in reference to various mediating factors: learner proficiency level (e.g., Mackey & Philp, 1998); L1 literacy level (e.g., Bigelow et al., 2006); instructional context (e.g., Sheen, 2004; Lyster & Mori, 2006); targeted linguistic structures (e.g., Mackey et al., 2000); and feature of recasts (e.g., Philp, 2003).

Clarification requests in themselves do not offer grammatical alternatives to the learners (i.e., positive evidence) nor information about the source of ungrammaticality in L2 learners' utterances (i.e., negative evidence). However, clarification requests may play a facilitative role in L2 acquisition because clarification requests provide L2 learners with the opportunity to pay attention to ungrammatical aspects of their utterances. Furthermore, clarification requests are likely to elicit learners' self-repairs or modified output. McDonough (2005) addressed this issue, examining the impact of clarification requests and learners' modified output in response to corrective feedback on L2 development. L2 development was operationalized as advancement through the developmental stages of English question formation (see Mackey, 2006). Participants performed a series of communicative tasks with native speakers of English in the following four conditions: (1) enhanced opportunity to modify (providing feedback with stress and rising intonation and opportunity for learners to modify their initial utterances); (2) opportunity to modify (providing feedback only without stress and intonation and opportunity for learners to modify their initial utterances); (3) feedback without opportunity to modify (providing feedback with stress and rising intonation but no opportunity for learners to modify their initial utterances); and (4) no feedback. Participants carried out three treatment sessions and then completed four oral production tests over an eight-week period. Statistical analysis showed that learners'

what they had originally written. During the noticing stage and stimulated recall stages, the students expressed their beliefs about the target language and often talked themselves through understanding why the changes had been made by the reformulator. For example, in their story, Nina and Dara had written *"Il est maintenant 6:01 et elle s'endore sans bruit"* ('It is now 6:01 and she fell asleep without a sound'). The reformulator changed this into *"elle s'endore dans le silence"* ('she fell asleep in the silence'). Nina and Dara's version put the emphasis on how the girl falls asleep (i.e., without a sound), whereas the reformulator's version highlighted the state of the room (i.e., silent). During the stimulated recall, Nina and Dara noticed this difference, and Nina said that "I think *sans bruit* is more, she, she fell asleep and she didn't make any noise. But silence is like everything around her is silent." It seems that they were not willing to incorporate the reformulation into their original story, because they felt that the reformulation changed their intended meaning. Later when interviewed, Nina said "Some of them [the reformulations], they seemed like they changed the story sort of and it wasn't really ours." These noticing and stimulated recall protocols suggest that Nina and Dara wanted to preserve their own meaning when receiving corrective feedback in the form of reformulation. In fact, when they were asked to rewrite their story individually, they used the lexical item (*silence*) that the reformulator had proposed, but in a way that preserved their meaning. These data show that the students reflected on the linguistic differences between their original story and its reformulated version, resulting in a deeper understanding of the proposed changes by the reformulator. Here, we can see how a learner engages in languaging about language to mediate L2 learning (Swain, 2006).

Private speech

Private speech is an important construct when it comes to considering the role of interaction in L2 acquisition. Vygotskyian sociocultural theory claims that learners initially use language to engage in communicative interaction with their interlocutors and, eventually, this interpersonal speech takes on an intrapersonal function in which the speech is directed to the self. Interpersonal (social) speech can have an intrapersonal (private) function (Lantolf, 2006). However, such theoretical discussion is not our aim here. What is important in this chapter is that several researchers, for example Ohta (2001), place importance on this intrapersonal (private) speech in L2 acquisition.

Ohta (2001) collected 34 hours of audiotape which was recorded through individual microphones from 10 learners of Japanese as a foreign language in a university class in the US. In her study, private speech was identified "by its (a) reduced volume, (b) because it was not in response to a question / comment directed specifically to the individual by the teacher or another student, and (c) because it did not receive a response by the teacher or a classmate" (p. 38). Ohta found that learners often "vicariously" responded to recasts intended for someone else, as exemplified in the following excerpt:

1 T: Kon shuumatsu hima desu ka? Hyun-san
Are you free this weekend, Hyun

Error → 2 H: Um (..) iie (.) um (.) uh:: (.) hima- (.) hima: (.) hima nai
Um (..) no (.) um (.) uh:: (.) free- (.) free (.) free-Neg

Recast → 3 T: Hima Ja ^ arimasen
You are not free

Uptake → 4 H: Oh, ja ^ arimsen
Oh not free

Uptake → 5 C: him ja^ arimasen (whispered and overlapping H)
(Private speech) *not free*

6 T: Hima ja arimasen (.) ii desu ne (.) Eh:to ja S-san kon shumatsu hima desu ka?
You are not free (.) well done (.) Uh, so, S, are you free this weekend?

In line 1, T asks H whether he is free this weekend. In line 2, H made an error, leaving out *ja*. When T provides a recast in response to the error in line 3, H uptakes it in the form of repetition. Interestingly, C covertly repeats the correct response in line 5. As can be seen in this excerpt, C is a peripheral participant in this interaction. That is, C produces a repetition (i.e., uptake) in the form of private speech. One function of such repetition is the consolidation of linguistic knowledge that learners have not fully internalized (Ohta, 2001). According to Ohta, C later "uses the form correctly in peer interaction, as well as when, in subsequent teacher-fronted practice, she covertly corrects classmates who use the wrong form" (p. 59). Ohta's study provides evidence that private speech during communicative interaction is a source of language acquisition (Lantolf, 2006).

Pedagogical Implications for Communicative Language Learning

Based on the research literature we have reviewed in this chapter, few would doubt that participation in communicative interaction is a source of L2 acquisition. However, the primary focus of SLA research reviewed here is on how languages are learned, not how languages are taught. Therefore, direct application of this research into classrooms may be unwise and even premature. Nevertheless, we believe that it is important to draw some pedagogical implications of SLA research, especially in the context of corrective feedback and output, that might be helpful for teachers' pedagogical decisions in communicative L2 classrooms (see also Ellis, Chapter 31 this volume; Pica, Chapter 37 this volume).

First, implicit feedback (e.g., recasts) may not be as helpful as expected in L2 classrooms (Ellis & Sheen, 2006). Although practical reasons, empirical evidence, and theoretical arguments have suggested the effectiveness of implicit feedback in L2 classrooms (e.g., Leeman, 2003; Carpenter et al., 2006; Long,

2006), explicit feedback (e.g., metalinguistic explanations) appears to act both on explicit and implicit knowledge, while implicit feedback does not necessarily do so (e.g., Lyster, 2004; Ammar & Spada, 2006; Ellis et al., 2006). Thus, in communicative L2 classrooms, teachers might consider making greater use of explicit feedback techniques (Ellis, Chapter 31 this volume; Seedhouse, 1997).

Second, the research shows the important role of output that pushes learners to make use of their resources and stretch their limited linguistic capacities to their fullest (Swain & Lapkin, 1995; Swain, 2005). When corrective feedback is given, the active participation of the learner through the production of a modified version of his/her original utterance is an important part of L2 learning processes (e.g., Ohta, 2001; Loewen, 2005; McDonough, 2005).

Third, the growing literature on languaging – exploring through the use of language the means and tools needed to express one's intended meaning – is of considerable importance (Swain & Lapkin, 2002; Swain, 2006). Teachers might wish to give their learners many opportunities to write together while encouraging them to language about the many rich and complex resources that the target language has in order to build the meanings they wish to express.

NOTE

We are grateful to Rod Ellis, Shawn Loewen, and Alison Mackey for their insightful comments on this paper.

REFERENCES

Aljaafreh, A. & Lantolf, J. P. (1994). Negative feedback as regulation and second language learning in the zone of proximal development. *The Modern Language Journal, 78*(4), 465–483.

Ammar, A. & Spada, N. (2006). One size fits all? Recasts, prompts, and L2 learning. *Studies in Second Language Acquisition, 28*(4), 543–574.

Bigelow, M., DelMas, B., Hansen, K., & Tarone, E. (2006). Literacy and the processing of oral recasts in SLA. *TESOL Quarterly, 40*(4), 665–689.

Carpenter, H., Jeon, S., MacGregor, D., & Mackey, A. (2006). Recasts and repetitions: Learners' interpretations of native speaker responses. *Studies in Second Language Acquisition, 28*(2), 209–236.

Ellis, R. (2005). Measuring implicit and explicit knowledge of a second language: A psychometric study. *Studies in Second Language Acquisition, 27*(2), 141–172.

Ellis, R. & Sheen, Y. (2006). Re-examining the role of recasts in L2 acquisition. *Studies in Second Language Acquisition, 28*(4), 575–600.

Ellis, R., Basturkmen, H., & Loewen, S. (2001). Learner uptake in communicative ESL lessons. *Language Learning, 54*(2), 227–275.

Ellis, R., Leowen, S., & Erlam, R. (2006). Implicit and explicit corrective feedback and the acquisition of L2 grammar. *Studies in Second Language Acquisition*, 28(2), 339–368.

Erlam, R. (2006). Elicited imitation as a measure of L2 implicit knowledge: An empirical validation study. *Applied Linguistics*, 27(3), 464–491.

Gass, S. & Mackey, A. (2006). Input, interaction and output in SLA. In B. VanPatten & J. Williams (eds.), *Theories in Second Language Acquisition: An Introduction* (pp. 173–196). Mahwah, NJ: Lawrence Erlbaum.

Hulstijn, J. (2005). Theoretical and empirical issues in the study of implicit and explicit second-language learning: Introduction. *Studies in Second Language Acquisition*, 27(2), 129–140.

Krashen, S. (1985). *The Input Hypothesis: Issues and Implications*. London: Longman.

Lantolf, J. (2006). Sociocultural theory and L2 development: State-of-the-art. *Studies in Second Language Acquisition*, 28(1), 67–109.

Leeman, J. (2003). Recasts and second language development. *Studies in Second Language Acquisition*, 25(1), 37–63.

Loewen, S. (2005). Incidental focus on form and second language learning. *Studies in Second Language Acquisition*, 27(3), 361–386.

Long, M. (1983). Linguistic and conversational adjustments to nonnative speakers. *Studies in Second Language Acquisition*, 5(2), 177–193.

Long, M. (1996). The role of the linguistic environment in second language acquisition. In W. C. Ritchie & T. K. Bhatia (eds.), *Handbook of Second Language Acquisition* (pp. 413–468). San Diego, CA: Academic Press.

Long, M. (2006). Recasts: The story so far. In M. H. Long (ed.), *Problems in SLA* (pp. 75–116). Mahwah, New Jersey: Lawrence Erlbaum.

Loschky, L. (1994). Comprehensible input and second language acquisition: What is the relationship? *Studies in Second Language Acquisition*, 16(3), 303–325.

Lyster, R. (2004). Differential effects of prompts and recasts in form-focused instruction. *Studies in Second Language Acquisition*, 26(3), 399–432.

Lyster, R. & Mori, H. (2006). Comparing interactional feedback across instructional contexts. *Studies in Second Language Acquisition*, 28(2), 269–300.

Mackey, A. (2006). Feedback, noticing and instructed second language learning. *Applied Linguistics*, 27(3), 405–437.

Mackey, A. (2007). Introduction. In A. Mackey (ed.), *Conversational Interaction in Second Language Acquisition: A Series of Empirical Studies* (pp. 1–26). Oxford: Oxford University Press.

Mackey, A. & Goo, J. (2007). Interaction research in SLA: A meta-analysis and research synthesis. In A. Mackey (ed.), *Conversational Interaction in Second Language Acquisition: A Series of Empirical Studies* (pp. 407–452). Oxford: Oxford University Press.

Mackey, A. & Philp, J. (1998). Conversational interaction and second language development: Recasts, responses and red herrings? *The Modern Language Journal*, 82(3), 338–356.

Mackey, A., Gass, S., & McDonough, K. (2000). How do learners perceive interactional feedback? *Studies in Second Language Acquisition*, 22(4), 471–497.

Mackey, A., Philp, J., Egi, T., Fujii, A., & Tatsumi, T. (2002). Individual differences in working memory, noticing of interactional feedback and L2 development. In P. Robinson (ed.), *Individual Differences and Instructed Language Learning* (pp. 181–209). Philadelphia: John Benjamins.

McDonough, K. (2005). Identifying the impact of negative feedback and learners' responses on ESL question development. *Studies in Second Language Acquisition*, 27(1), 79–103.

McDonough, K. & Mackey, A. (2006). Responses to recasts: Repetitions, primed production and linguistic development. *Language Learning*, 56(4), 693–720.

Nassaji, H. & Swain, M. (2000). A Vygotskian perspective on corrective feedback in L2: The effect of random versus negotiated help on the learning of English articles. *Language Awareness*, 9(1), 34–51.

Ohta, A. S. (2001). *Second Language Acquisition Processes in the Classroom: Learning Japanese*. Mahwah, NJ: Lawrence Erlbaum.

Philp, J. (2003). Constraints on "noticing the gap": Nonnative speakers' noticing of recasts in NS-NNS interaction. *Studies in Second Language Acquisition*, 25(1), 99–126.

Robinson, P. (2003). Attention and memory. In C. J. Doughty & M. H. Long (eds.), *The Handbook of Second Language Acquisition* (pp. 631–678). Malden, MA: Blackwell.

Schmidt, R. (2001). Attention. In P. Robinson (ed.), *Cognition and Second Language Instruction* (pp. 3–32). Cambridge: Cambridge University Press.

Seedhouse, P. (1997). The case of Missing "No": The relationship between pedagogy and interaction. *Language Learning*, 47(3), 547–583.

Sheen, Y. H. (2004). Corrective feedback and learner uptake in communicative classrooms across instructional settings. *Language Teaching Research*, 8(3), 263–300.

Storch, N. (2002). Patterns of interaction in ESL pair work. *Language Learning*, 52(2), 119–158.

Swain, M. (2005). The output hypothesis: Theory and research. In E. Hinkel (ed.), *The Handbook of Research in Second Language Teaching and Learning* (pp. 471–483). Mahwah, NJ: Lawrence Erlbaum.

Swain, M. (2006). Languaging, agency and collaboration in advanced language proficiency. In H. Byrnes (ed.), *Advanced Language Learning: The Contributions of Halliday and Vygotsky* (pp. 95–108). London: Continuum.

Swain, M. & Lapkin, S. (1995). Problems in output and the cognitive processes they generate: A step towards second language learning. *Applied Linguistics*, 16(3), 371–391.

Swain, M. & Lapkin, S. (1998). Interaction and second language learning: Two adolescent French immersion students working together. *The Modern Language Journal*, 82(3), 320–337.

Swain, M. & Lapkin, S. (2002). Talking it through: Two French immersion learners' response to reformulation. *International Journal of Educational Research* 37(3&4), 285–304.

Swain, M., Brooks, L., & Tocalli-Beller, A. (2002). Peer–peer dialogue as means of second language learning. *Annual Review of Applied Linguistics*, 22, 171–185.

Tomlin, R. S. & Villa, V. (1994). Attention in cognitive science and second language acquisition. *Studies in Second Language Acquisition*, 16(2), 183–203.

40 Classroom Discourse and Interaction: Reading Across the Traditions

LESLEY A. REX AND
JUDITH L. GREEN

In this chapter, we present a broad range of traditions that have shaped new directions in the study of classroom interaction as a discursive process. From this perspective, discourse – language above the level of single utterance or sentence – is central to the study of teaching and learning interactions. Although some researchers investigate classroom interaction without discourse as a theoretical or methodological tool, and others examine classroom discourse as texts, we present those traditions that view discourse as language-in-use and that seek to make visible how the linguistic and discourse choices of participants in classroom interaction are consequential for student learning in classrooms.

An Overview of Distinctions between Classroom Interactions and Classroom Discourse

Historically, the study of classroom discourse and the study of classroom interaction have different theoretical roots and methodological logics. Classroom discourse studies seek to make visible how everyday life in classrooms is constituted in and through the linguistic and discourse choices of participants; how language brought to and constructed in classrooms is consequential for social and academic knowledge construction; and, how language use shapes, and is shaped by, processes, practices, and content demands of the curriculum. In contrast, studies of classroom interaction generally examine behaviors and strategies used by teachers and students, with the notable exception of research grounded in ethnomethodology and conversation analysis. Classroom interaction researchers generally investigate which behaviors and strategies correlate with student performance measures or student learning indices.

Recent reviews of different traditions, their epistemological bases and theoretical orientations, make visible how the naming of phenomena such as discourse and classroom interaction leads to different understandings of what is accomplished in classrooms. In a recent review, Rex, Steadman, and Graciano (2006) identified seven research perspectives between 1960 and 2005. Each had a different theoretical and epistemological history and purpose: process-product; cognitive; socio-cognitive, situated cognition and activity theory; ethnographic; sociolinguistics and discourse analysis; critical; and teacher research. All of these programs of research purport to study classroom inter-actions, but not all focus on discourse. Further within and across all of these categories except process-product, discourse, where used, is approached dif-ferently according to the conceptualization of classrooms and the phenomena of interest in those disciplines.

A review by Green and Dixon (2007) examined the roots of classroom inter-action, classroom discourse, and situated learning, locating early beginnings of classroom interaction research (1920–60) in work in social psychology and sociology. Across these traditions, classroom interaction was viewed as behavior, and language as a marker of psychological processes (e.g., affective and cognitive), indicative of social variables needed to improve learning (e.g., authoritative versus democratic, effective teaching practices) (e.g., Dunkin & Biddle, 1974). This work was known as research on teaching, process-product research, or interaction analysis in classrooms. A priori coding systems were used (e.g., Rosenshine & Furst, 1986) and language was opaque, viewed as representative of pedagogical/cognitive behaviors.

By 1974, the focus of this work expanded to include advances in theory and methodology in fields such as linguistics, child language, conversation ana-lysis, ethnomethodology, ethnography of communication, psycholinguistics, sociolinguistics, and sociology. Grounded in these disciplinary traditions, education researchers conducted studies of relationships between language in the home and school, disciplinary demands of language use in classrooms, and linguistic, social, and cultural presuppositions that shaped language use by students and teachers. Today, education researchers bring traditions of discourse together with sociocultural and critical theories to explore a broad range of phenomena, including identity, knowledge construction, power rela-tionships, policy impact, literacy practices, and disciplinary knowledge (e.g., Hicks, 1995; Luke, 1995; Mercer, 1995; Knobel, 1999; Cazden, 2001; Wells, 2002; Rex, 2006). In the following sections, representative contributions of different traditions are presented to make visible the rich body of work currently avail-able on the study of classroom interactions and classroom discourse.

Fluidity of Society: Growing Diversity and Education

To understand why these discourse-based studies became critical to the study of learning in classrooms, post-WWII social contexts of schooling need to be considered. This period marked a change that continues today. Post-WWII, demographic characteristics of nations changed as people became more mobile and national populations more fluid (Bauman, 2000). Today, people move from town to town, and from country to country. With these moves schools, classrooms, and other social institutions become sites with greater linguistic, social, and cultural diversity. Further, in the US, laws and policies changed, initiating an ongoing period of desegregation of schooling by race and a need for schools to be responsive to the growing diversity of language learners. In other countries, similar social and political changes have also occurred, influencing directions of research in classrooms.

To help educators respond to these changing and diverse student groups and to the complexity of society, researchers grounded in discourse-based traditions constructed new, often interdisciplinary, approaches. These approaches are being used to understand how discourse processes and practices, as well as language use in classrooms, supports and constrains equity of access to academic institutions and to academic and social knowledge. As a consequence, rather than the earlier focus on language behavior, form, function, or deficit, these new interdisciplinary approaches provide ways of exploring discourse as constituting and constitutive of social contexts, social and academic identities, academic knowledge, disciplinary practices, as well as teaching and learning as social and discursive phenomena both in and out of school. These approaches also provide new ways to examine the complex cognitive processes involved in student oral, written, and graphic performances across events, times, and contexts for learning.

Major Theoretical Traditions Framing the Study of Discourse and Classroom Interaction

Traditions in this section represent clusters of programs of research that over the past four decades have become central to the work on classroom discourse and interaction. We have clustered traditions with overlapping or concordant assumptions about the nature of discourse and interaction. Though in their home disciplines each tradition is distinct, educational researchers often combine traditions to address complex issues in teaching and learning, a practice that has led to the construction of interdisciplinary approaches. Each cluster of approaches provides a theoretical language and set of methodological practices for conceptualizing, understanding, and studying particular educational issues. These approaches are further made possible by a series of technological advances that support in-depth analysis of classroom talk. These methodological and theoretical advances have recently led to contrastive analyses that demonstrate what the different traditions provide, what questions each addresses, and how each methodology affords researchers the ability to examine particular phenomena (Green & Harker, 1988; Hornberger & Corson, 1997;

Koschman, 1999; Goldman et al., in press). Additionally, as new traditions and approaches have developed, education researchers have begun to reexamine their data using new theoretical traditions, making visible how different theories influence what they can know about classroom discourse and interaction (Barnes & Todd, 1995).

The child as language user and language learner

A collection of theoretical and methodological developments about human language ability across disciplines advanced understandings of classroom discourse. This work, grounded in fields such as psycholinguistics, child language, linguistics, and applied linguistics brought to the fore the creative and learned nature of language for children and adults alike. As the fields of child language and psycholinguistics developed, researchers began to examine closely how children learned the grammar and meanings of language, focusing on the expressive purposes of language and their relationship to language acquisition and development (e.g., Cazden, John, & Hymes, 1972). Research in these fields focused educators' attention on how children learn language and what was involved in learning how to use the conventional system of grammar; on the forms and functions of the language of the home, and how this language was similar to and differed from the language of the school; as well as on how children acquired knowledge needed for reading, writing and speaking in classrooms (e.g., Cazden, 1972; Heath, 1983).

These traditions focused the attention of researchers, teacher educators, and teachers alike on the knowledge of language that children brought to school and how this knowledge was observable in children's oral and written communication. They also brought new understandings about how children learn to communicate through the language systems in which they were enculturated prior to beginning formal schooling, and how these systems formed communicative resources for students. Drawing on advances in linguistics and related fields, language-oriented researchers in education were able to frame studies of how children, in and through their interactions with others across educational contexts (home, school, community), acquired the rules of language, the sound systems, and their meanings in their contexts of use. These approaches focused on the moments of language use, creating the need for a shift in the study of classroom interaction from a behaviorist and language-as-opaque approach to research on discourse and language-in-use in classrooms and its consequences for student learning *of* language and *about* language (e.g., Green & Wallat, 1981; Halliday, 1985). This work led to explorations of how students learn to read and write in classrooms and to new ways of assessing students' reading, writing, and speaking performance. (e.g., Chomsky, 1972; Genishi & Dyson, 1984).

This early work examined the repertoires for language use students brought to and learned in classrooms. It also shifted educators' understandings of the creative nature of language and led to new approaches to systematic exploration of language use and the contextual nature of meaning (Mishler, 1979). By the late 1970s, educators and researchers alike turned their attention to the language of diverse groups of learners, many of whom spoke English as a second language, frequently used code-switching, or spoke a dialect other than school English (e.g., Labov, 1972; Rampton, 2000). Furthermore, as classrooms became linguistically and culturally more complex, new questions arose about ways of understanding language used by students and teachers in classrooms. Classroom discourse, rather than behavior, became a focus of research and theoretical re-examination within and across disciplines (e.g., Cazden, 2001).

From this perspective, classroom discourse was understood as a situated phenomenon, in which students draw on linguistic, contextual, and social presuppositions gained from interactions in other social milieus and groups to participate in and interpret the communications of others (Gumperz & Cook-Gumperz, 1986). This perspective led to the development of research approaches that enabled systematic descriptions of language-in-use. These approaches drew primarily on the use of transcriptions of actual talk rather than on a priori coding systems. These traditions raised questions about what constituted knowledge of language in classroom discourse and interactions. Researchers explored questions about how classroom language (as well as language in other contexts) is learned, what it means to know a language, how first and second languages develop, and what constitutes language learning across semiotic systems in classrooms (reading, writing, speaking). This work has led to reconceptualization of classroom discourse and new challenges for classroom teachers and researchers across disciplines.

Classroom discourse practices and processes in the construction of classroom life

Concurrent with research on child as language learner was the development of research traditions examining language in use in classrooms and how language use shaped and was shaped by the ways teacher and students communicated within and across events. These studies led to new understandings of teaching and learning as constituted in and through the discourse choices and communicative practices of teachers and students. This body of work is known as microethnographic and sociolinguistic studies of discourse-in-use in classrooms and other educational settings (Bloome et al., 2004; Erickson, 2004). This work expands the concept of meaning in context to explore how within and across the face-to-face and moment-by-moment interactions, teachers and students construct a language of the classroom (Lin, 1993), which in turn shapes who can say and do what, when and where, for what purposes, in what ways, under what conditions, and with what consequences or outcomes (e.g., Erickson, 1986; Hymes, 1996; Duff, 2002).

Drawing on work reconceptualizing context (e.g., Duranti & Goodwin, 1992), education researchers have undertaken microethnographic research in classrooms (e.g., Green & Wallat, 1981; Athanases & Heath, 1995; Bloome et al., 2004). These studies provided new understandings of classroom discourse as situated in moment-to-moment interactions and in over-time, intertextually-tied contexts (e.g., Bloome & Egan-Robertson, 1993). These studies show how social, historical, linguistic, cognitive, and cultural patterns of practice in class-rooms shape and are shaped by the discourse and communicative patterns constructed by members, creating a need to examine micro–macro relation-ships inside and outside of classrooms); how ways of knowing, being, and doing are constructed in classrooms; and how academic and social identities are socially constructed across times, events, and actors (Heller & Martin-Jones, 2000).

The theoretical and methodological traditions within ethnographic and socio-linguistic research have contributed important understandings of classroom discourse and its impact on what students and teachers construct in class-rooms (Cazden et al., 1972; Heath, 1983). These approaches support examina-tion of not only what was said and the actions that accompanied the speech, but also consideration of what Gumperz (1992) calls *contextualization cues* – pitch, stress, pause, juncture, eye gaze, gesture, proxemics, kinesics, lexical items and grammar. Contextualization cues were central to studying meaning and identity construction as well as assessment of academic and social ability (e.g., Cook-Gumperz & Gumperz, 1992). Such research was instrumental in providing alternatives to deficit models of language and in moving beyond difference models to models of how language use, within and across cultur-ally, socially, and lingistically diverse groups, involves wide variations of performance across time, events, and actors (e.g., Collins, 1986; Foster, 1995; Cook-Gumperz, 2006). These studies illustrated that *difference in language use is the norm* in classrooms and led to new understandings of how the language resources classroom members bring to classrooms are, or are not, supported.

Further, the micro-ethnographic approach made visible how *common know-ledge* (Edwards & Mercer, 1987) is constructed and how it guides participation and knowledge construction in subsequent times and events. The microethno-graphic approach raised new awareness about the units of analysis used to represent ways members construct extended stretches of interaction, patterns of interaction, demands for participating, responses to what is said and done, as well as academic content. Researchers grounded in discourse-based ethno-graphic studies often bring different theoretical and methodological traditions together to examine complex layers and historical patterns of communication and interaction, depending on the type of text being examined (e.g., oral, written, graphic) (e.g., Green, Harker, & Golden, 1987; Gee & Green, 1998).

Collectively, microethnographic work provided new understandings of discourse as both a process and a product of local interactions and as inter-textually tied to past and future events constituting human activity. Language is both a resource for communication and an outcome of communication across time and events. Prior uses of language (and literacy) are understood to be material resources members draw on to communicate with others, to read and interpret what is occurring in the present event under construction, and to support and constrain both the opportunities for learning and what is learned (e.g., Tuyay, Jennings, & Dixon, 1995; Vine, 2003). Additionally, this approach makes visible how disciplinary knowledge is discursively constructed within and across events (e.g., Castanheira et al., 2001; Brown, Reveles, & Kelly, & 2005; Street, Baker, & Tomlin, 2005); how curriculum is socially constructed (e.g., Weade, 1987; Chandler, 1992); the status of different languages in linguistically diverse classrooms (e.g., Collins, 1986; O'Connor & Michaels, 1993; Orellana, 1996; Lee, 1997; Willet, Solsken, & Wilson-Keenan, 1999; Champion, 2002; Genishi & Gluczynski, 2006); and discourse practices, funds of knowledge and participation structures of indigenous groups (e.g., Philips, 1982; Moll et al., 1992).

From discourse as object to discourse as social processes

Concurrent with the development of microethnographic studies, researchers grounded in sociology turned to developments in sociology and the study of everyday social practices constructed through discourse. This work exerted powerful influences on the study of education as a social, discursive phenomenon. Everyday conversations became the site to study situated social practices. Some sociologists developed methodologies for close analysis of talk-in-action (e.g., Watson, 1992). Others closely observed and described local situated discourse to develop an approach to sociology of language in society (e.g., Goffman, 1981) and in classrooms (e.g., Bernstein, 1975, 1996). With these approaches, researchers began to link local productions of teachers and students to broader social structures in schools and society. This work supported examination of how patterns of classroom life were interactionally produced, how school structures were constituted and configured, and how these related to what students were able to access (e.g., McDermott & Roth, 1978; Mehan, 1979; Heap, 1980).

Within this movement, Garfinkel's ethnomethodology (1967) provided an alternative to then current analytical sociological abstractions, such as *the class system*, for observing classroom schooling in relation to society. Ethnomethodology explained why members of society routinely acted as they did by observing concrete everyday actions of people as they created social order on their own terms. With its focus on investigating how ordinary, situated actions produce, replicate, and transform social institutions, ethnomethodology provided a means for examining how practices and outcomes of schooling are interactionally constituted (Mehan, 1979). Garfinkel's approach was complemented by Goffman's theorization of the role of talk in everyday life (1959). His theory on face-to-face behavior introduced constructs for analyzing classroom discourse that included frame theory, footing and alignment, and different forms of talk (1981).

Educational researchers adopted conversation analysis (CA), which emerged from ethnomethodological thinking, as a systematic approach for empirically describing classroom talk-in-interaction. Applying the CA approach, researchers examined the sequential interrelated conversation moves of teachers and students by noting the discursive mechanisms they used. By observing turn taking, use of names, and ways members oriented and held each other accountable to what was occurring in patterns of adjacent turns, researchers analyzed how knowledge, identities, and social relationships were interactively produced as social forms. They explored which knowledge was socially meaningful and the ways learning and teaching were enacted. By examining each turn in a sequence as placing a demand for a response on the next, patterns of reflexive actions of teacher and student interactants, and of constituent elements of their interaction, were identified. For example, in the US Mehan (1979) observed a patterned sequence of contingent turns in teacher–student interactions (I-R-E initiation-response-evaluation), which were similar to patterns identified by linguists (Sinclair & Coultard, 1975) in the UK. These interaction patterns were found to be common during instruction and consequential for student participation and knowledge construction, resulting in a particular type of schooling.

This situated perspective on classroom discourse framed empirical accounts of what counted as context, engagement, diversity, gender, productivity, and achievement, among other social conditions, processes and practices, within and across different local settings and circumstances. Macbeth's (2003) review of naturally occurring classroom discourse research credits this naturalistic inquiry approach with being the central innovation in classroom studies in the last 30 years. He also reaffirms the particular contribution of sequential analysis in telling us about the work of instruction, citing the value of understanding successes and failures of "lived orderliness" in minute interactional detail. Such research has described the roles students play in classroom order (e.g., Davies, 1983), reading positions and practices (e.g., Baker & Freebody, 1989; Freebody, Luke, & Gilbert, 1991), differential access to literacy instruction (e.g., Baker & Luke, 1991), and effects of testing practices (e.g., Poole, 1994).

Ideology, power, and different orders of scale

While ethnomethodology and CA focused attention on the social order under construction in local discursive situations, Bernstein sought to develop a broad sociological theory to explain the role of classroom discourse in what historically had been an intractable societal class hierarchy in the UK. He theorized ways in which curriculum and pedagogic practices acted selectively on those who acquire them (Bernstein, 1975; Bernstein et al., 2001; Atkinson, Davies, & Delamont, 1995; Sadovnik, 1995). Bernstein's theories, along with theories supporting exploration of negative practices of schooling for particular student groups, influenced new directions in classroom discourse research, particularly in the UK and Australia.

Beginning in the 1980s, building on Bernstein's critical sociological theory, linguists and sociologists in education began to explore relationships between local discourse practices and hierachical institutional practices and their consequences for and impact on classroom discourse. Academic, or official institutional, verbal and written school genres were observed to serve gate-keeping functions through which those in power made decisions. For example, by bringing Bernstein's theories together with the Systemic Functional Linguistics of Halliday (1985), researchers engaged in genre studies to explore how classroom exercise of socially dominant language structures marginalized some students and privileged others. Genres of speech as well as written genres considered appropriate in school were observed to be relatively fixed structures. Students from communities in which dominant schooling genres were practiced were more successful in classroom interactions than were students who practiced less privileged discourse genres. These studies led to new research and pedagogical approaches to teaching genres of power (e.g., Lemke, 1990; Hodge & Kress, 1993; Christie, 1995; Rex & McEachen, 1999).

In the 1990s, critical discourse analysis approaches (CDA) were developed that made possible studies of the relationship of discourse to power and ideology in classroom interactions and texts (e.g., Fairclough, 1995). From these perspectives power could be viewed in two ways: in terms of asymmetries that exist between participants in discourse events, and in terms of unequal capacity to control the production of texts and how they are distributed and consumed. CDA provided both a theoretical perspective and a methodological approach for examining power–ideology relationships in sociocultural contexts. CDA was applied to observe relationships between texts constructed in local discursive events (oral and/or written) and those created beyond that event (e.g., media, technological, graphic), and others (Ivanic, 1998).

By assuming critical situated perspectives, educational researchers from a broad range of traditions have examined different scales of situation – from segments of sequential oral or written discourses to larger units including narratives, genres, and patterned structures across oral and written texts. Such studies have explored how smaller units related to macro structures and how local discourse choices of speakers/writers are drawn from and reinforce discourses within broader sociocultural contexts (e.g., Gee, 1999; Maybin, 2006). These researchers have identified a range of properties of discourse practices and texts they regard as potentially ideological, including features of vocabulary, metaphors, genres, grammatical conventions, style, and discourse strategies (e.g., turn taking, politeness conventions, and topic appropriateness). They illustrated how discourse choices writers or speakers make in constructing texts begin to shape, and then are shaped by, the connected text(s) being constructed such that the writer/speaker/group inscribes an ideological position within the local situation. Issues of choice among discourses, of consciousness of decisions, and of who has access to these choices, for what purposes, and in what ways were shown to be consequential for social naturalization of language and identities. Educational researchers applying related critical theories have illuminated discrepancies in official schooling discourses and those who become marginalized and disenfranchised (e.g., Gutierrez, Baquedano-Lopez, & Tejeda, 1999).

Conclusions: Some Philosophical and Epistemological Distinctions

Understandings of classroom discourse and interactions have changed across disciplines and time as new theories developed. Today, an extensive body of research exists. This wealth of information brings new challenges, however. The concept of expressive potential (Strike, 1974) provides a way of distinguishing among these contributions. The expressive potential of each tradition is defined by its questions, by its descriptive and evidentiary processes, and its claims and results through particular language and genres. Each tradition, therefore, constitutes a particular language and area of study, affording researchers and educators particular knowledge and approaches for studying classroom discourse. The challenge facing educators is to examine how these different traditions may be used in complementary ways to construct new understandings of the consequences of classroom discourse and interactions.

REFERENCES

Athanases, S. Z. & Heath, S. B. (1995). Ethnography in the study of teaching and learning of English, *Research in the Teaching of English*, 29(3), 263–287.

Atkinson, P., Davies, B., & Delamont, S. (1995). *Discourse and Reproduction: Essays in Honor of Basil Bernstein*. Cresskill, NJ: Hampton.

Baker, C. & Freebody, P. (1989). *Children's First School Books: Introductions to the Culture of Literacy*. New York: Blackwell.

Baker, C. & Luke, A. (eds.) (1991). *Towards a Critical Sociology of Reading Pedagogy*. Philadelphia, PA: Benjamins.

Barnes, D. & Todd, F. (1995). *Communication and Learning Revisited: Creating Meaning through Talk*. Portsmouth, NH: Boynton/Cook, Heinemann.

Bauman, Z. (2000). *Liquid Modernity*. Cambridge: Polity.

Bernstein, B. (1975). *Class, Codes, and Control: Theoretical Studies towards a Sociology of Language*. New York: Schocken Books.

Bernstein, B. (1996). *Pedagogy, Symbolic Control and Identity: Theory, Research, and Critique*. London: Taylor & Francis.

Bloome, D. & Egan-Robertson, A. (1993). The social construction of intertextuality in classroom reading and writing lessons. *Reading Research Quarterly*, 28(4), 305–333.

Bloome, D., Carter, S. P., Otto, S., & Shuart-Faris, N. (2004). *Discourse Analysis and the Study of Language and Literacy Events: A Microethnographic Perspective*. Mahwah, NJ: Lawrence Erlbaum.

Brown, B., Reveles, J., & Kelly, G. (2005). Scientific literacy and discursive identity: A theoretical framework for understanding science learning. *Science Education*, 89, 779–802.

Castanheira, M., Crawford, T., Green, J., & Dixon, C. (2001). Interactional ethnography: An approach to studying the social construction of literate practices. *Linguistics and Education*, 11(4), 353–400.

Cazden, C. (1972). *Child Language and Education*. New York: Holt, Rinehart & Winston.

Cazden, C. (2001). *Classroom Discourse: The Learning of Teaching and Learning* (2nd edn.). Portsmouth, NH: Heinemann.

Cazden, C. B., John, V. P., & Hymes, D. (eds.) (1972). *Functions of Language in the Classroom*. New York: Teachers College Press.

Champion, T. (2002). *Understanding Storytelling among African American Children*. Mahwah, NJ: Lawrence Erlbaum.

Chandler, S. (1992). Questions when viewing classroom learning from a sociocultural curriculum perspective. In H. Marshall (ed.), *Redefining Student Learning: Roots of Educational Change* (pp. 33–58). Norwood, NJ: Ablex.

Chomsky, C. (1972). Stages in language development and reading exposure. *Harvard Educational Review*, 42(1), 1–33.

Christie, F. (1995). Pedagogic discourse in the primary school. *Linguistics and Education*, 7, 221–242.

Collins, J. (1986). Differential treatment in reading instruction. In J. Cook-Gumperz (ed.), *The Social Construction of Literacy* (pp. 138–164). New York: Cambridge University.

Cook-Gumperz, J. (1986). *The Social Construction of Literacy*. New York: Cambridge University Press.

Cook-Gumperz, J. (2006). *The Social Construction of Literacy*. Cambridge: Cambridge University Press.

Cook-Gumperz, J. & Gumperz, J. (1992). Changing views of language in education: Implications for literacy research. In J. Beach, J. Green, M. Kamil, & W. Shanahan (eds.), *Multidisciplinary Perspectives on Literacy Research* (pp. 151–179). Urbana, IL: NCTE.

Corsaro, W. (1994). Discussion, debate, and friendship processes: Peer discourse in U.S. and Italian nursery schools. *Sociology of Education*, 67(1), 1–26.

Davies, B. (1983). The role pupils play in the social construction of classroom order. *British Journal of Sociology of Education*, 41, 55–69.

Duff, P. A. (2002). The discursive co-construction of knowledge, identity and difference: An ethnography of communication in the high school mainstream. *Applied Linguistics*, 23(3), 289–322.

Dunkin, M. J. & Biddle, B. J. (1974). *The Study of Teaching*. New York: Holt, Reinhart, & Winston.

Duranti, A. & Goodwin, C. (eds.) (1992). *Rethinking Context*. New York: Cambridge University.

Edwards, A. D. & Mercer, N. (1987). *Common Knowledge*. London: Methuen.

Erickson, F. (1986). Qualitative methods in research on teaching. In M. Wittrock (ed.), *Handbook of Research on Teaching* (3rd edn., pp. 119–1611). New York: Macmillan.

Erickson, F. (2004). *Talk and Social Theory*. Cambridge: Polity.

Fairclough, N. (1995). *Critical Discourse Analysis*. New York: Longman.

Foster, M. (1995). Talking that talk: The language of control, curriculum, and critique. *Linguistics and Education*, 7, 129–150.

Freebody, P., Luke, A., & Gilbert, P. (1991). Reading positions and practices in the classroom. *Curriculum Inquiry*, 21, 435–457.

Garfinkel, H. (1967). *Studies in Ethnomethodology*. Englewood Cliffs, NJ: Prentice-Hall.

Gee, J. (1999). *An Introduction to Discourse Analysis*. New York: Routledge.

Gee, J. & Green, J. (1998). Discourse analysis, learning, and social practice: A methodological study. *Review of Research in Education*, 23, 119–170.

Genishi, C. & Dyson, A. (1984). *Analyzing the Language of the Young Child*. Norwood, NJ: Ablex.

Genishi, C. & Gluczynski, T. (2006). Language and literacy research: Multiple methods and perspectives. In J. L. Green, G. Camilli, & P. B. Elmore (eds.), *Handbook of Complementary Methods in Education Research*. Mahwah, NJ: Lawrence Erlbaum.

Goffman, E. (1959). *The Presentation of Self in Everyday Life*. New York: Doubleday.

Goffman, E. (1981). *Forms of Talk*. Philadelphia: University of Pennsylvania Press.

Goldman, R., Pea, R., Barron, B., & Derry, S. (in press). *Video Research in the Learning Sciences*. Mahwah, NJ: Lawrence Erlbaum.

Green, J. L. & Dixon, C. (2007). Classroom interaction and situated learning. In M. Martin-Jones & A.-M. de Meija (eds.), *Encyclopedia of Language Education: Discourse and Education* (pp. 1–12). The Netherlands: Springer.

Green, J. L. & Harker, J. O. (eds.) (1988). *Multiple Perspective Analyses of Classroom Discourse*. Norwood, NJ: Ablex.

Green, J. L. & Wallat, C. (eds.) (1981). *Ethnography and Language in Educational Settings*. Norwood, NJ: Ablex.

Green, J. L., Harker, J. O., & Golden, J. M. (1987). Lessson construction: Differing views. In G. W. Noblit & W. T. Pink (eds.), *Schooling in Social Context: Qualitative Studies* (pp. 46–77). Norwood, NJ: Ablex.

Gumperz, J. (1992). Contextualization and understanding. In A. Duranti & C. Goodwin (eds.), *Rethinking Context* (pp. 229–252). New York: Cambridge University Press.

Gumperz, J. & Cook-Gumperz, J. (1986). Interactional linguistics in the study of schooling. In J. Cook-Gumperz (ed.), *The Social Construction of Literacy* (pp. 50–75). New York: Cambridge University Press.

Gutierrez, K. D., Baquadano-Lopez, P., & Tejada, C. (1999). Rethinking diversity: Hybridity and hybrid language practices in the third space. *Mind, Culture, & Activity*, 6(4), 286–303.

Halliday, M. A. K. (1985). *An Introduction to Functional Grammar*. London: Arnold.

Heap, J. L. (1980). What counts as reading? Limits to certainty in assessment. *Curriculum Inquiry*, 10(3), pp. 265–292.

Heath, S. B. (1983). *Ways with Words: Language, Life, and Work in Communities and Classrooms*. New York: Cambridge University Press.

Heller, M. & Martin-Jones, M. (eds.) (2000). *Voices of authority: Education and linguistic difference*. London: Ablex.

Hicks, D. (1995). Discourse, learning and teaching. In M. Apple (ed.), *Review of Research in Education, 21* (pp. 49–95). Washington, DC: AERA.

Hodge, R. & Kress, G. (1993). *Language as Ideology*. New York: Routledge.

Hornberger, N. & Corson, D. (1997). *Research Methods In Language And Education*. Boston, MA: Kluwer.

Hymes, D. (1996). *Ethnography, Linguistics, Narrative Inequality: Toward an Understanding of Voice*. Philadelphia, PA: University of Pennsylvania Press.

Ivanic, R. (1998). *Writing and Identity: The Discoursal Construction of Identity in Academic Writing*. New York: Benjamins.

Knobel, M. (1999). *Everyday Literacies: Students, Discourse, and Social Practice*. New York: Peter Lang.

Koschmann, T. (1999). The edge of many circles: Making meaning of meaning making. *Discourse Processes*, 27(2), 103–117.

Labov, W. (1972). *Language in the Inner City: Studies in the Black English Vernacular*. Philadelphia: University of Pennsylvania Press.

Lee, C. D. (1997). Bridging home and school literacies: Models for culturally responsive teaching, a case for African American English. In S. B. Heath & D. Lapp (eds.), *A Handbook for Literacy Educators: Research on Teaching the Communicative and Visual Arts* (pp. 334–345). New York: Macmillan.

Lemke, J. (1990). *Talking Science: Language, Learning and Values*. Norwood, NJ: Ablex.

Lin, L. (1993). Language of and in the classroom: Constructing the patterns of social life. *Linguistics and Education*, 5(3&4), 367–410.

Luke, A. (1995). Text and discourse in education: An introduction to critical discourse analysis. In M. Apple (ed.), *Review of Research in Education*, 21 (pp. 49–95). Washington, DC: AERA.

Macbeth, D. (2003). Hugh Mehan's *Learning Lessons* reconsidered: On the differences between the naturalistic and critical analysis of classroom discourse. *American Educational Research Journal*, 40(1), 239–280.

Maybin, J. (2006). *Children's Voices: Talk, Knowledge and Identity*. Basingstoke, UK: Palgrave.

McDermott, R. & Roth, D. (1978). The social organization of behavior: Interactional approaches. *Annual Review of Anthropology*, 7, 321–345.

Mehan, H. (1979). *Learning Lessons*. Cambridge, MA: Harvard University Press.

Mercer, N. (1995). *The Guided Construction of Knowledge: Talk amongst Teachers and Learners*. Clevedon, UK: Multilingual Matters.

Mishler, E. G. (1979). Meaning in Context, Is There Any Other Kind? *Harvard Educational Review*, 49, 1–19.

Moll, L. C., Amanti, C., Neff, D., & Gonzales, N. (1992). Funds of knowledge for teaching: Using a qualitative approach to connect homes and classrooms. *Theory into Practice*, 31(1), 132–141.

O'Connor, M. C. & Michaels, S. (1993). Aligning academic task and participation status through revoicing: Analysis of a classroom discourse strategy. *Anthropology and Education Quarterly*, 24(4), 318–335.

Orellana, M. F. (1996). Negotiating power through language in classroom meetings, *Linguistics and Education*, 8, 335–365.

Philips, S. O. (1982). *The Invisible Culture: Communication in Classroom and Community on the Warm Springs Indian Reservation*. New York: Longman.

Poole, D. (1994). Routine testing practices and the linguistic construction of knowledge. *Cognition and Instruction*, 12, 125–150.

Rampton, B. (2000). Continuity and change in views of change in applied linguistics. In H. Tappes-Lomax (ed.), *Change and Continuity and Applied Linguistics* (pp. 97–114). Clevedon, UK: Multilingual Matters.

Rex, L. A. (ed.) (2006). *Discourse of Opportunity: How Talk in Learning Situations Creates and Constrains*. Cresskill, NJ: Hampton.

Rex, L. A. & McEachen, D. (1999). "If anything is odd, inappropriate, confusing, or boring, it's probably important": The emergence of inclusive academic literacy through English classroom discussion practices. *Research in the Teaching of English*, 34(1), 65–129.

Rex, L. A., Steadman, S., & Graciano, M. K. (2006). Researching the complexity of classroom interaction. In J. L. Green, G. Camilli, & P. B. Elmore (eds.), *Handbook of Complementary Methods in Education Research* (pp. 727–772). Mahwah, NJ: Lawrence Erlbaum/AERA.

Rosenshine, B. & Furst, N. (1986). The use of direct observation to study teaching. In R. Travers (ed.), *Second Handbook of Research on Teaching* (pp. 122–183). Chicago: Rand McNally.

Sadovnik, A. (ed.) (1995). *Knowledge and Pedagogy: The Sociology of Basil Bernstein.* Norwood, NJ: Ablex/Greenwood.

Sinclair, J. M. H. & Coulthard, R. M. (1975). *Towards an Analysis of Discourse: The English Used by Teachers and Pupils.* New York: Oxford University Press.

Street, B. V., Baker, D., & Tomlin, A. (2005). *Navigating Numeracies Home/School Numeracy Practices.* The Netherlands: Springer.

Strike, K. (1974). On the expressive potential of behaviorist language. *American Educational Research Journal*, 11(2), 103–120.

Tuyay, S., Jennings, L., & Dixon, C. (1995). Classroom discourse and opportunities to learn: An ethnographic study of knowledge construction in a bilingual third-grade classroom. *Discourse Processes: A Multidisciplinary Journal*, 19(1), 75–110.

Vine, E. (2003). My partner: A five-year-old Samoan boy learns how to articulate in class through interactions with his English-speaking peers. *Linguistics and Education*, 14(1), 99–121.

Watson, D. R. (1992). Ethnomethodology, conversation analysis, and education: An overview. *International Review of Education*, 38(3), 257–274.

Weade, G. (1987). Curriculum 'n' instruction: The construction of meaning. *Theory into Practice*, 26(1), 15–25.

Wells, G. (1999). *Dialogic Inquiry.* Cambridge: Cambridge University Press.

Wells, G. (2002). The role of dialogue in activity theory. *Mind, Culture, and Activity*, 9, 43–66.

Willet, J., Solsken, J., & Wilson-Keenan, J. (1999). *Linguistics and Education*, 10(2), 165–218.

41 Computer Assisted Language Learning

CAROL A. CHAPELLE

Foundations

The use of computer technology for language learning crosscuts many of the topics and issues discussed in this handbook because technology underlies forms of communication responsible for increasing language contact and globalization, which in turn affect language education. In many parts of the world, learners engage in communication with peers and pursue their academic goals through the use of information and communication technology. Some educators portray technology as the solution to problems and others see it as a plot to divert attention from the real aims of education, but the day-to-day reality for teachers and learners is that technology presents some new opportunities and challenges. The pervasive effects of technology on language use outside the classroom affect learners' knowledge and expectations for technology use in the classroom. Whereas 20 years ago teachers using computer technology to help learners with their language study were seen as innovative and unconventional, today teachers who fail to draw upon technology in language teaching are likely to be considered at least out-of-date.

Many applied linguists study issues of technology and communication that have changed the language landscape inside and out of the classroom, but the area of computer-assisted language learning or technology and language learning denotes a more focused set of issues pertaining directly to language teaching and learning: the question is how computer technologies can be introduced and used to help learners to develop their second language ability.

At the crux of the issue is a research–practice relationship as new teaching practices are explored and evaluated. On the practice side, technology prompts some fundamental changes in the way that second or additional languages can be taught and learned. In many places in the world today it is difficult to discuss language pedagogies without considering the options offered by CD-ROMs accompanying textbooks, electronic resources such as dictionaries and corpora, the communication and information offered on the Internet, and online learning materials and assessments. On the research side, technology-based innovations raise thorny issues about evaluation of teaching practices. How can learning be measured and attributed to the amorphous combination of technologies that may come into play in language learning? At a time when most students arrive in the classroom with conceptions about technology and its use for information and communication, issues about how to use and how to evaluate technology for language learning are central to language teaching today.

Core Themes

The core themes emerging from research and practice in CALL center around the learning opportunities afforded by technology use. First, technologies themselves as well as how they are constructed and configured to create opportunities for language learning are central issues which evolve rapidly with changes in technology. Such changes have directed attention to the issue of how learners can use technology beyond the classroom to develop their autonomy as language learners and learn autonomously beyond their exposure to formal classroom teaching. Changes in learning opportunities and learners' needs in turn create a new set of challenges and opportunities for teacher education.

Configuring learning through technology

Technology affords so many novel opportunities for language learning that simply understanding the options and using them to structure learning for students is a challenge for all language teachers. However, it is a challenge worth tackling in view of the opportunities afforded by new language learning tasks that can be developed through technology (Doughty & Long, 2003). Computer-mediated communication through the Internet provides a means for connecting language learners in different parts of the world to practice their language and learn about their peers beyond their own classrooms. Extensive language and cultural materials are available through the Internet; teachers can structure information hunting activities through the use of search engines. Search engines and search tools specifically designed for language study, such as dictionaries, concordancers, and translation tools, can also be used by students to seek answers to linguistic questions.

Multimedia and other forms of interactive CALL provide focused input and interaction that can be selected to fit the learners' level and provide evaluation of learners' responses. Such learning activities provide controlled opportunities for linguistic input for the learner (i.e., texts to read or videos to watch and listen to) and interaction with the computer. Interaction occurs as the learner clicks to have a response evaluated, to move forward, or to request additional information such as word definitions or cultural notes about the input. These types of interactions provide learners with immediate knowledge about correctness of responses or help in comprehending the language of the input, both of which have been found to be beneficial to learning. In many online learning materials, assessments serving as diagnostic or achievement tests are included to provide the learner with feedback on performance.

These electronic materials organized within a course delivery system, such as WebCT or BlackBoard (Siekmann, 2000), have expanded the possibilities for distance learning courses for additional languages. Distance learning predates the use of technology, but technology has expanded dramatically its utility for language instruction. The combination of multimedia and communication tools along with consumers who are accustomed to obtaining goods and services online have made distance learning an important new growth area for language, with important implications for traditionally low enrollment language courses.

Technology-supported distance learning provides a means for distributing expertise for less commonly taught languages including endangered languages. For example, an online class can connect the four people who are interested in learning Cree at one point in time despite the fact that they are scattered across Alberta, Nebraska, Oklahoma, and California. Courses for traditionally low enrollment languages and advanced level classes can draw enrollment from a wide area, thereby increasing the financial viability of language courses that were once impossible to offer. A second, implication is the changing role that distance learning implies for learners. "We can think of learners not so much as *entering* a course or learning environment, but as *constructing* the course according to the affordances of the learning environment and their own contributions as learners" (White, 2003: 88, emphasis in original). The reliance on the learner to construct his or her own language course raises important issues of learner autonomy.

Learner autonomy

Changing language learning opportunities are rejuvenating interest and research on how best to develop learner autonomy. On the one hand, a successful distance learning student is one who can work with some degree of autonomy. On the other hand, most learners do not know how to work autonomously to their best advantage. Instead, they need guidance from appropriately designed learning materials and teaching. Appropriately tailored individual instruction has been a stated goal of many software developers throughout the history of CALL: CALL "can be made sensitive to the learner's pace, pattern of responses, and so on, and can adjust the linguistic material to the needs of the individual" (Ahmad et al., 1985: 5). Despite this goal, such CALL materials that are individualized with the aim of providing guidance for autonomous learning are not the norm today. Over 15 years later, Benson pointed out, "there is an assumption that technology can provide learners with the kinds of support they need in order to develop the skills associated with autonomy," but the validity of this assumption depends on the characteristics of the activities the technology supports (2001: 140).

In particular, it might be argued that materials are needed to support the autonomous learner in ways that adapt to the learners' needs. According to instructional designers in education, "adaptive instruction prescribes the methods for changing the form of instruction to suit the needs or desires of individuals" (Jonassen & Grabowski, 1993: 35). For language learning this idea has been referred to more generally as "learner fit," defined as "the amount of opportunity for engagement with language under appropriate conditions given learner characteristics" (Chapelle, 2001: 55). Attempting to achieve good learner fit requires attention to at least four areas. The first is the need to identify and address precisely the linguistic difficulties that particular types of learners have. The second is the need to teach the language of the specific content areas that are relevant to learners. The third is the need to present material and interact with the learners in a way that enhances their learning style. The fourth is the use of assessment of learners' abilities during the course of instruction to make them aware of what they know and do not know and to recommend specifics for additional study.

A larger issue that extends beyond a language course and CALL materials is the need to develop the learners' strategies to help them make use of the extensive language and linguistic resources available on the Internet. If learners become accustomed to using electronic resources in their language classes, they should ultimately be able to draw upon the enormous resources of the Internet. Ideally, learners would develop the metacognitive sophistication that takes them to linguistic examples on the Internet as a means of answering their questions. For example, the learner who stops mid-sentence in an email because he doesn't know how to ask for advice about the best course to take should immediately think of the Internet, where a search of the British National Corpus for the word "advice" will turn up examples of "advice on" and "advice about" something, but not "advice in" or "advice for" something. Examples of lexical collocations that reflect the normal way of expressing something rather than possible ways of saying something are an area where continuous learning is needed, and where it is possible to accomplish much with the help of the Internet. In language classes, if learners have been working with such data, they will have been learning the strategies that will serve them well for the rest of their lives. But if learners are to develop their linguistic-Internet strategies, teachers need an expanded set of skills to help them do so.

Teacher education

The changes in language learning brought about by technology have profound implications for the knowledge required of a language teacher and therefore the content of a teacher education curriculum (Hubbard & Levy, 2006). The reality of many language teaching situations is that technological options and imperatives are intermingled with other teaching issues. In the novel contexts of language classrooms it is very unlikely that teachers will be teaching in the same way that they learned languages. Moreover, the face-to-face classroom methods and techniques drawn from the evolution of reflection and practice in language teaching do not provide the basic education teachers need to navigate the new landscape. Instead, this new landscape requires "teachers with basic technological skills who understand the capabilities and limitations of technology in teaching, and who accept responsibility for critically examining the options and their implications" (Chapelle & Hegelheimer, 2004). In other words, teachers need to know how to use technology and to understand why they are doing so.

The "how" of technology consists of both general purpose technology issues such as use of authoring tools, and those more specific to language study such as the use of computational analysis tools for language. In the past, prospective or practicing language teachers took a general educational technology course but in view of the scope and significance of specific tools for language study, most professionals in educational linguistics would agree that language teachers need education directly focused on technology for language education if they are to help their learners benefit from technology.

The "why" of technology use is at least equally complex for beginning teachers, many of whom need to somehow mesh their professional knowledge about face-to-face classroom teaching with the potentials they can see for technology. How should multimedia materials be integrated into what learners are studying in class? What is the teacher's role when learners are working on such materials? What benefits can learners gain through Internet communication tools? What kind of structure should the teacher place on such communication activities? How can the use of CALL materials in class help learners to prepare for taking high-stakes tests on the computer?

To respond to these basic questions that teachers raise about technology, teachers need to have some depth to their understanding of why they are using technology. Issues in applied linguistics that these questions entail include the varieties of languages found in Internet language (Herring, 1996; Crystal, 2001; Posteguillo, 2003), strategies for learning language through technology (Hubbard, 2004), and assessment of language through technology (Chapelle & Douglas, 2006). Teacher education in these and other technology-related areas is one of the driving forces behind research on CALL.

Research–Practice Relationships

Research on CALL has been prompted by practical concerns such as the need for updating teacher education, the desire to understand new pedagogies developed through technology, and the quest to develop better, more efficient learning activities. The imperative for knowledge that can be put into practice has shaped the research goals. In turn, research on CALL offers opportunities for the profession to engage with research-based knowledge about teaching and learning more generally. Language teachers, program designers, and learners ask applied linguists for concrete guidance. They want to be informed about what applied linguists have learned about the use of technology for L2 learning. This pull from those involved in language teaching and learning practices has guided what and how applied linguists have studied CALL for over 20 years.

Descriptive studies of technology use

In technology studies for language learning, like other areas of educational technology, the foremost research issue is to understand how learners work with technology for learning, and therefore descriptive research has been a priority (Knupfer & McLellen, 1996). Methodologies used for obtaining descriptive data range from survey research to interaction and discourse analysis to ethnography. Interaction analysis examines learners' strategies and working styles as they engage with interactive software (e.g., Chapelle & Mizuno, 1989). Discourse analysis including conversation analysis documents the language and types of exchanges that occur as learners engage in language learning tasks through technology (e.g., Chun, 1994; Kern, 1995; Negretti, 1999; Schwienhorst, 2004; Warner, 2004), and ethnography examines technology use within the broader context of language use (e.g., Warschauer, 1999; Lam, 2000).

The research motivation in all of these cases is to better understand learners' functioning in a new medium in which the teacher does not have direct knowledge of learners' actions unless they are documented in research. The remoteness of the teachers from language learning through technology makes results from descriptive research very important for understanding what technology is actually capable of adding to instruction. Findings have revealed the need to develop learners' strategies for engaging with language learning software, discourse moves for participating in online communication, and motivation for seeking out opportunities for language practice on the Internet. Moreover, such research can identify how and why learners develop areas of communicative competence that typically do not develop through classroom conversation (Belz, 2003; Belz & Kinginger, 2003). These insights meet critical needs for teacher education, but the primary motivation for educational research is to evaluate instructional strategies relative to alternatives, and this is done through evaluative research.

Evaluative research

Evaluative research is conducted to find evidence about the quality of learning, which, for technology-based learning, is interpreted by many to mean evidence about the comparative results obtained from learning online and learning in a traditional classroom. Such research is notoriously difficult to design because the researcher tends to attempt to make the classroom and CALL learning conditions the same in order to detect any difference the computer makes. But then, as Garrison and Anderson (2003) put it, "Why would we expect to find significant differences if we do exactly the same thing [in the two modes of learning] . . . ?" (p. 6). Despite the logical problem of designing such research and many papers arguing the limited insight to be obtained by research addressing this question, CALL classroom comparisons using experimental and quasi-experimental research designs remain a mainstay in technology research.

The comparative research that has proven fruitful investigates the outcomes of two real options for pedagogical tasks or curricula for a purpose rather than attempting to address the intractable issue of computer effectiveness. For example, many language programs have the option of doing more or less of their course materials online or individual learners have an option of taking a course in face-to-face classes or through distance learning (e.g., Warschauer, 1995/1996; Chenoweth & Murday, 2003; De la Fuente, 2003) . Generalizability of results from such studies is possible, but the scope of generalization is to the language program or learning activities rather than to the computer. In other words, the research is centrally about pedagogy rather than about technology.

Perhaps the greatest strides forward for evaluative CALL research come from comparisons of specific design features of instructional software. Comparisons of reading and listening software that provides annotations for vocabulary with that which provides no annotations tends to favor annotations for vocabulary learning (Borrás & Lafayette, 1994; Chun & Plass, 1996; Plass et al., 1998). Comparisons of software with more specific versus less specific feedback on learners' errors favor more specific feedback (Nagata, 1993). In short, the cognitive benefits of these software features that would be hypothesized by interactionist SLA (Gass, 1997; Ellis, 1999) have been borne out in research.

Not all evaluative research adopts an experimental or quasi-experimental design. Many studies using discourse analysis or what appear to be descriptive methodologies go beyond description to look for instances of language and strategic language use that the teacher intends and that is hypothesized to be valuable for second language acquisition. Such research has sought to document negotiation of meaning, self-correction, other correction, and other instances of focus on form during the process of communication online in pedagogical tasks (e.g., Lamy & Goodfellow, 1999; Blake, 2000; Kitade, 2000; Pellettieri, 2000; Kötter, 2003).

Findings indicate that such language related episodes appear in such tasks, even if they are less frequent than in oral, face-to-face communication tasks (García & Arbelaiz, 2003), but that the design of online tasks makes a difference. Moreover, when online communication takes place through writing, learners' cognitive challenge is different than in oral communication in that the communication stress is reduced, the opportunity for noticing linguistic form is increased, and the need for precision in production is heightened. All of these conditions should prove valuable for strengthening linguistic accuracy. Such research comes from studies that fall within the broad categories of description or evaluation, but today an important and distinct third view of technology use is revealed through critical perspectives.

Critical perspectives

Critical research encompasses a range of objectives arising from a desire to construct an understanding of technology use for language learning that goes beyond a neutral description or an evaluation of predefined objectives and outcomes. The classic critical works on educational computing are Bowers (1988, 2000), critiques that argue that the way technology is used narrows the potential of intellectual inquiry of professionals in education and reduces the scope of students' learning. In language learning, Warschauer (1998) argued the need for critical research agendas whose goal is to discover who chooses which technologies and for what purposes and why, and conducted a study that linked technology use to teachers' beliefs (Warschauer, 1999). Thorne's (2003) critical analysis several years later focused on learners' choices of technologies among the options they had for language practice through communication.

Based on cross-cultural communication among learners of French and learners of English, Kramsch and Thorne (2002) argue that current conceptions of communicative competence in applied linguistics fall short of capturing the social and cultural genres of communication required for global communication. In short, the marriage of critical analysis which looks beyond existing paradigms and frameworks in applied linguistics with new forms of technology-enabled learning, information access, and communication suggests that technology and language learning will remain an interesting and unpredictable area of educational linguistics.

Conclusion

Research and practice at the intersection of technology and language learning prompts fundamental changes in L2 pedagogies, research on learning, and the goals of language instruction. In fact, research on CALL offers opportunities for the profession to engage with research-based knowledge about teaching and learning and to expand possibilities for developing autonomy and conceptions of communicative competence. In this environment, the knowledge, skills, and perspectives language teachers need to develop is a critical area of concern for educational linguistics.

REFERENCES

Ahmad, K., Corbett, G., Rogers, M., & Sussex, R. (1985). *Computers, Language Learning and Language Teaching.* Cambridge: Cambridge University Press.

Belz, J. A. (2003). Linguistic perspectives on the development of intercultural competence in telecollaboration. *Language Learning and Technology,* 7(2), 68–117.

Belz, J. A. & Kinginger, C. (2003). Discourse options and the development of pragmatic competence by classroom learners of German: The case of address forms. *Language Learning*, 53(4), 591–648.

Benson, P. (2001). *Teaching and Researching Autonomy in Language Learning*. Harlow, UK: Pearson Education.

Blake, R. (2000). Computer-mediated communication: A window on second language Spanish interlanguage. *Language Learning and Technology*, 4(1), 120–136.

Borrás, I. & Lafayette, R. C. (1994). Effects of multimedia courseware subtitling on the speaking performance of college students of French. *The Modern Language Journal*, 78, 61–75.

Bowers, C. A. (1988). *The Cultural Dimensions of Educational Computing: Understanding the Non-Neutrality of Technology*. New York: Teachers College Press.

Bowers, C. A. (2000). *Let them Eat Data: How Computers Affect Education, Cultural Diversity, and the Prospects of Ecological Sustainability*. Athens, GA: The University of Georgia Press.

Chapelle, C. A. (2001). *Computer Applications in Second Language Acquisition: Foundations for Teaching Testing and Research*. Cambridge: Cambridge University Press.

Chapelle, C. A. & Douglas, D. (2006). *Assessing Language through Computer Technology*. Cambridge: Cambridge University Press.

Chapelle, C. A. & Hegelheimer, V. (2004). The English language teacher in the 21st Century. In S. Fotos & C. Browne (eds.), *New Perspectives on CALL for Second Language Classrooms* (pp. 297–313). Mahwah, NJ: Lawrence Erlbaum.

Chapelle, C. A. & Mizuno, S. (1989). Students' strategies with learner-controlled CALL. *CALICO Journal*, (7)2, 25–47.

Chenoweth, N. A. & Murday, K. (2003). Measuring student learning in an online French course. *CALICO*, 20(2), 285–314.

Chun, D. M. (1994). Using computer networking to facilitate the acquisition of interactive competence. *System*, 22(1), 17–31.

Chun, D. M. & Plass, J. L. (1996). Effects of multimedia annotations on vocabulary acquisition. *The Modern Language Journal*, 80, 183–198.

Crystal, D. (2001). *Language and the Internet*. Cambridge: Cambridge University Press.

De la Fuente, M. J. (2003). Is SLA interactionist theory relevant to CALL? A study of the effects of computer-mediated interaction in second language vocabulary acquisition. *Computer Assisted Language Learning*, 16(1), 47–81.

Doughty, C. & Long, M. (2003). Optimal psycholinguistic environments for distance foreign language learning. *Language Learning and Technology*, 7(3), 50–80.

Ellis, R. (1999). *Learning a Second Language through Interaction*. Amsterdam: John Benjamins.

García, M. F. & Arbelaiz, A. M. (2003). Learners' interactions: A comparison of oral and computer-assisted written conversations. *ReCALL*, 15(1), 113–136.

Garrison, D. R. & Anderson, T. (2003). *E-learning in the 21st Century: A Framework for Research and Practice*. London: RoutledgeFalmer.

Gass, S. (1997). *Input, Interaction, and the Second Language Learner*. Mahwah, NJ: Lawrence Erlbaum.

Herring, S. C. (ed.) (1996). *Computer-Mediated Communication: Linguistic, Social, and Cross-Cultural Perspectives*. Amsterdam: John Benjamins.

Hubbard, P. (2004). Learner training for effective use of CALL. In S. Fotos & C. Browne (eds.), *New Perspectives on CALL for Second Language Classrooms* (pp. 45–67). Mahwah, NJ: Lawrence Erlbaum.

Hubbard, P. & Levy, M. (eds.) (2006). *Teacher Education in CALL*. Amsterdam: John Benjamins.

Jonassen, D. H. & Grabowski, B. L. (1993). *Handbook of Individual Differences, Learning, and Instruction*. Hillsdale, NJ: Lawrence Erlbaum.

Kern, R. G. (1995). Restructuring classroom interaction with networked computers: Effects on quantity and characteristics of language production. *Modern Language Journal*, 79, 457–476.

Kitade, K. (2000). Second language learners' discourse and SLA theories in CMC: Collaborative interaction in Internet chat. *Computer Assisted Language Learning*, 13(2), 143–166.

Knupfer, N. N. & McLellen, H. (1996). Descriptive research methodologies. In D. H., Jonassen (ed.), *Handbook of Research for Educational Communications and Technology* (pp. 1196–1212). New York: Macmillan.

Kötter, M. (2003). Negotiation of meaning and codeswitching in online tandem. *Language Learning and Technology*, 7(2), 145–172.

Kramsch, C. & Thorne, S. (2002). Foreign language learning as global communicative practice. In D. Cameron & D. Block (eds.), *Globalization and Language Teaching* (pp. 83–100). New York: Routledge.

Lam, W. S. E. (2000). L2 literacy and the design of the self: A case study of a teenager writing on the Internet. *TESOL Quarterly*, 34(3), 457–482.

Lamy, M.-N. & Goodfellow, R. (1999). "Reflective conversation" in the virtual language classroom. *Language Learning and Technology*, 2(2), 43–61.

Nagata, N. (1993). Intelligent computer feedback for second language instruction. *The Modern Language Journal*, 77(3), 330–339.

Negretti, R. (1999). Web-based activities and SLA: A conversation analysis research approach. *Language Learning and Technology*, 3(1), 75–87.

Pellettieri, J. (2000). Negotiation in cyberspace: The role of *chatting* in the development of grammatical competence in the virtual foreign language classroom. In M. Warschauer & R. Kern (eds.), *Network-Based Language Teaching: Concepts and Practice* (pp. 59–86). Cambridge: Cambridge University Press.

Plass, J. L., Chun, D. M., Mayer, R. E., & Leutner, D. (1998). Supporting visual and verbal learning preferences in a second-language multimedia learning environment. *Journal of Educational Psychology*, 90(1), 25–36.

Posteguillo, S. (2003). *Netlinguistics: An Analytic Framework to Study Language, Discourse and Ideology in Internet*. Castello de la Plana, Spain: Universitat Jaume I.

Schwienhorst, K. (2004). Native-speaker/non-native speaker discourse in the MOO: Topic negotiation and initiation in a synchronous text-based environment. *Computer Assisted Language Learning*, 17(1), 35–50.

Siekmann, S. (2000). CALICO Software Report. Which web course management system is for me? A comparison of WebCT 3.1 and Blackboard 5.0. *CALICO*, 18:3, 590–617.

Thorne, S. (2003). Artifacts and cultures-of-use in intercultural communication. *Language Learning and Technology*, 7(2), 38–67.

Warner, C. N. (2004). It's just a game, Right? Types of play in foreign language CMC. *Language Learning and Technology*, 8(2), 69–87.

Warschauer, M. (1995/1996). Comparing face-to-face and electronic discussion in the second language classroom. *CALICO*, 13:(2&3), 7–25.

Warschauer, M. (1998). Researching technology in TESOL: Determinist, instrumental, and critical approaches. *TESOL Quarterly*, 32(4), 757–761.

Warschauer, M. (1999). *Electronic Literacies: Language, Culture and Power in On-Line Education*. Mahwah, NJ: Lawrence Erlbaum.

White, C. (2003). *Language Learning in Distance Education*. Cambridge: Cambridge University Press.

FURTHER READING

Butler-Pascoe, M. E. & Wiburg, K. M. (2003). *Technology and Teaching: English Language Learners*. White Plaines, NY: Pearson.

Chapelle, C. A. (2003). *English Language Learning and Technology: Lectures on Applied Linguistics in the Age of Information and Communication Technology*. Amsterdam: John Benjamins.

Egbert, J. (2005). *CALL Essentials: Principles and Practice in CALL Classrooms*. Alexandria, VA: TESOL Publications.

Egbert, J. & Petrie, G. (eds.) (2005). *Research Perspectives on CALL*. Mahwah, NJ: Laurence Erlbaum.

Fotos, S. & Browne, C. (eds.) (2004). *New Perspectives on CALL for Second Language Classrooms*. Mahwah, NJ: Lawrence Erlbaum.

Kern, R. (2006). Perspectives on technology in learning and teaching languages. *TESOL Quarterly*, 40(1), 183–210.

Levy, M. & Stockwell, G. (2006). *CALL Dimensions: Options and Issues in Computer-Assisted Language Learning*. Mahwah, NJ: Lawrence Erlbaum.

Lomicka, L. & Cooke-Plagwitz, J. (eds.) (2004). *Teaching with Technology*. Boston: Heinle.

Ortega, L. (1997). Processes and outcomes in networked classroom interaction: Defining the research agenda for second language computer-assisted classroom discussion. *Language Learning and Technology*, 1(1), 82–93.

Swaffar, J., Romano, S., Markley, P., & Arens, K. (eds.) (1998). *Language Learning Online: Theory and Practice in the ESL and the L2 Computer Classroom*. Austin, TX: Labyrinth Publications.

Thoren, S. & Payne, S. (2005). Evolutionary trajectories, Internet-mediated expression, and language education. *CALICO*, 22(3), 371–397.

Warschauer, M. & Kern, R. (eds.) (2000). *Network-Based Language Teaching: Concepts and Practice*. Cambridge: Cambridge University Press.

Zhao, Y. (ed.) (2005). *Research in Technology and Second Language Learning: Developments and Directions*. Greenwich, CT: Information Age Publishers.

42 Ecological-Semiotic Perspectives on Educational Linguistics

LEO VAN LIER

Introduction

Educational linguistics (EL) is a sub-category of applied linguistics. As such, it explores the uses and functions of language in educational settings. These include language classes (first, second, foreign), but also (potentially at least) all occasions and contexts of language use in, around, and about educational institutions, policy-making entities, families with stakes in educational matters, and so on and so forth. All in all this comprises a very wide and varied area of concern.

In this contribution I will look at EL from an ecological and semiotic perspective. I will first provide an overview of and rationale for an ecological perspective, and then outline its main areas of focus, such as the action/perception complex, the nature of language as part of semiotic systems of meaning making, the educational context as an ecosystem, and a view of the teaching/learning process as holistic and action-based.

Ecology

The discipline of ecology is traditionally linked to biology, environmental studies, and the nature of the environment. It refers to "the totality of relationships of an organism with all other organisms with which it comes into contact" (Haeckel, 1866, in Arndt & Janney, 1983). Its etymology goes back to the Greek word *oekos*, which means 'household'. It is worth emphasizing that ecology, in Haeckel's definition, can in principle apply to any field of study that deals with "organisms" whose relationships and interactions with one another are of importance, and this includes all human and social sciences. Nevertheless, ecology has traditionally been applied primarily to biology and environmental studies, and some of its well-known terms such as ecosystem, biodiversity, habitat, "Umwelt," and so on may be applicable to the human sciences primarily in more or less metaphorical ways.

From its beginnings in biology, the concept of ecology has gradually spread to other areas of investigation. Most famously this includes the work of the anthropologist Gregory Bateson, who connected the concept of ecology to mental activity as well as to human social activity. In psychology, early work with an ecological focus included that of Roger Barker, Kurt Lewin, and Urie Bronfenbrenner (see van Lier, 2004, for further details). As can be expected, this work has a strong focus on context and contrasts with types of research, whether qualitative or quantitative, that decontextualize data and evidence (such as experimental research or randomized trials).

A major force in ecological psychology has been the work of James and Eleanor Gibson on visual perception. This work takes a radically different direction from the approaches to ecological psychology and social science mentioned above, and is based in decades of experimentation. I will briefly review the Gibsons' theory of ecological perception, and its relevance for educational linguistics in the next section.

Perception and Action

In his early work (in the 1950s and 1960s) James Gibson criticized the prevailing theories of visual perception that were modeled on a static perceiver watching a picture or scene presented on a screen. This view can be referred to as the *picture theory* or *enrichment theory* of perception. In this view, sense data are "fleeting fragmentary scraps of data signaled by the senses" (Gregory, 1991). These unreliable, fuzzy, and incomplete sensory impressions are interpreted and enriched by a powerful cognitive apparatus that is primed to interpret sense data in accordance with mental categories, schemata, scripts, and so on. A prime example of an enrichment theory with direct impact on educational linguistics is information processing, which focuses on the ways in which "input" is processed cognitively.

Instead, James Gibson and Eleanor Gibson elaborated a *differentiation theory* of perception. On this view sense data are rich, well specified, and differentiated. Perceptual development consists in increasing effectiveness in terms of detecting new information and of varied responses to physical stimuli (J. J. Gibson, 1979; E. Gibson & Pick, 2000). The Gibsons' ecological theory of perception is distinct from other theories (constructivist, information-processing, enrichment theories) in three major respects. In the words of Gibson & Pick:

> One is the concept of *affordance*, the user-specific relation between an object or event and an animal of a given kind. A second is the concept of *information*, how events in the world are specified for perceivers in ambient arrays of energy. Third is the process of *information pickup*, how the information is obtained by an active perceiver and what is actually perceived. (2000: 15)

The notion of affordance ties perception together with action. While being active in the learning environment the learner detects properties in the environment that provide opportunities for further action and hence for learning. Affordances are discovered through perceptual learning, and the effective use of affordances must also be learned. Perceiving and using affordances are the first steps on the road toward meaning making.

One further property of perception/action in an ecological perspective is *reciprocity*: first, reciprocity between perception and action, second reciprocity between the perceiver (the self) and the perceived (the affordance). Gibson noted that other-perception is always accompanied by self-perception (1979). Awareness of self and awareness of other therefore go hand in hand.

The connection between perception and action also means that perception is not purely visual or auditory (etc.), rather, it is multisensory, involving all the senses. Gesture, movement, and speech go hand in hand, and the body is holistically and organically involved in perceptual activity. This was already noted in the classic anthropological study of the Balinese cockfight by Clifford Geertz (2005, originally published in 1972) in which he discusses the notion of "kinesthetic perception:"

> The use of the, to Europeans, "natural" visual idiom for perception – "see," "watches," and so forth – is more than usually misleading here, for the fact that . . . Balinese follow the progress of the fight as much . . . with their bodies as with their eyes, moving their limbs, heads, and trunks in gestural mimicry of the cocks' maneuvers means that much of the individual's experience of the fight is kinesthetic rather than visual. (pp. 84–85)

The interconnectivity between perception and action, and the multisensory nature of perception, point to a view of learning that is action-based and holistic. In a later section I will develop this notion of teaching and learning further. Meanwhile, the nature of language itself must also be seen to involve not just words and syntax, but also all other sources of meaning making that are available in the environment. This will be the topic of the next section.

Language as Semiotics

Language educators need a theory of language so as to anchor their work in firm principles leading to consistent and well-informed practices. This does not have to be a rigid, abstract theory that is full of tightly argued empirical facts and irrefutable logic, but rather a clear vision of what language is and does, and a coherent set of working metaphors for language learning and teaching.

There is a tendency of many current theoretical linguists and departments of linguistics to eschew connections with the practical concerns of language education and to regard applied work as somehow being irrelevant to or undermining the theoretical integrity of their work. It is not surprising, there-fore, that programs of applied linguistics, educational linguistics, or second language acquisition tend to be housed outside of departments of linguistics, often with scarce contact or collaboration between them. I have argued elsewhere that this territorial separatism is damaging both to linguistics and to educational linguistics (van Lier, 1994). Instead, theoretical linguistics needs to be concerned with real-world relevance, and educational linguistics needs to be concerned with solid theoretical underpinnings.

An ecological perspective on language learning sees language as part of larger meaning-making resources that include the body, cultural-historical artifacts, the physical surroundings, in short, all the affordances that the physicial, social, and symbolic worlds have to offer. The totality of these meaning-making resources is captured in the term semiotics, or the totality of sign-making and sign-using processes and practices. Thus, any act of language use incorporates far more than the mere words that are spoken (or written, for that matter). First of all, there is the inherent dialogicity of language itself, as brilliantly demonstrated by Bakhtin (1981). Utterances spoken or written carry with and within them not just the thoughts and intentions of the utterer, but they are also variously animated by the words of others. Before Bakhtin, the founder of modern semiotics, C. S. Peirce already emphasized the dialogical nature of semiotics and, indeed, of all thought: "All thinking is dialogic in form. Your self of one instant appeals to his deeper self for his assent" (as cited in Chandler, 2002: 34).

The dialogical nature of all language and language use has profound implica-tions for language learning. At once the nature of language is changed from a *product*, a static system that can be described in terms of its inner structure and components (structuralism), to a *process* of creating, co-creating, sharing, and exchanging meanings across speakers, time, and space.

Importantly, as indicated above, language does not act alone in this meaning-making process. The surrounding world plays a constitutive part as well, including the physical world of objects and spatio-temporal relationships, the social world of other meaning-making and meaning-sharing persons, the symbolic world of thoughts, feelings, cultural practices, values, and so on – in short, the whole mind-body-world complex of resources that is involved in any communicative act.

Education as an Ecosystem

According to some cognitive theories learning is something that happens primarily inside the head of each individual student (the mentalist position). More socially or environmentally oriented theories place the locus of learning in the environment (the environmentalist position). In between these extremes are theories that explore the relationships between environmental and cog-nitive processes (the interactionist position). The latter include sociocultural theory, language socialization, the ecology of language learning, and other approaches that might all fit under a more general umbrella of sociocognitive theories (Atkinson, 2002).

From an educational linguistics perspective, environmental and cognitive processes interrelate and both play a role in second language development. A sociocultural theory perspective adds the notion that higher mental functions arise from social interaction with peers and more knowledgable others. Practical concepts established in social activity and mediated by tools of various kinds, are gradually transformed into abstract concepts mediated by signs, as captured in Vygotsky's oft-quoted remark that every mental function appears twice, first on the social plane, and then on the psychological plane (Vygotsky, 1978). An ecological perspective looks particularly closely at how meaning making evolves from perceptual activity to iterative processes such as recognition, comparison, manipulation (including mental manipulation), representation, and interpretation, roughly equivalent to the Peircean semiotic processes of iconicity, indexicality, and symbolicity (van Lier, 2004).

Educational linguistics investigates the circumstances in which such language growth can flourish, and the purposeful actions and contexts that can be created to stimulate and instigate it. After all, to educate, *educere*, means a purposeful approach to rear, lead, or bring up others. In practical terms, then, educational linguistics investigates all the educational activities that occur, whether by purpose or by accident, in settings that are oriented toward language education. By this definition, it includes institutions of schooling as well as language education in the family, on the street, and in a multitude of other places. However, here I will focus on educational institutions that engage in language education.

The language classroom is not an island unto itself. Whatever happens in the classroom is connected in multiple ways to issues in the school, the family, the community, local educational authorities, governmental agencies, ideological and cultural pressures of the moment, and so on. Investigating these connections requires a theory of contextualized learning and over the years a number of models of contextual analysis have been developed to conduct such investigations in a systematic manner. Of particular interest from an ecological perspective are those models of context that focus not only on category systems, but primarily on processes of interaction and relationships of influence.

These include activity theory (Engeström, 1999), systems theory (Checkland, 1981), developmental systems theory (Oyama, Griffiths, & Gray, 2001), dynamic systems theory (van Geert, 1994), and Bronfenbrenner's nested eco-systems (Bronfenbrenner, 1979). Although they come from different traditions and employ different research methodologies, all these theories and models have a great deal in common, particularly in their endeavor to systematically link macro and micro levels of analysis.

A quite different and expressly critical theory is Basil Bernstein's sociology of education, as most recently put forth in his fifth volume of the "Class,

Codes and Control" series (2000). Bernstein has probed pedagogical relationships in terms of the creation and maintenance of boundaries (classification or power) and the controls on pedagogical communication (framing or control). The structures and relations created by these institutional processes regulate the transformation of knowledge into pedagogic discourse, as well as the formation and legitimacy of voice and identity in educational settings.

Any of the contextual theories can be used to examine educational issues in detail from an ecological perspective. In a priori terms there is no way of determining whether one contextual theory is more powerful or effective than another. Only practical application will show the strengths and weakness of each individual theory. As an example, one might take just a small strip of interactional talk from a classroom, and tease apart all the relational aspects influencing its occurrence and interpretation. Such an exercise would in some ways be similar to Geertz' thick description (1973), or Sacks' conversation analysis (1972). Here is one such example, taken from van Lier 2003:[1]

    A: Aaaaw! You lost my picture!
    B: Sorreeee! . . . Am I smart?

Here, two fourth-grade girls are working together on a web-based poetry book, sharing the computer and composing pages together. A has been away from the computer a while and B continued working, but something went wrong and when A came back, it turned out that a picture A had made was gone. A was clearly upset, and B was clearly distraught. This little incident is not very revealing unless we have more information about the context in which the two children are working and the relationships that are established. For example, one might be told that A is Anglo (and very familiar with computer use) and B is Latina (and not an experienced computer user). Furthermore, one might learn that B is classified as a special education student, and this may help elucidate the "Am I smart?" comment. Using any of the above-mentioned contextual theories, further relationships and practices can be unraveled and can be shown to have an impact on moment-to-moment interaction and meaning making in the setting.

From an ecological perspective, all communicative acts in a learning environment have multiple reasons, causes, and interpretive potential, depending on all the relationships between and among all the participants in the setting, as well as the evolving setting itself. In this way it can be said that the pedagogical setting is an ecosystem, embedded in other ecosystems along different temporal and spatial scales. Changes at any scale can have repercussions at other scales; however, as in biological ecosystems, cause–effect relationships are extremely hard to pinpoint. For this reason an ecological perspective is closely related to a chaos/complexity view of scientific work (Larsen-Freeman, 1997).

Pedagogy as Activity

As mentioned above, an ecological perspective on language learning places perception and action (or perceptual action) in the center of the educational process. The learner is an agent who is engaged in multiple ways in the pedagogical landscape. Most importantly, the learner picks up affordances and creates meaningful signs in the pursuit of some purpose. The learner does not passively receive environmental stimuli and only then actively (though perhaps not consciously) process them in the brain, creating linguistic structures, cognitive schemata, and the like, or activating a pre-existing blueprint or universal language organ.

Language learning happens in a context of purposeful action. It was Vygotsky who first proposed an inseparable connection between cognition and volition, or between intellect and affect, and argued that these form the basis for the genesis of consciousness, and ultimately for the development of all higher mental functions (1987).

In many educational settings today (as in past times, to be sure), students work very hard to amass the facts and the strategies that allow them to pass the all-important tests that serve as admission tickets to higher education, and at the same time provide a quantitative boost to the school's standing in the various annual performance indices that control their fate and their finances. However, these test scores, while achieving the immediate goal of numerical success, may in actual fact turn out to be no more than ephemeral knowledge and skills that evaporate soon after the test is over, the sorts of things Alfred North Whitehead, the great educational philosopher of the early twentieth century, called "inert knowedge" (1929; Miettinen, 1999).

Lasting, generative, and creative abilities require the involvement of mind, body, and emotions, and a persistent attitude of social engagement and environmental exploration. This is the essential human attitude of agency, which in ecological terms means that an organism learns and grows so long as it actively engages in and with its environment. In educational linguistics terms this means that the teaching and learning environment should be so structured as to invite and enable the learner to be active within it. This means active with all the senses (multisensory), the whole body, encountering meaning-making resources of all kinds (multimodal).

Language education then shifts from inputs provided to the learner and outputs required from the learner to activity, task, and project-based learning (Beckett & Miller, 2006), where learner agency becomes the focal point and activity the unit of analysis. This action-based, whole-body learning comes from a long tradition of reform-oriented pedagogues such as John Dewey, Lev Vygotsky, Jean Piaget, Johann Pestalozzi, and Maria Montessori. In Germany this approach goes by the name of *Handlungsorientierter Unterricht*, or action-based teaching and learning. As Finkbeiner (2000) points out, action-based learning "includes learners' hearts, bodies and senses" (p. 255). Neurological research (Damasio, 1994) and first-language acquisition research (Kuhl, 1998) strongly supports the ecological validity of such a stance towards learning.

Critical and Concluding Comments

An ecological perspective on educational linguistics expands the notion of learning from a primarily cognitive process to a whole-body process involving perception and action in complex integrative ways. It also expands the notion of language by incorporating it into semiotics, or the totality of meaning-making sources and resources. The teaching-learning environment must be rich in affordances, that is, opportunities for perceptual learning, and must engage learners in meaningful activities.

There have been many language teaching methods proclaiming to offer solutions to the complexities of language learning, and history tells us that there are many roads to success as well as to failure. Why add another one? In answer to this very reasonable question one can point to a very long tradition of educational thought (going back at least as far as Jan Comenius in the seventeenth century) that has advanced the main tenets of the ecological view of language and language learning I have outlined. To the extent that these educational views have been implemented (almost always on the periphery of the educational landscape) there is strong support for their success, although not necessarily in statistical terms. Of course, if success is measured in terms of test scores, approaches based on the transmission of facts to be memorized and displayed on test questions are likely to be more effective. However, we see time and again that such memorized material is not a measure of true competence, and its acquisition is not indicative of the quality of educational experiences or their lifelong value.

NOTE

1   In that study I analyzed the exchange in terms of Bronfenbrenner's nested ecosystems.

REFERENCES

Arndt, H. & Janney, R. W. (1983). The duck-rabbit phenomenon: Notes on the disambiguation of ambiguous utterances. In W. Enninger & L. M. Haynes (eds.), *Studies in Language Ecology* (pp. 94–115). Wiesbaden: Franz Steiner Verlag.

Atkinson, D. (2002). Toward a sociocognitive approach to second language acquisition. *The Modern Language Journal*, 86(4), 525–545.

Bakhtin, M. (1981). *The Dialogical Imagination*. Austin, TX: University of Texas Press.

Beckett, G. H. & Miller, P. C. (eds.) (2006). *Project-Based Second and Foreign Language Education: Past, Present, and Future*. Greenwich, CT: Information Age Publishing.

Bernstein, B. (2000). *Pedagogy, Symbolic Control and Identity: Theory, Research, Critique* (revised edn.). Lanham, MD: Rowman & Littlefield.

Bronfenbrenner, U. (1979). *The Ecology of Human Development*. Cambridge, MA: Harvard University Press.

Chandler, D. (2002). *Semiotics: The Basics*. London: Routledge.

Checkland, P. (1981). *Systems Thinking, Systems Practice*. New York: Wiley.

Damasio, A. (1994). *Descartes' Error: Emotion, Reason, and the Human Brain*. New York: Putnam's.

Engeström, Y. (1999). Innovative learning in work teams: Analyzing cycles of knowledge creation in practice. In Y. Engeström, R. Miettinen, & R.-L. Punamäki (eds.), *Perspectives On Activity Theory* (pp. 377–404). Cambridge: Cambridge University Press.

Finkbeiner, C. (2000). Handlungsorientierter Unterricht [Holistic and action-oriented learning and teaching]. In M. Byram (ed.), *Routledge Encyclopedia of Language Teaching and Learning* (pp. 255–258). London: Routledge.

Geertz, C. T. (1973). *The Interpretation of Cultures*. New York: Basic Books.

Geertz, C. T. (2005). Deep play: Notes on the Balinese cockfight (1972). *Daedalus*, Fall, 56–86.

Gibson, E. J. & Pick, A. D. (2000). *An Ecological Approach to Perceptual Learning and Development*. Oxford: Oxford University Press.

Gibson, J. J. (1979). *The Ecological Approach to Visual Perception*. Hillsdale, NJ: Lawrence Erlbaum.

Gregory, R. (1991). Seeing as thinking: An active theory of perception. In Eleanor J. Gibson (ed.), *An Odyssey in Learning and Perception* (pp. 511–519). Cambridge, MA: MIT Press.

Haeckel, E. (1866). *Allgemeine Anatomie der Organismen* [The General Anatomy of Organisms]. Berlin.

Kuhl, P. (1998). Language, culture and intersubjectivity: The creation of shared perception. In S. Bråten (ed.), *Intersubjective Communication and Emotion in Early Ontogeny* (pp. 297–315). Cambridge: Cambridge University Press.

Larsen-Freeman, D. (1997). Chaos/complexity science and second language acquisition. *Applied Linguistics*, 18, 141–165.

Miettinen, R. (1999). Transcending traditional school learning: teachers' work and networks of learning. In Y. Engeström, R. Miettinen, & R.-J. Punamaki (eds.), *Perspectives on Activity Theory* (pp. 325–344). Cambridge: Cambridge University Press.

Oyama, S., Griffiths, P. E., & Gray, R. D. (eds.) (2001). *Cycles of Contingency: Developmental Systems and Evolution*. Cambridge, MA: MIT Press.

Sacks, H. (1972). On the analyzability of stories by children. In J. J. Gumperz & D. Hymes (eds.), *Directions in Sociolinguistics* (pp. 325–345). New York: Holt, Rinehart & Winston.

van Geert, P. (1994). *Dynamic Systems of Development*. New York: Harvester Wheatsheaf.

van Lier, L. (1994). Educational linguistics: Field and project. In James Alatis (ed.), *Georgetown University Round Table on Languages and Linguistics 1994* (pp. 199–209). Washington, DC: Georgetown University Press.

van Lier, L. (2003). A tale of two computer classrooms: The ecology of project-based language learning. In J. van Dam & J. Leather (eds.), *The Ecology of Language Acquisition* (pp. 49–64). Dordrect: Kluwer Academic.

van Lier, L. (2004). *The Ecology and Semiotics of Language Learning: A Sociocultural Perspective*. Boston: Kluwer Academic.

Vygotsky, L. S. (1978). *Mind in Society*. Cambridge: Cambridge University Press.

Vygotsky, L. S. (1987). *Thinking and Speech*, trans. N. Minick. In *The Collected Works of L. S. Vygotsky, Volume 1: Problems of General Psychology*. New York: Plenum Press.

Whitehead, A. N. (1929). *The Aims of Education*. New York: The Free Press.

43 The Mediating Role of Language in Teaching and Learning: A Classroom Perspective

FRANCIS BAILEY, BEVERLEY BURKETT, AND DONALD FREEMAN

Introduction

In many classrooms around the world where students and teacher do not fully share a common language for classroom instruction, a double bind can develop. For students, the language of the classrooms can seem *opaque*: rather than providing an accessible medium to work with new academic content, the language itself can introduce a formidable barrier. For their teacher, on the other hand, the language of instruction can seem a relatively *transparent* medium through which teaching is done. So the 'double bind' comes down to students working to learn the language as they are trying to learn the content, while teachers work to teach the content while they are actually de facto teaching the language.

To capture this bind in this chapter, we argue that language mediates class-rooms on a metaphorical continuum from transparent to translucent to opaque. For students who understand and control the medium of instruction, language can be a relatively transparent window into the content, social processes, and relationships in the classroom. For those who do not, it can be corres-pondingly opaque, indeed an obstacle to access in these areas. For most students however, we will argue that language is 'translucent': the content, social processes, and relationships are more-or-less 'visible' to both teacher and students depending on the content and on how participation in the tasks and activities is organized and orchestrated.

The following two scenarios illustrate our point. They are constructed from observed classroom interactions, and edited for the purposes of this chapter.

The first scenario, which comes from Burkett's work (Burkett & Landon, 2004), is drawn from a middle school mathematics class in rural South Africa.

Scenario 1: "What's an obtuse angle?"

The teacher, like the students, is Xhosa-speaking, but the language of instruction in this basic geometry lesson is English. Twenty-four students sit in groups of four at small tables. A pair of students has just been at the blackboard demonstrating a right angle by holding up their arms bending at the elbows to create the requisite 90°. The teacher now works with another boy, who is standing at the blackboard at the front of class.

The teacher asks, "What is an obtuse angle?"

The boy lifts up his arm and tries to demonstrate an angle in the crook of his elbow; he does not speak. He watches the teacher's face for an indication of whether he is doing the right thing.

The teacher looks to the rest of the class, "Can anybody help him? What is an obtuse angle?" There is an uncomfortable shifting in seats and several blank looks; no one responds.

The teacher repeats the question in English, "What is an obtuse angle?"

A seated student begins to speak, "It is . . . it has . . ." He uses his hands to illustrate an angle of more than 90 degrees and he then breaks into Xhosa saying it is a 'bigger' angle. The teacher nods and replies in English, "Yes, how else can we say that and in English?"

The second scenario comes from an English language arts classroom in a US high school and is based upon the portfolio work of one of Bailey's graduate students. In this 'newcomer' school, Liberian students, even though they are native speakers of a West African dialect of English, were placed in the ESL program in order to address serious issues of literacy and interrupted education.

Scenario 2: "What's peer editing?"

The teacher is working with a small group of 'ESL' students as they study an abridged version of the American classic novel, *The Adventures of Tom Sawyer*. She has given out the written task, which the students are now poring over.

A Liberian student asks, "Miss, I don't know what you mean by 'peer editing'?"

The teacher responds, "Okay, Lek, what is 'to edit' a paper?"

A Thai student answers quickly, "Oh, you can mistake, . . . um, correct mistake in paper . . ."

The teacher continues, "Exactly, when you edit a paper, you correct all the mistakes like spelling or grammar mistakes. So what is 'peer edit'?"

A Columbian student answers a bit uncertainly, ". . . another students correct you paper?"

The teacher: "Yes, another student corrects your paper. And, you will correct one of your classmates' papers."

Having followed this exchange, the Liberian student counters, "I don't want someone messin' with my paper. What if he's wrong? Do I have to do this?"

In contrasting educational linguistics with the theoretical or applied versions, Spolsky (1978) argued that this new undertaking should be a "problem-oriented discipline" which focuses primarily on educational practice and is informed by relevant academic fields, including many subfields of linguistics. We agree and argue that, as these two scenarios illustrate, the central problem that teachers face is how to engage with language as part of teaching and learning. We refer to this engagement as "thinking and acting linguistically," which we unpack in the classroom. We begin by summarizing where language is part of the classroom, or using Spolsky's terms, where might the 'problems' of language be located. Then we look at the teacher's stance in response to these problems through three lenses – thinking, teaching, and assessing – and we ask: *What do teachers need to know in order to 'think linguistically' and how do they learn it?* Then given this broad knowledge-base, *what skills and practices are involved in 'teaching linguistically'?* These two perspectives focus on the teacher however, who is only part of the classroom equation; so to broaden the focus, the third lens addresses teaching in relation to learning by asking, *what role does language play in assessing classroom learning?* All of which analyses return us to the two classroom scenarios and how language is part of the processes of teaching and learning.

Classrooms as Language Environments

Classrooms are, first and foremost, language environments. If classrooms are laboratories and teaching largely a matter of constant experimentation, then we see language as the medium, in a biological sense, in which those experiments are 'cultured' and grown. In this section, we examine how language 'shows up' in the classroom in its social processes, interactions, and relationships in three broad and overlapping domains: among students, between students and teacher, and between home and school.

Arguably the key classroom social process broadly put is that of socialization (Cazden, 1988; Rogoff, 2003), as the two scenarios illustrate. In each instance, the teacher engages in bringing students into the assumptions and requirements not simply of the dominant language, but of how that language works in the classroom. In the South African scenario for instance, while the student can state what an obtuse angle is in colloquial terms in Xhosa, he is not able to give a 'mathematical' definition, much less say it in English. Thus what looks like language learning is, in fact, much more than that: by moving the students' knowledge of geometry, whether it is partial or complete, out of their language, Xhosa, and into English, the teacher is in essence re-teaching the content. And as a Xhosa speaker herself, there are ways the teacher can be relatively certain that her students are developing parallel understandings in both languages. In the second scenario, however, that socialization process is less transparent, as we discuss later.

Language lies at the very heart of teaching and learning. Through it concepts are conveyed, competence assessed, behavior managed, identities formed, relationships forged, and the complex and messy business of constructing knowledge takes place (Bloome et al., 2004). Mastering the institutional forms of talk used in classrooms and schools can have a direct impact upon student success. In order to participate in classroom life, students must have not only a working understanding of the dominant language used in the schools, but must also know how to use that language in order to participate in classroom instruction.

The problem is that classroom participants generally do not appreciate how deeply embedded teaching and learning are in language use. Like water for the fish, language is so fundamental and encompassing in classroom settings that it becomes transparent. When content teachers talk about their classes, they typically focus on the knowledge that they want their students to learn and the activities and materials they have designed to support such learning. Where teachers see concepts, educational linguists see language; where educational linguists see language processes, teachers see activities and lessons. Of course, second language students are all too aware of the role of language in their learning. Language often creates a formidable barrier to their school success: it can obscure and make complicated content to be learned through readings and lectures; it can make classroom activities and tasks difficult to participate in and learn through; and it can distort formal testing of these students' competence.

Underlying these challenges of classroom practice are some core constructs that are distilled from an extensive research literature on the language of the classroom. We suggest that these constructs can provide guidance to teachers about how language works in classroom teaching and learning.

Interaction, in or out of the classroom, is a process of rule-governed language use

Classroom discourse has been extensively studied, which provides a rich literature for teachers to build their professional practice upon (Philips, 1983; Shultz, Florio, & Erickson, 1982; Wong-Fillmore, 1985). As Mehan's (1979) research on linguistic patterns revealed, classrooms are worlds in which knowledge is constructed through talk; teachers engage with learners not only through formal lectures but also interactive oral linguistic processes such as the ubiquitous initiation-response-evaluation, or I-R-E, sequence. These interactions are, as Green (1983) argued, at the heart of how classroom learning socializes: "Rules of conversational participation and discourse construction have been shown to be culture specific and learned from interacting with others" (p. 174).

Because classroom activities are themselves linguistic events, second language learners often struggle to understand what they are expected to do in academic tasks and the underlying purpose of such activities. Innovative learning activities, like cooperative group work or brainstorming, create their own language/participation demands that can overwhelm a struggling second language student (Cohen & Goodlad, 1994). Often the linguistic processes used in the classroom, while transparent to teachers and students who share the language of the classroom, can be opaque to second language students.

Meaning comes from context

The meanings constructed by teachers and students in classroom interactions rely on verbal as well as non-verbal information, and on the discourse of the wider school setting. The contexts of the classroom and the school are not simply physical settings however; they are equally what Cazden (1988: 89) called "contexts in the mind," constructed by participants through interaction (Erickson & Shultz, 1981) and experience. Such meaning making requires skillful guessing, since words themselves do not have fixed meanings, but take on their meanings from how and when they are used (Gee, 1990).

The problem is that these meanings are not transparent for a number of reasons. Academic work requires a level of vocabulary and sophisticated grammatical and discourse skills that second language learners often do not fully possess, particularly if they have not developed these skills in their first language. Teachers need to recognize that these students have a double learning load: they must not only learn new content, but also the complex linguistic systems that are used to convey that subject matter. This can place a tremendous cognitive load for students to process, as we outline later (Sweller, van Merrienboer, & Pass, 1998).

Classrooms are cultural sites

Classroom learning and teaching processes cannot be separated from the broader sociocultural contexts in which they occur (Freire, 1970). This can create certain incompatibilities since culturally and linguistically diverse students often come to school from homes and communities with their own educational traditions, which often differ markedly from their school settings (Scollon & Scollon, 1981; McKeon, 1994; Hollins, 1996). The research literature documents many examples (e.g., Willis, 1977; Heath, 1983) of how teaching is inevitably grounded, as Canagarajah (1999) points out, in "the preferred ways of learning and thinking of the dominant communities and . . . this bias can create conflicts for learners from other pedagogical traditions" (pp. 15–16).

Consider constructivist educational practices, for example, which often ask students to develop an individual point of view about the world, to question and challenge their teachers, and to see mistakes as a natural part of the learning process (Brooks & Brooks, 1999). While these may be powerful educational principles, they can run counter to the accepted educational practices in many communities (Bailey & Pransky, 2005). Thus in such situations, teachers become de facto cultural mediators as they bridge – successfully or not – classroom expectations and practices with those of students' homes and communities.

Thinking: *What Do Teachers Need to Know in Order to 'Think Linguistically'? How Do They Learn It?*

Arguing as we have that classrooms are language environments, we turn now to teachers and how they learn to work in these settings. We refer to this process as 'thinking linguistically', by which we mean how teachers come to understand language as an integral element in the content they teach, the contributions that their students' sociocultural and educational backgrounds make in the classroom, and how these students participate in lessons and activities. In this section, we examine briefly the roots of the idea of thinking linguistically and then turn to the tensions involved in how the idea is understood and learned by teachers. We argue that this frame undergirds learning to 'act linguistically' as a teacher in the classroom, which we elaborate in the following section.

It is important to recognize that the very notion that teachers *can* think linguistically is quite recent; its provenance goes back only about 25 years to the advent of research on how teachers think in the process of teaching (Clark & Peterson, 1986; Calderhead, 1987). This stream of research helped to establish that teaching is more than simply behavior or activity, that it is rooted in the teacher's background and beliefs as well as in the knowledge gained through professional training. In the field of language teaching, teacher cognition has only become a central part of the research conversation since the mid 1990s (Freeman, 1996; Woods, 1996; Borg, 2003). Thus the argument that teachers need to learn to think linguistically is founded in the powerful supposition that classroom practices are socio-cognitive and behavioral undertakings (Johnson, 1999; Lampert, 2001). Further, it suggests that language is not simply one element of those classroom practices, but rather *the* central organizer of what is taught, how it is taught, and correspondingly what is learned and how.

This central place of language is very evident when one looks at how content works in classroom lessons. In the conventional view of teaching and learning, teachers 'package' content in methods and activities to convey it to students in much the same way as Reddy's famous 'conduit' metaphor of communication (1979), which portrays speakers as packaging meanings in language to deliver them to listeners. This view is hardly adequate to the complexities of classroom teaching and learning for the reasons outlined in the preceding section. Further, research on teacher cognition has contributed to this complexification by arguing that content involves not only what students see and hear in the lesson but also what their teacher knows and understands about what is being presented. This view of content as blending thinking and acting has been operationalized in several ways, as pedagogical content knowledge (Shulman, 1987), content representation (Loughran, Mulhall, & Berry, 2004), and knowledge for teaching (Ball & Bass, 2003). Each of these concepts focuses on how teachers use what they know about the broad subject-matter domain of the discipline to instantiate or represent that knowledge as content to particular students in particular classroom lessons or activities. Until recently that process of conveying content, however it was accomplished, was seen as largely language-neutral and the mediating role that language plays for both teacher and the students was not directly addressed; in short, language was taken as a transparent medium. As Ball and her colleagues (Ball, Hill, & Bass, 2005) noted in their work on knowledge of mathematics for teaching:

> It should come as no surprise then that an emergent theme in our research is the centrality of mathematical language and the need for a special kind of fluency with mathematical terms. In both our records from a variety of classrooms and our experiments in teaching elementary students, we see that teachers must constantly make judgments about how to define terms and whether to permit informal language or introduce and use technical vocabulary, grammar, and syntax. (p. 21)

The peer-editing scenario offers a clear example of this complexity of language-in-content in action. When asked by the Liberian student to define 'peer editing', the teacher must decide how to respond. The question can be understood on two levels: as a problem of lexical definition, or as a pedagogical query. Arguably the student, who speaks Liberian English, understands the words *peer* and *editing* separately. Thus the confusion may come pedagogically in linking *peer*, or 'fellow students', with *editing*, particularly when the fellow students in the ESL class are less fluent in English. However, the teacher responds by building a lexical definition of 'peer editing' by soliciting meanings of its component parts:

TEACHER:	What is "to edit" a paper?
STUDENT (Thai):	Oh, you can mistake, . . . um, correct mistake in paper . . .
TEACHER:	Exactly, when you edit a paper, you correct all the mistakes like spelling or grammar mistakes. So what is "peer edit"?
STUDENT (Columbian):	. . . another students correct you paper?
TEACHER:	Yes, another student corrects your paper. And, you will correct one of your classmates' papers.

The teacher addresses the student's question as a query about the lexical meaning and not about the social and linguistic processes embedded in the pedagogy.

Often thinking linguistically is seen uniquely in terms of content, as this scenario illustrates. Teachers see, and are generally trained to see, student confusion as primarily a function of not understanding the meanings of content vocabulary. This view seems rooted in, and indeed promotes, a deficit view of learning (Delpit, 1995). In essence the teacher's role is to provide the meaning so the student can participate on par with his or her peers from the dominant culture. In this scenario, the Liberian student is English-fluent, however the teacher addresses his question as if he were not, defining the language problem as not knowing what the words mean and building definitions through a classic classroom I-R-E structure. The well-intentioned motivation is to provide access to the content by defining terms and thus making the language as transparent as possible, even though to the Liberian student, having fellow students who are learning English edit his paper makes no pedagogical sense. His question engages the social processes inherent in the pedagogy of peer editing; when he concludes, "I don't want someone messin' with my paper. What if he's wrong? Do I have to do this?", he explicitly challenges the teacher's authority and the relative educational value of the activity.

This scenario elaborates the deep-seated complexity for teachers of thinking linguistically in the classroom. In responding, the teacher treats the student's question as a request for lexical definition, while arguably it is a pedagogical challenge to the activity itself. The Liberian student is asking for clarification of role, authority, and ultimately the learning benefit to him of participating in peer editing with non-native speakers of English. The exchange exposes the layering of influences that shape teacher decisions in thinking linguistically. These layers are multiple, beginning with the socio-institutional and educational definition of the students as an 'ESL class'; the teacher's professional identity, background, and training as an 'ESL teacher' responsible for the English language learning of these students; the different Thai, Colombian, and Liberian Englishes (Kachru, Kachru, & Nelson, 2006) among the students; and the pedagogical activity itself (peer-editing) which assumes a distributed level of literacy expertise among students. So a complex activity, which aims, as Calkins (1986) outlines it, to have students as writers "interacting with one's emerging text . . . to ask questions and help . . . the work-in-progress" (p. 119), is recast by this teacher as 'correcting mistakes'. This response is fueled, we would argue, by a way of thinking about language in the classroom that is circumscribed by deficits, that sees meanings as misunderstood, rather than querying the student's intent as a speaker.

In contrast, the teacher might look at why the student is asking the question "Miss, I don't know what you mean by 'peer editing'?" to see it as type of classroom speech event (Hymes, 1974). Focusing on the function of the question instead of the language form can lead to an examination of *how* teachers and students as classroom interlocutors use language to accomplish particular ends. When teachers think linguistically in this descriptive way, they realize that learning itself is a linguistic process, and that they need to be fully aware of the structure of their learning activities and how these impact upon student learning. Thus mediation is more than simply managing students' access to what words mean; it involves how language sets up classroom participation as, for example, the teacher's instructions do in the peer-editing scenario. Inherent in this broader grasp are the layered issues of power, and how language contributes to and authenticates social positions through whose language is valued in the classroom (e.g., Willet, 1995; Hawkins, 2005), as well as interaction, and how language shapes social processes in classroom teaching and learning.

The challenges to thinking linguistically in this way are multiple. Broadly speaking, most of us have not been socialized into a view of language as mediating force, so when people come to teaching they tend to fall back on their normative views of language as a transparent medium that 'packages' content. Because the mediating role is generally poorly understood, language problems in teaching are often assigned to specialist teachers and this can create several dilemmas in practice. Perhaps because their role is professionally defined as preparing students to participate in 'mainstream' classrooms, these specialists often seem to approach language problems from a deficit/remediation view, as in the peer-editing scenario. To focus on the perspective of mediation and social participation requires specialist teachers to have an ongoing, daily involvement that can be difficult to sustain in how schools are usually structured. Further, as demographics change, particularly in English-medium school systems around the world, there is a growing shortage of these trained language specialist teachers.

One common policy response has been to equip a wider range of grade-level and content-area teachers with skills to address language issues in their own classrooms. There is an irony in classroom practice that develops here, however. As greater numbers of teachers are introduced to pedagogical practices that address the place of language in teaching, these practices can seem more commonplace and non-specialized. In their ordinariness, such practices are often referred to as 'just good teaching'. There may be a small element of truth in this view, inasmuch as 'good teaching' generally focuses on learning and what students bring, use, and need in order to be successful. But equating language-sensitive teaching with usual classroom practices is a broad over-simplification, as we discuss in the next section.

Teaching: *What Skills and Practices Are Involved in 'Teaching Linguistically'?*

Arguing that thinking linguistically involves habits of mind (Sizer, 1997) that shape what teachers do, we turn in this section to the key skills and practices that enact such thinking in the classroom. As we have said, in some ways 'teaching linguistically' appears similar to what is generally regarded as sound instructional practice and classroom management. Often, in brief observations, there may be little outward manifestation of the teacher's language sensitivity or overt attention to the role of language. But this is the tip of the iceberg. Underlying the visible activity and teaching practices, planning is done, pedagogical decisions are made, and instructional practices are implemented with differing awareness, rationale, and attitudes. When teachers are teaching linguistically, the same things may be done for different reasons and with a more conscious application.

At its core, teaching linguistically involves an understanding of how language works to create specific meanings in particular subject areas and teaching-learning situations (Wong-Fillmore & Snow, 2000). This involves teachers consciously using concepts of academic genres and classroom pragmatics to design curricula and classroom lessons (Mohan, Leung, & Davison, 2001). Academic genres address characteristics of how language is organized to represent content meanings; lab reports or historical essays might be two common examples at the secondary school level. Pragmatics examines how interactions are organized to convey meaning; successful participation in a science lab team or presenting a history report might be examples. It is at this level that the skills and practices of what we might call 'language-sensitive teaching' become evident.

We suggest that there is a loose progression as teachers become sensitive to the language dimension of teaching. Initially they may carry out their usual practices with a greater awareness of how meaning making works in the content, materials, lessons, and social processes in their classrooms. In fact, many of the practices identified with content-sensitive language teaching methodologies such as the Cognitive Academic Language Learning Approach (Chamot & O'Malley, 1994) or Sheltered Instruction Observation Protocol (SIOP) (Echevarria, Vogt, & Short, 2000) follow this logic. These methodologies focus on how teachers' attention to language can open greater access to content. At the same time, there are parallel efforts to promote language-sensitive content teaching by grade-level content teachers (e.g., Clegg, 1996; Burkett et al., 2001). In a sense, these approaches reverse the focus by urging teachers to attend to the role of content in scaffolding second language learning. Content-Based Instruction (Snow & Brinton, 1997) or Content and Language Integrated Learning (Marsh, 1994; Marsh & Langé, 2000) are examples of this strategy.

In some senses, contrasting the language-into-content versus the content-into-language approaches poses a false dichotomy since, like an Escher print, content and language are two sides of the same coin. Teaching linguistically involves planning curricular activities and undertaking task analyses in order to provide optimal access to concept development and curricular content. This blending can be approached from several standpoints. Gravelle (2000) provides a framework from the perspective of the learning task that takes into account the social, linguistic, and cognitive knowledge and skills that the students bring and compares this knowledge with what the task demands. The aim is to surface the degree of alignment or mismatch between student

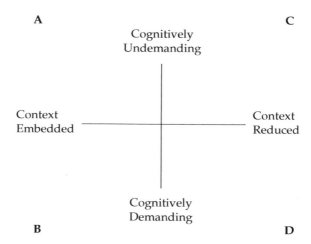

Figure 43.1   Cummins' quadrants (Cummins, 1984; reproduced by permission of the author)

knowledge and task demand so that the teacher can plan appropriate instructional support.

Similarly, Cummins (1981) offers a classic synthesis of this balancing act of student-task-language-content, suggesting a framework which relates two sets of factors, cognitive demand and context embedding, that interact in classroom language use. Arraying the factors on two axes, he uses the vertical to illustrate the range of the cognitive demand, or thinking skills, required of students to perform a task. These cognitive skills range from copying, labeling, or narrating to more complex thought processes such as inferring, hypothesizing, or synthesizing ideas. The horizontal axis illustrates context embedding, or the extent to which support for meaning is provided by the situation or context. This support might include pictures, diagrams, demonstrations or hands-on activities, and so on. Although sometimes overlooked, context embedding can also include gestures, facial expressions as well as tone, repetitions and clarifications, and other pragmatic strategies that characterize face-to-face interactions since these also enhance meaningfulness.

The two axes form bisecting continua so that cognitive demand runs from demanding to undemanding and learning context runs from embedded to reduced, thus creating quadrants which categorize four general situations of classroom language use. Most school tasks require the use of academic language that is cognitively demanding, in a situation that is context reduced. For example, students read a textbook explanation of the 'greenhouse effect', which presents the information in a context-reduced manner. Then, if they are asked to hypothesize about the potential impacts on the region where they live, the task requires high-cognitive demand since students are expected to apply information in an abstract manner. To strengthen the meaning context, textbooks will often include illustrations and diagrams, however these two-dimensional, visual representations that are meant to capture complex processes are themselves complex and opaque for many students. To reduce the cognitive demand, the teacher may try to oversimplify the task, for example eliciting I-R-E exchanges from students about local climate changes (e.g., "Is it hotter in the summer now than it used to be?"), instead of maintaining the challenge while increasing the support for meaning construction (e.g., Tharp & Gallimore, 1988; Mercer, 1995). By taking account of the role of language in materials and in the pedagogic and social processes in the classroom (Cooke, 1998), teachers can support their learners in the move from performing cognitively demanding but contextualized tasks to those that involve higher-order thought processing in decontextualized situations. Teachers need to work in ways that provide support for meaning construction in cognitively challenging tasks and then, once the language is well established and the processes familiar, to move to context-reduced tasks (Fu, 1995).

While the concept of cognitive demand looks at learning from the student's perspective, the notion of cognitive load (Sweller et al., 1998) examines the learning implications of the task itself. From a linguistic point of view, cognitive load involves assessing the task or activity from the standpoint of the specific vocabulary and topic as well as the meta-levels of genre and pragmatics discussed earlier. As teachers identify the oral and written genres of particular subject areas (Derewianka, 1990; Cope & Kalantzis, 1993; Martin, 1993) they can work explicitly with students to unpack the schematic organization of information and the specific lexical and grammatical forms that characterize the genre. As Unsworth (2001) argues:

> Students will be in a better position to both understand and critically interpret and to create and manipulate texts . . . when they understand that: different genres or text types exist; . . . are a means of achieving different social purposes; . . . [and] are typically structured in particular ways; . . . [with] characteristic grammatical features. (p. 127)

The challenge is to develop these genres, both orally (through classroom participation) and in written work. In oral genre development, teachers guide classroom talk from informal and colloquial language to the specialist and technical, and from the specific to the general (Gibbons, 2002). In the geometry scenario for example, the teacher tries to move students from describing an obtuse angle as "bigger" than a right angle, to defining it in mathematical terms as an expression of degrees, and ensuring that they are able to do this in English as well as Xhosa. The aim is to move students to appropriate and durable definitions that will help them grasp not only the immediate concept but also the broader subject matter as they encounter it throughout their school careers. With each of these practices, the teacher will be working toward increasing the transparency of language in the classroom setting that supports conceptual understanding and thus enhances the learning processes.

Assessing: *What Is the Role of Language in Assessing Classroom Learning?*

Thus far, we have sketched a view of educational linguistics that starts from viewing classrooms as language environments in which social processes, the content of lessons, and the dynamics of power and relationships are framed by, and indeed depend on, language. From this standpoint, the teacher's central challenge is to think and act in ways that engage that language environment so that students can have transparent access to what is being taught. We call these ways 'acting and thinking linguistically' to coin a shorthand that encompasses not only certain skills and practices, but also, perhaps more fundamentally, an orientation, awareness, and disposition in approaching teaching-learning situations from a language-sensitive perspective. This analysis focuses in large measure on the teacher, however. Missing, and indeed central to relating teaching to learning, is the question of assessment, which connects what has been taught to what has been learned.

Arguably the relationships among learning, instruction, and assessment are complex even under the most ordinary of classroom circumstances. When one introduces the dimension of language into these relationships, their contingency becomes even more apparent. Consider, for example, the geometry scenario in which the mathematical content is the distinction between right and obtuse angles. Some students, perhaps with the teacher's encouragement, demonstrate that they 'know' the difference by flexing their elbows appropriately, but no one defines it verbally. There are two languages in use here: Xhosa, which is shared by students and teacher; and English, which the latter uses and the former are learning. When the teacher asks in English, "What is an obtuse angle?" though several students demonstrate with their hands and arms what appears to be the correct answer, no one responds in either language. This situation frames the basic classroom assessment dilemma: What is the aim of the lesson? Is it to learn what an obtuse angle is? Or is it to learn what an obtuse angle is and be able to express that understanding in the language of instruction? And if students do not respond, where does the confusion lie? Is it in their understanding of the concept or their knowledge of the language, or perhaps some combination? (Gebhard, Haffner, & Wright, 2004).

This scenario illustrates that assessing what students are learning, while always a complicated undertaking, becomes even more so when teachers have not clearly identified the role of language in what they are teaching. This raises the key question: *What is the role of language in assessing classroom learning?* The following simple typology outlines a way of thinking about the basic response. Language is present in the assessment process in four basic ways. First, and perhaps most apparently, language is central in the assessment itself. Whether it is a paper-and-pencil test, an oral question-and-answer as in Scenario 1, or another form, the assessment is a linguistic text in both the broad and the specific senses, and it requires linguistic processes of thinking, writing, and speaking in order to complete. Second, the students' perform-ances in relation to the assessment are largely linguistic, even though they may be accompanied by other symbolic systems as in math or chemistry for example.

Third, when teachers mark classroom assessments, whether a formal test, a quiz, or a student paper, they engage in the linguistic process of using the student's language to understand what she or he has learned. Teachers read student answers; they listen to student explanations, as in the scenario; and they often respond with narrative comments to student texts. These processes of understanding and response are all language-based. Finally, students use these teacher evaluations of their performance to help them understand their own competence in what is being assessed. Teacher written comments on a test, essay, or lab report, oral comments that evaluate the student's response to a query (as in the classic I-R-E sequence), can occur in language that the student may or may not fully understand. Thus each of these four areas is fraught with problems for students who are second language learners and for teachers trying to assess what these students have learned.

In a sense, the problems of assessing classroom learning through language recast the classic Chomskian (1969) distinction between competence and performance. Returning to the metaphor of the visibility of language in the teaching-learning process, if its language is assumed to be relatively transparent, then the assessment can be seen as gauging students' underlying competence in the content. If, on the other hand, the language is assumed to be relatively opaque, and thus students' access to the content and even understanding of the assessment itself may be limited, then the assessment is, in essence, an evaluation of their performance in response to the task itself and less a meas-ure of the knowledge that task is intended to represent. Research (LaCelle-Peterson & Rivera, 1994) and practice strongly suggest that there is really no such thing as a classroom in which language functions entirely transparently, as a window into content and a clear guide to classroom interaction and learn-ing processes. Instead, in every teaching-learning situation, language is medi-ating knowledge; it is inextricably bound up with the underlying concepts being taught and is central to participants' ability to function and learn in classroom contexts. Thus for many students, regardless of background, lan-guage is a translucent medium at best and from time-to-time even an opaque one. Given this reality, assessing what students have learned in and through language is highly problematic.

A seeming solution to this dilemma is to move to other semiotic forms through which students can demonstrate their understandings, which seems to be what the teacher does in the geometry scenario when she has students 'show' an obtuse angle with their arms. These performances do not remove the role of language, however, they simply provide a richer context for it. When the content and the language – or what the student does and what she or he writes or says – match, the assumption is that the student is demonstrat-ing learning. But since both language and classroom activity are highly social, it is difficult to untangle what is social participation, the student acting like his or her peers, saying and doing what classmates are saying or doing, from what is individual mastery of a particular point of content. At the level of ongoing, day-to-day assessment in the classroom, these issues are constant and real ones. Often the dilemma is cast as *how* to assess what second language students are learning. It is thus rendered as a question of skill, technique, and resources. We would argue that there is a more basic dilemma: *What* is being assessed when teachers are trying to assess their students' learning? Because language *is* content, and not simply a vehicle for its transmission, that dilemma is a central one in any classroom.

Changing Classroom Demands: *The Role of the Language Specialist*

The field of education, globally, is faced with a truly vexing set of problems in understanding how to support the complex needs of students being taught and expected to learn through a language that is not their native tongue. The 'problem orientation' of the field of educational linguistics that Spolsky (1978) identifies provides a promising basis on which to conceptualize the nature of these challenges and begin to work with teachers to improve current class-room practices. In this final section, we return to the role of classroom teachers to suggest that their professional roles, within the United States and indeed around the world, are evolving. Shifting demographics in who students are and the backgrounds they bring, combined with evolving demands in cur-ricula and instructional practices that redefine what students need to learn and how they are to learn it, are reshaping the professional requirements and the role of second language teachers. Where general professional training in teaching language has largely been seen as adequate, given students, curricu-lum, and expected outcomes, we foresee an increasing demand for individuals trained in the specialist knowledge and practices of educational linguistics, who have the ability to support learning of diverse student populations.

In a sense, these global changes in students, curricula, and expected out-comes bring both ends to the middle. Grade-level and content teachers are increasingly expected to be able to teach language to students from diverse backgrounds in their classrooms. At the same time, second language teachers are expected to support these students' learning across all curricular areas. English, for example, is expanding as a language of instruction even in countries in which it is not the dominant language (Turkey is a case-in-point), and as a second language at more educational levels for many speakers (in Singapore for example) (Graddol, 2006). This proliferation of second language demands is mirrored in English-speaking countries as well, where there are major efforts to improve curriculum and instructional practices so that English language learners have the opportunity to gain fuller access to the academic curriculum. The policy aim that 'all' students will progress through the compulsory educational system and meet certain standards for graduation requires widespread educational retooling. Whether the instruction is termed 'Sheltered' or 'Structured' English Immersion (Freeman & Riley, 2005), the former, in which English language learners are taught content with language, and the latter, in which grade-level or content teachers teach both English-fluent students and English language learners side by side, second language students are expected to make progress in both English and content areas simultaneously.

However, language is not merely the vehicle through which students access content to learn subject matter. Rather, the use of highly literate forms of language is a primary desired goal of modern education (Scollon & Scollon, 1981). As the discussion of angles in the Xhosa classroom illustrates, the goal is not merely to help students understand the concept of an obtuse angle, which could be demonstrated physically, but to expand students' competence to express these concepts linguistically. As Stephen Pinker (1997) has argued, language allows us to capture abstractions of the world that no visual image can match. While an image of a triangle can only represent a specific triangle, language can create a representation that holds true for *all* triangles. Herein lies the challenge of moving teaching and learning fully into language.

At the school level, the person who is supposed to address this challenge is the conventional language-support or English to Speakers of Other Languages (ESOL) teacher, as the individual with professional training and often with direct experience with cross-cultural education and second language learning. These teachers are assigned primary responsibility to teach the core elements of pronunciation, vocabulary, grammar, and the functional language required for students' academic and social purposes. Within compulsory education, these language-support teachers often function as advocates for more sensible and effective educational practices and policies for their students, as well as professional liaisons between students' schools and families. With the best of intentions, however, this conventional role has often focused essentially on remediation, on supporting students who are learning the language of instruction until they can function like their fluent peers (Freeman, 2004). The deficit logic underlying this approach has generally led to a focus on language in teaching and learning as a problem to be solved, as illustrated in the peer-editing scenario for example, and not as a permanent feature of the classroom landscape.

These demands are pushing the field of second language teaching, and ESOL in particular, to redefine the knowledge base and professional competencies at both the conceptual and pragmatic levels. If working effectively with second language learners is framed as simply 'good teaching', then what is the role of the trained second language or ESOL teachers? In addition to direct instruction, these teachers often have to take on new roles as curriculum adapters and teacher trainers, as well as less formal work as peer mentors and instructional coaches to their colleagues. As increasing numbers of teachers find themselves responsible for language, these new roles and responsibilities need to be addressed, since being a skilled language teacher will not de facto make one a skilled teacher trainer or mentor of peers. Likewise, a teacher prepared to teach second languages will not necessarily be qualified to teach a content area or grade level.

As school systems around the globe grapple with the complexities of educating ever growing numbers of second language learners, there will be an increasing demand for language specialists who do have differentiated knowledge and who are trained to work with the specific populations of culturally and linguistically diverse students. Their students may be English language learners as conventionally understood, but these students are just as likely to speak varieties or dialects of English. As others have argued (Adger, Snow, & Christian, 2002), these language specialists must have a rich and expansive conception of language, not simply its structure but also how language mediates students' access to content, classroom learning processes, and assessments. Fundamentally, they will need to be able to articulate these understandings in order to be effective in their evolving roles as de facto teacher educators, curriculum designers, and material developers at the school level. They will work side by side with content and grade-level teachers to collaboratively adapt curriculum and classroom instruction to meet the specific needs of the second language students in these teachers' classrooms.

The growing global demands for access for all students to a quality education are going to require this shift in the profession of teaching. There is clearly much to be learned about how best to integrate language and content learning for second language learners. Therefore, a sustained focus on the complex relationship of language, culture and disciplinary knowledge as these play out in the classroom is an absolute necessity. As Spolsky (1978) noted:

> Whatever else the goals of a school system, there must be a first one: to make it possible for all children to function effectively in the domain of school. Unless the language barriers to education are overcome, a large proportion of the world's population is denied full access to education. (p. 16)

The 'problem orientation' of educational linguistics is ideal to bring educators together as they grapple with the complex global issues of educating diverse students and communities in the twenty-first century.

REFERENCES

Adger, C. T., Snow, C. E., & Christian, D. (eds.) (2002). *Teachers Need to Know about Language*. Washington, DC: Center for Applied Linguistics.

Bailey, F. & Pransky, K. (2005). Are "other people's children" constructivist learners too? *Theory into Practice*, 44(1), 16–28.

Ball, D. L. & Bass, H. (2003). Toward a practice-based theory of mathematical knowledge for teaching. In B. Davis & E. Simmt (eds.), *Proceedings of the 2002 Annual Meeting of the Canadian Mathematics Education Study Group* (pp. 3–14). Edmonton, AB: CMESG/GDEDM.

Ball, D. L., Hill, H., & Bass, H. (2005). Knowing mathematics for teaching. *The American Educator*, Fall, 14–46.

Bloome, D., Carter, S. P., Christian, B. M., Otto, S., & Shuart-Faris, N. (2004). *Discourse Analysis and the Study of Language and Literacy Events: A Microethnographic Perspective*. Mahwah, NJ: Lawrence Erlbaum.

Borg, S. (2003). Teacher cognition in language teaching: A review of the research in what teachers think, know, believe and do. *Language Teaching*, 36(2), 81–109.

Brooks, J. & Brooks, M. (1999). The courage to be constructivist. *Educational Leadership*, 57(1), 18–24.

Burkett, B. & Landon, J. (2004). Introducing an additive model of bilingual education in a rural Xhosa-speaking area of Eastern Cape Province, South Africa: Preparing the ground. Paper presented at the American Association of Applied Linguistics.

Burkett, B., Clegg, J., Landon, J., Reilly, T., & Verster, C. (2001). Developing language-sensitive subject-teaching in South African secondary schools. *Southern African Linguistics and Applied Language Studies*, 19(3&4), 149–161.

Calderhead, J. (1987). *Exploring Teachers' Thinking*. London: Cassell.

Calkins, L. (1986). *The Art of Teaching Writing*. Portsmouth, NH: Heinemann.

Canagarajah, A. S. (1999). *Resisting Linguistic Imperialism in English Teaching*. Oxford: Oxford University Press.

Cazden, C. (1988). *Classroom Discourse*. Portsmouth, NH: Heinemann.

Chamot, A. & O'Malley, J. M. (1994). *The CALLA Handbook: Implementing the Academic Cognitive Language Learning Approach*. New York: Longman.

Chomsky, N. (1969). *Aspects of the Theory of Syntax*. Cambridge, MA: MIT Press.

Clark, C. M. & Peterson, P. L. (1986). Teachers' thought processes. In M. C. Wittrock (ed.), *Handbook of Research on Teaching* (pp. 255–296). New York: Macmillian.

Clegg, J. (1996). *Mainstreaming ESL: Case Studies in Integrating ESL Students into the Mainstream Curriculum*. Clevedon, UK: Multilingual Matters.

Cohen, E. & Goodlad, J. (1994). *Designing Groupwork: Strategies for the Heterogeneous Classroom*. New York: Teachers College Press.

Cooke, S. (1998). *Collaborative Learning Activities in the Classroom*. Leicester, UK: Resource Centre for Multicultural Education.

Cope, B. & Kalantzis, M. (eds.) (1993). *The Powers of Literacy: A Genre Approach to Teaching Writing*. London: The Falmer Press.

Cummins, J. (1981). The role of primary language development in promoting educational success for language minority students. In *Schooling and Language Minority Students: A Theoretical Framework*. Los Angles, CA: Evaluation, Dissemination and Assessment Center, California State University, Los Angles.

Cummins, J. (1984). *Bilingualism and Special Education: Issues in Assessment and Pedagogy*. Clevedon, UK: Multilingual Matters.

Delpit, L. (1995). *Other People's Children: Cultural Conflict in the Classroom*. New York: The New Press.

Derewianka, B. (1990). *Exploring How Texts Work*. Sydney: Primary English Teaching Association.

Echevarria, J., Vogt, M., & Short, D. (2000). *Making Content Comprehensible for English Language Learners: The SIOP Model*. Boston: Allyn & Bacon.

Erickson, F. & Shultz, J. (1981). When is context? Some issues of theory and method in the analysis of social competence. In J. Green & C. Wallat (eds.), *Ethnography and Language in Educational Settings* (pp. 147–160). Norwood: Ablex.

Freeman, D. (1996). The "unstudied problem": Research on teacher learning in language teaching. In D. Freeman & J. C. Richards (eds.), *Teacher Learning in Language Teaching* (pp. 351–378). New York: Cambridge University Press.

Freeman, D. (2004). Teaching in the context of English-language learners: What do we need to know? In M. Sadowski (ed.), *Teaching Immigrant and Second-Language Students* (pp. 7–20). Cambridge MA: Harvard Education Press.

Freeman, D. & Riley, K. (2005). When the law goes local: One state's experience with NCLB in practice. *Modern Language Journal*, 89(2), 264–268.

Freire, P. (1970). *Pedagogy of the Oppressed*. New York: Herder & Herder.

Fu, D. (1995). *My Trouble is My English: Asian American Students and the American Dream*. Portsmouth, NH: Heinemann/Boyton/Cook Publishers.

Gebhard, M., Haffner, A., & Wright, M. (2004). Teaching English-language learners: "The language game of math." In M. Sadowski (ed.), *Teaching Immigrant and Second-Language Students* (pp. 33–46). Cambridge MA; Harvard Education Press.

Gee, J. (1990). *Social Linguistics and Literacies: Ideology in Discourses*. London: Farmer.

Gibbons, P. (2002). *Scaffolding Language, Scaffolding Learning: Teaching Second Language Learners in the Mainstream Classroom*. Portsmouth, NH: Heinemann.

Graddol, D. (2006). *English Next: Why Global English May Mean the End of "English as a Foreign Language."* London: British Council.

Gravelle, M. (2000). *Planning for Bilingual Learners. An Inclusive Curriculum*. Stoke-on-Trent, UK: Trentham Books.

Green, J. (1983). Research on teaching as a linguistic process: A state of the art. *Review of Research in Education*, 10, 151–252.

Hawkins, M. (2005). Becoming a student: Identity work and academic literacies in early schooling. *TESOL Quarterly*, 39(1), 59–82.

Heath, S. (1983). *Ways with Words*. Cambridge: Cambridge University Press.

Hollins, E. (1996). *Culture in School Learning: Revealing the Deep Meaning*. Mahwah, NJ: Lawrence Erlbaum.

Hymes, D. (1974). *Foundations in Sociolinguistics: An Ethnographic Approach*. Philadelphia: University of Pennsylvania Press.

Johnson, K. E. (1999). *Understanding Language Teaching: Reasoning in Action*. Boston, MA: Heinle & Heinle.

Kachru, B. B., Kachru, Y., & Nelson, C. (eds.) (2006). *The Handbook of World Englishes*. Oxford: Blackwell.

Lacelle-Peterson, M. & Rivera, C. (1994). Is it real for all kids? A framework for equitable assessment policies for English language learners. *Harvard Educational Review*, 64(1), 55–75.

Lampert, M. (2001). *Teaching Problems and the Problems of Teaching*. New Haven: Yale University Press.

Loughran, J. J., Mulhall, P., & Berry, A. (2004). In search of pedagogical content knowledge in science: Developing ways of articulating and documenting professional practice. *Journal of Research in Science Teaching*, 41(4), 370–391.

Marsh, D. (1994). *Bilingual Education and Content and Language Integrated Learning*. Paris: International Association for Cross-cultural Communication, Language Teaching in the Member States of the European Union (Lingua) University of Sorbonne.

Marsh, D. & Langé, G. (2000). *Using Languages to Learn and Learning to Use Languages.* TIE-CLIL: Jyväskylä & Milan.

Martin, J. R. (1993). Genre and literacy: Modeling context in educational linguistics. *Annual Review of Applied Linguistics*, 13, 141–172.

McKeon, D. (1994). Language, culture, and schooling. In F. Genesee (ed.), *Educating Second Language Children* (pp. 15–32). Cambridge: Cambridge University Press.

Mehan, H. (1979). *Learning Lessons: Social Organization in the Classroom.* Cambridge, MA: Harvard University Press.

Mercer, N. (1995). *The Guided Construction of Knowledge: Talk amongst Teachers and Learners.* Clevedon, UK: Multilingual Matters.

Mohan, B., Leung, C., & Davison, C. (2001). *English as a Second Language in the Mainstream.* New York: Longman.

Philips, S. (1983). *Invisible Culture.* New York: Longman.

Pinker, S. (1997). *How the Mind Works.* New York: W.W. Norton & Co.

Reddy, Michael J. (1979). The conduit metaphor: A case of frame conflict in our language about language. In A. Ortony (ed.), *Metaphor and Thought* (pp. 284–324). Cambridge: Cambridge University Press.

Rogoff, B. (2003). *The Cultural Nature of Human Development.* Oxford: Oxford University Press.

Scollon, R. & Scollon, S. (1981). *Narrative, Literacy and Face in Interethnic Communication.* Norwood, NJ: Ablex.

Shulman, L. S. (1987). Knowledge and teaching: Foundations of the new reform. *Harvard Educational Review*, 57(1), 1–22.

Shultz, J., Florio, S., & Erickson, F. (1982). "Where's the floor?": Aspects of the cultural organization of social relationships in communication at home and school. In P. Gilmore & A. Glatthorn (eds.), *Children in and Out of School: Ethnography and Education* (pp. 83–123). Washington, DC: Center for Applied Linguistics.

Sizer, T. (1997). *Horace's School: Redesigning the American High School.* Boston: Houghton Mifflin.

Snow, M. A. & Brinton, D. M. (eds.) (1997). *The Content-Based Classroom: Perspectives on Integrating Language and Content.* New York: Addison-Wesley Longman.

Spolsky, B. (1978). *Educational Linguistics: An Introduction.* Rowley, MA: Newbury House.

Sweller, J., van Merrienboer, J. J. G., & Paas, F. G. W. C. (1998). Cognitive architecture and instructional design. *Educational Psychology Review*, 10(3), 251–296.

Tharp, R. & Gallimore, R. (1988). *Rousing Minds to Life.* Cambridge: Cambridge University Press.

Unsworth, L. (2001). *Teaching Multiliteracies across the Curriculum: Changing Contexts of Text and Image in Classroom Practice.* Buckingham, UK: Open University Press.

Willett, J. (1995). Becoming first graders in an L2: An ethnographic study of L2 socialization. *TESOL Quarterly*, 29(3), 473–503.

Willis, P. (1977). *Learning to Labour: How Working Class Kids Get Working Class Jobs.* Farnborough, UK: Savon House.

Wong-Fillmore, L. (1985). When does teacher talk work as input? In S. Gass & C. Madden (eds.), *Input in Second Language Acquisition* (pp. 17–50). Cambridge, MA: Newbury House.

Wong-Fillmore, L. & Snow, C. (2000). *What Teachers Need to Know about Language.* Washington, DC: ERIC Clearinghouse on Language and Linguistics.

Woods, D. (1996). *Teacher Cognition and Language Teaching.* New York: Cambridge University Press.

44 A Research Agenda for Educational Linguistics

PAOLA UCCELLI AND CATHERINE SNOW

Our task was to respond to the papers in this volume by suggesting what the most pressing research agenda within educational linguistics might be. Given the wealth of evidence and ideas already presented, it may seem superfluous to develop a further agenda for research activity. But consider the representation of knowledge in any domain as a circle, set in a field that represents the unknown. As knowledge accumulates, the circle grows in area. But the circumference of the circle – representing the questions at the boundary between the known and the unknown – also increases in length, such that adding to knowledge inevitably means generating new questions and reaching new touchpoints with the unknown. Thus it seems appropriate to respond to the wealth of insights accumulated in this volume by identifying the new questions and problems revealed.

Furthermore, educational linguistics, like educational research in general, suffers from inadequate resources in the face of pressing need. Under such circumstances, identifying the most promising and the most urgent issues to attend to can help us use resources wisely, thus demonstrating most effectively the value of pursuing work in this area.

Research in educational linguistics shares a number of challenges with its mother field, research in education. Educational research is a somewhat ill-defined domain. It encompasses work that has disciplinary bases as disparate as neuroscience and anthropology, economics and developmental psychology, demography and discourse analysis, history and political science. What has traditionally brought these many strands of work together? Unfortunately, all too often very little. Perhaps the studies made reference to educational settings, or were carried out by researchers working in schools of education, or were published in educational journals, or were presented at one of the several, large meetings of educational researchers, such as those sponsored by the American Educational Research Association or by the European Association for Research on Learning and Instruction. In other words, these strands of research cluster sociologically, but do not necessarily share common features or defining characteristics.

The lack of a shared definition for educational research might account in part for its lackluster reputation. There are two major complaints about educational research: its poor quality, and its limited effectiveness in helping solve the problems of educational practice. The complaints about quality may be inevitable in a field that encompasses disciplines with very different methodological histories and proclivities. Quality is relatively easy to identify and to maintain in a field where the standards of proof are uniform, but if everything from ethnography to psychometrics, from qualitative analysis of interview data to hierarchical linear modeling are accepted methods, the criteria for rigor are inevitably less shared.

Even within the subfield of educational linguistics, the nature of evidence and standards of proof accepted by various members of the field differ greatly; quantitative sociolinguists and language acquisition researchers present data of quite a different sort from that accepted by experimentally inclined psycholinguists or by discourse analysts. While all those methods have the potential of illuminating educational questions in complementary ways, some greater clarity about the relation of methods chosen to the nature of the data available and the questions being asked would at least help educational researchers counter the claim that their enterprise lacks rigor.

A more important and, we argue, more serious charge against educational research is that it has not contributed sufficiently to the improvement of educational practice. Why is this so? One reason is the absence of procedures to ensure that research-based knowledge about effective educational practice can accumulate. Researchers in older, more prestigious, and more 'scientific' fields see their job as contributing to a growing body of knowledge. The entire enterprise moves forward as researchers use prior studies to define what is not known and thus decide where their energies should be focused. Educational research tends all too often not to proceed in a forward direction determined by what we know. Instead, 'knowledge' swings back and forth, dominant understandings replacing rather than building on each other. For example, educators go back and forth from Thorndike to Dewey, from Piaget to Vygotsky, from skills-focused to constructivist notions of learning, from experimental to interpretive methods, from biological to transactional explanations of development. As long as educational researchers are arguing about such basic notions as whether reading requires using information from print or constructing representations of text (when, of course, in fact it requires both), we can hardly hope to be taken very seriously by classroom practitioners.

Furthermore, we argue in this chapter that educational research writ large, and educational linguistics more specifically, would benefit from taking more seriously the implications of being educational. Research should not be characterized as educational simply because it involves school-aged children, or because it is conducted in schools. We argue for the importance of locating the questions that guide educational research in schools. Any teacher formulates in the course of any day dozens of insights and questions about learners and learning, yet teacher knowledge is not taken very seriously by researchers. Serious attention to those insights and questions would not only improve the teacher's effectiveness, but might also lead researchers to deeper understanding.

That so many questions of relevance to teachers have been formulated and addressed in the work reported in this volume is heartening. Indeed, much of the work on second and foreign language acquisition (Huhta, Chapter 33, this volume; Pica, Chapter 37, this volume) as well as on computer-assisted language learning (Chapelle, Chapter 41, this volume) constitutes a model of what we advocate: research that is practice-embedded and practice-inspired, thus practice-relevant by design rather than as a result of retro-fitting. In this chapter, we highlight examples of such work and suggest ways in which other subfields of educational linguistics might benefit from more central attention to the questions generated by practice. The work presented in this volume ranges widely, and in its range attests to the vibrancy of the field of educational linguistics. It may be time, though, to narrow the range of what we define as *educational* linguistics, in order to ensure that the relevance of knowledge about language to the improvement of educational outcomes be maximized.

The Main Streams of Work in Educational Linguistics

It is worth noting, as a starting place, the major lines of work that comprise educational linguistics. Indeed, the table of contents of Part II of this volume provides a good overview of these lines of work. We would characterize these domains (deviating somewhat from the names provided by the volume editors) as follows:

- using language in classrooms,
- literacy development,
- language learning,
- planning language use in educational settings,
- assessing language knowledge.

Clearly, the role of educational linguistics in each of these domains is somewhat different. In the first three domains, the primary customer for linguistic insight is the classroom teacher, who would benefit from knowing how his/her own language use facilitates or interferes with student learning, from understanding the linguistic challenges inherent in texts and classroom discourse, from valuing (while also decreasing) the linguistic variability displayed by student language users, from understanding how to shape classroom discourse to promote active engagement, critical thinking, and rapid learning, and from specific techniques to promote language and literacy development. In the last two domains, the primary customer is the ministry of education or the local educational authority, responsible for decisions about which language to use in schools, what standards for use of that language to impose, and how to assess whether those standards are being met.

Furthermore, work on educational linguistics will inevitably have varying priorities in different parts of the world. Each region faces unique challenges, and educational researchers need to attend to those challenges with a genuine focus on the specificity of each situation. In some places, for example, issues of educational language planning hardly arise. Yet, whether the focus is on the 781 million illiterate adults in the world (http://portal.unesco.org/education), on the need to prepare students for tertiary education beyond national boundaries and thus often in a second language (http://www.uis.unesco.org/ev.php?ID=6028_201&ID2=DO_TOPIC), or on the design of education for either indigenous or immigrant students who do not speak the national language (http://www.cal.org/topics/ell/), certain fundamental questions arise:

1 What should we be teaching our students about language to prepare them for academic success, for professional success, for their broader intellectual challenges in adult life?
2 What do teachers need to know about language in order to be effective in promoting the desired linguistic outcomes with the full range of students in their classes?
3 Once we have identified the desired linguistic outcomes of education and the required teacher knowledge, how do we go about fostering them?

In the sections that follow, we use these three questions both to organize the knowledge accumulated across the various chapters and as a first cut in specifying more precisely the most urgent questions for the future.

What Are the Desired Educational Outcomes?

What are the desired educational outcomes at each level of schooling, and how can we adapt them to diverse populations without abandoning high standards, yet taking into consideration the range of circumstances under which learning must occur? Lo Bianco (Chapter 9, this volume) insightfully lists eight overarching goals that display the range of secondary linguistic socializations schools aspire to produce. This enumeration of goals illustrates in great detail the complexity of the multiple tasks involved in socializing students into various modes of communication. The complexity only increases if we take into consideration that these eight discrete goals frequently overlap in the reality of many educational institutions, as language minority issues, multilingualism, disciplinary linguistic knowledge and language-related special needs are often coexisting factors that instruction needs to address.

Two tensions seem to lie at the core of defining what the educational out-comes should be in various contexts. The first one is the tension between homogeneity and diversification. Defining the 'standard language' to be used at school is challenging as student bodies become increasingly diverse and successful communication outside the classroom often calls for alternative language forms. Indeed, Nekvapil (Chapter 18, this volume) argues that "the standard" should move toward a polycentric nature, formed by mixed home languages, and accessible to all, not only the elites. While this might con-stitute a controversial claim, it points to a core definitional feature that cannot be overlooked in establishing educational outcomes related to language. The increasing mobility of the world population, which is generating contact among more languages and more cultures than ever before, raises to promin-ence the following questions: *What is (are) the standard language(s) to be taught at school? What is the best way for students to have access to it (them) in harmonious coexistence with their primary forms of discourse?* Recent projects that seek to develop dialect awareness (Wolfram, Schilling-Estes, & Hazen, 1997; Reaser & Wolfram, 2005) and strategies to help language minority students recognize and switch to academic English features (LeMoine, 2001) offer initial insights on the integration of language varieties in the classroom (see Reaser & Adger, Chapter 12, this volume). There is, however, a long road ahead for research that seeks to identify the optimal outcomes and the best instructional strategies for different populations under a variety of conditions.

The second related tension deals with centralization versus local control. North (Chapter 16, this volume) points out that for foreign language teaching a legitimate question is whether learning can be expected to progress in the same order across a variety of contexts. This is a concern that can easily be extrapolated to the discussion of standards for oral and literate school language as well. Should we have common centralized standards at differ-ent levels of schooling regardless of students' characteristics, or should we develop different sets of standards taking into account students' linguistic characteristics? As pointed out by Davies (Chapter 34, this volume), recent research has highlighted the need for adapting standards and assessments to the characteristics of certain populations, such as English language learners and students with special needs (Bailey & Butler, 2004). How to set realistic standards that attempt to close the achievement gap in the most efficient possible way is still a challenging task that deserves further attention. In dis-cussing the Common European Framework for foreign language instruction, North (Chapter 16, this volume) describes it as a metasystem to be used not as a direct implementation tool but as a reference point from which elaboration and adaptation to local circumstances are necessary. As he points out, whether some categories of this model can prove relevant in the context of school language education more broadly defined remains to be seen.

Finally, the "textually mobile world" (Hull & Hernandez, Chapter 23, this volume), characterized both by rapid shifts in populations and languages and by technological innovations occurring with unprecedented speed, requires redefining desired educational outcomes toward greater flexibility, a more global perspective, and the development of critical thinking. Students in school today need to be prepared to face not yet identified social and intellectual demands. While pragmatic orientations are gradually replacing traditional ones, in this attempt to promote more functional goals, we need to consider how explicit and how inclusive educational objectives ought to be. Hull and Hernandez (Chapter 23, this volume) highlight the rapidity of technological changes, inviting us to redefine what literacy means in a digital world. Shin and Kubota (Chapter 15, this volume) ask "how might one envision and practice a more linguistically and culturally responsive education in the postcolonial and globalized schools of today?" To this valid concern for a *responsive* education, we would add that of a *responsible* education. Communication skills should promote respectful dialogue, and literacy skills should allow for entry into deep contact with remote ideas, cultures, and people. We believe that an important aspect of language and literacy pedagogy should be to promote understanding and deep knowledge of our globalized and multicultural world by encouraging reading that emphasizes perspective-taking and by fostering language skills that focus on communication and lead to real dialogue.

What Do Teachers Need to Know about Language?

The issue of what teachers need to know about language is, of course, a burning and recurrent problem for educational linguists. There is a very long list of 'need to knows', for example:

- understanding the difference between non-standard dialects, second language characteristics, and language disorders (see Reaser & Adger, Chapter 12, this volume);
- understanding the inevitability of variation in language use, and the identity work such variation accomplishes (Mesthrie, Chapter 6, this volume);
- understanding the characteristics of normal language development, in both first and second language speakers, and how to measure it (Huhta, Chapter 33, this volume);
- understanding how oral language both relates to and differs from written language, and what (meta)linguistic skills children need to be explicitly taught in order to make the transition from oral to literate comprehension;
- understanding what constitute normal developmental errors in spelling and in writing, and which student errors should be responded to with explicit instruction;

- knowing enough about etymology and morphology to be able to explain the meanings of words and their morphological and etymological neighbors.

This brief list could be greatly extended (see Fillmore & Snow, 2002; Valdés et al., 2005). Most notably, though, this list primarily reflects declarative knowledge, whereas in fact an additional long list of linguistic knowledge items could be added that fall more in the domain of enacted knowledge, for example:

- knowing what kinds of questions to ask to generate productive classroom discussions;
- using sophisticated vocabulary words frequently in the course of interactions with students;
- understanding what aspects of written text are likely to be confusing to students;
- understanding how to respond to student writing to make it more sophisticated;
- being familiar with many literary and expository texts of potential interest to students.

The difficulties of providing teachers with sufficient declarative knowledge about education are clear; ensuring the availability to them of enactable knowledge is even more challenging (see Snow, Griffin, & Burns, 2005, for a further discussion of the distinction between declarative and enacted knowledge). Various teacher education programs have tried sending their students to courses in the linguistics department, or hiring in a linguist to teach pre-service teachers about language; such experiments are not notably successful (Burling, 1971, gives a charming account of the difficulties of this model from the linguist's perspective) for many reasons, including of course the multiplying list of competencies teacher certification programs must provide access to.

This array of challenges thus generates the following sorts of research questions: What is the minimal level of linguistic understanding needed by teachers engaged in initial literacy instruction? By teachers working with older students? By teachers whose students include second language learners? When is it most effective and most efficient to provide instruction in educational linguistics to teachers; are these matters better dealt with as part of professional development than as part of preservice programs? And what language skills and domains of linguistic knowledge should be considered as admissions criteria to teacher education programs? What would be the effect of teaching more linguistics in secondary grades on the knowledge and skills of teacher education students? In addition to specifying what teachers need to know, the question arises: How can this knowledge be made accessible and permanent without having folk language theories reemerge and replace educated theories?

How Do We Foster the Desired Linguistic Outcomes for Students and Teachers?

Fostering the desired linguistic outcomes – both declarative knowledge and enactable skills – among students and teachers requires both learning more about the processes of language and literacy acquisition, and figuring out how better to implement what we know. We discuss these challenges under four headings: in the first section we discuss a new way of doing educational research including educational linguistics, and in the remaining sections we present some specific domains where such research could be focused.

Enriching research–practice relationships

A theme alluded to in many chapters is the one already noted above: the value of embedding research in the realities of practice. It is worth noting that the articles in Part III: Research–Practice Relationships in this volume focus mostly on second language acquisition. The predominance of work on second language learning and language teaching over that on first language and content-area learning reflects the current reality in the field of educational linguistics, and derives from the obvious role of language in second/foreign language teaching. We argue, though, that more attention needs to be devoted to the role of oral language skills in the accomplishment of literacy and of academic skills, a domain where the linguistic factors may be less obvious, but are no less important.

If, as several of the chapters in this volume agree, researcher–practitioner collaborations are productive in improving the quality both of research and of practice, then the burning questions become: How do we build researcher–practitioner collaborations so that they are feasible, robust, and mutually informative? How do we get teachers – in particular content-area teachers – interested in, aware of, and reflective about language in their daily practices? Attempts to create educational settings that function like teaching hospitals, where clinicians and researchers work side by side, have been launched. Professional development schools (see http://www.ncate.org/public/ pdswhat.asp?ch=133) are one example. The Strategic Educational Research Partnership (SERP; Donovan, Wigdor, & Snow, 2003) has established 'field sites' in collaborating school districts in which practitioners nominate issues of concern and co-construct solutions with researchers who see themselves as engineers constructing tools to solve problems of practice. The need for educational linguists to work within such settings is obvious, since many of the problems of practice being nominated are deeply language related. For example, in the SERP field site established in the Boston Public Schools, the burning issue of concern is middle school students' reading comprehension, in particular their vocabulary knowledge, and their capacity to understand the discourse of content-area texts.

If research is truly to be informed by practitioner knowledge, then systematic ways must exist for researchers to learn what practitioners think and what they want to know. SERP, for example, has launched a pilot survey to collect information about middle school teachers' literacy-related beliefs and questions (www.serpinstitute.org); some data from a practitioners' survey of unanswered questions about Computer Assisted Language Learning is available at http://www.stanford.edu/~efs/callsurvey/index.html.

In addition to formulating questions based on practitioners' concerns, researchers need to think about how to design data collection and analyses that are beneficial to all participants involved. Practice-oriented research studies on second or foreign language teaching offer valuable examples. As described by Pica (Chapter 37, this volume), the field of second language acquisition has recently moved toward closer teacher–researcher collaborations that illustrate the type of practice-inspired and practice-relevant approach we advocate here. The strategies implemented, and the lessons learned in these studies, are relevant beyond the field of SLA and can inform research on the language of schooling and on literacy more broadly. In discussing instructional techniques, Pica proposes four basic principles that seem relevant as guidelines for practice-relevant research, independent of the specific curricular content selected. Following her basic principles, we think effective collaborations will be those that focus on *authentic tasks, the least complex implementation possible, areas where students need additional targeted instruction,* and *noticeably successful outcomes.* Successful partnerships would result in a bi-directional relationship, in which research informs practice, and theories are reformulated and refined based on their encounters with real-life challenges. Given that recent research on second language acquisition attests to the feasibility and fruitfulness of this reciprocal influence (see Pica, Chapter 37, this volume), other subfields of educational linguistics can use these principles as starting points to forge theory and practice relationships. In this collaboration, policy making needs to be involved for successful results. Connecting the standards used across instruction, assessment, and policy making is a key requirement for an efficiently integrated system that offers feedback to its different components. As discussed by King and Benson (Chapter 24, this volume), for instance, not only are various definitions of literacy used in different parts of the world, but these definitions tend to be narrow and simplistic in some policy circles. An elaboration of the commitment to practice-embedded research is the pragmatic orientation embraced by Davies' discussion (Chapter 34, this volume) of the design of the PISA, with its focus on measuring knowledge required in everyday tasks beyond the school setting. Davies also proposes studies of the impact of language assessment on the quality of instruction and on the quality of the standards proposed. This approach emphasizes the degree to which good language teaching exploits information from assessment to inform better instruction and set more clearly defined educational objectives.

The two areas into which Hudson (Chapter 5, this volume) divides *theory* are of great relevance to thinking about how researchers (including linguistic theorists), practitioners, and policy makers might enter into a more fruitful dialogue. Hudson distinguishes between *ideas* and *models*, the former being much less controversial than the latter. He defines *ideas* as concepts about the nature of language, which for the most part represent "issues on which linguists can agree." For instance, all linguists agree that language skills continue to develop into adulthood, although they might disagree on why and how these skills change; they also all agree that various language skills (phonology, vocabulary, grammar, pragmatics) are separable and perhaps even uncorrelated. Models "exist at the frontier of research" as they provide alternative explanations that are controversial by nature. As pointed out by Hudson, linguists are concerned with models, and their debates about models often obscure their agreement on big ideas. Whereas linguists and developmental psychologists can argue about the specifics of varied theoretical models, the job of educational linguistics is not to seek proofs for theoretical formulations, but to generate relevant ideas for educational practice. If elucidating what teachers, students, policy makers, and other educational participants need to know about language to achieve successful outcomes is the goal, then focusing on ideas instead of models offers a wise solution. Ideas, as Hudson points out, however, are not easily inferred from theoretical linguistic writings; linguists could contribute to education by spelling out the key ideas clearly. Indeed, collaborations among theoretical and educational linguists could prove mutually advantageous as ideas relevant to educational practice are identified, and as real data from students challenge those ideas and offer evidence on which more comprehensive linguistic models might be built.

Of course, many of the "big ideas" commonly assumed to be true in the community of educational linguists need to be made more particular if they are to influence educational practice. For example, the claim that L1 instruction has a positive effect on L2 literacy acquisition, or that advanced literacy skill is related to oral language comprehension, are generally accepted as true, but what do they actually mean for classroom practice?

Reaser and Adger (Chapter 12, this volume) review attempts to unravel specific language-related factors that explain why the mismatch between vernacular and standard languages constitutes such a challenge in school. Reaser and Adger review studies carried out by Labov and his colleagues, showing that there is a complex relationship between vernacular languages and reading. For example, some features of African American English – introduced when reading aloud standard English texts – are more likely than others to constitute reading errors.

The more specific and practice-relevant research questions get, the more they can generate other relevant questions and make significant contributions to the improvement of students' instruction and learning. An example of such a question based on the research Reaser and Adger reviewed is: "Why is it that knowledge of Standard English is so variable in the low SES population . . . and what are the mechanisms by which increased knowledge of Standard American English favors learning to read?" Answers to this type of question have great potential to provide specifically targeted and useful advice for educational practice.

Another level at which research needs to be made relevant to practitioners is in the dissemination of findings. As Reaser and Adger (Chapter 12, this volume) foreground, communication of linguists' important insights to educational researchers requires different approaches than communication to linguists. Moreover, educational linguists should tailor their message to their various audiences – educational researchers, teachers, policy makers, and other practitioners. The dimensions of language in which each of these groups is interested, and the terminology and illustrative examples that will appeal to each, differ in important ways.

In a truly fruitful dialogue, then, linguists would articulate their big ideas, practitioners would request specific implications for practice, and linguists would track the effectiveness of those practical implications in order to hone their big ideas. In a fruitful dialogue, both participants have much to learn.

The value of sharing insights across first and second language acquisition research

Another theme encountered across chapters is the value of research on first language acquisition as a resource to educational linguists, and, in particular, as a basis for thinking about both research and practice in second/foreign language acquisition (Huhta, Chapter 33, this volume). As evidenced across chapters in this book, there are some areas in which SLA has a longer trajectory of accumulated knowledge in relation to research on L1, such as the research–practice collaborations discussed above (Pica, Chapter 37, this volume). Conversely, there are other fields in which research on L1 has deeper resources and better articulated theories, such as early literacy assessment (Huhta, Chapter 33, this volume). We celebrate the contributions of first language research to second language instruction, but note that the vast literature on first language acquisition is almost exclusively devoted to describing natural, untutored acquisition, and emerges from a commitment to constructivist views, in which the child is seen as spontaneously using input data to invent language anew. Despite recently increasing efforts to improve students' vocabulary skills via explicit instruction (Beck, McKeown, & Kucan, 2002; Carlo et al., 2004; Biemiller & Boote, 2006), there is still scarce research on the role of implicit or explicit instruction in first language acquisition, even though recent findings have documented enormous differences among normally developing children in language skills (e.g., Hart & Risley, 1995), and are beginning to document the effects of language skills on content-area learning and assessment (Abedi, 2003; Butler et al., 2004).

It is also striking that, while research on first language acquisition is a source of inspiration to educational linguists, there is very little problematization within educational linguistics of crucial questions of practice related to first language learning. Given huge differences among children in the language skills available to them at entry to schooling, and the demonstrated consequences of those differences for later school success (Tabors, Roach, & Snow, 2001; Tabors, Snow, & Dickinson, 2001), it seems as if educational linguists need to focus on questions about how to enrich language learning opportunities in early childhood. For example: What practices should we recommend to parents and preschool teachers to ensure optimal early language development? How does exposure to different activities and activity structures (peer play, book-reading discussions, pretend play, etc.) promote the development of language, especially the foundation for academic language?

Ironically, then, educational linguistics draws deeply on research about early language acquisition, but attends only minimally to the consequences of variation in early acquired language skills for educational outcomes and has, for the most part, not exploited advances in foreign/second language teaching methods to inform instruction in vocabulary and academic language for monolinguals. It would be unwise not to take advantage of insights from well-researched areas, such as vocabulary instruction for L2, to explore how to bring them into the mainstream of education practices. Are components identified as crucial in second language research, such as metalinguistic awareness (Ellis, Chapter 31, this volume), or "languaging" (Swain & Suzuki, Chapter 39, this volume), also factors positively associated with more broadly defined school language and literacy skills? North (Chapter 16, this volume) even asks if a common framework developed for the teaching of foreign or second languages could be applied in primary school to the teaching of the mother tongue. As he points out, we should not lose sight of the intrinsic differences distinguishing these two learning processes and minimize the value of simple extrapolations from one field to another. Still, well-replicated findings in SLA or FL research generate hypotheses about language learning more broadly defined that deserve attention. These findings might be of particular relevance to issues that arise when classrooms serve children from multiple language backgrounds, for example those that emerge in thinking about Walter's (Chapter 10, this volume) question about what happens when the child does not speak the language of the classroom.

The global question about language acquisition that might be at the center of a systematic research agenda for educational linguistics is the following: What is the nature of the knowledge about language available to a proficient speaker at different stages of development of oral and literate skills? A corollary of this global question is the following one: How can we define and assess the more advanced language skills typically developed during middle childhood and adolescence? If we had the answers to these questions, then many other troubling issues (e.g., What new language skills are needed to process academic or disciplinary texts? What are the possibilities for transfer from a first to a second language and/or literacy system? How should teachers respond to non-standard dialects? What constitutes good classroom discussion?) would become much more tractable.

Despite the enormous value of the basic work done on language acquisition to educational linguists, it is important to emphasize that improvements in domains such as language teaching and language assessment cannot wait for more data and better theories about either first or second language acquisition. The problems of practice are too large and too urgent, as emphasized by Jones and Saville (Chapter 35, this volume), for solutions to be postponed until all the data are collected. Indeed, one of the contributions of practitioners to research is to provide candidates of excellent practice that can then be subjected to further study and evaluation, and whose success or failure might inform theory.

The challenge of instruction and assessment with more advanced learners

Language development researchers, as noted above, have focused primarily on young children and the major advances in language skills achieved between ages 1 and 3–4 years. Their work is directly relevant to the practice of early childhood educators and has informed and improved the design of preschool and parent-involvement programs. Most educators, though, take those early accomplishments for granted, and concern themselves with later language development – development of the capacity to engage in classroom discussion, to produce extended discourse orally and in writing, to acquire sophisticated vocabulary, and deploy complex grammar. Understanding these later developmental challenges, for students operating in their first language and for those acquiring a second language, is a task with which educational linguistics could help. As Hull and Hernandez (Chapter 23, this volume) point out, adolescent literacy has lately received more attention; however, there are still numerous gaps to fill in to fully understand how to better serve older students.

As both Jones and Saville (Chapter 35, this volume), and Davies (Chapter 34, this volume) discuss, language proficiency becomes broader and more multi-dimensional at later ages/grades. Therefore the challenge of assessing these more sophisticated language skills also increases. Yet, in the accountability-driven world of education, developing assessments for these more sophisticated language skills is key, because if they are not assessed, they are unlikely to be attended to in the classroom. Furthermore, decisions about placement of second language learners in mainstream classrooms should depend on valid assessments of their ability to comprehend and produce the academic language needed for success in those classrooms; it is still the case that second language proficiency tests often focus on basic rather than academic language skills, and thus, exit students who are unprepared for the tasks they will face in mainstream classrooms (Kieffer, Lesaux, & Snow, 2006).

Particularly when thinking about older learners, for whom language and literacy skills are the gateway to all learning, the need to integrate instruction and assessment becomes urgent. We agree with Huhta (Chapter 33, this volume) on the need to develop diagnostic assessments that inform teacher practice and allow for ongoing feedback between teacher and students. If, as claimed by Reaser and Adger, it is true that linguists and educational linguists are becoming interested in collaborating with educators to produce practical assessments and materials for classroom use, then the gap that currently exists in the availability of materials on language variation could be filled productively. Indeed, recent collaborations among linguists, educational linguists, and practitioners in the design and production of instructional materials and assessment have started to produce successful results (Labov and Baker, 2001, quoted by Reaser and Adger, Chapter 12, this volume).

Questions that arise, then, include the following: What are the key characteristics of academic language needed for success in the middle and secondary grades? How can these language skills best be taught? Do students benefit from instructional attention to these skills as oral language in the primary or even preschool years? Do students who have acquired academic language skills in a first language transfer useful knowledge of them to a second language, and if so, under what circumstances and for what combinations of first and second languages?

Beyond language as skill: Motivation and identity in language learning

A recurrent issue in language teaching is the motivation of learners. Motivation is a complicated issue in foreign language classes, in which the lack of a positive reason to master the language might well be compounded by all sorts of negative motivations, e.g., embarrassment, fear of making errors, loss of self-esteem, or difficulty of an honorable self-presentation during the early stages of language learning (see McKinney & Norton, Chapter 14, this volume). Motivation can also play a role in learners' willingness to shift from a non-standard to a standard dialect (see Mesthrie, Chapter 6, this volume), or to adopt the academic language features desired for classroom discussion and for literacy.

There has been considerable research done showing the impact of motivation on second/foreign language learning and exploring the interaction between types of motivation and social setting in determining outcomes. However, the extension of these ideas to issues of identity construction within a first language has not yet happened. Within the various content areas, there is growing attention to important questions of the form: What does it mean to speak/write like a historian or a scientist? What language skills are involved, and how distinctive are they for the different content areas? The motivation-related question that accompanies these is: How do we create classroom conditions under which students are motivated to acquire academic identities and the language skills associated with them?

Raising issues of identity and motivation also alerts us to the degree to which research in educational linguistics has focused on some populations and language varieties to the exclusion of others. The research agenda would not be complete without an urgent call for the inclusion of those neglected populations and language varieties, as highlighted by various authors in this volume:

• Reaser and Adger (Chapter 12) for non-standard varieties beyond African American English;
• Supalla and Cripps (Chapter 13) for deaf children;
• McCarty, Skutnabb-Kangas, and Magga (Chapter 21) for endangered languages in different parts of the world;
• King and Benson (Chapter 24) for indigenous languages;
• Hull and Hernandez (Chapter 23) with a more general call to study diverse cultures, ethnicities, social classes, and gender.

As evidenced by these various calls, there is still a long list of populations awaiting researchers' attention.

Conclusion

The richness and breadth of the work presented in this volume emphasize the value of greater clarity about the definition of educational linguistics, its goals, and the fundamental questions with which it should grapple. Educational linguistics lies at the intersection of research on education and research on applied linguistics (see LoBianco, Chapter 9, this volume). While Applied Linguistics is the branch of linguistics that uses linguistic theory to address real-world problems, Educational Linguistics is the branch of Applied Linguistics that addresses real-world problems in education. By far the largest subfield within educational linguistics has always been the study of second language acquisition and second language teaching, and the rich accomplishments of that subfield are reflected in the several chapters devoted to it in this volume. However, educational linguistics is much broader in scope than just second/foreign language teaching. In fact, as argued by van Lier (Chapter 42, this volume), it should encompass all academic learning mediated by language in one form or another.

We have argued that educational linguistics needs on the one hand to narrow its focus to pay particular attention to the most pressing real-world educational problems, and on the other hand to expand its focus beyond language teaching/learning to an understanding of how language mediates all educational encounters. Furthermore, in studying the role of language in all learning and teaching, it is extremely helpful to remember the continuum proposed by Bailey, Burkett, and Freeman (Chapter 43, this volume): from learning situations in which the language used is transparent to all concerned (teacher and students share a language and students control the academic language of the classroom) to situations were language use is opaque (students are still learning the basics of the classroom language, even as learning through that language is expected). Intermediate points on that continuum, where most students and teachers probably find themselves, represent differing degrees of translucency – i.e., students and teacher share a language but not necessarily all the specific linguistic features that characterize disciplinary, metacognitive, or classroom language use. Identifying the situations where lack of shared language knowledge interferes with learning, and characterizing helpful approaches to those situations, in the form of pedagogical strategies, curricular adjustments, student commitments, or reorganization of learning settings, is the common and urgent challenge for educational linguists.

NOTE

Support for the preparation of this paper came from the Institute of Educational Sciences, US Department of Education, through grants numbered R305G050201 and R305G050029, as well as from the Spencer and Hewlett Foundations through the Strategic Education Research Partnership Institute.

REFERENCES

Abedi, J. (2003). *Impact of Student Language Background On Content-Based Performance: Analysis of Extant Data. CSE Report.* Los Angeles, CA: National Center for Research on Evaluation.

Adger, C. T., Snow, C. E., & Christian, D. (eds.) (2002). *What Teachers Need to Know About Language.* Washington, DC/McHenry, IL: Center for Applied Linguistics/Delta Systems Co., Inc.

Bailey, A. L. & Butler, F. A. (2004). Ethical considerations in the assessment of the language and content knowledge of U.S. school-age English learners. *Language Assessment Quarterly* 1(2–3), 177–193.

Beck, I., McKeown, M., & Kucan, L. (2002). *Bringing Words to Life: Robust Vocabulary Instruction.* New York: Guilford Press.

Biemiller, A. & Boote, C. (2006). An effective method for building meaning vocabulary in primary grades. *Journal of Educational Psychology,* 98(1), 44–62.

Burling, R. (1971). Talking to teachers about social dialects. *Language Learning,* 21, 221–234.

Butler, F. A., Bailey, A. L., Stevens, R., Huang, B., & Lord, C. (2004). Academic English in Fifth-Grade Mathematics, Science, and Social Studies Textbooks. CSE Report 642. Los Angeles, CA: Center for Research on Evaluation Standards and Student Testing, CRESST.

Carlo, M. S., August, D., McLaughlin, B., Snow, C. E., Dressler, C., Lippman, D. N., Lively, T. J., & White, C. E. (2004). Closing the gap: Addressing the vocabulary needs of

English-language learners in bilingual and mainstream classrooms. *Reading Research Quarterly*, 39(2), 188–215.

Donovan, M. S., Wigdor, S., & Snow, C. E. (eds.) (2003). Strategic Education Research Partnership. National Research Council, Washington, DC: National Academies Press.

Fillmore, L. W. & Snow, C. E. (2002). What teachers need to know about language. In C. T. Adger, C. E. Snow, & D. Christian (eds.), *What Teachers Need to Know About Language.* (pp. 7–53) Washington, DC/McHenry, IL: Center for Applied Linguistics/Delta Systems Co., Inc.

Hart, B. & Risley, T. (1995). *Meaningful Differences in the Everyday Experience of Young American Children.* Baltimore: Brookes.

Kieffer, M., Lesaux, N., & Snow, C. E. (2006). Promises and pitfalls: Implications of No Child Left Behind for defining, assessing, and serving English language learners. Paper prepared for Civil Rights Project Conference, Washington, DC, November.

Labov, W. & Baker, B. (2001). Testing the effectiveness of an individualized reading program for African-American, Euro-American and Latino inner city children. Poster presented at the meeting of Interagency Educational Research Initiative Project. Washington, DC.

LeMoine, N. R. (2001). Language variation and literacy acquisition in African American students. In J. L. Harris, A. G. Kamhi, & K. E. Pollock (eds.), *Literacy in African American Communities* (pp. 169–194). Mahwah, NJ: Erlbaum.

Reaser, J. & Wolfram, W. (2005). *Voices of North Carolina: Language and Life from the Atlantic to the Appalachians.* Raleigh, NC: NC State University.

Snow, C. E., Griffin, P., Burns, M. S., & NAE Subcommittee on Teaching Reading (2005). *Knowledge to Support the Teaching of Reading: Preparing Teachers for a Changing World.* San Francisco, CA: Jossey-Bass.

Tabors, P. O., Roach, K. A., & Snow, C. E. (2001). Home language and literacy environment final results. In D. K. Dickinson & P. O. Tabors (eds.), *Beginning Literacy with Language* (pp. 111–138). Baltimore: Paul H. Brookes Publishing Co.

Tabors, P. O., Snow, C. E., & Dickinson, D. K. (2001). Homes and schools together: Supporting language and literacy development. In D. K. Dickinson & P. O. Tabors (eds.), *Beginning Literacy with Language* (pp. 313–334). Baltimore: Paul H. Brookes Publishing Co.

Valdés, G., Bunch, G., Snow, C., Lee, C., & Matos, L. (2005). Enhancing the development of students' language(s). In L. Darling-Hammond & J. Bransford (eds.), *Preparing Teachers for a Changing World: What Teachers should Learn and Be Able to Do.* San Francisco, CA: Jossey-Bass.

Wolfram, W., Schilling-Estes, N., & Hazen, K. (1997). *Dialects and the Ocracoke Brogue.* Raleigh, NC: NC State University.

Author Index

Aasen, I. 297
Abedi, J. et al. 512, 636
Abrahamsson, N. 426
Adegbija, E. 271
Adger, C. T. 168, 171, 622
Ager, D. 116, 233, 269
Agha, Asif 83, 84, 93
Ahai, N. 275
Ahmad, K. et al. 587
Aijmer, K. 544
Akamatsu, T. 185
Aksu-Koç, A. 393
Al-Sulaiti, L. 540
Albertini, J. A. 174
Albó, X. 348, 351
Alderson, J. C. et al. 224, 225, 464, 469,
    471, 472, 473, 474, 477, 478, 479, 480,
    497, 504
Alexander, N. 342, 347
Alidou, H. 208, 345
Aljaafreh, A. 564
Allen, L. 448
Allington, R. L. 337
Allwright, D. 526
Almond, R. G. 496, 498
Alvarez-Torres, M. J. 527
Amastea, J. 150
Ammar, A. 561–2, 568
Anaya, A. 51, 348
Andersen, E. S. 148
Andersen, R. W. 389, 390, 392–3, 394,
    417

Anderson, B. 324
Anderson, T. 590–1
Anderson, S. R. 17
Andrews, R. 56
Angelil-Carter, S. 195
Annahatak, B. 404, 406
Aparici, M. 386
Appadurai, A. 208, 214, 334
Arbelaiz, A. M. 591
Arndt, H. 280, 596
Arthur, J. 267
Aston, G. 540, 541, 546, 547, 548
Athan, R. G. 510, 511, 515
Athanases, S. Z. 576
Atkinson, D. 600
Atkinson, P. 578
Atwell, E. 540
Auerbach, E. 197, 198, 344
August, D. 459, 512
Augustine, Saint 356, 362–3

Bachman, L. F. 464, 471, 473, 480, 496
Bäckman, L. 430
Bailey, A. L. 483, 486, 490, 512–13, 514,
    515–16, 630
Bailey, F. 610
Bailey, K. M. 526
Bailey, N. 387t
Baker, B. 170, 639
Baker, C. 130, 135, 149, 344, 578
Baker, D. 577
Baker, D. P. 321

Baker, F. T.   171
Baker, K.   137
Bakhtin, M. M.   70, 193, 335, 599
Baldauf, R. B., Jr.   21, 103, 233, 234, 235, 237, 238, 239, 240, 241, 242, 282, 283
Baldegger, M.   224
Ball, D. L   612
Bamgboṣe, A.   276
Banfield, A.   86
Baquedano-López, L.   149, 154
Baquedano-López, P.   149, 401, 406
Baquedano-Lopez, T.   580
Bardovi-Harlig, K.   387, 391, 392, 394
Barker, R.   597
Barlow, M.   55, 543, 544
Barnes, D.   574
Bartlett, T.   306
Barton, D.   268, 332
Bass, H.   612
Basturkmen, H.   560
Bates, E.   416, 417
Bateson, G.   597
Batstone, R.   439
Battison, R.   179
Baugh, J.   78, 120
Bauman, Z.   573
Baxter, S.   345
Bayley, R.   149, 400, 406
Baynham, M.   123
Bazilashe, J.   348
Bebian, R.-A. A.   176
Beck, I.   636
Beckett, G. H.   602
Belazi, H. M.   49
Bell, A.   71
Bellugi, U.   178, 182
Belz, J. A.   544, 590
Benati, A.   448
Benavot, A.   321
Benson, C.   348, 350
Benson, P.   587
Benton, R.   299
Bergeron, S.   208
Berkely, A.   92
Berman, P. et al.   459
Bernardini, S.   548
Bernstein, B.   77, 78, 404, 577, 578, 579, 600–1
Berry, A.   612

Bhabha, H. K.   195
Bhatia, T. K.   42, 43f, 44, 44f, 49
Bialystok, E.   149
Biber, D. et al.   539, 541, 542, 543, 545, 547
Biddle, B. J.   572
Biemiller, A.   636
Biewer, C.   549
Bigelow, M. et al.   563
Billig, M.   121
Birdsong, D.   45, 426, 427, 429, 430, 432
Black, P. et al.   470, 471, 474, 475, 476, 479, 480
Blackburn, L. A. et al.   186
Blake, R.   591
Bley-Vroman, R.   426, 527
Bligh, D. A.   168
Block, D.   209
Blomberg, D.   361–2
Blommaert, J.   83, 98, 110, 266
Bloom, B. S.   470–1, 473, 474
Bloome, D. et al.   164, 575, 576, 609
Blot, R.   90
Board of Education (England and Wales)   314
Boldt, R.   478
Boli, J.   324
Bond, T. G.   501
Bongaerts, T.   426, 433
Boote, C.   636
Bopp, M.   275
Borg, S.   611
Borrás, I.   591
Botley, S.   548
Bourdieu, P.   121, 193–5, 404
Bowen, J.   412
Bowers, C. A.   592
Bowker, L.   549
Boyd, S.   286, 287
Braine, G.   212
Brandt, D.   333
Braslavsky, C.   321
Brennan, M.   178
Brentari, D.   178, 185
Bresnan, J.   418
Breton, R. J. L.   273
Brice-Heath, S.   76–7
Brindley, G.   485, 510
Brinton, D. M.   615

Brito, I. 198
Broadfoot, P. 510
Bronfenbrenner, U. 597, 600
Brooks, A. 54
Brooks, J. 610
Brooks, L. 564
Brooks, M. 610
Brooks, P. 384
Brown, B. 577
Brown, G. 464
Brown, J. D. 210
Brown, R. 41, 385–6, 385*t*, 399
Brumfit, C. 11, 12–13, 16, 18
Brunot, F. 122
Bruthiaux, P. 11, 14, 349
Brutt-Griffler, J. 212
Bryant, P. et al. 56
Bucholtz, M. 86
Buck, G. 477–8
Buckby, A. 225
Buckingham, T. 11, 12
Bull, W. 79
Burkett, B. et al. 607, 615
Burling, R. 632
Burnard, L. 540, 547
Burns, M. S. 632
Burt, M. 386, 387*t*, 413, 545
Bush, G. H. W. 511
Bush, G. W. 512
Butler, F. A. 483, 512–13, 514, 515–16, 630, 636

Cadierno, T. 448
Cairney, T. 153
Calderhead, J. 611
Calkins, L. 613
Calvet, L.-J. 21, 281, 284
Cameron, D. et al. 209, 306
Canagarajah, A. S. 210, 212, 214, 216, 241, 262, 361, 610
Carlo, M. S. et al. 636
Carpenter, G. R. 171
Carpenter, H. et al. 563, 567
Carroll, J. B. 20
Carroll, S. 449, 450*t*
Carter, R. 55, 542, 545, 546, 547
Castanheira, M. et al. 577
Castellon-Wellington, M. 513
Casterline, D. C. 177

Cazden, C. 85, 572, 574, 575, 576, 608, 610
Čermák, F. 540
Cha, Y.-K. 313, 323
Chakrabarty, D. 216
Chamberlain, C. 179
Chambers, A. 547
Chamot, A. 615
Champion, T. 577
Chandler, D. 599
Chandler, S. 577
Channon, R. 178, 180
Chapelle, C. A. 588, 589, 590
Charity, A. H. 164
Chartier, R. 333
Chaudron, C. 526
Checkland, P. 600
Cheng, W. 544
Chengappa, S. 48
Chenoweth, N. A. 591
Chipere, N. 56
Chomsky, C. 574
Chomsky, N. 55, 62, 77, 398, 399, 619
Christian, D. 110, 622
Christie, F. 16, 579
Christie, J. 154
Chua, S. K. C. 237
Chumbow, B. S. 266
Chun, D. M. 590, 591
Clahsen, H. 222, 225, 427
Clancy, P. M. 401
Clapham, C. 464
Clark, C. M. 611
Clark, J. L. 223
Clegg, J. 615
Clinton, W. J. 511
Clouser, R. A. 363
Clyne, M. G. 243, 266
Cobb, T. 548, 556
Coelho, E. 164
Cohen, A. D. 480, 497, 498
Cohen, E. 610
Cole, M. 148, 330–1, 344
Collier, V. 129, 135–40, 136*t*, 138*t*, 144, 345, 517
Collins, J. 90, 576, 577
Comajoan, L. 389
Comber, B. 196
Committee on the Prevention of Reading Difficulties of Young Children 164

Committee on the Swedish Language 258
Comrie, B.   388
Connor, U.   542, 547
Conrad, A. W.   314
Conrad, R.   174
Conrad, S.   539, 542, 545
Cook, G.   549
Cook, V.   412, 428
Cook-Gumperz, J.   332–3, 407, 575, 576
Cooke, S.   617
Cooper, R. L.   3, 233, 235, 282, 347, 357, 360, 361
Cope, B.   336, 367–8, 617
Corder, S. P.   413
Cormier, K.   178
Coronel-Molina, S. M.   300
Corsara, W. A.   407
Corson, D.   1, 20, 57, 236, 573
Cortés, M.   386
Costa, A.   48
Coulmas, F.   341–2
Coultard, R. M.   578
Coulter, G. R.   178
Coxhead, A.   546
Crago, M. B.   404, 406
Craig, H.   162, 163, 170
Crawford, J.   120, 299–300
Cripps, J. H.   186
Croneberg, C. G.   177
Crookes, G.   527, 529
Crooks, T.   497, 498
Crouch, B. A.   175
Crystal, D.   209–10, 313, 589
Cummins, J.   79–80, 135, 215, 216, 514, 517, 616, 616f
Curtiss, S.   41
Cushman, E.   331

Dahl, Ö.   391
Damasio, A.   603
Daneš, F.   252, 254, 256, 260
Daniel, D.   345
Dante Alighieri   115
Daoud, M.   234
Darling-Hammond, L.   462
Davies, A. et al.   2, 15, 464, 471, 489
Davies, B.   578
Davies, J.   356, 361, 362

Davies, M.   555
Davis, P. M.   135, 142
Davison, C.   615
De Bot, K.   38, 420
De Houwer, A.   43
De Kleine, C.   165
De Klerk, V.   540
De la Fuente, M. J.   591
De la Piedra, M.   153
De León, L.   405
DeKeyser, R. et al.   394, 428, 437, 438, 440, 448, 449
Delamont, S.   578
Delandshere, G.   470, 480
Delpit, L.   613
Derewianka, B.   617
Detwyler, J.   168
DeVincenzi, F.   478
Dewey, J.   602
Dhorsan, A.   348
Díaz, G.   386
Dickinson, D. K.   637
Dietrich, R.   386, 387, 389, 392
DiGello, E.   186
Dittmar, N.   387
Dixon, C.   572, 577
Donley, K.   547
Donovan, M. S.   633
Dorian, N.   346
Dorsey-Gaines, C.   152, 331
Doughty, C.   437, 441, 443, 445, 527, 528, 529, 586
Douglas, D.   465, 589
DPEP (District Primary Education Program)   343
Dreier, O.   95
Dualy, H.   386, 387t
Duff, P. A.   575
Dulay, H.   413, 545
Dunkin, M. J.   572
Dunn, C. D.   403
Duranti, A.   83, 84, 575
Dussias, P. E.   45, 48
Dutcher, N.   135, 345
Dutro, E.   510, 511, 515
Dyson, A. H.   148, 335, 574

Eastman, G. C.   177
Ebel, R. L.   480

Ebert, R.   533, 534
Echevarria, J.   615
Eckert, P.   73, 75, 83, 86, 90–1
Eckstein, K.   32, 34
Economist, The   298
Edelenbos, P.   475–6
Edwards, A. D.   576
Edwards, C.   300
Edwards, J.   73, 282
Egan-Robertson, A.   576
Eggington, W.   285
Egkoff, G.   241
EIB en Bolivia   292
Eisenstein, E. L.   333
Elder, C.   485, 490
Elias-Olivares, L.   150
Elley, W.   56
Ellis, N.   57, 416, 437, 439, 440, 441
Ellis, R.   412, 414, 437, 440, 441, 442, 443,
    444, 449, 451*t*, 529, 560, 561, 562, 563,
    567, 568, 591
Ellsworth, E.   196
Engeström, Y.   600
Epstein, E. H.   129
Erickson, F.   84, 86, 87, 575, 609, 610
Erikson, E.   363
Erlam, R.   443–4, 448, 449, 451*t*, 561, 562
Erting, C. J.   176
Ervin-Tripp, S.   150
Eskey, D. E.   11, 12
Espy, K. A.   32
Eurydice   314, 319
Evans, J.   445, 447*t*
Eversole, R.   343

Fader, A.   404
Fafunwa, A. B.   135
Fairclough, N.   166, 579
Fairfield, S. L.   364
Fanon, F.   207, 211
Farde, L.   430
Farris, K. S.   404, 406
Fasold, R.   79
Fathman, A.   526
Felser, C.   427
Ferguson, C. A.   10, 362
Fettes, M.   241
Fiebach, C. J. et al.   35
Field, M.   401, 404, 405, 406

Fiez, J. A.   433
Figueras, N. et al.   228
Fill, A.   280, 281
Fillmore, L. W.   632
Finkbeiner, C.   602
Firth, J. R.   540
Fischer, J. L.   69
Fischer, K.   164
Fishman, J. A.   21, 68, 79, 156, 252, 268,
    300, 304, 307, 314, 347
Fiske, E. B.   140
Flege, J. E.   426, 428
Fletcher, W. H.   549
Florio, S.   609
Flowerdew, J.   547
Flowerdew, L.   542, 544, 547
Fohtung, B.   273
Foster, M.   576
Fotos, S.   444, 445, 529
Fowler, J.   363
Fox, C. M.   501
Fradd, S. H.   517
Frawley, W.   497
Freebody, P.   578
Freedle, R.   477, 478
Freeman, C.   208
Freeman, D.   611, 621
Freire, P.   148, 195, 331, 610
Frenck-Mestre, C.   427
Friederici, A. D.   31, 32, 34
Friedrich, M.   31, 32
Frisbie, D. A.   480
Fromkin, V.   42
Frye, D.   200
Fu, D.   617
Fuchs, D.   474
Fuchs, L.   474
Fulcher, G.   490
Furst, N.   572
Fuss, D.   195

Gal, S.   98–9, 100
Gallimore, R.   617
Gándara, P.   109
García, F.   290
García, M. F.   591
Gardner, H.   108, 109
Gardner, S.   476
Garfinkel, H.   84, 484, 485, 492, 577

Garner, M.   282
Garrett, M. F.   42, 49
Garrett, P.   149, 399, 401, 406, 407
Garrison, D. R.   590–1
Garvin, P.   255, 260, 267
Gaskell, D.   548
Gass, S.   440, 527, 558, 559, 591
Gathercole, V. C.   390
Gavioli, L.   546, 548
Gebhard, M.   618
Gee, J. P.   17, 329, 332, 335, 344, 576, 579, 610
Geertz, C. T.   598, 601
Gellner, E.   116
Genesee, F.   44, 110, 149
Genishi, C.   574, 577
Gerken, L.   31
Gfeller, E.   274
Giacalone Ramat, A.   390, 392
Gibbons, P.   474–5, 617
Gibson, E. J.   597
Gibson, J. J.   597, 598
Gibson, K.   105
Gilbert, P.   578
Giles, H.   49, 71
Gill, S. K.   214
Gillette, B.   431
Glaboniat, M. et al.   224
Glaeser, E. L.   101, 102, 108
Gluczynski, T.   577
Goffman, E.   83, 84, 484, 492, 577
Goke-Pariola, A.   267
Golden, J. M.   576
Goldman, R. et al.   574
Goldschneider, J. M.   394
Goldstein, H.   485
Goldstein, T.   211
Gomez, R. L.   31
González, N.   149, 151, 155, 156
Goo, J.   558
Goodfellow, T.   591
Goodlad, J.   610
Goodluck, H.   541
Goodwin, C.   575
Goody, J.   330, 356, 358
Gootman, E.   106
Gordon, R. G.   152, 275, 325n
Gort, M.   150–1
Gough, K.   342

Grabowski, B. L.   588
Graciano, M. K.   572
Graddol, D.   123, 244, 620
Graff, H.   332
Granger, S.   543, 544
Grant, A.   300
Gravelle, M.   615
Gray, R. D.   600
Green, D. W.   48, 427
Green, J. L.   572, 573, 574, 576, 609
Greene, J. P.   137
Greenfeld, L.   116
Greenleaf, C. L. et al.   335
Gregory, E.   148, 152
Gregory, R.   597
Grenoble, L. A.   76
Griffin, D. M.   164
Griffin, P.   491, 632
Griffiths, P. E.   600
Griggs, P.   449, 452
Grigorenko, E. L.   472
Grimes, B. F.   131
Grin, F.   348
Grosjean, F.   45, 74
Gumperz, J. J.   70, 85, 86, 215, 399, 575, 576
Gutierrez, K. D.   580

Haarmann, H.   242
Haberzettl, S.   418
Haeckel, E.   596
Haertel, E.   510, 520
Haffner, A.   618
Hahne, A.   32, 34
Hakansson, G.   418
Hakuta, K.   149, 150, 459, 512
Hale, K.   298, 307
Hall, D. E.   166
Hall, R. A.   253
Hall, S.   192, 195
Halliday, M. A. K.   13, 17, 55, 60, 63, 68, 367–8, 574, 579
Ham, S.-H.   313
Hambleton, R. K.   501
Hamilton, L.   518
Hamilton, M.   332
Hammond, J.   343
Hanlon, C.   41
Hansen, B.   178

Hansen, J.   414
Harker, J. O.   573, 576
Harklau, L.   211
Harley, B.   528, 532
Harmon, D.   298
Harris, K.   545
Harris, R.   209
Hart, B.   636
Hartig, M.   280
Hary, B.   540
Hasan, R.   148, 367–8
Hasselbring, S. A.   270
Hasselgren, A.   544
Hastings, J. T.   470–1, 473, 474
Hatch, E.   526
Hau, C. S.   234
Haugen, E.   280–1, 357, 360
Hausenblas, K.   255
Hauser, R. M.   459
Haverkort, M.   28
Haviland, J. B.   401
Havránek, B.   252, 253, 254, 256
Hawkey, R.   491
Hawkins, E.   57
Hawkins, M.   614
Hawkins, R.   57
Hayhurst, A. B.   178
Hazen, K.   168, 630
He, A.   87–8, 405, 406
Heap, J. L.   577
Heath, A.   485
Heath, S. B.   78, 331, 333, 337, 401, 404, 406, 407, 574, 576, 610
Hegelheimer, V.   589
Heilman, E. E.   107
Heller, M.   90, 209, 215, 576
Hennoste, T. et al.   540
Herman, J.   510, 520
Hernandez, G.   336
Herring, S. C.   589
Herron, C.   442
Heubert, J. P.   459
Hicks, D.   572
Hill, H.   612
Hillocks, G.   56
Hinton, L.   155, 307
Hirvela, A.   548
Hobsbawm, E. J.   116
Hodge, R.   579

Hollins, E.   610
Holm, J.   165
Holm, W.   308
Homoláč, J.   255
Honda, M.   58
Honig, B.   100, 108
Hornberger, N. H.   10, 13, 16, 17, 18, 19, 20, 124, 235, 243, 268, 280, 282, 283–4, 289, 291, 300, 334–5, 342, 347, 350, 573
Horvath, B. M.   267
Hough, D. A.   306
Housen, A.   438, 438t, 445, 447t, 544
Houtondji, P. J.   306
Hovens, M.   348, 350
Howard, K. M.   407
Howatt, A. P. R.   10
Hroch, M.   116
Hubbard, P.   588, 589
Hübschmannová, M.   262
Hudson, R.   53, 54, 58, 63, 166
Hughes, R.   545, 546
Huhta, A.   473
Hull, G.   334, 335, 337
Hulstijn, J.   561
Hult, F. M.   13, 16, 17, 19, 258, 286, 287
Hundt, M.   549
Hunston, S.   539
Huntington, S. P.   357
Huss, L.   287
Hyltenstam, K.   426
Hymes, D.   12, 17, 84, 85, 86, 331, 398, 399, 574, 575, 576, 613
Hyon, S.   369

Ibrahim, A.   198
Ide, N.   540
Ijalba, E.   48
Indefrey, P.   33
Ingram, D. E.   240, 383
Inhelder, B.   46
International Bureau of Education (IBE)   314, 324
Irvine, J. T.   98–9, 100
Isahara, H.   540
Ivanic, R.   332, 579
Iwashita, N.   527
Izre'el, S.   540

Jackendoff, R. S.   40
Jaffe, A.   86, 91–2, 404
Jake, J.   49
Jakobson, R.   86, 253
Janks, H.   196–7
Janney, R. W.   280, 596
Jarvis, S.   415, 419
Jefferson, G.   399
Jennings, L.   577
Jernudd, B. H.   258, 262
Johannson, A.   253
Johansson, S.   541
John, V. P.   574, 576
Johns, A.   369
Johns, T.   548
Johnson, J.   429
Johnson, K. E.   611
Johnson, N. K.   213
Johnson, R. E.   176
Johnson, S.   73
Jonassen, D. H.   588
Jones, K.   335
Jones, N.   229, 504
Jones, R.   547
Josephson, O.   288
Julca, F.   290

Kaan, E.   32
Kachru, B. B.   212, 613
Kachru, Y.   212, 613
Kaftandjieva, F.   222
Kaiser, S.   244
Kalantzis, M.   336, 367–8, 617
Kamanä, K.   304
Kamhi-Stein, L. D.   212
Kandel, I. L.   314
Kane, M. T.   497, 498
Kang, H. S.   528, 529
Kaplan, R. B.   11, 21, 233, 234, 235, 237,
   238, 239, 240, 242, 282, 283
Karchmer, M. A.   174
Kawaguchi, S.   418
Keane, W.   355, 356, 359
Kellerman, E.   414, 415, 420
Kelly, G.   577
Kemmer, S.   55
Kendrick, M. et al.   198, 199
Kennedy, C.   548
Kennedy, G.   539

Kenner, C.   154, 335
Kern, R. G.   590
Ketteman, B.   547
Kieffer, M.   638
Kiesling, S.   86, 92
Kilgarriff, A.   541
Kim, A.   34
King, K.   300, 342, 347, 348, 350
Kingdon, J. W.   100
Kinginger, C.   590
Kitade, K.   591
Klein, W.   386, 387, 389, 392
Klima, E.   178, 182
Knobel, M.   572
Knupfer, N. N.   590
Kondo, K.   155
Kormos, J.   420
Koschman, T.   574
Kostin, I.   477, 478
Kötter, M.   591
Kramsch, C.   209, 212, 402, 405, 592
Krashen, S.   46, 120, 386, 387t, 413, 440,
   557
Krauss, M.   75, 297, 346
Kress, G.   199, 334, 579
Kroll, J. F.   38, 45, 48
Kroskrity, P.   84, 91, 400
Kubanek-German, A.   475–6
Kubota, R.   192, 209, 210, 211
Kucan, L.   636
Kučera, K.   540
Kuhl, P.   31, 603
Kulick, D.   73, 403, 405, 406, 407
Kumaravadivelu, B.   209, 211, 214
Kutas, M.   30
Kymlicka, W.   106

Labov, W.   12, 68, 69, 70, 77–8, 120, 163,
   166, 170, 369, 575, 639
LaCelle-Peterson, M.   512, 619
Lacey, C.   502
Lado, R.   412
Lafayette, R. C.   591
Lakoff, R.   72–3
Lam, W. S. E.   334, 590
Lambert, W. E.   135
Lampert, M.   611
Lamy, M.-N.   591
Landon, J.   607

Lane, H.   175
Lang, H. G.   174
Langé, G.   615
Lankshear, C.   195, 335
Lantolf, J. P.   472, 473, 474, 476, 479, 489,
   497, 558, 564, 566, 567
Lapkin, S.   528, 529, 558, 564, 565–6, 568
Larsen-Freeman, D.   425, 601
Larson, M. L.   135
LaSasso, C.   185
Lawson, D. S.   33
Lawson, S.   49
Lawton, D.   502
Le Page, R. B.   71–2
Leap, W.   76, 79, 80
Lee, B.   86
Lee, C. D.   577
Lee, D.   541, 556
Leech, G.   541, 548
Leeman, J.   562–3, 567
Lemke, J.   579
LeMoine, N. R.   169, 630
Lenneberg, E. H.   41, 428
Leonard, L.   349
Leopold, W.   45
Leow, R.   444, 449, 451*t*
LePage, R.   342
Lesaux, N.   638
LeTendre, G. K.   321
Leung, C.   209, 475, 476, 477, 489, 615
Levelt, W.   42, 49, 418, 420
Levy, M.   588
Lewin, K.   597
Lewy, A.   470
Li, D. C.-S.   99, 235
Li, G.   155
Li, M.   235, 238, 239, 240
Li, W.   243
Lichter, M.   103
Liddell, S. K.   176
Liddicoat, A. J.   233
Lightbown, P.   445, 447*t*, 526
Lillis, T.   199
Lima, A.   198
Lin, A. et al.   210, 213
Linacre, J. M.   224
Linn, R. L.   511, 516, 518
Lippi-Green, R.   166–7
Litteral, R.   275, 276

Littlebear, R.   298
Liu, S.   428
Lo, L.   342
Lo Bianco, J.   115, 118, 123, 271, 344
Locher, M.   84
Lockwood, A. T.   140
Loewen, S.   449, 451*t*, 559–60, 561, 562,
   564, 568
Lomawaima, K. T.   300, 301
Long, M.   46, 420, 425, 426, 438, 443,
   529, 532–3, 557, 558, 562, 563, 567–8,
   586
Long, S.   148, 152, 154
Loomba, A.   206, 207
López, L. E.   289, 290, 291, 292, 351
Loschky, L.   527, 558
Loughran, J. J.   612
Low, G.   19
Lucas, C.   178
Lucka, B.   541
Luke, A.   110, 195, 210, 337, 572, 578
Lumley, T.   491
Luo, S. H.   155
Luykx, A.   150, 151, 290
Lyman, R.   104
Lynch, B.   491
Lyster, R.   442, 445, 446*t*, 449, 451*t*, 559,
   561, 563, 568

Ma, Q.   540
McAnally, P. L.   176
McArthur, T.   165
Macauley, J. I.   135
Macbeth, D.   578
McCandliss, B. D.   433
McCarten, J.   546
McCarthy, M.   542, 545, 546, 547
McCarty, T. L. et al.   237, 299, 300, 301,
   307, 308
McClelland, J. L.   433
McConell-Ginet, S.   75
McDermott, R.   577
McDonald, J. L.   417
McDonough, K.   527, 559, 560, 563–4,
   568
Macedo, D.   208
McEnery, A.   547, 548
McEnery, T.   539
McGee, P. L.   517

McGroarty, M.   21, 103, 105, 108, 109
McHenry, E.   333
MacKay, I.   426
McKay, S.   195
McKee, C.   176, 177, 181, 184, 186
Macken, M. et al.   369, 370
Macken-Horarik, M.   370
McKeon, D.   610
McKeown, M.   636
Mackey, A. et al.   527, 558, 559, 560–1, 563
McKinney, C.   196, 199–200
McLaren, P.   195
McLaughlin, J.   34
McLellen, H.   590
McLuhan, M.   330, 333
MacMahon, M. K. C.   177
McNamara, T.   465, 466, 489, 491
McNeill, D.   41
MacSwan, J.   49, 162–3
MacWhinney, B.   416, 417, 418, 433
Madaus, G. F.   470–1, 473, 474, 518
Madden, C.   387*t*
Maffi, L.   298
Magga, O. H. et al.   299, 300, 301, 306
Maher, J.   177
Mahiri, J.   334
Maller, S. J.   184
Mann, C.   237
Marckwardt, A. H.   171
Marinova-Todd, S. H.   426–7
Markee, N.   10, 12, 13, 15, 349
Marko, G.   547
Markowicz, H.   178
Marley, D.   214
Marschark, M.   174, 184, 186
Marsh, D.   615
Marsh, F.   615
Martin, J.   19, 369, 370, 412, 617
Martin, P. W.   213
Martin-Jones, M.   50, 335, 576
Martinez, C.   162–3
Martinez-Roldán, C. M.   150
Mathesius, V.   253, 254
Mathiot, M.   267
Mattheier, K. J.   260
Mauranen, A.   549
Mavrognes, N.   56
Maxwell, M. M.   184

May, S.   109, 192, 266, 267, 299, 304
Mayberry, R. I.   179, 184
Maybin, J.   579
Mayer, C.   185
Mazrui, A. A.   266
Mazrui, A. M.   266
Mead, M.   399
Mehan, H. et al.   76, 83, 93, 577, 578, 609
Mehrotra, S.   345
Meier, R. P.   178, 184
Meinhof, U. H.   73
Meisel, J. M.   43, 44, 222, 225
Melander, B.   258
Menezes de Souza, L. M.   344, 350
Mercer, N.   572, 576, 617
Messick, S.   460, 491, 496
Mesthrie, R.   70, 76, 79, 80
Metzger, M.   185
Meyer, C.   539, 549
Meyer, J. W.   321, 323, 324, 325
Miceli, T.   548
Michaels, S.   577
Miettinen, R.   602
Milani, T. M.   286
Miller, C. P.   269
Miller, D.   108
Miller, P.   406
Miller, P. C.   602
Mills, D.   547
Mills, D. L. et al.   31, 33
Milone, M. N., Jr.   174
Milroy, L.   72, 73
Mishler, E. G.   575
Mislevy, R. J. et al.   496, 498, 502, 506, 507*f*
Mitchell, R.   490, 543, 544
Mizuno, S.   590
Modiano, N.   135
Moffat, L.   198
Mohamed, N.   444
Mohan, B.   475, 477, 615
Moll, L. C. et al.   150, 156, 577
Möllering, M.   547
Montanelli, D. S.   184
Montessori, M.   602
Montrul, S.   392
Moore, H.   483
Moore, L.   406
Moores, D. F.   177

Morgan, B. 196
Morgan, D. 186
Morgan-Short, K. 448
Mori, H. 559, 563
Moritz, M. 406
Morren, Ronald 141*t*, 149
Moss, B. 332
Mottez, B. 178
Moyer, A. 428
Mufwene, S. S. 282
Mühlhäusler, P. 209, 280, 281, 283
Mulhall, P. 612
Müller, M. 224
Munro, M. 426
Murday, K. 591
Murphy, E. 119
Murray, N. L. 497
Musau, P. M. 268
Mushengyezi, A. 199
Mutua, K. 307
Myers-Scotton, C. 48, 49, 74, 75
Myles, F. 543, 544

Nassaji, H. 564
National Council for the Accreditation of
    Teacher Education (NCATE) 167
National Council of Teachers of English
    (NCTE) 167
National Institute for Educational
    Research (NIER) 314
Nebeská, I. 255
Negretti, R. 590
Nekvapil, J. 262
Nelson, C. 201, 613
Nelson, M. 334
Nesselhauf, N. 543, 549
Nettle, D. 76, 268
Neustupný, J. V. 259, 262
Neville, H. J. 33, 34–5
New London Group 197, 336, 367
Newkirk, T. 335
Newmark, L. 412–13, 415
Newport, E. 35, 184, 429
Ningiuruvik, L. 404, 406
Nissan, S. 478
Nitko, A. J. 469, 471, 479
Nkrumah, K. 208
Noreen, A. 253
Norris, J. 57, 394, 441, 442, 445

North, B. 220, 222, 223, 224, 227, 229,
    497
Norton, B. 192, 194, 198
Norton Peirce, B. 194
Noyau, C. 386, 387, 389, 392
Nunan, D. 527

Oakes, L. 286
Obanya, P. 345
Oberecker, R. 32
Obler, L. K. 48
O'Brien, J. 197
Ochs, E. 148, 149, 398–400, 401, 402–3,
    406
O'Connor, M. C. 577
Odlin, T. 411, 414, 415
Odora Hoppers, C. A. 307
OECD (Organization for Economic
    Cooperation and Development)
    115, 486–7
Oh, J. S. 155
Ohta, A. S. 566–7, 568
Oikennon, S. 448
Oliver, R. 527
Olshtain, E. 414
Olsson, J. 56
O'Malley, J. M. 615
O'Neil, W. 58
Ong, W. J. 330, 333, 356
Ooi, V. 547
Orellana, M. F. 577
Ortega, L. 57, 394, 441, 442, 445
Osterhout, L. 34
O'Sullivan, Í. 547
Ouane, A. 350
Ovens, J. 541
Oyama, S. 600

Paas, F. G. W. C. 610, 617
Padden, C. 174, 186
Pahl, K. 334
Pakir, A. 118, 237
Pallier, C. et al. 432
Palmer, A. S. 464, 471, 496
Palmer, F. 540
Palmer, J. D. 12
Palozzi, V. 101–2, 107
Paradis, J. 44
Paradis, M. 440

Park, J. S-Y.　216
Parker, C. S.　129
Parks, S.　363
Partington, A.　539
Passeron, J.　194–5
Patrinos, H. A.　348
Patten, A.　106
Paugh, A.　401, 403, 407
Paul, P. V.　174, 185
Paulston, C. B.　267
Pavlenko, A.　192
Pearson, J.　549
Pearson, P. D.　337
Pease-Alvarez, L.　149, 150
Peirce, C. S.　599
Pellettieri, J.　591
Penfield, W.　428
Pennycook, A.　19, 209, 210, 212, 215,
　282, 334
Pestalozzi, J.　602
Peterson, P.　485–6
Peterson, P. L.　611
Petitto, L. A.　184
Philips, S.　404, 577, 609
Phillipson, R.　10, 14, 209, 210, 284
Philp, J.　558, 559, 563
Piaget, J.　46, 363, 602
Pica, T. et al.　526, 527, 528, 529
Pick, A. D.　597
Pienemann, M. et al.　222, 225, 393, 416,
　418, 532
Pierrard, M.　438, 438t, 445, 447t
Piller, I.　431
Pinker, S.　41, 181, 429, 621
Pisoni, D. B.　42
Plass, J. L. et al.　591
Platt, J.　342
Poehner, M. E.　472, 473, 474, 476, 479
Pollitt, A.　497, 499
Poole, D.　578
Posey, D.　298
Posteguillo, S.　589
Postovsky, V.　45
Poulisse, N.　45
Powesland, P. F.　71
Prabhu, N. S.　527
Prah, K. K.　271
Pransky, K.　610
Pravec, N. A.　544

Pravidla . . .　256
Prensky, M.　367
Price, C. J.　28
Prodromou, L.　549
PROEIB-Andes　289, 290, 291
Prop. 2005/2006:2　287–8
Prys Jones, S.　149
Purpura, J. et al.　459

Quigley, S. P.　174, 176, 184, 185
Quinto-Pozos, D.　178

Ramanathan, V.　196
Ramey, D. R.　345
Ramirez, F. O.　324
Ramirez, J. D.　345
Rampton, B.　75, 83, 87, 90, 209, 405,
　407, 575
Ramsey, C.　174, 186
Ranta, L.　442
Rassool, N.　343, 344
Raz, N.　430, 431
Read, P.　300
Read-Dickins, P.　476–7
Reaser, J.　168, 630
Reddy, M. J.　611
Reder, S.　545
Reibel, D.　412–13, 415
Reich, R.　106, 107, 108, 109
Remez, R. E.　42
Renou, J.　57
Reppen, R.　539, 540, 545, 547
Resnick, D. P.　333
Resnick, L.　333
Reveles, J.　577
Rex, L. A.　572
Reyes, I.　150, 152–4, 155
Rhydwen, M.　271
Ricento, T.　109, 235, 266, 280, 343
Richards, J.　342
Rickford, J. R.　169
Riley, K. C.　400, 405, 407, 621
Ringbom, H.　415
Risley, T.　636
Ritchie, W. C.　43f, 44, 44f, 47, 49
Rivera, C. et al.　512, 519, 619
Rivers, R.　186
Roach, K. A.　637
Roberts, L.　428

Robinson, P.   438, 558
Roever, K.   466
Rogers, H. J.   501
Rogers, R.   93
Rogoff, B. et al.   155, 608
Romaine, S.   74, 76, 80
Römer, U.   545
Romero-Little, M. E.   299, 308
Romo, H. D.   153
Rosa, E.   449, 451*t*
Rose, S.   176
Rosenshine, B.   572
Rosenthal, J. W.   241
Roskos, K.   154
Rossell, C. H.   137
Roth, D.   577
Rothery, J.   18, 19, 369, 370
Rowan, B.   323
Rowsell, J.   334
Rubal-Lopez, A.   314
Rubin, E. J.   33
Ruge, J.   153
Ruiz, R.   118, 267
Rulon, K. A.   529
Rymes, B.   83, 84, 87–8

Sabourin, L.   33, 34, 427–8
Sachdev, I.   49
Sacks, H.   84, 399, 601
Sadembuo, E.   274
Sadler, D. R.   475
Sadovnik, A.   578
Sahni, U.   197–8
Said, E.   207, 210, 216
Salaberry, M.   445, 446*t*
Salaberry, R.   389, 392, 393
Samarin, W. J.   359, 360
Sandiford, H.   546
Sandler, W.   181
Sanz, C.   445, 446*t*, 448, 449, 450*t*
Sapir, E.   17
Sarmento, J.   348
Sasnett, M.   314
Sato, E.   516
Sauro, S.   528, 529
Saussure, F. de   253
Saville, N.   225
Saville-Troike, M.   45
Sawyer, J. F. A.   357, 358, 359, 361

Sayer, P.   150
Scarborough, H. S.   164
Schachter, J.   419
Scharnhorst, J.   257
Schecter, S. R.   149, 400, 406
Schegloff, E. A.   399
Schieffelin, B. et al.   84, 91, 148, 149,
   398–400, 402–3, 405, 406
Schiffman, H. F.   235, 285
Schilling-Estes, N.   167, 168, 171, 630
Schissler, H.   321
Schmidt, D.   416
Schmidt, R.   439, 452, 558
Schmidt, R. Sr.   100–1, 108
Schmitt, B. M.   30
Schmitt, D.   546
Schmitt, N.   546
Schneider, G.   220, 222, 224
Schultz, J.   86, 87, 610
Schultz, K.   337
Schumann, J. H. et al.   5, 430
Schwartz, B.   46, 416
Schwienhorst, K.   590
Scollon, R.   286, 610, 621
Scollon, S.   286, 610, 621
Scott, F. N.   171
Scovel, T.   426, 547
Scribner, S.   148, 328, 330–1, 344
Scriven, M.   469, 470
Secada, W. G.   140
Seedhouse, P.   568
Seidlhofer, B.   544, 548, 549
Selinker, L.   411, 413
Sepmeyer, I.   314
Serra, M. et al.   384, 385, 386
Seton-Watson, H.   115
Setzler, K.   545
Shaker, P.   107
Shanmugaratnam, T.   119
Sharwood Smith, M.   443, 444*t*
Sheen, Y.   433, 559, 562, 563, 567
Shin, H.   210
Shirai, Y.   390, 392–3
Shohamy, E.   21, 99, 235, 239–40, 347,
   348, 349, 350, 466, 475, 490, 510
Shohat, E.   208
Short, D.   615
Shulman, L. S.   612
Shultz, J.   609

Shuy, R.　12, 13–14
Sichra, I.　289, 301
Siegel, J.　276
Siekmann, S.　587
Silver, R. E.　118
Silverstein, M.　83, 84, 86, 87, 90, 91, 98, 399
Simpson, A.　196
Simpson, J. M. Y.　357, 358
Simpson, R.　540, 541
Simpson, S.　276
Sinclair, J. M. H.　546, 547, 578
Singleton, J. L. et al.　174, 184, 186
Sizer, T.　614
Skehan, P.　414
Skilton-Sylvester, E.　268, 283
Skutnabb-Kangas, T.　209, 284, 298, 299, 300, 301, 306, 346, 347, 350
Slabakova, R.　392
Slobin, D. I.　392, 399, 417
Smith, A. D.　116
Smith, B.　421
Smith, G.　307
Smith, L. T.　208, 307
Smith, R. C.　14
Smitherman, G.　78, 164, 171
Snow, C. E.　615, 622, 632, 633, 637, 638
Snow, M. A.　615
Snyder, L. S.　184
Sokalski, K.　448
Sokoya, A.　135
Solsken, J.　577
Sorace, A.　424
Sorenson, A.　45
SOU　287
Soysal, Y. N.　321
Spack, R.　300
Spada, N.　437, 445, 447t, 561–2
Spencer, P. E.　186
Spender, D.　73
Spiekermann, H.　260
Spivak, G. C.　207, 211
Spolsky, B.　1, 2, 10, 11, 14–15, 16–17, 19, 20, 21, 98, 99, 114, 222, 223, 233, 234, 235, 266, 282, 313, 323, 343, 349, 356, 357, 456, 469, 474, 480, 486, 496, 608, 620, 622
Spring, J.　121
Sprouse, R.　416

St John, E.　547
Staddon, S.　117
Steadman, S.　572
Stein, P.　198–9, 336
Stein, S.　108
Steinberg, L. S.　496, 498
Stern, H. H.　223
Sternberg, R. J.　472
Stevens, R.　514
Stevens, S. S.　499
Stocker, K.　86, 92
Stockwell, R.　412
Stokoe, W. C.　177
Stone, M. H.　501
Storch, N.　564, 565
Stowe, L. A.　28, 33, 427–8
Streeck, J.　407
Street, B.　83, 92, 329, 332, 334, 344
Street, B. V.　577
Strevens, P. D.　10, 13
Strike, K.　580
Stromquist, N.　344, 349–50
Strong, M.　185
Stroud, C.　268
Stubbs, M.　1, 57, 356, 540
Supalla, S. J.　176, 181, 183, 184, 186
Sutton-Spence, R.　178
Swadener, B. B.　307
Swain, M.　449, 450t, 526, 528, 529, 558, 564, 565–6, 568
Swales, J.　540
Swaminathan, H.　501
Swan, M.　421
Sweetland, J.　169
Sweller, J.　610, 617
Swords, R.　169

Tabors, P. O.　637
Tabouret-Keller, A.　71–2
Tadadjeu, M.　274
Taeschner, T.　43
Takala, S.　222
Talleyrand, C. M. de　122
Talmy, S.　211
Tan, C.　235
Tang, K. L.　478
Tarone, E.　414, 526
Task Force on Aboriginal Languages and Cultures　298–9

Tatsuoka, K.   477–8
Taylor, D.   148, 152, 331
Taylor, L.   490
Teasdale, A.   476, 489
Tees, R. C.   31
Tejada, C.   580
Teleman, U.   258, 286
Tembe, C.   348
Thal, D. J. et al.   33
Tharp, R.   617
Thesen, L.   196
Thomas, G. M.   324
Thomas, W.   129, 135–40, 136*t*, 138*t*,
    144, 345
Thorne, S.   209, 592
Tinio, V. L.   234
Tocalli-Beller, A.   564
Todd, F.   574
Tognini-Bonelli, E.   539
Tollefson, J.   21, 211, 213, 236–7, 266
Tomasello, M.   55, 384, 442
Tomlin, A.   577
Tomlin, R. S.   558
Tono, Y.   544–5
Toohey, K.   194, 196
Toribio, A. J.   33
Torrance, H.   485, 486
Towell, R.   57
Trim, J. L. M.   222, 225, 226, 280,
    506
Trudell, B.   274
Trudgill, P.   70
Tsuda, Y.   284
Tsui, A. B. M.   213, 236–7
Tucker, R.   135
Tupas, T. R. F.   208
Tuyau, S.   577
Tyack, D.   107

Uhlířová, L.   261
UNDP   348
UNESCO   79, 266, 297, 314, 324, 341,
    342, 343, 344, 345, 346
Unsworth, L.   369, 379, 617
Upton, T.   542, 547
Ur, P.   526, 527, 529
Urzúa, A.   103
US Bureau of Education   314
Uylings, H. B. M.   32

Vail, L.   357, 361
Vaillancourt, F.   348
Vainikka, A.   416
Valadez, C. M.   162–3
Valdés, G. et al.   632
Valli, C.   178
Van Cleve, J. V.   175, 177
Van Ek, J. A.   222, 224, 225, 506
Van Els, T.   233, 234, 235, 239
Van Geert, P.   600
Van Leeuwen, T.   369, 370, 379
Van Lier, L.   16, 18, 19, 282, 285, 597,
    599, 600, 601
Van Merrienboer, J. J. G.   610, 617
Van Pletzen, E.   199–200
Vandaele, S.   445, 447*t*
VanPatten, B.   445, 446*t*, 448, 449
Varela, E.   443, 528
Vasquez, V.   197
Vaughn, P.   267
Vawda, A. Y.   348
Ventureyra, V. A.   432
Villa, V.   558
Vine, E.   577
Vinokur, G.   253
Voegelin, C.   1, 280, 281
Voegelin, F.   280, 281
Vogt, M.   615
Volk, D.   148, 152
Volterra, V.   43
Vygotsky, L. S.   148, 330, 335, 564, 566,
    600, 602

Waldinger, R.   103, 104
Wall, D.   464
Wallace, C.   200–1
Wallat, C.   574, 576
Wallerstein, N.   197
Walter, S. L.   139, 140, 141*t*, 142, 346
Ward, B. A.   101, 102, 108
Warner, C. N.   590
Warner, S. L. N.   304
Warren, M.   547
Warschauer, M.   590, 591, 592
Washington, J.   162, 163, 170
Watahomigie, L. J.   307
Watson, D. R.   577
Watson-Gegeo, K. A.   114
Watt, I.   330

Watt, J. M.   364
Weade, G.   577
Weber, H.   342
Weber, M.   73
Weber-Fox, C.   34–5
Wee, L.   118
Weedon, C.   192, 194
Weick, K. E.   323
Weiler, K.   196
Weinreich, U.   360, 411, 412
Weir, C.   497, 498, 499
Weist, R.   387
Wells, G.   185, 572
West, M.   485–6
Whaley, L. J.   76
Wheeler, R.   169
White, C.   587
White, J.   445, 447*t*
White, L.   46, 416
Whitehead, A. N.   602
Whitmore, K. F. et al.   148
Widdowson, H. G.   2, 12, 14, 18–19, 22n, 549
Wigdor, S.   633
Wiggins, G.   472
Wilbur, R. B.   178, 184
Wilen, D. K.   517
Wiles, J.   186
Wiley, T. G.   161, 342, 345
Wiliam, D.   470, 471, 474, 476, 480
Wilkins, D.   245
Willet, J.   577, 614
Williams, A.   154
Williams, E.   329
Williams, J.   439, 445, 447*t*
Williams, R. S.   400
Willis, J.   527, 548
Willis, P.   610

Wilson, A.   539, 548
Wilson, W. H.   304
Wilson-Keenan, J.   577
Wiseman, R. L.   155
Wix, T. R.   186
Wixson, K. K.   510, 511, 515
Wolfram, W.   166, 167, 168, 630
Wolk, S.   174
Woll, B.   178
Wollaston, I.   356, 361, 362
Wong, G.   237
Wong, S. C.   195
Wong-Fillmore, L.   609, 615
Woods, D.   611
Woolard, K.   84, 91, 400
Wortham, S.   83, 84, 89, 90, 93, 403, 404, 406
Wright, B. D.   501
Wright, M.   618
Wright, S.   99, 122
Wurm, S. A.   346
Wyse, D.   56

Yon, D. A.   195
Yoon, H.   548
Yoshinaga-Itano, C.   184
Young, M. Y. C.   235, 237
Young-Scholten, M.   416
Yuen, S. D.   345

Zentella, A.   150, 155, 405, 406, 407
Zepeda, O.   301, 308
Zeshan, U.   178
Zieky, M. J.   501
Zobl, H.   417
Zorzi, D.   547
Zwarts, F.   28

Subject Index

AAAL (American Association for
    Applied Linguistics) 11
ability 463–5, 500–1, 502
academic language use 514–15, 545,
    615–17, 616f
    see also English for Academic Purposes
Academic Performance Index (API) 486
access policy 235, 238, 246t
accommodation 4, 49, 71
accomplishments 389
accountability 483–92
    and assessment 460, 520, 638
    definition 484
    and standards 483, 484–5
    see also English language learners
    (ELLs) in US; standards
achievements 389
ACTFL see American Council on the
    Teaching of Foreign Languages
action-based teaching and learning
    602–3
action verbs 389
activities 389
adolescents 198–9
adult learners 200–10
AERA see American Educational
    Research Association
affordance 597, 598
African American English
    dialect 77–9, 169
    literacy 163–4, 169, 170, 333
    oral language development 162–3,
    170–1

age of acquisition (AoA) 425–7, 428,
    429
agency 148, 235, 598, 602
aging 429–31
AILA see Association Internationale de
    Linguistique Appliquée
ALTE Framework 227, 228, 497
American Association for Applied
    Linguistics (AAAL) 11
American Council on the Teaching of
    Foreign Languages (ACTFL) 11,
    458, 489, 497
American Educational Research
    Association (AERA) 462, 503
American National Corpus 540
American Psychological Association
    (APA) 462, 503
American Sign Language (ASL) 174,
    177–8
    language acquisition 35, 184
    and reading achievement 186
    structure 179–83, 180f, 182f, 184
Andes: bilingual intercultural education
    (EIB) 288–92
AoA see age of acquisition
APA see American Psychological
    Association
API (Academic Performance Index) 486
applied linguistics 10–14
    critical applied linguistics 19
    inter-/multidisciplinarity and
    transdisciplinarity 13
    and linguistics 1–2, 11–13, 15

applied linguistics (*cont'd*)
  mediating function 11
  scope 13–14
ASL *see* American Sign Language
aspect 387–9, 392, 393, 394–5
aspect hypothesis 389, 392–3
Assembly of Alaska Native Educators 308
assessment
  absolute/relative decisions 456–7
  accountability 460, 520, 638
  alternative assessment 472, 476
  aspects of language ability 463–5,
    500–1, 502
  benefits 461–2
  CEFR 227–30
  certification decisions 459–60
  comprehension skills 477–8
  consequences and fairness of decisions
    3, 348–9, 460–3
  content and construct 478–9
  criterion-referenced tests 457–8
  definitions 469–72
  diagnostic assessment 459, 469–70,
    471, 472–4, 473*f*, 475–6, 478–80
  diagnostic competence 475–6
  dynamic assessment 472, 473, 474–5,
    479
  effects on learning 474–5
  formative assessment 459, 469–74,
    473*f*, 475–7, 478–80, 520, 639
  in general education 470–1, 476
  more advanced learners 638–9
  norm-referenced tests 457
  placement/readiness decisions 458–9,
    471, 638
  policy 235, 239–40, 247*t*
  proficiency *vs.* achievement 464
  role of language 618–20
  second/foreign language assessment
    456–66, 471–2, 474–6, 477–9
  selection decisions 458
  standards 488–92
  "strong"/"weak" performance 465
  summative assessment 459, 470, 476
  uses of tests 456, 458–60
  validity 495, 496–7
  see also accountability; English
    language learners (ELLs) in US;
    frameworks; scales; standards

Asset Languages 505
Association Internationale de
  Linguistique Appliquée (AILA)
  10–11, 14
Association of Language Testers of
  Europe (ALTE) 471–2, 491, 504
  Framework 227, 228, 497
attainment stages 497
attention 533, 558, 560, 563
audience design 71
audio-lingualism 119–20
Australia 240–1, 299, 300, 343, 490
authenticity of texts 529–31
awareness 57, 439, 452, 533, 534, 558,
  598, 637
Aymara 290, 291

BAAL (British Association for Applied
  Linguistics) 11
Bank of English 541
basic interpersonal and communicative
  skills (BICS) 514, 516, 517
bidirectional learning 147, 152–3
bilingual intercultural education (EIB)
  288–92
Bilingual Syntax Measure (BSM) 545
bilingualism 74, 149–57
  adult bilingualism 44–6, 47*t*
  and biliteracy 124, 149–51, 350–1
  Canada 79, 90
  home and school practices 151–4
  and identity 154–6
  key questions 38–9
  modes of language use 46, 47–50
  national policy 118–19, 237
  psycholinguistics 38–9, 42–50
  sequential childhood bilingualism
    44–6, 47*t*, 79–80
  simultaneous acquisition 43–4, 43*f*, 47*t*
  see also multilingualism; ultimate
    attainment
biliteracy 124, 149–51, 350–1
Black English 77–9, 92
Black Stylized English (BSE) 198
Bolivia 291–2, 348
brain development 32
brain imaging techniques 28–30
British Association for Applied
  Linguistics (BAAL) 11

British National Corpus   540, 541, 555
British Sign Language   177
Broca's area   27–8
BSM (Bilingual Syntax Measure)   545
Buddhism   356, 360–1

C/ALP *see* cognitive/academic language
    proficiency
CA *see* conversation analysis
CAL *see* Center for Applied Linguistics
CALL *see* computer-assisted language
    learning
Cambridge ESOL   225
Cameroon   273–5, 347
Canada   79, 90, 99, 300, 304, 404
Canadian Language Benchmarks (CLB)
    505
CANCODE corpus   545
Catalan   386, 386*t*, 388, 389
CDA (critical discourse analysis)   579
CEFR *see* Common European Framework
    of Reference for Languages
Center for Applied Linguistics (CAL)
    10, 14, 486
China   99, 235, 238
Christianity   355, 356, 358, 359, 360, 361,
    364–5
citizenship   57–8, 107–9, 115, 121–2
clarification requests   563–4
classroom discourse and interaction   57,
    76–7, 571–80
  child as language user and language
      learner   574–5
  discourse as object/as social processes
      577–8, 590
  diversity   572–3
  ethnomethodology   577–8
  ideology, power and scale   578–80
  interaction as rule-governed language
      use   609–10
  microethnographic and sociolinguistic
      studies   575–7
  theoretical traditions   573–80
classrooms: mediating role of language
    57, 76–7, 606–22, 640–1
  assessment   618–20
  classrooms as language environments
      608–11
  cultural sites   610–11

  interaction as rule-governed language
      use   609–10
  meaning from context   610
  role of language specialist   620–2
  socialization   607–8
  teachers thinking linguistically
      611–14
  teaching linguistically   614–17
cloze passages   532
code-mixing/switching   48–50, 67, 74–5,
    131, 150, 405
  teaching   169
  in teaching   50
codification   254–5, 260
Cognitive Academic Language Learning
    Approach   615
cognitive/academic language proficiency
    (C/ALP)   514, 516, 517
cognitive demand   617
cognitive linguistics   63
cognitive load   617
*Collins Cobuild English Language
    Dictionary*   546
colonialism   208, 210, 299, 307, 357
Common European Framework of
    Reference for Languages (CEFR)
    220–30, 506, 630
  aim   220–1, 505
  assessments and examinations   227–30
  competence   226
  Decision Tables   228–9, 229*t*
  descriptive scheme   220, 221–2
  empirical validation   228–30
  external validation   504
  goals   224–6
  learning order   222
  levels   220, 222–6, 227, 227*f*, 506
  local goals and central framework
      226–30, 483, 490
  specification   228
  standardization   228, 504
  validity in context   221–3, 480
communal language teaching   243
Communication Accommodation Theory
    49
communication-focused instruction   437
communicative competence   398, 399,
    496, 514, 590, 592
  see also linguistic competence

communicative language teaching   120
communicative process   255
Communities of Practice   75
community language schools   243
community policy   235, 239, 247*t*
Competition Model   416–17, 418
comprehension skills: assessment   477–8
computer animation   374–5, 375*f*, 378, 380*f*
computer-assisted language learning (CALL)   585–92
  critical perspectives   592
  descriptive studies   590
  evaluative research   590–1
  learner autonomy   587–8
  learning through technology   586–7
  research–practice relationships 589–92, 634
  teacher education   588–9
concordancers   541–2, 542*t*
Confucius Institute   244
congruence   390
consciousness-raising (CR) tasks   442, 444
Content and Language Integrated Learning   615
Content-Based Instruction   615
context of situation   368
contextualization   86–7
contextualization cues   71, 576
contrastive analysis   169, 412
convergence   71
conversation analysis (CA)   399, 400, 578, 601
copula deletion   77–8
corporate language teaching   244–5
corpus linguistics   539–49
  class activities   547–8
  computer-assisted analysis techniques 541–2
  concordancers   541–2, 542*t*
  corpora   540–1, 549
  corpus-based teaching materials 545–7
  course design   547, 549
  dictionaries   546
  effects of use in instruction   548, 549
  empirical analysis of patterns   540

future in language instruction   548–9
  and language instruction   543–8
  learner corpora   543–4
  quantitative analysis/qualitative interpretive techniques   542–3
  and second language acquisition 543–5
  websites   555–6
corpus planning *see* language cultivation: developed contexts; language cultivation: multiple language contexts
corrective feedback   41, 46, 559–60, 561–2, 564, 568
Corsica   91–2, 404
CorTec   556
Council of Chief State School Officers 512
Council of Europe   115, 220
covert prestige   49–50, 70
CR tasks *see* consciousness-raising (CR) tasks
creative construction hypothesis   413
criterion-referenced tests   457–8
critical applied linguistics   19
critical discourse analysis (CDA)   579
critical literacy   195–6, 197, 199–201
critical pedagogy   195–202
  adolescents   198–9
  adult learners   200–1
  post-secondary students   199–200
  practice   196–202
  theory   195–6
  young learners   197–8
critical period hypothesis   32, 33, 41
critical thinking   18–19
cross-linguistic influence *see* interlanguage and language transfer
crossing   75, 87
cultural capital   194–5
cultural identity   75, 195
curriculum   116–17
  dialect awareness   167–9
  human capital based   118
  humanist intellectualism   119–20
  impact of English   313–26
  nationing/citizenship   121–2
  policy   235, 239, 246*t*
  religion/social ideology   120–1

secondary linguistic socialization
113–14, 122
skills 117–19
Czech Republic 255–7, 260–2, 540

deaf children and linguistic accessibility
33, 35, 174–87
language impairment framework 176
reading instruction 174–5, 186–7
reform in deaf education 174, 187
signed language 175–7, 178–9, 185,
186–7
speech therapy and auditory training
176–7, 185, 187
description 53–4, 59
developmental pragmatics 399
developmental psychology 363–4
DfES 505
diachrony 60
diagnostic assessment 459, 469–70, 471,
472–4, 473f, 475–6, 478–80
diagnostic competence 475–6
DIALANG 472, 473, 478
dialect density 162
dialect mixture 69
dialects 59, 68–9, 78, 167–9, 170–1
dictionaries 542, 546
difference 192–3, 194, 195, 196, 572–3
differentiation theory of perception 597
diffusion 71
discourse 332, 414
see also classroom discourse and
interaction
discovery learning 167–8, 548
distance learning 245, 587
distributional bias hypothesis 392–3
divergence 71
domain 68, 84, 92–5
Dominica 403
dopamine 430
Dual System Hypothesis 43, 44
dynamic assessment 472, 473, 474–5,
479

EAP *see* English for Academic Purposes
early exit programs 131
East Timor 348–9
Ebonics 78–9, 80
ecological perception 597–8

ecology 280, 596–7
ecology of language 280–93
Andes: bilingual intercultural
education (EIB) 288–92
and educational language planning
and policy 282–5
principles 280–2
semiotics 598–9
Sweden: multilingualism 286–8
Ecuador 341, 350
education as ecosystem 599–601
education systems 113, 121–2
and educational linguistics 114–16
research/practice 122–4
secondary linguistic socialization
113–14
educational linguistics
core themes 116–22, 628–9
definition 1–2, 4
ecological-semiotic perspectives
596–603
and education systems 114–16
focus 16
foundations 113–16
history 14–16
nature 16–20
policy 20–1
practice 18
problem-oriented approach 17, 18
research agenda 626, 627–41
research/practice 109–10, 122–4
scope 20–1
transdisciplinarity 17, 18–20
educational outcomes
access and participation 140
centralization *vs.* local control 630
cognitive outcomes 137–40
flexibility and globalization 630–1
homogeneity *vs.* diversification 630
educational reform 510, 511, 520
see also English language learners
(ELLs) in US
Educational Testing Service 487
EEG (electroencephalograms) 29
EIB (bilingual intercultural education)
288–92
elaborated codes 77
eloquence 119–20
ELP *see* European Language Portfolio

ELTDU (English Language Teaching
  Development Unit) scale   224
empowerment   197–8, 306
encephalographic techniques   29
endangered languages   75–6, 282,
  297–308
  concerns   298–9
  definition   297
  evaluation of present measures
    307–8
  future   308
  grass roots initiatives   304
  international efforts   302–3, 304–5
  national language policies   3, 303
  reasons for   299–301
  role of Indigenous peoples and
    organizations   305–6
  role of NGOs   305
  role of researchers   306–7
  role of schooling   299–300
  submersion education   300–1
English: impact on school curriculum
    313–26
  data   314–15
  dominant foreign languages   315,
    317–18t
  English as first foreign language   314,
    315–19, 316f, 317–18t
  English education as institution
    321–4, 322t
  regional variations   319–21, 320t
English as a lingua franca   549
English for Academic Purposes (EAP)
    199, 544, 545, 546, 547, 548
  see also academic language use
English language learners (ELLs) in US
    510–20
  academic language use   514–15, 516
  ELL proficiency and grade level
    517–18
  NCLB (No Child Left Behind) Act
    512–13
  NCLB standardized testing   518–20
  NCLB Title III   513, 514, 515, 516,
    517–18
  standards   515–16
  state policies   519–20
"English profile"   225
enrichment theory of perception   597

epistemology   362–4
erasure   99, 100–1
Eritrea   141, 142–3, 143t
ERPs (event-related potentials)   29–30,
    31, 36, 427–8
ethics
  curriculum   120–1
  and language tests   3–4
  and standards   491–2
ethnic groups: terminology   343
ethnic minority: terminology   343
ethnicity   70, 73, 195
ethnography of communication   331,
    332, 590
ethnography of speaking   399–400
ethnomethodology   577–8
etymology   60
Eurocentres   224–5, 226, 228, 229
Eurocentres Scale of Language
    Proficiency   224
Europe   115–16
*European Charter for Regional and Minority
    Languages*   302
European Language Portfolio (ELP)
    223, 226
European Union   244
evaluation policy   235, 239–40, 247t
evidence centred test design   496–7
exchange errors   42
explicit knowledge   114, 440, 561–2

FFI see form-focused instruction
field   368, 373–6, 374t, 375f
Finland   303
Finno-Ugric languages   300
fMRI (functional magnetic resonance
    imaging)   28–9, 427, 432
focusing   71–2
foreground   394
foreign language teaching   56–7, 107,
    119–20
form   60, 84–90
form-focused instruction (FFI)   57,
    437–52
  awareness   439, 452, 534
  definitions   437–41
  explicit FFI   438, 438t, 439–40, 441t
  focus-on-form   438–9, 560
  focus-on-forms   438, 439

implicit/explicit L2 knowledge   440–1
implicit/explicit learning   439–40
implicit FFI   438, 438*t*, 439
   pedagogy   437
   proactive explicit FFI   441–2, 443–9,
      446–7*t*
   reactive explicit FFI   442–3, 449–52,
      450–1*t*
   theory   437
formative assessment   459, 469–74, 473*f*,
      475–7, 478–80, 520, 639
fossilization   413, 420, 430
frameworks   495–7, 504–7
   linking educational assessments
      506–7, 507*f*
   types   505
   utility   505–6
   see also scales
France   99, 122, 175, 176
free variation   69
freedom of choice   4
French: L2 acquisition   388, 389
French Academy   257
French Sign Language *see* Natural Sign
function   60, 254
functionalism   253, 313–14, 321
funds of knowledge   149
'future-person' ideology   115–16

Gallaudet University   177
gender   70, 72–3, 140–3, 192, 197, 198,
      404
generative grammars   62
generative linguistics   62
generic structure   369
Genie   41
genocide   301
genre   369, 615–17
   in narrative   369–72, 380
global English   115, 540–1
globalization   206–16, 631
   from below   214
   colonial discourses   210
   and colonialism   208
   cultural dimensions   208
   in language education   209–11
   literacy   334
   spread of English   209–10, 284, 313
glossolalia   360

grammar   40, 56
grammar communication tasks   529–30,
      530*f*, 531–2, 531*f*, 533
grammatical structure   61
"Great Divide" theories   330
Guatemala   140–1, 141*t*, 142*t*, 143–4,
      144*t*, 291, 348

haemodynamic (blood flow) techniques
      28–9
Hawaiian   304
heritage language programs   131
heritage language schools   243
historical linguistics   69
home-based learning   243
human and minority rights   268–9, 287,
      301, 302–3, 304, 341, 345–6
humanism   119–20, 194

IAEP (International Assessment of
      Educational Progress)   487
iBTOEFL *see* Internet-Based Test of
      English as a Foreign Language
ICLE (International Corpus of Learner
      English)   544
iconicity   99, 100–1
identity   192–202
   and bilingualism   154–6
   critical pedagogies   196–202
   cultural identity   75, 195
   and linguistic behaviour   71, 73, 86,
      93–4, 639–40
   sexual identity   201
   theorizing identity   194–5
   theorizing language   193–4
   theorizing pedagogy   195–6
identity politics   195
IEA (International Association for the
      Evaluation of Educational
      Achievement)   487
IELTS (International English Language
      Testing System)   489
ILO *see* International Labour
      Organization
ILTA (International Language Testing
      Association)   491
imagination   197–8
immersion programs   304, 307–8, 621
implicit knowledge   440, 561–2

in-service corporate language training
    245
indexicality   68, 91
indigenous: terminology   343
indigenous languages   115, 299, 300,
    304
    see also endangered languages;
        vernacular/indigenous literacies
indirect freestyle   86
Indonesia   239
inflections   61
information and communications
    technologies   124, 242, 245, 333–4,
    336, 367
    see also computer-assisted language
        learning (CALL)
information gap tasks   527, 529
information pickup   597
Inhibitory Control Model   48
Initial One-system Hypothesis   43–4,
    44*f*
initiates   148
Input Processing Instruction   445, 448–9
inter-/multidisciplinarity   13, 18
Inter-Agency Round Table (IAR)   489
interaction   70–2, 557–68
    attention   533, 558, 560, 563
    awareness   558
    clarification requests   563–4
    corrective feedback   559–60, 561–2,
        564, 568
    explicit and implicit knowledge
        561–2
    languaging   565–6
    negative and positive evidence   562–4
    noticing   558–61
    pedagogical implications   567–8
    private speech   566–7
    recasts   562–3, 567–8
    role in L2 learning   557–8
    as rule-governed language use
        609–10
    scaffolding   564–5
    through technology   586–7, 590
    uptake   559–60
    working memory   560–1
    zone of proximal development   564
    see also classroom discourse and
        interaction

interactional sociolinguistics   70
interculturalism/interculturality   120,
    289
    see also bilingual intercultural
        education (EIB)
interdependence hypothesis   79–80
interference hypothesis   163
interlanguage and language transfer   45,
    411–21
    constraints   413–18
    definitions   411–12
    early developments   412–13
    language distance and psychotypology
        415
    linguistic factors   415–16
    methodology   419–20
    pedagogy   420–1, 548
    performance models   420
    processing accounts   417–18
    psycholinguistic accounts   416–17
    sociolinguistic and task effects
        414–15
interliteracy   150–1
International Assessment of Educational
    Progress (IAEP)   487
International Association for the
    Evaluation of Educational
    Achievement (IEA)   487
International Corpus of English   540–1,
    549
International Corpus of Learner English
    (ICLE)   544
International English Language Testing
    System (IELTS)   489
International Labour Organization (ILO)
    302, 305, 343, 345–6
International Language Testing
    Association (ILTA)   491
International Second Language
    Proficiency Ratings (ISLPR)   489
internet   245, 586, 588
Internet-Based Test of English as a
    Foreign Language (iBTOEFL)   457,
    458
interval scales   499
investment   194–5, 196
IRE (Initiation, Response, Evaluation)
    76
Islam   243, 355, 356, 358, 359, 364, 406

ISLPR (International Second Language Proficiency Ratings) 489
Israel 99, 235
Italian: L2 acquisition 388, 392, 424
item banking 501, 501*f*, 502
item response theory (IRT) 501

Japan 239, 401, 403
Japan Foundation 244
JET (Japan Exchange and Teaching) 245
jigsaw tasks 529, 530, 531–2, 531*f*, 533, 534
Judaism 355, 356, 358–60

Key Word in Context (KWIC) 541–2, 542*t*
kinesthetic perception 598
knowledge about language (KAL) 39–40, 54–6, 631–2

L1 interference hypothesis 34, 35
L1/L2 130
LAM *see* language acquisition management
LAN (Left Anterior Negativity) 30, 34, 35, 427
language
  creativity 40
  neurobiology 27–8
  as semiotics 598–9
  as social practice 193–4, 215
  in use 86–90, 92–3
language acquisition 383–95, 384*t*
  acquisitional stage 383
  aspect 387–9, 392, 393, 394–5
  congruence 390
  correction 41, 46
  delayed exposure effects 32–3, 35
  initial state (universals and L1) 390–2
  input 392–3
  instruction 393–4
  L1 development 31–2, 40–1, 384–6, 385*t*, 393
  L2 acquisition 33–5, 222, 225, 386–7, 387*t*, 388–9, 392–5, 427–8
  lexical knowledge 31
  morpheme studies 384–7, 385*t*, 386*t*, 387*t*, 391, 394

multiple factors 394–5
neurobiology 30–2, 427–8
one-to-one principle 390
phonology 30–1, 34, 414
readiness 393
relevance 390
research 636–8
sentence production and comprehension 41–2
syntax 31–2, 34, 35, 384–5, 385*t*
tense 387–9, 392, 393, 394–5
see also bilingualism; form-focused instruction; interlanguage and language transfer; language acquisition management (LAM); language socialization; ultimate attainment
language acquisition management (LAM) 20–1, 233–48, 347–8
  access policy 235, 238, 246*t*
  communal language teaching 243, 246–7*t*
  community policy 235, 239, 247*t*
  curriculum policy 235, 239, 246*t*
  evaluation policy 235, 239–40, 247*t*
  industrial language teaching 244–5, 246–7*t*
  medium of instruction 236–8
  methods and materials policy 235, 239, 247*t*
  other language teaching (OLT) 241–8
  personnel policy 235, 238–9, 246*t*
  promotional agencies 243–4, 246–7*t*
  resourcing policy 235, 239, 247*t*
  schools 236–40
  second/foreign language selection 238
  teacher-led policy 235, 240, 247*t*
  tertiary study 240–1
  vernacular/indigenous languages 347–8
Language Across the Curriculum 57
language and cultural promotion agencies 243–4, 246–7*t*
language and literacy practices 148–9, 151–4
language campaigns 243
language contact 74

language cultivation: developed contexts
251–63, 630
  concept   251–3
  Czech Republic   255–7, 260–2
  developed contexts   252
  goals   252–3
  origin   253–5
  postmodern era   259–62
  Sweden   257–9
language cultivation: multiple language
    contexts   266–77
  Cameroon   273–5
  community-based decision making
    267, 271–2
  cultivation processes in local
    communities   272–3
  impact of language cultivation   269
  language diversity policy   268–9
  languages   267–8
  national level policies   266–71, 283–5
  organization and planning   273
  Papua New Guinea   275–6
  participation   270
  resources   269–70
language–culture nexus   399, 401
language destandardization   260
language education
  colonial discourses   210
  globalization   209–11
  linguistic repertoires   215–16
  local knowledge and postmethod
    pedagogies   214–15
  local languages as media of instruction
    213–14
  NNS teachers   212–13
  othering   210–11
  post-colonial appropriation and
    resistance   211–15
  post-colonialism   210–16
  World Englishes   212
  see also language of instruction (LoI)
language education policy see language
    acquisition management
language for specific purposes (LSP)
    117–18, 465
language ideologies   84, 91–2, 98–110,
    400
  in classroom interaction   578–80
  future directions   109–10

"future-person" ideology   115
  and identity issues   154–6
  invisibility of   166–7
  and sociopolitical conditions   98–9
  US political influences   100–2
  in US workplaces and schools   102–9
  vernacular/indigenous literacies
    349–50
language modernization   252
language of instruction (LoI)   129–45,
    236–8, 637
  access and participation   140
  cognitive outcomes   136*t*, 137–40,
    138*t*
  cost effectiveness   143–4, 144*t*
  definitions   130–1
  educational dimensions   135–44
  instructional strategies   130–1
  L1/L2   130
  language of wider communication
    (LWC)   130
  and national development   133–5,
    134*t*, 135*t*
  primary language   131–5, 132*t*, 134*t*,
    135*t*, 213–14
  subject of instruction (SoI)   130
  submersion programs   139–40, 300–1
  urbanness and gender   140–3, 142*t*,
    143*t*
language of wider communication
    (LWC)   130
language "organ"   55, 62
language planning   75
  see also ecology of language; language
    acquisition management; language
    cultivation: developed contexts;
    language cultivation: multiple
    language contexts; status planning
language policy   2, 3–4, 75
  bilingualism   118–19, 237
  for Indigenous/minority languages
    303, 347–8
  see also ecology of language; language
    acquisition management; language
    of instruction
language proficiency   496, 502–3, 514,
    516, 517
  see also frameworks; scales; ultimate
    attainment

language socialization   148–9, 398–407
  across the lifespan   402–3
  dialogic process   70, 403–5
  diversity of contexts   405–7
  future research   156–7
  home and school practices   151–4
  socialization through and into
    language   401–2
  theoretical approach   398–400
language spread   361
  English   209–10, 284, 313
language system   40
language transfer *see* interlanguage and
  language transfer
language universals   390–2
Languages Ladder   505
languaging   565–6, 637
late exit programs   131
learner autonomy   548, 587–8
learner fit   588
learning styles   198–9, 548, 598
  see also multiliteracies; multimodality
letters   61
lexemes   61
lexical aspect   388
lexical (aspectual) categories   388
lifelong learning   241–2, 505
linguistic anthropology   83–96, 399
  domain   68, 84, 92–5
  form and use   84–90
  identity   86, 93–4
  ideologies   84, 91–2
  power   90–2
  trajectory   93, 95
  transcription conventions   95–6
linguistic capital   118
linguistic competence   39–40, 49, 193–4,
  226, 398, 399
  see also communicative competence
linguistic instrumentalism   118
linguistic minorities   56, 116, 151–2
  see also minority/minoritized languages
linguistic performance   39–40
Linguistic Society of America (LSA)   11,
  79
linguistic structuralism   253
linguistic theory   53–63, 634–5
  description   53–4, 59
  and education   53, 54–8

  form/function   60
  ideas   54, 59–62, 635
  knowledge about language (KAL)
    39–40, 54–6, 631–2
  lexemes/inflections   61
  models   54, 62–3, 635
  prescription   59
  punctuation/grammatical structure
    61
  sounds/letters   61
  synchrony/diachrony   60
  texts/systems   60
  variation/uniformity   59–60
  words/meanings   61
linguistic variables   70
linguistic variation *see* variation
linguistics   12, 17, 598–9
literacy   328–37
  concepts   148, 328–9, 337, 343–5
  critical literacy   195–6, 197, 199–201
  cross-cultural/cross-national contexts
    334–5
  and development   335–6
  historical view   332–3
  history   329–32
  and linguistic theory   62
  PISA Project   483, 486–8, 634
  and power   283–4, 331–2
  research/practice   123–4, 148–9,
    336–7, 638
  syncretic studies   148
  technology   333–4, 630–1
  see also multiliteracies; narrative;
    religious literacy; vernacular/
    indigenous literacies
locutio prima/secondaria   115
LoI *see* language of instruction
loi Toubon   99
London/Oslo-Bergen (LOB) Corpus
  541
Longman Grammar of Spoken and Written
  English   547
LSA *see* Linguistic Society of America
LSP *see* language for specific purposes
LWC (language of wider
  communication)   130

Macao   237
Malaysia   214

Manually Coded English (MCE)   179, 183–4, 183*f*, 185
Māori   299, 304, 307
Markedness Model   48
Matrix Language Frame (MLF) model   49
Mayan   92, 140–1, 141*t*, 142*t*, 342, 405
meanings   61
measurement scales   499–500, 502
MEG (magnetoencephalograms)   29
mental grammar   40
metalanguage   368
metalinguistic explanation   443, 444*t*, 445, 448
metapragmatic awareness   400
Methodical Sign   175–6, 178, 185
methods and materials policy   235, 239, 247*t*
Michigan Corpus of Spoken Academic English (MICASE)   541, 555–6
Michigan Protocol for African American Language   170
minority/minoritized languages   266
   see also endangered languages; indigenous languages; linguistic minorities
missionaries   243, 357, 360–1, 403
MLF (Matrix Language Frame) model   49
mode   368–9, 373, 378–9, 379*t*
models   54, 62–3, 635
modularity   40
Monash University, Australia   117–18
monolingualism
   language use and acquisition   39–42, 399
   and monoliteracy   346–50
moribund languages   297
Morocco   214
morpheme studies
   L1 development   384–6, 385*t*, 386*t*, 391
   L2 acquisition   386–7, 387*t*, 394
mother tongue teaching   55–6, 79, 119
motivation   639–40
multiculturalism   106
multilingualism   38, 73–6, 79, 115–16, 281, 335
   see also bilingualism; ecology of language; language cultivation: multiple language contexts

multiliteracies   367–9
Multimedia Adult ESOL Corpus   545
multimodality   198–9, 334, 336, 344, 367, 548
   narratives   370, 372, 374–5, 377–8, 380–1
multiplex relations   72
multisensory perception   598

N400   30, 31, 34, 35, 427
narrative   369–81
   field   368, 373–6, 374*t*, 375*f*
   foreground   394
   generic stages   369–72, 370*t*, 371*f*
   genre   369–72, 380
   mode   368–9, 373, 378–9, 379*t*
   multimodality   367, 370, 372, 374–5, 377–8, 380–1
   register   369, 372–9, 380
   social purpose   370, 370*t*
   tenor   368, 373, 376–8, 376*t*, 377*f*
   themes   378
National Assessment of Educational Progress (NAEP), USA   518
National Council of Teachers of Mathematics, USA   517
National Council on Measurement in Education (NCME)   503
National Research Council, USA   517
National Standards in Foreign Language Project   496, 505
nationalism   73–4, 98–9, 115, 121–2
nativism   55
Natural Sign   175, 176
negative evidence   562–4
networks   72–3
neurobiology of language   27–8
neurobiology of language learning   27–36
   aging   429–31
   brain development   32
   brain imaging techniques   28–30
   delayed exposure effects   32–5
   of first language acquisition   30–2
   future directions   36
   of second language acquisition   427–8
New Literacy Studies   329, 332, 334, 336, 344
New Zealand   3, 4, 299, 304, 307

NNS (non-native speaker) teachers
212–13
nominal scales   499
norm-referenced tests   457
North Carolina Language and Life
Project   168
Northern Ute   76, 80
Norway   300, 303
noticing   439, 548, 558–61, 591

Occupational English Test (OET)   459–60
one-to-one principle   390
ordinal scales   499
Orientalism   207, 216
orthography   256, 260, 272, 274
overt prestige   70

P600   30, 32, 34, 35, 427
Papua New Guinea   148, 275–6, 402, 403
pedagogy
as activity   602–3
multimodal   198–9, 334, 336
postmethod pedagogies   214–15
see also critical pedagogy
peer support   152–4
perception and action   597–8, 602
Permanent Forum on Indigenous Issues
(PFII)   305, 307
personnel policy   235, 238–9, 246*t*
Peru   289–90, 347, 349
PET (positron emission tomography)
28–9
phonological development   30–1, 34,
414
picture theory of perception   597
PISA project   483, 486–8, 634
popular culture   198, 200
Population Reference Bureau   274
positive evidence   562–4
post-colonialism   206–16
and globalization   208
and language education   210–16
(neo)colonialism   208
Orientalism   207, 216
postmethod pedagogies   214–15
social inequality   216
post-secondary students   199–200
poststructuralism   193, 194, 195, 196
postvocalic *-r*   69–70

power
in classroom interaction   579, 613–14
and difference   78, 192–3, 194
empowerment   197–8, 306
endangered languages   299, 306
and identity   195
and ideology   90–2
literacy   283–4, 331–2
practice-based accounts   90–1, 330–1
Prague School   253–5, 257
preschool programs   243, 304
prescription   59
prestige   70
primary education   76–7
private speech   566–7
problem-posing   200
Processability Theory (PT)   418
professional development schools
633
proficiency scales   497
Profile Deutsch   224
psycholinguistics   38–50
bilingualism   38–9, 42–50
monolingual language use and
acquisition   39–42, 399
punctuation   61

Quechua   290, 291, 300, 301, 347, 349
Queer theory   201

Rasch modeling   501
rating scales   497
ratio scales   499
reading
African American English   163–4, 169,
170
applied research   170
critical reading   197, 200–1
deaf education   174–5, 186–7
errors   163–4
PISA Project   487
recasts   562–3, 567–8
reciprocity   598
register   57, 68, 369
in narrative   372–9, 380
religious literacy   355–65
divine speech   355
education and faith development
120–1, 362–5

religious literacy (*cont'd*)
  education and language   107, 243,
    360–2
  language   355–6, 357–9, 364
  religious codes   359–60
  sacred texts   356, 358–9, 364
  war memorials   356
research–practice relationships   626,
    627–41
  advanced learners   638–9
  computer-assisted language learning
    (CALL)   589–92, 634
  desired educational outcomes   629–31
  educational research   122–4, 626–8
  enriching research–practice
    relationships   633–6
  language acquisition research   636–8
  literacy   123–4, 148–9, 336–7, 638
  motivation and identity in language
    learning   639–40
  second language acquisition (SLA)
    525–7
  teachers' knowledge of language
    631–2
  see also corpus linguistics; task-based
    teaching and learning
resourcing policy   235, 239, 247*t*
restricted codes   77
reversal errors   42
Romance languages   388, 389
Romani   261–2
Russia   3, 303, 324

Saami   300, 303, 306
Samoa   148, 401, 402–3
scaffolding   152, 154, 388, 564–5
scales   495–504
  construction   499, 502
  examination levels   497
  item banking   501, 501*f*, 502
  item response theory (IRT)   501
  measurement scales   499–500, 502
  for objectively-marked tests   500–1,
    500*f*
  proficiency scales   497
  rating scales   497
  stages of attainment   497
  standard setting   503–4
  for subjectively rated skills   501–3

  test validity model   498–504, 498*f*
  validity   496, 497, 499, 502
  see also frameworks
schools
  dual-language   155–6
  language acquisition management
    236–40
  United States   105–9, 155–6
  see also curriculum
second language acquisition (SLA)
  and corpus linguistics   543–5
  research and practice relationships
    525–7
  see also form-focused instruction;
    interaction; interlanguage and
    language transfer; language
    acquisition; task-based teaching
    and learning; ultimate attainment
secondary linguistic socialization
  113–14, 122
Self and Other   210–11
semantic development   31, 34, 35
semiotics   368–9, 598–9
sensitive period hypothesis   32, 33–4
sentence production and comprehension
  41–2
Seoul English Village   210
SERP (Strategic Educational Research
    Partnership)   633–4
sexism in language   72–3
sexual identity   201
signed languages   174–87
  American Sign Language   35, 174,
    177–83, 184, 186
  ASL structure   179–83, 180*f*, 182*f*, 184
  British Sign Language   177
  and deaf education   175–7, 178–9, 185,
    186–7
  linguistic status   177–9, 304
  Manually Coded English (MCE)   179,
    183–4, 183*f*, 185
  and reading   174–5, 186–7
Simultaneous Communication   185
Singapore   118–19, 235, 237
SIOP (Structured Instruction Observation
    Protocol)   615
skills   117–19
SLA *see* second language acquisition
social class   69, 70, 76–7

social dialectology 68–9
social network theory 72–3
social practices 147, 193–4, 215
social relations 83–4, 86–7
social transformation 121
sociolinguistics 12, 66–80
  application of research 166–71
  definition 66–8
  and education 76–80
  research on vernacular varieties
    161–71
sociology of education 600–1
Sociology of Language 68
sounds 61
South Africa 347
South Korea 239, 323–4
Spanish 386, 386*t*, 388, 389, 391–2
speech acts 71
speech errors 42, 420–1
speech/language services 170–1
Speech Production Model 418, 420
spot the difference tasks 529, 530, 530*f*,
  531–2, 534
stages of attainment 497
stakeholders 484
standard language 251–2, 254, 484–5
standards 484–92, 630, 634
  and accountability 483, 484–5
  educational standards 485–6, 490,
    496, 515–16
  and ethics 491–2
  as goals 488–91
  language assessment 488–92
  PISA Project 483, 486–8, 634
  standard setting 504
  see also frameworks; scales
stative verbs 389
status planning 251, 252, 257, 259,
  283
storyboards 372, 372*f*, 377, 377*f*
Strategic Educational Research
  Partnership (SERP) 633–4
strategic essentialism 195, 211
structured heterogeneity 69
Structured Instruction Observation
  Protocol (SIOP) 615
stylistic norms 255
subject 194
subjectivity 194

submersion programs 131, 139–40,
  300–1
summative assessment 459, 470, 476
Sweden 257–9, 286–8, 303
Swedish: L2 acquisition 392
Sydney School 369
synchrony 60
syntax
  L1 development 31–2, 384–5, 385*t*
  L2 development 34, 35, 414
systemic (functional) linguistics 63,
  368–9, 579
systems 60

Taiwan 244, 404
Tanzania 90
target language use (TLU) domain
  463–4
task-based teaching and learning
  525–36
  authenticity 529–31
  cloze passages 532
  consciousness-raising (CR) tasks 442,
    444
  ease of production and
    implementation 531–2
  focus 532–4
  grammar communication tasks
    529–30, 530*f*, 531–2, 531*f*, 533
  information gap tasks 527, 529
  jigsaw tasks 529, 530, 531–2, 531*f*,
    533, 534
  language transfer 414–15
  learning outcomes 534–5
  practice activities 442
  research and practice relationships
    525–7, 634
  spot the difference tasks 529, 530,
    530*f*, 531–2, 534
  tasks in teaching and research 527–9
teachability hypothesis 393
teacher education 58, 588–9, 631–2
teacher-led policy 235, 240, 247*t*
teacher talk 76–7
teachers
  non-native speakers (NNS) 212–13
  responsibilities 525
  role of language specialist 620–2
  teaching linguistically 614–17

teachers (*cont'd*)
  thinking linguistically   611–14
  see also research–practice relationships
teacher–student exchanges   76, 578
teaching *see* foreign language teaching;
  mother tongue teaching
tenor   368, 373, 376–8, 376*t*, 377*f*
tense   387–9, 392, 393, 394–5
tertiary study: language education policy
  240–1
TESOL (Teachers of English to Speakers
  of Other Languages)   11, 486, 515,
  517
texts   60
themes   378
thinking skills   18–19, 58
threshold hypothesis   79
TLU (target language use) domain
  463–4
TOEFL (Test of English as a Foreign
  Language)   489
Total Communication   185
total linguistic fact   83–4
transdisciplinarity   13, 17, 18–20
Transfer to Somewhere Principle   417

UG (Universal Grammar)   415–16
UK
  educational standards   485, 490
  language socialization   404, 405
  National Qualifications Framework
    505
  Voluntary Service Overseas   244
ultimate attainment   45, 424–33
  age of acquisition (AoA)   425–7, 428,
    429
  approximating L1 learning context
    432–3
  cognitive and biological aging   429–31
  definition   424
  factors   428
  future directions   431–3
  L2 dominance   432
  levels   424
  nativelike ultimate attainment   425–8
  psycho-social variables   431
  ultimate understanding   433
Unitary System Hypothesis   43–4, 44*f*
United Nations   301, 304–5

Universal Grammar (UG)   415–16
uptake   559–60
urbanness   141–3
USA
  deaf education   175–7, 179
  educational standards   485–6, 496,
    515–16
  Elementary and Secondary Education
    Act (ESEA)   511, 512
  ESL classes   211
  Goals 2000   511
  Improving America's Schools Act   512
  individualism   108–9
  language education policy   236–7
  language socialization   148, 401, 403,
    404, 405
  linguistic ideologies   100–9
  nationally mandated testing   511–12
  Native Americans   299–300, 303,
    306–7, 308, 401, 404, 405
  NCLB (No Child Left Behind) Act
    105, 349, 486, 490, 512–13, 520
  Peace Corps   244
  political influences   100–2
  schools   105–9, 155–6
  vernacular language varieties   161–71
  workplaces   103–5
  see also African American English;
    English language learners (ELLs) in
    US

Vai   330, 344
values   4
variants   70
variation   59–60, 66–7, 68–70, 77–9, 167
  see also dialects
vernacular: terminology   342–3
vernacular/indigenous literacies
    341–51, 634
  ideology   349–50
  international policy and research
    163–5, 170, 345–6
  language education policies   347–8
  language in the public space   349
  language policies   347
  language tests   348–9
  monolingualism and monoliteracy
    346–50
  terminology   342–5

vernacular language varieties: research
161–71, 630, 635–6
application of research 166–71
literacy 163–5, 170
oral language development 162–3,
170–1
vocational education 241, 245

Wernicke's area 27, 28
West African Pidgin English 165
words 61
working memory 560–1
World Bank 244
World Commission on Culture and
Development 299

World Council for Indigenous Peoples
305–6
World Englishes 212
World Resources Institute 298
writing
critical approach 199
and grammar teaching 56
orthography 256, 260, 272, 274
systems 330, 341–2
vernacular 164–5

young learners 197–8

zone of proximal development (ZPD)
154, 472, 564

Made in the USA
Lexington, KY
20 December 2011